THE ECONOMIC MIND IN AMERICAN CIVILIZATION

VOLUME THREE

1865–1918

Also by JOSEPH DORFMAN

In REPRINTS OF ECONOMIC CLASSICS

THE ECONOMIC MIND IN AMERICAN CIVILIZATION,
I & II [1946]; IV & V [1959]
THORSTEIN VEBLEN AND HIS AMERICA [1934]

Edited by JOSEPH DORFMAN

TYPES OF ECONOMIC THEORY BY WESLEY C. MITCHELL,
I & II [1967, 1969]

THE ECONOMIC MIND IN
AMERICAN CIVILIZATION

VOLUME THREE
1865-1918

BY

Joseph Dorfman

REPRINTS OF ECONOMIC CLASSICS

Augustus M. Kelley · Publishers
NEW YORK 1969

First Edition 1949

(New York: The Viking Press, 1949)

Copyright 1949 by Joseph Dorfman

REPRINTED 1969 BY

AUGUSTUS M. KELLEY · PUBLISHERS

New York New York 10001

By Arrangement with THE VIKING PRESS

. . . .

S B N *678-00111-1*

Vol III 678 - 00539 - 7

L C N *64 - 7664*

. . . .

PRINTED IN THE UNITED STATES OF AMERICA

by SENTRY PRESS, NEW YORK, N. Y. 10019

Contents

Part IV: The Promise of the New Century

Preface

AFTER commerce, industry. Foreign commerce, the keynote of early American economic development and thought, gave place to industrial expansion in the period ushered in by the Civil War. The first two volumes of *The Economic Mind in American Civilization*, which traced the years from 1606 to 1865, were focused on the spirit of foreign commerce, for this brought the treasure, the goods, and the profits—the visible signs of the importance of a nation in the world. Agriculture, domestic industry, and internal commerce were all directed toward the expansion of foreign trade.

America had inherited from Europe a hierarchic, ordered social organism. The merchant—cosmopolitan, agile and sophisticated—could manage in such a society rather comfortably. But the free functioning of commerce was inherently opposed to the principles of arbitrary rule and political privilege manifested by such a society; and the struggle opened the way for the infiltration of democratic ideals. The very growth of democracy, as symbolized in the names of Jefferson and Jackson, was involved in the contest.

Between the Revolutionary War and the Civil War "aristocratic," or "monopolistic," law-created privileges were gradually diminished and eliminated. Enlightened opinion maintained that a government with too great powers created sinecures and parasites: such had been the historic experience. Liberal-minded men were concerned with restraining the growth of government in order to enlarge economic opportunity. Laissez faire and the aspirations of the common man merged in the conflict against aristocratic tradition. The liberals were, therefore, not anti-capitalistic, but rather anti-"feudal." They knew, of course, that unrestrained individualism was not always desirable, but they firmly believed that any evil effects would be checked by the enterprising individuals in the great rivalry of wealth-seeking. Though there were certain exceptions, the domestic economy did not appear to require much overseeing.

The period after the Civil War maintained a good deal of continuity with earlier economic concerns, but these were subject to fresh emphases. The money problem remained prominent, although the issues and parties were not precisely the same. The elimination of depression and unemployment and the proper methods of running the money economy were the subject of much controversy in the business community. That the farmers and, to a lesser extent, labor groups were also interested in these controversies there is no question, but there is little to indicate that they supplied much of the leadership.

In matters other than currency and the tariff, the age was indeed new. All too rapidly a vast domestic economy rose and proliferated. The growth of large business units was accompanied by striking inequality of wealth, and a large and permanent wage-earner class developed. This had not been foreseen by liberal opinion, and even conservative economists had thought that the United States might escape the sight of great wealth for the few alongside poverty for a goodly number. It was believed that a rough equality would generally prevail. Now some writers began to argue that great wealth would stimulate the rise of a leisure class, which would impart culture and taste to the lower classes—a European rather than a native tradition.

As these new economic problems grew to threatening proportions, the practice of going to the government for help was revived and intensified. From a substantial part of the business community, as well as from farmers and laborers, came demands for "cheap" money. Small business wished the government to curb large business, and many interests clamored for high tariffs. Shippers asked the government to prevent the extortions and inequities of the railroads. Labor organizations demanded that the government limit immigration, legalize the eight-hour day, and establish bureaus of labor. Farmers asked for agricultural education, for experimental stations, for the elimination of competing imports; some bankers yearned for a more adequate central banking system. And the underlying humanitarian spirit was irked by child labor and pressed for protection of women in industry. Each of these groups was not wholly homogeneous within itself. This was particularly true of the business community, where interests often conflicted. And always there was the traditional feeling that State power was by nature mechanical and despotic in tendency and could not achieve that moral regeneration of man so essential to the efficient, harmonious working and progress of society. The growth of governmental controls was tortuous and gradual. Only in times of stress was the increase in the number of restraints noticeable; and at no time could the process be said to be going fast; caution was always the keynote, with England rather than the so-called "bureaucratic" countries on the continent of Europe as the model of action. New bureaus and offices were regarded askance. The government was hesitant and groping. Only as knowledge increased and as means of action became more adequate did government gain confidence. With the support of public opinion, government found it possible to moderate the excesses of individualism in one area after another. Evils which had been considered inevitable came increasingly to be regarded as subject to positive remedies. In our own century government became readier to confront the problems of depression and unemployment, responding in no mean measure to the advice and demands of reformers.

These reformers were a miscellaneous lot—railroad regulators, anti-monopolists, conservationists, tax reformers, monetary reformers, anti-tariff agitators, Christian Socialists, bank critics, labor leaders, agrarian crusaders, and some economists. They did not belong to the same class or have similar aims. Many were concerned with reform in only one particular field, ignoring the need in other areas. Now and then large groups of otherwise unrelated interests joined together to achieve a common end. However, a number of reformers were active on a variety of fronts, recalling the old conception that a country comprised a variety of interests, each of which was entitled to consideration in achieving a balance. And even in these cases reform was essentially empiric and flexible rather than tightly systematic, moderate rather than radical.

The earlier period had witnessed a number of radical movements aimed at demolishing and reconstructing society. Young America had offered the greatest opportunity for experimentation. Colonies of many hues were tried out—Owenite, Fourierite, and anarchistic, let alone the many strictly religious ones. These idealistic communities were escapes from society, and yet their essentially sanguine promoters hoped that the colonies would provide an example for the reconstruction of society. Their relatively brief existences hardly affected the course of events; but the literature they produced contained some of the most incisive and passionate critiques of the money economy.

In the post-Civil War period radicalism merged with reformism, particularly with respect to the growing labor movement. Many clergymen became more articulate in proposing social measures. Another feature was the gradual loss of interest in community experiments. At the start there was a strong infiltration of European currents, notably that which is generally called Marxian. Specific radical movements, however, attracted relatively few. The label "socialism" was itself a serious drawback. It was rather Henry George's *Progress and Poverty* and Bellamy's *Looking Backward*, the effects of which reached far beyond the United States, that gave a foundation to widespread native radicalism. But the atmosphere of America turned this radicalism into reform channels. By the turn of the century the interest in sweeping social reconstruction had declined. But the various movements had highlighted evils and helped to infuse reform with a certain sharp earnestness.

In all this the economists of the United States played an active role. They were, by and large, better trained than those in the pre-Civil War period, and yet they remained fresh in their approach. A group of progressives in each new generation carried the ideas of their predecessors a step forward, bearing witness to the need of change and adaptation in a dynamic economic order. They were perhaps always a minority in the profession, but they deeply influenced the history of America.

By the end of the period there was a definite recognition of the importance of sophisticated, professional economic thought for the intelligent operation of society. From the most specialized investigations of marginal analysis to the broadest study of business cycles, disinterested inquiries elaborated the structure and functioning of economic life, and new techniques of research were developed. The progress of his science endowed the economist with a greater objectivity, though times of crisis, one must admit, put a great strain on it, and he seemed to follow blind "instinct." Professionalism had its price, not the least of which was the deprecation and lessening contribution of the brilliant and self-taught amateur.

One enduring predilection, however, colored the thinking of many influential economists. While they realized that large units had the value of great material efficiency, they felt that a scheme of small units and close personal relations was more desirable. The question was how to attain the benefits of large units without losing all the social advantages of small ones. They quieted their misgivings by assuming that large-scale units would reach a point beyond which they would prove inefficient. Although that point seemed always to recede, they remained confident that an effective solution would be found. There was also an influential though declining number of economists who considered the growth of combinations and monopolies as inevitable in the march of progress. These men considered government control coercive, and they were among the most forceful critics of "excesses of democracy." They clamored for a stronger executive power at the expense of the legislative power, for while they felt that the mass of men could not be trusted with their political destinies, they could manage their economic tasks without government help. The community, however, detected in this philosophy a nostalgia for aristocracy, and economists began to regard monopoly as too complex to be dismissed as inevitable by means of old abstractions.

I have attempted in this book to catch the ideas that expressed the popular as well as the technical, the side currents as well as the dominant stream. The conservative tradition, the reform and liberal spirit, are examined. The germination, the slow growth, and the clash of ideas—those which are now taken for granted and those which are still in controversy—are traced. The various economic ideas are presented in their social setting; the meaning and evolution of important thinkers, whether professional economists or not, are clarified. The rise of new viewpoints both in theory and practice is portrayed. Passion and emotion played a role in economics alongside reason, and I have tried to look beyond the rhetoric to the positive and practical course of theory and policy.

A considerable amount of personal correspondence has been used as well as public and private collections throughout the country, little-known published works, newspapers, and periodicals. Government documents, including hearings, have also been examined, and authors of anonymous works have in many cases been tracked down.

A sequel volume will carry the story nearer to our own day, possibly to the beginning of World War II.

This book is not clear of debt. A number of friends were of great aid, practically and spiritually. A grant from the Council for Research in the Social Sciences of Columbia University has made possible the extensive research involved. Dr. Nathan Savitsky's warm and exceptionally generous counsel sustained me in the effort to go on. In discussions with Professor Sidney Weintraub of St. John's College many a knotty point became clearer. Several parts of this book have benefited from the shrewd reactions of my colleague Professor Carter Goodrich. Professor Solomon F. Bloom of Brooklyn College, with characteristic generosity, helped clarify specific parts of the manuscript and draw together the manifold threads. Mr. DeWitt Hardy aided in editing the final draft of the manuscript. Miss Mary Barnard laid aside her own work to prepare the index. My wife, Sarah Sorrin Dorfman, seconded me with effective collaboration and unflagging confidence.

It is a grief to me that as this volume went to press my revered teacher, Professor Wesley C. Mitchell, passed away. His faith, encouragement, and guidance presided over my labors for nearly a quarter of a century.

JOSEPH DORFMAN

Columbia University
November 1948

There were other supporters of gradualism. Horace White, the financial editor of the influential *Chicago Tribune* and later editor-in-chief of the powerful *New York Evening Post*, declared that the best way to return to specie payments would be to allow the country to grow up to the volume of the existing currency rather than to shrink the currency to the actual size of the country—a process involving panics and bankruptcy.[25] George Opdyke, New York private banker and economist, who had been an early proponent of government inconvertible currency, also argued that the country's growth would in time require the "excess" currency, at which time the greenbacks would become automatically convertible.[26]

Other men of prominence, however, wanted no change. Silas M. Stilwell, a wealthy lawyer and businessman and a former Whig officeholder, flatly supported greenbacks. He had been one of the most active sponsors and promoters of the national banking system. In a lecture before a group of New York capitalists he declared that any substantial contraction of greenbacks would check, if not entirely suspend, the progress of all our great enterprises; for, as reserves, they were in fact the basis of bank issues and credit. Should the legal tenders be withdrawn, the banks would have to be supplied with an adequate amount of cash or suspend. He hoped that Congress would not be influenced by the "stereotyped" ideas in the money centers. If Congress would leave gold for foreign commerce and legal tenders for local business, we should be emancipated from British rule and thus be a truly independent country.

When leading financiers and businessmen of Michigan appealed to Stilwell to suggest remedies for the depressed "trade and extortionate rate of interest" in "accord with settled principles of economic laws," Stilwell amplified his paper-money stand. The great amount of our indebtedness to Europe, he wrote, must be paid for by shipments of gold and produce. Consequently not for years would the exchange rate be equalized and the gold premium eliminated. This he considered all to the good: the high rate of gold would benefit all the nation's great interests, enabling farmers to obtain a high price for their export produce and aiding domestic manufactures by acting as a tariff barrier. The law of commercial exchange would compel the country to abandon gold as a currency, and it would be wise, therefore, to leave its movements to the great law of demand and supply until we paid our foreign debts with gold and produce and became a creditor instead of a debtor nation.

Domestic trade, according to Stilwell, would be in a precarious position if our credit and solvency depended upon the quantity of gold or of any article subject to foreign demand. The price of gold was controlled by the price of foreign exchange, and the price of exchange was governed by the foreign indebtedness. Our paper currency, not being an article for export, like gold, was not depreciated or increased in value by the price gold bore in our markets.

The principles laid down in books on political economy, he explained, did not apply to the United States, because the balance of trade in a broad sense was against the United States. He proposed that the amount of greenbacks should always be equal to the amount of national bank notes, for then the banks could always redeem their notes with money. The limitation on the amount of national bank notes, moreover, must be eliminated, for restriction or "monopoly" checked business expansion.[27]

Hard-money advocates sharply criticized this selfish opposition by business and financial interests to the resumption of specie payments. Charles Francis Adams, the eminent diplomat and pre-Civil War financial writer, the son of one president and grandson of another, expressed great mortification that a multitude of the best people should fear that they would suffer heavy losses if the nation returned to specie payments. His noted son, Brooks Adams, asserted that the opposition to the national banks arose from the fear that contraction would reduce profits.[28] Dr. Henry Bronson, eminent student of the early history of paper money in Connecticut, pointed out that among the great gainers from depreciated greenbacks were the railroad companies, because of their large outstanding issue of bonds. And he thought that businessmen were especially ignorant of the principles of international trade in that they believed that the huge and increasing foreign indebtedness rendered impossible for some time to come a return to the specie standard.[29]

Gamaliel Bradford, Boston private banker and learned student of economics, neatly summed up the whole state of affairs. "The great mass of men," he wrote, "whether engaged in trade or not, have but little faith in the existence of any principles or laws governing the movements of the currency and monetary affairs. They look upon inflations and contractions, upon stagnations and crises, as the results of the blind working of some unseen power; and when the tempest overtakes them in its course, they are inclined, like the

Mahometan, to bow their heads, with the exclamation, 'Allah is great!' " [30]

The Panic of 1873 and the subsequent sharp decline of prices intensified the monetary controversy. When the panic occurred, the New York financial community, led by Cornelius Vanderbilt, spearheaded a successful demand that the government reissue the greenbacks which it had withdrawn from circulation.[31] This accelerated the demand for more issues, although many critics were reiterating that panics could not be cured by legislation. Representative Alexander Mitchell of Wisconsin declared: We can never "overrule the irrevocable, inevitable laws of political economy [so] as to enable those who live beyond their incomes 'to make both ends meet,' or to insure profitable returns to those who invest their means in undertakings which can never pay interest. . . . The more commercial a nation is, the more sharp and general will these revulsions be." [32]

Thomas W. Olcott, president of the Mechanics' and Farmers' Bank of Albany, New York, and opponent of greenbacks, complained in 1874 that "we have too many cooks to have good financial broth at Washington. How can it be otherwise when bankers and merchants and economists are so divided and conflicting in their views?" The New York City bankers, with all their experience and intelligence, could not agree on fundamental principles, not even on what was a usable reserve: "We all know that a large reserve in the banks in that city is indispensable, and yet what nonsense to call that a reserve which is legally locked up and unavailable." [33]

David A. Wells, shortly after the panic, offered an interesting explanation of unemployment. He believed that the chief cause of the unemployment was technological advance, which caused overproduction in the sense that labor was in excess of "any present demand." Heretofore, he said, the laborer always had the alternative of taking up public land, whereby he quickly could become a capitalist. But with that recourse just about gone, and with the growth of highly efficient labor-saving devices, the country would be faced with a permanent pauper class unless new wants could be found whose satisfaction would increase the field of employment for labor. Wells' solution again was to lower or eliminate tariffs on raw materials and semi-finished materials, on the ground that the sale of such goods in the United States would enable the countries supplying them to purchase our surplus factory production.[34]

Congress, in 1875, endeavored to placate one faction of the easy-money school by removing all limits on the total volume of national bank notes and to placate the hard-money advocates by ordering specie payments resumed in 1879 and fractional paper currency replaced by silver coins. This came about largely because the dominant sentiment of the people of property had apparently crystallized around resumption in gold. The powerful *Chicago Tribune* became adamant against greenbacks when the demand for redemption of the government debt in greenbacks became the great political issue of the campaign of 1868. And when Carey went beyond his original limits for greenbacks, a large number of Pennsylvania industrialists, including Joseph Wharton, who had formerly supported Carey and his disciple Kelley, denounced both. Certainly in the financial capital it appeared that sentiment was strongly in favor of resumption. Stilwell bitterly complained in March 1875 that the powerful New York newspapers no longer would print his communications: "If I am right, and I know I am, then is it not un-Christian, and cruel to our idle and starving poor for a great Christian journal to suppress testimony, where the Truth is so important? . . . I have 47 papers edited by honest, able, and fair men who go for Truth. These papers are always open to me. But the *Herald, Tribune,* and *Times* drive the Truth from their doors." [35]

The ardent greenbackers were naturally dissatisfied with the legislation and continued to push forward a variant derived from the pre-Civil War proposals of the New York merchant Edward Kellogg. They would make the greenbacks the sole currency, but prevent any "excess" or deficiency by making them interconvertible with government bonds, bearing the low interest rate of 3.65 per cent.[36] Among the more eloquent advocates of this movement was Wendell Phillips, a leader in many diverse reform movements, who saw in the greenback scheme the solution of all the nation's economic ills. Under the system then in force, he declared, the control of the currency was vested in a few irresponsible bank directors; the elastic greenback plan would rightly place control in the hands of businessmen, who by the nature of our institutions could be entrusted with this great power. Just as the businessmen knew how many commodities to make at any moment, so they could best decide how much currency was needed at any moment by the people. They would keep it in the form of bonds or draw it forth in greenbacks as the hour dictated.[37]

In 1876 the scheme was taken up by the new Independent Party, more popularly known as the Greenback Party, as the primary means of achieving the "full development of all legitimate business." Their presidential candidate was the New York philanthropist, iron magnate, and protectionist Peter Cooper. According to Cooper, overproduction was caused by underconsumption. His reasoning followed this line: the policy of contracting government credit induced contraction of all other credit; this, in turn, led to a diminution of enterprise and the consequent lowering of earnings; smaller earnings led to underconsumption, which was the true end result and not the superficially obvious overproduction.

The Greenback Party polled approximately only 1 per cent of the vote, but the continuance of the depression increased the strength of the greenback cause. In 1878 Congress ordered the retirement of the greenbacks stopped, but the original House provision, removing the requirement of inconvertibility, was dropped, and the existing amount of $346,681,016 was made permanent. In the same year the different varieties of greenback leaders got together and organized the National Party, which later changed its name to the National Greenback-Labor Party. The obscure character of its chief plank testified to the miscellaneous groups involved. Its convention demanded that government provide money "adequate to the full employment of labor, the equitable distribution of its products, and the requirements of business, fixing a minimum amount per capita of the population as near as may be, and otherwise regulating its value by wise and equitable provisions of law, so that the rate of interest will secure to labor its just reward." A little more definite was the statement of William A. Carsey, secretary of the General Committee of the party, who described his business as a "bricklayer and sometimes an editor." He bluntly stated that new issues would be used partly as loans to would-be settlers on the public lands, but largely for a vast system of internal improvements to relieve unemployment. This, he declared, would lead to a desirable inflation of prices, in view of which all speculative men would invest in business and give employment. He acknowledged that inflation was usually followed by a panic, but he considered panics and depressions inevitable: "I want ten years of prosperity, and by the time a period of depression comes around, we will not care about it." [38]

In the presidential campaign of 1880 the chief plank was still obscure, simply stating: "All money, whether metallic or paper, should be issued by the government, and not by or through banking corporations, and when so issued should be a full legal tender for all debts, public and private." Despite additional planks covering almost every reform, presidential candidate General James B. Weaver of Ohio received a vote of only 300,000.

More enduring was the "free silver" movement, which included some opponents of greenbacks as well as supporters. Their demand was the restoration of the bimetallic standard. This standard had disappeared by default with the passage of the Coinage Act of 1873, which, by eliminating the coinage of the silver dollar, in effect established a single gold standard. It became an issue after the enactment of resumption legislation in 1875. Henry C. Carey now joined the free silver forces, though this was in direct contradiction to his former position.[39] In 1876, in view of the panic in the London silver market in July of that year and the continued decline of the price of silver, his disciple Kelley submitted a bill calling for the restoration of the old "double standard" as it had existed before the Act of 1873, that is, with the silver dollar freely coined and full legal tender at 16 to 1.

Congress appointed an eight-man commission, composed of three members each from the House and Senate and two experts, to hold hearings and report on the entire question. The chairman was a protectionist from the silver state of Nevada, Senator John P. Jones. In testifying before this body, I. Smith Homans, Jr., wanted to go even further than Kelley, demanding the ratio of the Latin Monetary Union—15½ to 1.[40] The majority report, signed by Chairman Jones, Senator Lewis V. Bogy of Missouri, Representatives Richard P. Bland of Missouri and George Willard of Michigan, and expert William S. Groesbeck of Ohio, favored free silver. It stated that the decline in the value of silver was due not to the heavy production of silver but to its demonetization by the United States and continental European countries; that the shortage of money in the face of increasing business transactions resulted in falling prices, which, in turn, led capitalists to hoard their money rather than invest, since falling prices could not be expected to cover original costs. For the same reason, the report went on, enterprisers feared to borrow, and their previous debts became a crushing burden. The result was stagnation of business with all its fearful consequences for the laboring class.

The report therefore recommended the restoration of the double standard, which would supply the basic prerequisite, steadiness in the value of money. The law authorizing the interchangeable use of the two metals as money would establish and maintain their market and legal ratio. Upon the slightest divergence between the two, the law of the double standard would create a new and constant demand for the cheaper metal, thereby suspending the demand for the dearer one, and, until equivalency should be restored, would furnish a supply of the dearer metal to the markets of the world. It thus operated on demand and supply, which were the sole factors of value. The report significantly expressed no sympathy with greenbacks.

The three remaining members submitted two minority reports. Professor Francis Bowen of Harvard and Representative R. L. Gibson of Louisiana argued that it was impossible to maintain a given double standard, for the market ratio would inevitably vary from the legal ratio; consequently, according to Gresham's law, a traditional principle of economics, the overvalued or cheaper metal would drive out the undervalued or more expensive metal. The other minority report came from George S. Boutwell, formerly Secretary of the Treasury under Grant, and at the time senator from Massachusetts. He agreed with the majority that a bimetallic standard was desirable, but he wanted it to be international; and he believed, in any event, that the introduction of silver as a currency should be postponed until the effort to secure the co-operation of other nations had been faithfully tried.[41]

The ideas of the majority report found much support among publicists. John Philip Phillips, wealthy New Haven physician and lawyer and former greenbacker, advanced in *A Primer of Political Economy* (1879) the idea that the principle of the bimetallic standard be obtained by requiring that in all future contracts gold and silver be made semi-legal tenders; that is, all coin debts should be legally payable only by delivering one-half their amount in gold dollars and one-half in silver dollars.[42] And there were some highly respectable individuals who maintained that even if the bimetallic standard led to an exclusive silver currency, this would not be undesirable. Thus, for example, Thomas W. Olcott declared that silver was intrinsically more valuable than gold, was more gradual in its production, and commercially commanded the market of the world. True, silver was cumbrous and heavy, but so were clothes in winter, and the inconvenience could be readily endured as a guard against impending dangers which far outweighed all consideration of cheapness and inconvenience in handling. His remedy was to remonetize silver and prohibit gradually the circulation of all paper money worth less than twenty dollars. His most significant argument for this was that since the precious metals had given us a special prominence and power in turning the wheels which moved the machinery of the world, we should pause before losing one-half of it by demonetization.[43]

Congress partially placated the silver forces by passing in 1878, over President Hayes' veto, the Bland-Allison Act. This restored the old silver dollar as full legal tender; in place of unlimited coinage it provided that the government should purchase for coinage from two to four million dollars of silver monthly. This legislation, together with the resumption of specie payments and the return of prosperity, quieted the interest in monetary questions for the time being. Besides, other serious problems were demanding attention. These spread far beyond the establishment of a satisfactory monetary and fiscal policy into the whole organization of our industrial society.

PROBLEMS OF INDUSTRIAL RECONSTRUCTION

As might be expected of an expanding capitalism, the character and method of investment was of real public concern, and there was a considerable outcry against the evils of stock-market speculation. The very respectable *Boston Daily Advertiser* compared unfavorably the current practices of the New York Stock Exchange with those of its early days, when cases of overreaching and fraud had been rare. "It would be perhaps saying too much," it admitted, "that the members were not possessed of the same speculative traits that exist at the present day"; but in those days the occurrences were not treated by the "body politic as shrewdness and bold financial schemes, as now, but were branded as fraud and punished as such." On the matter of remedies, however, the predominant opinion was well expressed by the San Francisco *Mining and Scientific Press*. Public sentiment was opposed to stock-market speculation, it editorialized, but there was no agreement among the "ablest jurists" as to the means of stopping it. Perhaps it would be best to let the thing run in the hope that it would ultimately wear itself out.[44]

The monopolistic practices of the railroads were also attracting public attention. The growth of the railroads brought many advantages, but also created a number of problems. The government encouraged expansion by offering vast land grants to the companies. To the first railroad corporations that jointly spanned the continent, the Union Pacific and the Central Pacific, the government extended in addition a loan of government bonds. The opportunities for profit-making were increased as the promoters organized separate companies to handle construction, and the construction company for the Union Pacific, the Crédit Mobilier, was involved in a national scandal when a congressional investigation in 1873 revealed that the outgoing vice-president, Schuyler Colfax, and such prominent congressmen as Kelley and James A. Garfield, had been given shares of stock.

The "modern" financing methods which were widely used by railroad companies gave rise to widespread complaint that promoters or controllers of the companies had engaged in "stock-watering" and other forms of financial manipulations. In the West the railroads were accused of charging exorbitant freight rates; in the East they were accused of discriminating in rates between shippers and between localities. The consolidation of railroads and the use of "pools" to apportion traffic which would otherwise be competitive raised charges of monopoly. The complainants included such diverse groups as Western farmer organizations, the Chicago Board of Trade, and the New York Chamber of Commerce.

Concrete legislative action against the railroads was first taken in the West. A national farmers' organization, the Patrons of Husbandry, more popularly known as the Grange, led the movement. The Grange, established in 1869 to better social life among the farmers, had originally been a secret society, but it soon developed into an effective political force. As a result of its efforts, states in the Midwest passed acts fixing maximum rates for the railroads. The companies appealed to the courts with the old cry that such acts attacked the sanctity of charters.

David A. Wells, who was now prominent in the railroad world, declared that the Supreme Court would hold unconstitutional legislation hostile to the railroads. Such legislation, he declared, violated the Fourteenth Amendment, which provided that no state should deprive a person of life, liberty, or property without due process of law. A charter was an executed contract, and no state legislature had the power to "exercise the attributes of ownership" over property which it did not own or possess.[45] But in 1876 the Supreme Court, in *Munn* v. *Illinois*, upheld the Granger Acts. In upholding Illinois' right to fix grain elevator charges, the Supreme Court declared that state legislatures had authority to regulate "private property 'affected with a public interest'" and that property became "clothed with a public interest when used in a manner to make it of public consequence."

The implications of this decision did not go unchallenged. A dissenting judge, Associate Justice Stephen J. Field, complained that the decision practically destroyed "the guarantees the Constitution intended for the protection of the rights of private property." [46] A leading writer on constitutional law, Thomas McIntyre Cooley, Chief Justice of the Michigan Supreme Court and Dean of the University of Michigan Law School, later a railroad receiver and a member of railroad pools, also took issue. He granted that the state had the right to regulate property and business. But if this power were unlimited, freedom would be precarious. What, then, were its limits? In colonial days, he said, public regulation of prices was common, but was eventually abandoned because wise men, from observation and reflection, concluded that the laws determining prices were inherent in the nature of civilized society, and that their operation would not be improved by legislative interference.

The word "monopoly," Cooley asserted, had an ominous sound to American ears, and whatever found itself called such was already condemned in the public mind. He contended that a monopoly obtained by virtue of the exceptional location and special advantages of one's business, or by an exclusive ownership of something having a public demand, was lawful. Even if a single individual owned all of some essential metal, the state would be violating the general principle of democratic government if it attempted to fix the price of that metal. He applied the same principle of freedom to the widespread monopolies effected by the combination of all those who had required wares or services to sell. To illustrate the point he used trade unions. Whatever might be thought of the wisdom of trade unions, he declared, so long as they attempted only to regulate their own charges the state should abstain from interference. If these unions let others alone, they must be let alone by others. The state could not say that their members should take less than they would voluntarily consent to take. The principle which must apply to trade unions in general, Cooley concluded, must be applicable to other peaceable combinations.

Perhaps the most significant feature of Cooley's analysis was his attempt to establish definitely that profits were as much a property as the physical thing itself, that to deny that profits were property was to make a mockery of the constitutional protection of property. After citing Bentham's "idea of property" as consisting in "an established expectation; in the persuasion of power to derive a certain advantage from the object, according to the nature of the case," Cooley went on to say that the "capability of property, by means of the labor or expense or both bestowed upon it, to be made available in producing profits, is a potential quality in property, and as sacredly protected by the Constitution as the thing itself in which the quality inheres." [47] In a later period, when Cooley was chairman of the Interstate Commerce Commission, he found himself in action questioning his conception of property, but by that time the courts had gone a long way toward accepting it.

The foremost student of railroads, Charles Francis Adams, Jr., a brother of Brooks Adams, although recognizing the evils in the existing situation, opposed any "coercive" government control of railroads. In 1869 he wrote so striking an essay on the antics of the notorious "railroad barons"—Cornelius Vanderbilt, Jay Gould, and Daniel Drew—with the Erie Railroad that it became a classic on high finance. These upstart geniuses in railroad promotion, finance, and warfare were to him a "knot of adventurers, men of broken fortune, without character and without credit," who took possession of an "artery of commerce more important than was ever the Appian Way," and made "levies, not only upon it for their emolument, but, through it, upon the whole business of a nation." He wrote his friend Wells: "The old robber barons were children in the art of thieving—it is only now reduced to a system; poor old Rob Roy must hide his diminished head before Drew, or Vanderbilt, or Jay Gould."

But government ownership, Adams always maintained, would destroy the advantages of competition; government regulation of rates and profits would destroy the incentive of companies to develop their business and, worst of all, would lead to greater corruption. "He who owns the thing knows that he must also own the legislature which regulates the thing." In every case the "man who owns will possess himself of the man who regulates." The most effective regulation, therefore, would be through a state commission, which would rely on publicity and the power of public opinion rather than on compulsion to force the railroads to make desired changes. In accordance with Adams' views, Massachusetts established in 1869 the Board of Railroad Commissioners, with the power to insist on uniform accounting methods for the railroads.

For a while Adams advocated one form of state interference: that Massachusetts should obtain the benefits of competition without the evils of combination or cutthroat competition by extending and becoming sole owner of one large road in which it already had a heavy investment. He granted that this proposal did not accord with the general principles of the science of political economy; but, after citing the "greatest of living economists," John Stuart Mill, on the principles of laissez faire, he said that the system of rail transportation was an exception. His argument was that the cotton factory and the shoe factory were exempt from all government interference because these businesses were completely subject to the laws of supply and demand and of competition. If their owners obtained an inordinate return others would enter these businesses, and the profit would speedily fall to the average rate. If capital and industry were free to enter and withdraw, no monopoly could exist. Competition prevailed where the competing forces were too numerous to combine. It assumed large and free demand and many sources of supply. But the very nature of railroad traffic excluded such a possibility except in very special cases. The best route was of necessity already occupied, and a new line must be costlier. The shortest, safest, and the speediest route only the old line could supply; and the fact that it could also supply it cheapest would usually deter capital from intrusion.

Therefore, except at the few competing points for through traffic, the points where the railroads converged, railroad transportation was an absolute monopoly. The statute books, said Adams, bulged with futile laws to stop the practice of charging more for a shorter than for a longer distance. Railroad men frankly justified this extortion at local points on the ground that it was necessary if their roads were to live. If they hauled for bare costs to competing points, then they had to receive double profits at the local points where no competition existed. In other words, while ordinary competition resulted in reduced and equalized prices, railroad competition resulted in local inequalities and arbitrarily raised and depressed prices. But if the state owned one road the competition and comparison existing between the public and private lines would keep pure the administration of each and induce the most efficient management.[48] In practice, however, the Massachusetts legislature refused to follow Adams' advice, and by 1876 Adams had accepted pools as the only sound remedy, provided they were coupled with state advisory public service commissions. As other railroad men acted in like manner, businessmen in the great railroad centers of Chicago and New York began complaining that the discriminatory rates set by the pools enabled less favorably situated commercial centers to obtain the Western traffic. Adams tried to explain through the columns of the *Atlantic Monthly* that the source of the trouble lay in the fact that, because pooling arrangements were not enforceable by the courts, they frequently broke down; that this led to a revival of cutthroat competition, which was followed by greater and more complete monopoly in accordance with the law of the survival of the fittest.

The misguided populace, according to him, attacked the pools and combinations on unsound economic grounds. They asserted that combination, even when formed to hold ruthless competition in check, if not to end it, must eventually raise prices. But he contended that despite "what ought to be, or what the economical treatises tell us ought to be," practical experience increasingly showed "that there are limitations even to the economical working of the principle of competition in trade." True, competition had forced the railroad system up to its present high state of efficiency, but it was achieved at such an excessive cost and by the creation of such excess capacity that the process could not be continued indefinitely. Where competing roads existed, each jealous of its petty independence, the extreme competition brought about their own destruction and the derangement of the community. At the same time Adams informed the "wild" Grangers that since in the case of railroads the number of competitors necessarily was limited and none could withdraw, competition resulted in the absorption of the weaker by the stronger, with the competition merely a "phase of evolution."

With his experience as a railroad and pool official behind him, Adams informed Congress in 1880 that while national railroad regulation was desirable, such regulation should take the form of a legalized pool or federation, with the government holding only advisory powers. Federation, he said, was the only means of restraining the pace of the consolidating movement, for unregulated competition would eventually lead to one big monopoly, whereas the federation system would enable the weak to survive. Any attempt by Congress to impose "coercive" regulation would fail. On one side were the corporations, wielding immense power through their wealth and manifold connections, and on the other was the community at large, a mass of unorganized individuals. In wealth, in organization, in power of obstruction, in power of terrorism, it might be said, one was infinitely greater than the other.[49] And Colonel Albert Fink, the outstanding leader of the organization of pools, pushed this logic to an extreme by calling for a "corporation of corporations" that would embrace the entire railroad system.

Closely connected with the railroad "monopoly" problem was the cry of monopoly now raised against two other important industries, anthracite coal and oil. The Pennsylvania anthracite railroads owned most of the former, and special railroad rebates were very helpful to John D. Rockefeller's operations in the latter. Adams felt that these combination movements merely indicated that the natural trend of many industries was toward this form of organization. Thus, in defense of the Pennsylvania coal combination, he argued that a responsible combination, even of monopolies, insuring a steady supply at regular prices was preferable to the chaos previously existing.[50]

The popular publisher, playwright, and author O. B. Bunce defended such combinations more elaborately. Spasmodic production, he argued, hurt the consumer, because it made prices uneven and inflicted cruel injury upon labor and operators. Unregulated and unrestrained production disarranged the complex machinery of modern society, stirring the whole energies of the people into producing at one period and arresting them at another. The resulting cessation of production created unemployment, reduced consumption, and hence rendered "recovery the very labor indeed of Sisyphus." The only apparent remedy was for the producers, by joint action, to adjust production to the means possessed by the community for exchanging goods and services.[51]

As industries began to combine, so also did labor. During the mid-seventies an authentic large-scale labor movement first became apparent. The developing factory civilization of the United States found itself face to face with the characteristic problems of such a social and economic order, and many of these problems had to be reckoned with in terms of workers who were rapidly becoming conscious of the advantages of organized self-interest. These problems were highlighted in 1877 by the great national railroad strike against a reduction in wages. Violence resulted, and for the first time federal troops were used in a labor dispute.

A most incisive statement of dominant opinion was that expressed by R. G. Eccles, a distinguished doctor and journalist. "Men must seek for the highest remuneration without combination, compulsion, or restriction," he declared. "Businessmen must seek the highest prices in the same way. . . . Ask the state to do nothing [for the laborer] or you will impose extra burdens upon the worthy and sink them to pauperage. Teach the workingmen to live more economically and practice self-restraint. . . . Teach them that they bring down their own wages, and that this is not their employer's doings. Show them that if their wages descend slowly and steadily, it will avoid a crash of business, and, making goods correspondingly cheap, do them good rather than harm in the end." [52]

Nevertheless, there was a growing sympathy for trade unions. The highly respectable Albert S. Bolles, a distinguished student of public finance and banking and editor of the *Norwich Morning Bulletin*, not only supported trade unions but contended that if employers would reveal the state of their business affairs much of the antagonism between employers and laborers would disappear.[53] Dr. William Elder, one of the many disciples of Carey, admitted the need for trade unions as a counterweight to the power and combinations of employers, but he felt that their "unnatural" insistence upon fixing wage rates showed that the workingmen apparently intended to take the rule of the world's business into their own hands, for their own benefit.[54]

In addition, agitation was growing for a law establishing an eight-hour working day. This movement had gained impetus during the Civil War under the leadership of Ira Steward, a machinist.[55] He based his arguments on the orthodox economics of John Stuart Mill; namely, that wages ultimately were determined by the standard of living of the workingmen. Given the leisure an eight-hour day provided, he said, the workingmen could develop new tastes. This would lead to such a concentrated demand by the workingmen for higher wages that it could not be resisted by the employers, and the higher wages would not raise prices because the greater market for goods would lead to the substantial economies of mass production.

Proponents of the eight-hour day also claimed that such legislation would raise wages because the supply of labor in relation to the demand would be reduced. In the absence of such legislation, they argued, great technological advance would prove to be a curse to labor because it would cause considerable unemployment and thereby depress wages. W. Godwin Moody, whose latest venture was in the printing business, carried the Steward logic a step further in a paper that came to be widely discussed. He demanded the establishment of a national commission to adjust hours from time to time so as to provide full employment, claiming that otherwise machinery which should uplift the people would further oppress them by creating surplus labor and depressions. He maintained that agriculture no longer could absorb the surplus labor created by technological improvement, because agriculture was one of the businesses most thoroughly revolutionized by machinery and was already one of the most uncertain and unprofitable of callings. Later, in 1883, Moody proposed that the working day be reduced to six hours to provide full employment and thus increase "the number of consumers, the amount of consumption, and demand for additional production." [56]

Carey, however, complained that measures limiting the working day constituted despotism and injured labor by causing a withdrawal of capital. Such laws, he wrote, assumed the erroneous notion that labor and capital were naturally hostile to one another. Beginning with this fear of capital, the trade unions proceeded to another error, the "fear of competition in their own class for employment," because they thought the market for labor would become overcrowded. This was not so, for "in the nature of things . . . there is no possibility that labor shall ever fail of its opportunities if its market be kept free and fairly balanced. There has never yet been a day in the world's history when the productive industries were at all adequate to the wants of consumers. . . . There is possibly a limit to the consumption of food, as there is to the area and fertility of the earth; but their respective limits are providentially adjusted to each other step by step through all the stages of their growth; whereas, with respect to all other industries, supply creates demand." [57]

Out of this controversy some action developed. A few states passed limited eight-hour laws, stipulating that other hours could be arranged through specific contracts. Congress in 1868 reduced the working day of federal employees to eight hours, but as interpreted by government authorities the act involved a corresponding reduction of wages. It was only after years of agitation that Congress finally decided in favor of reduced hours without wage cuts.

These were hesitant steps, but other social legislation was not moving at all. Factory legislation was still in its infancy. The problem of child labor was causing considerable concern, but the prevailing attitude seemed to be that progress must of necessity be slow. Thus Atkinson expressed the opinion that child labor would be eliminated through the forces of invention and competition. Then he asked what to him was a rhetorical question: "But will that time come soonest if by so-called charitable legislation they [children] are forbidden to work at all?" [58] But people were not so certain that nature should take its course. Perhaps the clearest manifestation of the community's growing concern with improving the conditions of labor was the establishment in a number of states of bureaus of statistics to inquire into labor conditions, the constantly increasing demands for a national bureau, and, above all else, the appointment in 1878 of a congressional committee to inquire into the depression of labor and business. The House of Representatives, in appointing this committee, declared that since labor and the productive interests of the country were suffering severely from causes not yet fully understood, and since "our real and permanent prosperity" was founded and depended "upon labor as the source of all wealth," it was the duty of Congress to ascertain the causes of the prostration and to submit proper measures for relief at the next session.

The committee held extensive hearings and listened to practically every shade of opinion. Horace White, who was at that time considered the foremost student of commercial crises, told the committee that crises did not arise from so-called scarcity of money but from inevitable speculative activity. Economists, said White, generally held that speculative eras arose because the world's enormous productive machinery resulted in surplus production over consumption. This surplus tended to reduce profits to a minimum, that is, less and less every year. Capitalists therefore experimented with new and distant investments, thus causing an era of speculation.

Asked if a public works program was feasible, White declared: The trouble is "there is no place for it to stop. There is nobody to say what employment I shall be engaged in, or how much money I shall earn. I may want to build a railroad to the Pacific, and . . . have I not as good a right to the government means and credit as anybody else has?" [59] Along similar lines George Walker, previously mentioned as an opponent of greenbacks, testified that he was hostile to "non-interference or laissez faire so generally advocated by English economists," but that such a government interference as relieving unemployment through public works was a communist idea which would induce dependence upon government and take away from the workingmen the healthy effect of personal exertion and responsibility.

Walker's presentation of the law of all commercial crises was a little sharper than the usual one. "There are ups and downs of business," he said, "and they are to a certain extent periodical. After a period of great depression there begins gradually a period of activity, which grows . . . until at last it becomes uncontrollable, and a crisis is inevitable. . . . The crisis is caused (to begin at the end of the cycle, in order to lay the foundation for starting again) by an overabsorption into fixed capital of that ready capital which is necessary in order to do business."

Walker held to the usual view of a panic occurring every ten years; White held to a twenty-year interval. Their explanations as to why the Panic of 1873 did not precisely fit the period, since the last serious one had occurred in 1857, were quite diverse. Walker explained that the existence of greenbacks had delayed the appearance of the panic but had increased its intensity. White said that the panic had occurred four years ahead of time because of the great destruction of property during the four-year Civil War.

This confusion of counsel was multiplied by others. Chairman Abram S. Hewitt, a wealthy ironmaster and Peter Cooper's son-in-law, summed up the situation thus: "Many people think the cause [of depression] is too much currency; some think it is too little." Later White admitted that economists themselves were not "sufficiently agreed upon the fundamental principles of commercial crises to command strict attention from the unprofessional classes." [60] Not all the witnesses before the committee even agreed that unemployment was a serious evil. Lyman J. Gage, eminent Chicago banker, and later McKinley's Secretary of the Treasury, declared that there undoubtedly always would be a large number of unemployed persons in all large cities. Unless there was a surplus of labor, the price of labor would be constantly enhanced by the demand for it. The surplus kept the price steady. Fortunately, by the time the committee was ready to submit its report in 1880, the business horizon was bright, so the committee simply recommended that the immigration of Chinese labor be restrained.[61]

But even a wave of prosperity could not solve the social and economic problems raised by the emancipation of the slaves. Emancipation destroyed not only a Southern tradition but an American tradition as well. The Negro had been regarded as an institution; now he had to be considered as a man. The dominant factions in the anti-slavery movement since Jefferson's day had never envisaged the blacks remaining in the South or, for that matter, in any settled part of the Union. Southern whites, having regarded the blacks as inferior for over two centuries, could not tolerate them as equals. Consequently every plan for emancipation had been based on the principle of exporting the blacks. Now, faced with the brute fact that the Negroes must remain, the country was in utter confusion over the steps necessary to secure to them the exercise of their freedom.

The Northern victors were divided. The Republicans were the majority party, and under their banner the war had been waged. But President Lincoln's assassination shortly after the peace led to the accession of Andrew Johnson, a former Democrat from Tennessee, who, along with the Democrats, maintained that the Confederate states should be restored to the Union with their political structures substantially intact. The majority of the Republican Party held that under such conditions the Negroes would not have political and civil rights. The refusal of the Southern states to grant the Negro these rights, and their enactment of vagrancy laws that actually meant servitude, furnished ammunition for the "radical" Republicans. Since they were victorious in the congressional elections of 1866, they were able to override Johnson's vetoes and carry out their plans. These included the retention of federal forces in the South as well as of the Freedmen's Bureau, which was the economic arm of the federal govenment's intervention.

During the war Congress had established the Freedmen's Bureau to take care of the ever-increasing number of slaves freed by the advance of the Union armies. The Bureau was to engage in humanitarian work, relieve immediate distress, adjudicate legal matters, and whenever possible allot the Negroes small farms from abandoned estates on a rental basis. These lands they could buy after a three-year tenancy. After the war Congress extended the work of the Freedmen's Bureau, but this and other Reconstruction measures evoked tremendous opposition from Southern whites. A writer in *DeBow's Review*, the outstanding commercial organ of the South, declared that the Negro population was incapable of self-government and if left to its own devices would rapidly "degenerate into barbarism." [62] One of the leading contributors, George Fitzhugh of Virginia, who before the war had described slavery as ideal communism and capitalism as cannibalism, now declared that a severe black code including "vagrancy laws" was necessary to govern the Negro and preserve white supremacy. He suggested that the burden of supporting the weak and aged blacks should be thrown exclusively on the Negro groups by taxing the income of the strong and healthy Negroes. He disposed of the notion that Negroes be given an education by saying that learning would result in making them idlers. And he warned that whites were resolved never to give up their farms or to grant the blacks the suffrage. [63]

Some confusion arose when a group of South Carolina newspapers, alarmed at the "exorbitant demands" of a state labor convention, suggested to property holders that land be sold to the Negroes who had the means because then "their interest and yours become identical." In this way, they believed, in less than three years every landowner, white or black, who did not "feed on official pap" (the Freedmen's Bureau) would be in the "same ranks of opposition to extravagance, corruption, high taxation, and labor strikes of ignorant men, encouraged by designing demagogues." Such a proposal for economic equality, however, got hopelessly tied up with social rights, and Southern newspapers were indignant when Negroes, having been refused service in white restaurants, sought court action. They denounced the insolence of the Negroes in demanding "what they cannot have, that is, social equality," and as a way to defeat social equality they welcomed white immigration so that they could "beat Sambo at the polls." [64]

The discontent in the South was intensified by the rise of a class of whites whom the plantation aristocracy regarded as white trash. [65] The South's leading literary journal, the *Southern Review*, went all out and denounced American democracy, "the sovereignty of the people," as the source of all evil. It did not even spare the memory of Jefferson, for "Mr. Jefferson, the sage of Monticello," was the mouthpiece of an "unreasoning radicalism." How often in the world of fanatical reformers, complained its editor, the Reverend A. T. Bledsoe, was "the moral freedom of mankind . . . sacrificed in the mad pursuit of personal or civil freedom?" Moral freedom was the freedom sought by the Christian religion—the freedom of man himself from "ignorance, error, vice, from all manner of imperfection and evil, and his restoration to the image of his Maker." He felt that it was the duty of the state to help develop this moral freedom by expedient means, including, if necessary, "the use of personal servitude, or civil despotism itself." The role of slavery had always been to "promote the moral emancipation and freedom of its patients."[66]

Some Southern thinkers asserted that while free labor was always more efficient than slave labor, it could operate only for the welfare of the former slaves so long as the whites controlled the state of affairs. Bradley T. Johnson, a Virginia jurist and a former Confederate general, contended in 1875 that ardent defenders of slavery, among whom he included himself, had never questioned that free labor would produce more and develop the country's resources faster than slave labor, but they had not believed the "negro was sufficiently advanced in civilization as yet to become his own master; and we were convinced that the ordeal of free labor and free competition would be a fiery ordeal for him, and we relied on slavery as a great conservative safeguard in a Democracy." According to Johnson, the "new system" achieved great material advance in Virginia and the whole South wherever the "superior race" was allowed to control affairs.[67] These advocates finally had their way. With the departure of federal troops from South Carolina and Louisiana in 1877 white supremacy was completely restored throughout the South, and the race problem, in both its political and economic aspects, was as far as ever from solution.

From this confusion few significant generalizations can be made. The modernity of many of the arguments is striking, but few were worked out continuously and logically enough to compose a significant economic doctrine. They tended to be opportunistic and superficial. In part this was caused by the scarcity of economic data the economic publicist then had to work with. The Census did not include much usable information; businesses did not publish accurate reports; the current analyses and summaries of trade and price figures were far from adequate. In consequence the publicist had to draw conclusions from his own experience, and these tended to change with his experience, so that, arguing from a different set of circumstances, he was very likely to modify, and might contradict, in his later writings what he had said earlier.

As at the close of all great wars, this was a period of uncertainty and change. The emerging industrial society was taking form with the growth of large-scale business enterprise and the development of monopolistic practices, with the formation of labor unions, with a speculative stock market, and with a new economic order emerging in the South. In that industrial society the role of government was not yet set, but already it was being pulled in two directions, one to promote the new industrial enterprise by tariffs and a favorable monetary and banking policy, the other to remedy the most obvious evils by social legislation. In this era monetary policy was thought to be the key to business prosperity, so most economic writing centered upon it.

In a period when so little was settled and so much open to question, attacks on any specific pattern of business activity were not considered subversive. The arguments outlined in this chapter, however dogmatic they might be, were in general carried on by respectable members of the business community, who did not feel that they were betraying any natural order of things. There were, however, a few radicals who felt that any arguments about the best measures for directing current economic development were futile, since what was needed was basic reorientation. The times were such that on occasion even they obtained a hearing.

CHAPTER II

The Radical Movements

A S BEFORE the Civil War, there continued to be several movements working toward a radical reconstruction of society. Some were new, and some were continuations of older movements. For example, the old movement for land reform was still pressing its program. It now demanded that the large land grants to the railroads be revoked, that these lands, together with those still held by the government, be reserved for actual settlers, and that the government enable the settlers to get started through the issue of greenbacks.[1]

Something of a new twist was given the movement by Edward Thomas Peters of the Treasury's Bureau of Statistics. The usual land reform policy, he wrote in 1871, benefited only a few agriculturalists; it could not aid the mass of laborers in the ever-growing cities and towns who were unable to take advantage of the lands. Building on John Stuart Mill's arguments for land reform, Peters went on to demonstrate the evils of land ownership in all cases: "The 'unearned increase in the value of land' is not a mere growth in value which enriches the landowner without impoverishing others, but . . . represents the increased tribute which circumstances enable him to levy upon those who use the land or its products. . . . Even when the higher value is attended by greater advantages, these advantages are such as naturally arise from the association of human beings in the community—advantages which in society men mutually confer and receive and for which they therefore should not be compelled to pay tribute to one who has done nothing to create them." [2]

Such an analysis led logically to a radical solution, but Peters did not push it that far. Other reformers, however, were not content simply with the demonstration of evils—they presented strong remedies.

PHILOSOPHICAL ANARCHISM

At one extreme among these radicals stood the non-violent or "philosophical anarchist" movement. Its leadership consisted mostly of New Englanders and New Yorkers of good family and education, and occasionally of substantial wealth. The movement had begun before the Civil War under the leadership of Josiah Warren, a descendant of the Warren who fell at Bunker Hill. Warren's scheme was based on the abolition of all coercive authority—the State—and on the "Sovereignty of the Individual," complete individual responsibility in all relations. In economic matters, he argued, this would achieve the free working of the beneficent principle of free competition. Each individual producer would receive a price for his product equivalent to the time and other sacrifices incurred; then the equitable principle of price limited to "cost" would operate. The degree of pleasure and pain or net pain would be the measure and limit of price. As equilibrium required, compensation for each occupation would be so adjusted to the relative amount of disagreeableness of an occupation that there would be no preference for one or the other at the price affixed to it.

According to Warren's plan, money would be "labor notes." Under the current system, he maintained, the producer was oppressed and crises ensued because the circulating medium was monopolized by the holders of specie and bank charters. He therefore proposed to substitute labor notes, which each of the "laborers" would issue and which would promise a "definite quantity of labor of a specified kind." [3] Warren's disciples and fellow anarchists converted Warren's vague labor note schemes into systems of "free banking," in which any individual or group of individuals could issue paper money provided it was not legal tender. The free competition in banking, they argued, would destroy the oppression of capital by driving the rate of interest down to the mere cost of supplying the paper.

This obtained some notoriety, but the scheme enjoying most popular approval was that of "mutual banking," advanced by the wealthy Boston anarchist, former Army officer, philosopher, mathematician, theologian, and lawyer, Colonel William B. Greene (1819–1878), who "could produce to order almost any revolution out of the Massachusetts Bill of Rights." [4] He avowedly modeled his plan on the colonial Massachusetts land bank scheme, and on the "People's Bank" of Warren's European counterpart, Proudhon. Greene proposed that the Massachusetts legislature pass a law authorizing groups of individuals to establish non-specie-paying "mutual" banks of issue. The members would pledge any valuable property, be permitted to borrow up to one-half the market value of the pledge, and would pay no more than one-half per cent interest on loans to cover expenses (in reality, then, the real rate of interest would be zero), and would agree to accept the mutual bank money at par in payment of debts.[5]

While most of the anarchists stressed the money monopoly as the most important evil, Ezra H. Heywood, editor of the New England anarchist organ *The Word*, placed first among the "impositions" of capital its extortion of rent. He declared that land was really a gift of nature and therefore ground rent amounted to the heaviest tax on business and labor. In the same category, and equally indefensible, was the ownership of mines, forests, and waterways for what they would yield. The second "imposition" of capital was the credit monopoly; then came the right of eminent domain, and finally the subjection of women.[6]

With more emphasis than Heywood, Joshua K. Ingalls placed land control in the center of his economic theory. He was one of the original group which had spearheaded the successful drive for the Homestead Act. His theory of land use went far beyond the scope of this act. He contended that the unrestrained private appropriation of land, which led to monopoly rent, was the source of all economic evils, especially those terrifying periodical crises that afflicted the country every decade by deranging the stability of business and ruining the frugal and "industrious man of business as well as the reckless and extravagant." The "capitalistic class as distinguished from the industrial or commercial classes" controlled the ownership of land, and by extorting a forced tribute in rent disabled the community's ability to purchase the goods produced. Although the complete remedy, either through the efficient limitation of private property in land or full government control of the land, required the concurrent action of the several states, and this was impossible, the federal government could enact measures which would at least moderate the pernicious effect of land ownership. Such measures should primarily aid the active, or industrial, as against the passive, or financial, capitalist. When the former placed his property in an industrial or commercial concern, he accompanied it with his personal effort in administration and other useful services. He took risks and responsibilities which justly entitled him to share liberally in the real product, but the mere lender who had security for his investment was no more entitled to a share in the results than if he had placed his gold in a safe deposit company where he would have been compelled to pay instead of receiving a premium. It was risk capital employed in business or lent without perfect security that was swallowed up in a business convulsion, whereas fully secured capital was relatively increased. This did not make for a sound or just economic organization of society.

From this standpoint Ingalls called on the federal government to require the states to adhere to a uniform inexpensive bankruptcy system and to prevent the collection of debts above the principal. He added that something should be done about the patent laws, for they injured commerce and industry. They did not serve so much to encourage useful inventions as to foster monopoly and combinations, which used them to terrorize legitimate business through fears of vexatious and costly litigation. The patent laws, therefore, should be repealed or modified so as to render impossible monopoly arising from the manufacture or trading of patented articles. This could be done without "interfering in any way with the regular course or competition in any business," by allowing the inventor to collect from the maker or seller a limited fee.

In later years he increasingly deprecated the importance of the monetary question. The question of money or credit, he said, was of no interest to the wage earner. It was simply a question between debtor and creditor. So long as labor remained unable to employ itself or to have its rights in the general social wealth produced, metallic, fiat, or commodity money could only modify, not essentially change, the fundamental injustice; because however scarce or plentiful the money, he had nothing to obtain it with. Furthermore, the usual anarchist proposal of lowering the interest rate would merely aggravate evil, for it would raise land values and increase speculation. This would be so because land values represented the capitalization of the rent at the going interest rate.

In these later writings he performed an excellent service to students of economics by pointing out that one of the great difficulties in social studies was the equivocal nature of some of the terms employed. For example, the term "competition" was used by the traditional economists to denote a great regulator of human affairs without which society would collapse. The same term was used by the socialists as describing all that was depraved and vicious in industrial and human life. Actually each side was pursuing divergent lines of thought with no possibility of ever joining forces or even of rationally attacking each other's position. To economists the word meant the pursuit of a livelihood by equals under freedom of opportunity, i.e., a striving for something to which access was assumed to be free and of which there was an abundance. To socialists it meant the forced struggle of men barred from opportunity, i.e., a struggle for something to which there was no freedom of access. Consequently the socialists stressed the importance of morals, religion, and the State, while the economists demanded a "let alone" policy.[7]

Ingalls considered himself an anarchist and was so considered by his colleagues, because while he appeared to stress government control, he felt that such control should be essentially designed to free the individual for perfect competition. Nevertheless, his concrete land reform view tended to dilute the purity of his anarchism; only a few could be consistently anarchist.

The most lucid as well as one of the most able of these was the New Englander Benjamin R. Tucker, who, while he saluted Warren as friend and master and translated the works of Proudhon, for the most part followed Greene. He declared that the anarchists were simply "unterrified Jeffersonian democrats." Since the capitalist groups could defraud labor only because legal privileges or monopoly enabled them to charge more for their capital than the cost of handling and transferring which the natural law of competition would permit, he advocated absolute free trade, both domestic and foreign, and waged war upon monopolies in money, land, tariff, and patents.

Among the greatest heresies, declared Tucker, was the socialist doctrine that society should take the instruments of production and administer them through its organ, the State, on the principle of majority rule. This doctrine disregarded individual choice and must therefore culminate in the government's managing all the affairs of men, for it was "the tendency of power to add to itself." The nation would be transformed into a vast bureaucracy, and every individual into a State official. Its constitution would have but one article: "The right of the majority is absolute." Having the responsibility, the community through its majority expression would insist more and more on prescribing the conditions of health, wealth, and wisdom, thus impairing and finally destroying individual independence, and with it all sense of individual responsibility.

He insisted that the notion that competition meant war rested upon exploded fallacies. Competition meant war only when it was restricted, either in scope or intensity, so that it was not perfectly free competition; for then its benefits were won by one class at the expense of another, instead of by all at the expense of nature's forces. Universal and unrestricted competition meant the most perfect peace, and the truest co-operation and competition became simply a "test of forces resulting in their most advantageous utilization." When the demand for labor exceeded the supply, and everyone could get work easily at wages equaling his product, it was for the interest of all (including his immediate competitors) that the best man should win; in other words, where freedom prevailed, competition and co-operation were identical. And the only way to make the demand for labor greater than the supply was through competition in the supply of money or use of credit.

Tucker defended the classic law of supply and demand as the root of all good. He thought it would give people what they wanted, at prices close to cost. The first and necessary condition was to free competition. "This done, the constant and habitual practice of right, though prompted by selfishness, will bring people to a realization of the intrinsic beauty of their conduct, evil motives will gradually be replaced by good ones, and Nature will thus furnish a new proof of her economy by making selfishness its own destroyer."[8]

The anarchists condemned all labor legislation. They denounced bureaus of labor statistics as parasitic, and held that state regulation of working hours denied citizens the right to make their own contracts. They denounced trade unions because such combinations worked against the principles of competition. Heywood explained to the working classes that the competition of the "free open market" encouraged those producers most fit to survive. More broadly, he declared that the labor problem would be solved by "unrestricted liberty to create and equitable exchange the world over." For much the same reasons he denounced the attempts of the Grangers and trade unions to eliminate the middleman by establishing co-operatives. To him the middleman was as serviceable and necessary as the end man. In fact, in their attacks on producers' co-operatives the anarchists seemed to accept the existing system of business enterprise, distinguished from then current financial enterprise, as the most desirable.

The wage system, explained Greene, had the advantage of that complete and centralized authority of the manager necessary for the skillful buying of raw materials, the selling of the finished goods, and the paying of wages according to the varying capacity and industry of the workingman. The theory that the wage system was *de facto* slavery was therefore foolish. Capital, free of law-created privileges, was innocent enough. The employer had a just right to charge something for his risk and for the labor of initiating and superintending the enterprise.[9]

As was true in all reform movements, some leading anarchists had notions strangely out of place in the general anarchist philosophy. Stephen Pearl Andrews, one of the patriarchal figures in the movement, was the most extreme example with his "Pantarchy" scheme. It had an authoritarian flavor, and Andrews was the "Grand Pantarch." "Integralism" was the "complete all-sided philosophy of the Pantarchy." The meaning of this philosophy was perhaps most clearly revealed when Andrews first presented it, just before the Civil War, as the peaceful solution of the slavery question. In a pronouncement issued by the "Political Department of the Pantarchy" to the "inhabitants . . . of the world at large," he declared the abolitionists should learn that there were slaveries more widespread, subtle, and cruel than chattel slavery, and should preach to the rich that they were in the same logical category as the slaveholders and could retain their wealth with a good conscience only if they investigated social evils in the light of all science. This they could best accomplish by aiding the "priesthood of the new philosophy" in their experiments with every promising scheme of social amelioration. By such scientific investigation the slaveholders would become in fact "Patriarchs, Patricians, Patrons of the Slave." The plantation would become profitable to themselves and the "earthly heaven of the slave." After the end of slavery the chief objects of Pantarchy were avowedly reduced to two: first, to support Andrews, financially and otherwise, while he completed his series of "scientific and philosophical discoveries known as the science of Universology and the Philosophy of Integralism"; and, second, to enable him to lead the way into a practical system that would result in a great and beneficent revolution.[10]

Because of the freedom and elasticity of their thought these philosophical anarchists, bizarre as some of their policies were, contributed much to strengthening democratic tradition. They supported the general principle of human freedom in a variety of issues, even when such action allied them with programs and persons clearly opposed to anarchist thinking. Their predominantly New

England heritage stood them in good stead, for, like their ancestors who had successfully matched wits with the Crown, they displayed their learning in court, public forum, and press.

They caused no little annoyance in the community, but some leading businessmen listened and even expressed sympathy with many of their views. One was Charles Moran of New York (1811-1895), prominent in the mercantile and banking world, publisher of the *New York Commercial Advertiser*, and respected by academicians. Moran followed Herbert Spencer in wanting government power limited simply to the protection of life and property; in fact he wanted government limited to mere local government, to protect the minority against the rapacious majority. Like the anarchists, he opposed tariffs, patent laws, and usury laws, and declared that if the post office were operated by private enterprise it would be more economically and efficiently run. He opposed an income tax, reduction of hours, and labor legislation of any sort, and even deprecated any form of public relief. On the central question of money Moran agreed in general with the anarchists that banks should be as free from government restraint as other useful businesses, and should be given the right to issue inconvertible notes. But he thought that the anarchists erred in their scheme by not limiting collateral for note issues to short commercial paper. After the resumption legislation was passed, Moran opposed greenbacks but ardently supported bimetallism.[11]

Anarchism was more nearly in agreement with predominant business thought than was the other radical group, the socialists. The latter were a more miscellaneous group and at times included anarchists.

SOCIALISM

Unlike the philosophical anarchists, the socialists had a foreign flavor and were definitely identified with the name of Karl Marx. But, like earlier imported radical movements, they soon adjusted to the atmosphere of America. Within a few years after Marx founded the International Working Men's Association in London in 1864, German immigrants established sections of the Association in the United States, primarily in New York, and other groups soon followed. Most flamboyant was the "native American" Section 12, organized in New York City in 1871. Its leaders, the glamorous sisters Victoria C. Woodhull and Tennie C. Claflin, early attracted attention and profits by establishing a stock-exchange house that had the benefit of advice from the elderly Cornelius Vanderbilt. They published in their journal, *Woodhull & Claflin's Weekly*, communications from Brigham Young in defense of polygamy and the first American edition in English of the Marx-Engels *Communist Manifesto*, which appeared under the title "German Communism— Manifesto of the German Communist Party." [12] The issue containing the *Manifesto*, like most of the others, carried on the front page advertisements of brokerage houses, including that of the sisters "Woodhull, Claflin & Co., Bankers and Brokers." And such announcements as "Tennie C. Claflin will make her debut on the rostrum upon the subject of 'The Ethics of the Relations of the Sexes; or, Behind the Scenes in Wall Street,'" were not unusual. Since the sisters received considerable help with their journal and speeches from Stephen Pearl Andrews, their work naturally reflected the anarchist viewpoint. But they were heretical on money. They favored greenbacks, the Kellogg scheme, rather than free banking, doubtless in good part because Victoria's current husband, Colonel James N. Blood, was an ardent and lifelong greenbacker. [13]

The German sections were annoyed by the antics of Section 12, particularly in propagating matters that seemed to have little to do directly with labor problems. They themselves were engaged in translating appropriate extracts from Marx's *Das Kapital* for distribution at eight-hour day demonstrations. [14] They complained to the General Council in London, and in 1872 the Council ordered the suspension of Section 12. The sisters shortly afterward went to England, where Tennie C. married the wealthy Francis Cook, whom the King of Portugal made Viscount de Montseirate, and Victoria married John Biddulph Martin, member of a leading banking family. [15]

Indicative of the broadly reformist character of the American division of the International, even after the suspension of the "anarchists" in Section 12, was the manifesto it issued in New York City in October 1873 in connection with the depression. It told the workers to demand that the authorities relieve their sufferings (1) by providing employment to those willing and able to work, at the usual wages, and on the eight-hour plan; (2) by advancing produce or money for one week's sustenance to distressed laborers and their families; and (3) by prohibiting eviction for non-payment of rent from December 1, 1873, to May 1, 1874. [16] But personal and doctrinal differences among the American leaders of the International led to bitter struggles and secessions. The wounds were somewhat healed with the dissolution of the International Working Men's Association in 1876 and the formation of the Working Men's Party of the United States, which became in the following year the Socialistic Labor Party of North America, and, finally, in the nineties, the Socialist Labor Party.

Its policy, according to the testimony of its leaders, was to promote a society of the future having few laws and a maximum of individual liberty. Industry would be operated by laborer-producer co-operatives, which would fix prices and wages.[17]

C. Osborne Ward, native-born ex-machinist and teacher and spokesman for the Brooklyn Section, stated that differences in reward were justifiable at present but would be very slight in the ideal State. This state was to be achieved not by force but by educating the public. He emphasized that as members of a labor party he and his fellows believed that there must be a conversion to true Christianity, to the end of overthrowing the predominating "competitive, monopoly-begetting idea" of acquisitiveness. When most of the people had been Christianized and the party possessed a majority, the co-operative society would be voted in.[18]

Such utopianism was clearly a long way from the "scientific socialism" of Karl Marx. The ignorance of Marx's work, common to the native socialists, was repaired by German immigrants when they joined the party. They presented his views to the public, or what they took to be his views, for Marx might have had some difficulty recognizing his disciples. Chief among them was the able New Jersey kindergarten teacher, Adolph Douai, who was a graduate of a German university. In 1876 he began a series of articles on Karl Marx's *Das Kapital* in the *Socialist* with the statement that this first attempt to render *Das Kapital* into English in a concise and popular form would be too difficult unless arranged differently from the author's order and complemented by some of his other writings.[19]

As a result of such ventures into journalism Douai gained some reputation as a student of economics and in 1878 was asked to testify before the congressional committee investigating the depression. In his analysis of the depression he attributed the main cause of business stagnation to "planless production." Production, he said, was being carried on by private capitalists who did not consider the needs of the world, and this capitalistic production took advantage of a situation where the laborer was free in person but did not possess the necessary instruments of labor, which must be furnished by some capitalist. The laborer was therefore forced to sell his labor power to the capitalist employer at the market rate and, in consequence, to leave a surplus value in the hands of the employer. This led to "overproduction" or "underconsumption." If the laborer sold his working force to the capitalist for only a part of its worth, the laborer must become poorer. As long as employers had a constant market for their products, wages might be high enough, but soon there would be only a few great capitalistic countries competing in the world's market, and there would no longer be a market for all the goods produced; at that time purchasing power would fall so low that production would be reduced.

Stated another way, the capitalistic system assumed the shape of overproduction; first the middle class would be impoverished, then the small capitalists, until at last nothing would be left but a very "small class of very large capitalists or share societies [corporations]." By that time the laborers' purchasing power would have been so reduced that capital could no longer obtain a return. Then, as profits fell to zero in the next five or ten years, Douai held, contrary to Marx's teaching, the capitalists would be willing to sell out to the community and the community would give them an annuity.

Later, before another congressional body, Douai pointed out that after the socialist state had been created it would meet the problem of overproduction by planning. By means of statistical data it would obtain exact knowledge of the demand for the current year and produce accordingly, plus an additional store as security against famine. In this way the crises occurring every five years or less, characteristic of the capitalistic system, would be cured.

Douai in this same testimony raised an important question about the intrinsic worth of capitalism. In denying that capital added to value by intelligently directing blind labor, he declared that capital did not employ its own intelligence because it had none. It employed scientific men, technical men, and skilled laborers of all kinds, experts who seldom received adequate payment, for the largest share went to capital, and even their intelligence was misused by the suppression of useful inventions and discoveries. Supposing there were some intelligent capitalists and supposing they paid the technicians liberally, the latter still should not be considered the sole owners of their valuable technologies. The human mind had developed them over a long period; each individual scientist and inventor added but a little to all that which had already been invented for the benefit of mankind.

Douai, as a spokesman for the Socialistic Labor Party, proposed certain reforms which would facilitate a gradual transition to a co-operative republic: a constitutional amendment limiting labor to eight hours; bureaus of labor statistics, both state and federal, for their investigations into profits would show the workers that they were being exploited and would enable them to determine how best to help themselves, whether by reforming society or insisting on higher wages; following these was a series of social and political demands, even less connected with a radical reconstruction of society, including the abolition of the contract system, both in prison and government work; the prohibition of child labor below the age of fourteen and free education up to that age; stringent employers' liability laws for injuries sustained by employees; the prohibition of the importation of Chinese contract labor; direct popular legislation enabling the people to propose or reject any law; minority representation in all legislative elections; and recall at any time of any public officer by the election of his successor. Two important reforms Douai left for enactment after these first demands had been met: one, that all indirect taxation be replaced by a progressive income tax; and two, that government operate all banking and insurance. However, for the present, he said, the party regarded savings banks as commendable.[20]

Originally the Socialistic Labor Party sharply opposed the Greenback Party. Ward stated in 1878 that the Greenback Party believed in competition, whereas the Socialistic Labor Party held that competition was the source of all evil. He called upon workingmen to oppose the election of greenbackers, for they sought to inflate the "normal value of the product of their labor," and this, in turn, would be filched by the monopolist.[21] For the presidential campaign of 1880 the Socialistic Labor Party swallowed its principles and supported the candidates of the Greenback-Labor Party.

Midway between the socialists and the extreme anarchists stood the ex-Chartist John Francis Bray, who had enjoyed the friendship of that "whole-souled and good man" Robert Owen. He was now busily occupied with perfecting a plan of "industrial partnership" to solve the problems of unemployment and excessive inequality of wealth. Under his scheme government would lend greenbacks at cost to partnerships of labor and capital. His theory promoted the establishment of such partnerships in all occupations, to be organized under general laws which would permit conditional self-government but no despotic central authority and no governmental supervision of workshops.

Thus society would become an industrial republic, with the only government tie being a national board of trade to supply statistics on the nature and extent of demand for commodities.

In this way the "usurer and financial vampire" would be eliminated and labor set free from the domination and extortion of capital. For a time, at least until we progressed further, there would be a system of "graded wages." As a partner, the laborer would demand and obtain an equitable share of the profits in addition to wages; that is, he would share in all future accumulations. The universal partnership of all industries under general laws, he concluded, would prevent "present ruinous competition, low wages, disputes between labor and capital, bankruptcies, gluts, losses, and business confusions." Capital would increase and labor would have a "stake in the world." [22]

By and large the radical movements were fluid. Though each sect at times castigated the others as reactionary, the lines between them were so loose in fact, though not necessarily in theory, that a man might at one and the same time be a member of a number of organizations that seemed on the surface to be opponents. Thus Bray was vice-president of the anarchist American Reform League and an honored figure at the gatherings and in the journals of the Socialistic Labor Party. Similarly, Ward saluted both Lassalle and Proudhon as the great authorities on socialism. Douai gave equal credit to Lassalle and Marx as the founders of modern socialism. And he served with George Gunton, the ex-labor leader and disciple of Steward, among the associate editors of the socialist *Labor Standard*. Further evidence of the mixed nature of radical thought was the policy set forth by the short-lived National Labor Union, which tried to please a mixture of labor leaders and reformers of all sorts: on the one hand it espoused greenbacks as its chief plank, on the ground that they were necessary to provide sufficient currency to animate business and eliminate the need for trade unions, and on the other, it sent a delegate in 1869 to the Basle Congress of the International Working Men's Association and expressed its desire to co-operate with that organization in the "common cause." The general situation was nicely summed up by the *Socialist*, which declared that many socialists associated themselves with all movements which tended to move society a step forward. "But they are not finalities. The student of social affairs is well aware that no natural basis of society can be established but by and through a long series of experiments." [23]

Although the respectable journals carried innumerable articles to

the effect that the country would soon be in the hands of the socialists, the socialist leaders complained that it was hard to make headway
in America because the mass of Americans still entertained the super-
stition that under the existing system everyone in industry had a good
opportunity to acquire a competence, if not great wealth. The socialists had hit upon a basic truth, for, as Wendell Phillips pointed out
when he dismissed the fear of communism in America, the strongest
safeguard against communism was the fact that the majority of the
people possessed property. "Three-fifths of Americans have something
to lose [by communism], and half the rest hopes soon to have." [24]

At this time too there was a heightening of that attitude which denounced any and all reforms as communistic. The *Public*, a New York
organ devoted to business and finance, complained that the communistic spirit was not understood even by many intelligent writers and
influential property owners. Actually, communism stood for the impairment of capital, it wrote, not just for violence as most people
thought. In fact, in so uncertain a democracy as the United States,
the violent form was less dangerous than the form which sought
change by law and the machinery of elections. Where the "habit of
submission to the rule of the majority is strong," it stated, "there is
always more danger that all the rights of property may be impaired
and even the foundations of civilization undermined by an ignorant
majority and bad laws, than by any form of revolutionary violence.
Is it not plain that the Granger, the Repudiator, the Inflationist, and
the bank-hater have in the aggregate power enough to do more mischief in the country? Granger railroad laws, scaling of debts, Bland
silver bills, convertible bond schemes, and war against banks and bondholders are all merely phases of Communism in America." [25]

So-called radical thinking was diverse and often confusing. It was
hardly revolutionary in any immediate sense. Part of it was of native
origin, and most of the rest was stripped of foreign content by the
requirements of American conditions. The land reformers were, of
course, merely continuing a pre-Civil War movement, and the power
of their ideas was revealed in the following period by the tremendous
appeal of Henry George's *Progress and Poverty*. Philosophical anarchists were, after all, traditional individualists, simply carrying their
logic to an extreme. Their emphasis on currency and a zero rate of
interest reflected in good part a demand, almost as old as America
itself, for a cheap and plentiful supply of the pervasive instrument

of expanding enterprise—money. American socialists, it should be remembered, despite some of their bizarre ideas, presented a goodly
number of reform measures that were eventually recognized as necessary for the efficient functioning of democracy in the new America.

CHAPTER III

The General Academic Temper

ALTHOUGH many of the publicists and the radicals cited in
the first two chapters had keen appreciation of economic
practices, derived from their business connections, with the
exception of such men as Carey, Wells, and Cardozo they were not
in the usual sense professional economists. Those to whom the study
of political economy was a full-time scientific investigation were usually teachers, although not by that circumstance completely isolated
from practical affairs. For, since the economic thought of American
political and business leaders throughout the period from 1865 to
1880 was usually conservative, and only occasionally liberal or radical, and the same proportion seemed to hold for the doctrines taught
by professional economists, they were welcome witnesses in Washington. At this time, too, the public was becoming more aware of the
fact that important national problems were fundamentally economic
in nature, and this gave them a wider audience than they had formerly had. These men contributed extensively to both the popular
press and the learned journals; they testified before government commissions and advised many leading officials, including presidents of
the United States.

A NEW ENGLAND CONTINGENT

As was the case before the Civil War, most of the popular American treatises came from New England. Those which had the widest
circulation during this period—*The Elements of Political Economy*
by the Reverend Francis Wayland, *The Science of Wealth* by Amasa
Walker, and the *Elements of Political Economy* by Arthur Latham
Perry—were in the laissez-faire tradition,[1] native to that section and
made up of its doctrinal mixtures. Both Amasa Walker and Perry

found their intellectual fatherhood, not in the writers of the main English classical tradition, but in the Frenchman Frédéric Bastiat, whose theoretical logic in *Economic Harmonies* "proved" that traditional laissez faire would yield a perfect harmony of interests. Yet both their books owed their popular appeal largely to their lengthy discussions on current practical controversies such as the tariff, government finance, money, and banking.

Amasa Walker was an outstanding figure in the financial, political, and academic worlds. His *Science of Wealth* was extremely popular both at home and abroad. Economics, wrote Walker, was primarily a "business science" requiring but "common sense and a good knowledge of the English language." It reduced basically to this: that government was best which governed least. The wants of a people were the only proper motives for production, and producers, whether laborers or capitalists, were the best judges of the means to gratify such wants. Economics taught the relation of man to those objects of desire which he could obtain only by effort. The first fact of the science was that man had wants; the second was that those wants could be supplied only by effort; the third was that the objects or satisfactions obtained by those efforts were collectively called wealth. Wealth included only those objects having value, and value was the exchange power of one commodity or service in relation to another. "Value never exists in an article unless someone is willing to give labor, in some form or other, in exchange for it."

Wages, asserted Walker, were high in proportion to the disposition of those possessing wealth to pay it out for labor; this disposition depended largely upon the security and profitableness of capital in production and upon the enterprise of the people. The laborer should save; for then he could overcome the "natural advantage" of the capitalist, and he could wait to obtain a "fair price." Upon labor associations Walker took the position that the law should not suppress them, for the laborer was not obligated to act as an isolated individual any more than was the capitalist. If the individual capitalist was permitted and even encouraged to combine with others to increase the power and profits of capital, as, for instance, in a corporation, the laborer had an equal right, and the legislature had an equal duty to give him any "facilities for doing this he may justly demand." But the labor associations economically desirable were those described as "friendly societies," those which helped members to obtain employment, provided sick benefits, and engaged in education and temperance reform.

He doubted the usefulness of associations to raise wages, i.e., the trade unions. He did not question their legality so long as they were purely voluntary, but he did question their right to punish those who refused to join them, and he viewed unfavorably the principle of the strike. In the last analysis, he felt strikes could not raise wages permanently. Laborers through their unions might extort an increase during periods when commodities were in great demand, but when trade became dull, they were certain to be placed again in the power of the employer. Such unions, moreover, endangered labor's necessary liberty of action; to prevent damaging its condition or production, what it needed was freedom, protection, and justice. With freedom the laborer could work for whom he would; with the ballot, he could insure himself and his interests protection and justice.[2]

Walker, however, placed little reliance on law to improve the laborer's condition. Legislative fixing of hours he considered unsound economics, and in 1868 he sharply attacked the law establishing an eight-hour day for federal employees as setting a bad example. An eight-hour day in private industry, he argued, would reduce the production of labor, and the subsequent reduction of profits would reduce the capitalist's funds for labor. In addition, the government "has no rightful control over the labor of free men, who must dispose of their services at all times, in such quantities, and at such rates as they can get, in the great competition of industrial pursuits. . . . All attempts to interfere with the laws of value must be ineffectual."[3]

Without governmental interference, however, there might be some remedial changes. There were some advantages in consumers' co-operatives, though little in producers' co-operatives. Feasible profit-sharing would create the ideal system of co-operative partnership, since this did not call for employers to relinquish in any degree the control and management of their business affairs. Only basic charity was a community responsibility. And in the United States it was not so serious a problem as in Europe, because land here was so cheap and labor so much in demand that no able-bodied man need be a pauper. If the government must grant some aid, this might take the form of local workhouse relief. Each community would then have an active interest in diminishing its pauperism.

Walker sharply opposed immigration restrictions on the ground that the influx of foreigners had favorably affected the physical condition and social position of the native. The general intelligence and enterprise of the native population being far above that of the immigrant seeking employment, the natives had taken the lead in industrial undertakings. The overseers and managers in the large factories were seldom foreigners. Formerly American children and young girls had been the mill operatives; now the immigrants had replaced them, and children of American descent held better positions with increased compensation. Thus immigration had both hastened the development of our natural resources and improved the rewards of the native. He accepted the commonly held idea that immigrants, because of different ethnic characteristics, differed in physical and moral quality and that some were far more desirable as settlers and citizens than others. "But American institutions receive all, tolerate all; must educate and elevate all, fusing the whole if possible into a homogeneous, enlightened, and prosperous people. Such is the grand experiment upon which, for weal or woe, the American republic has entered." [4]

Having thus disposed of wages and labor, he went on to the uses of capital. Interest, he said, had its justification in the right of property and in the reward for self-denial. Since interest was governed by the law of supply and demand, usury laws or government interference with the free play of the money market could only have the effect of raising the rate of interest above its natural level. This could only impede the free flow of capital, a vital characteristic of the system. If there were a surplus of capital, assuming that production itself did not expand in the meantime, the excess in a given line would be transferred to other branches of industry or withdrawn for personal gratification. The same would be true for special occupations. When the limit of profitable production was reached, the amount of capital employed could not well be increased. The product being generally in the form of circulating capital, it flowed to other businesses or was turned to purposes of adornment and culture. This was true also, though more rarely, of the general industry of a country. In practice, the limits of industry did not remain the same. As wants expanded, capital, relieved from its former employments, went to new efforts.

But it must be remembered, he warned, that the United States could not expect everywhere and at all times such rapid progress as it was then witnessing. This was a new country, conscious of new and pressing needs, and eager to satisfy those needs. Capital, like population, had its checks: a disinclination of capital to emigrate, the lessening power of personal supervision from a distance, and a distrust of the administration of foreign laws. Another constant force against the increase of cápital was the fall in its rate of return. "The desire to spend is just as truly in human nature as the desire to earn, and can be as accurately calculated. Hence, . . . as the desire to earn loses power by capital becoming plenty and cheap, the desire to spend gains force." [5]

Having laid the theoretical foundation of his argument, Walker now came to the important public questions of the day: the tariff, government finance, and banking. He did not consider the public debt a blessing because the taxes necessary for its payment depressed industry and reduced this country's ability to compete with other nations. But the suggestion that the debt should be redeemed by issuing depreciated greenbacks distressed him. Even if it be granted that the bonds were originally bought with the depreciated greenbacks, they should be repaid in coin, because the bondholders were not to blame for the depreciation. This was only one argument in his general case against greenbacks. Although he had, while in Congress during the war, supported their issue and had even proposed that the bond interest be paid in the notes instead of in coin, he now argued that legal tender credit currency had been an unwise, shortsighted step. Such currency was always issued in excess, unsettled business, and by raising prices caused the government a greater loss than the gain it reaped by the "forced loan."

Those who opposed the return to specie payments were to his mind usually people engaged in speculative operations. So long as the circulating medium was made plentiful by expansion, prices would constantly rise. Consequently those purchasing in anticipation of a rise would make a profit. These speculators made great fortunes at the expense especially of labor and were able to force Congress to stop the contraction of the greenbacks. In opposition to their propaganda, he argued that contracting the currency would not hurt trade. Prices would all decline to the same extent because wages would decline, and trade would go on as usual. In fact, manufactures would gain by having better export markets.

Walker was more consistent in his attitude toward bank notes. He held to his original contention that bank notes should have a 100 per cent specie reserve. Before the Civil War he had argued that the power of the state banks to issue currency beyond their specie reserves—the mixed currency system—must result in a panic. Deposits, he had pointed out, were far more important than bank notes in causing panics and suspensions of specie payments; under the system of fractional reserves, deposits would rise to an important and unsafe magnitude partly because banks compelled borrowers to leave a part of their loans as a sort of permanent deposit. Such deposits were artificial, for they did not arise from the legitimate wants of trade. So, although agreeing that the national banking system was preferable to the old state bank systems in many ways, he still objected to its note-issue power. In fact, before the Panic of 1873, he suggested that the government alone issue convertible notes, which would be merely an extension of the gold notes issued for deposit of specie. In turn, the national banks should be relieved of all taxation and restrictions. Afterward he argued that before this could be done, the greenbacks would have to be withdrawn. He agreed with the theoretical soundness of what he called the "Western" contention, that national bank notes should be the first to be withdrawn because if any paper money was used, the country as a whole rather than private corporations should have the profit. But while this argument was theoretically conclusive, he asserted that Congress would never agree to it and therefore it need not be considered. The banking interest was too powerful to permit elimination of bank note circulation, and the people strongly though erroneously believed in bank issues. Therefore greenbacks should be contracted first. But the resumption of specie payments, he wrote in 1869, must be a gradual one, for immediate resumption ignored the law of supply and demand.

Perhaps his most significant contribution on monetary matters was his insistence that deposits were the most important part of the currency, were created by loans, and from the standpoint of the currency were identical with bank notes. These truths, he said, were not easily recognizable. "It took me ten years to get a complete analysis of deposits." [6]

Walker's attack on the mixed currency system made him the outstanding exponent of what had long been known in England as the "currency principle." One of the most fertile aspects of his analysis was a differentiation between panics and crises. Depressions would occur but they would not degenerate into panics if the mixed currency system were abolished. There were, he insisted, "natural tides in business," but the mixed currency system intensified these tides until they ended in a panic or ruin. These tides were "calculable and healthful." They were the test of business character. They might continue to the extent of exposing bad concerns but they never destroyed good ones. When they occurred, money would be wanted to pay debts, but when one debt was paid, the same amount of money would remain to pay others. The pressure would not annihilate any part of the currency. The receiver of the payment would not secrete the money in vaults until the crisis passed. The means of payment could be reduced only by the specie exported.[7]

On the tariff Walker argued that "protection" hindered the beneficent functioning of natural competition. His basic technical thesis was a crude form of an argument long before developed in England, the doctrine of comparative advantage. As an example in practical terms, he observed, the United States had greater natural facilities and advantages for manufacturing iron than any other country, but the domestic article could not be produced so extensively and so cheaply as to exclude the foreign article. This came about because the United States could do better in agriculture, thanks to the relative extent and cheapness of our land. The infant industry argument he thought sophistical. Each branch of legitimate industry "comes full-grown and full-armed into life. . . . There is no infancy so far as completeness or robustness of life is concerned."

Walker was so much a free-trader that he even deprecated a tariff for revenue. Customs duties, he said, were a convenient and profitable source of revenue, but, like all indirect taxes, they were very unequal, unjust, and expensive. He considered the income tax the ideal tax and bemoaned its demise. As private revenue rose or fell, he said, so should the contribution to the public revenue. Were it to supersede all other forms of taxation, perfect equality would be established; property and labor would each bear its just share of the public burdens.

Walker's humane interests broadened his writing beyond what was then considered pure economics. In the last analysis these did not lead to any real break with the hard core of his traditional laissez-faire attitude, but they did testify to his concern that the boundaries of the science should not be narrowed. He was particularly insistent that consumption should not be eliminated from economics. He thought, for example, that Simon Newcomb, a "sagacious and generally correct writer," had gone too far when he stated that "if a laborer is willing to work all day for a quart of whiskey to get drunk upon, political economy does not question his wisdom." True, any author had the discretion to confine his inquiries to any limits that he might set and to erect them into a consistent system, but such a system could not inspire that interest which attached to a scheme concerning the industrial welfare of man as a whole. "It may be a science of political economy, but not *the* science." After all, what the laborer did with his money made a difference to society. By right consumption every people could be rich, free, and hopeful. He even included in proper consumption compulsory public education, because it would prevent pauperism and crime and bring about general economic betterment, especially of the workingman.[8]

Another aspect of consumption was the economy of the war system. War was not a moral but a political necessity, he declared, and it would end when all nations should establish a code of international law and institute a high court of appeal for adjudicating disputes. The current system conflicted with the simplest dictates of common sense and the highest interests of mankind. One nation increased its vast armament only because another did, and still they were as relatively defenseless as ever. The changes continually occurring in the machinery of war were so great and frequent that no nation could ever hope to be fully prepared. The mind stood aghast at the awful possibilities of the future if the current senseless and inhuman competition in war preparations should continue. And with Walker the attainment of world peace was no mere academic matter; he spent much of his time and money for the cause, and attended world congresses on the subject. In spite of a number of inconsistencies, Walker was for his time the outstanding American economist. And the tremendous popularity of his treatise, *The Science of Wealth*, and its abridgment, did much to develop an intelligent appreciation of economic questions among the general public.

Walker died in 1875, but the technical tradition he stood for was carried on and extended by his close friend, Arthur Latham Perry of Williams College. Perry was a distinguished and extremely popular elaborator of Walker's views; few teachers of the day held as important a position in the classroom and in the outside world.[9] He numbered among his admirers leading government officials and public figures. McCulloch valued Perry's support of his financial program. He considered Perry's treatise the best book on economics—as well he might, since many of the conclusions Perry, as a "scientific economist," reached on production, labor, money, and credit, he said, accorded with those he himself had reached by experience and observation in managing large banking institutions. President Cleveland wanted to appoint Perry Secretary of the Treasury.[10]

Perry's conception of economics was consciously limited to the market place. Economics was the science of values and as such was exclusively the science of buying and selling, including material commodities, personal services, and commercial credits. If a term were needed to express the sum of all valuable things, that term, he said, should be not wealth, which was vague and meaningless, but property, which "denotes a right of possessing, using, enjoying, selling, and destroying anything"—in short, as the Roman jurists defined it, anything which could be bought and sold.

Perry granted that Adam Smith was the great historical name in the science, but Smith, he declared, limited the meaning and scope of value to commodities only, i.e., concrete things, and thus confused utility and value. Perry also asserted that Adam Smith's successors, by following this notion and resorting to ingenious mathematical formulas, had deduced the dismal Ricardian law of rent and the Malthusian doctrine of population. These were vicious, materialistic doctrines, he argued, because they led to the conclusion that land ownership was a monopoly and rent receivers were non-productive.

But Bastiat, said Perry, cleared away the uncomfortable disharmony by the use of the magic word "services," for services referred to persons rather than to things, and each person in a free exchange served the other. Best of all, Bastiat's conception of value removed from economics the stigma of being a dismal science. The science of value was, therefore, a social science, for it began and ended not in dead matter, but in the living force that activated man. He who dealt successfully with value was bound to become a successful businessman: he would know man's wants, the probable changes of fashion, and the thousand and one subtleties that made up mercantile sagacity. "Your man of business must be a man of brains. The field of production is no dead level of sluggish uniformity like the billowy and heavy sea"; its navigation "requires foresight, wise courage, and a power of adaptation to varying circumstances." Since only services were sold, the competition of those ready to render them eliminated the influence of God's free gifts on value and resulted in value reflecting only irksome labor.

Using human effort as the basis of economic rewards, he made human labor the center of his system and common sense the means of its success. But this did not lead him to conclusions different from those of other laissez-faire theorists. In his system economics was primarily concerned with buying and selling, in which all engaged, and since the great advantage of the power of introspection was possessed by every man, woman, and child, it was easy to deduce sound economic principles. "Almost everybody watches the action of his own mind enough to see what are the *motives* in buying and selling." Hence, no law or encouragement was needed to induce any person to trade; on the other hand, any law or obstacle hindering two persons from trading who would otherwise do so not only interfered with a sacred right but prevented an inevitable gain that would otherwise accrue to both parties. Introspection would thus break up economic fallacies.[11]

Whatever disharmonies occurred, Perry said, arose not within the sphere of exchange but from the interference with free exchange by such human institutions as usury laws, trade unions and labor legislation, paper money and protective tariffs. The popular proposals for remedying low wages, such as trade unions, a legal minimum wage, and the concentrated pressure of public opinion on employers, violated the doctrine that naturally fixed wages—i.e., the wage-fund doctrine. The wage fund was that part of capital devoted to the payment of wages. "If we call this portion of capital . . . a dividend, and the number of laborers a divisor, the quotient will be the general average rate of wages at that time and place. This principle invariably determines the current rate of wages in any country." The more capital there was, the greater was the demand for labor. "If, in the division between capital and labor at the end of any industrial cycle, profits get more than their due share, these very profits will wish to become capital and will thus become an extra demand for labor, and the next wages fund will be larger than the last. If capital gets a relatively too large reward, nothing can interrupt the tendency that labor shall get, in consequence of that, a larger reward the next time." [12]

Similarly, he upheld in an extreme form the traditional argument, derived from J. B. Say, against the possibility of a "general glut"; namely, that the supply constitutes the demand.

In Perry's eyes paper money constituted a major heresy. Like Amasa Walker, he originally opposed not only greenbacks but any form of bank currency, because unlike specie it had no natural limitation of supply. He went further than Walker in that he even questioned the worth of a currency backed by a 100 per cent reserve. He argued that sound banking demanded that banks be prohibited from issuing paper money and be limited to dealing in debts and deposits and lending the national coined money.

Credits, however, including book credits, bills of exchange, corporation bonds, and, above all, bank deposits, were the great instruments of advance, Perry held. They gathered up the driblets, economized exchanges, spared the use of money, and even utilized the future to contribute productive services. Following the British economist and former banker Henry Dunning Macleod, he contended that the use of credit, especially bank credit, created a new capital, a new purchasing power, something in the world of values in addition to what had existed before. This addition was limited because of the uncertainties of the future, but it was extensive because credit rights to future products had a ready value.

Other economists and bankers protested Perry's idea that credit could create capital, insisting that the relation of debt to credits did not involve anything more than an exchange between two parties of titles to certain tangible goods, and consequently that "incorporeal property," such as bank deposits, mortgages, etc., was neither wealth nor capital. But Perry contended that if his point were granted that rights were property, then new rights were new property, and therefore new capital had been created by credit. The excess of a banker's average deposits over his average reserves was a creation of new credit, a new resource of production, a purchasing power available to the banker that had not previously and practically been available to anybody.

Credit, however, had one disadvantage to his mind, in that when it was used freely in addition to money and increased purchases went on in all departments at once, there was a general rise of prices and a universal spirit of speculation. Everyone seemed to make great gains and extended his operations to the limit, so that indebtedness was multiplied on every hand. Eventually, on the realization that the granting of credit had been overdone, speculative purchases ceased, banks became cautious in discounting paper, borrowers attempted to sell their goods at any price in order to raise funds to meet their obligations, and prices fell. A panic followed, which was more irrational, if possible, than the previous overconfidence. Then inflated credits and commodities collapsed in the hands of their holders; the sacrifices were inadequate to meet the debts, and business failed. The banks could not or thought they could not help. Consequently widespread disaster resulted. Thus crises had swept the country in 1837, 1857, and 1873, and doubtless would occur in the future. They always arose from disordered credits and, though not necessarily connected with credit or bank paper, were most likely to present themselves as currency problems.

But if the strong and conservative banks would maintain their or-dinary condition, they could prevent or abate a panic. The banks need not place more money in circulation or extend credit; it was merely required that they be in a position to offer credit on approved securities when the occasion arose; the mere knowledge that abun-dant credit could and would be given should suffice to solve a finan-cial crisis. Therefore, when a panic seemed imminent, banks should have the power to extend discounts. It had been done in England, when the Bank of England was given government permission to vio-late the Bank Act of 1844, and thereby the ragings of a "commercial storm" had been stilled. Of course banks must raise their discount rate under these circumstances, and for this reason usury laws should be abolished.

Especially interesting was Perry's analysis in 1871 of the future of interest rates. Historically, he declared, the rate of interest had de-clined as capital increased, but this would not go on indefinitely, for at around 2 per cent there would be almost no motive for lending. This historical decline came about, in part, because of the following factors: The price for the use of money, like other prices, was deter-mined by supply and demand. The supply was large because "we are a capital-loving people and the practice of hoarding has but little Ḱold upon us." Almost everybody made money in some form and had something to lend in some form. This tended to depress the rate of interest. Also, the desire of foreign investors to realize a higher in-terest in the United States than at home tended to do the same. But, on the other hand, our people were fond of great enterprises, most of which were executed with borrowed capital. This created a de-mand. Capital was productive in the United States, owing to the lavish gifts of nature, which also made for demand. Though these influences somewhat explained the past, they could not predict the future.

He hedged by saying he did not know whether supply would out-strip demand, or demand the supply. If the money remained sound and we were sure of its future, the historical tendency of decline would be the prospect; that is, if the money were gold and silver only, or sound bank or government paper instantly convertible into specie, rates would fall. On the other hand, if the money were to continue to be paper currency exclusively, especially legal tender, and by natural consequence a good deal of it, the interest rate would rise. Speculators would absorb the money no matter how large the quantity. Fearing that the country would not have a sound national money in the immediate future, and fearing that the habit of the people to borrow inordinately would continue, he declared the rate of interest would be not less than 6 per cent.[13]

Perry outdid Amasa Walker in defending the income tax and free trade. Free trade came to absorb more and more of his attention. In fact it came close to monopolizing all his economic thought and teaching. He devoted considerable space to the subject in his textbooks, and he wrote innumerable articles for free-trade organs and gave over two hundred speeches throughout the country on the subject. He attacked the protective tariff on all levels: it was unsound economics; it violated the right of property, the letter and spirit of the Ten Commandments as well as of the New Testament. A protective tariff was really stealing for the benefit of a few privileged men at the expense primarily of the Western farmer. Not only did the farmer have to pay higher prices for manufactures, but the market for his product was restricted, since manufacturing countries, unable to sell their goods, were compelled to reduce their food imports.[14]

In the end his attacks on protectionism were so vigorous that a petition signed by some Williams College alumni and headed by the signature of a Cleveland ironmonger, George H. Ely, was sent to the college authorities, complaining that Perry had committed the college to a support of free-trade views. The memorial stated that this was inexpedient, unwise, and unjust. "It is true that an institution of learning is bound to ascertain, establish, and teach truth throughout the domain of morals and science. But absolute scientific truth cannot be predicated on any question of social science or political economy. . . . We deprecate . . . everything in the administration of the college which tends to place it in the position of advocate or defender of any controverted politico-economic question." Perry valiantly stood his ground and declared that at Williams free trade was taught. Those college professors who proclaimed that they taught neither protection nor free trade, he said, were at best foolish, because this in fact denied that the science they professed to teach was a science at all. The position furthermore surrendered what Jefferson called the self-evident rights of man, the rights of man to liberty and the pursuit of happiness.[15]

So determined was Perry over free trade that in protest against the Republican Party's extreme "protectionism" he left the party and joined the Democrats. Like the Federalist and Whig Parties before it, he wrote in 1882, the Republican Party was a party of privilege;

it lived and moved and had its being in privilege and consequent corruption.[16]

In spite of this indignant stand upon free trade, he did his economic enemies justice on other grounds. Thus, interestingly enough, he found himself in agreement with the underlying social philosophy of Henry C. Carey. "Of course," he wrote, "Carey and his followers are all protectionists," and "they are all friendly to paper money, . . . and some of them have no objection to irredeemable paper money," but these features were to his mind not indigenous to Carey's system. Among the central truths Carey enumerated, and Perry agreed upon, were these: that the real interests of classes and individuals were essentially harmonious; that there was a constant tendency to increase in the wages of labor, and toward a similar increase in the aggregate profits of capital, although at a lower rate; and that the well-being and advancement of society corresponded to the degree of association and liberty in it.

Perry was, however, somewhat doubtful of the optimism characteristic of Carey and other writers on economics. It was ironic that Perry traced the failure to develop "sound" economic thinking on the part of the American people and the American government to that very optimistic faith in economic freedom which his works unconsciously breathe. Ever since the establishment of the national government, he wrote, a succession of public questions involving economic principles had stirred the mind of the nation, questions relating to money and banking, the public debt, and the tariff. Offhand one would have thought that under these circumstances the people would, by then, be uncommonly well trained in economics. But unfortunately this was not so. The country had never had a generally accepted national textbook such as the English had had for a century in the work of Adam Smith. In addition, the American people had never been driven by the pressure of want, or by medieval burdens, to study the science; the people had not been burdened with politically privileged classes, standing armies, and frequent wars. Cheap and fertile land had offered an escape to persons crowded by competition or the pressure of numbers. Consequently "the enormous losses of their commercial crises, and of their protective tariffs, make far less impression on them than . . . on a people less fortunately placed." Such conditions were more a matter for thankfulness than for optimism. Yet he could not see the beam in his own eye, for he was an early nineteenth-century optimist himself. He proudly called himself a democrat. "A democrat," he said, "in his fundamental belief and active sympathies, whatever party ticket he may be constrained to vote, has a vast moral advantage in teaching the civic studies over another man, who either theoretically or instinctively is drawn to favor classes privileged by law." [17] His strength and weaknesses flowed from the assumption that the country had undergone no fundamental changes since Jefferson had laid down the economic canons for the democracy of his day. Consequently democracy meant to him precisely what it had meant in Jefferson's day.

Another outstanding New England writer and teacher of the pre-Civil War generation was Francis Bowen. But he was not of the same school of thought as Walker and Perry. Bowen felt that the exponents of evolution, especially Darwin and Spencer, who had furnished the basis for free trade, were not only "at war with all morality and religion, but with the institution of property, the family, and the State, on which the whole fabric of modern civilization" was based. He identified Darwinism with Malthusianism and the German philosophy of Pessimism. From the latter sprang the leaders of the German democracy, whose highly educated men, he said, despaired of society and wanted to destroy it. He called on the "aristocracy of wealth and intellect" to propagate their numbers, lest the earth be completely "occupied by the progeny of the ignorant and debased, . . . the dangerous classes of society." [18]

In his original pre-Civil War treatise, *The Principles of Political Economy* (1856), Bowen had said that he was attempting to lay the foundation of an American system of political economy. In truth, his writings, as a protectionist, were neither more nor less "American" than those of the free-traders Walker and Perry, who claimed the benefit of speaking in universal principles. The chief feature of the new edition in 1870, called *American Political Economy*, was indicated by its subtitle: "Including Strictures on the Management of Currency and the Finances since 1861." Here Bowen outdid Perry and Walker in his caustic criticism of the greenbacks, the national debt, and the national banking system.

National debts were vicious, he wrote, and the way the American debt had increased during the war was especially bad. The government had borrowed huge sums in heavily depreciated paper dollars but had agreed to repay them with an equal number of gold dollars. It had bound itself to pay interest in coin, at the full market rate—6 per cent for most of the bonds—and this rate could not be reduced except by a breach of public faith. So Bowen advocated refunding the debt in the form of short-term annuities, with the entire issue to be paid off within twenty-five years, or within the lifetime of the generation that contracted the obligations.

The national banking system was unsound, he argued, for it was based on the erroneous notion that banks could not exist without the privilege of issuing their own paper. This, of course, unjustly yielded enormous profits to a few, at the expense of the mass who used the notes. Bowen even argued in 1867 that if the bank notes were withdrawn the greenbacks would rise to par; and since they would then be supported by gold reserves in the Treasury, and the Secretary could then exchange gold for notes at par or vice versa, "we should have the best currency in the world." [19] He urged that the small bank notes be eliminated or taxed at least 7 per cent, so that the profits from their emission might be enjoyed by those who used them, the masses. An indirect consequence of such a tax, he declared, would probably be that the national banks would no longer oppose a resumption of specie payments.

Paper money, he stated in the 1877 minority report of the Monetary Commission, had led to the crisis of 1873. A revival of business would probably have begun in less than a year had not the Treasury reissued part of the withdrawn greenbacks, and had it not seemed likely that the remainder would be reissued. At that time no one had known what to expect. Confidence had broken down entirely; capitalists had preferred to keep their funds idle rather than make loans which might be repaid in depreciated dollars. What might have been a temporary convulsion turned into a general paralysis of trade. Although all this was true and condemned paper money, he thought that immediate restoration of the specie standard, even if possible, was not expedient. Large amounts of gold would be needed, the drastic fall in prices would distress merchants and producers, and debtors would suffer as much as creditors had suffered from the depreciation. Therefore restoration should be gradual. Citing Ricardo, he argued that the Treasury should begin redeeming the paper in gold, at the market value, and then advance this price at short intervals.

As for bimetallism, Bowen had been an advocate of the gold standard even before the Civil War. And in his minority report he declared that since there was a large output of silver, it should be used for subsidiary coinage. Unlimited legal tender silver coinage might cause not so much a depreciation of the standard of value as fluctuations in the value of the standard. The resulting uncertainty would depress legitimate enterprise. Both metals had been falling in value, he declared, but while the fall of gold had been so slow and gradual as to be detected with difficulty, the depreciation of silver had been sudden and very great.

These views were disturbing to certain groups of the business community. Boston hard-money men, objecting to Bowen's proposal that the national debt be paid in gold, not at par but at a considerable discount, raised a fund to bring lecturers with "sound views" to Harvard. And President Charles Eliot finally removed economics from Bowen's teaching load in 1871 and appointed to a separate professorship of political economy the cautious free-trader and sound-money man Charles Franklin Dunbar (1830–1900), former publisher of the influential *Boston Daily Advertiser*.[20]

Dunbar's writings held views that Bowen and Carey likened to the pessimistic doctrines of the British classical school. Writing in 1876, Dunbar declared that as "our condition approaches more and more to that of old countries, our ability to rely upon the increasing abundance of our resources to cure all mistakes will disappear." Statesmen, therefore, must follow sound economic theory if disaster was to be avoided.[21] No remedial measures by government would be adequate. People who demanded an eight-hour law were under the delusion that it was possible by "artificial regulation to fix the value of labor," but he advised that the men who were "sincerely and honestly engaged in the movement should be patiently and candidly heard" by the legislature.

His theory could not face all the facts, however. It is important to note that after a fire in a textile mill had caused serious loss of life, he thought that some qualifications must be attached to the basis of political economy, which heretofore had assumed that in the long run private interest would be synonymous with public safety and that the instincts of capital were the surest guide in all matters pertaining to the regulation of business and the distribution of wealth. This principle still held as to the disposition of capital to provide for its own safety, but its regard or disregard of the safety of others was quite another matter.[22] Beyond this he would not go.

He was especially pessimistic about the possibility of legislative action eliminating depressions. He asserted in 1874 in the midst of a severe depression that the "great tides in our commercial affairs which culminate in periodical crises and panics are not to be explained merely as phenomena of currency or the effects of this or that tariff. . . . The causes of our panics like that of 1873 lie too deep for legislative remedy, and recovery from them, always looked for with the same impatience which is now witnessed, is and must be slow and painful."

But he did feel that there was an urgent need for banking reform. Banking was his main interest, and he cogently presented what came to be considered enlightened banking opinion, especially in *Chapters on Banking* (1885). He contended that bank deposits were just as much a circulating medium as bank notes; in fact, compared to deposits, bank notes were relatively insignificant and unimportant. Presenting these views to the public after resumption of specie payments, and after the beginning of the repayment of the national debt, Dunbar drew the practical conclusion that the issue of national bank notes should be based on the assets of the issuing bank rather than on the disappearing national debt. This would provide "asset currency," convertible, however, into specie. This elastic note issue would vary with the requirements of business. The banking habit was firmly rooted in the business community, and the banks would find a medium of exchange in the amount needed. The medium should be in the form and proportion most convenient for the community, and this question of proportion could not be determined by any combination of counselors, public or private. No legislature or conference of bankers could say that the people required any given amount of notes for managing their exchanges. Left to itself, the country would settle this problem of proportion in a natural way, by the demand which each individual using a credit currency of any kind would make for notes or for a deposit account.[23]

This banking theory is his most significant contribution to American economic thought. As one of Dunbar's students put it, although the idea of a substantial identity between bank issues and bank deposits was not original with Dunbar, "he gave it such a cogent and lucid exposition that it may now be regarded as a part of our general stock of beliefs, thereby having no small influence on the thinking of the day."[24] He also performed an enduring though minor service when he launched and supervised the *Quarterly Journal of Economics* in 1886.

The great spokesman of the New England school of laissez-faire economy came not from Harvard but from Yale. William Graham Sumner (1840–1910) made New Haven the rostrum for his extremely conservative general social philosophy. He embodied a New England opinion which held that Jefferson and Jackson had brought low that fine aristocratic culture and "balanced government" intended by the Founding Fathers. After graduating from Yale in 1863, Sumner studied at Geneva, Göttingen, and Oxford to prepare for the ministry. On his return he spent three years as a Yale tutor and then served as an Episcopal minister for an equal time, first as assistant in the fashionable Calvary Church in New York and then as rector at the equally, or perhaps more, fashionable church at Morristown, New Jersey. In 1872 he returned to Yale to the newly created professorship of political and social science. Sumner at once showed himself to be a powerful teacher and an able controversialist. Almost every popular journal contained products of his pen on current issues.

His general economic philosophy was presented in his course on the history of finance, politics, and political economy. Relatively early in his lectures he told his students: "You need not think it necessary to have Washington exercise a political providence over the country. God has done that a great deal better by the laws of political economy." [25] In subsequent lectures he hammered the point home. Although his formal teaching followed the methodology laid down by the last great classical economist, John E. Cairnes, its content followed Herbert Spencer's more extreme laissez faire and evolutionism. Sumner declared that the millionaires, like the great statesmen, scientists, and military leaders, were a product of natural selection, which, acting on the whole body of men, picked out those who could meet the requirements of certain work to be done. They received high wages and lived in luxury, but the bargain was a good one for society, for the intense competition guaranteed that their function would be performed at a minimum cost and brought about "discipline and the correction of arrogance and masterfulness." [26]

Sumner's views were rooted specifically in a strong acceptance of the Malthusian doctrine of population and the old Federalist traditions of John Adams. When population was relatively scarce in relation to the land, he wrote in 1878, the standard of living was relatively high, approximate equality prevailed, and the competition of man with man was lax. Error and vice on the one hand, and painful exertion on the other, did not bring their proportionate penalties and rewards. In other words, little poverty and misery existed, and consequently there was no social problem of class antithesis.

But when the population grew dense, and the struggle for self-preservation became intense, competition for life, in turn, became severe. The rewards for extraordinary talent, skill, and energy rose high, and vice and error brought a heavy penalty. In other words, great poverty and misery and class antagonism came to prevail. Hereditary virtue and vice weighed heavily because it became far more difficult to pass from one social condition to another; and the starting point, as regards health, mental vigor, talent, early training, tradition, and capital, which the father fixed for the son, became a decisive advantage. The main instrument of that advantage was "capital," and the inequality in the distribution of capital was "at once the proof and reward of unequal effort and virtue." Any direct measure to ameliorate the lot of labor, even poor relief, any interference with traditional laissez faire, would simply spell retrogression and destruction. He told Congress that government could do nothing to assist labor.[27] In fact, so stark was his Malthusianism in *What Social Classes Owe to One Another* (1884) that one reviewer declared that through Sumner's eyes "the laboring class and 'the poor' in general . . . are regarded as sheer intruders and cumberers of the earth." [28] Sumner paid them the honor, however, of fearing them. The very growth of capital and inequality, he declared, showed the need to revise the democratic structure and to maintain the increasingly delicate industrial mechanism against the envy of the masses. Unfortunately our inherited institutions of civil liberty looked toward the executive power, as if from that organ alone danger could come, whereas the task was to devise institutions which would protect civil liberty against popular majorities as embodied in the legislative power. More concretely, Sumner suggested that elections be held less frequently and that the executive have absolute power to appoint and dismiss administrative officers.[29]

Sumner had a wide contemporary influence on economic thought, but his lasting fame rests on *Folkways* (1906), which he published after he had formally transferred to the field of sociology, but which was the outgrowth and elaboration of his economic works. *Folkways*, with its overwhelming illustrations of the force of custom and convention in creating the standards of truth and conduct in a given society, was an important contribution to the literature of social science.

He practiced the individualism he preached. If he believed in them, he courageously espoused movements which might be unpopular. He fought vigorously to reduce the hold of theology in the colleges and demanded reforms which would allow more room for the physical and social sciences. He waged a sharp battle with President Noah Porter over his right to use Spencer's *Study of Sociology* as a textbook in his courses when Porter prohibited its use on the ground that it substituted evolution for theology. He not only denounced the protective tariff as stealing, but even went on to mention by name great and influential corporations instrumental in pushing the measure through. Then, too, although Sumner did not think very highly of those fathers of the Democratic Party, Jefferson and Jackson, he on more than one occasion showed his displeasure with corruption in the Republican Party by voting the Democratic ticket, much to the dismay of the admirers of his economics. And who can forget his downright courage in denouncing the Spanish-American War?

A VOICE OF THE MIDDLE-ATLANTIC STATES

Reinforcements for the New England tradition came from New Jersey. At the College of New Jersey (now Princeton University) economics was taught by the Reverend Lyman H. Atwater, professor of logic and moral and political science. Atwater, by virtue of his numerous articles in influential journals, and the number of his students who later became prominent in public and business life, was a force in public opinion only slightly below Sumner.

Atwater was a decided follower of the prevailing philosophy in the American academic world—that of the Scotch school of Common Sense. This philosophy was called Common Sense by its eighteenth-century founders, said Atwater, because they "rejected all philosophic fictions contradictory to the intuitive judgments" of mankind. He considered economics *a priori* in the sense that its premises were to be found in what "we know from experience to be the longings, views, and volitions of human nature in regard to material utilities, and the easiest method of gaining them." It could not be a science of prediction, but of determining tendencies toward certain events which occur in the absence of counteracting tendencies.

The student should not overlook the harmony of the universe that economics teaches, Atwater continued. "As the science of Political Economy centers on labor and exchangeable labor and products, so it finds the culmination in the ever-increasing division and diversity of labor. An increase of external wealth to man is but the symbol of the growing wealth of his interior being." In the body politic, each member must serve the other and the whole, and it "advances in excellence, dignity, prosperity, and glory as its labor becomes diversified." This harmony he felt was to be achieved, at least as far as labor was concerned, through free competition, which provided the only "permanent equilibrium," that of the equality of supply and demand.

In the last analysis, he wrote, strikes, like trade unions which generally resorted to them, would be impotent unless the strikers could forcibly prevent others from taking their jobs. To do this, they must use measures which invaded the rights of their fellow men. Since strikers had no justification for their actions even if employers came to an agreement to reduce wages, so long as the latter violated no previous contracts, gave due notice of the intended reduction, and used no coercion to compel parties to work at such rates, the strong arm of the law must be invoked to crush these "conspiracies" against the "laws of God, the Rights of man, and the welfare of society." He was particularly bitter against the Railroad Strike of 1877. Such strikes, he said, must be suppressed by the national power as obstructing interstate commerce. And no "wire-drawn theories" of states' rights should be allowed to interfere with the exercise of federal power.

He could see only harm in trade unions. He accused them of being the greatest single factor responsible for the financial and industrial distress. Their opposition to wage cuts in a falling market had prevented the resumption of full production and employment, whereas with reduced wage rates they would have been able to exchange their labor for lower-priced commodities. And, finally, through the agency of trade unions and strikes, subversive agitators were constantly invading the rights of capital and infecting the vast "proletarian mass" with agrarian and communist ideas. The growing communist spirit was reinforced by the importation of the "dregs of Old World populations" and by the emancipated millions of "ignorant and improvident blacks." He accepted no compromise. A national arbitration bureau, he declared, would be both unconstitutional and unsound, because its awards in favor of labor would reduce, and even at times destroy, the value of property and thus constitute confiscation.

Atwater, with notable consistency, dreaded public poor relief as an attempt by the people to live in whole or in part on the unfair seizure and consumption of the earnings and savings of others. The State, it is true, he said, must support those who would otherwise starve, but they must be treated as paupers. And every able-bodied pauper should earn every meal he ate at the public table by breaking stone or by some work with pickax and shovel to improve the public streets and highways. There was always the danger that poor relief of any kind would tend to increase the idleness of the people and, like a legal reduction of hours, completely consume the source of "wages-capital."

Atwater was not so ruthless as some of this sounds; he wavered somewhat on the subject of labor. Employers, for instance, by bettering the lot of their laborers should wean them away from the trade unions. He even suggested that corporations set up joint welfare funds and share the profits remaining after paying wages, interest on capital, compensation for risk, insurance, and superintendence. More radical yet, a corporation could attain the objectives of a producer's co-operative by having its employees buy shares with their savings and thus identify themselves with its prosperity. The ultimate solution of the labor question was for the laborer to become a capitalist, and this he could easily do by refraining from wasting his wages in drink and the like. And while Atwater flatly declared that labor could not "ameliorate its condition by any mere legislation whatever," still the great law of liberty or free competition was subject "of course . . . to any qualifying exception in behalf of such legislation as may prevent the overstraining of the young, or secure their proper mental education or industrial training, and to tentative efforts to introduce new branches of industry."

He also changed his theory to meet the problem of the railroads, where he thought "reckless competition" was an evil. He agreed with Charles Francis Adams, Jr., in wanting no "compulsory" governmental regulation of the railroads. Government power must be used to protect property, and neither state nor national power should be used to regulate the control of property. But the situation demanded some changes. He hoped especially that the railroads would take steps to eliminate the practices of their managers in fleecing the stockholders. He denounced the practice of setting up separate companies to filch the profits of the railroads; such companies were extravagant, ridden by nepotism, and burdened with officials who continued their own high salaries while insisting that their laborers take cuts. For the welfare of the stockholders and the general public, the frauds of managers or parasites must be eliminated, and the companies must be put on a strict and rigid business footing. As a remedy, Atwater felt that "due publicity" would be sufficient.

Upon the currency question Atwater did not remain consistent either. Though he had strongly supported the greenbacks during the Civil War, he now felt that such inconvertible paper should never have been issued. He granted that government currency was the ideal paper money, but the temptation would always be strong for the government to issue it in excess and to make it inconvertible. Under existing conditions he considered the bond-secured national bank notes by far the best. Later, after resumption began, Atwater realized that with the government redeeming the public debt, the basis for the national bank notes would eventually disappear. He then expressed some sympathy with the idea of an asset currency. His form was that the bank notes be based on one-half to two-thirds a bank's capital and be a first lien on the assets.

Atwater considered heretical Perry's notion that credit rights were capital, though he admitted that some "intangible values" were a kind of capital. The qualifying test lay in the possibility of reducing an intangible to a material equivalent. For example, the good will of a store gave it actual dynamic force; it had a real function, like that of a motor which turned machinery; the good will increased the productiveness of labor and capital. Turning to the free silver issue, he shifted to high moral ground. The free silver supporters were both bad economists and of questionable morality, he thought. In effect, they were seeking to defraud creditors by paying them in a depreciated metal.[30]

ECONOMISTS OF THE WEST

As the rest of the country is heard from, the verdict in favor of laissez faire seems to be unanimous; for Western economists, by and large, appeared to be just as firm in their laissez-faire views as the Easterners. Typical was the Reverend Julian M. Sturtevant of Illinois College, who declared that the foundation of all free society was that great law of human nature, the law of competition. This law, by starving out those unable to survive, would assure the succession of the race from the best physical, moral, and mental stock, and thus place "the race on an ascending . . . plane."

The problem of monopolies, he went on, would solve itself if the natural laws of economics were permitted to play their part. The Pennsylvania coal monopoly would end if the prohibitive tariff on coal imports were reduced to a revenue tariff. The petroleum monopoly would quickly break down because the high price would reduce demand and stimulate the search for other methods of illumination and other sources of supply. As for the railroad monopoly, the public ought to find protection not in State interference, but in the "sagacity, integrity, and wisdom" of the men who managed the great railway lines. In the last analysis, huge fortunes were the results of real labor. The Vanderbilts and the Astors of the world, he declared, were not mere laborers, but "laborers of gigantic strength, and they must have their reward and compensation for the use of their capital" if the world was to have their services.

Since public revenue fell outside the sphere of free contract, Sturtevant, interpreting public finance narrowly in its contemporary sense, denied that it had a place in a treatise on the principles of economics. He declared that the revenues, or "wages," of government were not determined by economic laws: "it receives whatever it demands." In some cases government would take the position of a partner and accept as compensation a certain percentage of profits; however, the share would not be determined by an agreement between all partners but by the will of this one. Although the government was all-powerful here, it could not oppose natural economic law. He strongly denounced the moves to remonetize silver. In relation to money, he declared that government's sole function was to make and enforce laws compelling the fulfillment of contracts in that money which experience had already established. "It is a mischievous delusion," he wrote in 1879, "for government to enact that debts may be paid in silver dollars, each worth only ninety cents. The experience of the civilized world will still make gold money, though our laws may drive it from circulation; and our exchanges with the human race must, in spite of our senseless and tyrannical legislation, be adjusted in the money of the rest of the world." For the same reasons he opposed greenbacks.

Going further, he opposed the national banking system as well as greenbacks. He felt that banking matters could be managed best by private bankers, because they were subject to unlimited liability. "Those vast lines of confidence and exchange, which rank among the grandest characteristics of modern civilization, are controlled by private bankers, who owe nothing to any legislative tinkering or favoritism." They were, according to him, "capable of furnishing to the individual merchants and travelers of all countries, all the substantial conveniences and advantages which have ever been supposed to be derived from banks and paper money." [31]

Sturtevant's absolutism was somewhat modified by his fellow Middle Westerner, the Reverend Aaron L. Chapin (1817–1892), president of Beloit College and professor of history and civil polity, in his popular revised edition of Wayland's treatise. Chapin noted in a concluding hortatory chapter that "a mighty power is . . . concentrated in the hands of a few managers," a power which could be used against the interest of the corporations and the public. The promoters swindled the small security holders who supplied all the funds, bribed legislatures, and played fast and loose with the companies for the sake of stock-market speculation. This needed a remedy, but he would not accept a "blind Granger movement of open hostility" against the great corporations. Abuses could not be remedied by legislation, but only by a sound public sentiment that rested upon an intelligent regard for the fundamental principles of political economy. [32]

In his attitude toward labor Chapin was more completely orthodox. He stated in his high-school textbook that combinations of laborers or employers to prevent free competition could not materially influence the rate of wages. Such attempts "interfere with the natural law of supply and demand, which is the grand regulator of wages for the best interest of all." If capital had gained an advantage by special legislation, this could not be counterbalanced by special legislation fixing working hours and wages of labor, but rather by united protests against all special legislation, insisting on freedom as the fundamental law of productive industry.

In his mind the great wrong to labor arose from the fluctuating currency, which was in the hands of the capitalists. Private banks, with the note-issue power, did not in his eyes have special privileges, but were the agencies of a country's prosperity. As an example he cited the favorable credit of the great city of Milwaukee, which was due, he declared, to the steadying influence of an early institution established, almost by an evasion of law, as an agency of credit to meet the ever-pressing need of industrial development. When fraudulent and wild speculation had created hostility to paper currency, and the banks of issue had been forbidden generally throughout the Western country, the Wisconsin Marine and Fire Insurance Company had issued certificates of deposit. These went into general circulation because they met a pressing need. The company performed all the functions of a bank without the name. Public confidence had nothing to rest upon but the honor and integrity of the managers, who invested some real capital, but there was a "basis of solid capital and much Scotch honesty and thrift in the management." Its operations were sound, the promises were made good, and the institution greatly aided the rapidly unfolding wealth of the state and region. It became the leading banking institution in the state and brought wealth to its owners, and this was a fit reward for its aid in increasing the wealth of the community.[33]

The school of thought represented by protectionism and bimetallism was by no means absent from the West, though as elsewhere it was less prevalent in the academic institutions. At Chicago University an ardent Careyite, Van Buren Denslow (1834–1902), taught economics. He was an outstanding protectionist journalist. His general social philosophy was indicated by the title of an address he gave before the Philosophical Society of Chicago in 1879: *A Plea for the Introduction of Responsible Government and the Representation of Capital into the United States as Safeguards against Communism and Disunion.* Obviously he would be extremely skeptical of democratic rule and bitterly opposed to any government regulation of railroads, any check on the drift toward monopoly, any ameliorative labor legislation, and any relief to the unemployed. Yet he wanted government to establish a high tariff, free silver, and paper money.

He was a fierce defendant of the business system as it then was; government was to be used only to promote it. He even approved wars for its sake. Great wars, he declared, averted crises by removing the glut of unsalable products. "They call for large expenditures of money, but they frequently manufacture most of the money they call for." By adding to the volume of paper money they raised prices and induced that feeling of profit and success in all occupations which stimulated efforts. At the same time they stilled, at least temporarily, the discontent of the poor.[34]

Not many would follow his thought to such an extreme. The protectionist and bimetallist the Reverend John M. Gregory (1822–1898) of Illinois Industrial University (now the University of Illinois) was mild in comparison. In his *New Political Economy* (1882) the distribution of wealth was described as of a primary and a secondary type. The primary division was into wages, including all salaries, sums paid for services, interest on capital used or invested, rent on land and buildings, and finally profit, the payment for risk. All of these entered into every article of value produced. But after wealth had reached the persons who had created it, i.e., laborers, capitalists, and managers, there was a secondary distribution of wealth, a division into a part to be consumed and a part to be saved. Only by the thoughtful and provident was this division intelligently made at the outset. In most cases it was created by accident and seemed to depend on chance. Yet it appeared with a certain regularity and in a definite proportion when large populations were involved. The latter part of secondary distribution of wealth, the part that went into savings, naturally sought investment. Only in the earlier and less settled state of society were men disposed to hoard their savings for fear of robbery and confiscation. These investments were subject to two counterbalancing laws: the law of safety and the law of profit. Investment was influenced by the business experience of the investor as well as by the social and other advantages in the investment, but the laws of safety and profit were the chief controlling factors in directing the flow of funds.

Five years later, while visiting in England, Gregory made some interesting suggestions on unemployment. He declared that widespread unemployment was a necessary result of our gigantic industrialism. Consequently the workers must be compelled to realize that periods of unemployment belong to the regular phenomena of industrial life, and to count upon the certainty of periods of enforced idleness, just as the farmers counted upon the winter. The instinct of prudence must be aroused, so that the workers would make provision for these periods. Once this instinct was developed, then society or government might help by establishing well-devised postal savings systems or other savings banks, made safe by public guaranty. They might institute plans of cheap and safe insurance against non-employment, accident, and sickness, and give aid by free dispensaries, hospitals, and asylums, to which employers and workers alike would be compelled to contribute.[35]

Although surprisingly few, there were some economists to support the Western agrarian movement. One of the most liberal was James H. Canfield of the University of Kansas, a militant Republican free-trader. He was somewhat sympathetic to the agrarian and labor movements and encouraged his students to read the "radical" literature of the day. He advocated a tax on land alone, assessed at the value of unimproved lands in the immediate vicinity, because this would discourage speculation and the withholding of lands from productive use. This, naturally, was not popular with the dominant interests. In fact, in the nineties, when he was chancellor of the University of Nebraska, "there was talk that the faculty were urging the Regents to dismiss him," ostensibly because of his advanced views.[36]

SOUTHERN NOTES

The general disruption of society in the South after the war naturally gave little opportunity for the development of anything like an objective body of economic doctrine. It was bound to be influenced by the environment of disaster. As was quite to be expected, therefore, much was said about the desirability of returning to the pre-Civil War economic order. George Frederick Holmes, professor of history and literature and acting professor of political economy at the University of Virginia, proclaimed that a "fever of anarchy and revolution" was now characteristic. "The passionate desire of communities . . . to substitute the license of the mob . . . for established rule and cheerful obedience is abundantly manifested in every movement of the age." If this "turbulent insubordination" and the lust for equality were not suppressed, the result would be the ruin of industry and the decay of civilization. "It is an instinct, not an accident of language," Holmes stated, "which has applied the designation of Master, alike to the owner of Slaves and to the Employer of Free Labourers. The repudiation of the term does not alter, and scarcely disguises, the character of the relation." [37]

From a college for Negroes, where such a disguised defense of slavery would scarcely be acceptable, came an open defense of economic inequality. T. Tileston Bryce of the Hampton Normal and Agricultural Institute (now Hampton Institute) of Hampton, Virginia, presented an extremely individualistic philosophy in *Economic Crumbs* (1879). He denounced the protective tariff and greenbacks, but, most of all, he castigated strike leaders and trade unions as tyrants over the workingmen as well as over the community in general. "Perfect equality would be a perfect stagnation," he declared. If all men were equally good lawyers, where would be the clients? If all were merchants with equal stocks, where would be the customers? That some men should have more capital was no more unjust than that "one man should be stronger, taller, or more healthy than another." Critics of this natural order were vicious, improvident, and lazy. Wages of all kinds depended on the beneficent principle of freedom of exchange. This was equally true where a man agreed to give a dollar a month to a boy in exchange for his services as a bootblack, and where a railroad agreed to give a man $25,000 for his services. In fact every man bought and sold labor. "Mr. Vanderbilt, the great owner of railroads, hires a multitude of men, but is hired by another multitude to carry them and their merchandise on his cars."

Some strong sentiments in opposition were stated by Confederate veteran Colonel William Preston Johnston (1831–1899). He was the son of the famous Confederate general Albert Sidney Johnston, and had been educated at Yale. His teaching career began at Washington and Lee University, and he later became the first president of Tulane University. He was quite aware of the post-Civil War deficiencies in the higher learning and pointed out that "true scholarly prestige . . . is the recognition of scholarship by scholars. At present, unfortunately, the South is almost outside the pale." To him, Southern universities should be for the benefit of the poor, not nurseries for rich men's sons. "No, my friends," he declared at a commencement of the University of Texas, "the university is not the rich man's school. The rich man can take care of himself. It matters little to him whether you have a university at all, so far as his son is concerned. He can smile serenely and send his son to Yale, or to Oxford, or to Berlin." [38]

Johnston's liberalism showed itself most strikingly in some poems, privately printed in 1894, that bore the general title *My Garden Walk*. Thus, one of them, "The Farmer's Grange," declared that the Grange would no longer permit the "swindling, murd'rous band" of railroads to rule the land:

> We have prayed in vain for peace
> To the men who rob and fleece;
> We are bound to have release,
>   Says the Farmer's Grange.

All stout-hearted men—wearing "blue mixed with grey"—would meet and join together

> On the Field of unreaped wheat,
> In the barn and in the street,
>   . . .
> No Craydee Mobiliay *
> Will suit our time of day,
>   Says the Farmer's Grange.

In another and later poem, "The Strike Ended," he had "A Voice from Homestead" express his sentiments on the Homestead strike:

> King Capital hath won the day,
> And set his heel on Labor's neck,
> And Wealth resumes her ancient sway;
> The vanquished worker must obey,
> Low crouching at her beck.
>   . . .
> Your masters loudly, proudly, tell
> That ye are free, nor scourge, nor rod
> With force the body can compel,
> Where dwells, as in a citadel,
> The soul—a spark from God.
>
>   . . .
> Since ye are free, be ye content
> With filthy rags and mouldy crust;
> By freedom—to the poor—is meant
> Toil till the upright soul is bent
> And sink into the dust.

Symbolic of the past greatness of the South in the realm of eco-

* Crédit Mobilier.

nomics was the passing of J. N. Cardozo in 1873, the ablest pre-Civil War economist of the country, at the age of eighty-seven. He was intellectually vigorous and continued writing almost to the end. The generation immediately following him spoke, if it spoke at all, in a vein similar to that of the Tory Radicals in England. If its voice had not been so weakened by its malnutrition, the South might have offered valuable criticism of the industrial North.

THE TARIFF ISSUE

As the previous pages have indicated, there was general agreement in the academic world on most major issues. The one exception was the question of the tariff, but even here, by the end of the period, only one leading Eastern institution and a few Midwestern state universities could be said to be clearly protectionist. The one was the University of Pennsylvania, where the Reverend Robert Ellis Thompson (1844–1924), professor of social science, held to Carey's views throughout, even on money.[39]

At Cornell, to be sure, an early economist, the Reverend William Dexter Wilson, was a Careyite, but President Andrew D. White, although himself a protectionist, arranged for special lectures by free-trade sympathizers, justifying the presentation of both sides on the ground that political economy was not an exact science.[40] After 1885 the regular economist was a free-trader, and the special lecturers presented protectionism.

The views of the teachers, however, were not necessarily absorbed lock, stock, and barrel either by the students or the communities. James Burrill Angell, when teaching at the University of Vermont, confessed that he had never met a sheep farmer who understood how necessary it was to combine imported wool with domestic wool. "What is worse, I have grave doubts whether I ever convinced one of the fact." [41]

Considering the general picture in the colleges during this period, and considering, too, that the three most popular works among other than college students were those of Adam Smith, John Stuart Mill, and Arthur Latham Perry, it is obvious that traditional views still had a strong hold on the minds of Americans. *Publishers' Weekly* offered a prize in 1876 to subscribers and their employees for the best list of the ten "most salable works on political economy" arrayed in rank. Thirty lists were received, and the "popular vote" for the leading works was: [42]

John Stuart Mill, *Principles of Political Economy*	30
Adam Smith, *The Wealth of Nations*	30
A. L. Perry, *The Elements of Political Economy*	23
John E. Cairnes, *Some Leading Principles of Political Economy*	20
Henry Fawcett, *Manual of Political Economy*	19
Amasa Walker, *Science of Wealth*	17
Francis Wayland, *Elements of Political Economy*	17
Horace Greeley, *Essays Designed to Elucidate the Science of Political Economy*	14
Francis Bowen, *American Political Economy*	13
W. Stanley Jevons, *The Theory of Political Economy*	11

Indicative of the same trend was the fact that the history of economic thought most generally used was the American translation of Jerome Adolphe Blanqui's *Histoire de l'Economie Politique en Europe* (*History of Political Economy in Europe*, 1880). Wells, who wrote the preface, stated that the publication of Blanqui in the United States was most opportune, for the people must be continually told the truth: that labor, exercised conjointly with skill and frugality, was the only path for the permanent attainment of material abundance, and that "all attempts to increase the production and equalize the distribution of wealth by establishing through legislation fiat money or fiat property by interfering with and restricting exchanges, by arbitrarily regulating the price of money or other commodities and services, and by instituting inquisitorial, vexatious, and unnecessarily multiple taxes, invariably tend to encourage the spirit of speculation rather than of production, to . . . weaken popular morality, and to impair . . . a healthy national development." Such schemes were at odds with natural laws and had always resulted in disaster. "And in presenting evidence in support of these propositions, derived from unquestionable historic precedents and experiences, and in such a manner as admits of ready comprehension, the history of Political Economy by M. Blanqui is calculated to perform a service the value of which cannot well be overestimated."

Wells was so enamored of Blanqui's views that he provided in his will for the establishment at Harvard of the David A. Wells Prizes. The prizes "shall be paid in gold coin of standard weight and fineness," or in the form of a medal of gold of corresponding value.

"No essay shall be considered which in any way advocates or defends the spoliation of property under form or process of law; or the restriction of commerce in times of peace by legislation, except for moral or sanitary purposes; or the enactment of usury laws; or the impairment of contracts by the debasement of coin; or the issue . . . by government of irredeemable notes . . . as a substitute for money." [43]

Often these academic economists had accurate insights; and there is little question of their serious concern with the national welfare; but the excitement of the times and the terrific hold of tradition made them peculiarly impervious to the stresses and strains developing in the American economy.

These works unwittingly laid the theoretical foundations for the private economic empires that were built in the last quarter of the nineteenth century. It was a period of hope, and the vigorous captains of industry were the symbol of the great material advance of the nation. The three outstanding writers of textbooks of the day, Perry, Walker, and Bowen, were skeptical of the Malthusian doctrine of population and the Ricardian theory of rent primarily because they felt that these doctrines were unfairly pessimistic.

CHAPTER IV

New Currents

THE main theses of American economic theory had by 1870 been so long accepted and so often reiterated that they had the character of a tradition. They were so firmly established that they could not be overthrown, but they could be modified. Two new schools, the "mathematical" or "marginal utility" school and the "historical" school, which had already become the center of advanced European economic thought, were to force such modifications in the next few decades. As American economists read the new views being developed abroad, they redeployed their theory either to attack or absorb them. It was not always, or even most often, a case of choosing sides, but no economist of this period could afford to ignore the new developments.

Economists first attempted to render the fundamental propositions of the main tradition more precise by reformulating them in the language of mathematics. The English economist W. Stanley Jevons [1] was foremost in this field. In *The Theory of Political Economy* (1871) he conceived of mathematical reasoning in economics as simply a more rigorous presentation of deductions. Since economics "deals throughout with quantities, it must be a mathematical science in matter if not in language. . . . The theory consists in applying the differential calculus to the familiar notions of wealth, utility, value, demand, supply, capital, interest, labour, and all the other notions belonging to the daily operations of industry. As the complete theory of almost every other science involves the use of that calculus, so we cannot have a true theory of Political Economy without its aid." In other words, Jevons attempted to treat economy "as a Calculus of Pleasure and Pain" and developed a theory of value which had its formal immediate foundation in demand, or, more precisely, the "final degree of utility," rather than in the cost of production, as the classical school held.

Jevons did not deviate very far from the classical tradition in his premises, logic, and conclusions. But since most economists were unfamiliar with higher mathematics, especially calculus, they were skeptical of his methods. Not until almost a decade later was his work generally accepted. By that time a substantially identical theory in non-mathematical form had been presented by Jevons' contemporaries, notably by the "Austrian" group—Carl Menger, Eugen von Böhm-Bawerk, and Friedrich von Wieser—and by the American John Bates Clark. Jevons' theory was then incorporated into the main tradition of the English-speaking world under the name of "marginal utility," a term translated from Austrian usage.[2]

THE NEW THEORY OF VALUE AND TRADITION

From its early beginnings one American thinker strongly supported the mathematical school, Simon Newcomb. His influence was both broad and profound; his counsel was asked on all major issues by both business and government.[3] He had an international reputation as an astronomer and was professor of mathematics in the United States Navy and Johns Hopkins University, but he also wrote extensively on economics. He was a frequent contributor to the leading popular journals and was a prominent reviewer and editorial writer for the *Nation*. In these articles he accused the old-fashioned economists of criticizing the mathematical method primarily because they lacked a knowledge of mathematics and had to use more cumbersome literary methods to express much the same ideas.

In the *North American Review* in 1872 Newcomb recommended Jevons' treatise on the ground that any attempt to introduce a precise mathematical mode of expression into economics was worthy of encouragement. To his mind, however, it was inferior to the forgotten French work, *Researches into the Mathematical Principles of the Theory of Wealth* (1838), by Augustin Cournot. The basis of Jevons' work, he wrote, was a theory of utility which "may well supersede the old distinction of value in use and value in exchange. The utility of every article we possess, or rather the utility of an increased supply of that article, diminishes with the quantity we have on hand and vanishes when we have all we want to use." Jevons' theory of utility is very valuable, he continued, because it enables "us to understand what we see in the commercial world, but it does not furnish sufficient means for investigating it. We cannot get at the law of utility *a priori*." Later, in his own textbook, he accepted Jevons' "improved theory of value" as an explanation of market value. "Consider a man in a situation where the command of food is difficult or uncertain. A daily supply of a pound of bread would be of the greatest value to him; to obtain it he would give all his time if necessary." It would be of equal utility, because it would prevent him from starving. The supply of a second pound would be of less utility and value. As additional units were supplied, a point would be reached where he would prefer something else to food, perhaps clothing. Similarly, the utility of successive supplies of clothing would diminish. "A point would thus arise in the case of each and every commodity at which the utility of an additional portion would be so small that it would be indifferent whether a person did or did not undergo the labor or privation necessary to command it. . . . Thus final utility [as Jevons calls it] is synonymous with value, which is measured by price. Now, what is ordinarily bought and sold in the market are not sums total comprising the whole of any commodity which exists, but little portions each of which is insignificant alongside of the whole. It is therefore with final utilities alone that the operations of commerce and the laws of economics are commonly concerned."

Newcomb pointed out that the working logic of the orthodox critics of the mathematical method was in fact the same as that of the mathematical economists. But Jevons himself was wrong, he said, in attempting to found a "Calculus of Pleasure and Pain." "We may make the acts of man undertaken with a view of gaining pleasure and pain the subject of a calculus, but this can hardly be considered as measuring pleasure and pain themselves." The degree of feeling could not be expressed in numbers, he added, but only the phenomena which give rise to these feelings.[4]

Newcomb's interest in mathematics led him, under the impact of the passage of the Bland-Allison Silver Act in 1878, to make some fruitful suggestions in the use of statistics. In 1879 he pointed out that, habituated to measuring variations in wealth by dollars or other denominations supposed to be units of value, people assumed that the monetary unit was stable in value. Its purchasing power might alter, but people would only tardily become aware of this change in its value, because it could be determined only by a painstaking, difficult, factual investigation, and even when people understood the fact, it was difficult for them to realize that the change was in the value of the dollar itself and not in the value of the commodities. The first effect of an actual depreciation of the standard was therefore a feeling of prosperity. This led to hazardous, unprofitable enterprises, to extravagant expenditures, and to a long depression from which the community recovered but slowly.

An appreciating dollar was also disturbing. Nominal values having shrunk to, say, one-half, the average man felt that one-half his nominal wealth was gone, though in reality he might be as rich as ever. This imaginary evil became real when the people endeavored to combat it. The laborer, unmindful that the price of necessaries was much lower than his wages, fought against the continual diminution of his nominal pay.

Newcomb wanted a dollar of uniform value as measured by the average of commodities; that is, its "purchasing power" or "absolute value" should remain invariable. The idea had already been suggested in England under the name of "tabular standard" in connection with the payment of long-term debts, but Newcomb's idea was a little more precise. He wanted the legal tender dollar defined as a quantity of something, no matter what, sufficient to purchase, in the public market, at average wholesale prices, a definite quantity of commodities. The amount of metal in the dollar could be changed from time to time to compensate for the change in prices. This scheme could be made effective by issuing a paper currency redeemable not in gold dollars of a fixed weight, but in such quantities of gold and silver bullion as would be necessary to make the required purchase. Similarly, to obtain the advantages of a coined money system, the government could change the metal content of the dollar from week to week or month to month.

Realizing the complexity of his plan, since different commodities would give different results, he considered that an average would be best. To avoid doubt and dispute, he conceived of an exact procedure. He asked for a permanent commission of experts to collect and publish regularly the changes in the values or purchasing powers of the precious metals, measured by the average of prices in the public markets.

At the time Newcomb first proposed the scheme he was convinced that prices had not fallen very much and would soon return to their former level. When they failed to do so, he sought an explanation. Being so wrapped up in maintaining the gold standard, so adamant against the free silver movement, he jettisoned his tabular standard notion and reformulated his position in terms of labor as the ultimate standard. In this way the fall in prices was explained by increased labor efficiency, due to technological improvements. This avoided a source of error in drawing conclusions from the old statistical table which was more easily recognized than avoided; for example, regardless of falling prices as revealed by his old tabular standard, the continuous improvement in manufactures meant that goods cost even less when measured in terms of human labor, which is the proper ultimate standard, and prices by this standard had really risen. Under such circumstances he became especially insistent that statistical investigation be considered "applied, not pure economy, and . . . at best only an application of principles of political economy to be otherwise learned."

Neglecting for the moment this ambiguity occasioned by the free silver controversy, he returned to his tabular standard for a discussion of the variations of the purchasing power of money. This led him to a clear enunciation in 1886 of what he called the "equation of society circulation," or what has more recently been called the "equation of exchange." This equation in its vulgarized form was the familiar quantity theory of money, but the mathematical type that Newcomb developed was elaborated by successive theorists into a key tool of monetary analysis. In Newcomb's formulation the equation was V × R = K × P. In simple language, the equation denoted that the quantity of currency in circulation—including money, bank notes, and bank credits—multiplied by its velocity of circulation (V × R) equaled the total amount of business transacted expressed in the current scale of prices (K × P).

All four of the quantities in the equation of exchange would be subject to change. However, if the "volume of currency be increased, all other things being equal, money will be cheaper relatively to goods, and thus the scale of prices will be increased in the same proportion."

This was more effective as a tool of analysis than as the basis of immediate practice. For most economists Newcomb probably made his most suggestive explanation of depression by distinguishing between a "fund" as relating to a point of time and a "flow" as relating to a period of time. He attempted to show how a contraction in the monetary circulation of the means of payment produced a corresponding effect on the industrial circulation of goods and services which consumers were anxious to receive and producers to render, and how this was accentuated by relatively rigid prices. His concern, however, with the "viciousness" of strikes and trade unions and his belief in the beneficence of extreme laissez faire were so overpowering that he developed his insights only so far as they could be used to demonstrate his practical views. He left to others the theoretical exploitation of the rich vein he had uncovered.

Above all, he maintained to the end the importance of the mathematical method in economics. In fact he wrote that the science of public and individual prosperity would not be solved until it was taken up by the mathematicians.[5] Until that time he, like others, would be forced to resort largely to traditional common sense in solving problems. It was unfortunate for economics that Newcomb's primary interest was in astronomy. His talents were such that he might easily have been the outstanding contributor to economics in his time.

THE HISTORICAL SCHOOL

The other "new" method, that of the German "historical school," caused an even greater furor. The historical method was not entirely new to Americans. It had, in fact, been practiced by some arch-conservatives, but not with the detailed exactness applied by the Germans. Its significance was enhanced by Germany's sudden rise to greatness after the Franco-Prussian War and by the exaggerated respect for all German scholarship then developing. The "method" first came prominently before the American public in 1875, not through reading of original German treatises, but rather because of what was said about it in the popular journals. Thus, for example, an editorial in the *Commercial & Financial Chronicle* praised the leader of the school, Wilhelm Roscher, professor of political economy at the University of Leipzig. The editor had obtained his information, not from Roscher's treatise, *Grundlagen der Nationalökonomie*, but from an article in an English publication written by an Irish follower of the school, Thomas Edward Cliffe Leslie, professor of political economy and jurisprudence in Belfast.

The *Chronicle* declared that Roscher's fundamental principle was that every stage of national development, every system of positive law which prevailed in any country, required for its harmonious working a corresponding economic system. Consequently Roscher severely attacked the English economists of the last quarter of the century as unworthy successors to Adam Smith, for they discussed political economy as if man were "merely an exchanging animal," or as if human society were led by a blind, selfish pecuniary interest, removed from all the varying conditions of time and place, of national and social organization. "In this country as in Germany," said the *Chronicle*, "we want to investigate man as he is; and not as he might be under some Utopian economy of society where he might be more free than we see him, and more prone to follow the selfish tendencies of pecuniary interest." Germany was attracting many students in economics, it continued, since political economy was the science which treated of the forces that caused a nation to grow in wealth, and Germany was the nation in which these forces were exhibiting the most extraordinary activity. German works were so well adapted to the wants and views of American economists, concluded the editorial, that it hoped that translations would be made of Roscher and of his followers, especially Gustav Schmoller of the University of Strassburg (later of Berlin).[6]

Perhaps the *Chronicle* should also have quoted from Leslie to the effect that Roscher had asserted that Marx and Lassalle were not sound followers of the historical method. Properly used, according to Leslie, this method would make its disciples "distrustful of reforms which do not seem to be evolved by historical sequence, and the spontaneous births of time. . . . No revolutionary or socialist schemes have emanated from its most advanced Liberal rank." [7]

Interest in the historical school was stimulated by another eulogy of its tenets which appeared at the time in the *Revue des Deux Mondes* and which was widely read in the United States and England, being later translated into English in the *Bankers' Magazine* under the title "New Tendencies in Political Economy." It was written by the eminent Belgian economist, political scientist, and historian Émile de Laveleye of the University of Liége. Laveleye, a bimetallist and protectionist, was essentially a believer in individual initiative and private enterprise, but he also believed that "excessive individualism" must be curbed.

This latter characteristic was most prominent in his review. It stressed that this great new school led by Roscher opposed the optimism, selfishness, cosmopolitanism, and belief in natural laws of the old English classical economics. It attacked "Manchesterthum," or the sect of Manchester, and its variant, "the mathematical school" of Jevons and his continental contemporary Léon Walras, and held that the unsound views so prevalent in Europe were logically derived from the English free-traders. The main trouble with this sect, he said, was its optimistic belief that man was inherently good, and that social phenomena were regulated by natural laws which, but for the vice of institutions, would lead to happiness. Not the least of the consequences of believing in natural laws, in his eyes, was the fact that it strengthened the opposition to bimetallism and protectionism, both of which were essential to business prosperity. It overlooked the value of obligatory military service along with obligatory education in making a country civilized and powerful.

The new school, which was composed of university teachers, had been nicknamed "Katheder-Sozialisten"—"Socialists of the Chair"— by its enemies in Germany, but Laveleye pointed out that it was not to be confused with the actual socialists, the Marxists. In fact the new school more effectively safeguarded the social fabric from the Marxists than the optimistic school of the ardent free-trader Frédéric Bastiat, because the Marxists used Bastiat's procedure of exclusive reliance on abstract formulas and "natural laws" to break down the social order and demand its essential reconstruction.[8]

The *Nation*, which advocated free trade and the gold standard, feared that the approval given the historical school by the *Commercial & Financial Chronicle* and the Laveleye article would influence the "well informed." Its editor, Edwin L. Godkin, asserted that the new group of German economists, though very erudite university teachers, were young men with little public experience and long accustomed to accepting militarism and bureaucracy. In fact they were socialists, for they acclaimed the power of the State. But a number of prominent *Nation* readers had read Roscher in the original and were quick to inform the *Nation* that it was quite wrong as to the views of the school.[9]

The *Nation*, in consequence, modified its position somewhat. The next editorial was written by James Morgan Hart, who was a philologist and had studied canon and civil law at the University of Göttingen. Hart granted that the German school was not socialist, for the socialists proper were "rude and . . . illiterate demagogues" who would convert the State into a sort of employment bureau and bring everyone down to the same "glorious equality of besotted ignorance." The "Katheder-Sozialisten" were men of science, but with the exception of Schmoller they had been blinded by their resentment against the incidental wild speculation of the prosperous era which unification and Bismarck's policy of internal free trade had brought to Germany. Because of the speculation, stock jobbers and the like had risen to great wealth, power, and influence, and the professors, living on fixed income, saw themselves being reduced to poverty and insignificance. Like the followers of Congressman Kelley's interconvertible bond scheme, Hart continued, they foolishly called on the State to curb the speculation instead of "trusting to the relief which comes with time, good sense, and hard work." Fortunately for Germany, he said, mere theorists had but little influence on the government, since its great emancipator of trade, Bismarck, was no theorist, no omnivorous reader of books, but knew the history of his people, their deference to enthroned authority, and their penchant for casuistry and hair-splitting. The Chancellor used their submissiveness as a working tool and ignored theory.[10]

The following year Charles Francis Adams, Jr., praised the "new school" and used it to support his views on railroads. He explained in the *Atlantic Monthly* that the faulty teachings of extreme traditional laissez-faire economics had wrought havoc in the railroad industry, and that the German thinkers provided the true method. Protectionists in the United States, he said, had mistakenly claimed these German thinkers as allies, but the latter were fundamentally free-traders who rightly declared that the principles of free trade were not of unlimited application; that, on the contrary, experience had shown that in the "complex development of modern life functions are more and more developed, which, in their operation, are not subject to the laws of competition or the principles of free trade." [11]

Adams' interpretation of the German historical school as essentially based on orthodox free trade and hard money economics turned out to be accurate when the first English translation of Roscher's work appeared in 1878 under the title *Principles of Political Economy*. The translator was John J. Lalor, who worked on Horace White's *Chicago Tribune*. The translation revealed that Roscher defended most of the tenets of the English classical tradition, especially Ricardo's theory of rent, Nassau Senior's theory of interest as the reward of abstinence, and Malthus's doctrine of population. Roscher stated that the workingman's condition could improve only if his numbers increased less rapidly than the capital destined for wages, although he qualified these propositions with the aid of a mass of historical footnotes.

For the American edition Roscher supplied additional chapters on "Paper Money," "International Trade," and the "Protective System." He attempted to show that while protection was a necessary step in the transition from medieval to modern economy, free trade was nevertheless sounder for advanced civilized nations, especially the United States. While he allowed for the infant industry argument, he castigated Carey for advocating a perpetual tariff. Similarly, hard money should be the medium of exchange in civilized societies. This still allowed for gold or silver, depending on the circumstances. Differing monetary standards had one advantage: the fact that some countries were on a gold standard and others on a silver standard restricted extreme fluctuations of prices.[12]

The *Nation's* reviewer of the American edition now considered that Roscher's doctrines were those of the classical school with some differences, but he was none too clear as to what the differences were. Sumner, the reviewer, and others of his group—Wells, W. E. Foster, R. L. Dugdale, and G. H. Putnam—increased the confusion when they drew up a popular reading list, *Political Economy and Political Science*. Roscher's book, they said, "deserves mention as representing the so-called historical school of the Germans." It varied somewhat from that of the great authority Mill, but the uninformed reader would not be likely to find any important differences of either doctrines or method between Roscher and Mill.

The *Bankers' Magazine* in its review applauded the new method. But it followed this review with one equally eulogistic of an English "old school" treatise which the publisher of the magazine, I. Smith Homans, Jr., had just reprinted in the United States. This was Henry Dunning Macleod's *Economics for Beginners.* Macleod defined economics as a "science of exchanges or commerce," i.e., "the science which treats of the laws which govern the relations of exchangeable quantities." He concluded that it was not only a physico-moral science, but the "only moral science capable of being raised to the rank of an exact science." This juxtaposition did not disturb the reviewer, who said that he did not think it inconsistent to recommend both Macleod and Roscher; that although Macleod belonged to the opposite school so far as his definition of political economy was concerned, his book taught a neophyte about to enter the domain of practical life what he must learn; that the book might fitly be denominated a manual of business definitions gathered from the treatises on commercial law and the usages of merchants and bankers, as well as from the more scientific and technical writings on political economy; and that these were not matters of controversy but the sure fruits of experience and learning.[13]

It is clear that the historical school was not at first taken seriously in this country. Economists, learned and popular, were interested in concrete issues, and labels were generally thrown about for persuasive purposes rather than for exact definition. But as the rising interest in the wider scope of the historical school did allow for broader and more liberal economic thought, the colleges began to understand and value it. Colleges devoted to the humanist tradition were now willing to open their curricula to it. On the ground of having studied economics for two years under the "ablest teachers of the science in Germany," Richmond Mayo-Smith, a graduate of Amherst, was appointed to give instruction in economics at Columbia College, where heretofore the subject had been taught by the professor of philosophy and English literature, Charles Murray Nairne. Perhaps Mayo-Smith's greatest significance lay in the fact that, as a leader in the invasion of the higher learning by the German historical method, he pioneered in the teaching of statistics in the social sciences.

Somewhat earlier this German thought had moved into the West, where such leaders as William Watts Folwell of Minnesota and

Bernard Moses of California claimed it was as essential as the deductive method of the classical school. Folwell (1833–1929), president and instructor in political economy at the infant University of Minnesota, used the historical method primarily to handle controversial issues, especially the tariff and the currency.[14] In this development the kind of influence the historical school had can be clearly seen.

Though as a student at Geneva College Folwell had been deeply influenced along protectionist lines by the Reverend William Dexter Wilson, later of Cornell, he soon began to have his doubts. About the time he began teaching economics in 1872, the powerful protectionist Industrial League of Philadelphia sent him a circular letter asking what textbook he used and how protectionism was taught. Folwell replied that he used Amasa Walker's book, but with reservations. While assigning the book as a general guide to the work of the class, "I am careful to inform them that upon some very important topics there are various opinions held and ably advocated. . . . I have drifted far from the old 'Henry Clay-Whig' doctrines in which I was trained, and do not now believe that 'protection' can be defended upon general principles. Doubtless it can be, as a rare, special, and elementary thing. Nevertheless, I do not teach any such matters *dogmatically*. The historical method is the only fair one and the only safe one." [15]

A few years later, in setting forth "the True Method of Political Economy," he amplified on this historical procedure by dividing his course into two parts: first, political economy, and second, national economy. To the latter he relegated the "considerable body of vexatious practical questions, such as the tariff, greenbacks, and transportation, which must be solved by practical statesmen, not only in the light of political economy, but with the help of jurisprudence, ethics, and experience." Thereby, he claimed, a teacher of political economy could consent to practical measures of national economy which found their justification outside the science—the tariff, for instance. Economics as a science must assume men to be equally free to consume, to produce, and to exchange, he granted, but at the same time it must agree that a government might, for reasons of state, curtail and regulate industry and commerce, and even abolish certain lines of trade and labor.

He went on to assert that political economy had become a human science, that it discussed not colorless abstractions, not laws dogmatically arrived at by deductive logic, but man the producer and the exchanger. Folwell stated, as did the orthodox generally, that the motive of all human efforts lay in the wants, real or fancied, of the human being. The study of these phenomena, he declared, fell under the traditional title of consumption and led to the inference that consumption tended to increase indefinitely, at least in an advancing society. By studying production in connection with consumption, one arrived at the law that supply varied as demand, or that production varied as consumption; hence production tended toward an indefinite increase, except for such modifying circumstances as diminishing returns.

The principle of competitive distribution was accepted by the most enlightened nations, for it was favorable to industry and personal liberty. The law of distribution as historically worked out was simply, "Let each party in production have a share as may be consistent with the equal rights of all others," or, more concretely, "competition may be moderated but it cannot be abolished." The share to labor was subject to the law of competition, the harshness of which was being mitigated as modern civilization discouraged the increase of population beyond the number which could be supported in comfort and decency. As for the wage fund, Folwell rephrased the proposition to read that there was no wage fund apart from the number and character of laborers; in other words, the wage fund was "in mathematical language properly a function of production." Labor and wages were interdependent variables. He accepted the theory that laborers were not merely manual operatives but also superintendents and professional classes. Interest was the share of those furnishing the circulation capital. Rent was the reward for fixed capital.

If occasionally the result of production, after meeting the payment of capital and labor, was greater or less than expectations, that is, if a "margin plus or minus" occurred, these losses need not be considered, for if the margin was generally a losing one, production soon would be reduced to a minimum. The prospect of this undetermined margin of gain was the great stimulus to production, and the margin of gain over and above the ordinary and expected net returns of production was called profit. Profit must fall to the capitalist, who alone could take the chances of gain and loss. No mere entrepreneur or middleman without capital could receive profit; he received only wages of superintendence.

Then, turning to exchange, Folwell declared that exchange must be "spontaneous and naturally self-directive." Only the exchanges in a free open market could be of scientific interest to the political economist. In discussing the instrument of exchange—money—Folwell used anthropological literature to show how money originated and why no scheme to float inconvertible paper money could ever succeed. The habit of civilized men to use specie, he said, was too strongly held to be overcome. "The theory, the philosophy, of money" was "wholly an afterthought."

Consistent with this anthropological point of view, though not with the issue that had occasioned it, was Folwell's much later defense, in 1924, of the government's right to issue greenbacks. Though he had not been sympathetic with them and though he felt the Constitution barred government from issuing paper money, still he insisted that the Supreme Court in upholding their issue had simply done what "reasonable and practical men had to do," for greenbacks had been essential for the maintenance of the nation's existence. And then Folwell gave one of the most eloquent presentations of the doctrine of the Constitution as a dynamic phenomenon: "Constitutions are not all made; they grow. The splendid and admirable document left us by the grand convention was but the embodiment, the codification, of means of government then long ancient. In deference to the public sentiment of the day they endeavored to organize a government of unlimited vigor, within a limited range. To this government they gave the purse and the sword. The main frame of the Constitution will probably remain for a long time as it was put together out of the timbers remitted to them from the old time before them. Unchanged in interior arrangement, in external adornment and enlargements, it cannot remain. Each new generation will accommodate the fabric to itself. This is inevitable and doubtless beneficial." [16]

Although Folwell did not differ fundamentally from the classical school, he made so many qualifications in his views that he rightly considered himself progressive and liberal as compared with the dogmatic group represented by Sumner and Atwater. [17] In general, this broadness was the most distinguishing characteristic of the historical school. Its protagonists were forced by their major premise to face the illogical development of history, upon which few dogmas could be established.

This very tolerance, however, allowed the historical school to shelter many odd companions. At the outstanding institution of higher learning in California, and, indeed, in the Far West, the University of California, the tone was sharply conservative. Its president declared in his 1881 report that the distinguishing feature of his institution's liberal arts course was the prominence given to history, political economy, and political theories. This was to combat, in his words, a situation where "political and financial theories that have been tried again and again, and have again and again failed, are constantly forced anew upon our people, often by honest but ill-informed lawmakers. Views regarding the rights of property, communistic in their tendencies, if not professedly communistic, are not uncommon." It was, therefore, the duty of colleges and universities to do all within their power to acquaint the young men who would "be the future leaders of the country with the history of these failures and the harmfulness of these views, that our people may be saved from their constant repetition." [18]

California's professor of history and political economy, Bernard Moses (1846–1931), more than filled the requirements for sound doctrine. He was of New England birth but received his undergraduate training at the University of Michigan and his doctorate from Heidelberg. At the start he armed himself with the statement that the economist must use a variety of methods in arriving at his conclusions. He must use the deductive method of the English classical school and the historical method of Roscher; he must consider both the "facts of history and the facts of consciousness." From the "facts of history we form generalizations, which are then confirmed deductively by starting with some axiom, or some universally accepted principle, of human nature." An example of this was Gresham's law. We know from history its past truth, but "how do we know . . . that it will hold in the future?" Simply by "referring to the axiomatic proposition that men in trade act from self-interest, and that they may gain something by paying with inferior money and hoarding the superior for other use."

Moses was sharply critical of ameliorative social measures that threatened the beneficent spirit of free enterprise. He contended in 1880 that the recent German compulsory workmen's accident insurance law, which provided that employers pay the larger share of the premium, would in the end be maintained at the expense of the workers. The employer, he wrote, asks himself, "Out of what fund shall we take this new tax? Shall it be out of our own insurance upon the capital invested, or out of profits, or out of wages?" Was there any doubt that they would deduct it from the latter? All wages would be reduced, but the workmen who had no accidents would pay damages and pensions to those who did, or to their families—not voluntarily, but through the intervention of the government.

Moses was naturally a staunch defender of the Malthusian doctrine of population. Even if it could be shown that many communities had advanced more rapidly in wealth than in population, this would only prove, according to him, that these nations were in the stage of industrial development where an increase of labor brought about a proportionate, or more than proportionate, increase of product. But as this process could not be shown to go on indefinitely, it did not satisfactorily refute the law of diminishing returns and did not disprove the Malthusian theory.

As for socialism, he warned that in seeking to achieve simultaneously private liberty and social equality, it was trying to reconcile the incompatible. Socialism must necessarily sacrifice the freedom of the individual and exercise a government control as absolute and arbitrary as that existing in Czarist Russia. To him, Czarist Russia was a good example of realized socialism in the modern world,[19] and he used the "historical" approach to explain the Christian "communism" of the ancient world. He said that, living in the degenerate, debauched Roman empire, early Christians accepted the social ideal of a community of goods in great part because of their belief in the approaching end of the world. In their unworldliness were the seeds of a great social revolution—principles which, if carried out, would have "annihilated that order of things on which our material prosperity is based, and of that individuality which is the basis of social progress." This consequence, he said, was not realized in western Christendom because of the triumph of the German race, which furnished the essential and predominant element of the progressive society of the West.[20]

In the nineties, as the nation drifted toward imperialism, Moses proclaimed the inevitable end of the democratic experiment. Because of the natural right of property, he declared, the democratic form of society would disappear under normal social development. His argument was this: "With no restrictions placed upon the movements of the individual members" in the original state of democratic equality, the "fittest in the several lines of activity acquire positions of advantage and the less fit fall behind or are crowded to the wall."

Every step away from the simplicity and equality of the early democratic agricultural state toward the complexity of modern urban society is marked by an increased inequality of material conditions. "As a result of free social progress, society in the course of time . . . becomes undemocratic," even though the law does not recognize the existence of classes.[21] In the end, it seems, his conservatism carried him so far that it became radical reaction.

THE INGENIOUS ALEX. DEL MAR

One of the most ingenious figures of the period, unallied to either school but influenced by both, was the adventurous Alex. Del Mar (1839–1926). Having been born Alexander Delmar, he used in the course of his career a variety of pseudonyms, including "Emile Walter," "Atlanticus," and "Kwang Chang Ling." Although he never held a regular academic post, he lectured on political economy at various universities, including the University of California. He was a combination of mining engineer, journalist, politician, and entrepreneur, and had a fertile mind and a strong intellectual bent. He was connected, as editor or contributor, with such influential organs as Hunt's *Merchants' Magazine* and the *Commercial & Financial Chronicle;* he was active in the New York Chamber of Commerce, and he served as the first head of the Bureau of Statistics established in the Treasury Department in 1866. A decade later he was statistician and corresponding secretary of the United States Monetary Commission, i.e., the Silver Commission of 1876. He next moved to California, where he invested in mines and offered his services as a mining expert. Later, for a time, he had his mining headquarters at London. In the nineties he returned to the United States.

Through his extensive writings Del Mar acquired a reputation as an outstanding historian of money, with definite leanings toward bimetallism, but this was not his most individual contribution. His originality was best revealed in his works on prices and interest. Very early he presented the notion that all prices of specific goods did not rise and fall simultaneously with the variations in the money supply but followed a definite, predictable order. He demonstrated the order or "law of the precession of prices" by a detailed statistical study which reflected the governing "natural law of marketa-

bility"; this meant that the order in which the prices varied depended on the degree of organized markets existing for the goods.
Thus securities, raw materials, finished goods, and labor changed in
just that order.[22] This variability in price changes has since become
a leading factor in the study of prices. Along with this he developed, early in his career, an explanation of interest rates which has
since been called the "organic productivity" theory of interest. He
contended that the governing factor of true interest was the net
rate of increase in the organic world, i.e., primarily the growth of
plants and animals.[23]

Unfortunately Del Mar was so occupied with his numerous ventures that he had little time to develop fully his economic ideas.
Instead, he generally used them immediately for financial ends. He
set up his very suggestive notion of the "law of the precession of
prices" as an infallible guide to would-be investors. His organic
theory of interest he used in an even more personal fashion. After
calculating that the true rate of interest was 3 per cent, he contended that the difference between that rate and the market rate of
10 per cent arose from the risk in investing capital. He therefore
suggested that a large insurance company could be profitably organized to insure risk on capital investment. But he found no backers.[24]

With all his vagaries, however, Del Mar never lost his faith in the
overwhelming importance of statistical or inductive work. He consistently argued that economic phenomena could, through the use of
such methods, evolve true laws of prediction. This, he declared,
was evidenced by the statistics on murders and suicides in various
countries. "Of all things these actions would be considered the
most arbitrary and irregular in their manifestations. Yet when taken
as the average of human actions, governed by the prevailing state
of society and other social considerations, they show a remarkable
regularity and precision of movements. . . . Hence the inference
that these movements are amenable to law is almost irresistible." [25]

As head of the Treasury's Bureau of Statistics he contributed no
small part to the development of statistics. He was in good part justified in writing, upon completing his annual survey of imports in
1868, "The public now knows all about the statistics of our foreign
commerce, and (whoever may complete them in the future) is so
well informed in regard to their technique that no such systematic
deception as they were made the vehicle of in the past can ever

again be successfully repeated." [26] And all this, it should be remembered, came from a man who claimed that Bastiat was the soundest guide in economics.[27]

Although, as has been said, these economic theories were quickly turned by Del Mar to practical account, they had a stimulating influence upon the development of our economic thought. The same cannot be said for his work on bimetallism, which, though widely read and quoted, was more opportunistic than permanent. His defense of it became enmeshed in the political campaign for free silver. He made speeches and added chapters to his treatises for the cause. He contended that there was no argument on the point that a sound monetary system must provide stable prices. However, this could be ideally accomplished only with paper money, that is, a "purely numerary money," leaving the gold and silver to be collected by the Treasury for use in foreign trade or diplomacy. Unfortunately, owing to the frailty of human nature as revealed by experience, paper would be issued in excess. It was theoretically the best, but practically an impossible, medium of exchange.

On this basis he had opposed the greenbacks, though he considered the current monetary system inadequate. The demonetization of silver had in his figures reduced by at least one-half the scanty support upon which the stupendous superstructure of the world's commerce, contracts, and expectations depended. Gold was especially bad for the United States, because whatever gold was obtained departed quickly for Europe, where its velocity of circulation was greater. But, if silver were coined at the ratio of 16:1 as a national rather than an international money, the monetary supply would be in effect regulated so as to discourage exportation, hoarding, and melting. In his words, silver money "will stay with us; it will stimulate the now paralyzed industry of the Nation; and even to moneylenders and their agents it will afford better and safer returns on capital. A circulating silver dollar is better than two dollars of idle gold."

In practice, Del Mar contended, universal money, as involved in the single gold standard, would simply result in raising the material comfort of the Eastern countries at the expense of the advanced Western countries, by equalizing the economic condition of all. For example, the approach to a universal money was already resulting in a higher standard of living for the peasant, the ryot tenant, of India. "As a moralist," he commented, "I rejoice in this improvement of the ryot's condition in such an alleviation of his grievous burdens;

as an Anglo-Saxon, I would inquire into its effect upon Western labor ... agriculture, ... commerce, ... capital, and ... civilization. Europe and America possess certain advantages, such as geographical position, climate, coal and iron reserves, a sturdy and intelligent population, mechanical skill, aptitude for the sea, fondness for commercial adventure, and a vast sum of capital seeking employment. . . . These advantages have cost our race many centuries of effort, they have embroiled us in hundreds of wars, they are the fruits of endless sacrifices." He questioned whether Europe and America were "prepared to relinquish these advantages, by adopting in common with other States a system of money which might tend to level all economical conditions."

As the silverites lost face and following toward the end of the century, Del Mar began to vacillate in his apologies for their platform and finally abandoned them entirely. In 1905 he declared through the columns of the *Bankers' Magazine* that great new supplies of gold had removed any fear of a money shortage. This increase in sound money—and "what can be sounder than gold coin?"—was a certain harbinger of increased commerce and exchange, higher prices, augmented production, and a moderate distribution of wealth, opportunities, and honors, which alone could offer an adequate reward to the genius of man. He fully redeemed his previous record by the ecstatic statement that the new supplies of gold promised a period of brilliant social advancement and prosperity, rivaling the halcyon period of the Elizabethan Age, which had set in with the great discoveries of American treasure.[28]

Because he overplayed his hand, it has too easily been assumed that Del Mar did not hold some good cards. His statistical analysis of the shortage of money was not negligible, and his final allegiance to gold was not necessarily the contradiction it seemed. The skittishness of his life and some of his writings should not be allowed to obscure the worth of his views on interest and prices, and especially his strong reinforcement of the historical school's emphasis on statistics.

GENERAL FRANCIS A. WALKER: REVISIONIST

What Del Mar was doing almost incidentally, certainly without sustained and serious effort, Francis A. Walker, the son of Amasa Walker, was doing sincerely and devotedly, spending his life at it. He was rewarded with a wide public following and a wealth of prestige, both here and abroad, and with the satisfaction of knowing that after him economic theory could never be the same.

Walker (1840–1897) attended Amherst and after graduating in 1860 entered a law office.[29] With the outbreak of the Civil War he went into battle and rose to the rank of brevet-brigadier general. After the war he spent a few years as a journalist and teacher in an academy; then, in 1869, David A. Wells, who at the time was Special Commissioner of the Revenue, had the twenty-nine-year-old youth appointed as his deputy and placed in charge of the Bureau of Statistics.

As superintendent of the ninth census, that of 1870, he helped to develop that survey into an organ which would mirror the country's development. It was no easy task; he had great difficulty in "securing authority and appropriation in the face of State's Rights, public parsimony & Congressional indifference, for an enumeration which shall answer reasonably well to the demands of modern statistical science."[30] His integrity was apparent in his quick acknowledgment of errors, and in his valiant attempt to select census takers on the basis of their fitness rather than their political connection. He soon was known as the first statistician of the land. His plea that a detailed and comprehensive enumeration of occupations be included as part of the census testified to his broad vision. Such a survey, he contended, would give an accurate and striking picture of the nation's economic condition, industrial capacity, and even its civilization, "for in the occupations of the people, . . . we find their habits, their tastes, their ruling appetites, their social patterns, and their moral standards, more truthfully revealed than ever in any book of travels or history."[31]

In 1872 Walker was appointed professor of political economy and history at the newly organized Sheffield Scientific School, which was then only loosely connected with Yale College. Walker taught with Sumner in the Yale Graduate School and inaugurated a course on the statistics of industry. Although he resigned from government service at this time, he retained his interest in statistical work and even directed the next census. As a result, he had some definite advantages over other teachers; his work on the census made him more aware of the vast complexities of the American economic organism, and consequently he had less of the dogmatic assurance of his contemporaries in the academic world. It also gave him more prestige.

Because of the authority with which he spoke, Walker's conception of money, among other things, became the accepted one in the tradition. He defined money as "that which passes freely from hand to hand throughout the community, in final discharge of debts and full payments for commodities." This included specie, inconvertible currency, and bank notes, but did not include bank deposits and other credit instruments. While he did not like greenbacks or any inconvertible currency, he felt that they must be considered money, since they did the work of money. "The bank deposit system," he declared, "allows the mutual cancellation of vast bodies of indebtedness which would, without this agency, require the intervention of an actual medium of exchange; but deposits are not such a medium. In a word, deposits, like every other form of credit, save the use of money; they do not perform the function of money." [32]

In this respect, Walker was not as advanced as were such students of banking as Charles F. Dunbar and Gamaliel Bradford, who noted that deposits did exercise the function of money and were created by the banks in good part in the process of making loans. Thus Bradford pointed out: "With regard to these deposits there are three facts just beginning to be recognized and which must form the basis of any sound regulation of banking. First, they are money, and while they exist are the exact equivalent of notes and gold. Second, they are money created by the banks, and just as much an addition to the circulation as if the banks issued so many additional notes. Third, they are money created to an indefinite extent by means of promises to pay on time, and cancelled by payment of those promises." [33]

Walker held that the demonetization of silver by the leading commercial nations had been bad for business, since it reduced the monetary supply and thus artificially raised the burden of debt and fixed charges, both public and private. Furthermore, the steady enhancement of the purchasing power of money between the time labor and material were purchased and the goods marketed and paid for, reduced the profits of the entrepreneur or man of business. Since profit was the motive for production, an employer who could not see his way clear to make a profit would neither buy materials nor pay wages, and industry would begin to decline.

A contracting currency, he said, was particularly serious in times of business depression. When production had collapsed in consequence of some shock, the steady unremitting pressure of a contracting circulation must retard recovery. It would check the forward impulse and increase the chances of loss; and, in "the initial adventure of reviving production, must strongly tend to prolong the period of suspense, and create an industrial valetudinarianism" from which the nation might not soon recover. Thus, under a contracting currency, depression would last longer and be more serious than it might otherwise have been. Following this line of thought, he concluded that silver should be used to expand the currency. But he did not approve of remonetization at the old rate. He held that only repudiationists and inflationists wanted the old rate reestablished, for it would reduce their debts. Nor did he think that the United States should undertake remonetization alone, for this would simply result in a loss of all its gold.[34]

Walker's independence of mind, so marked in the silver issue, was also apparent in his sharp attacks on the pervasive wage-fund doctrine. He maintained that the doctrine had been accepted mainly because it "afforded a complete justification for the existing order of things respecting wages" and demonstrated the futility of trade unions and strikes as a means to increase wages. In opposition to this he contended that the value of the product, not the amount of wealth which the employer possessed or could command, determined the amount of wages which could be paid. The prospect of profit in production determined whether labor would be hired; the anticipated value of the product determined how much he would be paid. The product, therefore, and not the capital, furnished "at once the motive to employment and the measure of wages." Wages must in the long run be less than the product by enough to give the capitalist his due returns, and the employer, as distinct from the capitalist, his "living profits." This new concept, Walker insisted, taught the workers that by better production and by zealously pursuing their economic interest, they could improve their condition.

Walker's theories had two significant ramifications. First, he emphasized the "fact" that the captains of industry, the entrepreneurs as distinct from the capitalists, were the chief agents of production. They were the great engineers of industrial progress, for they directed the efficient functioning of labor and capital. Profit, as distinct from interest, was the reward for their industrial success.[35] They need not have capital, for by possessing the higher qualifications of technical skill, commercial knowledge, and administrative power, they would readily obtain capital through credit. They were small in number because fierce competition sifted the courageous entrants, so that only the fittest could survive. They might be unamiable and uninteresting persons, but they possessed a certain hardness which was necessary for successful business. The great mass of employers were really small businessmen engaged in a difficult and dangerous struggle for survival, who, because of their hard lot, had the sympathy of the public and of labor. Yet they were the greatest tax on the laboring class; lacking qualifications for business, their operations were not profitable, and consequently their laborers received low and uncertain wages.

Second, Walker's attack on the wage-fund doctrine led him to support limited State interference on behalf of labor. Those who opposed State interference assumed, he said, perfect competition; but where imperfect competition existed, State interference was justified in order to bring about perfect competition, which would mean a free, easy, and sure resort to the best market, whatever the object bought or sold. Under these conditions the result would be an equitable division of all burdens and a diffusion of all benefits throughout the industrial society. Under imperfect competition, when the ability of one individual class to respond to the impulses of self-interest was seriously reduced by ignorance, poverty, or whatever cause, while the classes with which it was to divide the product of industry were active, alert, and highly mobile, the most mischievous effects would follow. In the case of merchandise, the difference of one additional penny of profit would determine where a commodity would be marketed; but labor could not move with the same ease to the market where a higher wage was paid, man being bound by strong attachments to his locality, weighted with daily burdens almost to the limit of his strength, and beset with both reasonable and superstitious fears.

Granting these premises, legislative enactments for the benefit of labor could be deemed sound only if they helped labor to obtain a substantial and not a nominal freedom of movement. Laws in restraint of trade, or interfering with the times and methods of employment, with wages, and prices, were not mischievous because they violated a theoretical self-sufficiency of labor or freedom of contract, but because they diminished mobility. On the same canon, Walker argued that ameliorative legislation for labor might go so far as to insist on the thorough primary education of the entire population, provide a sound system of sanitary administration, and secure by special precautions the integrity of savings banks. Also, the State might, in the interests of health, pass factory acts prohibiting labor beyond the terms which physiological science accepted as consistent with health; it might restrict within limits the employment of children and even of women, inasmuch as they were denied the suffrage; and it might provide for frequent sanitary inspection of the workshops.

In this doctrine of imperfect competition he also found justification for strikes, and to some extent for trade unions. Strikes were insurrections, he asserted, and the wage-earning class was happiest when it had "acquired that individual and mutual intelligence and that activity of industrial movement" which put them "beyond the necessity of such a brutal resort"; but strikes were of unquestioned utility in the "first stages of the elevation of masses of labor long abused and deeply abased." Thus the early strikes in England had been necessary to destroy the hold of custom and fear on the minds of the working classes, "habituated to submission . . . unaccustomed to concerted action, illiterate, jealous, suspicious, tax-ridden, and poverty-stricken."

Though Walker could not wholly approve of trade unions as organizations for conducting strikes and related operations, he sharply assailed legislation against labor combinations. "Selfish and proscriptive as the modern trade union has been, it has curbed the authority of the employing class, which sought to domineer, not in their own proper strength, but through a cruel advantage given them by class legislation, by sanitary maladministration, and by laws debarring people in effect from access to the soil." But he doubted that the laborers could gain any long-lasting benefit from restrictions denying access to the trades in any "country where education is general, where trade is free, where there is a popular tenure of the soil, and where full civil rights, with some measure of political franchises, are accorded to workingmen." [36]

Thus, as far as practical conclusions on trade unions and strikes in this country were concerned, Walker did not differ too much from his conservative contemporaries. But the difference in tone, in the willingness to judge cases on their merits, and, more important, his ultimate formal principle, held out the possibility of liberal development.

Though he believed that the classical tradition furnished the skeleton foundation for sound economics, he castigated the reigning "orthodox" economists for their extreme conservatism and laissez-faire position. He observed their neglect of historical and inductive methods, and their overemphasis upon an *a priori* method which achieved a simplicity in classification to which the subject matter was not susceptible. These factors, he said, had cost the science of economics public regard, especially among the laboring classes. As a remedy for this the historical school, it seemed to him, offered the greatest promise. "The economists of Germany, Italy, Belgium, and France," he wrote in 1879, "are doing the work which Adam Smith began, in his spirit but with larger opportunities and a wider and ever-widening view." [37] With some justice he wrote: "When I first started out in 1874, I suffered an amount of supercilious patronage and toplofty criticisms [from the established economists] which was almost more than I could bear. Downright abuse would have been a luxury. I have hit the Economic Harmonies pretty hard, I fancy, from the squirming, but all this is only destructive and should clear the way for serious careful productive work in economics." [38]

Walker's views, however, grew rather conservative during the eighties, when the reform movements went beyond anything he considered desirable. His position can be seen in his popular textbook, *Political Economy*, published in 1883, and in later writings. Although the book was more liberal than others, he furiously denounced Henry George's single tax as "steeped in infamy," and when *Looking Backward* swept the country, he denounced its doctrine of equal distribution as the "grossest violation of common honesty." The aim of a national organization of labor to combine all labor into one big union was, in effect, he said, an effort to subject employers to a parliament of labor in hiring and firing, wages and hours. He thought that foreigners were responsible for strikes, and that the new sources of immigration from Eastern Europe were not altogether desirable.[39]

In testifying before a congressional committee in 1883, Walker contended that American laborers "received very nearly if not quite all that the normal operations of economic laws could bring to them from the products of their industry." Even though he still vigorously attacked the wage-fund doctrine, his argument was less liberal than in the seventies. Some economists, he wrote in 1884, still clung to the wage-fund doctrine on the ground that it provided a "barrier against foolish and mischievous claims" by the laboring classes for raises in wages or reduction of hours, but his doctrine that production furnished at once the motive and measures of wages did the same thing by discountenancing all demands made on behalf of labor which were made "merely under the impulse of compassion, or philanthropy, or the enthusiasm of humanity." [40]

He then went on to elaborate a theory of profits and wages that was considered reactionary and erroneous even by some conservative economists. Profit, he maintained, was the return for exceptional natural abilities measured from the level of those employers barely subsisting. This "no profits line" was like the no-rent margin of land, and profits, being in the nature of rent, did not enter into price. Under free competition, therefore, the reward of a successful employer would be exactly measured by the amount of wealth he produced beyond that produced by employers of the lowest industrial, or no-profits, grade, using the same amount of labor and capital.

From this he argued that the landowner, capitalist, and employer received shares from the product which were respectively determined by Ricardo's law of rent, by the prevailing rate of interest, and by a law of business profits analogous to the law of rent. Since these shares were settled, each by its own limiting principle, labor became the "residual claimant"; residual in the sense that labor gained by every cause which increased production of industry without giving the other elements in production a claim to increased reward. Under "free" or "perfect competition," labor would gain by "purely natural laws," not only by increases in production resulting from their efficiency and industry, but even by gains resulting from invention.[41] It was quickly enough pointed out by critics that Walker's new view led to the very conclusion that he had ascribed to the wage-fund doctrine; namely, that no combination of labor could better labor's condition.

Walker's theory of profits came to be characterized as one of the "wildest creations of nineteenth-century economic thought," [42] and his related theory of wages was subjected to similar criticism, but his stubborn and continuous defense of these doctrines, to which he devoted the last twenty years of his life, was a strong factor in causing economists to reconsider the classical doctrines. He allowed nothing to interfere. When in 1881 Walker became president of the Massachusetts Institute of Technology, he continued his deep interest in economics and valiantly attempted to meet all criticism of his doctrines.

He did not, however, consider himself a good polemicist or, for that matter, a superior theorist. He summed up his own weakness and strength when he wrote later: "I have not an analytical mind" because of a "great weakness in the matter of abstract reasoning. Whenever I say that a rise of prices means that the value of money has fallen, I have to stop to think it over, to be sure that this is what I mean." With characteristic modesty he added: "I shall be sorry to see the body of economists shut up within my own limitations." But "any advantage I may have in economic discussion comes from the degree of clear force with which I apprehend things concretely. . . . I have often said that I was like a navigator before the discovery of the compass and other instruments. I cannot put thought out to sea and sail a course for weeks knowing that after just so many miles, I shall sail straight into a harbor. I have to *coast* along and run from point to point that I can see." [43]

But such was his stature that even men whom he would have characterized as extreme followers of the "analytical" method admired him as resembling the "older classical economists who kept in touch with practical life and had no idea of making their science a collection of refinements remote from the business of the world." [44] And so wide was his influence that many of his concepts were even adopted in England.

Walker's early views on the entrepreneur and wages were quickly picked up by other economists and by popular lecturers. But even though they used a more radical rhetoric than Walker's, they were often less liberal. The Reverend Joseph Cook of Boston, for example, in a lecture on socialism, asked his audience to condemn State interference because it ignored the distinction between perfect and imperfect competition. As a result of the imperfections in labor-market competition, all workingmen should keep the spirit of self-help alive. It was self-help that would give the working class building societies, trade unions, co-operatives, and industrial partnerships. "The political demagogues who would lead us away from these measures, to support of schemes of State help, are the enemies of social progress." [45]

Although Walker's doctrines were often twisted in this way, their partial acceptance by economists augured a new era in economic thought. The need for economists to concern themselves more with an objective analysis of the economic order and less with rationalization of the current beliefs was becoming more apparent. More courage was called for, and that courage they were beginning to manifest. Walker's thought and his influence were the end product of the ferment brought in by the new European doctrines. He was a pioneer in the attempt to reconcile the new facets which the new schools had discovered, and which subsequent economic theory could not ignore.

PART II

The Expansion of Economic Thought

CHAPTER V

The Turbulent Eighties

DURING the 1880's many of the issues which had been simmering since the Civil War came to a boil. For the first time since 1856 the Democratic Party came to power. The scales of political control fell into delicate balance, where an unfortunate phrase, such as "Rum, Romanism, and Rebellion," might lose an election. This sharpened the political temper of the times, but it was not politics that caused the trouble, it was economics. Serious violence broke out, and such events as the Haymarket Riot resulted. This was the more disturbing because it seemed to be the product of a fundamental economic war, preached by a heretical school of theorists. Violence was simply the rare explosion in an atmosphere of mounting tension. Part of this may have been due to a clearer understanding of economic problems and the consequently more vigorous proposals for their solution.

The explosive issue of pre-Civil War times, the tariff, did not contribute to the violence, although politically it was still a leading campaign issue. In spite of the prospect, for the second time in our history, of a surplus revenue, reformers could not get an effective reduction in the tariff. Protection was firmly entrenched, and all they could do was to hold the most extreme advocates of high rates in check. They could, and did, write and talk at length, but with little success, for although the traditional free trade party, the Democrats, won the election of 1884, enough Democrats in the new Congress voted with the Republicans to defeat any attempt. President Cleveland himself limited his message to Congress in 1887 simply to demanding tariff reduction. The Democratic House did pass a bill for reduction, the Mills bill; but by that time the Senate was Republican. Republican victory in 1888 foreshadowed extension of the protective principle, and in 1890 the McKinley tariff bill was passed.

MONEY

Upon the question of money there was a sharp division of senti-ment and a much stronger belief in the vital importance of the problem. Tempers shortened as the controversy lengthened, and the possibility of compromise became fainter as the advocates became more doctrinaire. At one end were the proponents of the view that all government money should be eliminated and that the national banks should replace the sub-treasuries as depositories for govern-ment funds;[1] at the other end were those greenbackers who wanted the abolition of national bank notes as well as specie currency. It became more and more difficult to balance between extremes.

A popular type of greenbackism was that suggested by a retired Western businessman, N. A. Dunning, in *The Philosophy of Prices* (1887). His plan aimed to prevent falling prices. It provided that the government make certain that a supply of money equal to fifty dollars per person should be outstanding at all times. This money should be partly gold and silver certificates and the remainder green-backs. After all, such a procedure, he stated, accorded with the view of almost every economist that the "volume of currency in circulation determines the level price of labor and its products."[2]

In a similar vein, and with the same lack of effect, that forceful leader of farmers' movements Ignatius Donnelly proclaimed in his anonymous utopia, *Caesar's Column* (1890), that the scarcity of money killed off enterprising businessmen. Hard money, therefore, should be abolished, except for small payments. The money should be regulated by government currency at a fixed ratio to popula-tion. The world, released from its iron band, would then leap toward marvelous prosperity, and no financial panics would occur, for there could be no contraction.

This plea for a fixed ratio of money to population, whether specie or paper, enjoyed some popularity but had no enduring effect. An ultimately more successful argument for paper money approached the same problem of elasticity from a different angle: the ratio of money to business activity. Hugo Bilgram, the Philadelphia builder of manufacturing machinery, asserted, in *Involuntary Idleness* (1889), that to prevent unemployment and encourage the enterpris-ing businessman, as against the inert, passive capitalist, the govern-ment should issue an unlimited amount of credit money to those able to supply the proper security. The risk involved in accepting securities other than national bonds would be met by a rate sufficient to cover the possible loss. "In the absence of an arbitrary limit the volume of money would be free to expand in proportion to the effective demand, and the rate of interest being reduced to the rate of risk only, interest proper for the use of the money would cease." To be sure, capital as well as money when lent would continue to bring a return, but under the free operation of the law of supply and demand capital's true return would be based on risk and the deterioration of the capital.

A simplified form of the argument for elastic currency gained wide support in the one greenback treatise that appears to have enjoyed a tremendous audience—that of the old greenbacker S. F. Norton of Chicago, editor and publisher of the *Quarterly Sentinel* and *Monthly Sentinel*. His delightful pamphlet, *Ten Men of Money Island*, sold, it is claimed, well beyond 100,000 and was even serialized in the *New York World* and reprinted in England. As the publisher pointed out, the secret of its success was that it "makes the very vexed money question not only so plain and simple that any person can understand it, but . . . as interesting as a novel."

The book told, in a romantic, fictional form, of ten adventurers and their families—Plowem, Reapem, Foreplane, Sledgehammer, Dressem, Grindem, Pickaxe, Makem, Discount, and Donothing—who went off to an island in the Pacific Ocean. Discount and Donothing, because of their extensive knowledge of finance and politics, hoodwinked the community into accepting as the medium of exchange specie and convertible bank notes. As a result of the inelasticity of the currency the island was soon in the throes of depression and starvation. Discount, the banker, was of course forced to close the doors of his bank, but he "retired to private life and lived upon the property which he had so discreetly and kindly transferred to his wife when business was prosperous with him." The community saved itself by having the government supply inconvertible paper as the only money and make loans directly to the people at a low rate of interest. Prosperity now reigned. "The poor house has been converted into a museum for the preservation and exhibition of a large collection of curious things and valuable relics of the past—among the latter being a few gold and silver coins and one of Discount's specie bank notes."

Since silver seemed to combine a specie base with "elasticity" and, moreover, had a powerful political bloc—the silver-producing states

—behind it, the demand for free silver led to the most serious monetary struggle. The popular assumption that the decreased supply of precious metals was the cause of the world-wide depression helped to give the movement impetus. The movement gained enough strength so that the Republican Congress in 1890 passed the Sherman Silver Purchase Act requiring the Treasury to buy four and a half million ounces of silver a month, with Treasury notes redeemable in either gold or silver at the government's option. Significantly enough, this was approximately the whole product of domestic silver mines.

But the monetary problem continued to be an important political issue, connected as it was in men's minds with the terrifying phenomena of depression. As in the past, the business community supplied a large part of the contestants. The easy-money people, whether greenbackers or free silverites or a combination, had their most ardent champions as well as critics there. After all, the more fundamental forms of greenbackism derived from the pre-Civil War views of the two New York merchants Kellogg and Opdyke. And silver had a number of supporters even in the financial group; for example, the *Commercial & Financial Chronicle* heartily denounced David A. Wells for his enthusiastic and exclusive support of a gold standard and demanded international bimetallism. What obscured the situation here, as so often before, was the vast amount of polemics and the fact that dominant academic opinion opposed the silverites of all sorts, but it should be noticed that practically a reverse situation was occurring in Europe.

The current greenback schemes went much further than their founders had proposed. Opdyke had specified $10 per capita; now the demand was for $50. Kellogg had proposed an interconvertible bond scheme with the paper money lent on real estate; now the emphasis was on an absolute increase of the amount, with almost any "valuable" asset, as well as real estate, as the security. Greenbackers generally agreed that the most important objective was low interest rates; they were not always explicit on another and related objective, to raise, or, as they preferred to call it, "stabilize," prices. None of the popular schemes was ever "leveling," not even to the extent of proposing direct government aid to public works. Such schemes might be advocated, but they got short shrift. The popular schemes clearly had a business animus, and their protagonists viewed them as instruments for stimulating business enterprise.

Silver in preference to greenbacks got ahead. It was something "real"; it had the backing of the silver-producing states; it had been used as a standard; and it did not raise the problem of what interests or groups were to get the notes, which would involve consideration of a tremendous diversity of interests.

An additional factor in the situation was the farmer, who began to have considerable enthusiasm for these movements, especially when these were tied up with crops and farms as security for the loan issues of greenbacks. Such farming features were easily and quickly added to the new greenback schemes, as was done by that old greenbacker and successful Oklahoma real-estate promoter Colonel Samuel Crocker, in his anonymous utopia, *That Island* (1892).[3] But, as before, such schemes ran up against the problem of who was to get the greenbacks. The people in the agricultural area were no more homogeneous a class than the business community. Here, too, silver in the end made a more definite impression, since it was not only real but conflicted little with that demand for "economy" in government that ran through the pronouncements of all farmers' organizations, and it was not as easily attacked as were the greenback proposals.

MONOPOLY

The battle over monetary policy was repeated in the fight over monopoly regulation. But here action by the government was more novel and therefore appeared more dangerous. The anti-monopoly cause enlisted many gifted and influential writers. The financial editor of the *Chicago Tribune*, Henry Demarest Lloyd, a Columbia College graduate, created a furor with an article in the *Atlantic Monthly* attacking the "Lords of Industry." He described Standard Oil as "the greatest, wisest, and meanest monopoly known to history," whose strength was due in good part to another great monopoly, the railroads. His theme was that the forces of capital had outgrown the control of the people and had become its masters. "Our strong men are engaged in a headlong fight for fortune, power, precedence, success. . . . They ride over the people like Juggernaut to gain their ends. . . . The common people, the nation, must take them in hand. . . . There is nobody richer than Vanderbilt except the body of citizens; no corporation more powerful than the transcontinental railroad except the corporate sovereign at Washington." The power of the people, he said, must be used for its industrial life as it was used for its political life, or the people would perish.[4]

This article and others like it were especially disturbing to big businessmen because this writing reached a wide audience of substantial men of property. C. E. Perkins, president of the Chicago, Burlington & Quincy, complained that thanks to articles like Lloyd's in the popular monthlies—*Atlantic, Harper's, North American Review*, and *Scribner's*—the ignorance on transportation and monopolies was as dense among businessmen, lawyers, and legislators as among the farmers. The only way to counteract the ignorance was to reply in the same journals, rather than to write for farmers' organs and the like, for the readers of the former were the influential interest, the "property interest," and once they could be made to see that the "let alone" policy was the best, then, he concluded, "we shall have a great many helping to educate the voters, men who are now dead set the other way." [5]

Perhaps one of the most ironic aspects of the situation was that the supporters of pools and trusts had to attack Ricardo and classical economics, while their sharpest critics rushed to his support. Thus those favoring combinations said Ricardo was wrong, because, in industries requiring large permanent investment, competition forced prices below cost. The pig iron industry and railroads were cited as notable examples. On the other hand, James F. Hudson of the influential *Pittsburgh Dispatch* contended that concerns having the latest equipment made a slight margin of profit even during depression. Only the old-fashioned or badly located ones suffered and were finally forced out.[6]

The confusion over the treatment of trusts in current opinion was well revealed by the difficulties of leading respectable organs in dealing with the issue. For example, the *Nation* objected strenuously to the statement of the Republican presidential candidate, James G. Blaine, in 1888 that "trusts are largely private affairs, with which neither President Cleveland nor any private citizen has any particular right to interfere." [7] But it also contended that whether a trust was a monopoly and harmful depended on the circumstances involved in each particular case. The *Commercial & Financial Chronicle* was even more circumspect. The majority of writers, it said, charged that trusts were a great commercial conspiracy; a few writers said that they were the natural outgrowth of modern business conditions and embodied no special evils. Neither extreme was correct to its mind. As if in answer to Hudson, it contended that the effects of competition in regulating the price of manufactures was not wholly satisfactory. Competition might prevent average prices from going too high or too low, but it did not prevent wide fluctuations which resulted in heavy losses to both the producers and the public. A man would not invest in an industry unless he believed he could obtain a satisfactory return. However, once he had built a plant, he must continue operations even if he merely covered operating costs and failed to cover maintenance charges, let alone derive a return on the investment. As a matter of fact, he would compete the more actively when prices were below cost, as long as he had funds.

Thus, instead of setting a natural or normal standard of prices, the journal continued, competition established two different standards—one determined when new capital would enter the industry and the other when old capital would be driven out. Now, those concerns surviving a depression would have a temporary monopoly in the boom that followed; then the high returns would entice new people into the industry; goods soon would be thrown on the market and competition made ruinous. The efforts by pools to prevent cutthroat competition were therefore natural and justified to a certain extent. But the law did not sanction them. The trust was devised to give the pools stability, without promoting consolidations, by checking price fluctuations and waste of capital. In ordinary competition each man sought to extend his market and to be as efficient and economical as possible, so that his prices might be such as to command a large sale. This assured the public efficient service. The managers of trusts, however, generally preferred to do a relatively small business at high prices. This not only hurt the public but led to ruinous competition by enticing capital into the industry. Furthermore, a monopoly tended to oppose improvements of plants; the gains of stable prices were then offset by losses in efficiency.

Curiously enough, both the *Nation* and the *Chronicle* made an exception of the trust that was the center of current controversy, the Standard Oil Company. The *Chronicle* claimed that Standard Oil had wisely kept prices low enough to discourage overwhelming competition; the *Nation*, in an unsigned editorial by Horace White, argued that oil prices had fallen simply because there had not been, and could not be, a monopoly in the oil industry and that Standard Oil never had been a monopoly.[8]

Loose and uncertain as most of these arguments were, they served to convince a large part of the public that monopolies should be controlled. And in 1890 Congress attempted to settle the controversy by passing the Sherman Anti-Trust Act, which declared illegal "every contract, combination in the form of trust or otherwise, or conspiracy, in restraint of trade or commerce among the several states, or with foreign nations." Three years earlier, in 1887, it had acted in the pivotal railroad field with the beginnings of a policy of national control. A Supreme Court decision of 1886, denying to individual states the right to fix rates on shipments going beyond their borders, had brought the issue of national control sharply to the fore. And public opinion finally wrote the Interstate Commerce Act into the law.

Company spokesmen, as might be expected, had been adamant against any form of outside compulsory regulation. Jay Gould stated that in general the freer you allowed things, i.e., the more they were left to the law of supply and demand, the better they regulated themselves, but this did not apply in the railroad field. For there "the bigger fish would sooner or later swallow up the other if they were alongside. They have to do it as a matter of self-preservation." Colonel Albert Fink, the outstanding manager of pools, declared that combinations notwithstanding, rates were fixed by competition—by water competition. The system of pooling, of self-government, accorded, he said, with the spirit of our institutions. The railroads must combine lest their excess facilities lead to cutthroat competition.[9] But these men did not convince the community that an effective pooling system would not give the railroad companies a tremendous power, or, as James F. Hudson put it, "a power over business vaster than either the United States government, or any other under a representative system, ever possessed."[10]

The act, when finally passed, provided for a permanent national commission, the Interstate Commerce Commission, to supervise the railroads. It declared that rates should be reasonable, and it prohibited pooling arrangements. Discriminatory rates, defined as "undue or unreasonable preference or advantage" to any particular person, business unit, locality, or particular kind of traffic, were also forbidden. A higher rate could not be charged for passengers or freight under "substantially similar circumstances and conditions" for a shorter distance than for a longer run, if the former was in the same direction; but the Commission might suspend this "long and short haul" clause. Railroad rates must be filed with the Commission and posted for public inspection at all stations; and no rates could be increased without ten days' notice. A basic provision required annual reports and uniform accounts. But, since no enforcement arrangements were made, these rules remained "little more than an expression of legislative opinion favorable to general publicity."[11]

Even though the act was mild as compared with other proposals set forth in Congress, it was hotly denounced by the railroad heads. Senator Leland Stanford of California, himself a railroad magnate, called it an attack on ownership and the value of property, for the essence of ownership was control, and the value of property was its "income-producing capacity."[12] Believing, as they did, that the act contradicted a natural law, they were prepared to violate it.

Fortunately the first chairman of the Commission was Judge Thomas McIntyre Cooley. He was conservative and had been a pool official, but he also possessed fearlessness and high intellectual integrity.[13] Though the act in many respects ran counter to his views, he set out to enforce it with such vigor that he found his earlier writings being cited against his actions. Court decisions stripped the Commission of much of its effectiveness, but at least a beginning had been made in coping with the problem.

AGRICULTURE

The lead in these campaigns against monopoly and "tight" money had been enthusiastically followed by the farmers, and they were not satisfied simply with paper victories. Their discontent was rising to a high pitch. It was charged that while farm prices were declining, costs were remaining much the same. Loud complaints were made of extortionate and discriminatory practices of the banks, mortgage companies, milling companies, elevators, railroads, and other "middlemen." One writer in the *St. Paul Pioneer Press* wanted to know in January 1886: "How long even with these cheap and wonderfully productive lands can . . . any agricultural community pay such enormous tribute to corporate organizations in times like these without final exhaustion?"

In the Middle West the National Farmers' Alliance (more popularly called the Northwestern Alliance) was a powerful political factor. It demanded a host of reforms, especially government loans in greenbacks on farm lands, these loans to be made for half their value at 2 per cent interest, with the borrower having the privilege of repaying the loan within twenty years. The Southern organization, the National Farmers' Alliance and Industrial Union (generally known as the Southern Alliance), crystallized the rising discontent of the farmers in 1890. They demanded very definite reforms. The government should abolish the national banks and be the sole issuer of paper money by means of the famous sub-treasury plan. As formulated in its most definite form a year before, the plan stated that the government was to establish sub-treasuries or depositories throughout the country. Here borrowers would deposit cotton, wheat, oats, and corn and receive greenbacks to the amount of 80 per cent of their market value. They would also receive negotiable warehouse receipts, stating the amount borrowed. The loan was repayable at the end of a year at 1 per cent interest. It was contended that this scheme would provide a sufficient and elastic currency, at a low enough rate of interest, profitably to move the crops at harvest time. In more general language, it was said that when the farmer returned the warehouse receipt, he would return the paper money; and being canceled, it would disappear from circulation. Thus the system provided a perfectly automatic and elastic currency, expanding when demand expanded, and contracting when demand contracted. The following year, in order to induce the northern group to combine with the Southern Alliance, the plan was expanded to include as security non-perishable farm products, and also real estate, with proper limitations upon the quantity of land and the amount of money; and the rate of interest was raised to 2 per cent rent. This latter demand was especially popularized by Senator William A. Peffer of Kansas, former publisher of the *Kansas Farmer*, in *The Farmer's Side* when he asked for government short-term loans on crops and long-term loans on real estate.

Besides the free coinage of silver, the Southern Alliance also demanded that, all told, the circulating medium should be increased to no less than $50 per capita; that Congress prohibit dealings in futures of all agricultural and mechanical products; that alien ownership of land and land holdings by large corporations in excess of their actual needs be prohibited and such excess land now held be reclaimed for settlement. It further demanded a graduated income tax and economy in government. National and state control of the means of communication and transportation should be tried, and if they should prove unsatisfactory, then outright government ownership should follow. These demands were definite and radical, and their proponents meant business.

Picturesque figures, such as Mrs. Mary E. Lease, who told large audiences of farmers to "raise less corn and more hell," and "Sockless Jerry" Simpson, felt they were leading a crusade and acted accordingly. They got some results, although not far-reaching enough to still their agitation. The Department of Agriculture was raised to full cabinet status, and its head was now called Secretary instead of Commissioner. Legislation was enacted taxing oleomargarine and providing for the inspection of imported livestock and the exclusion of diseased animals. The original Morrill Act of 1862, providing for extensive public land grants to each state for establishing agricultural and mechanical colleges, was supplemented in 1890 by the second Morrill Act, which provided cash grants in addition. But the farmers still strenuously complained of the practices of railroads, heavy interest charges, and low prices for farm products.

LABOR PROBLEMS

To large property holders these farm crusaders seemed to be revolutionists, but at least they were in an American tradition. The new labor movement, however, seemed not only revolutionary but somewhat sinister, an intolerable foreign conspiracy. During the seventies unionization had been growing, and by the eighties had become a major economic problem, which the government had to face. In 1883 Congress held extensive hearings on the relation of labor and capital and in 1884 established a landmark in the country's development by creating the Bureau of Labor in the Department of the Interior. Four years later the Bureau was given a somewhat higher and independent, though not cabinet, status as the Department of Labor.

Carroll D. Wright (1840–1909),[14] a man of deep social sympathies and a keen appreciation of the value of statistics, was appointed head of the Bureau with the title of Commissioner. He had been a patent lawyer and at the time of his appointment was director of the Bureau of Statistics of Labor of his native state, Massachusetts. While he did not believe in direct labor legislation, he did believe in arbitration and trade unions. He considered unemployment largely an outgrowth of the economic structure rather than a phenomenon of natural depravity. Statistics, he thought, would help remedy the situation, but they were not going to be easy to compile. The number of states with bureaus of labor statistics had increased, but there was one serious defect that was generally applicable. As the Commissioner of Labor Statistics of Minnesota pointed out: "I regret very much that the [state] bureau was launched with a fund commensurate with the small opinion which the average legislator has of its utility." [15]

Trade unions, although they had grown in strength until their presence was felt by the government, were still in disrepute with a large group of businessmen. Joseph Medill, publisher of the *Chicago Tribune*, declared that the trade unions were composed of foreigners, who kept out natives. Jay Gould, who controlled the Western Union Telegraph Company as well as several railroads, added that strikes came from the poorest sort of people. "Your best men," he informed the congressional committee, "do not care how many hours they work or anything of that kind. They are looking to get higher up; either to own a business of their own and control it, or to get higher up in the ranks." The general manager of the Atlas Works of Pittsburgh, Thomas M. Miller, on being asked what might be done to raise the wages of people earning seventy-five cents a day, replied that nothing could be done. The law of the "survival of the fittest" governed that, and the poor and the weak had to go to the wall to some extent. [16]

After the strike on the Chicago, Burlington & Quincy Railroad was broken in 1888, Thomas M. Cooley, chairman of the Interstate Commerce Commission, asked the company to give the men a few concessions, but, as he noted in his diary, the president was on his high horse and the company would yield nothing. [17] Such company action was supported by the statements of many influential economists, among them Edward Atkinson. William Ashley, then a fellow at Oxford, was sharply critical of a paper delivered by Atkinson on American labor associations. Atkinson, he wrote, "laid down the law right and left. . . . I suppose he is a great statistical authority, but why don't people take the trouble to learn the elementary facts of social life! . . . He [Atkinson] lumped all the labor movements of America together, speaking of them all as 'cranks'; his objection was not only to socialism, but to the very principles of T[rade] Un[ion]s, the joint action of associations instead of individual contract." [18]

Meanwhile the trade union movement moved ahead. The Knights of Labor, organized in 1869, was the most important. Its basic principle was "one big union of all producers," and it excluded from membership only bankers, lawyers, professional gamblers, stockbrokers, and liquor dealers. It considered co-operatives the ultimate solution of the social problem and invested large sums in such enterprises. It gained great prestige when it emerged victorious, from a strike over a wage cut, against Jay Gould's powerful railway companies in 1885, and its membership rose to over 700,000. However, when it lost a second strike the following year against that same magnate over charges of discrimination against the Knights, a permanent decline in the order set in.

The organization was bitterly attacked as subversive, but a good number of prominent and earnest humanitarians rallied to its defense. *Our Day*, edited by the Reverend Joseph Cook, declared that "Christian men should not be in haste to join the hue and cry raised by politicians and capitalists against the Knights of Labor." Local assemblies, it said, might have made mistakes, but the head, Terence Powderly, was a "conservative and Christian" leader, and the organization continued to hold up a knightly Christian ideal in its name and declaration of principles and in its constitution. "Indeed," it continued, "there are few principles in their ideal which are not in the platform of the chief Christian reformers of the day. In working toward such an ideal they should have only kindly criticism from those who believe, with Hon. Carroll D. Wright of the National Bureau of Labor, 'that in the adoption of the philosophy of the religion of Jesus Christ, as a practical creed for the conduct of business, lies the surest and speediest solution of those industrial difficulties which are exciting the minds of men today, and leading many to think that the crisis of government is at hand.' " [19]

One serious drawback to the successful operation of the Knights of Labor appears to have been the lack of a clear-cut policy on objectives of immediate concern to wage earners. By way of illustration, take a curious treatise on economics authorized by the Massachusetts State Assembly of the order for the use of the Knights and circulated publicly. It was prepared by a member who was also the publisher, Hiram W. K. Eastman, and was called *The Science of Government: A True Assay of the Crude Ore of Political Economy* (1888). In this treatise Eastman supported Carey's views in denouncing free trade, interest, socialism, and in demanding an exclusively government currency based on the volume of exchanges. But at the same time he urged measures which were anathema to Carey. He called for the nationalization of railroads and the telephone and telegraph. Also, he wanted the enactment of a graded income tax, with incomes under $500 exempt from taxation since they were barely sufficient for subsistence. Incomes from $500 to $1000 should be taxed ½ per cent, and the tax on every additional $1000 income should rise 1 per cent; all incomes in excess of a 50 per cent tax should be confiscated. This graded income tax would prevent the growth of inequality and the accumulation of that idle purchasing power which reduced employment. An active purchasing power could be obtained by higher wages. The resulting sense of security would cause proportionately increased consumption, rapidly rising values, and a larger return to the businessman. Eastman finally suggested that employers should join the Knights and fight "shoulder to shoulder their common foe, the monopolists of their government's power, functions, and duties."

Such wishful thinking was less freely indulged in by a new national labor organization rising to prominence in 1881. The Federation of Organized Trades and Labor Unions of the United States and Canada (later the American Federation of Labor) was composed of autonomous skilled craft unions. It proved more effective than the Knights of Labor, for it clearly emphasized that the primary interest was in immediate remedies—for wages, hours of work, and labor conditions—rather than in an ideal future society. Although the Socialist leaders had in effect talked the same way, many respectable citizens were more willing to give a sympathetic ear to the Federation, as one congressman put it, so long as they did not present a "foreign point of view." The Federation leaders capitalized on this sentiment. Samuel Gompers, president of the organization, declared that the trade unions were neither communistic nor socialistic. Even the majority of the Socialists in the organization said: " 'Whatever ideas we may have as to the future state of society . . . must remain in the background, and we must subordinate our convictions . . . to the general good that the trades union movement brings to the laborer.' " [20]

Adolph Strasser, previously a prominent Socialist, demonstrated that stratagem before the Senate Committee hearings on Labor and Capital in 1883:

Strasser: I look first to the trade I represent; . . . to the interests of men who employ me to represent their interests. . . . We have no ultimate ends. We are going on from day to day. We are fighting only for immediate objects—objects that can be realized in a few years.

Senator Wilkinson Call: You want something better to eat and to wear, and better houses to live in?

Strasser: Yes; we want to dress better and to live better and . . . become better citizens generally.

Chairman Henry W. Blair: I see that you are a little sensitive lest it should be thought that you are a mere theorizer. I do not look upon you in that light at all.

Strasser: Well, we say in our constitution [of the International Cigar Makers' Union] that we are opposed to theorists, and I have to represent the organization here. We are all practical men.[21]

Some of the leaders were quite adept at manipulating traditional economics. For example, Frank Foster stated: "Even accepting the doctrine of the orthodox school of political economy, that labor is . . . a commodity, . . . the supply of any commodity in the market is not a fixed quantity, but is, or may be, regulated by combination," as in the case of the Standard Oil Company. "We claim . . . the same right" for labor. At the same time, in order to give a better theoretical foundation for the demand for an eight-hour day, the Federation circularized academic economists as to the effect of such a measure. It also engaged George Gunton, a former labor leader who was a contributor to the academic journals, to prepare a pamphlet, *The Economic and Social Importance of the Eight-Hour Movement* (1889).[22]

Gunton pointed out that consumption by the masses was the foundation of the market, and that the "success of the employing class depended on the extent of the consuming class." Consequently the failure of the wage-receiving classes to consume, which enforced idleness implied, undermined the prosperity of the whole community and laid the base for recurrent industrial depressions. Failure to recognize this fact sprang from the popular economic heresy of regarding the laborer as a factor in production and ignoring him as a factor in consumption. This led to the mistaken policy of absorbing the greatest possible amount of the laborer's energy and time in production; such an absorption seriously restricted, if it did not destroy, his opportunity for developing consumption. Thereby the growth of consumption had been limited, and that of enforced idleness—the greatest of all social evils—had been promoted.

The first step to prevent enforced idleness, he argued, should be toward a reduction of hours. Not only would shorter hours increase wages by reducing .enforced idleness, but it would have a more permanent effect by creating new wants, and this would raise the standard of living. Moreover, the reduction of hours would increase profits rather than reduce them. The capitalist was not concerned so much with the rate of profit as the aggregate amount of profit. He wanted not so much a larger proportion as a larger actual amount of wealth, which could be economically accomplished only by increasing the aggregate consumption. Low wages resulted in small consumption, limited use of capital, and slow methods of production. Even at a high rate of profit this made a large aggregate income impossible.

For example, a shoe manufacturer, in order to live according to the accepted standard of his class, must charge a profit of ten cents on each pair of shoes. If by investing a larger amount of capital and using improved machinery, he could make the shoes at two-thirds the former cost, and double his sales, he could reduce the price, increase wages, and yet make larger aggregate profits. This, however, would be possible only when the aggregate demand for shoes was increased. Thus the larger production consequent upon the increased consumption by the masses would make all classes actually richer.

Commissioner Carroll D. Wright agreed that the growth of the labor movement, along with the growth of employers' organizations, was the solution to depressions and labor problems. To Wright the increase of productive capacity was greatly in excess of demand. "This full supply of economic tools to meet the wants of nearly all branches of commerce and industry," he said, "is the most important factor in the present industrial depression." True, the discovery of new manufacturing processes would continue and would act as an ameliorating influence, but it would not provide for as marked an extension as had occurred during the past fifty years, or afford profitable employment for the vast amount of capital created during that period. Prices would continue low regardless of costs. The day of large profits was past. There might be room for further intensive, but not extensive, development of industry in the present area of civilization.

The remedy, Wright felt, was the complete organization of each industry. Manufacturers said, he pointed out, that if employers in each industry would combine in an association, the regulation of the volume of production with demand would be placed on a scientific foundation, and depressions and labor troubles ended; and workingmen argued that if they could organize on a strong comprehensive basis, they could so regulate wage rates as to achieve the necessary uniformity and stability in the hours of labor. Wright thought that the manufacturers held a correct position, and that the position held by the workingmen would also be sound if, as some did, they embodied the amount of production in their views. If complete organization on each side was achieved, each force would treat with the other through intelligent representatives, thereby eliminating the passion, excitement, and other ills occurring when a large body of individual men endeavor to treat with single proprietors. With specific disputes treated by representative bodies, and manufacturing reduced to a scientific basis, "so-called overproduction," in his view, would be eliminated and employment equalized.

Wright felt that this proved there was no contest between laborers and capitalists as such. The contest was over the proportion of the profits each side should receive for its respective investment. The interests of capital and labor, while not identical, were reciprocal, and the wise comprehension of the reciprocal element could be fully achieved only by a complete organization through which each party would feel itself to be an integral part of the working establishment. Public sentiment could encourage each side to treat with the other so that production could be regulated by demand rather than by the ill-advised eagerness of men to emphasize the worth of their individual contribution. In consequence, Wright maintained that one of the important services rendered by the federal Bureau of Labor was to supply statistical information to the captains of industry, thus enabling them to consider output more scientifically and to eliminate some of the haphazard methods of production.

Later Wright rephrased his main argument, with modifications, in terms of underconsumption and contended that industrial education was the most effective mode of action; that by increasing the skill and consumption of the lower classes it would raise their standard of living and thus their consuming power.[23]

The unsophisticated underconsumption theory enjoyed some attention in respectable journals, such as the *Atlantic Monthly*, from prominent figures; for example, Uriel H. Crocker. Crocker, a Harvard graduate, prominent Boston lawyer, assiduous economic journalist, and son of an outstanding New England railroad magnate, argued that instead of reducing production to avoid crises, consumption should be raised. He wrote in 1886 that the recent successful strikes of the Knights of Labor were working toward this desirable goal—if the Knights did not go too far—for the rise in wages would bring increased consumption and the machinery of production and distribution would go into full action, thus providing full employment. However, "it is much to be feared that excessive demands by the laboring classes . . . will tend to check enterprise and to frighten capital, and will thus, by reducing the demand for labor," bring about an actual reduction of wages.[24]

THE CRY OF OVERPRODUCTION

Such views as those of Wright and Crocker were indicative of the increasing number of able non-academicians who were questioning a central position of "orthodox" economics; namely, the impossibility of general overproduction. Furthermore, their analyses went far beyond the mere monetary mechanism. These men came from various professions. There was Frederick William Henshaw (1858–1929), a graduate of the University of California and later an Associate Justice of the State Supreme Court, who thus described the course of general business: "Trade passes from a state of quiescence to one of activity; there is growing confidence, prosperity, excitement, speculation, over-production, revulsion, pressure, stagnation, and distress, ending again (or again beginning) with quiescence." This was the problem to be attacked. To Henshaw the causes of recurring crises were these: Commercial distress came about when the production of important commodities, requiring vast capital and thousands of laborers, exceeded demand; prices then fell below a point where the dealers derived a profit. As a result the unfit were eliminated. Unless one wished to destroy credit, which as a matter of fact could not be done, there was no way to prevent revulsions. "They are of mental origin," he said; "they spring from excessive hopefulness; they are caused, as it were, by a diseased confidence; and until an all-wise system of government or education shall render it impossible for men to be knaves or fools, crises will hold their place in the business world."

While the primary cause of panics was psychological, a secondary cause, he found, was the conversion of an excessive amount of circulating capital into fixed capital. This constituted an attempt to expend in fixed capital more than the savings of the community. Added to this was another difficulty, the too rapid increase of circulating capital itself. England furnished a good example. In producing fixed capital, she was practically at a standstill, for she had enough for many years. In factories, ships, machinery, buildings, her annual outlay was a fraction of her vast wealth. The various forms of circulating capital were, therefore, of increasing importance for her prosperity. But with the increment of money and commodities the difficulty of finding a market for them arose, and resulted in those secondary and more immediate effects, a tendency toward minimum profits and the temptation to engage in speculative enterprise.

He concluded with the statement: "The theory has been advanced that . . . [the] occurrence [of crises] will become increasingly frequent 'till at length business will move under one continuous crisis; that instead of successive taps, there will be the long roll; in place of occasional heavy blows, one strong pressure. Time alone can test this theory, but until a measure can be found to quench man's inordinate thirst for gain . . . it is undoubtedly true that crises will occur." [25]

Henshaw's analysis ran much along established lines, but others opened new paths. Frederick B. Hawley (1843–1929), for instance, was much less orthodox. He graduated from Williams College in 1864, and spent the next two years studying law. Then he entered his grandfather's lumber business in Albany. In 1876 he became a cotton broker and merchant in New York. He was a keen student of classical economics, but from his experience he concluded that the classical doctrine of the impossibility of general overproduction, or, as he called it, "over-accumulation," was erroneous.

Hawley in 1882 presented his position elaborately in *Capital and Population*, and for the benefit of the temporary Tariff Commission he neatly summarized its essential principles in a paper that same year. He informed the Commission that capital had a persistent tendency to press upon its limits, which were determined by population and the state of the arts; that is, a community could not continue accumulating capital beyond the amount that could be profitably utilized in employing labor. Any permanent addition to capital beyond this amount required either an increase in the number of laborers, or a diversion of some labor from industries using little to those using a greater amount of capital, in proportion to the labor employed. "For," he said, "if . . . a further addition is made to capital, i.e., to the funds actively engaged in or reserved for productive employment, the competition of such capital lowers the rate of profit." Consequently industrial activity and employment would be reduced. Thus any policy which opened new avenues for investment, by maintaining the rate of profit and the amount of employment and productive efficiency, allowed such accumulations as the new investments justified to be saved from the products of labor which would otherwise not have been employed.[26]

Hawley had gone even further in earlier articles. He had argued that depressions could not permanently be eliminated until the inequality of wealth was reduced, as a result of which the powers of consumption would be increased. For instance, Vanderbilt spent only about 2 per cent of his annual income; if that income were distributed among men of average fortunes, about 50 per cent would be spent. But while the too rapid accumulation of wealth should be discouraged for the capitalists' own benefit, he warned, "any remedy which greatly disturbs vested interests or individual freedom attacks principles more fundamental to progress than the elimination of the evil of excess of capital," for individual property and consequently inequality of wealth were essential to civilization. He declared that second to a tariff scheme the most desirable remedy would be for the rich to spend lavishly on elegant residences, museums, parks, etc. The government could erect buildings and the like to draw away excessive accumulation, but such expenditures, when met by taxes, would reduce the powers of consumption.[27]

Hawley's emphasis on the entrepreneur as the great dynamic force was particularly stimulating to academic economists. He had a "risk theory of profit," in which enterprise or "risk taking" was ranked with land, labor, and capital as one of the four fundamental divisions of the productive forces, and profit, its reward, was classed with rent, wages, and interest as one of the four distinct forms of income. "Enterprise, or the assumption of risk, was the distinguishing function of the entrepreneur," and profit was the reward for services rendered by assuming industrial risks. More specifically, since industrial risks would not be assumed without the expectation of a compensation exceeding the actuarial value of the risk, profit was the income arising from the chance of the gain being greater than the loss, in the risks assumed. Hawley granted that profits might include monopoly profits, but such monopoly gains, he contended, were also attached to the other incomes from productive factors and were largely due to the "friction or insufficiency of competition." [28]

Perhaps Hawley's most conspicuous service was his criticism of the kind of statistics with which Edward Atkinson was flooding the country, proving that labor received practically all the product of industry. Atkinson did not take Hawley's criticisms too kindly, and Hawley declared: "I am not an anarchist, a communist, or even a socialist, despite Mr. Atkinson's suspicions. . . . By association, education, and sympathy I belong to the capitalist or employing class; but I do not believe . . . in a policy that misleads. . . . And when a widely read book . . . appears, which asserts that laborers now receive 95 per cent of all that is produced, and that the utmost . . . a more even distribution could effect for the poor man would be to give him one more glass of beer a day, I believe great harm is being done. . . . [The masses] are sure to suspect the truth and even the honesty of such statements, which in the end must breed distrust and opposition."

Was Hawley's alternative much better? "The right appeal," he said, "is to show that society is an organism, and that increasing differentiation is the one condition absolutely essential to its progress or even to its continued existence. It is to show that the highest social functions can be adequately performed only by the favorites of fortune, and then to recognize and enforce such functions, not only as the special duties but as really the best privileges of the rich." [29]

Along lines developed by Hawley, George Basil Dixwell (1815–1885) of Boston defended the tariff, and, like Hawley again, his analysis went beyond the tariff. Dixwell came of a distinguished New England family and passed most of his active life in China, where he held prominent commercial and diplomatic positions, such as consul general for Russia at Hong Kong and chief municipal officer of the International Concession at Shanghai. After "great commercial successes and reverses," Dixwell returned to this country in 1875 at the age of sixty, "freed from the cares of business through an ample inherited fortune."

To the free-trade argument that industry was limited by capital, Dixwell replied that, on the contrary, the increase of both industry and capital was limited by the "field of employment." The field of employment, in turn, was limited by effective demand. Take for example, the shoe industry; men's desire for shoes was itself limited, even if these shoes were given away. Interpose difficulty of attainment, the necessity for effort or sacrifice, and fewer would be used. The demand would be further narrowed if a portion of the community was unemployed. "Evidently," he concluded, "only a certain number of shoes can be profitably made at any cost you choose to fix upon. Reduce profits ever so low, and still the manufacture has its limits. Increase now the aggregate means of the community for the purchase of shoes, whether by increasing the population or by increasing the proportion of the population which can find a sale for its labor, and the demand for shoes will increase, their exchangeable value will rise, the profits of the manufacture will augment," and consequently more shoes would be made to meet the changed conditions. The new limits would now be in the production, which again would reduce the exchangeable value of shoes to that point where the profits fell to the rate usual in the community. The moment profits enabled the manufacturers to add to their capital a greater annual percentage than that by which the population increased, they would increase their production faster than the population; when profits were lower, they would allow the population to gain upon the production. There was evident to him a limit, though somewhat flexible, to the field of employment open to this industry.

This was true, he said, not only of the manufacture of shoes but of all commodities and services. The normal condition of a progressive community, then, was that skill, dexterity, judgment, and machinery were constantly diminishing the sacrifice by which men could procure commodities, and were constantly increasing the amount of unemployed capital. This capital naturally sought new commodities and services which might tempt the capitalists to increase their consumption and thereby keep pace with the increasing capacity for production. Each new commodity, convenience, and amusement furnished a new market for existing industries and enlarged the effective demand. The field of employment was increased, the people were more fully occupied, the gross annual product was augmented, and the opportunities for utilizing additional fixed and floating capital were multiplied.[30]

By far the most popular work along these heterodox lines was done by the usually orthodox David A. Wells. His *Recent Economic Changes* (1889) was largely a compilation of previous articles dealing with economic disturbances since the panic of 1873. Wells asserted that while there had been disagreeable accompaniments to the vast industrial changes, still, on the whole, considerable progress had been made. In the long run the disturbing features would disappear in accordance with the principles of traditional economics.

At the same time Wells contended that the fall in prices, which the bimetallists attributed to the demonetization of silver, was in fact caused by the improved facilities of production, which resulted in an increased supply in the world markets disproportionate to the increase in population. He was disturbed by the fact that large-scale enterprise in competitive society would continue to function even when prices were not sufficient to cover cost of production and a fair profit. Thus, for example, though several joint stock companies had made no profit and paid no dividends for years, they continued operations. "Under such circumstances *industrial overproduction*—manifesting itself in excessive competition to effect sales and a reduction in prices below the cost of production—may become chronic."

In a somewhat similar analysis the previous decade Wells had stressed tariff reduction as the remedy; now he concluded that the solution lay in combination. This was the gist of Wells' argument, but running through it were those same doubts as to the value of the ultimate harmony that he had expressed to his friend Atkinson while preparing the book. He appealed to Atkinson to help him out of some serious intellectual difficulties, but not in an "offhand manner." The result of technological progress was to economize on labor with temporary displacement and to increase production in excess of current demand. In the process of time there would be adjustment, but he wanted to know how. Take, for example, copper. The reduction in the price had resulted in a 25 per cent increase in consumption. This should have increased the number of wage recipients. Yet actually some of the mines suspended work by reason of the low prices. "I have got the facts, lots of them like these—but I don't come out quite clear in my conclusions." The point of it all, he declared, was in the assertion of their mutual friend, Charles Nordhoff, that it was not enough to show that those things would ultimately adjust themselves; the problem was "how shall we treat labor grievances now?" [31]

Certainly by supporting the doctrine of general overproduction Wells discarded a cherished axiom of orthodoxy.[32] In fact, the orthodox economists considered this view the one blemish on Wells' reputation. One eulogist said of Wells: "In his *Recent Economic Changes,* one of the most effective books of its kind, he was led astray by the overproduction fallacy, although that lapse had little to do with the real value of the volume." The reviewer for the *Nation* declared that it would have been improved had Wells used throughout, "as he does occasionally, the terms 'disturbance' in place of 'depression,' and 'cheaper production' in place of 'overproduction.' As he shows by manifold proofs, there has been no depression, but a vast increase of trade in the period of which he treats, and he recognizes the truth that universal over-production is an absurd idea. There is some reason to think that the author himself has been unconsciously affected by this confusion of terms." [33]

Yet in giving some respectability to the doctrine of general overproduction, Wells helped to turn serious attention to the whole problem of what in a later era became known as "business cycles." These, as Francis A. Walker had earlier commented, had not been considered a problem of economic theory.

THE OLD RADICAL CURRENTS

These unorthodox theories were fairly widely read but little acted upon. The general public was still rather apathetic toward theoretic solutions to its practical needs. It listened to the theories of overproduction and the like, which had an obvious kinship to radical doctrines, but the more thoroughgoing types of radicalism in their old forms could scarcely even collect an audience. Judson Grenell of the *Detroit Free Press,* a Socialistic Labor Party leader, complained of this to John F. Bray in 1883: "Education is such a slow process in peaceful times, that I often wish for *revolution,* when the mind as well as the pulse quickens and ideas spread with lightning rapidity. The people are dead. They eat and drink and sleep and hope for the opportunity to 'get rich' all of a sudden. Delusive hope! If that could only be taken away from them by impressing upon them the fact that not one in a hundred thousand has such a chance, why then we could see progress in right ideas." [34]

And there were some prominent defections that added to the discouragement. Grenell's fellow Socialist and labor leader of Detroit, Joseph A. Labadie, began to think that the government by impeding the natural workings of competition was the cause of all economic evil.

"I have tried," he wrote, "to look in the direction of governmentalism for the cure of social and industrial ills, but the longer I look in that direction the more hopeless and gloomy do the prospects get. Competition is to economics what gravitation is to physics, and anything that tends to interfere with its natural and legitimate working will ultimately result in evil. What, it seems to me, is necessary to create harmonious social relations and reach the highest and most perfect economy in the production and distribution of wealth, is to gradually remove the barriers that the state has placed between the producer and the *natural* means of production. The state assumes to do too much, and it is a botcher." [35]

Under such circumstances it is not surprising that the socialists became opportunistic. In its attempts to keep within the climate of American opinion, the Socialistic Labor Party found it necessary to shift its idiom from time to time. Thus in 1884 it proclaimed that the current industrial competition was resulting in "monstrous monopolies . . . subversive of all democracy, injurious to the national interests, and destructive of truth and morality." Three years later, however, it declared that this competitive system "carries within itself the germs of a new organization of humanity. . . . By the evolution of this system to its highest pitch, the dispossessed working masses will at last become opposed to a comparatively few despotic chiefs of industry, and by reason of the unbearable uncertainty of existence, the former will find themselves compelled to abolish the wage system and establish the co-operative society."

The society advocated by the Socialistic Labor Party would substitute public ownership for private ownership in the instruments of production, and with it "co-operative production and a guarantee of a share in the product in accordance with the service rendered by the individuals to society." Governments and lawmaking bodies must assist the change toward co-operative society by proper legislation, in order to avoid a class conflict. The party stated: "For that purpose we strive for the acquisition of political power with all appropriate means." [36]

But until that time should come they tried to pursue obtainable, practical goals. One branch of the Socialistic Labor Party, that of

Minneapolis, canvassed academic economists in an effort to find a meeting ground on what constituted sound political economy for the laborers. A committee, whose actual guiding spirit was W. G. H. Smart, formerly of Boston, wrote Professor William W. Folwell of the University of Minnesota in 1888 that it had been "instructed to examine the national platforms of the political parties now asking for the votes of the workingmen with a view to discovering the bearing of each on the interest of said class." The members of this committee expressed great surprise that the Republican and the Democratic Parties, holding as they did diametrically opposing views on the great economic issues, had not appealed to the economics professors, whose domain, after all, was to deal authoritatively with those questions about which the "two great parties are quarreling, and in regard to which *one* of them, *at least*, must be entirely in the wrong."

Folwell, as the "chief official authority in this State on questions of political economy," was asked to answer the following questions briefly and categorically from the standpoint of his science in its most recent expressions:

1. Is or is not the the so-called "iron law of wages," as enunciated by Ricardo and accepted by Marx and other distinguished economists —namely, "The natural rate of wages is that price which is necessary to enable the laborers in competition one with another to subsist and to perpetuate their race without increase or diminution"—the true law of wages under the present economic system of the civilized world?

2. If your answer to the above question is in the affirmative, will what is called the "American system of Protection" prevent the operation of that law and thus act as the "bulwark of wages" to American labor?

3. Still supposing your answer to the first question to be in the affirmative, will the operation of what is called the "Mills Bill" for reducing the tariff, or will the abolition of a protective tariff altogether, prevent the operation of said "iron law of wages," and permanently benefit the working classes by reducing the cost of living without proportionately reducing their wages?

4. Are the large combinations of capitalists and corporations known as "trusts" a logical and therefore proper development of the present economic system, or are they abnormal excrescences that can and should be eradicated by legislation?

5. Would "the abolition of the saloon remove burdens, moral, physical, pecuniary, and social, which now oppress labor and rob it of its earnings" (as one political party [Prohibition Party] asserts), while the other conditions of the working classes remain as they now are?

Folwell's reply, apparently not too clear, was "unfavorable to their hopes and expectations." [37] From William Graham Sumner, as they must have expected, they received a "decisive and uncompromising reply." These sources proving so unco-operative, they turned to Folwell for "any other authoritative names here or in Europe" to whom they should send the questions. "Of course," they added, "we would like names of those most likely to favor our views, as a set-off to those we have already addressed and those free from the bias arising from sordid national politics." [38]

The discouraging prospect, which led some radicals to seek compromise and slow reform, led others to recommend change by force. A new variety of anarchism, coming from Europe, aroused some short-lived interest by its doctrine of violent revolution. It insisted that only force could bring about such requisite fundamental changes in society as the abolition of property. Its proponents argued that the dominant capitalist class had used, and would continue to use, force to maintain itself in power; and force must be met by force. These anarchists were known as the "anarchists of the deed," to distinguish them from the philosophical anarchists. Their most prominent exponent in America, Johann Most, was a German who had been expelled from the Marxian Social-Democratic Party of Germany. He called himself an "anarchistic-communist," or better, an adherent to "communistic anarchism." He declared that the anarchists were socialists because they wanted radical reform, and they were communists because they believed that community of property was the only basis of such a reform. [39]

On May 4, 1886, the Haymarket bomb episode blew open an economic issue the pressure of which had been rising for years. The death of several policemen attempting to disperse a peaceful labor meeting caused fear and hatred to run rampant throughout the nation. The press was practically hysterical. As a result every kind of socialism was confused with "anarchism of the deed." In Kansas City, Missouri, the central labor union expelled socialist members and "adopted strong resolutions against socialism and anarchism," and a local Knights of Labor Assembly was suspended for socialistic tendencies. [40]

Seven anarchists were sentenced to death for the bombing and one to life imprisonment. William Dean Howells and a host of other liberals protested against what is now viewed as judicial murder, but to little avail. The sentences of two were commuted to life imprisonment, and one committed suicide. The only native American of the condemned group, Albert A. Parsons, died pleading, "O, men of America, let the voice of the people be heard." Around the scaffold crowds sang the "Marseillaise." [41]

Probably the most glowing tribute paid to the condemned men was that of the American philosophical anarchist Benjamin R. Tucker just a few days before the execution: "I differ with them vitally in opinion; I disapprove utterly their methods; I dispute emphatically their anarchism, but as brothers, as dear comrades, animated by the same love, and working, in the broad sense, in a common cause, than which there never was a grander, I give them both my hands, and my heart in them. Far be it from me to shirk in the slightest the solidarity that unites us. Were I to do so, for trivial ends, or from ignoble fears, I should despise myself as a coward." [42]

So the eighties drew toward their close with society forced to reassess or reassert its basic assumptions. The Haymarket Affair was a climax in deeds of the growing differences radical economists had been spelling out in words. But it was only the most dramatic, perhaps because the most destructive, deed of the decade; there were other acts, constructive in their aim, that had a more lasting effect. The beginnings of legislation to control monopolies and the railroads, the establishment of the federal Department of Labor, the passage of legislation for the purchase of silver, and the creation of governmental machinery to aid the farmer—all indicate that the turbulent controversies of the time affected practice; that what the reformers were saying was not just sound and fury, but signified something. The country was by now alert to economic questions, and it was willing to take action; perhaps not fast enough for some, but it was not standing still. The monetary problem remained paramount as the key to prosperity and depression in men's minds. The legislation passed, the Sherman Silver Purchase Act, was heavily attacked and open to serious criticism, but at least it meant positive action, in a situation where even the great majority of active anti-silverites contended that something needed to be done, but could not agree among themselves as to the specific remedy.

Perhaps the most significant development of the decade was the emergence of labor as a new power in the country. Although its enemies spoke as firmly and loudly as ever, an increasing number of respectable voices were rising to its defense. The power of organized labor should not be exaggerated, however; the movement was still viewed with suspicion by the dominant groups. As its words and actions moved more directly toward the concrete ends of improving wages and working conditions, it gained more strength within itself and wider public approval.

CHAPTER VI

Popular Radicalism

THE traditional arguments of the socialists and the philosophical anarchists drew a small audience. They seemed to be losing what effectiveness they had had as critics; now that their theories were found not to be contagious, they were benignly tolerated. However, any revolutionary doctrine threatening a deep or wide infection, such as the Haymarket Affair, which was attributed to "anarchists of the deed," was to be treated as a plague.

Yet this same period witnessed the emergence of a widely read radical literature that appeared to add greatly to the turbulence of the times. Henry George's *Progress and Poverty* and Edward Bellamy's *Looking Backward* were such books, one would suppose, as might have been criticized out of existence by the powers they attacked. That they were not is a historical contradiction that requires much explanation. First, the books caught the discontents of the hour so effectively that nearly all persons with some complaint against the current system—and these were many—could find aid and comfort in them. Second, both authors were able in their writing to convey their deep sincerity and their intense love of humanity in such a way as to disarm the opposition. They had a broad humanitarian social philosophy that transcended their specific proposals for reconstruction and reform. Third, their writing was in such a form as to seem once removed from practical, immediate action. Fourth, their books gave a sense of humane direction to many persons who were made uncomfortable by the cold logic of traditional economics, without making them feel that inhumane means were necessary to gain their ends. Last, both writers wrote directly for the popular mind, by-passing the irritable temper of economic doctrinaires. In this way, perhaps because neither had had much formal education, George and Bellamy, without hardening their hearts to temper their minds, were able to awaken professional economists to their own deficiencies.

HENRY GEORGE

From the viewpoint of economic theory Henry George is the more important of the two; his influence to the present time has been subtle and extensive. He was born in Philadelphia of respectable parentage.[1] His formal education ended as he approached fourteen, but was supplemented by attendance at popular lectures and extensive reading, largely of the type indulged in by able journalists. He worked as an errand boy and clerk, then went to sea, and finally became a printer. Hoping to better his fortunes on the Pacific Coast, he worked his way to California in 1857. He joined the gold rush to British Columbia in 1859, but arrived too late. So he spent the next two decades in California, earning a precarious living in journalism mixed with Democratic Party politics.

George was an ardent free-trader and was deeply impressed with Wells' work for tariff and revenue reform, especially with Wells' report in 1871 as chairman of the New York State Commission on tax reform. At that time George was beginning to develop his ideas on the single tax; and he was wrought up over the iniquities of the California tax system, which, he wrote Wells, was worse than New York's. Wells in his report, of which George received advance sheets, advocated the abolition of the general property tax, which, he contended, was both inequitable and easily evaded by personal property. Instead, the state should tax all corporations holding state franchises which were in the "nature of a monopoly," e.g., gas companies; tax all land and buildings; and, as an equivalent for a tax on personal property, tax every individual an amount equal to three times the rent or rental value of the home or place of business he occupied.[2]

Along with this his humanitarianism led George to study labor reform. He early protested against the views expressed by Atkinson that the eight-hour day was an attempt to substitute a statute for the steam engine. On the contrary, he wrote Wells in 1871, it was an attempt to "utilize for the masses some portion of the benefits of the steam engine, and I do not think that large production depends so much upon the number of hours of human labor as upon the intelligence and economy with which that labor is directed."

All in all, he came to the conclusion that economics and politics could not be separated. He hoped that it would be possible to make a square fight on the chief economic questions, especially the tariff, for their importance far transcended that of current political questions, important as the latter might be. "I am not certain that the time has not come for a new political organization, and I am quite certain that in some way co-operation between the liberal, free-trade wing of the Republican party and the like wing of the Democratic Party, should be secured prior to the next election." A fusion did take place, but it failed to live up to George's expectation, and it quickly fizzled out.

George was not completely at ease in the realms of economic theory, but his sense of mission carried him on. Despite his keen recognition that he was on the "outskirts, intellectual as well as geographical," he had a high spiritual quality that more than made up for any intellectual deficiencies. In encouraging Wells to continue his efforts for tariff and tax reform despite defeats, he wrote: "Turn light into the caverns of ignorance, and the bats will whirr about your ears. Offer to lay hands upon vested wrongs, and you arouse the most bitter, the most unscrupulous assailants. I know the sickening part of it—how the very men you are doing your best to serve often turn upon you in their ignorance or worse. . . . Sometimes I feel disheartened when I see how little the people, and especially the laboring classes, appreciate their true interest, how easily they are deluded with words and led by demagogues, . . . and my habitual view of the future of the nation is far less rose-colored than it once was, but for all that the earnest honest man, who would do what he can in his day and generation, must go on.[3]

In 1879 George finished *Progress and Poverty*, the book which made him famous. His thought had its origin in two experiences. On a visit to New York he had been moved by "the shocking contrast between monstrous wealth and debasing want." In California he had been impressed by the unused land held for speculative purposes. In the latter phenomenon he saw a fundamental cause of the former, and of depressions. As the subtitle of the book states, it was "An Inquiry into the Cause of Industrial Depressions and of Increase of Want with Increase of Wealth."

Beginning like the traditional economists, George ruled out historical and statistical investigations as unessential to economics. Economics as an exact science should trace by infallible logical analysis the workings of the axiomatic principles of common sense, "truths of which we are all conscious and upon which in everyday life we constantly base our reasoning and our actions." In consequence, George's theory of value was quite similar to that originally developed by Carey as the doctrine of the cost of reproduction. Things had value "in proportion to the amount of exertion which they will command in exchange," was his definition in the posthumously published *The Science of Political Economy*. The great mass of goods being reproducible, value was in effect fixed by the efforts of present labor, the cost of reproducing them. This held for the goods called capital as distinct from land, and the return to capital, that is, interest, he justified on the basis of a theory similar to Del Mar's organic productivity theory.[4] Interest sprang from the "power of increase which the reproductive force of nature, and the, in effect, analogous capacity for exchange, give to capital. . . . It is not the result of a particular social organization, but of laws of the universe which underlie society."

Since, as he pointed out, land was non-reproducible, its value was fixed solely by demand, as formulated in Ricardo's law of rent, which George called a geometric axiom. As George interpreted this law, it read: "The rent of land is determined by the excess of its produce over that which the same application can secure from the least productive land in use." This would, of course, be the point where no rent is paid. More significant was George's alternative conception of this law: "The ownership of a natural agent of production will give the power of appropriating so much of the wealth produced by the exertion of labor and capital upon it as exceeds the return which the same application of labor and capital could secure in the least productive occupation in which they freely engage." In other words, declared George, "to say that rent will be the excess in productiveness over the yield at the margin, or lowest point of cultivation, is the same thing as to say that it will be the excess of produce over what the same amount of labor and capital obtains in the least remunerative occupation." This payment for rent, therefore, represented no aid to production, but merely the monopoly power of securing a part of production, from the producers, for the right to produce.

Carrying this argument further, he said that the law of rent was also the law of interest and wages, for marginal—i.e., no rent—land fixed wages and interest. Wages were the average produce of labor at the margin of cultivation, or the point of lowest return. The relation between wages and interest was determined by the average power of increase which attached to capital from its use in "reproductive modes." Wages and interest would thus vary inversely with rent. As rent increased, wages and interest would fall. Laborers and capitalists were really co-partners in misery because of the workings of the vampire rent.

"What has caused rent to increase?" asked George. The answer lay in the growth of social forces to which the recipients of rent contributed nothing but their permission to produce. Population increase was an important factor, for this increase led to a lower margin of cultivation, and thus to an increase of rent, but total production itself was increased through the resulting economies of production, division of labor, and increasing exchange. This applied most significantly in the cities, where the huge land values were but evidence of the progress in wealth as a consequence of increasing population and co-operation.

A second factor leading to an increase of rent, according to George, was improvement in the industrial arts. By producing more wealth and increasing the labor supply, these improvements necessitated more land and thus a lower margin. "While the primary effect of labor-saving improvements is to increase the power of labor, the secondary effect is to extend cultivation and, where this lowers the margin of cultivation, to increase rent." But the most important cause for increased rent was, in his eyes, land speculation. In all progressive countries, he said, the steady increase of rent created a confident expectation of a further rise. Thus land was held for a higher price than it would normally bring. Withholding land from use forced the "margin of cultivation farther than required by the necessities of production."

Herein also lay the cause of depressions. This extension of the margin beyond the normal limit forced labor and capital to cease producing in self-defense, for it meant the reduction of their accustomed returns. The slackening of production at any one point in the closely interwoven economic fabric reflected itself at other points in a cessation of demand. Hence a depression. This depression continued until (1) the speculative advance in rents was lost; (2) the increase in labor efficiency owing to the growth of population or advance in the arts enabled the normal rent line to overtake the speculative rent lines; (3) labor and capital became reconciled to producing for smaller returns. "Or, most probably, all three of these causes would co-operate to produce a new equilibrium, at which all the forces of production would again engage, and a season of activity ensue; whereupon rent would begin to advance again, a speculative advance again take place, production again be checked, and the same round be gone over."

Thus the cause of depression and increasing poverty lay in the fact that, with the increasing productive power of labor and capital, rent tended to increase even more, thereby forcing down wages and interest. This being so, for George the real solution could be arrived at by the State's appropriating rent. Businessmen would then be relieved of taxes, and the monopoly of the natural opportunities of labor would be destroyed.

Since everyone would then have an opportunity to make a comfortable living, society would "approach the ideal of Jeffersonian democracy, the promised land of Herbert Spencer, the abolition of government. But of government only as a directing and repressive power." In place of its repressive functions, government would with ever-increasing revenues from the single tax on land, toward the progress of society, operate the telegraph and railroads, gas, heat, and water concerns, universities, and other public activities. "We would reach the ideal of the socialist but not through government repression. Government would become the administration of a great co-operative society."

George seems to have been well acquainted with those two laissez-faire critics of land ownership, John Stuart Mill and Herbert Spencer.[5] And he quickly recognized that Edward T. Peters in his 1871 articles was sketching the broad philosophy that was to be the basis of his own position on the appropriative nature of land values. But George had certain advantages over others in the field. He not only offered a simple remedy, but he also wrote with a brilliance that matched his passionate sincerity. One admirer well said: "The wonderful poetry with which he succeeded in popularizing what before him was with truth called the 'dismal science,' will win men's hearts before their reasoning is even touched, and it is through the heart that the people is conquered." Another forcefully stated: "More than any other man, Mr. George aided in refuting the vulgar notion that the reform movement in America was an importation from king-cursed, army-ridden foreign nations, brought in by ignorant ne'er-do-wells and criminals. . . . He injected into the reform movement an element absolutely essential to its preservation from sourness and dry rot: the element of moral earnestness and religious feeling." [6]

William Lloyd Garrison, the son of the great anti-slavery leader, expressed it well when he explained why he had become a single taxer: "How can we make men and women sober and self-respecting who breed together in slums and swarming tenements because natural opportunity for work is denied them? With land rescued from speculation and easy of access to everyone who wishes to use it, who doubts that improved conditions of living would lessen depraved appetites and brutality? . . . [Single tax] reconciles with justice, a universe which without it seems irreconcilable and makes existence sweeter and more hopeful for mankind." Even some of its sharpest critics had to admit that *Progress and Poverty* was a "brilliant book, glowing with a noble philanthropy, courage, and self-devotion." [7]

Ironically, the object of the book—to furnish a cure for depression —became unimportant, and George eventually stood out primarily as a social reformer and propounder of an ethical creed. George's great contribution was perhaps neither his panacea nor his specific analysis, but rather his vivid presentation of his belief that the material progress of society was the outcome of the growth of society, that the greatest gains had come to the possessors of strategic resources, rendered valuable by the progress of society, not by the contributions of the possessors.

The book had an especially profound effect on the young college generation. It was in sharp contrast to the dreary textbooks; that some professors warned students to avoid it merely whetted their appetites, and the book was "bootlegged" among them. Abroad, too, the book turned able young minds to serious consideration of economics. Thus the Reverend Philip H. Wicksteed, then a somewhat heretical British Unitarian minister, and later an outstanding British economist, wrote George: "I have been for years an occasional student of Political Economy and long ago I became profoundly convinced that some great fallacy or fallacies lay at the root of the science, especially its utter inability to explain not only the cause but the nature of commercial depressions. I lost no opportunity of speaking to friends who were well versed in the science but could get no kind of satisfaction. [Your book] has given me the light I vainly sought for myself . . . [and] has made for me 'a new heaven & a new earth.' " [8]

By and large, the mass of professional economists were disturbed by the book. After all, as one acute supporter of George put it, "the discoveries of the economists as to the nature of rent lie at the base of George's plan." The difference between the professional economist of the day and George was on the question of justice, and that was, he added, not strictly within their province as economists.[9] Nevertheless, George's emphasis on the ethical basis of any economic system brought a broader outlook to the study of that subject. After him, it was difficult, if not impossible, to dismiss economics without relating it to the structure of the society within which it operated.

The socialists, who had always maintained this and had therefore insisted upon changing the framework, naturally welcomed the wide popularity of George. Marx viewed George's book as significant because it was a first if mistaken attempt to loosen the bonds of orthodox political economy. However, he considered *Progress and Poverty* a "last attempt to save the capitalist regime. Of course, this is not the meaning of the author, but the older disciples of Ricardo —the radical ones—fancied already that by the public appropriation of the rent of land everything would be righted." The single-tax proposal, in other words, belonged to "bourgeois political economy" and was in the last analysis a "frank expression of the hate which the industrial capitalist feels for the landed proprietor who appears to him as useless and superfluous in the system of bourgeois production." [10]

Marx's avowed followers in the United States, however, originally included George's proposal in their popular expositions of Marxian socialism. Thus the Socialist journalist Laurence Gronlund declared, in *The Co-operative Commonwealth* (1884), "There is no need to devote more space here to discuss the supreme title of the State to land since the appearance of Henry George's book." The main socialist criticism of the book, he said, was that it pushed the land question—in our country a secondary question in importance—so much into the foreground that the main question was obscured. Here, where a large majority of the farmers worked their own property, the attack on all land titles would make a large portion of the workers to be benefited hostile to all social change.

Despite these misgivings, Gronlund and other Socialist leaders persuaded George to run for mayor of New York in 1886, under the banner of the United Labor Party. The respectable press and the opposition candidates, by now thoroughly aroused, pictured George as a robber, nihilist, communist, and bloody anarchist. But since George was an excellent orator as well as writer, he lost by only a narrow margin—too narrow a margin for the comfort of his opponent. The possibility of George's views capturing the imagination of the country was such that William Torrey Harris took time out from his task of promoting the Hegelian philosophy to denounce George for his woeful ignorance of statistics.[11] And a lawyer, on hearing that Professor Folwell planned publicly to attack the single-tax movement, wrote him that if it was true that the single tax would be unconstitutional Folwell should say so in order to quiet the fears of investors.[12]

By this time whatever conservative following George's free-trade views had recruited had fallen away. Soon after, he and the Socialists parted company, with the Socialists using conservative arguments against him. C. Osborne Ward declared that land taxation sufficient to provide fully for government needs would lead to anarchy, if not to violence and bloodshed. The enormous class of landowners would rise in rebellion. "Better to suffer the old system, bad as it is," he said, "until men see their way clear to introduce the more humane and democratic finality" to replace the "obnoxious competitive system." [13]

So George's theories, popular as they were, remained a great educational influence without a political party to put them into action.

EDWARD BELLAMY

It would seem fairly obvious that the social climate was not favorable to radical reform, for a similar fate befell another book that appeared immediately after the Haymarket episode. This book used the logic of the "unearned increment" to defend a comprehensive scheme of nationalizing industry. It was Edward Bellamy's utopia, *Looking Backward*, which, like George's book, became an integral part of the popular study of economics. George and Bellamy had much in common. Both came of devout parents, both were journalists, and both wrote well. Bellamy's formal education was only a little better than that of George; he was a student for a time at Union College. While George grew up in the commercial centers of Philadelphia and San Francisco, Bellamy developed in the important manufacturing center of Chicopee Falls, Massachusetts.[14] Yet Bellamy's book came from different sources and foretold a different future. George built on Mill and Spencer: Bellamy on Gronlund and the old French socialist literature.

In contrast to most utopians and reformers, Bellamy did not believe in fighting monopolies and the machine process. Rather, he made them the means of achieving the socialist State, or what he called "Nationalism." In the era of petty trade and handicraft, he declared, the competitive system may have worked passably well. Workingmen were constantly becoming employers, since a little capital or a new idea was all that was needed. But the innumerable small businesses were inefficient in an age of steam and telegraph and large-scale enterprise. Consequently they were forced to surrender the field to capital. The old handicraft scheme provided a greater equality of conditions with more dignity and freedom, but even if it could be restored, it would mean a return to the days of stagecoaches. The regime of the trust was oppressive, but its efficiency resulted in an undreamed-of increase in material wealth. Early in the twentieth century, according to his utopian history, the evolution was completed by the consolidation of the entire capital of the nation.

The inhabitants of his utopia found it beyond comprehension that Bellamy's contemporaries should leave the means of livelihood to a class whose interest was to starve the community. Looking backward, they saw that the profits system involved enormous waste. Mistaken undertakings resulted in the failure of four out of five enterprises. The field of industry was a battlefield, without mercy or quarter. Rising by the destruction of a competitor was considered admirable. Each businessman worked solely for his own gain at the expense of the community. Any increase in the wealth of the nation was incidental, for it was equally common and feasible to increase one's own fortune by injuring the community. A businessman would combine with those competitors he could not destroy, to war on the public by cornering the market. The one ambition of the nineteenth-century producer was to obtain absolute control over some necessity so that he might keep the community on the verge of starvation and thus command famine prices.

Finally, the existence of idle labor and capital were testimony to the imbecility of the profit system. Capitalists had to throttle one another to invest their capital, and unemployed and starving workmen rioted and burned. In the very nature of the system, depression was chronic. For every year of good times, there were two of bad times. Yet the dominant economists, after endless discussion had concluded that crises, like droughts and hurricanes, were inevitable.

In contrast to the existing system of business enterprise, Bellamy pictured nationalized industry as the triumph of common sense. In his utopia no leisure class of property existed, and consequently there was no competitive emulation, no subjection of women, and no necessity of fashions. There was none of the waste and deception of duplications and salesmanship, no separation of pecuniary symbols from the underlying industrial realities, no chronic depression with idle labor and capital. All lived in comparative luxury. No changes in human nature were required. "The conditions of life have changed and with them the motives for human action." Men were honored for efficient work instead of rewarded for competitive expenditures.

This was possible in utopia because of integrated organization. The effectiveness of a nation's working forces under the many-headed competitive leadership of private capital, he wrote, as compared with the results under a single head, might be likened to the military efficiency of a mob, or a horde of barbarians with a thousand petty chiefs, as compared with a disciplined army commanded by one general. With the perfect interworking of every wheel and every hand, all the processes interlocked so that industries were adjusted to one another and to the demand.

Bellamy argued that there should be equal distribution of the national income. He who with the same effort could produce twice as much as another, should, instead of being rewarded for doing so, be punished if he does not. As for the theory that every man was entitled to what he produced, Bellamy, in answering Laveleye's criticism, later questioned the natural right of property in any form. "All that a man produces today more than his cave-dwelling ancestor, he produces by virtue of the accumulated achievements, inventions, and improvements of the intervening generations, together with the social and industrial machinery which is their legacy. . . . Nine hundred and ninety-nine parts out of the thousand of every man's produce are the result of his social inheritance and environment. The remaining part would probably be a liberal estimate of what by 'sacred justice' could be allotted him as 'his product, his entire product, and nothing but his product.' . . . The human heritage must, therefore, be construed as an estate in common, essentially indivisible, to which all human beings are equal heirs. Hitherto this community and equality of rights have been disregarded, the heirs being left to scramble and fight for what they could individually get and keep." [15]

Although this was extremely radical in theory, Bellamy kept it on that level and never considered himself much of a practicing reformer. To the eminent literary critic William Dean Howells, one of his followers, he wrote: "I may seem to out-socialize the socialists," but a movement labeled socialism could never succeed in the United States, since it "smells to the average American of petroleum, suggests the red flag, and all manner of sexual novelties, and an abusive tone about God and religion." [16] Moreover, Bellamy did not believe in confiscation as a method at all, "except in special cases where obvious abuses may plainly justify it. Of course Nationalism aims at the ultimate substitution of common ownership of the means of production for individual ownership, but I see no reason why the change in tenure may not be effected without special hardship to any particular class of the people, and without serious derangements of the regular course of business." And his disciple Sylvester Baxter, of the respectable *Boston Herald*, stated that equal division was merely the ultimate aim; therefore it could be stated only as an ideal and was not a "feature of any immediate program." [17]

Bellamy's book, however, coming close on the heels of the vast popularity achieved by *Progress and Poverty*, revived socialism after the blow dealt it by the Haymarket episode. People who spurned a book that spoke favorably of socialism turned avidly to a book that presented somewhat similar ideas under the rubric of Nationalism. Farmers' organizations sent the book through the rural communities. Nationalist clubs sprang up throughout the country. A large number of newspapers and magazines supporting it were born, and the Nationalists even entered the political arena as a separate political party.

The aims of this Nationalist Party, however, were somewhat vague. It held that the principle of the brotherhood of humanity should be the one guiding truth, that the principle of competition was simply the application of the brutal law of the survival of the strongest and most cunning and must be replaced by the principle of association. But in "striving to apply this nobler and wiser principle to the complex conditions of modern life, we advocate no sudden or ill-considered changes; we make no war upon individuals; we do not censure those who have accumulated immense fortunes simply by carrying to a logical end the false principle on which business is now based." To them the combinations, trusts, and syndicates demonstrated the practicality of the basic principles of association.[18] Almost all sorts of reformers could join the movement under these terms. Henry Demarest Lloyd informed the Chicago Nationalists that an old slave song was being taken up by the workingmen: "We are coming, Father Abraham, nine hundred thousand strong!" [19] Gronlund became exceedingly enthusiastic over the scheme and filled many pages of the *Nationalist*, the first important organ of the movement, with elaborations. He even ordered the sale of his own *Co-operative Commonwealth* stopped, in order to push that of *Looking Backward*.[20]

Some enthusiasts, stressing those parts of the book that praised the efficiency of military organization and the appointment of officials by the retiring functionaries or elders, gave the movement something of a mystical, authoritarian turn. Burnette G. Haskell, a San Francisco lawyer and insurance agent, explained that as a believer in evolution he supported Nationalism. His duty, he said, was to "so shape my individual life that I shall fit in as one piece of the future social mechanism if I would survive. . . . Let us sink self in the State." The "silver voices of heroic bugles, the sweep of collective armies with 'broadening front clearing to the outer file,' the million gleaming bayonet points of the marching hosts of heaven above, the orderly pulse of the unseen atom, the absolute harmony of universal law," he declared, "all these teach me that I am myself too little to be an 'Anarchist' and *boss* of the world; and so, perforce—or no! by choice—I whisper: 'not *rights*, but *duties*,' and behold, I am a 'Nationalist.' " [21]

Since the objectives of the movement were vague and the membership was composed of such heterogeneous elements as theosophists, ex-Army officers, and all varieties of socialists, it was perhaps not surprising that the party soon broke up over the question of specific procedures. Socialists soon found that *Looking Backward* was unsocialistic. Gronlund in the preface of his second edition of the *Co-operative Commonwealth* (1893) warned that socialism should not be held responsible for Bellamy's notion of equal wages, which was both impracticable and unjust. Bellamy's influence went the way of George's: both became classics of the literature of dissent; though they animated the reform spirit, their practical programs were not accepted.

SOCIALISM AFTER BELLAMY AND GEORGE

The eloquence of Bellamy and George had one far-reaching and significant effect upon socialists. It convinced many of them that there was a great emotional need felt by the American people that could be turned toward social and economic reform. At the same time that Gronlund was denying that Bellamy's theory was socialist, he was adopting the spirit of his leadership. While still connected with the Department of Labor, Gronlund circularized academic economists to get their support for a new kind of all-embracing socialism, a secret society, the American Socialist Fraternity, which would be composed of young men. The only qualification for membership was a disposition to welcome the extension of the function of government. So disposed, the group would, by the turn of the century, be an effective force to make use of the "sentiment of expecting something extraordinary." [22]

According to the circular, Gronlund wished first of all to persuade the right kind of people that "socialism, under the auspices of the intelligence of the country, is *providentially destined* to be our future social system (not the socialism which is in the interest only of the weak and the inefficient, but that which will create *glad* and *willing* obedience in all—ORDER—and thus is even more in the interest of the competent)." These people, then would form the American Socialist Fraternity, a *"private* organization of intimate friends," who as instruments in the hands of the "Power behind Evolution," would realize this socialism. Gronlund stressed secrecy in order that no one's influence and usefulness should be jeopardized and lost to the movement.

In view of the tremendous power in organization, in *"unity,* especially when joined to a strong belief that the 'stars in their courses are fighting for us' . . . a thousand such young men, in the different centers of our country, can, by a persistent pull, IN CONCERT in the course of, say, 21 years, convert our people."

Another socialist movement, Christian Socialism,[23] was seeking to found socialism on an even deeper emotional base. Its outstanding promoter, the Reverend William D. P. Bliss (1856–1926) of Boston, and perhaps its most radical voice, declared at the close of the period that he was a Christian Socialist because "I was made a Christian by Karl Marx, and a Socialist by Jesus Christ." [24] If the religious-minded people of the country could be so captured, the social effects might well be revolutionary.

While a Congregational minister in 1885, Bliss became interested in socialism, in good part through reading Henry George. The following year he changed to the Episcopalian ministry, became a prominent member of the Knights of Labor, and began a long career of promoting organizations and journals for social reform. He published handbooks and delivered many lectures on the subject. Originally he tried to convince the workingmen in Massachusetts that they could achieve their ends only by political action as an independent party rather than by strikes, for political action would be more effective, permanent, and cheap. The reign of the strike was over, he asserted, and the democracy of politics for workingmen had begun.

True, he admitted, when the workers voted an independent labor ticket the capitalistic papers attributed their action to the cunning influence of one or two leading cranks or demagogues and denounced the movement as communism and anarchy. "The only red flags flying over this movement," he said in refutation, "are . . . the little red schoolhouses scattered over our hills and the red brick walls of the school buildings in our towns. The spelling book, not Karl Marx, is the real instigator of the movement." What handicapped the movement was the lack of means to put its knowledge into effect. Unfortunately, he observed, labor in Massachusetts did not have an independent labor ticket, but voted instead with that party which promised most for labor.[25]

After this political movement petered out, Bliss helped to organize in Boston the first Bellamy Nationalist Club of the country, and in the same year, 1889, with Bellamy's blessings, he organized the Society of Christian Socialists. The ideal of his Christian Socialism was a divine democratic brotherhood of mankind, and as means toward that end his group would aid through peaceful political action everything that looked in this direction—co-operation, profit-sharing, the eight-hour day, trade unionism, arbitration, the development of municipal socialism.

The Christian Socialists favored, first of all, he said, municipalization of light, heating, and transit companies, the nationalization of the telegraph and railroads, and the establishment of postal savings banks. More specifically, government control over public utilities should be extended preparatory to gradual municipalization and nationalization. The school age should be raised and child labor abolished. Taxation should be shifted from personal estates to real estate, with all land values taxed on a graduated principle. Also, a wise and carefully adjusted inheritance tax should be imposed to reduce the glaring inequalities of wealth.

Although he could not get the main group of Christian Socialists to follow him, Bliss proposed as the most immediate necessary reform that the State was in duty bound to supply work to the unemployed. This reform, he emphasized, touched the essence of the problem vastly more than the municipalization of gas or the nationalization of railroads. Such issues were of little importance to the very poor, who used no gas and rarely, if ever, patronized the railroads. But employment for the unemployed would help every poor man from Maine to California. This was all the unemployed asked, only a chance to work. Bliss suggested that state and local governments use the unemployed of that period to build houses which would be sold to artisans at cost. Later Bliss advocated state employment in necessary public works for one year at trade-union rates for trade-union hours. For the cities, such projects could be improvements for the most crowded quarters—baths, parks, model dwellings, and so on—and for the country, the building of good roads and the provision of cheap irrigation.[26] Bliss agreed with skeptics in his own party who felt that under current political leadership such a public works program would fail, as it had in the Paris of 1848, but he felt it was worth a try.

At the same time Bliss pushed the movement for the Australian, or secret, ballot. Once the people could exercise fully their political rights, then economic reform could be expected to follow quickly, he wrote. And on the burning question of money, he demanded that sufficient currency be issued, without the intervention of banks, to conduct business on a cash basis. The correct tactics for pushing these practical reforms, he felt, were not sermons in churches but a

series of inexpensive tracts presenting both sides of the current social issues. The topics to be presented in successive months were:

Is profit sharing advantageous?

Should cities and towns municipalize the supply of water, gas, elec-
tricity, and coal?

Should we nationalize our railroads?

Should we increase the taxation on land values?

What is an honest dollar? [the gold dollar, the gold and silver dollar,
the paper dollar]

Should we abolish the present national bank system?

Should we have a customs duty for revenue or protection? Or no duty
at all?

What shall we do with the saloon—license it, or prohibit or nationalize
it?

Are strikes justifiable?

What party should Christians vote for? [or as an alternative] Should
we adopt the eight-hour day?

Should women vote? [27]

In the nineties Bliss started a new organ, *The American Fabian*.
Its aim was to unite all social reformers and lead the way to a conception of socialism sufficiently broad to include everything of
value regardless of its source.[28] As its title suggests, it was to be the
organ of the American counterpart of the British Fabian Society.
Its program was broad enough to recruit the aid of such men as
Gronlund. Fabian socialism, said Bliss, did not differ from any other
socialism in its aims. In its economic analysis it would follow Jevons'
theory of value rather than that of Marx. In propaganda, it would
usually follow a progressive policy of advancing its principles
through any party where an opening might be found. The two
movements could almost be considered one. In his account Bliss
proudly stated that the English society "took its impetus from an
interest in social problems occasioned by the lectures of Henry
George in England, and the reading of *Progress and Poverty*," and
that its founders were brought together by Professor Thomas
Davidson of New York.[29]

This last assertion deserves some comment, for the career of
Davidson, although somewhat irrelevant, illustrated a basic difficulty
of socialist and reform organizations. Davidson, a Scotsman by
birth and education, was aptly described as a "wandering scholar."
He originally attacked "orthodox" political economy as materialistic, supported George's opposition to the private ownership of land,
and even expressed a strong interest in Bellamy's Nationalist move-

ment. But by the nineties Davidson had ceased to be any kind of a socialist or single taxer. "I soon found out the limitations of socialism," he declared. "Nations have been great . . . in proportion as they have developed individualism on a basis of private property. . . . The way out of our difficulties is not through any increase of state functions, but through a slow growth of the moral sense, and the social spirit." [30]

No such change of heart affected Bliss. He remained active in spreading Christian Socialism. Under his guidance, at Buffalo in 1899, the National Social and Political Conference—described as the "Conference of Unrest"—was held. This led to Bliss's last general reform organization—the Social Reform Union, with Bliss as president and Howells and Gronlund among the vice-presidents. A host of reformers, including several state governors, were listed among its supporters. Again, it was to provide a common ground for all varieties of reformers. As Bliss put it, it was composed of "socialists and individualists, single taxers and prohibitionists, men and women of all parties and of every school of thought."

Its objectives were:

1. Direct legislation [initiative and referendum] and proportional representation.
2. Public ownership of public utilities.
3. Taxation of land values and (for the time at least) of franchises, inheritances, and incomes.
4. Money (gold, silver, or paper) issued by government only and in quantity sufficient to maintain a normal average of prices.
5. Anti-militarism.[31]

To enlighten and educate the electorate, and thus promote the ultimate acceptance of this program, the Union established a "College of Social Science," in the nature of a correspondence school. Its faculty was composed of exiles from academic halls and possessed much ability. But, like all the other short-lived political movements sponsored by Bliss, the main contribution was to keep alive the spirit of Christian Socialism.

Bliss himself now turned toward economic movements, where as usual he took an advanced position. In 1906 he promoted in New York City the Garden City Movement, which had gotten under way in England. This was a movement to establish in rural areas planned industrial communities, which would combine the advantages of both city and country. Model factories would be constructed; and workers and other residents would occupy inexpensive, comfortable homes, each with a garden, and the entire area would be surrounded, if possible, by a belt of agriculture. A large tract would be bought at the beginning so that, even if operations began on a small scale, the whole tract could be developed in a carefully thought out and harmonious manner. At the same time, since the land would be bought at the low value of unimproved land, the large unearned increment arising from the development and growth of population would go to the community and not to private speculators and investors. To achieve these objectives the land would be bought by a company acting as trustee for the group with profits limited to 5 per cent. All profits from the sale or lease of land would be spent in improving the estate, constructing public buildings, and accumulating a sinking fund to pay off the original investment, and then the citizens would finally own the city and control their own lives.

This movement, too, was short-lived, but developments of succeeding decades have again revealed Bliss's pioneering insight, or at least his ability to grasp pioneering ideas. In the realm of thought he had a lasting value. Not least among his contributions was his widely used *The Encylopedia of Social Reform* (1897), which in 1908 was revised as *The New Encyclopedia of Social Reform*. It was in general character an encyclopedia of the social sciences, the first of its kind in the United States, and Bliss overlooked very few liberal spirits as contributors.

In small schemes of practical amelioration the sweeping generalizations of Bellamy and George, and the enthusiastic reform movements born from them, came to some sort of terms with their age. But it should be remembered that the influence of these two men, although to a certain extent unseen, was real and pervasive. Perhaps *Progress and Poverty* contributed more than any other single work to the growth of interest in economics. Men of quite different social views drew inspiration from it, some moving on to moderate socialism, others adapting their professional economic thought to meet the vital issues George had raised. These same influences were enhanced by *Looking Backward*. And both books contributed to the reformist fervor of men of good will, whom the Christian Socialist movement and its leader, Bliss, well represented.

CHAPTER VII

The Liberalism of the New Generation of Economists

AMONG the younger economists who were at work in the eighties there was a substantial body consciously intent upon liberalizing economics. Controversy abroad over the value of the European historical method had been renewed, and in disputing this issue these men reached a common point of view. The "movement" toward broadening the area of economics was not highly organized, but its force and consistency could be clearly seen. The supporters of the historical school in America were continuing the protest against extreme individualism. The traditions and scope of this school allowed for considerations of pressing social problems—especially the ever-present labor issue, which the "orthodox" were inclined to dismiss as the "so-called" labor problem. To many economists this willingness to face all the facts seemed basic, and on this basis they tended to band together. The members of the "new school" differed among themselves on both theoretical and practical grounds, but they agreed that the old economics could not supply sound principles of conduct for the community in general, or adequate training for prospective businessmen and government officials.

EDMUND JANES JAMES

The first important figure in the movement was E. J. James (1855–1925).[1] He was born and reared in Illinois and studied under Johannes Conrad at Halle, where he received his doctor's degree in 1877, with a dissertation on the tariff. He returned to the United States and taught for a number of years in the lower schools in Illinois. James came to public attention through his leading articles in the popular three-volume *Cyclopædia of Political Science, Political Economy and of the Political History of the United States*, edited by John J. Lalor. In 1883 he was appointed professor of public finance and administration at the Wharton School of Finance and Economy (now the Wharton School of Finance and Commerce) of the University of Pennsylvania; three years later he became its director.

James' support of bimetallism reflected the sentiments of a substantial part of the business community, especially in Pennsylvania, but his defense of labor unions, which was rather striking, indicated he was concerned with more than business issues. By our system of education, by the policy of our newspapers, and by example, he declared, we had inspired the laborer "with a desire to share more largely in the material benefits of an advancing civilization, without, however, securing to him a corresponding possibility of doing so under the action of our industrial system." The laborer's wants outran his means of gratifying them, and as he awakened to the misery everywhere, he saw luxury flaunting itself in his face. James even suggested in 1888 that the answer to communism and violent anarchism was to better the condition of the workingmen. He warned that all the Johann Mosts in the world could make no impression on the American workingman if conditions made him contented with his lot. But if conditions perpetuated discontent and bitterness, then socialism and anarchism would spring up naturally, like indigenous plants, even if the laborer had never heard of the socialists and anarchists. In his view the ruthless wealthy were actually the propagators of anarchism because they produced the discontent. Newspapers were equally at fault for they never failed "to utter words of contempt for every effort of the workingmen to better their condition, while passing over with the merest mention the flagrant outrages perpetrated on society by the wealthy and lucky scoundrel." These were much more to be feared than Most's *Freiheit;* for, "on the one hand they stir up the hatred of the laborer by their bitter words, on the other [they further] the very things which tend to make his condition more intolerable." [2]

James did not carry these thoughts very far or champion them vigorously for very long. He devoted most of his subsequent career to advancing commercial education and extension teaching, and to serving successively as president of Northwestern University and of the University of Illinois.

RICHARD T. ELY: CHRISTIAN SOCIALIST

More continuously active in the "new school" movement was Richard T. Ely (1854–1943).[3] Ely, born and raised in a New England Congregational settlement in upstate New York, had to work for his education. He was graduated from Columbia College in

1876, and was awarded a three-year fellowship to study philosophy in Germany. But he soon found that his training in the relatively naïve Scottish Common Sense philosophy offered inadequate preparation for understanding the subtleties of the idealist philosophies of Kant and Hegel, and he turned to the social sciences, majoring in economics. He studied under such leaders of the old historical school as Karl Knies at the University of Heidelberg.

Upon his return to the United States in 1880, with no academic position in view, he began writing on a variety of practical topics for a number of popular organs, ranging from the *New York Tribune* to the *Bankers' Magazine*. In 1881 he became the sole teacher of economics at Johns Hopkins University, with the rank of assistant in political economy. Besides teaching, he held office as a state tax commissioner, and he continued to publish a steady stream of pamphlets and newspaper and magazine articles calling for reforms in the social order. In 1884 he issued his polemic against "orthodox" economics in "The Past and the Present of Political Economy." [4] Even beyond these many activities he had ambitious plans; he wished to promote the writing of a history of American economic thought and to sponsor learned associations.

Like James, Ely denounced the "old school" political economy as deductive and mathematical rather than inductive and historical. He stressed the need to abandon extreme laissez faire and to humanize economics. Fundamentally Ely was a Christian Socialist; in fact most of the American Christian Socialists used his works as their guide. He warned the churches that they must regain the trust of the laboring mass by defending its just claims if a bloody class conflict was to be avoided. "The Christian Church," he said, "can do far more than political economists towards a reconciliation of social classes." He even urged ministers to join the Knights of Labor.[5] Like the original Christian Socialists of England, he advocated voluntary producers' and credit co-operatives as well as consumers' co-operatives. He felt that the State could do considerable good through factory legislation and regulation of public utilities.

Ely was skeptical of ameliorative experiments by employers. The much-lauded company town of Pullman, Illinois, he branded "un-American" because of its company spies, its strict control of the entire life of the employees, and its principle that all ameliorative devices, whether amusements or churches, must yield a return on the investment. And he opposed company-sponsored schemes of insurance, for they increased the power of the employers over the employees. The worst union practices, he felt, were not very different from those of business, and strikes could be avoided if employers were less arrogant. He was in many ways quite radical; he even praised Marx's *Das Kapital* as one of the "ablest politico-economic treatises ever written. . . . It is difficult reading, not because it is poorly written, but because it is deep." [6] But socialism and anarchism he deplored as atheistic, materialistic, and bloody.

Ely used such strong language in pleading for reform that he often found himself accused of being a socialist. His colleague, Simon Newcomb, in an unsigned review of Ely's *The Labor Movement in America*, described the book as the "ravings of an anarchist or the dream of a socialist," and added, "Dr. Ely seems . . . to be seriously out of place in a university chair." [7] Nicholas Murray Butler, then a tutor on the Faculty of Political Science of Columbia University, implied in another review that the book favored the abolition of private property, that is, the "socialistic programme." Ely replied that while he would not accuse the reviewer of malevolence, he was guilty of "culpable negligence" and was grossly careless. "The truth is, I point out many causes for the evils of present society as intemperance, imperfect ethical development of man, . . . unchastity, ignorance of the simplest law of political economy, extravagance, and in fact the wickedness of human nature." [8]

Wherever he turned, Ely seemed to step on somebody's toes. His friend President Andrew D. White of Cornell warned him that he must avoid the appearance of building up the German bureaucracy as the ideal toward which we should work, for, White said, this would "alarm even many of your best allies." [9] Perhaps because of this free-hitting style, his prolific writings and his lectures did much to create an interest in liberal economics. The *Indianapolis News* declared: "Few scholars are as fortunate as he in having the confidence of the laboring classes and their recognized leaders, and he is equally as fortunate in having many intimate friends and relatives connected with great corporations. He has the respect of prominent businessmen, as evidenced by the invitations he receives to address their organizations." [10] And his "ability to recognize and stimulate the possibilities of younger men" gained him an influential following.[11]

Of particular influence was Ely's textbook, *An Introduction to*

Political Economy (1889). The book was rather vague on concrete proposals for reform, but in comparison with the "orthodox" treatises of the day it was strikingly liberal. It contained a crude version of the marginal utility doctrine and the Ricardian doctrine of rent, but its significant feature was the attention it called to a variety of evils in the existing order.[12] Having a sale of more than thirty thousand copies in the course of a decade, it exercised a considerable influence on the thought of Americans.

HENRY CARTER ADAMS: THE PHILOSOPHER OF ECONOMIC LIBERALISM

Henry C. Adams (1851–1921) was another member of this younger group destined to be a most fertile thinker and writer.[13] He was the son of a Congregational missionary in the West, and after graduating from Iowa College (now Grinnell) in 1874, he began studying for the ministry at his father's old school, Andover Theological Seminary. But he soon lost all desire to become a minister and turned to journalism. This, too, he found unsatisfying. Fortunately Johns Hopkins had opened, and Adams obtained a fellowship, by which he was enabled to hear Francis A. Walker's lectures.

After receiving his doctor's degree in 1878, Adams was at loose ends. He obtained funds for a year's study in Europe, and on his return President White gave him a part-time position at Cornell. To make ends meet, and in accordance with White's suggestion that he take his time in obtaining a permanent post, Adams also taught part of the year at Johns Hopkins, and then a one-semester course in economics, in 1880, at the University of Michigan. By 1882 he was regularly dividing his time between Cornell and Michigan.

Adams was among the first to present Jevons' theory of value, in his *Outline of Lectures upon Political Economy* (1881), but at the same time, doubting that the existing competitive system could achieve the competitive ideal, he showed strong leanings toward the "historical method." According to Adams, this method did not consist, as many thought, in an appeal to history for the support of assumed premises; rather, its test was the judicial spirit with which one entered upon the task of analysis. He thought that political economy might be studied historically "(1) to learn more thoroughly the true nature of man . . . ; (2) to learn to study the present in a purely objective manner; and (3) to guard against the acceptance of inadequate reforms."

Adams believed that Jevons' theory of utility rightly determined the productive nature of exchange. The theory, he wrote, conceived of utility not as an intrinsic quality of things, but as an attendant quality which gave to commodities the power to prevent pain or increase pleasure. Economic quantities in this theory were not viewed as economically homogeneous but as quantities composed of successive increments, a distinction which led to the law of varying utility. He stated it thus: "As the quantity of any commodity decreases, the intensity of the utility—any part of that which remains—increases, until at last the utility of the commodity becomes indispensable, that is, the utility becomes infinite."

From this he obtained a formula for determining value. By comparing the visible supply of a given commodity with the fairly well-defined demand for it at a given time, "we shall discover the final degree of utility which it bears, viz., the utility of the last increment which is always the portion about to be sold." Similarly, "the utility of all commodities is unconsciously estimated and . . . a basis is secured for determining the ratio of exchange between them"; that is value. The law of value, then, is that "commodities placed upon a market for sale will tend·to exchange in a ratio inversely to their degree of final utility."

According to this theory, therefore, both individuals in an exchange gained, because each parted with a commodity of which the utility was less intense, for one of which the utility was more intense. In the case of goods already produced, exchange would cease to be productive when the degree of utility for a given unit of a commodity was the same as the degree of the corresponding unit of the other. But "while labor is no measure of value for the exchange of goods once thrown upon the market, the value of that procured by exchange, expressed in labor expended to secure the power of purchase, is that which determines the limit of production for exchange, of any commodity. This is something of a guarantee that goods will exchange in proportion to labor expended in production."

This meant, as Adams interpreted Jevons, that legislatures could not determine the rates at which commodities should exchange except by regulating supply and demand. Through such regulation, the government might block exchanges and so destroy production. In further accord with Jevons' view, Adams declared that the rate of interest depended upon the final increment of a product which sprang from the use of capital; that the rate of interest tended to fall in an economically progressive country because as industries passed from lower to higher grades of production the "increment of product, measured on the amount of capital last invested," tended to decrease; and this last increment determined the rate at which all returns to capital were computed.

Later Adams scrapped the marginal utility economics, at least its expansion into the area of distribution. He denied that there was any marginal producer and maintained that the later distinction between statics and dynamics was fruitless and illogical.[14]

But Adams by no means held that the current system was a perfectly harmonious one. On the contrary, he felt that the problems of labor relations and monopoly must be solved before an ideal competition could be achieved. In an address on labor, before the Cornell Engineering School in 1886, he declared that the student must look beyond the excesses committed by some of the labor organizations in the course of their agitation, to the underlying goal. Viewed historically, the labor movement was a step in the further development of individual rights and harmonized with the basic ideal of Anglo-Saxon institutions, that of equal rights. The religious reformation had secured for each man the right to maintain his own opinions in matters spiritual, a right that had naturally grown into the modern doctrine of the freedom of thought, speech, and press. The political revolution, which had been realized through the struggle for ministerial responsibility, had secured for men the right of self-government. The Industrial Revolution had as its objective that the exercise of industrial power be held to strict account; more concretely, that the irresponsible power of capital be checked and the rights of capital granted to individuals only on conditions of strict responsibility to society.

In the scheme of petty industry the ordinary rights of "personal freedom" secured to men the enjoyments of the fruits of their labor. But under the regime of great industries, Adams held, the laborer was dependent upon the owner of machines, of materials, and of places for the opportunity to work. The old theory of liberty, which placed the personal right to acquire property on the same footing as the right to security of life, was no longer applicable to modern society.

Since the structure of modern industry required concentration of capital, to his mind it followed that laborers must unite or they would surely get the worst of any bargain. Furthermore, underlying the laborers' demands was the "idea" that the laborers had some rights of proprietorship in the industry to which they gave their skill and time. This could be realized, he argued, by curtailing the traditional property rights of the possessing classes; that is, by imposing certain duties upon the holders of property. This was the unconscious purpose of the trade-union movement. Trade-union demands for arbitral tribunals implied proprietorship in industry, for arbitration was the machinery by which responsibilities could be imposed on the legal owners of capital. By tenure and by protection from arbitrary dismissal the laborers would get an industrial home. Promotion according to civil service rules would give them a vested interest in the industry.

If employees gained the right to be consulted as to whether their number or hours should be reduced in a period of depression, he wrote, they would secure the right to live in hard times upon the fund of capital they had created in prosperous times. Thus collective bargaining and the labor contract envisaged a "crystallization of a common law" of labor rights, and would ultimately result in the establishment of an Industrial Federation. Workmen would receive the benefits of industrial partnership without disturbing the nominal or legal ownership which existed; and a new law of productive property would arise. Thus the underlying purpose or guiding end of the labor movement was opposed to the tyranny of German socialists and was in full harmony with the development of Anglo-Saxon liberty. The solution of the labor problem therefore lay in the further development of property rights.[15]

Coming in the midst of the bitter railroad strike against the Gould system, Adams' address gave rise to some hysteria. Henry W. Sage, one of the benefactors of Cornell University, complained to the authorities that Adams was undermining civilization; Adams' part-time appointment was canceled. But President James Burrill Angell of Michigan was not disturbed; he gave Adams a full-time program with the rank of professor of political economy and finance. Cornell, in fact, wanted him back shortly afterward.[16]

In 1887 Adams presented a monograph, "Relation of the State to Industrial Action," which came to be a classic statement of the role of government in industry. A tyranny which sprang from the unregulated workings of self-interest was just as hard upon the individual, he argued, as that which sprang from political privileges.

Laissez faire was the dominant habit of thought and action, but its authority simply rested upon its *de facto* existence, that is, "the instinct of conservatism," which by "historical accident" operated against expanding the functions of government. In Germany, where the State rather than the individual was dominant in industrial society, the conservative tradition was opposed to individual initiative. The American view must emphasize the complementary relations of the State and the individual in the development of the social organism. "Both governmental activity and private enterprise," he explained, "are essential to the development of a highly organized society, and the purpose of constructive thought should be to maintain them in harmonious relations."

Failure to distinguish between laissez faire as a dogma and free competition as a principle, he felt, had caused considerable confusion. The benefits of free competition were those of industrial freedom, but industrial freedom was not the same as laissez faire or unrestrained competition. The free play of individual interests tended to depress the moral sentiment of any trade to the level of the worst man in the business, because the consumer was interested only in cheapness and not in the conditions of production. For example, most manufacturers, though aware of the social evils of overworked women and children, must act as did the unscrupulous minority, lest they be driven out of business.

The State, he claimed, might therefore give legal expression to the wishes of the majority of the competing businessmen by outlawing undesirable practices and thereby raising the plane of competition. Competitive action would not be curtailed, but the manner in which it should operate would be determined. But Adams carefully stated that this conception of the State's power to raise the plane of competition must not be applied to the vital struggle between employer and employee, lest legal liberty be destroyed.[17]

He maintained that the State also might interfere in business to secure to the public the benefits flowing from the inevitable organization of those "natural monopolies" which were the outgrowth of modern industrial development. He noted, moreover, that such monopolies were fast becoming more powerful than the State. In order to recognize the situation before it was too far advanced, he proposed what he considered an effective criterion for the existence of monopoly. If an increment in capital and labor yielded an increment in product, the increment of product must necessarily be less than, equal to, or greater than, the increment of labor and capital which brought it into being. In the first two instances, those of "constant" and "diminishing returns," the entrepreneur's struggle for superior success was a "struggle to depress the cost of rendering services rather than to raise the prices of services rendered." In the third category, that of "increasing returns," free competition was powerless to exercise a healthy regulative influence, because it was easier for an established business to extend its facilities to meet a new demand, than for a new industry to spring into competitive existence. Any competition in these industries was of a piratical, cutthroat, short-term kind, ending in monopoly, with the community paying the costs of the wasteful temporary competition.

Adams felt that the principle of increasing returns applied to only a few industries, the "natural monopolies" such as those of transportation, telegraph, gas, and water companies. The question, he said, was whether society should support an "irresponsible extralegal monopoly or a monopoly established by law and managed in the public interest." [18]

Adams also believed that "as countries became more populous, and the social and industrial relations more complex, the functions of government must necessarily extend to continually new objects." For example, the increasing necessity of forest conservation: the frequent recurrence of floods, the more rapid and marked alternations of drought and wet, the progress of farming toward the exhaustion of lands—all pointed clearly to the fact that the people of the United States must soon turn their attention to the cultivation of trees. But individuals would not enter such an enterprise because the returns in dividends were too remote from the first investment. [19]

Would not State control cause corruption? Adams denied that this would necessarily occur. He argued that corruption itself sprang from the fact that the State's power was limited; consequently there was a lack of correlation between the duties assigned to public officials and the functions performed by private individuals, so that the inducements offered were not of about the same strength in both domains of activity. Extension of the State's administrative functions, manned by an adequate well-paid Civil Service, would restore the harmony that should exist between State and private service, for it would bring social distinction, the chance to exercise one's talents, and the pleasure of filling well a responsible position.

Adams then went on to examine the corporation. This form of industrial organization, he declared, had intensified the monopoly problem, and through its aggregate power further threatened to corrupt democratic institutions. He found that the limited liability privilege had proved the source of vast public mischief. The corporation had violated the principle of modern society that responsibility should be commensurate with the liberty enjoyed. Under the corporate form the managers could and did engage in vast speculations and reckless activities from which they reaped the gains. The risks, however, rested on other members of the community or on the community as a whole. And this irresponsibility on the part of corporate management contributed greatly to panics and crises.

Economists, Adams declared, recognized that although competition might control industries when they were small and many, it was ineffective when industries became large and relatively few. Similarly, intercorporate competition was essentially different in its operation and results from interpersonal competition. In his words, "Not only has the industrial power of our day, generated by the organization of labor and the extensive use of machinery, fallen under the control of corporations, but these corporations assert for themselves most of the rights conferred on individuals by the law of private property, and apply to themselves a social philosophy true only of a society composed of individuals who are industrial competitors."

The remedy, to his mind, was certainly not the abolition of limited liability, for such a drastic step would deprive the community of the benefit of corporate organization. Rather, Adams suggested that the corporate form be limited to "natural monopolies." In fact such industries should be compelled to take the corporate form; as corporations, they should be required to make "reports which would enable the government, acting under rules prescribed by law, to direct their policy and control their administration." Holding a corporation which performed a public service to account, as an officer of the government was then held to account, could not be considered socialistic, he contended. At the same time all other businesses should be subject to inquiry though not to control, in order to determine whether or not they should be refused the liberty of incorporation or be required to assume corporate form.

Adams suggested, too, that states and municipalities should obtain the greater share of their revenues from taxing these incorporated natural monopolies. Inasmuch as the value of the monopoly increased with the growth of the society, he said, "increment of earnings is largely an unearned increment to the corporation and should be directed through the machinery of taxation to the benefit of the citizens from whom it accrues." [20]

Adams generally favored government control as against government ownership except possibly in the case of municipal public utilities, but for a moment in 1901 he was so upset by the threat of a trust to wipe out his investments in a wire company unless he sold out to it that he wrote: "I find myself impelled, against my will, to the extreme theory of State control, for . . . the time has come when the American people are obliged to choose between responsible control by means of relatively poor government administration, and better administration in the hands of private corporations, which recognizes in no sense any responsibility to the public. And when that alternative comes to be clearly recognized, it is merely a question of manhood and morality and not a question of industry that is to be decided." [21]

Originally Adams meant that municipal and local state powers, rather than federal powers, should be expanded—except in the instance of money and banking. The growth of the national power at the expense of the other forms of civil authority disregarded, he declared, the democratic idea that responsible power should be as close as possible to those upon whom it is exercised. But with the setting up of national control over the railroads in 1887, Adams moved to a sturdy defense of this expansion in government authority. And as chief statistician for the Interstate Commerce Commission he did some of his most constructive work.

His job was not easy because the Commission was under continuous fire. When critics asserted that the Commission was a failure, Adams quickly enough pointed out that its shortcomings flowed largely from the Supreme Court decisions stripping it of effective power. He asserted in 1893 that if the Commission was to administer speedy relief to a shipper who was being destroyed by the special contracts or rebates granted to a competitor, its findings in regard to the facts must be final. Otherwise the Commission merely increased the difficulty of which complaint was made, since, for all practical purposes, the Commission became just another court from which appeal could be taken. The decisions of the Court had also negated, he said, the intention of Congress that the Commission should have the "fullest liberty of investigating the books of corporations and of securing evidence from witnesses." Taking these things into consideration, he still said: "Control of railways by commissions is the truly conservative method of control. If it succeeds, we may look for a solution of all the vexed industrial problems in harmony with the fundamental principles of English liberty. If it fails, there is nothing for the future of our civilization but the tyranny of socialism."

Adams was among the first to point out that fixing a valuation to determine "reasonable" rates could have no meaning insofar as it was based on the existing railway income. His insistence that the physical valuation of company property be considered led to the formulation of a more tangible and effective basis for arriving at carrier rates. He logically argued that since the rates set must be high enough to permit the survival of roads operating under inferior conditions, those roads more favorably situated would enjoy a tremendous gain. Equity therefore demanded that the excess return or surplus profit accruing to such roads should be turned over to the State.[22]

Not the least of Adams' achievements was the establishment of the Statistical Bureau for the Interstate Commerce Commission. There he set up a model system of accounting. Though for years he was unable to secure the co-operation of the roads, and the Supreme Court ruled that the Interstate Commerce Act did not provide for the enforcement of uniform accounts, Adams was not completely discouraged. "The more despondent I become as to the outcome of the Commission idea . . . the more interested am I in doing what lies in a Bureau of Statistics and Accounts to realize that idea." [23]

Adams early pointed out that the standardization and examination of accounts was not only essential in the supervision of railway management, but would also serve as a model for controlling industries in which the principle of competition failed to work its normal results. Ever-increasing statistical activity by the government was essential not only for the sake of controlling naturally monopolistic industries, but also for the efficient functioning .of competition wherever possible. Collecting, compiling, and publishing of such commercial facts as were essential to safe business calculations would remove the chief obstacle to its efficient functioning, for the uncertainty surrounding business dealings would be eliminated. Only expenditure for public education, Adams asserted, was more vitally important to the interests of the State than that for statistical investigation.

It seems on the surface surprising that such a fertile and sensitive mind as Adams' was so little concerned with that burning issue of the times, the monetary question. In his published outlines of economics he did in a perfunctory manner disapprove of government inconvertible notes and supported international bimetallism. But he aptly summed up his view of the entire controversy when he said that the money question was the "perpetual motion problem of economics." [24]

But there was no question in his mind that the "constantly recurring periods of commercial depression" were the most serious economic evil and the greatest impediment to the "rapid development of individual well-being and national improvement." The conviction was growing, Adams insisted, that the cause of depressions was the maldistribution of the ownership of productive machinery, which resulted in such a distribution of the product of productive machinery that current product could not be currently consumed.[25]

In many ways Adams was one of the most effective economic thinkers in this period. His concept of "proprietary rights" became so common that its origin was lost. His emphasis on accounting as an instrument of social control was equally far-reaching. But most forceful was his conception of raising the ethical plane of competition. This exercised a considerable influence on his young fellow economists and the public and became the underlying intellectual basis of ameliorative legislation. In the course of time it was expanded beyond the limits he had set for it.

It was unfortunate that Adams never found time to elaborate and revise his classic paper, "Relation of the State to Industrial Action." He planned to do so, but almost as soon as he had finished the original monograph he began spending much of his time on investigations for the government and private organizations. While lucrative, these allowed him little opportunity for the sustained effort required by such a mighty theme.

Adams in the beginning of his work clearly stated the problem that is still the center of economics. "The great problem of the present day," he said in 1885, "is properly to correlate public and private activity so as to preserve harmony and proportion between the various parts of organic society." [26] This statement, taken with the views he held on specific issues, suggests that Adams was in a very real sense the philosophical parent of much of the political-economic legislation of the next fifty years. His influence was certainly both powerful and pervasive.

CHARLES SWAN WALKER: CONSCIENCE OF THE NEW ERA

Chief radical of this group was the Reverend C. S. Walker (1846–1933), professor of mental and political science at the Massachusetts Agricultural College (now the University of Massachusetts). He even upheld the labor unions' use of the boycott. He took for his example a shirt manufacturer who employed a large number of women at starvation wages and who imposed on them various indignities in the way of mistreatment, fines, and penalties. Having no practical protection from the courts, the women joined the Knights of Labor. Through a committee they appealed for justice. The manufacturer not only refused them justice, but further declared that unless they withdrew from the Knights of Labor he would discharge them. On their refusal he executed his threat and refused to listen to a committee of the Knights who wished to submit the matter for arbitration.

Thereupon the Knights, 700,000 strong, published to the world his injustice and said that they would not buy his shirts. They said the custom of 700,000 men and their friends was worth a great deal; it was theirs to give to whomsoever they chose. They determined to give it to those retailers who would not handle the shirts of the obnoxious manufacturer, who coined money out of woman's virtue and woman's blood. Arguing from this instance, C. S. Walker maintained that the workingmen had grasped the idea that their custom was of great value and that through organization they might control and use it for their own good instead of letting it enrich others.[27]

He also presented a powerful statement in defense of the great agrarian crusades sweeping the West. As he studied the plight of the Western farmers, he came to the conclusion that the city and the country formed two non-competitive groups, that the farmer traded perishable provisions and raw materials for the city's manufactures and for money. But while the former were compelled to throw their commodities upon the market all at once in the fall of the year, the city's commodities were easily controlled by their owners, who, he said, readily combining among themselves, could sell or hoard very much as they pleased. The farmer in all regions, then, was forced to sell his products to the city, year after year, when the market was glutted and prices were at the lowest point. At the same time he bought at a great disadvantage. Then, too, the farmers needed money to pay taxes and interest in the fall, but that was the very time when money, being a commodity in great demand, was very scarce and high. Again, in the spring the farmer was forced to buy seed and fertilizer, agricultural implements and labor. To be sure, money was cheap at that time, but the farmer, having no means of getting it, had to purchase in some form of credit. Consequently the farmer at all times was compelled to sell cheap and buy dear.

Added to this were excessive transportation costs. The farmer asked for cheap transportation between the farm and the market and was told that the rate from the elevator of the middleman to the ship of the foreigner was the lowest in history. If he still persisted in asking for cheaper rates from his country station to the city, he was told that the delicate intricacies of the modern railroad system were so great that to do what the farmer asked would bankrupt the roads. When the farmers joined together to build their own local electric lines, to carry their crops and themselves from the farm to the city, they were attacked at every point by the great railroad corporations, even to the extent of open war.

As the farmers' efforts resulted in villages springing up around them, then growing into cities, and thus increasing land values, it was true that a few farmers could sell building lots at a profit, but after paying off their debts to Eastern capitalists and meeting losses occasioned by the need to sell their crops below cost, they had little remaining. Yet the exceptional success of these few fortunate ones had stimulated the multitude to run more deeply into debt, in the hope that they could hold out until the "unearned increment" in the value of the land should make their fortune. For the average farmer, either the land did not rise in value, or just as it was about to happen the mortgage holder in the city foreclosed, taking with the farm the future unearned increment.

This was the picture as Walker saw it. To him, therefore, it was not surprising that the city grew richer while the country grew poorer, that city tenements rose story after story while farmhouses were steadily abandoned. Furthermore, he maintained, in the cities the burden of taxation diminished in proportion to the benefits enjoyed, while in the country the benefits enjoyed diminished as the burden of taxation became more crushing. He wrote: "It is an acknowledged fact that the great wealth of city fortunes easily evades taxation, and contributes only as much as the owners choose to appropriate with the expectation of collecting in the end from someone else."

To illustrate the decline in rural wealth he pointed to the rapid increase of tenant farming, to the number of alien landowners with holdings running into thousands of acres, to the vast land grants to railroads and other corporations, to the multiplication of mortgages, to the growth of the debtor class among agriculturalists, to the black farmer of the South, and to the importation of European peasants to take up the abandoned farms of New England. He pointed out that as economic power shifted, so did political power; as wealth and population concentrated in the city, the American farmer discovered that he was losing politically. Once the vote of the farming area had been decisive and its public opinion a power in legislative halls; but now the city supported an expensive lobby that effectively stopped the farmer from getting his bills passed. Just as the landed aristocracy of England had kept their pre-eminence by ennobling the leaders of the people and removing them from the House of Commons to the House of Lords where they became harmless, so during the past generation, as soon as a farmer had risen to "power and influence among his fellows," he had been courted and enriched, made a stockholder in some corporation, given a city residence, and so led at length to "forget the old homestead, and his brothers and sisters struggling with fate in the back districts." The manufacturing, the professional, the trading classes had as a rule concentrated in the cities, and, having interests in common, they had easily combined and acquired the wealth of the nation. Soon they controlled the press, school, and church, and dominated the caucus, the political convention, the legislative halls.

Because of this declining political power, and in the face of their declining economic self-sufficiency as individuals, he maintained, the farmers as a group must organize to work out their salvation. No one else would help them. When the farmer had in his dilemma finally turned to the scholar and asked of him a fair statement of the problem and a clear solution, based upon historical and economic grounds, said Walker, the scholar had been too preoccupied and prejudiced to give the question that painstaking investigation and careful and impartial decision which alone could make his answer of much practical value to the hard-pressed agriculturalist. The farmers, therefore, must rely on their own efforts, in spite of the difficulties. Though as a class they were proverbially conservative, and patient as the lowing oxen, and their strong individualism made organization a slow, difficult process, he showed that they had time and again evidenced their ability to organize and become masters of the situation. He pointed to the Granger movement as a good example, although of late years the Grange, composed of the more prosperous farmers, had been very conservative, keeping out of politics and devoting itself primarily to social and educational interests. He welcomed as its successor a new and more aggressive organization, the National Farmers' Alliance and Industrial Union.

Its particular measures—the so-called sub-treasury plan, the demand for the free coinage of silver, the abolition of national banks, and the substitution of legal tender notes for national bank notes, the issue of fractional currency, the prohibition of gambling in stocks and alien ownership of land, government ownership and operation of the means of communication and transportation—seemed to many, he admitted, nothing less than "absurd, foolish, wicked, and revolutionary. But let these questions be freely and fairly discussed," he pleaded. If they were as alleged, their true nature could easily be shown and they would never become accepted. But if these measures were rejected, then it became the true statesman to devise some other methods and measures by which the farmers of America might be saved from the fate of the agricultural classes of other lands and of other ages. In any event, he said, the concentration of the nation's wealth in the hands of a few had gone far enough; and if the farmers' movement should succeed in turning the public opinion of the nation to the "necessity of 'demanding equal rights for all and special favor for none,' and of suppressing personal, local, sectional, and national prejudice, it will atone for many mistakes and prove itself to be one of the great developments of a people's life. . . . A hundred years ago our fathers met and solved the problems of the new government. Degenerate sons of noble ancestry must we be, if we prove insufficient for the task of our day." [28]

JOHN BASCOM: CONVERT TO LIBERALISM

Throwing in his fortunes with this liberal wing was an eminent figure who had heretofore been considered one of the most conservative economists. This was the Reverend John Bascom, president of the University of Wisconsin. Before the Civil War, in his "deductive" *Political Economy* and in magazine articles, he had lashed out against labor unions and had declared that there was little danger of monopolies. And he had continued along these lines for a time after the war. But now, under the impact of a "wider outlook," he had become skeptical of the all-sufficiency of the deductive method in economics. He now claimed that labor unions must be recognized, and that the way to control them was by aiding them; for these organizations prevented social evils from passing beyond the point of remedy. Their errors, he found, were insignificant compared with the great gains of "untiring effort after progress." If the gains of such combinations had been much less and the dangers even greater than they were, deliberative united effort would still be the beginning of better things. "We must be content to pay the price of progress."

Bascom deplored that kind of criticism which saw only too clearly the convulsions of labor seeking its own, the extraneous and factitious mischiefs which attached to them, and which condemned these manifestations without appreciating the burdens of the workmen and their difficulties in removing them. "Workmen," he said, "will listen to those who feel the hardships of their position, not to those who disparage these hardships; not to those who are always impressed with the mischiefs of the remedy, and forever renew the council of patience as if it were given to children."

Capital, Bascom continued, was combining in many undesirable ways which must be repressed, for "liberty always is, and must be, associated with proximate equality in social conditions." The State must take these matters of injustice and inequity in hand. "The impotence of the State is now a favorite doctrine, under which the weak are left to the strong. Tyranny first asserted itself through law; now it asserts itself against law. The spirit is the same, the method only is different. The world belongs to those who can win, and organic resistance is said to be adverse to liberty, the liberty to plunder. . . . A community is never injured by the heroic legal temper, provided it is a thoroughly just and humane one. The motives and limitations of wise law are these very interests—just public and private liberty."

On succeeding his friend Perry at Williams College in the nineties, Bascom reiterated that "social strength in the end must be found in an equilibrium of the two tendencies, individualism and collectivism. We are suffering grievously by the excess of one of them [individualism]. Whatever danger may come to us from socialism will arise from an unreasonable resistance to the organic force which is pushing into our lives. . . . Growth must have its way. To refuse to walk lest we should be compelled to run, or to run lest we should be forced to fly, is not reason, and prepares the way for that violence which we most dread." [29]

ELISHA BENJAMIN ANDREWS: THE PHILOSOPHY OF SOCIAL CONTROL
AND MALTHUSIANISM

The problem of economic equilibrium between freedom and governmental restraint, which was so central to Bascom's later theory, was the theme for the school's variations. Some of the more interesting ones were those of a German-trained economist, who based his theory on the elaborated marginal utility doctrine of the "Austrian" economists. The Reverend E. Benjamin Andrews (1847–1917) was president of Brown University and the nephew of the philosophical anarchist Stephen Pearl Andrews.[30] He was a very popular teacher and was constantly in demand as a speaker. He wrote with facility and ease for both learned and popular journals, not only on economics but on all the social sciences, and his works had a wide audience.

Andrews heavily stressed morality and religion in his popular *Institutes of Economics* (1889) and expressed his obligation to both the German historical school and the socialists for their effective criticism of the old classical school. Following Cairnes, Andrews insisted first that "certain general laws of absolute and universal validity and no less 'natural' than those of physics, underlie the science of Economics"; and second, that in "all economic activity the presumption is in favor of individual liberty and free competition (laissez faire), rightfulness of public intervention in no case [being] admissible save after proof of its necessity."

Though Andrews stayed closely within the classical tradition, he cut into dominant practical problems more sharply than this general position would suggest. He considered the monetary question of prime importance. He became one of the leaders of the bimetallist movement and moved from schemes for the greater utilization of silver to an unqualified free silver position. He ultimately reversed his position, however. In 1903, while chancellor of the University of Nebraska, he publicly came out in support of the gold standard. He had, he declared, erroneously believed in the nineties that gold production had reached its high point.[31]

On the question of rent Andrews showed definite leanings toward Henry George.[32] And on the subject of monopolies he created something of a furor. He flatly declared that the competitive system was fast disappearing. It was giving way to trusts and combinations, except in some simple forms of manufacturing and retail trade. This system of combinations was not due to legislation. "It has sprung," he said, "from the very soul of our old laissez-faire competitive sort of industry." Such a state of affairs he called "laissez-faire monopoly."

He described its development as follows: In small and simple industries competition kept prices in line with the cost of production. This was not true of complex massive industries. Here the manufacturer who was first in the field could set his own price, far in excess of the cost and reasonable profit, because capital, always timid, would not immediately take the risk of competing. When competition did enter, prices would fall far below the normal figure, resulting in crisis and failures. Recognizing this fact, capitalists had preferred to co-operate. Eventually, as the competition for foreign markets became more severe, the larger producers of different exporting nations would combine. The general course of mammoth industry, as the world grew smaller, would be to rely on self-protection through international combination.

The assumption that monopoly could not occur in an industry where some competition existed was to him erroneous, for such competition was often more formal than real—a situation which he described as "tolerance of the market." To him the existence of a number of independent producers did not alter the fact that one large trust could charge more than the competitive price. A monopoly need not control the entire production, for immediate mastery of a decided majority meant in practice the mastery of all. Formal competitors actually shared, within large limits, in the profits of the monopoly without any of the responsibilities. These independent units were, in effect, parasites of the trust, lifted up and nourished by its power. "They are related," he said, "to the monopolists proper, just as rent-takers are to marginal cultivators."

Andrews granted, however, that combinations might after all be a net advantage to humanity. They forecast the demand and regulated supply accordingly, much as would be done under socialism. In providing the massed capital and centralized control, they offered incalculable advantages over the old haphazard method, and produced goods at less cost. The question was how much, if any, of the resulting saving went to consumers. Society should endeavor, he contended, to retain all the advantages of monopoly and to increase them if possible, while preventing the monopolist from receiving more than his just share. This could be accomplished by government regulation and eventually government price- and profit-fixing. Government regulation was justified because the government had the right to interfere for the "true and permanent weal of society," but he recommended that every device of control be tried before municipalization or nationalization was undertaken.

But Andrews was not quite satisfied with this solution in terms of restrained governmental control. Regulation would protect the public from exorbitant prices, but what would spur on the inventor of those improvements which had been the glory of competitive industry? Society would have all the good which combination, through the agency of great capital and orderly control, could bring it, but these benefits alone would not compensate for the loss of civil liberty and the decadence of genius in invention and initiative. That, obviously, was a question political economy could not answer, declared Andrews. "It brings us to one of the very numerous points where political economy abuts ethics." Moral betterment must first of all come to men to make the industrial age a blessing. "We must have more philanthropy, richer, more solid character, willingness in men to do for love what hitherto only money could induce."

Strangely enough, Andrews did not advocate direct government aid to ameliorate the position of the "brutish and ignorant" masses. Here he fell back on the "natural laws" of the Malthusian doctrine of population and diminishing returns. The "much ridiculed doctrine of Malthus" he accepted as substantially true, in that men's reproductive propensity needed control. Yet here, too, Andrews was more liberal than the older generation. He thought that the laboring masses should be inculcated with the desire for a higher standard of living, and should be imbued with the dignity of life so that they would not want their children, doomed by poverty, to live like brutes or slaves. This sentiment, once inculcated, would be a check upon population and at the same time would force from capital into the laborers' hands all that ought to go to them as wages.

This improved condition he would achieve through compulsory schooling for all children from two to fourteen years of age. With the best teachers and physical appliances in use, twelve years of such schooling would soon change the national conception of life. It would multiply intelligence and morality, rendering the laborers determined and able to stand together for all their just rights. And population would be voluntarily limited, so as to allow a decent plenty for all. All this would eventuate without any clash of social classes, since wealth would be immensely increased after the "ignorant work-population, ever the least productive economically, would be no more." [33]

Although Andrews' theoretical basis was essentially that of the great tradition in economics, his influence was to redirect it. He performed an eminent service in constantly reiterating that the time had come for American economists to depart from Bastiat and his "automatic economics," namely, that the free pursuit by each human being of his own welfare, as conceived by him, would result in the maximum social good. As he prophetically wrote in the *Andover Review* in 1886: "The historian will one day be astounded at the credit our bright age has given to the theory which makes of the State a mere policeman."

SIMON NELSON PATTEN AND THE NEW NATIONALIST ECONOMICS

Simon N. Patten (1852–1922), one of the most provocative figures of the group, was more critical of the older economic theory than Andrews.[34] Patten received a doctorate from Halle in 1878, with a dissertation on public finance. On his return to the United States he was forced to spend four years on the family farm in Illinois, then six years as a public school teacher. Not until 1889 did he get a college post, and then only through the friendship of his Halle classmate, E. J. James, who obtained for him the professorship of economics at the Wharton School.

Patten was a follower of the marginal utility economics, but, unlike most of the others in the school, he was an ardent protectionist.

He based his curious theory of protection on the conception that the nation's ills arose largely from faulty, unvaried consumption of agricultural products. The tastes of the American people, he held, must be adapted to those products which would bring about the best utilization of the soil, that is, to a variety of crops. The exclusive devotion of the soil in the South to tobacco and cotton, for example, had led to exhaustion. The development of variety had been prevented by free trade, for this restricted cultivation to the few products which could be transported long distances. As poorer land was brought into cultivation to meet the foreign demand, greater returns were attained by the "natural monopolies," such as rent, which depressed the condition of labor and capital. Low wages and low interest would thus result in large-scale monopolistic organization of industry. Free trade would achieve those pessimistic results envisaged by the Ricardian theory of rent and the Malthusian doctrine of population. However, if the country turned to home manufactures, these tendencies could be reversed by means of tariffs and the like.[35]

One graduate student, Henry R. Seager, later professor of economics at Columbia, wrote in his copy of Patten's *The Economic Basis of Protection* (1890) a succinct statement of Patten's tariff position as presented in class.

General Principles Given by Professor Patten, May 1891, U. of P.

1. A nation should employ its labor in those industries where it is most productive.
2. Often industries that give the greatest temporary return are not those that give the greatest permanent return.
3. A national policy is more necessary when the people are not inclined to save and work.
4. Differences in nature favor free trade.
5. Differences in men favor protection.
6. Cheapness of single articles not a criterion of industrial efficiency.
7. Some articles should be on the free list.
8. Some articles should have a duty.
10. Excluded from the class room discussion: the rate of the tariff.[36]

To the argument that protection destroyed the natural law of free competition, Patten replied, in his book *Premises of Political Economy* (1885), that the traditional laws of economics were not natural laws but social laws, developed by a non-progressive people. America required a different set of social laws to achieve fully that progress inherent in its rich material environment. The methods by which he came to such conclusions, he said, were both historical and deductive; perhaps less of the former than the latter, for historical work was less exciting and more tiring than theoretical work.[37]

His study of consumption was much more than a defense of the tariff; it opened up, he said in *The Consumption of Wealth* (1892), the most fundamental and deductive field; it yielded a theory which rested "upon the laws of pleasure and pain, modified by the social environment." He argued that the rich should open to the public their art collections and libraries; for this would increase the total amount of pleasure of the community without increasing the real psychic cost.[38] His theory also led him to pioneer for social welfare work and schools of philanthropy to raise the standard of living of the poor, and to plead for higher taxes to develop education, parks, and amusements. By thus promoting public ends, qualities which lay dormant under the "reign of individual selfishness" would be greatly strengthened.[39]

This emphasis on "public ends" led him to the notion of "economic freedom." The problem of economic freedom, he declared in *The Theory of Prosperity* (1902), was to find an equivalent for the rights that in earlier times went with land; that is, the workmen should have all that the landowners of the past enjoyed. Freedom consisted not merely of political rights, but was also dependent upon the possession of economic rights freely recognized and universally granted to each man by his fellow citizens. These rights measured freedom in proportion as there was mutual agreement concerning their desirability, and as complete adjustment made their realization possible. Only those rights that American conditions permitted, and the impulses which unimpeded activity might allow, could be properly considered ideal. There were a number of rights which satisfied these conditions in his time; consequently, he said, they must be incorporated in the national thought and become as clearly defined as political rights. As the conditions of adjustment to the American environment improved or as the environment changed, he foresaw that other rights could be added.

The achievement of these rights depended in the last analysis upon the growth of the social surplus. In modern nations, he declared, the productive power was more than sufficient to provide the minimum of subsistence. In this social surplus every worker had a right to share through the granting of economic rights. The right to comfort, for instance, was the right to share in the social surplus. This right was not a right to equality in the distribution of wealth but to the income necessary to secure to the worker the best physical conditions.

The right to leisure was a corollary to the right to comfort, and the right to recreation was an outcome of the narrow division of labor demanded by production on a large scale. Included, too, in his theory, was the right to cleanliness; that is, clear water, pure air, and clean streets were matters of public interest, and for these ends the social surplus should be freely used. In the general right he also included the right to scenery. Men should provide for their visual enjoyment with the same care as for other material conditions. Natural scenery must be preserved and restored; the demands of city life for corresponding advantages in its architecture, museums, and parks must also be met. Bad streets and glaring advertisements depressed men, reduced their productive power, and checked the growth of social feelings.

Besides the general rights belonging to every person in the industrial world, his discussion emphasized two exceptional rights that had grown out of special conditions. One of these was the right to relief. "The energy and the skill of each person," he said, "should be left free so that the reward for work can come to the worker; but misfortune is not an individual affair due to conditions that individuals make. The evil may lie in the environment, as in the case of a failure of crops; it may be due to accidents for which others are to blame; to the diseases and degradation of bad local conditions; or to social action. . . . The social surplus is more than sufficient to provide for all the exigencies that persons cannot control."

Second, there was the special right growing out of the peculiar position of women. Under the existing family arrangements and social conventions grave evils would continue until society gave to women workers an income large enough to insure their physical and moral well-being. The social surplus should therefore be freely used for women. No society could be safe, moral, and progressive until women had independent incomes. "The law should compel it if higher motives do not move men to compensate women for the evils to which they are liable, and from which they cannot escape without losing qualities that men admire."

Patten's concept of economic freedom was certainly broad and generous. His difficulty appears to have arisen largely through a somber, personal recognition of the weaknesses in human nature; in attempting to give due weight to human failings, he used a starkly realistic language which contrasted with the typically optimistic tone of the more liberal economists. In *The Theory of Social Forces* (1896) he criticized the philanthropy of "democratic ideals" which would give the benefits of civilization to all regardless of the merit or demerit of the individual. These ideals, he maintained, were "static elements," for they retarded the displacement of the less efficient classes and restricted the activity of the more efficient. He criticized the reformers for forgetting that the evils and pains of life came from the environment or from the defects of human nature, and not from the oppression of men, and also for keeping silent about "the pains and obstacles to progress which . . . represent the cost of nature's bounties."

For a more specific example of where this kind of thinking carried him, he declared, "we should more carefully exclude from society those who are tainted with pauper instincts and compel those who seek public support to live apart from the rest of the community." Empty jails, he added, were erroneously assumed to be a sign of progress. On the contrary, they showed merely that the public had not raised, as rapidly as its increased prosperity permitted, the minimum standard determining the point of exclusion from society. Jails, reform schools, almshouses, and asylums should increase, and the better condition of the innocent and worthy would cause a large increase of utility and improve the condition of society.[40]

In a similar way there was a reverse side to Patten's economic nationalism. While he emphasized the need of government intervention to develop the resources of the nation, he contended that this aid should not take the form of direct labor legislation, maximum price-fixing, or, for that matter, the direct outlawing of monopolies. In fact such activities would tend to impoverish the nation; and like the cry for free silver their popularity bore witness to people's inability to realize that by developing the country's many resources they could make it a great nation.[41]

This many-sided approach to his subject, contradictory as it seems in summary, often opened up significant lines of inquiry. For instance, he insisted that the factors of production must be distinguished from those of distribution. "The landlord," he said, "does not produce, yet he shares in distribution, while a teacher produces but may not share in the distribution." But before Patten had gone much further in his analysis, it became hard to see just what the distinction was. Capital as used in production, he continued, included "capital sunk in land, in men (skill) and instruments for production." But in distribution "capital sunk in land becomes rent, that sunk in men is labor, while the return for productive purposes is interest." [42] As with many other insights of his this needed further clarification.

Patten was at his best when he took his own advice, that "deductive economics need no longer seek for justification," and worked in what he called the "historical spirit." Thus he wrote of Ricardo that his importance and fame as an economist arose not from the breadth of his studies, but from his "happy selection of the right features of the English industrial life for study." What made Ricardo a stumbling block for further inquiry was that his followers tried to convince us that Ricardo's world was our world or that "we would be in such a world as soon as the force of inherited customs, habits, and laws became so weakened that their effects no longer obscured the working of the law of competition." [43] Economists generally agreed that it would be "excellent for economic thought if Patten could develop his ideas into a clear and logical system." As Ely put it, Patten needed someone to help him work out "into a systematic whole his various thoughts." [44]

To make matters more confused, Patten's procedure suffered from his penchant for devising new terms for old concepts. He continually picked up new terms from various fields, especially from philosophy and psychology, and manipulated them for his own purposes in economic discussions. But since he was not a close student of these other realms, such borrowing often tended to confuse his arguments. Each successive work contained so many novelties that it was difficult to see a continuity between the various books. Although these characteristics deflected the reader, they made Patten an excellent pedagogue. The variety of the information, the constant attunement to new terminology, the manipulation of new concepts, interested students and stimulated them. Consequently his students often elaborated his own doctrines along lines of which he did not approve, but he encouraged their intellectual adventures. Furthermore, some of his more important concepts, such as "economic freedom" and "social surplus," were such that students could easily forget the meaning Patten gave them and expand their use into areas which Patten would reserve for the distant future, if he would consider them at all. It is in great part due to Patten that so many University of Pennsylvania graduates became leaders in concrete movements for the amelioration of the masses and the restraint of business excesses.

Patten had high intellectual integrity. And a man who could write that "my present suffering is mainly from the thought that what I see before me and would like to do is beyond my powers" was just the sort of man who would give much of himself to develop the potentialities of his students. He exerted every effort to keep promising scholars close to the mark. Thus he wrote to one: "Don't get into any more 'humanity work.' You are well beyond that stage. Adjust your expenses to income and use your leisure to advance science." [45] No man, perhaps, illustrated more vividly the clash of old traditions and new sentiments than did Patten.

The figures who have passed in review in this chapter stood on common ground, but each developed in distinctly individual fashion. Ely's Christian socialism does not yield a systematic program comparable to that of Henry C. Adams; Andrews and Patten are generally less optimistic, and yet Andrews contributed to the clarification of monopoly and Patten developed a potentially explosive theory of social surplus. And C. S. Walker and John Bascom used their prestige to obtain a hearing for the claims of laborers and farmers. Taken as a group, they stood in the realm of policy for the position that Adams so well stated in 1883 in *Bradstreet's*, that in "the presence of strongly marked conflicting sentiments it frequently occurs that judicious compromise is all that either party can hope or expect."

CHAPTER VIII

John Bates Clark: The Conflict of Logic and Sentiment

THE most eminent of the "younger" generation of economists, dean not merely in age but in pre-eminent criticism of traditional economics, was John Bates Clark (1847–1938).[1] He was the third American figure to attain outstanding international importance. He was the father of what afterward became the main tradition in economics, and had a prominent role in founding the American Economic Association and in keeping economic thought open to every new influence, even when such influence sharply countered his own. Beginning as a moderate Christian Socialist, sharply critical of the excesses of the current regime of business, he emerged with what was the leading analysis of the economic drift of the country. Certain views, especially those on monopoly, were reflected in later legislation.

The future economist matured early in life because of heavy responsibilities. His father had been a successful official of the Corliss Engine Works in Providence, Rhode Island, but tuberculosis forced him to go to Minnesota and he called on the eldest son to manage the family affairs. Thus John Bates Clark left Amherst at the end of his junior year and entered the plow business in Minneapolis. Hard times for the farmers, he soon discovered, meant that to "sell" was one thing, to collect another. Driving around the state with horse and buggy, young Clark recouped from country storekeepers wherever practicable and made terms for delayed payments wherever it was advisable. At the end of 1871 he returned to Amherst, far more mature than the average student. There he displayed independence of mind by refusing to recognize "the absolute correctness" of the accepted philosophy and insisting on his own line of thought.

He had planned to enter the ministry after graduation, but on consulting his teacher in philosophy and the social sciences, the Reverend Julius Seelye (later president of Amherst), he decided on economics. Seelye, convinced of the overwhelming importance of economic problems, declared that if a student showed ability to deal soundly with them from the platform, "I encourage him to make that his profession." Of Clark's "remarkable aptitude" he had no doubt.[2] So after graduation Clark went abroad and studied for a while at Heidelberg and Zurich. On his return in 1875 teaching positions in the Eastern colleges were scarce. Being unable, despite his high recommendations, to teach there, he settled for a lectureship at Carleton College in Northfield, Minnesota. Classes had hardly begun, however, when illness forced him to take a two-year leave. During this period he did some tutoring, especially in Latin, at the University of Minnesota. After that he tried to obtain a fellowship in the newly opened Johns Hopkins University, but failed because he had no written work to show.[3] In 1877 he returned to Carleton, nominally as librarian and professor of history and political economy, but actually, as he put it, as "Professor of Odds and Ends," teaching everything from rhetoric to moral philosophy.

Clark moved East in 1881, where he taught first at Smith, then concurrently at Amherst and Johns Hopkins. In 1895 he went to Columbia University. He was about to take the "plunge into New York life and work," he wrote. "For a time it will be as strange to me as a journey in Russia; for though I have lived in cities I never worked in a city, or got entangled in its complex life." [4] In his teaching, as in his writing, Clark's high standard of free inquiry and intellectual integrity was maintained from the beginning. His favorite student at Carleton had been an intellectual misfit, Thorstein Veblen. Veblen's later fame was a source of great pride to Clark, a pride undisturbed by the fact that much of that fame rested on criticisms of the kind of economic theory he had developed.

Clark began his writing career in 1877, in the *New Englander*. He began with a flat assertion: "In the present state of the public mind, financial heresies receive a ready circulation, and if these false doctrines connect themselves . . . with fundamental errors of Political Economy, it is time that those errors were exposed and their teachers discredited." He proposed to set forth a "new philosophy of wealth," which would render "the classification of all labor as productive," both feasible and obvious, and make it "easy to place every variety of laborer in exactly the class of wealth-producers" in which he belonged.

Clark defined wealth as "relative well-being," pertaining to individual rather than community welfare. A good, in order to be wealth, had to possess "utility"—that is, satisfy a want; but its essential attribute was appropriability, which rendered ownership possible. That wealth was distributed as equitably as possible under the circumstances had been proved to his satisfaction by anthropological inquiry. As the institution of property acquired a moral basis, the nature of the competitive struggle changed. In the primitive state it had been a struggle to secure actual possession; in the civilized state it was a struggle to secure lawful possession, either by creating something of value, or receiving it from a previous owner by a voluntary cession. Political economy treated not of man the savage, but of man who through ages of unifying processes of social development had become a part of the social organism.

In 1881 Clark supplemented his "philosophy of wealth" with a "philosophy of value." Value was a "measure of utility." This utility was not "absolute," but "effective utility," the power to modify our subjective condition under actual circumstances, mentally measured by supposing something which we possess to be annihilated or something which we lack to be attained. But it was society, not the individual, whose estimate of utility constituted a social or market valuation. In the light of the pleasure-pain calculus, market value was "a measure of utility made by society considered as one great isolated being." The rewards society thought the producers entitled to were established through the "laws of property," these laws being "fixed principles of distribution" that society was not at liberty to violate. To be sure, values in use might be augmented if these naturally established market values could be arbitrarily changed. Indeed, he said, "better systems of social circulation may be before us in the future, if we can but wait for their development." But wholesale confiscation would mean violent revolution and would lead to a "chaotic condition fatal to the welfare of all."

This "philosophy of value" was the logical outcome of the main American tradition in economics as refined by Clark's liberalism. Under an ideal system of free contract, which he called "free competition," everyone received either what he produced or its equivalent. In the America of the eighties he saw a close approximation of this condition, constantly coming closer under the pressure of the principle of harmony inherent in the evolving social organism.

The guiding force, Clark insisted, was competition, its excesses prevented by the growth of moral character. It was the great force in production and was still needed in distribution. Even in the case of so-called monopolies and pools, competition was latent. For the standard of equity in the purchase and sale of commodities was set by the "normal action of supply and demand in the open market." Exchanges made at current rates in open market were equal exchanges and constituted justice. Unequal exchanges effected by refinements of force and fraud were of course reprehensible; or, as Clark characteristically put it, "What is ordinarily termed a good bargain is, morally, a bad bargain." But his theory did not condemn speculation as such. Buying articles cheap with a view to selling them later at a higher price was to acquire wealth by accretions of time utility—a category of production rather than of exchange. Thus was the merchant rewarded for producing time, place, and form utility.

The analysis was similar to Jevons' conception, but Clark was then unaware of the work of Jevons or of his continental contemporaries.[5] Instead of their term "marginal utility" or "final degree of utility," Clark used "effective utility" or "social effective utility." * With characteristic modesty he attributed them to suggestions made by his old Heidelberg teacher, Karl Knies.[6]

One very interesting concept Clark developed in this early period was that of "inappropriable utilities." Certain utilities, he noted in 1882, escaped their creator and diffused themselves among other members of the community. The builder of a beautiful house, for example, could not monopolize all its utility; its tasteful construction created an inappropriable utility which resulted in raising the price of adjoining property. More significant, the railroad created a value far greater than its projectors could realize in the increased value of land and higher returns to productive effort in the area it traversed. A railroad might even enrich a section while becoming bankrupt itself. The land grants to the railroad companies had their justification largely in the principle of inappropriable utilities. On the other hand, since the railroad corporation received no reward for the inappropriable utilities it created, it would "sacrifice them with impunity." Through the working of this principle much of the welfare of large populations was entrusted to corporations having no interest in promoting it. Until recently, indeed, the railroad company or its managers had often stood to gain considerably by sacrificing the welfare of the people in its district. Discriminatory rates as well as other abuses had recklessly made or marred the welfare of areas, and were tending to "hasten the time when only the assumption of railroads by the State can prevent evils too serious to be tolerated. The State only can secure to itself all the utilities which these agencies can create, and ensure their impartial distribution among those who are dependent on them."

Clark applied his principle of inappropriable utilities to every form of industry in which a community had an independent interest, especially education and religious institutions. Their tax exemption was a partial refunding of the value they diffused through the community.

In harmony with these views, he supported in "The Nature and Progress of True Socialism" (1879) a form of socialism that would not violate the natural ideal order of property. In truth, a "remnant of natural ferocity" existed in business institutions; the theory of the modern bargain appeared to be that of the medieval judicial combat: "Let each do his worst, and God will protect the right." Never-

* For detailed material on Clark's views on marginal utility, see Appendix.

theless, these institutions contained in themselves the germs of a progress that would break the limitations of the existing system, and "give us the only socialism that can be permanent or beneficial." Believing in this "natural development," he rejected the Marxian "political socialism" which, he declared, sought as an immediate practical aim that government own all capital and divide the returns according to principles of "abstract justice."

Further study convinced Clark that while more efficient machine production had led to the centralization of capital in great corporations approaching monopolies, the strategic inequality of labor engendered by this had been corrected at first by the availability of free land. And as that factor disappeared, a new one had materialized in the form of labor unions. Inasmuch as a few soulless employers would always attempt to take advantage of the few unemployed by engaging in cutthroat competition, thereby depressing wages temporarily below their normal level, this practice would be prevented by the growth of unions. True, the rise of the factory system had rendered unskilled labor a threat to skilled labor, but that problem was being met by a new type of union, the all-embracing Knights of Labor.

The solidarity of capital on the one hand and labor on the other might, he thought, bring into effect that moral law under which legitimate competition functioned automatically without the waste of higgling or the personal competition of handicraft days. The next step would be the voluntary arbitration of labor disputes, but since that might involve ceaseless litigation, a greater advance would be the profit-sharing co-operative, wherein the laborers would become entrepreneurs as well as laborers. The final state, Clark explained, would be the voluntary producers' co-operative, or "full co-operation," where industrial strife would be eliminated because the laborer would also be the capitalist. Consciously borrowing from the English Christian Socialism of the 1850's, which he described as "economic republicanism," he declared that full co-operation had the best chance of becoming the eventual ideal if it began with small producers. At that level the worker-capitalists, not yet compelled to borrow, could acquire the managerial experience necessary for larger operations.

Upon its ability to excel other systems of production, indeed, would depend the growth and survival of the co-operative system. Initial failures would not be decisive. If but one cotton mill on the co-operative plan should surpass other mills in economy of production, so that it could undersell them, all cotton mills might ultimately be compelled to adopt the co-operative plan. All economic institutions must be tested by competition; but whether arbitration, profit-sharing, or full co-operation would permanently supersede the now obsolete individualistic struggle, he concluded, should be determined by their success in action. The fittest would survive. The new political economy must recognize this special and higher competition by which the economic system is kept efficient.[7]

These ideas, revised and elaborated, appeared again in *The Philosophy of Wealth* (1886), whose predominant note was Clark's Christian Socialism. He appealed to the Church to take a more active interest in the masses; and to economists to extend economic inquiry beyond the narrow materialistic confines of the older system. He expressed the hope and even the expectation that the system of "full co-operation" would through the evolutionary competitive process of survival eventually replace the now outmoded system of individualistic competition. He flatly opposed the extreme individualism typified by William Graham Sumner.[8]

That the book was an important one was generally agreed, but some significant differences of opinion arose as to its nature. Franklin H. Giddings, then a newspaper editor, and later professor of sociology at Columbia, thought this new volume "by all odds the most original and helpful contribution to economic theory since Jevons." As Giddings understood it, "All true competition or rivalry must be between members of the same class and all bargaining must be between different classes. . . . Therefore the conditions determining profits and wages . . . are exceedingly complex, being determined partly by the competition within each class, and partly by the bargaining of each class in its dealings with others." To him, Clark had developed nothing less than a new statement of the law of distribution.[9]

On the other hand, Clark's friend from Minnesota days, William W. Folwell, was skeptical about his marginal utility analysis because the phrase "measure of utility" was not "exact as a figure." He was "firmly persuaded," nevertheless, that "a great deal of *speculative* work on Industrial Science" was needed. "You have put us under an obligation in the preparation of this thoughtful work," Folwell wrote. To which Clark replied that Folwell's doubts might be somewhat allayed on a second reading, for the value theory conveyed a different meaning when fully considered.[10]

More challenging was the analysis of Arthur Twining Hadley, head of Connecticut's Bureau of Labor Statistics, and professor of political science at Yale. In an unsigned review in the *Independent*, he praised Clark's theory of value but declared that the author had fallen into the "crudest socialistic fallacies" regarding the nature of wealth, especially in his estimate of trade. And when men like Henry C. Adams speak of it as a standard American work on economic science, it "becomes us to protest against a series of admissions [by Clark], which, if once allowed, would put the extreme socialists in the right, and everyone else in the wrong."

When Clark objected to this interpretation, Hadley replied that he knew Clark was no radical but that certain statements in the book encouraged readers to believe the two notions he (Hadley) had to fight every day—that "labor creates wealth all ʰut universally, and that trade is a gain of one party at the expense of another." Hadley admitted that he had misunderstood Clark's strictures on the ethics of trade. However, he went on, "what you say sounds so much like what Marx says on the same subject, that . . . reₐders will think that you object to speculation as such, and not merely to manipulation of the market." In fact, he said, "how can we decide between the two? If A has more special intelligence than B, B will commonly have more pressing necessities than A. When does A's advantage cease to be fairly due to his superior intelligence, and become unfairly due to B's pressing necessities? Of course, such a point does come, but I do not see any way of drawing the line to show where it comes." [11]

Horace White of the powerful *New York Evening Post* urbanely dismissed Clark's criticisms of business practice. White simply said the book did not fall within the "province of political economy. . . . The question what ought society to strive for is strictly a moral question." [12] But other reviewers lauded this quality. In writing of the spirit of the book as a whole, Woodrow Wilson, then associate professor of history and political economy at Bryn Mawr, praised the work's "moderation and its Christianity" He wrote Clark: "A sane, well-balanced sympathizer with organized labor is very dear to my esteem; and one who finds all the necessary stimulations of hope, not in chimeras or in hastened reformation, but in the slow process of conservative endeavor, is sure of my whole respect." Henry C. Adams also praised Clark for elaborating the "life-giving truth that society is an organism subject to the law of ordered change, and makes it the basis of his theory of value." C. S. Walker wrote: "I am pleased . . . with the candor joined with independence that marks your discussion of disputed questions. . . . Your knowledge of mental science has made you a better student of political economy. The real nature of man is an element in all problems of political economy of prime importance." [13]

As the reviews in general bore out, the primary strain in Clark's thinking at the time was a broad conception of economics that emphasized social reform; the secondary strain was to reformulate the theory of value to make it more logically consistent and at the same time give ethical validity to the underlying foundations of modern society. But shortly thereafter the secondary strain became the primary one, so that in the later and more famous *The Distribution of Wealth* (1899) the first strain is practically non-existent. This does not mean that Clark ceased to be concerned with social reform, but rather that he no longer considered it within the realm of economic theory; and his strong moral and intellectual conscience drove him further in search of what he called a scientific explanation for the substantial validity of the system of capital and wages. No more than before did he believe that the existing system was ideal; but he wanted to show that specific economic laws, laws that made for a substantial equity in distribution under the reign of property and contract, underlay the ever-closer approach to the ideal. This was accentuated at the particular time by the controversies raised by Francis A. Walker's theory of the laborer as the residual claimant of industry and Henry George's potentially dangerous single-tax doctrine.[14]

Clark presented in 1888–89 two of a series of basic papers that became the foundation for his international fame. The first, "Capital and Its Earnings," aimed to refute "agrarian socialism" by a reconsideration and redefinition of the nature of capital and rent in such a way as to eliminate the distinction between capital and land as well as the need of direct anti-monopoly legislation. Pure capital, he declared, was a "permanent fund of abstract value embodied in an ever-changing list of concrete things." [15] Capital included the value of land, for the "common consciousness" recognized that land was a productive instrument duly included in business inventories as capital. The earnings of the heterogeneous concrete instruments constituting capital Clark called "rent." Hitherto applied only to land by the outstanding authorities in economics, its laws applied in fact to all concrete things into which pure capital entered.

The law of market rent was the Ricardian formulation for land rent, expanded to include all instruments: "Rent equals product minus the product of the poorest instrument of the same class that is utilized with an equal outlay of labor and auxiliary capital." For example, take a ship, ascertain its product, and then search for the worst hull to which can be consistently entrusted as many men and as much auxiliary capital as are entrusted to the first ship being tested. "This is the no-rent ship, and its product . . . equals wages and interest on subsidiary capital." The rent of the good ship is its "product minus such wages and interest"; its earnings are "gauged by its power to increase the product of industry." Here Clark formulated an embryonic marginal productivity theory.

The normal rent as distinguished from market rent, Clark went on, was governed by the cost of production and also applied to all instruments as well as to land. If, for instance, the earnings of a ship were greater than those of a mill of equal cost, more ships and fewer mills would be built; the competition of ships would then reduce the earnings to the standard in other spheres of investment. In other words, the interest on the pure capital invested in an instrument determined its normal or permanent rent. Since pure capital gravitated to the point of greatest return, the earnings of capital would be equalized.

This primary law of the return on productive wealth was a "chief basis of an equitable system of distribution." "Pure capital," he said, "represents 'economic merit' or personal sacrifice incurred in the service of society." Ten thousand dollars as the fruits of twenty years' labor should command the same annual return in whatever form invested. So conceived, the whole income of society was composed simply of the rewards of labor and capital. True, an element of pure profit appeared from time to time, but that was a special premium for mechanical invention and for improving industrial organization; competition tended to eliminate it and yield to wages and interest the entire gain from social industry.

Clark granted that there was some element of "natural monopoly" in land, but it tended toward insignificance. The value of land was composed of four utilities. Three of these were produced by labor—the fertility secured by drains or irrigating canals, the fertility gained by enriching surface loams, and the accessibility secured by improvements in the means of transportation. But the fourth utility, based on literal proximity to markets and thus the result of general social growth, constituted a limited monopoly. However, this kind of monopoly tended to become relatively unimportant as the period of original occupation and exploitation disappeared, allowing land to be utilized in the normal way.

Clark recognized the seriousness of the general monopoly problem, and he by no means precluded State action. He urged as the most effective safeguard the unimpeded flow of capital, i.e., free purchase and sale to the points of large reward. As long as the State did not touch the value, the pure capital, it could safely shift the vehicle. Thus if land were anywhere dangerously monopolized, changes could be made so long as the land was paid for. Similarly, while pools could not and should not be suppressed, any tendency toward monopoly would be prevented if capital were free to flow to the point of highest return. Where patent laws tended to encourage monopoly, such laws could be amended as necessary. In short, guarantee the operation of natural law, and relatively little direct action need be undertaken by government.[16]

Having coped in his first essay with "agrarian socialism," Clark discussed in the second the "Possibility of a Scientific Law of Wages." Admittedly he was spurred by the Henry George theory that wages were determined by the product yielded on marginal or no-rent land because there alone could labor's separate product be reckoned.[17] While he considered this theory sound to the extent that wages tended to equal labor's product, he could not accept a "theory of 'squatter sovereignty' over the labor market." He pointed out that George's theory ignored the fact that all instruments had a no-rent margin. The theory therefore must also be extended to include all instruments in addition to land.

Expanding further the rent doctrine, Clark reformulated the law of diminishing returns to apply to all capital and labor. An increasing amount of labor applied to a fixed amount of pure capital yielded an ever smaller return. If capital were fixed and population increased, productive contribution per unit of labor would diminish. But if the laborers accepted what they produced, that is, their marginal product, they could find employment; thus could the market for labor be expanded indefinitely. In other words, the surplus labor pressed down the productivity margin, the final product of labor became smaller, and the general standard of wages lower. Earnings of capital were similarly determined; if the supply of labor were fixed and capital increased, each further increment of the latter added an ever smaller amount of total output. The law of diminishing returns was therefore two-dimensional: it applied to whichever agent of production exceeded the other in the "rate of its quantitative increase." A relative surplus of either agent created less wealth per active unit than had been produced with the smaller supply.

This "self-reversing" force, Clark declared, controlled the general division of the social income. As capital increased it "must push outward the margin of its field" and embody itself in improved instruments that tend to yield less return. Each reduction of the final product reacted on the general interest rate. In turn, with every fall in the rate of interest the poorest appliances in use and the least remunerative uses of better appliances would be abandoned. In other words, the no-rent or marginal line was relocated, the product of the final increment of labor was increased, and competition raised general wages to the new standard. Thus if competition were perfect, labor was not "robbed" by capital; the return of each was fixed in the same manner. "Each gets an amount gauged by the product of its own final increment."

Although trade unions were beneficent and necessary when they acted rationally, Clark added, to fight the law of "marginal valuation" or, as he later preferred to call it, "specific productivity," was not rational. Their attempts to restrict membership with a view to maintaining wages, in the face of an increasing labor supply, must end in a more than "normal depression" of the wages of their members. The eight-hour-day philosophy, especially, overlooked the fact that a rise in wages was governed by the marginal productivity of labor. "Higher wages for men means a larger amount of usable things due to the labor of men," said Clark. "When this comes about by natural causes, the good results in the way of larger production by machinery follow. Invention makes the marginal productivity of both labor and capital larger. Aside from that, [the] growth of capital in amount makes the marginal productivity of labor larger." By thus emphasizing "productivity," Clark felt that while he accepted the "traditional conclusion" of both the wage fund and Malthusian doctrines, he had rejected the process by which it had been reached.[18]

Clark was considerably disturbed by the disruptive effects of strikes and sought to work out principles for arbitration that would not violate the law of marginal productivity. While he opposed violence, he granted that if strikers used purely verbal persuasion in endeavoring to keep others from taking their places the road would be open for that very sinister personality, the strikebreaker, who, he said, "is ready, for high pay, to take for a time a high personal risk." A good-sized force of these could defeat the average strike, since the employer could afford to pay a high rate until enough of the regular workmen surrendered to make the remaining strikers despair of winning. Although the use of strikebreakers was decidedly unfair and should be prevented, he said, the community could not tolerate large-scale strikes which disrupted the industrial life of the nation. The remedy was arbitration tribunals whose awards would have to be accepted by the employers if they wished to continue the business, and by the employees if their positions were not to be taken over by non-union men.[19]

Clark felt it would be relatively easy for a tribunal to set fair wages. The "really natural standard of pay lies," he said, "between the amount that idle men may here and there consent to take and the amount that a union which guards its monopoly by force may be able to extort; and it lies at about the level of what a union that is extended and efficient but not monopolistic can get." Well-constituted tribunals would recognize this standard and could easily keep the pay of labor at least near "its natural level."

Clark warned that in a period of depression "a general union of laborers" should adjust its claims for wages with especial regard to the marginal product of labor. Otherwise it would increase the number of unemployed. In criticism, Professor George E. Barnett of Johns Hopkins asked what "the marginal product of labor" was, and Professor Thomas S. Adams of Wisconsin (later of Yale) asked whether the injunction had any real meaning beyond that "conveyed by the time-worn union maxim, 'Don't strike for an increase of wages in a falling market.' "[20]

Perhaps the most significant statements on the labor problem by Clark at this time were that capital and labor were each combining to do the same thing, and that both combinations might well act for their joint welfare provided they did not overstep the limits set by the law of marginal productivity.[21]

Each class of producers, Clark reiterated time and again, tended to get the wealth it brought into existence. Study of distribution revealed "the inherent honesty of a competitive economic system, provided only the competition is truly free. . . . Dishonesty comes through a perversion of this competitive system." These "certainties of economic science," he urged, should be "put within reach of boys and girls of high-school grade. In the good times coming, economics will be on a par with mathematics in having its elementary courses within the comprehension of grammar-school children, its more solid courses for pupils in high schools, and its college courses made possible by the early training of the students who take them." [22]

This conviction about "certainties" limited his theory's flexibility, but Clark was aware that he had not presented a complete theory of distribution. He knew that his "law," valid for the "static" State, must for the "dynamic" modern State be supplemented or modified. And when Henry C. Adams chided him for ignoring such factors as bargaining strategy and the role of the civil law, Clark replied that he hoped to treat them adequately in the division on Dynamics.[23] But he never quite got around to it.

Adams wondered whether Clark, after committing himself to the "mechanical reasoning" of the full-blown marginal utility school, could pass beyond its limitations.[24] Clark's strong social sense and kindly nature, however, proved far stronger than his formal methods might at first glance indicate. Satisfied that socialism was impracticable, he nevertheless wrote introductions for translations of able books that fed the current of socialism.[25] The reader should realize that socialism was undesirable and contrary to evolution, he pointed out, but heretical opinions should get a hearing.

It was characteristic of the man that what others might consider socialism he considered democracy. Thus he championed the referendum, promoted most vigorously by the socialists and laborites, on the ground that it was a safeguard for wealth itself and helped eliminate corruption. The worst ills of democracy, he declared, were caused by thwarting the will of the people, that the "reformatory spirit should make common cause with the present popular tendency." [26]

The extension of government power to include municipal ownership of gas plants and other utilities, if it came about "naturally as a result of experiment," was not socialism. If one town tried it and it worked well, why should not another follow suit? So say fair-minded men. If men pushed it with ulterior theoretical designs, he dubbed it socialism, for to the extent that these men were in it, it was so. A distinction must be made, he said, between the "natural enlargement of State functions and the doctrinarian policy of pushing such enlargements toward a goal. The last is what there is fear of on all sides."

Clark was somewhat annoyed with Ely for emphasizing frauds in government operations. "Shall we not play into the hands of our laissez-faire friends if we make much of such frauds? I am personally in favor of public ownership of gas, water, and electric-light plants, but I am able to see that it would inevitably lead to frauds upon the public." He wanted reforms presented to the public in a way that would show that they did not tread on the rights of important classes, or on any rights at all.[27] But such statements on reform, it should again be noted, Clark did not consider as a part of economic doctrine, as he had in the days of *The Philosophy of Wealth*.

In his later writings, therefore, Clark assumed that enlightened self-interest provided the sound ethical base to the economic system, and he limited his analyses to what he thought pure economics. In the nineties, for instance, one of the leading reform problems was the control of trusts. Assuming that trusts which were not monopolistic were ethical, he analyzed their economic functions. In his presidential address before the American Economic Association in 1894 he declared that the competitive form of society that evolution had achieved was a dynamic one.[28] Trusts accorded with competition and the dynamic progressive movement. The indiscriminate attacks on trusts failed to recognize that trusts embodied the efficiency of large units and were here to stay.[29] In other words, to Clark size was not to be attacked per se; but with the passage of time he came to feel that, since growth was often accompanied by monopolistic behavior, increasingly stringent measures should be taken to curb the latter.

At the turn of the century he was more explicit and presented a plan that would suppress monopolies yet retain trusts. Amassed capital, he declared, was beneficial since this natural and centralizing tendency indicated the survival of the most productive forms of business. Trusts could produce more cheaply and give better service than smaller concerns. They were especially essential in the contest between the United States and European countries for lucrative connections with the recently opened up areas of Asia and Africa. They were also essential for the subsequent contest between both America and Europe on the one hand, and Asia and Africa on the other, for command of the world's traffic. Victory would mean a leading position in the permanent progress of the world, with such positive wealth, high wages, and intellectual gains as could not be enjoyed by those developing less power.[30]

But Clark now went a step beyond reliance on potential competition as a safeguard, for potential competition was not enough, and too tardy, to prevent trusts from degenerating into monopolies. He said that by cutting prices below cost in one field or one product the would-be monopolist could crush the small competitors and sustain himself by charging higher prices in other fields and products. Akin to these resources for predatory warfare was the power of the trust to boycott customers who purchased also from independents, or, conversely, to make special rebates to merchants who dealt exclusively with it. Such practices should be eliminated, and toward this end the law should put all customers under a most-favored-nation clause. No other regulation would be needed.[31]

Clark declared before the Committee on Interstate Commerce in 1911 that under the Sherman Anti-Trust Act sufficient competition was possible. But while unfair practices by large corporations were prohibited, a trade commission should be established to see that these prohibitions were observed. It should be something like the Interstate Commerce Commission, but the latter, since it dealt with a naturally exclusive monopoly, must engage in price regulation. The trade commission would deal with what we were trying to rescue from the condition of monopoly. However, he said, "there is an ultimate contingency in which, after years of experience, . . . a very limited price-regulating power might be given to it. . . . I think I can count on the fingers of one hand all the cases in which it would be necessary to apply that measure." [32]

In any event, that new and "menacing institution," the holding company, he said, should be suppressed; and undue community of interest must be prevented even if it necessitated the "extremely radical and drastic regulation" that no man should have ownership in two competing corporations. Furthermore, if the trusts were broken up so that each unit was an "absolutely large and efficient company," the result would be not ruinous competition, as critics claimed, but, on the contrary, with certain conditions which could be created, there would be "tolerant competition, competition of the normal sort, more nearly akin to that which existed long before the trusts were formed in the days when competitors were numerous and fairly efficient."

The central economic problem for Clark became increasingly the control of trusts. Although interested, he did not study exhaustively the monetary problem or often engage in the polemics on it. When the silver controversy was at its bitterest in 1895–96, he did write several articles. On the assumed basis of his "natural law" of marginal productivity, he asserted that the appreciation in the value of gold did not increase the burden on debtors, for a steady appreciation or depreciation of the standard caused an adjustment of the interest rate in the opposite direction, thereby balancing the loss or gain in the principal. True, the "cyclical changes in business" introduced a disturbing factor, but by the "signs of the times, the coming of either . . . [boom or depression] ought to be measurably anticipated." [33]

With the increased emphasis on natural law his later writings lost most of his early Christian Socialist sentiment. Reflecting on this change of emphasis in his father's writings, his eminent son, Professor John Maurice Clark, has well remarked: "In an historical movement like the development of consolidations, concentration, and monopoly, there may be a first stage when it is new and people are alarmed by the prospective threat it presents. That stage might be represented by the concern shown in *The Philosophy of Wealth* about such things.

"There may come a stage when people find the world going on much the same as before in spite of the presence of the new factors, and their emphasis is toned down to a secondary qualification on a system primarily built around the older factors; as my father's later system is built around free competition with the assumption that the force of monopoly can be successfully 'contained.'

"Later still may come a stage at which the new factors have really developed their power, perhaps to the point of dethroning the older forces from their dominant position. The students may be forced to shift their emphasis, as I think we are forced today, and our appraisals may sound more like those of the people of the first period who were excited about what the new movement might do. Much the same might be true of the need of considering ethical factors." [34]

John Bates Clark was in more ways than one the grand old man of economics. Aside from his outstanding contributions to the elaboration and refinement of systematic marginal economics, he possessed a warm and tolerant personality that broadened the study of economics even as his own interests narrowed. Thus a large number of his contemporaries as well as a greater number of younger men acknowledged indebtedness to him. His influence has been very great down to the present, but not wholly as he would have liked; for many statements which he carefully qualified, such as, every man gets what he produces, have been taken by uncritical conservatives as rigid dogma. This made a great nineteenth-century liberal thinker into the symbol of twentieth-century reaction, but fortunately, in more recent years, greater recognition has been given to the more explicit humanitarian trend of *The Philosophy of Wealth.*

CHAPTER IX

The Union of the Economists

THE opposition of so many young men to the regnant extreme individualism of the eighties found a most effective outlet in the creation of the American Economic Association in 1885. E. J. James and Simon N. Patten set the ball in motion around 1884. They wanted a Society for the Study of National Economy, modeled after the German association of the followers of the historical school. Such a society would, they said, "combat the widespread view that our economic problems will solve themselves, and that our laws and institutions which at present favor individual instead of collective action can promote the best utilization of our material resources and secure to each individual the highest development of all his faculties." Among other things, they advocated national grants to the states for education, and the setting aside of a part of every locality for forests; they denounced the "arbitrary discrimination of our transportation companies," which prevented the development of a sound industry. But their emphasis on extension of the national power as against local power, their blunt assertion that the power of the national government was paramount over the states, and their support of a protective tariff, made it unlikely that many American economists would be interested in that specific society.[1]

Their efforts, however, paved the way for Ely's successful movement in the spring of 1885 to band together all the liberal economists in the pursuit of free inquiry; or, as Clark put it, to organize a "Political Economy Club on a rather progressive basis" by including the "younger men, who do not believe implicitly in laissez-faire doctrines, nor the use of the deductive method exclusively."[2] Ely's prospectus stated: "We regard the State as an educational and ethical agency whose positive aid is an indispensable condition of human progress." Individual initiative was necessary in industrial life, it said, but "the doctrine of laissez faire is unsafe in politics and unsound in morals." The conclusions of the political economists of the last generation were not to be trusted, it asserted, for political economy was in the first stages of scientific development and its advance was to be achieved not so much by speculation as by an impartial study of actual economic conditions. The new group was to "seek the aid of statistics in the present, and of history in the past," and asked for the united efforts of Church, State, and science, without which the conflict between labor and capital could not be solved. The prospectus banned any "partisan attitude" on questions of government policy, especially in regard to restrictions on trade and the protection of domestic industry, for the progressive development of economic conditions must be met by corresponding changes in policy.[3]

Ely felt that the organization would exercise an influence on public opinion, and that those interested in it would be conservatives rather than radicals. The need for individual initiative and effort and for competition would not be questioned. Ely wrote privately at the time: "What I would like to see is simply an association of the younger progressive elements, and the platform must be broad, yet it must not include men of the Sumner type, nor be used for partisan purposes either for free trade or protection."[4]

Patten, however, felt that the "very object of our association should be to deny the right of individuals to do as they please, and that, of course, is restricting trade. . . . We should give in some specific form our attitude on all the leading questions where State intervention is needed." [5] But he was willing to sacrifice his personal predilections to push the movement, and with James, Adams, and Ely as official sponsors a meeting was held in September 1885 for all those interested in the prospectus.

Most of the economists present at the original meeting thought that the condemnation of laissez faire and of the work of the old school should be modified. Clark declared that the "point upon which individuals will be unable to unite is, especially, the strong condemnation of the laissez-faire doctrine." Henry C. Adams stated that "the radical changes in society have forced new problems to the front for study and solution, but the claim to be historical students would be forfeited, should even a suggestion of isolation make its appearance." E. Benjamin Andrews declared that no impassable gulf separated Wagner, Roscher, and Knies from Adam Smith, Mill, and Ricardo. Even James insisted that the group should give no justification for the charge that they were "State socialists" or "professorial socialists." E. R. A. Seligman of Columbia, who very actively promoted the Association, summarized the general opinion when he said that modern economics had not yet attained that certainty in results which would authorize the group to invoke increased governmental action as a check to various abuses of free competition.

The statement of principles was accordingly modified; the strictures against laissez faire were eliminated, but the first principle, that "We regard the State as an agency whose positive assistance is one of the indispensable conditions of human progress," [6] still remained.

The man chosen as the first president was Francis A. Walker, a logical choice under the circumstances. Walker had an international reputation and was highly respected in almost all circles. He had been among the first to speak well of the historical school, and he had stated in his textbook that the classical school and the historical school were complementary. It was characteristic of the man's tolerance that he wanted the Association open to all groups of American economists. For a while a number stayed outside, especially the Yale-Harvard group, leading Walker to declare: "If my slipping down from the presidency would promote harmony and extend the usefulness of the Association, I shall cheerfully yield to anyone who may be named—even Sumner." [7]

The new organization contained a diversity of powerful figures, but they were able to work together fairly well. Between the Association and those on the outside, however, there was a good deal of friction. The Association group called itself the "new school" and derided the outsiders as the "old school." The magazine *Science* arranged for a debate in 1886 to be carried on through its columns by spokesmen of each school. Simon Newcomb, speaking for the old school, called his Johns Hopkins colleague Ely a socialist, and Ely hotly refuted the charge. The issue was nicely confused when both sides claimed the British economists Alfred Marshall and Jevons.[8] One writer well stated at the time: "Economists can ill afford to waste their energies in discussing theoretical refinements of method. They should rather husband all their resources for the purpose of grappling more successfully with questions that are at once pressing and outstandingly difficult." [9]

In 1887, eager to attract the young men of the old school, the Council of the Association toned down the constitution. All that remained of the old spirit was the statement that the first objective of the association was "the encouragement of economic research, especially the historical and statistical study of the actual conditions of industrial life." [10] Seligman denied that the change was made in "deference to a coterie." The idea was simply that the Association should chiefly agree on the lines of method, and that any emphasis on the historical and statistical method would be sufficient. Good men like Arthur Twining Hadley and Henry Farnam of Yale, he declared, would be willing to join if the platform were toned down.

Consequently by 1890 most of the leading academic members of the "old school," with the notable exception of Sumner, were members of the American Economic Association. Ely wrote at this time that the "old issues which divided the economists a few years ago . . . are no longer so important as they were and now is the time for a love feast! . . . What we want now is to bend all energies to make it an active progressive society." [11] To bring this about the Association sought agreement on the definition of terms. A committee on terminology was appointed, with Clark as chairman, to prepare a brief vocabulary of leading economic terms. Sharp differences immediately arose in the seemingly innocuous field of consumption, involving not so much the terminology as the function of consumption. Clark in his role of harmonizer made the following suggestions as a basis for agreement: "Are the men who say that consumption is not a part of the science of Political Economy and those who say that it is the most important in reality widely separated in thought? Do not the former mean that it is not a subject of *research* and the latter that it is among the most important *data?* Is it difficult to place beyond controversy the extent to which the consuming process lies within the field of research? Ought not the terms 'productive' and 'unproductive' consumption to be put through a course of criticism?"

This did not settle the issue. George Gunton and Frederick B. Hawley insisted, contrary to tradition, that the distinction between productive and unproductive consumption was misleading. Gunton declared that "unproductive consumption is an economic misnomer. Consumption is always productive because it furnishes the effective market basis for production. . . . There may be wise and unwise consumption, but there is no unproductive consumption." And Hawley added an amplification of his general theory: "The economic antithesis of consumption is not production but accumulation. Capital in gross is as subject to the law of supply and demand as any of its component parts. More [capital] . . . frequently is accumulated than can find satisfactory employment. Too rapid accumulation is checked, not by an increase of production . . . but by a decline in industrial activity. As [J. B.] Say affirms, the supply of commodities constitutes the demand, but demand is of two sorts—for consumption and for accumulation, and if these are disproportioned, if more is demanded for accumulation than can be satisfactorily utilized as capital, a glut results." [12]

In the face of such difficulties the whole matter of terminology was allowed to lapse. The committee reported to the Association that an authoritative usage would hinder original work, and where varying usages existed, a natural selection must determine which was to survive.[13]

Primarily the Association was, as Patten later asserted, a protest against the narrow conventional English economics as well as the traditional self-satisfied political and social ideas in America. Many economists regarded the formation of the American Economic Association as a declaration of emancipation from narrow economic dogmatism. A later generation of young economists might regard the original controversy over inductive and deductive methods as meaningless, but there was something to Ely's comment that the situation necessitated emphasis on the so-called historical method in order to balance the tendency in the other direction.

If the Association had accomplished nothing more, it had united the young economists in a determination to raise the standard of inquiry. George P. Garrison of the very new University of Texas wrote to Ely that he wanted to develop the study of social sciences in that institution: "We have, I think, special advantages for the study of the (farmers') Alliance Movement, the Negro question, Mexican Civilization, etc. Can you give me in a few lines any suggestions as to how I should direct inquiries, gather statistics, or to push investigations in any particular direction?" [14] In ways such as this the Association became a clearing house for research projects and information. As an information center it had international standing. The Association furnished the stimulus in good part for the formation of a similar society in Great Britain, the Royal Economic Society. In fact, for a time, William Ashley of Oxford led a movement for an English association which would be a part of the American association.

Along with this there developed at this time a number of important professional publications. The American Economic Association published articles, discussions of meetings, and monographs; Harvard started the *Quarterly Journal of Economics;* Columbia, the *Political Science Quarterly;* Pennsylvania, the *Annals of the Academy of Political and Social Science.* These organs helped to raise the level of discussion, and where popular controversial issues were presented, more attention was paid to consistency of argument and relevance to fact than had heretofore been the case. All these publications were broad in their policy; all presented articles in abstract theory, but practical issues and problems occupied most of the space even of the *Quarterly Journal of Economics.*

In this trend toward higher standards and the liberalization of economics there was one striking backward step. While leading conservative economists in the previous period had demanded the retention of the income tax, now practically all conservative and liberal economists opposed it. In a volume of papers, *The National Revenues,* written by leading economists from every region, old school and new school, the editor commented: "Several contributors would regard a national tax on private incomes as a desirable source of revenue; but none urges it as now feasible." [15]

Another conservative note was usually heard in discussions of national social insurance. Although much was said of Bismarck's establishment in Germany of national social insurance for the sick and aged, the dominant opinion in the United States was that expressed by the Reverend D. Collin Wells, of Phillips Academy (Andover): "In America it will be long before our condition will demand, or our temper permit, a compulsory national insurance." [16]

As the period closed, the prevailing feeling was that society in general and labor in particular had advanced and that the remaining pressing problems were gradually being solved. This was well expressed by Professor William Jewett Tucker of Andover Theological Seminary in a new course on social economics. Labor, he declared, had made great gains in the advance from slavery to serfdom, and from serfdom to the wage system. True, the school of Marx denied the advance and declared the laborer was still a slave. Such a denial, he said, was plausible at the time of the introduction of machinery and the factory system. Marx's chapters on "Machinery and Modern Industry" in *Das Kapital*, with their array of substantiated facts, were a "terrible indictment of the factory system in its earlier stages." But the improved condition since then was so manifest as to make such an indictment only historically accurate.

Much of the advancement, Tucker said, must be attributed to the industrial system itself, which was still consistent with the admission that the history of the system revealed great oppression, and that the system was still capable of tyranny and injustice. Industrialism had organized labor as well as capital, so that insofar as there was contention between the two, it was conducted on terms which were growing more nearly equal. The wage earner in many areas of industry had, in consequence, attained a position of comparative independence and power. He concluded: "The incidental questions affecting the health, comfort, and associations of the average operative have been settled or are in process of settlement by legislation." He had, however, to except the one question for which no satisfactory answer had been given, that of the adjustment of wages and profits.[17]

Despite this generally expressed optimism, however, the country passed into what has since been termed the "heartbreaking nineties." This temporary good feeling about the economic system was rudely shaken by a severe depression, by violent strikes, and by popular radical movements. In the face of this new outbreak of old problems in a new guise, the Association and the professional journals of economics became the principal forum for wide speculation, since practically all economists found their most understanding audience here.

PART III

The "Heartbreaking" Nineties

CHAPTER X

The Nineties: A General View

THE eighties had closed with the passage of some reform legislation and an extension of the field of economics, but few practical issues had been settled. The nineties opened in a state of unrest and continued that way. The monetary problem, which had been plaguing the country since the Civil War, reached its climax in 1896 and was settled, not by economists, but by gold miners. The organization of labor went on, in a hostile environment little alleviated by the economists. Lip service only was paid to the public control of railroads. The question of monopolies was discussed, and any decision postponed to the future. The decade's political activity, which was extremely turbulent, was tied up with these economic problems, made critical by a major depression, until the Spanish-American war proved a most effective stimulant to our economic system. All in all, in such an environment economic thought should have been wide-ranging and widely read, and it was. But it is significant that with such a favorable atmosphere for change, success for the time being came not to the liberals but to the conservatives.

The public control of railroads, for instance, that had been established on paper for a decade, got hardly anywhere because of unfavorable legal action. Supreme Court decisions rendered the Interstate Commerce Commission almost ineffective, putting it in a position that made rate regulation a nearly impossible process. In the famous case of *Smith* v. *Ames* (1897) it declared that "due process of law" required that rates be reasonable and that the Court was the final judge. It held that in determining "just compensation" and "reasonable rates" account must be taken of the "original cost of construction, the amount expended in permanent improvements, the amount and market value of its [the company's] bonds and stocks, the present as compared with the original cost of construction, the probable earning capacity of the property under particular rates prescribed by statute, and the sum required to meet operating expenses." All were matters for consideration, and were "to be given such weight as may be just and right in each case." Just how these different matters were to be weighed the Court did not say; nor did it indicate any machinery for investigating the facts. The solution to control of interstate commerce had to wait until the next decade.

TRUSTS AND MONOPOLIES

The attempt to control monopolies followed much the same course. As consolidations became more and more the order of the day, the problem of monopolies became more pressing. The old trust form used by Standard Oil, whereby stockholders of different corporations transferred their stock to trustees, was declared illegal, but it was replaced by outright consolidations, interlocking directorates, and holding companies. The Sherman Anti-Trust Act was stripped of much of its force when the Supreme Court in *United States* v. *E. C. Knight Company* (1895) limited it to agencies controlling transportation and excluded manufacturing concerns.

This did not reflect public opinion, which was strongly opposed to monopoly. Recognizing this strong protest, President Cleveland condemned the growth of monopolies as a threat to republican institutions. In his last message to Congress, on December 1, 1896, he declared that trusts did not necessarily bring reduced prices to the public. But even if they did, their social consequences were extremely dangerous for they degraded the laborer, the small businessman, and the farmer to the level of a "mere appurtenance to a great machine, with little free will, with no duty but that of passive obedience, and with little hope or opportunity of rising in the scale of responsible and helpful citizenship." He said the instinctive belief that such was the inevitable trend of trusts and monopolies explained the popular dislike of them, and added, "Whatever may be their incidental economic advantages, their general effect upon personal character, prospects, and usefulness cannot be otherwise than injurious." [1]

Congress tried to placate the popular dislike by appointing an Industrial Commission. One phase of its job was to devise ways and means to cope with the "trusts." But the notion of the trust was so elastic that individuals generally known as "trust makers" were often among the institution's most vociferous critics. The lack of a clear delineation as to where the benefits of large-scale industrial organizations ceased and the evils of monopoly began added to the confusion. In fact even farmer and labor organizations were by no means enthusiastic about an all out "trust-busting" campaign.

The grand master of the Grange wanted legislation that would eliminate all the evil practices of these so-called trusts and combinations but that would not cripple "legitimate enterprise and the development of the resources of our country." The secretary of the Farmers' National Congress, John M. Stahl, declared that the trust was inherently designed for more efficient production. "If so far it has wrought ten times as much harm as good to the people," he said, "that is not the fault of the trust, which certainly can exist without being a monopoly." A spokesman for the National Farmers' Alliance and Industrial Union of America declared that "trusts and combines if conducted on a strict business competitive system would be a blessing rather than a curse."

Organized labor approved of the trusts if they in turn would recognize the parallel role of trade unions. Henry White, general secretary of the United Garment Workers of America, declared that trusts had more efficient means of production than did small businesses and could give labor better terms. The attitude of organized labor toward them, therefore, would be determined by their willingness to treat with the unions. Samuel Gompers asserted that organized labor viewed apprehensively the many panaceas and remedies offered by theorists to curb the growth and development of industrial combinations. "We have seen those who know little of statecraft and less of economics urge the adoption of laws to 'regulate' interstate commerce, 'prevent' combinations and trusts, and we have also seen that these measures, when enacted, have been the very instruments employed to deprive labor of the benefit of organized effort. . . . The State is not capable of preventing the legitimate development or natural concentration of industry." He stated that the real evil of the trusts was their corrupting influence on politics, and this would be corrected only when the toilers were organized and educated to understand that the State was rightfully theirs.

The growth of trade unions, Gompers emphasized, was the counterpart of the growth of industrial combinations. In the early days of the capitalist system, when the individual employer determined the conditions in his shop, he said, the individual worker considered himself competent to protect his rights; as industry developed and employers formed companies, the workers formed unions; when industry concentrated into great combinations, the workers formed national and international unions; as industry became trustified, the toilers organized federations of all unions.

The Socialist leader and Chicago attorney Thomas J. Morgan, who had formerly been a machinist, was rather sarcastic about the critics of the trusts. They posed, he said, as the champions of personal liberty, of good citizenship, and of manhood. But what did the individual employer do before the days of corporations and trusts? He bought and exploited women and children. These individual businessmen organized the Manufacturers' Voluntary Association, brought the suit in which the Supreme Court declared in effect that an individual employer might drive the hardest bargain with a starving woman or girl, work her twelve or twenty-four hours a day and pay fifty to seventy-five cents compensation, and that all laws interfering with the rights of the individual employer were unconstitutional.

The views of the ex-labor leader and eight-hour-day philosopher George Gunton so strongly favored trusts that when he appeared as a speaker at the Chicago Conference on Trusts in 1899 the chairman had to threaten to clear the galleries if the hostile demonstrations of the spectators did not cease. Gunton wanted the federal government to grant national charters to corporations, giving them the right to do business, on a nation-wide scale, without government interference. He said: "This would be economic, in that it would give the market of the entire country to every business enterprise." [2]

The opposition to trusts and monopolies was due in good part to the traditional distrust of concentrated wealth, which was considered a threat to democratic government. The desire for rough economic equality characteristic of this country continued to make itself heard. It also appears to have been the underlying factor in the passage of the second income tax law in 1894. The first income tax law, long defunct, had been passed during the Civil War, essentially as a revenue measure. Now the income tax was expected to reduce the great inequalities of wealth as well as to provide for the probable loss of revenue resulting from tariff reform. The measure passed was extremely moderate, imposing a straight tax of 2 per cent on all incomes above $4000.

No sooner was the act passed, however, than it was attacked in the courts as unconstitutional and communistic. The Supreme Court by a five to four decision in 1895 declared the act unconstitutional on the ground that an income tax was a direct tax, and direct taxes, according to the Constitution, must be levied on the states according to population. But perhaps Justice Field's statement that the "present assault on capital is but the beginning" presented a more accurate picture of the opposition's attitude. Justice Harlan, in a minority opinion, declared that the decision gave aggregate wealth a position of favoritism. A position, it might be added, that no legislation of the decade did much to shake.

LABOR

Labor organization, which, as Gompers pointed out in his history, was developing the same kind of power in a different field, naturally caused considerable anxiety. There were a number of serious strikes. In 1892 a strike was called at the Carnegie Steel Company plant at Homestead, Pennsylvania. The strikers, apparently familiar with Henry C. Adams' conception of proprietary rights, declared: "The public and the employees . . . have equitable rights and interests in the said mill which cannot be modified or diverted by due process of law. . . . The employees have the right to continuous employment, in the said mill during efficiency and good behavior." [3] A bloody clash occurred between strikers and imported Pinkerton detectives, and the entire state militia was called out. When the anarchist Alexander Berkman attempted to kill H. C. Frick, one of the most hated anti-union employers in the country, newspapers became hysterical.

In 1894 the Pullman strike, sometimes labeled "Debs' Rebellion," was called. The Pullman Company had cut wages approximately 25 per cent but refused to reduce rents in the company-owned tenements, maintaining that the two businesses were entirely separate investments. Respectable organizations and leading citizens asked the company to arbitrate, but President George M. Pullman refused. The American Railway Union, to which some of the Pullman employees belonged, therefore forbade its members to handle

Pullman cars and equipment. The company obtained the assistance of the General Managers' Association, which determined the labor policy as well as other matters for the twenty-four railroads centering or terminating their operations in Chicago. A sweeping federal injunction was issued making the "very command" of the union leaders "to their striking men . . . an open defiance of the courts." The leading union officials, including the president, Eugene V. Debs, were arrested for conspiracy under the Sherman Anti-Trust Act and also for contempt of court in violating what they called the "untenable injunction." President Cleveland declared that a state of insurrection existed and sent federal troops into Chicago. Governor Altgeld protested this violation of state sovereignty and declared that he was ready to send state militia when requested by the local authorities. "In one hour," exclaimed Henry Demarest Lloyd, "[the Democratic Party] sacrificed the honorable devotion of a century to its great principle and surrendered both the rights of states and the rights of man to . . . centralized corporate despotism. . . ."

The American Federation of Labor, after calling Pullman a public enemy, declared that "against this array of armed force and brutal moneyed aristocracy" it would be "worse than folly to call a local or general strike in these days of stagnant trade and commercial depression." So the trial of strength was an unequal one, and the strike was broken. But it had widespread public reverberations. After the strike had been crushed, President Cleveland appointed an investigating commission with Carroll D. Wright at its head. The commission condemned the employers and the sweeping character of the injunction, and pointed to the General Managers' Association as an illustration of the "persistent and shrewdly devised plans of corporations to . . . usurp indirectly powers . . . not contemplated in their charters and not obtainable from the people or their legislators." It condemned the formation of organizations which fixed and imposed rates and wages and battled with strikers. The commission recommended that unions be recognized, that contracts forbidding union membership be declared illegal, and that arbitration be made compulsory.[4]

The influential *Harper's Weekly*, edited by Carl Schurz, declared that the commission's report constituted a most dangerous silent revolution. "The principles silently assumed" by the commissioners negated all those on which society had hitherto rested; they assumed that economics was not science but sentiment. "The society to which they look is not the Christian and Industrial civilization which embodies all that history has achieved for man, which reverences the moral law, and applies it by guarding vested rights as sacred, but is a vague dream of a socialistic community, in which every man has an undefined claim upon the property and labor of every other." [5]

Wright answered in an address before the American Economic Association that, on the contrary, the activities of the railway companies and other corporate interests denoted a "silent revolution." The railway companies, he said, were supporting an expensive lobby at Washington to secure a pooling measure supposedly in the interest of shippers, and inevitably the demand would arise for the government to take charge of the roads, and from the proceeds guarantee to the stockholders reasonable dividends. He followed with this statement: "Under such a seductive movement, the stockholders themselves, conservative men in this hall now, will vote for the striking of the blow. All this . . . will be at the demand . . . of the railroads and of the shippers, and not of the labor involved in carrying on the work of transportation." Wright wondered whether the pooling lobby would demand "the extension of the same principles to labor, and ask for their employees the status of semi-public servants." It would be inconsistent to demand government control in the one case, and laissez faire in the other. If the freight rates were to be fixed by the measure creating "one great trust" in the freight business, then the system should be completed "by bringing labor into the arrangement as well as the railways and the shippers." If in this pooling measure, he said, "as some claim, we are legislating the railroads out of State socialism, let us legislate labor out of State socialism as well." [6]

The problem to Gompers was much simpler. He shrewdly used the current economic situation to emphasize the need for large reserve funds in the unions. "We have seen," he said, "that when organizations have little or no funds and an industrial crisis comes, as it does under our economic conditions, periodically—there is a periodicity about our industrial crises that is very noticeable to the student—those workers little organized and lacking funds are the first to succumb to the constant reduction of wages, and when an industrial revival occurs, they are the last to receive any of its benefits." [7]

The general social aspect of the labor problem became a matter of acute public concern when times were bad. To a great degree, political action was demanded. Thus, as the depression that followed the Panic of 1893 witnessed the breakdown of private relief in the industrial centers, unprecedented in amount as it was, there arose a widespread demand for a government issue of greenbacks to relieve unemployment. In 1894 a march to Washington of the unemployed from all parts of the country was set afoot by a successful Ohio businessman, Jacob S. Coxey. Its demands were definite. The unemployed should be put to work on public works projects, which should be financed by issues of greenbacks. Any state or minor political unit which would undertake such a public improvement program should receive greenbacks from the federal government in return for its own bonds. These non-interest bearing bonds should be repaid at the rate of 4 per cent per annum. In addition, the federal government should issue $500,000,000 in greenbacks for road improvement. Such notes, it was contended, would supply actual cash in place of the national bank notes—mere "confidence money"—and thus relieve the "money famine" which had depressed business. Bellamy gave these famous Coxey's armies his blessing, and other sympathizers agreed that if "the banker and usurer class" who dominated the government could appear before congressional committees, "why not this 'living petition' of workingmen?" [8]

One of the most moving statements for Coxey's armies came from Morrison I. Swift, a Massachusetts journalist who held a doctorate from Johns Hopkins. He wrote an open letter to the Massachusetts congressional delegation in which he declared: "When some take this unusual means to arouse the conscience of the country to their wrongs and misery, walking hundreds of miles to solicit relief, it is an indication of excessive social strain. Let us not repeat the fatal error of trying to sneer them down or stamp them out by force. We who are interested in these problems in Massachusetts invite you therefore to meet the coming petitioners in a different spirit than that which was accorded to the unemployed here [in Massachusetts] when they went to their own State House and asked for help." [9]

This specific movement fizzled out, and with it a considerable force feeding the greenback crusade, without relieving the distress. In 1896 the Commissioner of the Kansas Bureau of Labor and Industry, William G. Bird, appealed to economists and labor leaders for their expert opinion on methods of ameliorating labor's condition. "From remotest times," he pointed out, "the hackneyed phrase of 'labor problem' has agitated all nations to a greater or less extent." Egypt solved the problem by erecting "those vast piles, the age-old pyramids"; Great Britain recently "attempted unnecessary public works on the Thames embankment." America now was faced with much the same problem, Bird continued. "Philanthropic schemes of many kinds have been energetically undertaken to assuage the suffering incident to our prolonged commercial depression." Political economists, students of our social system, and men prominent in the circles of organized labor had long sought some plan to relieve the depression, which was a serious matter involving the very existence of the republic.

Bird received a large number of replies, among which that of Edward Alsworth Ross, professor of finance and sociology at Stanford University, best summed up the situation. He, like others, had numerous proposals for alleviating the condition of the laboring people. But he called attention to these facts: "Nothing I have suggested affords a cure for unemployment. I confess frankly I am a good deal in the dark on that question and am looking for guidance to those who have made a more special study of that evil than I have." [10] But the general attitude was something like that expressed by the Massachusetts Railroad Commission. It pointed out that a panic occurred approximately every ten years, followed by a depression; but there was always a recovery. No one could precisely predict when the current depression would end and recovery begin, nor how rapid recovery would be. This depended largely on the wisdom and moderation of those making the laws and shaping the financial policy of the country. It concluded: "That the recovery will be complete no one will hesitate confidently to believe. The thing that hath been, it is that which shall be." [11]

GREENBACKS, SILVER, AND THE ELECTIONS OF 1896 AND 1900

Meanwhile the discontent of the public reached a climactic point with the organization of the People's Party, more popularly known as the Populist Party. Although strongest in the South and West, this was not exclusively a farmers' party. Its program was broad, with money at its center. Originally, in 1891, the national executive committee had demanded that the government lend money—greenbacks—at 2 per cent, limited in amount and on approved security. "The volume would be entirely self-regulating," for if there was in circulation more money than business required, borrowers would return the surplus to the Treasury; and in case of scarcity those having the security could borrow money from the Treasury. The People's Party of Massachusetts had a variant scheme: sufficient greenbacks to transact cash business should be issued, and these would be kept at par by being varied in volume by a commission, "according to a fixed rule in proportion to the population and the average market price of a given number of commodities." [12]

At the first national nominating convention of the party in 1892 the platform presented the greenback proposal by asking for the "sub-treasury plan of the Farmers' Alliance, or a better system." This scheme was characterized by the Republicans as the loan of public money on "haystacks, hogs, and hominy." The convention also demanded that the government issue greenbacks to pay for public improvements and that silver be coined in unlimited amounts at the current legal ratio of 16 to 1: so that, in all, the amount of circulating medium should be speedily increased to $50 per capita. It added to this a host of reformist measures. At one time the party thought of running Leland Stanford because he had two years earlier suggested in the Senate that greenbacks be issued on real-estate security, but California Populists destroyed the boom by calling him "an unprincipled monopolist." So they fell back on an old greenbacker, General James B. Weaver, as their presidential candidate. The General was still as strong for greenbacks as ever. He expressed his sympathy with the free silver forces, but he felt that the addition of silver would not create a sufficient currency, since there was not enough silver to relieve the financial distress. It could never be more than a "valuable auxiliary to our currency." It should be allowed, he said, to "take its place without hindrance in our trinity of finance, which, in the present state of public enlightenment, should consist of gold, silver, and full legal tender paper, issued in sufficient quantity to conduct the current business of the country on a cash basis." [13]

Although Cleveland was elected in 1892 the Populist Party gained so many seats in Congress that the old parties were disturbed. The new party had attracted outstanding liberal figures. Henry Demarest Lloyd, whose *Wealth Against Commonwealth* stirred the nation, accepted the party's nomination for a seat in Congress in 1894.

Lyman Trumbull, the author of the Thirteenth Amendment to the Constitution, supported him, thereby creating a national sensation.

Greenbackism seemed too radical for the financiers to swallow, but there was a widespread feeling among them that money should be loosened some way or other. Various proposals came from the banking community, as well as from economists, to eliminate the existing government notes and substitute national bank notes; and there were also proposals to reduce the cost to bankers of these notes by substituting as security bank assets for government bonds, because the advancing premium on these bonds reduced the profits on national bank notes. While there was general agreement as to the advisability of an "asset" currency to provide elasticity, the bankers could not agree on a specific scheme. Another related proposal strongly urged by bankers and economists was that state banks should be permitted to issue bank notes by removing the 10 per cent tax on such notes. The irony of this suggestion was that for years the same circles had pointed out that the chaotic condition in banking before the Civil War had been due to state bank issues and had finally resulted in the passage of the National Banking Act. Now such an eminent publication as *Rhodes' Journal of Banking* stated that the disasters and difficulties that resulted from the state banking system were, unfortunately, better remembered than the benefits. "A few wild-cat banks, in some of the outlying states and territories, are remembered much more vividly than the excellent institutions that did business under the laws of Massachusetts, New York, Pennsylvania, Maryland, Louisiana, Ohio, Indiana, and Illinois." [14]

The Populists were not impressed; they dubbed the whole scheme one to create rubber money. This widespread clamor for an increase in the amount of money shifted its base from greenbacks to silver. For the presidential candidate in 1896 the Populist Party turned down S. F. Norton, the choice of the greenbackers, and accepted the nominee of the Democratic Party, the silverite William Jennings Bryan, with free silver as the main issue.

Cleveland's monetary policy, along with the continued decline of prices, provided ammunition for the free silver forces. Cleveland blamed the panic of 1893 on the Sherman Silver Purchase Act and obtained its repeal by Congress. Then, in 1895, he arranged with a financial syndicate, headed by J. P. Morgan, for a loan of $65,000,-000 in gold to maintain the reserve requirements behind legislation to resume specie payments. The free silver faction and the American Federation of Labor denounced this as a betrayal of the country to the "gold bugs" of Wall Street.

Both sides had a number of persuasive writers to plead their cause. Brooks Adams, who had in the previous decade bitterly flayed the greenbackers, now, in *The Law of Civilization and Decay* (1896), told how the "producing" classes, typified by merchant adventurers, "bold, energetic, audacious," had been steadily crushed by that new aristocracy, the bankers, who lacked culture, manners, and learning. These usurers early in the century "conceived a policy unrivalled in brilliancy, which made them masters of all commerce, industry, and trade." They engrossed the gold of the world, and then by legislation made it the "sole measure of values." They began first with England and, by 1873, they were triumphant everywhere. "When the mints had been closed to silver, the currency being inelastic, the value of money could be manipulated like that of any article limited in quantity, and thus the human race became the subjects of the new aristocracy." [15]

An interesting newcomer in the monetary controversy was Arthur Kitson, an English businessman and inventor. He was temporarily living in Philadelphia, and in 1895 presented the silver issue in his popular *A Scientific Solution of the Money Question* (1895). "Free silver coinage," he wrote, "will enable this nation to again achieve national independence, which a body of men, either ignorantly or treacherously, sacrificed to the gold power during, and shortly after, the [Civil] war. It will increase the volume of money and enable debtors to meet their obligations honestly. Gold . . . creates debts, and then prevents men from settling them. It places mankind in perpetual bondage. It is a prison gate that only opens inward. Its victims are permitted to enter, but never to escape."

The most effective silverite writer, however, was William Hope Harvey of Chicago, more popularly known as "Coin" Harvey. In December 1893 he began publishing *Coin's Financial Series*, periodical publications in the form of dime novels which became extremely popular. One issue, *Coin's Financial School*, sold in its first year 400,000 copies. This book of 155 pages began with the statement that Coin, a young financier of Chicago, deciding that it was time for wisdom and sound sense to take the helm, had established a school of finance to instruct the youths of the nation in what had been considered an abstruse subject. Each chapter represented a day's lecture, and, according to the book, each day the attendance increased. The mythical students asked questions which Professor Coin always answered definitely. On the fourth day, when asked a question by Professor J. Laurence Laughlin, an "avowed mono-metallist," Coin so replied that Laughlin "arose to say that he was satisfied with the answer." Harvey's book was so well done that readers thought that such a school actually existed and that Laughlin had attended and been converted. In fact Laughlin, who was now head professor of political economy at the University of Chicago, and a zealous and prolific popular writer against free silver, was so outraged that he publicly denied attending a lecture in the mythical school.[16]

Harvey was quite clever in using that commonplace of traditional economics, the quantity theory of money, in defense of the cause. "All writers on political economy admit the quantitative theory of money," he said. "Common sense confirms it. . . . If the quantity of money is large, the total value of the property of the world will be correspondingly large as expressed in dollars or money units. If the quantity of money is small, the total values of the property of the world will be correspondingly reduced." Then quite adroitly he turned to the traditional form of the theory and argued that the "money of ultimate redemption," or "basic money," alone influenced prices.

Of the numerous attempts to answer "Coin" Harvey, certainly one of the most widely circularized was George E. Roberts' *Coin at School in Finance* (1895). Roberts was then publisher of the *Fort Dodge Messenger* and later vice-president of the National City Bank of New York. In this tract Roberts declared: "Hard times are admitted, but . . . Mr. Coin and his school of agitators made them hard, and are keeping them hard, by their show of strength in favor of radical changes. . . . Nothing can so retard the recovery for which all people . . . are anxiously praying as doubtful currency legislation. . . . All of the ideas presented by Coin, and most of his rhetoric, have been used before, and condemned. The entire financial world not merely distrusts these theories, but emphatically denounces them. . . . It is not enough that theorists shall approve a plan for business revival. It is necessary that it shall appear safe to the men who have capital. To attempt to revive business without their confidence and co-operation is foolish." But it was indicative of the mind of the country and the strength of Harvey's appeal that in Roberts' "school" the "lessons" in "sound" finance were presented not by a gold monometallist, but by an international bimetallist.

The free silverites were so skillful in manipulating traditional economics that their opponents declared in exasperation that the bimetallists were in fact calling attention to the "real inconsistencies which . . . exist in the writings of some first-class economists." Cleveland's cabinet requested Arthur Latham Perry to prepare a "short, sharp, logical, and popular demolition of the whole silver pretensions." [17] And Democratic Congressman Michael D. Harter of Ohio appealed to President Daniel Coit Gilman of Johns Hopkins University for all instances that would vindicate Gresham's law. He wanted from Gilman, he said, "every historical illustration you can recall of the cheaper money, iron, copper, silver, paper, shells, etc., driving the dearer out. Begin with the Grecian iron money, or earlier, and, if possible, omit no historical proof of this kind in any country or in any age, winding up with the Argentine Republic, Mexico, and all others in that condition today. . . . Kindly give name of history opposite each in which I will find full account." [18]

The most potent economic argument of the anti-silverites was that free silver would cut the value of the dollar to sixty cents and produce an upheaval in business from which there could be no recovery. Under these circumstances it came about that the 1896 presidential campaign was the first in our history to center on economic theory. While the Republicans in their opposition to free silver had on their side the majority of renowned academic economists, the Democrats had not only a number of younger economists just fresh from their doctorates, but also one of the oldest and most conservative of the pre-Civil War economists, Marcius Willson.[19]

Thirty-six-year-old William Jennings Bryan of Nebraska, the "boy orator of the Platte," obtained the Democratic nomination for president in a stirring speech that closed with the never-to-be-forgotten sentence: "You shall not press down upon the brow of labor this crown of thorns; you shall not crucify mankind upon a cross of gold." This, from a student of that ardent anti-silverite, the Reverend Julian M. Sturtevant of Illinois College! In Bryan the Democratic Party had a figure who appealed to the common man as no man had since the days of Lincoln. Bryan was deeply religious, of the evangelical type; he was frugal and saving, and he had the gift of conveying his seriousness and simplicity to the mass of voters. Many men of learning and substance, "intelligent and independent citizens," were deeply impressed with his sincerity and earnestness; they were aware of his "personal modesty, his deep sense of responsibility, his charity and absence of bitterness, and of the many qualities in his many-sided character that stand forth and justify his prominence and the hold which he has on the affections of the great common people." [20] The *Bankers' Magazine* wrote later of Bryan and this campaign: "In an age noted for political coward-ice, he was always politically brave and courageous. His political honesty was as undoubted as his political integrity. When great issues were at stake you always knew that he would be on one side of the fence or the other, not astride of it. When the issues were economic, he was probably on the wrong side; but there he was, proclaiming his views so clearly and persistently that no one could possibly mistake them. This is praise that can justly be bestowed upon few of his political contemporaries. In 1896, it will be re-called how long it took Mr. McKinley to speak out boldly in favor of the gold standard. Bryan from the outset of that memorable campaign plainly declared his purpose of putting the free coinage of silver into practice at the earliest moment he was empowered to do so." [21]

Even the technical aspects of free silver Bryan could discuss in such a homely fashion as to make them understandable to all. And Bryan had sufficient learning—he had a Master of Arts degree—to use shrewdly the statements of respected economists, living and dead, even when they might in fact be opposed to free silver. And there would be nothing wrong with his specific quotation. He ex-plained, for instance, in his speech accepting the Democratic nomina-tion, that the best-known law of commerce was the law of supply and demand and that he would build his argument upon this law. "We apply this law to money," he continued, "when we say that a reduction in the volume of money will raise the purchasing power of the dollar; we also apply the law of supply and demand to silver when we say that a new demand for silver created by law will raise the price of silver bullion. . . . The restoration of bimetallism will not only stop falling prices, but will—to some extent—restore prices by reducing the world's demand for gold. . . . The interests of society demand a financial system which will add to the volume of the standard money in the world, and thus restore stability to prices." In the last analysis, he said, the gold standard encouraged hoarding, because money was rising in value, and thus discouraged industry and paralyzed enterprise. But under bimetallism, with prices rising or steady, money could not afford to be idle in bank vaults.[22]

A rather ironical feature of the free silver issue was that Republican candidate William McKinley, governor of Ohio, had originally been a silverite. After all, bimetallism had had the support of a considerable segment of the business community and conservatives. Even such a sturdy Republican leader as Senator George F. Hoar of Massachusetts had worried lest the repeal of the Sherman Silver Purchase Act would lead to increased imports, and consequent loss of gold, thereby further distressing American manufacturers in the world markets.[23] But by now there was agreement in the business community, at least among the most influential group, that the gold standard was essential for business prosperity, and McKinley's new position simply reflected the change.

Much of this solidification of business sentiment was due to McKinley's guiding genius, Mark Hanna. In social philosophy Hanna was an ardent Hamiltonian, who believed that "some men must rule" and the "great mass of men must work for those who own." To him, "life meant war . . . on business associates, employees, on the State itself"; although he was at the same time quite friendly to organized labor.[24] Under Hanna's guidance and prodding "big business" openly supported McKinley as the advance agent of prosperity, and the wealthy deserted the Democratic Party in unprecedented numbers. Every conceivable pressure was brought to bear on debtors, employees, and hesitant businessmen. The Democratic leaders complained that their party was attacked by all the great trusts, corporations, syndicates, banks, and papers. "The very graveyards were robbed of the names on their tombstones to be enrolled as voters for an honest dollar." [25]

The Republican victory, together with the new gold discoveries first in South Africa and then in Alaska, marked the beginning of the end for free silver as a vital national issue. The Spanish-American War in 1898, foretold by liberals as a consequence of American investments in Cuba, brought a wave of prosperity. William Dean Howells exclaimed: "After war will come the piling up of big fortunes again; the craze for wealth will fill all brains, and every good cause will be set back. We shall have an era of blood-bought prosperity, and the chains of capitalism will be welded on the nation more firmly than ever." [26]

By 1900, therefore, the time was ripe to settle the monetary problem with legislation. The Gold Standard Act of that year definitely established the "dollar consisting of twenty-five and eight-tenths grams of gold nine-tenths fine . . . which shall be the standard unit of value, and all forms of money issued or coined by the United States shall be maintained at a parity with this standard." It also eased the terms upon which national bank notes could be issued.

In the campaign of 1900 the Democratic Party, with Bryan, who had raised a regiment for the Spanish-American War, again its standard bearer, now made anti-imperialism the main issue. The platform still contained the free silver plank, for Bryan found it hard to give up, even though he admitted that the "increased production of gold since 1896 had reduced the importance of the question." But by 1906 even Bryan gave up the issue. He asserted that the "unlooked-for and unprecedented" increase of gold production brought victory to both sides because it allowed the retention of the gold standard and at the same time secured the larger volume of money, which was the aim of the bimetallists.[27]

THE RADICALS

While in many ways the political writers were now using the language of the radicals, the radical movements produced no vital literature like that of the previous decade. Bellamy and George passed from the scene. The philosophical anarchists, typified by Tucker, continued to insist that "free money" was the fundamental solution of economic problems. Perfect freedom in finance would wipe out nearly all the trusts, or at least render them harmless and perhaps helpful. The money trust could be abolished, as Tucker said, only by "monetizing all wealth that has a market value." [28] Tucker, however, neatly pointed out in 1891 that the conservative element was proposing currency reforms along anarchist lines. He indicated particularly the "asset currency" scheme of Edward Atkinson, the "most orthodox and cocksure of American economists, who now swells with his voice the growing demand for a direct representation of all wealth in the currency." Atkinson proposed that the national banks be divided into districts, that each district designate a certain city as a banking center, that any bank could deposit with the clearing house satisfactory securities and receive in return clearing house certificates in the form of bank notes of small denominations to the extent of 75 per cent of the value of the securities deposited; that these certificates be redeemable on demand at the bank in legal tender money. Such a scheme, said Tucker, overlooked the fact that if any large proportion of the country's wealth should become directly represented in the currency, there would not be sufficient legal tender money to redeem it. But he welcomed the scheme "because here for the first time Proudhon's doctrine of the republicanization of specie is soberly championed by a recognized economist." [29]

Another reminder of the historic continuity of the radical tradition in America was the steady outpouring of the ex-Chartist John F. Bray, still intellectually vigorous in his eighties. He was still advocating industrial partnerships between labor and capital financed by greenbacks. But where several decades earlier he had foreseen the eventual disappearance of inequality in incomes, he now forcefully insisted that the wage system must be retained because the man who had devoted years to self-improvement and enlargement of his capacities would not be satisfied with the same payments as the "dull clump" whose thoughts had never been elevated above eating and drinking.

There is something of grandeur and pathos in the following recording in his log in June 1893:

"My birthday—84 years old! But nary a cannon has been fired all day, nor a bell rung, nor a demonstration! I must wait until my turn comes! Surely something will yet come of my labors for mankind! I did not work for money or fame, but by compulsion of the inner man! And I have had all the reward I expected! When did ever a Reformer work for or expect pay! I regret nothing that I have done, but only wish I could have done more! It makes one feel so good to fight against wrongs."

One of the few to remember the occasion was Gompers: "Letter and books from Gompers—speaks of my birthday and old times!" Toward the end of the year, as the discontent began to mount, he recorded that the "great social and industrial revolution I foresaw more than fifty years ago" seemed around the corner, and he expressed the wish to live a few years longer to see its beginnings. "I want to do something more for the world if possible, but what can

I do, old, ailing, obscure, an almost unknown reformer as I am, and no more work in me." [30]

The few remaining native anarchists received temporary aid from abroad in the figure of Michael Flürscheim (1844–1912), who practiced as a professional reformer in England, Australia, New Zealand, Polynesia, Mexico, and the United States. The United States had supplied much of the experience and inspiration for his ideas, and his last book, *The Economic and Social Problem* (1909), was published in this country. It also trained him in how to accumulate the means by which he pursued his reforming career, for Flürscheim, the son of a rich Frankfurt merchant, spent the five years from 1867 to 1872 in New York, learning banking. When he returned to Germany, he acquired a small ironworks business in Gaggenau, in the state of Baden, and in little more than a decade he developed it into one of the leading firms in the country.

His first interest in reform, which was awakened by *Progress and Poverty*, was in land nationalization, and he was soon actively engaged in popularizing the idea. He added, however, his own genealogy of economic sin. While he agreed with George that rent was the mother of economic distress, he held that interest was its father. He therefore concluded that the economic cure lay in a combination of land nationalization and free money along the lines of mutual banking proposals. He organized and gave financial backing to practical experiments, and eventually emphasized free money rather than land nationalization as the final cure.

Flürscheim's explanation of the cause of depression, which he offered as early as 1884 in *Auf friedlichem Wege*, was in some respects novel and interesting. This theory, which was known at the time as the "Flürscheim theory," he expounded in England in 1892 in his popular writings, particularly in *Rent, Interest and Wages*. In 1895–96 he presented it in the United States in its most succinct form through the columns of the radical organ, the *Twentieth Century*. The rich, he declared, neither consumed the larger part of their incomes nor invested them in equipment. Rather, they invested in money instruments, i.e., land, mortgages, bonds, etc., and thus loaded the producers with an increasing interest and rent debt. They thereby diminished the producers' purchasing power and disabled them from filling the gap which the non-exercise of the rich man's purchasing power had opened between productive power and consumption. The gap widened as productive power increased through technical progress. The increase in the production of precious metals could not keep pace with the money claims, which continued to grow through compound interest. Since metallic money could not be produced faster than the claims grew, these claims could not be met. Only a money based on all commodities could meet these claims.

Earlier theories of the insufficient purchasing power of the masses and the oversatiation of the wealthy minority were defective, declared Flürscheim, in that they did not explain adequately what became of the unspent incomes. Such theories held that the rich invested their unspent incomes in new machinery, or, rather, that they lent the money to others on good security to establish factories and mines. But this did not explain existing unemployment. Machines and railroads could not be made without labor. Even if the investments proved unprofitable, they created employment, for the incomes had been consumed. Instead of oysters and champagne, machines had been consumed. Such an explanation, therefore, did not meet the facts.

If recipients of rent and interest, however, invested in government bonds, lands, and the like, investments which continued to increase at compound interest, it could be seen that the claims eventually exceeded the means of payment and income. Thus a continually increasing proportion of incomes was invested in new tribute claims, which caused a constantly increasing gap between productive and purchasing power. The one steadily increased in consequence of technical improvements; the other, weakened by the new tribute claims, weighed upon the masses. If, therefore, capital found such investments closed to it, it would be forced into productive investments, which would set labor to work. Land nationalization and free currency, the latter obtained through co-operative stores accepting the exchange bank system, would accomplish this result and reduce interest for real capital to the risk premium. This, concluded Flürscheim, would result, not in State socialism, but in "free individualism," and economic crises would permanently disappear.[31]

Flürscheim's activities in the United States and his significant contribution to the literature of the depression problem have largely been forgotten and he is remembered primarily as a German land reformer. His experimental colonies, through which he hoped to combine all the advantages of socialism with those of individualism, failed in the New World as they had in the Old, and he returned to Germany for the last time in 1909, embittered, ill, his large fortune greatly depleted.

Unlike the anarchists, the socialists were gaining strength. This was in small part the result of a growing metropolitan proletariat. The old Socialistic Labor Party was still active under a new name, the Socialist Labor Party. It showed increasing strength for a time, its vote rising from 21,164 in the 1892 presidential election to 33,545 in 1896. A good part of the votes, however, came from New York, and it was considered more or less a New York party.

Out West, therefore, Eugene V. Debs ignored it and formed a new socialist party. He himself had become a socialist while serving a jail sentence in connection with the Pullman strike. Debs, like Bryan, had a homespun quality, and his socialism was characterized by wide humanitarianism. Debs, Lloyd, and others organized the Social Democracy of America in 1897. Its distinctive feature was its effort to organize co-operative colonies in one state at a time, working toward the political conversion of that state to socialism. This socialist state would then serve as a springboard for converting the nation into a co-operative commonwealth. But hardly had the party been organized when some of its most active promoters, led by Victor Berger of Wisconsin, were ready to drop the colonization scheme, and sought, though vainly, to obtain as editor of the party's organ, Daniel De Leon, the most influential figure in the Socialist Labor Party.[32]

The next year, at the first national convention in Chicago, a split occurred, with the majority insisting that the colonization scheme was of primary importance and the minority insisting on political action. Debs had originally sponsored the colonization idea, but he now sided with Berger and the minority. They seceded and formed a new party, the Social-Democratic Party of America.

Meanwhile the Socialist Labor Party also split up, partly because of a clash of personalities and partly because of the disagreement as to the role of trade unions in the movement. De Leon, whose past included a lectureship in international law and diplomacy at Columbia University and support of Henry George and Edward Bellamy, had worked for socialism within the American Federation of Labor and the Knights of Labor; but he now insisted that these organizations were interested only "in pure and simple trade unionism," and he wanted to set up a socialist labor organization to compete with the established unions. After a turbulent contest in 1899, the De Leon faction won control of the party. The "Kangaroos," as the opposition, led by the New York labor lawyer Morris Hillquit, was dubbed, set up their own organization, supported Debs for president, and in 1901 formally fused with the Debs group to form the Socialist Party of America. The new party differed little from the old Socialist Labor Party or the Social Democracy, though it added planks for national insurance of workers against accidents, and against unemployment and want in old age, and it called for the abolition of war and the introduction of international arbitration.

De Leon's Socialist Labor Party at its 1900 convention scrapped all specific resolutions and planks, retaining only the statement of principles. The committee on platform and resolutions declared that the "whole string of planks . . . remind us of the infancy of Socialists, when Socialists were still impressed with the idea that we must do something immediately for the working class." In any event, "those palliatives which . . . Socialists will advocate, or will push to the front wherever they have representatives in office, can be made through the Municipal Program." Rather oddly the national secretary explained that in good part the opposition had arisen from German-born members, who forgot they were no longer in some German village and were prejudiced against anything American; the renovated party was a truly American party, De Leon said, attuned to American conditions.[33] This statement was not supported, however, by political events. The De Leon party polled in the 1900 presidential election about as many votes as it had in 1896, and thereafter steadily declined.

Debs, however, obtained 94,000 votes in 1900. His relatively large vote testified in part to his personal popularity, the kind of native support De Leon's party was claiming, and in part to the breadth of his socialist viewpoint, which seemed to provide a place for almost any variety of dissent. As one of the outstanding intellectual leaders of the Debs group, the Reverend George D. Herron, said: "The international socialist program is broad enough for the widest variety of opinion as to detail, and as to the working out of principle. . . . We must remember that Marx's ideal was that of perpetually fluid and endlessly growing civilization, in which every element of life may find free and full expression. The elemental meaning of socialism is the liberty of each man to take a free look at life, to see truth for himself, and to speak his own mind about what he sees, without let or menace from any source." [34]

Perhaps the basis for this trend of socialism was most succinctly stated in *Elementary Principles of Economics* (1899), written by the Michigan socialist Charles H. Chase. It declared that while State socialism was the ultimate goal of all progress, "attempts now made to abolish competition . . . must temporarily fail; . . . because it [socialism] is not adapted . . . to man's present state of development." Acting upon that premise, socialist politicians had no compunctions about adopting a policy of political expediency. George Shibley, an economic adviser to the Democratic Party, condemned the Socialists in 1900 for talking like the Democrats. Until recently, he pointed out, they had not harped on the evils of monopoly but had stressed the evils of the competitive system. "In short, they have completely shifted their position and yet they retain their name!" [35]

This illustrates one of the significant developments of the decade. With the entrance of economic reform into political action the need for handy labels became evident, but it soon became equally evident that economic thought was not amenable to such crude handling. Instead of uniting economic theory and practice, a decade of political discussion seemed only to confuse the relations between them. Only a dispassionate and uninterrupted study of the facts could hope to clarify the situation, and this was vouchsafed only to academic economists. They increased their efforts to fit the old economic theory to the new social situation.

CHAPTER XI

The New Synthesis

IN RESPONSE to the new demands of the nineties, the economic thought of the academic world became more mature and complex. Within the profession, economic discussion was less marked by personal animosities; controversy was on a higher level, and generally opposition to any idea was presented dispassionately. Notable advance was made in the theory of marginal utility, and it became possible to consider the ideas of Marx in a sane fashion. Orthodox views continued to dominate the scene, but orthodoxy was no longer inflexible.

BROADENING THE SCOPE OF ECONOMICS

At the same time that economic thought was becoming more catholic it was reaching a wider audience. The subject was by now enjoying such popularity that even women were delivering lectures on it, and extension teaching of it was becoming a permanent feature of the intellectual life of the country. The leaders in the extension movement regretted that the audience did not include members of the working class but consisted rather of teachers, people of some leisure, members of art clubs and similar organizations, and the clergy. David Kinley of the University of Illinois opined that the workingmen failed to attend because they believed that they were being patronized. This was due, he thought, partly to the attitude of the lecturers and partly to the fact that the courses were given " 'for the working people' by those of a higher social station." The leaders of the movement, he argued, could rectify this by recognizing that the workingmen wanted not only mental training but information as well.[1] A more pointed explanation might be, one might well add, that the workingmen would hardly be encouraged to continue attendance after being told, as they were by one lecturer, that the chief obstacles to social progress were the law of diminishing returns and their own lack of the savings instinct.[2]

Regardless of class, however, the number of economics students increased. Schools of commerce were by now also swelling their number. The Wharton School at the University of Pennsylvania had been the first, and it was not immediately imitated, but now the Western universities took up the idea with California, Chicago, and Wisconsin establishing such schools. As a result, F. W. Taussig of Harvard suggested that a session of the American Economic Association's meeting for 1900 be devoted to the subject of specialized education for businessmen, because the movement toward such education was growing in strength.[3] This was done.

The business community, however, which was expected to supply a good part of the funds, was not too enthusiastic in supporting business education. William W. Folwell told a Minnesota Bankers' Association meeting that the indifference of businessmen to such education was due to the conservatism which had always and naturally distinguished the mercantile and banking classes and their dislike of changes and revolutions. "They have simply held on," he said, "to the old idea and the old way, while lawyers, doctors, engineers, and even some farmers have taken up with the new." [4] After these slow beginnings, however, the movement soon gained increasing momentum.

Further testifying to the popularity of economics was the discussion about teaching the subject in secondary schools. Critics asserted that economics was too broad and profound for the immature high-school student,[5] but supporters replied that it was the best discipline for citizenship. Charles J. Bullock of Pawtucket High School and later of Harvard felt that it would repress class hatred and extravagance. The growth of class hatred, he said, which was the result of economic ignorance, was one of the most menacing dangers of the present day. Those in the higher social scale failed to realize that their own progress was bound up with the progress of all other classes, even the lowest; on the other hand, the laboring classes must learn how dependent was labor upon capital, and how unfounded was much of their distrust of the capitalist. All failed, according to him, to recognize the need for social solidarity and all it implied. Economics would also teach the mass of the American people the evil of extravagant and wasteful expenditure, public as well as private, that wealth rapidly accumulated was lavishly expended in a barbarous manner. "The plain people," he declared, "attach too little importance to economy in the management of their own incomes, and are quite largely responsible for the existence of a public sentiment that would sometimes justify extravagance on the ground that it benefits trade."[6]

Besides this widening popular interest the professional future for academic experts looked on the surface extremely promising. The raging controversies over the tariff, Civil Service reform, and monetary issues created phenomenal demand for economics in the colleges, although the very sources of that demand raised problems in supplying it. Thus President R. H. Jesse of the University of Missouri wrote Ely in 1891 that a chair of history and political economy was to be created. Now the curators, he said, "personally . . . would take Democrat, or Republican, gold or silver man; but they are afraid that the man himself would have a hard time at the hands of the press and the University [would suffer] next winter before the Legislature unless he were something of a Democrat and favored some coinage of silver. . . . A *moderate* Democrat, who favored gradual revision of the tariff in the direction of free trade, and a limited coinage of silver—at least until international agreement confirm or forbid—would about fill our political want. Such a man would please nobody violently, nor displease any grievously. But such a man, with fine ability & good attainments, has not yet been found." [7] Such was the penalty of popularity.

In the light of the sensitiveness revealed by such a statement it is not surprising that the number of cases involving academic freedom should prove a disturbing factor in the progress of academic economics. In the forefront of public attention were the cases of Richard T. Ely at Wisconsin, E. Benjamin Andrews at Brown, E. W. Bemis at Chicago, and E. A. Ross at Stanford. The number of cases was in part a reflection of the tense social scene, and in part the retention of the old view that a professor's duty was to "teach established truth," not to engage in the " 'pursuit' of truth." [8]

Professor Charles H. Hull of Cornell gave perhaps the classic answer to this view in connection with Andrews' resignation over his free silver position: "We believe, having the experience of a millennium of educational history to back our belief, that the unfettered search for truth is the noblest discipline for the human mind, the truest incentive for right living. The truth itself is high, we may not attain unto it. . . . It is difficult to determine, changing, elusive, but the search for it, though strenuous, is practicable; it is the best that we can do, and we lose that best when authority prescribes either the course or the specific goal of the search. . . . For the search is education, the find is stagnation." [9] Unfortunately such high principles were not always consonant with the necessities of authority.

But there were also more peaceful developments. At this time the fight between the "old school" and "new school" came formally to an end. The American Economic Association eliminated the statement of principles, and Charles F. Dunbar, who had denounced the group in 1886, was chosen to succeed Francis A. Walker as president in 1892.[10] In fact even such an outstanding spokesman for the historical method as William Ashley, then professor of economic history at Harvard, purposely abstained from open controversy on the matter of method, but he said privately that "before we try to *explain* the economic world, we must *know* it. So many theorists seem to think that they all imbibe a sufficient knowledge from the atmosphere. But the fact is that we don't know the actual structure of economic society as it is." [11]

Another ground for agreement was the feeling expressed by Folwell that "statistics will at length give to political economy the character of a quantitative science, in some degree at least." [12] But even this was not unanimously endorsed. Some economists felt that information on such matters as capital could never be accurately obtained and wanted government efforts along these lines stopped. In reply, Thomas G. Shearman, a New York single taxer and lawyer, acutely noted that some of these same people wanted the government to continue to collect statistics on wages, even though it was conceded that such statistics had been compiled in a most dubious fashion. He contended that if wage statistics were still to be taken, then, in all fairness, statistics of capital and profits should also be obtained. "There is no subject," he said, "upon which statistical information is more desirable than that of the distribution of wealth, its causes and effects." [13]

Along with the need for accuracy the economists recognized the need for breadth. As large departments of economics were established, interest grew in the related field of sociology, which was quite often taught by men who had considerable interest in economics. Thus Columbia University established a separate chair of sociology in 1894, and the incumbent was John Bates Clark's collaborator, Franklin H. Giddings, who continued to write for the professional economic journals and to attend the meetings of the American Economic Association. And at Harvard the Department of Economics included courses in sociology.

Unfortunately this broadened the field for possible disagreement. Giddings, Patten, and Albion Small (head of the Sociology Department at the University of Chicago) carried on lengthy controversies as to the proper realm of each. William Ashley wisely declared in the course of one of these controversies that "the great thoughts which have affected men's minds, and determined our intellectual attitude, have usually come from men like Darwin or Maine who have cared but little about the classification of the sciences." [14] But this was not oil enough for the troubled waters. The argument continued in spite of the fact that economists in the United Kingdom were contending that America was further ahead in economic study because she was using the broader methods that were essential in handling serious economic problems. In 1892 Section F—Economic

Science and Statistics—of the British Association for the Advancement of Science felt strongly enough about this to appoint a committee, composed largely of "orthodox" economists, to examine the state of economic learning both at home and abroad in an effort to improve the admittedly low state of training in the United Kingdom.[15]

This committee's special reports on economics training in the United States should have encouraged the economists and sociologists to forget their differences. E. C. K. Gonner noted how far ahead in popularity and scope of the subject the Americans had gone. He declared that America was zealously pursuing economic studies and wisely recognizing the need for "inductive inquiry and training." He noted with approval extensive lists of courses in applied subjects, pointing out that economics in the United States was connected with political science, history, and even general sociology. The committee found that the unsatisfactory condition in the United Kingdom was attributable primarily to the "omission of many teachers to recognize adequately methods of empirical study." [16]

The eminent classical economist Professor C. F. Bastable, in his presidential address before Section F in 1894, declared that the stricter economists had fostered the error that political economy differed from other social sciences in the rigor of its logic and the certainty of its conclusions. They regarded "such types of precision as geometry and logic as the proper models in the pursuit of this 'exact science.'" The mistake committed was twofold: first, the solidity of economics was overestimated, and second, economics ceased to be treated as part of a comprehensive whole, including social science, politics, jurisprudence, and social ethics.

Bastable said that the need for a broader treatment of economics became glaringly apparent when one observed the character of the socialistic movement that was passing over Western civilization. The ordinary antithesis between socialism and individualism, or, as it was often conceived, between self-sacrifice and selfishness, was misleading; for "the struggle is rather one between two distinct types of social organization, one resting on the exaltation of the relatively modern institution of the State, the other deriving its principal force from the oldest and most enduring element of human society—the family." That socialism could not be an effective social organization was a lesson that only the study of social science in all its branches would most effectually teach. The broad treatment of economics in the United States, he said, was a shining example of the necessary future development in economics.[17]

MARGINALISM BECOMES CLASSICAL

As their interests ranged farther afield, the American economists did not fail to cultivate their own garden. There marginal analysis was now definitely in the foreground. As the liberal-minded Emily G. Balch of Wellesley College put it: The "most important contemporary work in economic theory is that based largely . . . on the conception of marginal utility," and she described it as tending toward psychological analysis and mathematical expression.[18] The main difficulty, others thought, aside from the validity of a psychological analysis based on sensations, was the very fact that utility was not measurable, that there was no unit of happiness. Thus men on different sides of concrete questions claimed to base their views on the marginal utility doctrine, and naturally enough neither side was convinced. Students arrived at the doctrine from varied directions.

The most extreme exponent of the supremacy of the marginal utility doctrine was a man who early gave promise of making a significant contribution to American history. This was Sidney Sherwood (1860–1901) of Johns Hopkins. While teaching economics at the University of Pennsylvania in 1891, he delivered in Patten's seminar a paper on Locke's views of political economy. In this paper Sherwood pointed to Locke as the fountainhead of the philosophy of the American Revolution. Patten, wrote Sherwood to his former teacher Ely, "was especially exercised by the claim I made quite incidentally that Locke exerted a direct influence upon the political thinking that accompanied the American Revolution. . . . In spite of what Professor Patten has said, I haven't the slightest doubt that Locke was read and studied here during the quarter of a century preceding our revolution. But I mean to look into the writings of Jefferson and others to see if I cannot find positive evidence. . . . Our revolution was the logical outcome of the political struggles in England during the 17th century—culminating as they did in the English revolution of 1688. And that the man who voiced the achievement of the liberal party in England was unknown and unregarded by the thinking men of the American revolution, I do not believe." [19] Unfortunately for history, Sherwood dropped such inquiries and devoted himself to elaborating conventional views of economics, especially on banking, trusts, and the philosophy of marginal utility.

Sherwood asserted that the doctrine of marginal utility was the key to inquiry not only in economics but also for all the other social sciences, and he went on to claim for it even the entire realm of philosophy. The new theory of value, he declared, showed that no practical measurement of motive existed but in human choice, and thereby the scope of economics extended to the whole range of human motive. In elaborating this view, Sherwood stated that such an application of the "theory of utility, and the theory of margins, or of marginal utility, is nothing more than a certain form of thought. . . . It is perfectly possible to study not only certain phenomena of the market, but to study all phenomena of society from this standpoint . . . [because] with whatever conditions the individual is confronted and whatever the social forces which shape the life of the individual . . . and his action, the actual choice of the individual may be expressed in terms of the utility to the individual of the result of different lines of action. . . . If the mastery of society over the individual amounts to such a control that life becomes intolerable—I go to even that extreme—we may express in terms of utility this condition which confronts the individual. And if it is intolerable, the motives which drive a man to suicide, out of the society, out of the life, this is also capable of being expressed in terms of utility, or of a negative utility, if you choose." [20]

The sole, able, undiluted follower of the classical school was Silas Marcus Macvane (1824–1914) of Harvard, who was born and educated in Canada. Macvane taught in the Department of Economics under Dunbar for five years. Later, in 1878, he was appointed to a professorship in history. Macvane's writings on economics began with his transfer, yet they comprise practically all his publications. Stranger still was the fact that he had no "sympathy with the historical tendency." Indeed, as one critic put it, he hardly allowed it to influence his opinion. [21]

Macvane's time was taken up with the economic controversies of the day. While he was opposed to bimetallism, he did not get as hysterical as did many another academic economist as to the possible effects of silver legislation. He argued in 1884 that the Bland-Allison Act was foolish but not immediately dangerous; that until the country had more than enough greenbacks, national bank notes, and silver certificates in circulation to occupy the whole field of currency, some gold must be used as money, and as long as this continued, no real premium on gold could result. Such a premium could arise, he said, only from a depreciation of the currency, which, in turn, could result only from inflation. The only source of inflation at the time was, in his view, the coinage of silver dollars, fortunately limited to $2,000,000 a month. The entire currency, including gold, was therefore only slightly, if at all, greater than the country needed. This might be inferred, he said, from the fact that the gold, "having largely come to us from abroad, has shown a marked and decided tendency to remain with us."[22]

Besides engaging in the monetary controversies of his day, Macvane carried on a running battle in the academic journals against the marginal utility doctrine, especially in its more elaborate form as presented by the "Austrians"—Böhm-Bawerk and von Wieser. His keen thrusts evoked detailed replies and led to clarification of the doctrine. To the Austrians, wrote Macvane, the cost of any given commodity was not to be found in the process of producing the commodity itself, but in the value of the other products that might have been produced by the same means of production. For example, they held that the demand for wool for coats created costs in the production of blankets, and the existence of blankets was responsible for the costs in the production of coats. If people had no use for wool, except as material for coats, it would not be an item in the cost of production of coats. Thus they looked for the conception of cost as occurring outside the production of the very thing whose cost people wished to determine. Cost in their view, said Macvane, "insists on being something or belonging to something that might have been, but is not. When you try to grasp it, to attach it to a real commodity, and to measure it as a definite tangible quantity, it eludes you and retires to the region of the might-have-beens." The classical theory of cost, continued Macvane, might have flaws, but at least it had the merit of attaching itself to those features of production that "men must always and everywhere *feel* as cost." Cost and value as the Austrians treated them, he declared, became indistinguishable and led to their reasoning in circles.[23]

Macvane insisted on what is now known as a "real cost" doctrine, namely, that cost was composed ultimately of the burden of labor and the burden of waiting which accounted for the capitalist's return. He substituted the term "waiting" for "abstinence" because it clearly brought out the fundamental fact that time must elapse between the outlay of labor and the finished product, and thereby supplied the economic answer to the argument that labor was the whole burden of production.[24]

The period of waiting, Macvane emphasized, varied with industries, but that it constituted a real element in the cost of production could not be doubted if one bore in mind "human impatience." The possessor of capital assumed the burden of waiting on behalf of the wage worker. When the employer advanced wages to the laborer, he was in reality discounting the future rights of the laborer. If the laborer would submit to nature's terms and wait for the finished product to emerge, the whole product would belong to him. In some cases, where the waiting was necessarily long, this might be physically impossible, but more commonly the will rather than the ability was lacking. Here, again, it was not the absolute hardship of the waiting element that counted in the cost of production, but rather men's estimate or opinion of that hardship. A general change of opinion regarding the sacrifice of waiting acted on the values of commodities in all cases where the length of waiting was different. As men came to think more lightly of waiting, there would occur a fall in the value of commodities involving the longest waiting period.[25]

The champions of labor who claimed the whole product for labor claimed the impossible, said Macvane, for they demanded the product before nature could give it. This was true, too, he declared, of those writers (like Francis A. Walker) who argued that wages were paid from the proceeds of present labor. The finished commodities that were streaming into the reservoirs of trade at that moment to become the wages of the labor then being expended were not for the most part products of recent labor. They were the final results of labor spread over years past, much of it over many years.[26]

Meanwhile Macvane also chastised Walker for minimizing the role of the capitalist in favor of the entrepreneur, and, after pointing out flaws in the logic of Walker's doctrine, complained that Walker went too far in idealizing the entrepreneur. He said: "Men grow rich by producing much, but they also grow rich without producing anything. . . . It might be a great comfort to our Vanderbilts, Goulds, and Fisks to be told that their gains represent wealth of their own creation—if they could be got to believe it!" [27] His defense of the growth and control of wealth went further. When it came to trusts and combinations, Macvane contended in his extensively used *The Working Principles of Political Economy* (1890), the community had in general little to fear from these types of economic organization. Any attempt on their part to interfere with the natural course of production and trade was likely to bring losses. After all, since few commodities were absolutely necessary and without tolerable substitutes, the monopolist would find it to his advantage to charge not an extortionate price, but a price corresponding most nearly to the natural price, i.e., the cost of production. In all this he came close to saying that whatever is, is right.

A man who spent most of his life as an official of charity organizations could scarcely accept this analysis, and such was the background of David I. Green (1864–1925). Green received a doctorate from Johns Hopkins in 1893.[28] There he gained the knowledge of marginal utility economics with which he opposed Macvane.

In an article in 1894, "Pain-Cost and Opportunity-Cost," Green disputed Macvane's contention that true cost was comprised of pain by the laborer and waiting by the capitalist. Rather, cost consists of "sacrifice of opportunity," he said. For example, an individual whose alternative opportunities were limited would work hard and late for a dollar, but when an increased demand for his special abilities opened other opportunities, he would ask for better terms. A person would not keep books at $100 a month when he could earn $200 a month as a shop superintendent. Then, too, a laborer stopped working at a certain hour not because he was tired, but because he desired some time for pleasure and recreation. People insisted on being paid for sacrificing profitable opportunities rather than for the pain involved in the work.

The pain in a day's work, therefore, had little to do with power in exchange. "The subjective feelings of different individuals," he said, "are not easily compared, but the economic opportunities which a man sacrifices by pursuing a certain course of action are more capable of objective measurement. These sacrifices of opportunity . . . constitute the principal part of the costs of production which determine normal exchange values."

Even if through the progress of society the direct painfulness of labor were eliminated, productive effort would still involve sacrificing certain opportunities for others, and the "ratios of exchange would still tend to correspond to the sacrifices of production," he continued; for we must always economize our opportunities. Right and duty demanded that we refuse to yield our opportunities without adequate compensation for the task in hand. This demand, he concluded, for "an adequate return for opportunities sacrificed is the . . . basis of our ratios of exchange."

Rational behavior demanded, as Green developed his theory of it, not only that time and action be economized, but also commodities, capital, and natural resources. Before utilizing these resources for a specific purpose, he said, we must weigh the other uses to which they might be put; and the most "advantageous opportunity which we deliberately forego constitutes a sacrifice for which we must expect at least an equivalent return." Certainly the sacrifice of waiting, which a number of writers attempted to establish as a justification of interest, said Green, was of this character. Green chose as an illustration an individual who, desiring to protect the future of his family, took out insurance and paid the premium. The insurance company invested this wealth in a mortgage, and interest would be paid on this mortgage, because the earning potentialities of capital was an opportunity which the company was unwilling to forego without a legitimate reward. If the opportunity was not utilized, the "best welfare" of society as well as of the company would suffer. "The hardships incident upon excessive saving," therefore, affected the supply of capital; but, he said, the interest paid was gauged by the opportunities foregone rather than the pain endured.

Similarly, though there was some truth in the contention of the classical economists that rent did not enter into cost and price, he pointed out that it was not always easy to find the no-rent margin or to be sure that price was determined there. The problem could be solved by his method of considering the opportunities sacrificed in diverting factors to a definite use. Every businessman viewed the rent he paid as an expense of business. In starting a new business, he chose between higher rent and less labor or lower rent and more labor; between more capital or more labor; between fewer laborers of great skill or a greater number of unskilled laborers; and each choice was made with the view of keeping the cost of production as low as possible in order to compete successfully with rival producers. The use of a piece of fruitful land for a particular purpose was as much a sacrifice to the entrepreneur or to society as the employment of labor, if both the land and the wages could be otherwise profitably employed. If all labor was included in cost, the use of land must also be included, for labor cost was principally an opportunity-cost rather than a pain-cost.

The common element in all opportunities, Green maintained, was the power to satisfy want. Utility, in connection with limitation of supply, explained why one man earned more than another with the same exertion; why one plot of ground rented for more than another; in short, why the expenses of production and the ratios of exchange did not correspond with pain-costs. In the case of a homogeneous factor, such as a group of laborers of uniform efficiency, the pay of all would be the same, not because of an equality of pain but because any one of them would presumably be sacrificing an equal opportunity to earn "simply the marginal utility rate of pay," the identical alternative earnings.

Green concluded from his analysis that doctrines of the classical school led to those of the Austrian school. "The values of the factors of production," he said, "are imputed to them [the factors], on account of their marginal utilities. . . . The utility of the means of production depends upon the utility of the products. . . . The commonly accepted view that the normal values of goods . . . produced under free competition correspond with the relative expensiveness of their production will doubtless remain the most ready means of accounting in a general way for the ratios of exchange, but the sacrifices of opportunity which determine the expenses of production must find their explanation upon the side of utility."

Green pointed out that in the modern economic system the wants first satisfied were not those most urgent but those represented by the largest purchasing power. Thus the "so-called marginal utility to society" was not a definite utility, but a "definite amount of money which would be offered for the last increment of the supply." However, duty to take advantage of opportunities did not "justify the extortion which unbalanced competition often renders possible." [29]

Böhm-Bawerk accepted Green's concept of opportunity cost as a more elegant statement of the position of his own Austrian school on cost as a sacrifice of utility.[30] But Green himself objected to certain phases of the Austrian formulation. He asserted that in the first place the Austrians, by overemphasizing demand, neglected the forces fixing the supply of the elements of production. Second, they ignored the need to calculate the surplus of utility over discomfort and to formulate rules for increasing that surplus. Finally, and most significantly, he criticized the Austrians for failing to treat monopolies. Green admitted that monopoly was a matter of degree and that every form of private property had an element of monopoly, but he contended that the general characteristics of the two groups were sufficiently distinct. "The action of monopolies is not without system," he said, "and the rules which prevail in the establishment of monopoly prices are of increasing importance to the theory of value." [31]

Green feared for this competitive balance. He felt it was being endangered by the growth of class antagonism and combinations. "Capitalists and wage workers, becoming distinct classes of society, are often contending with each other to the detriment of both, while each side is alarming the other with the strength of its combinations. What power can cope with the great oil monopoly, or the Western Union Telegraph Company, or what resistance could be made if all the poor people should unite in the demand for a redistribution of wealth?" His solution of social problems lay in the growth of the scientific spirit and patient research; and, above all, in universal education, for this will "carry new vitality to the sluggish members of society, awakening ambition and giving a taste for higher things." [32]

Following Green's lead in explaining classical theory in terms of the new concept, a number of economists insisted that the marginal utility doctrine did not disparage Ricardo and the old cost of production or labor theory; in fact the two doctrines supplemented each other. The marginal utility theory, they said, merely reiterated in a more refined and subtle way what all economic theory had said of value, that marginal utility was equal to marginal disutility, which was nothing more than marginal cost.[33] And a new *Principles of Economics* (1890) gave tremendous impetus toward this reconciliation of the development of marginal utility with the old classical tradition.

This book was written by the outstanding British economist Alfred Marshall of Cambridge University, and was eventually to supersede Mill's treatise as the authority in the main tradition in the English-speaking world. It attempted to combine both the marginal utility school, emphasizing demand, and the classical school, emphasizing the cost of production; but it definitely gave primacy to the older classical tradition. Marshall discarded the customary separate treatment of value and distribution and attempted to study the "causes that determine the distribution of commodities among different classes as one."

The distinguished leader of the moderate wing of the German historical school, Adolph Wagner of the University of Berlin, wrote a lengthy review article of the book in the Harvard *Quarterly Journal of Economics*. He condemned the younger more extreme followers of the historical school for their disparagement of the classical economists, and praised Marshall for following in the path of Ricardo. He contended that Marshall had established the "continuity between the classical English political economy and the science as it must stand to satisfy the demands of the present. It [Marshall's book] marks no revolution, but a progress made with true regard to every advance in the science." [34] Arthur Burnham Woodford, who had just completed his doctorate under Ely at Johns Hopkins, declared in the *Dial* that the volume, in its clear "exposé of the evolutionary character and the importance of time in industrial life and institutions," brought economics up to date. And he praised the "hopeful human tone pervading even this most purely theoretic part." [35] These two views reflect fairly accurately the calm which was succeeding the storm blown up by the introduction of the marginal utility doctrine.

By and large the exponents of the marginal utility economics were rather progressive in their social outlook, and were interested to some extent in, or at least not adverse to, social reform. Even Sherwood was rather sympathetic to Henry George's social views. There was one outstanding exception, however, W. G. Langworthy Taylor (1846–1941), professor of economics and sociology at the University of Nebraska, who was an extreme conservative as well as a convinced marginalist.[36]

He consciously thought of society as an organism. "The absurdity of a *legal* scale of prices," he said, "is glaringly manifest to one once imbued with the conviction that social life is as highly organic as is vegetable life." On the other hand, he contended that the modern corporation, instead of being the means of throttling competition, was really a form of its growth. Although the capital at the manager's disposal was great, the world of capital was greater still. Therefore, even if the manager was enabled to gain a temporary advantage for those who had entrusted him with their capital, he feared to excite a reaction which might ruin him and them. In Taylor's words: "Obstinately to maintain an advantage in prices at the expense of the consuming public will gradually, and sometimes very swiftly, arouse forces of competition that will . . . ruin him. The problem of the successful manager is that of so judiciously adjusting his tariffs as not to arouse the avenging arm of the giant Capital. On the other hand, the system of credit allows the individual investor easily to withdraw from the enterprise, and thus to control the manager's relations with him. The spectacle presented is . . . therefore . . . one of ever-increasing delicacy of adjustment and of competition."

In fact a good thing about economic crises, Taylor argued, was that they led to a deeper understanding of production and distribution, that competition was no longer understood as the rivalry of small business concerns. He even suggested that there be one universal trust. If consumers were free to purchase as they chose, "precisely the same forces would exist to compel this universal monopoly of production to proportion the prices of the different wares to the public demands." He recognized, however, that because of psychological and biological reasons such a universal trust was impractical.

The spirit of the times, according to Taylor, was for all interests to unite, each in his own domain, and thus to form separate guilds or economic classes. The consolidation of the laboring classes into national trade unions on the one hand, and of numberless manufacturing interests into national and international trusts on the other hand, was an evidence of this spirit. Similarly, legislation enabling the banks to combine into a national guild with control of the note issue and free from government paternalism was in accord with this modern spirit. Finally, the protective tariff agreed with the trend of political expansion by including new areas and population and thereby solidifying nationality. The fact that the United States had always been in a condition of active expansion had kept it constantly in the protectionist line.

As might have been expected, Taylor was unsympathetic to the free silver views of his fellow townsman William Jennings Bryan. If there had been any appreciation of the circulating medium, he declared, "it has been arranged by society to compensate capitalists for the great losses they have sustained through ignorant anticapitalistic legislation." [37]

MARX IS DISCOVERED

In strong contrast to Taylor's outline for the supervision of society by large business was the growing appreciation of Karl Marx. Serious study of Marx's theory was slow to develop; not until 1887 was *Das Kapital* (the first volume) translated into English. Such Marxist phrases as "surplus value" were being commonly used, but with the connotation that every class shared in the surplus created by the progress of industry.[38] The revolutionary impact of his writing was disregarded.

Charles William Macfarlane, a Philadelphia capitalist, engineer, and keen student of marginal utility economics, asserted that the Marxians contributed much to economic theory. The importance of the work done by the socialist writers, he wrote, lay largely in their "vigorous protest against the assumption of an economic man, the iron law of wages, etc. The accent which they have thrown upon the intimate connection that exists between the phenomena of value and price on the one side, and the phenomena of distribution on the other, is important, too. . . . It was Marx who first recognized the important distinction between labor in the form of spinner, weaver, etc., and labor conceived as an abstract mobile fund. The similarity between capital and labor in this respect, Marx, of course, failed to notice, but he did have some grasp of these two conceptions of labor. These are the conceptions which J. B. Clark has developed with such skill and clearness."[39]

There seemed to be no knowledge of Marx but as just another economic theorist to be fitted into their systems. Seligman declared that the social point of view in connection with the theory of value was first advocated by Marx, but was emphasized in an incorrect way. He pointed out that Marx, moreover, was entirely ignorant of the marginal utility doctrine.[40] Only in such offhand remarks as these do we get an inkling that a revolutionary formula had been drawn up which would change the history, if not the economic theory, of modern times.

Academic economists at this time also showed more interest in such related matters as the broad heresy of oversaving, namely, a prevalent notion that unregulated savings by individuals had pernicious consequences and that universal thrift was no remedy for social ills. A formulation widely popularized in England by John A.

Hobson, a liberal economist of the Left, came across the Atlantic with such impact that at the 1895 meeting of the American Economic Association the subject was brought up. Henry R. Seager (1870–1930) of the University of Pennsylvania and later of Columbia ably presented what he called the "orthodox" case. Modern theorists, he said, denied that savings might lead to overproduction. They held that a certain amount of savings was necessary to maintain the existing fund of capital, which was constantly being depleted by accident, miscalculation, and fraud, by overspending by individuals, and by the needs of a growing population. As savings exceeded the limits set by these "normal needs of the industrial organism," the interest rate fell. Lower interest rates, by decreasing costs, led to lower prices. Thus accumulation was checked by weakening the motive to saving, and at the same time the fall in prices stimulated consumption to keep pace with increased production, so that oversaving and overproduction were automatically checked. To which Edward W. Bemis, a critic, replied that a fall in the interest rate instead of diminishing savings, might increase it. "Savings may even be stimulated by a desire to retain a fixed income and by the development of foresight and of the desire for social prestige and power." [41]

EDWIN ROBERT ANDERSON SELIGMAN: PIONEER IN PUBLIC FINANCE

An area of economics that had heretofore been largely neglected now was considerably developed—that of public finance. Henry C. Adams had published some notable studies in this field, but it was E. R. A. Seligman (1861–1939) of Columbia who gave it the greatest distinction.[42] Seligman had been actively interested in organizing the American Economic Association and in a variety of reform movements. For example, he was the first of the prominent economists to broach the doctrine of a living wage. Writing in the *Gunton Institute Bulletin* in March 1898, he declared that while there were insuperable difficulties in achieving a living wage through government wage-fixing in every trade, still a beginning could be made if all units of government—national, state, and municipal—would insist that in all work done for them the contractors pay a living wage. This would not interfere with competition but would raise the plane of competition to a high level. This specific development would "not revolutionize the world," and in fact would accomplish very little, but that little would "be in the direction of progress and social peace."

Seligman's interest in such matters was, however, secondary to his sustained interest in the field of public finance. A number of his works, especially his monographs *The Shifting and Incidence of Taxation* and *Progressive Taxation*, helped to make public finance a subject of theoretical as well as practical importance. His activities centered largely on tax reforms, particularly in connection with the general property tax and progressive taxation.

He was an ardent opponent of Henry George's single-tax proposal, but George was in good part responsible for Seligman's elaboration of the canon of "faculty" or "ability to pay." The elements of faculty, he declared, were twofold, those connected with acquisition or production and those connected with consumption. It has been well said that his inclusion of the distributional criterion of taxation under the category of "faculty" was a "master stroke of practical wisdom." The "happy ambiguity" of the canon enabled Seligman to support relatively heavy taxation of land, franchises, and the like, and to advocate new forms of taxation which he considered necessary if more radical tax demands by the people were to be staved off.[43] Seligman always carefully circumscribed the application of the canon. Thus, while he approved the theory of progressive taxation, he advocated caution in putting it into practice. His reservations led his friend Ely to comment caustically in 1893 on those economists who cautioned us "not to make progress too rapidly." The danger, Ely said, was not that "we shall go too rapidly, but that we shall not go at all."

Although an exponent of a progressive inheritance tax, Seligman denied that it was a just instrument for checking the growth of large fortunes and diffusing wealth. He justified it on his theory of "faculty." "An inheritance," he said, "is simply a fortuitous income, a chance accretion to property, which augments the faculty of the individual and which, just because of its accidental or unearned nature, is a most fitting subject of taxation." [44]

Yet Seligman took a relatively radical step in supporting the income tax law in 1894. He argued that it was in accord with the democratic trend throughout the world. "It seeks to correct the growing conviction among all masses of the population that our present tax system largely exempts those that are best able to pay." He was skeptical, however, of a progressive income tax, because while a progressive tax corresponded to the demands of ideal justice, it was impracticable. This was so because the two methods of paying an income tax were either in a lump sum by the taxpayer or by stoppage at the source. The former method had failed, at least in Anglo-Saxon countries; the second method was not susceptible to graduation since it might involve a number of sources.

After England adopted the "progression" principle, in 1910, Seligman recognized its possibilities for the United States. He insisted, however, that first a proportionate income tax must be imposed. "After the [proportionate] tax had been in operation for some time, it might be possible cautiously to introduce the principle of graduation." Once the administrative provisions for the stoppage-at-source income tax were in full operation, and the government assured of its desired revenue, "there would perhaps be no insuperable objection to requiring a compulsory declaration of entire income from all individuals whose income exceeded, let us say, ten or twenty thousand dollars and assessing a somewhat higher rate of tax upon them. . . . But unless graduation be utilized only as a supplementary principle, it would, under actual conditions, in all probability play havoc with the entire scheme of the income tax from the point of view of both revenue and justice."

With the passage of the extremely moderate progressive income tax act in 1913, Seligman declared that it was significant that the principle of progressive taxation evoked almost no discussion. "The legitimacy of the theory was taken for granted, and in the few cases where it was mentioned, it was assumed to be a corollary of the theory of ability to pay. This shows," he said, "the development which has taken place since the discussion of the law of 1894." [45]

CONSOLIDATION OF GAINS

After the turn of the century such advances were possible, but in the nineties economics was trying to consolidate its gains, not make new advances. For example, Richard T. Ely, that outstanding leader of the "rebels," grew increasingly conservative. He moved in 1892 from Johns Hopkins to Wisconsin with a newly created title of professor of political economy and director of the School of Economics, Political Science, and History. The following year he issued a new popular textbook, *Outlines of Economics* (1893). Ely asserted that this text differed from the earlier *Introduction to Politi-*

cal Economy in that it was somewhat more advanced and more "theoretical." Perhaps the main formal difference was in the elaborate presentation of the marginal utility doctrine, and in the statement that the constructive work of the Austrian school was fundamental.

In the first edition, Ely was still a staunch follower of the Ricardian theory of rent, and in other writings at the time he accepted, to a certain degree, its practical implications as to taxation. But in later revisions of the treatise (in which he had as collaborators Thomas S. Adams, Max O. Lorenz, and Allyn A. Young), he declared that the confiscation of pure economic rent, as distinguished from the return of improvements, would never appeal to the conscience of the American people, that such a policy further illustrated the danger of basing social reasoning on any theory of "natural rights." From there he ultimately went on (1916) to accept completely Clark's view of land as a species of capital.

Ely's conservative trend was particularly noticeable in a series of extension lectures he gave on socialism in 1892 in which he enumerated more than twenty "valid objections" to socialism.[46] But this did not save him from popular attack. When labor troubles raised the temperature of Wisconsin politics to near hysteria, Ely was accused by the State Superintendent of Public Institutions of justifying and encouraging strikes and boycotts, of giving advice and aid to striking printers in Milwaukee, of entertaining an agitator or "walking delegate" from Kansas City who had come to assist the strikers, and of upholding socialism in his works. The University authorities immediately ordered an investigation of Ely's teachings, and he replied that if the charges were true, they would unfit him to hold his post. But he denied every one of these "base and cruel calumnies." "I have maintained," he said, "that even could socialism be organized and put in operation it would stop progress and overthrow our civilization."[47] Leaders in the academic world rallied to Ely's defense with testimonials, and Ely was absolved by the Board of Regents.

Popular judgment notwithstanding, Ely is a good example of the way in which old economic reformers were moderating their zeal. By this time the marginal utility theory had become orthodox and was combined with the old classical doctrines in such a way as to discredit neither. Social sympathies which had seemed so dangerous previously were now largely in the ancillary study of sociology.

The emphasis upon statistics brought about an increasing drive to make the collection of such material, especially in connection with the Census, both more accurate and more comprehensive. Even some of the socialist emphasis upon human values could be recognized as a factor in the new equation. All in all economics was trying with some success to establish an equilibrium among the theories that had seemed so explosive in the eighties.

CHAPTER XII

The Younger Traditionalists

THE synthesis which was being made between the classical economists, following the English school, and the historical and marginal utility schools of the Continent was put together in many different ways. The most authoritative combination in this country was conservative; upon the basic framework of the classical school of Adam Smith and John Stuart Mill was grafted a simple and restricted version of marginal utility. This was the final outcome, but the three greatest leaders of this time, Arthur Twining Hadley of Yale, F. W. Taussig of Harvard, and J. Laurence Laughlin of Chicago, did not consciously attempt to reach such a solution. Hadley thought he had repudiated classical economics; Taussig thought he had made only a few modifications in it; and Laughlin was convinced he had never left its preserves. Yet all three were perhaps among the greatest builders in America of a new foundation for further economic study.

ARTHUR TWINING HADLEY

Hadley (1856–1930) [1] was a man of versatile interests and culture. He had a lucid pen and was abreast of the latest developments in economics and practical affairs. He was a graduate of Sumner's Yale and had studied for two years under Wagner at the University of Berlin. On his return to the United States in 1879, he combined teaching at Yale with journalism, and for a while he was also Commissioner of Connecticut's Bureau of Labor Statistics (1885–87) and editor of the Department of Foreign Railroads for the *Railroad Gazette* (1887–99). He capped his academic career by becoming president of Yale University in 1899. As an economist he had a wide influence in his day. His treatise, *Economics: An Account of the Relations between Private Property and Public Welfare* (1896), succeeded Francis A. Walker's as the most popular one in the colleges. It was urbane and comprehensive; by means of footnotes and qualifications it obtained a catholicity that Francis A. Walker would have considered downright radical.

Hadley accepted the marginal utility theory of value as fundamentally sound, for it carried, he said, the commercial theory to its logical conclusions. According to this theory, as he interpreted it, the value of an article was the price which it would command under a system of free and open competition, as distinct from one which was the result of special bargaining or fraudulent concealment. But he felt that those economists who were devoting their energies to analyzing and developing the intricacies of the marginal utility theory were engaged in useless or irrelevant activity. In its simple form, the theory explained more clearly than previous ones the psychological motives which determine the direct relation between utility and price under the existing commercial system. But those economists engaged in elaborating it were stepping over into the domain of psychology, because their work was only remotely related to the practical problems of business and legislation. By their excessive use of psychological terms and conceptions and their neglect of purely commercial ones, these economists had made economics a science not for statesmen and men of the world, but for schoolmen.

Hadley accepted the doctrine of natural selection as the other renovating force in modern economics. He adapted this doctrine to support the view that titles to property, "are more likely to be productive than not, because if men fail to use their capital for things the community needs, they lose money and are eliminated from control of the next period of production." He added: "To the medieval economist the businessman was a licensed robber; to the modern economist he is a public benefactor. . . . So confident are we of the substantial identity of interest between the businessman and the community as a whole, that we give our capitalists the freest chance to direct the productive resources of society to their own individual profit."

Hadley's early reputation was based on his book *Railroad Transportation*, which came out in 1885. In effect, this book brought the analysis of Charles Francis Adams, Jr., up to date. In it he stated that in a business with large fixed capital the Ricardian law that businessmen would cease producing when prices fell below the cost of production was false. "It very often involves worse loss to stop producing than to produce below cost," he pointed out.[2] More specifically, he said that thoroughgoing competition would result in rates which would leave no income to meet fixed charges. Only by combination could cutthroat competition be eliminated. Combination would result in any event, but much of the waste of cutthroat competition could be avoided, especially in the case of railroads, if the State would sanction such devices as pools. Hadley had little sympathy with such "coercive" regulating devices as the Interstate Commerce Commission, for such government interference, to his mind, did more harm than good. Potential competition. he said, must be relied upon to keep the combines from obtaining exorbitant profits.[3]

In elaborating this theory that combination was inevitable for a large part of modern industry, Hadley threw considerable light on the problems of heavy fixed investment. He considered that the investment of fixed capital had caused more radical changes in manufactures and transportation than in agriculture. In the first place, factory production had increased faster than farm production. This was to him the natural course of events. The amount of food obtainable from a given area, he said, could not be indefinitely enlarged. No amount of additional capital, for instance, could increase agricultural production a hundredfold. Consequently no one farm, however large, could ever supply more than a minute fraction of the world's consumption, and competition would continue to exist between different agricultural producers. Nor did he consider the interest and maintenance charges of fixed capital a dominant factor in the cost of producing food. In this field the theory of normal price was applicable, he stated, and in the majority of cases, competition would protect the consumers and do justice to the producers.

He then pointed out that the conditions in manufacturing were radically different. Here the units of capital, he held, were much larger. Each producer could expand output with a gain in economy. As his sales increased, his expenses for wages and materials would increase only slightly, if at all, but the share of the charges on fixed capital which each unit of product must pay would decidedly decrease. "There is no fixed standard of cost," he said, which could be considered as the normal price because the "cost per unit of product depends on the quantity sold, falling as sales increase."

Furthermore, he said, the price which would entice new competition into the field would be much higher than that which would induce old firms to withdraw. No concern would leave the field so long as it could meet an appreciable part of its interest charges. "It is better to lose part of your interest on every piece of goods you sell," he wrote, "than to lose the whole of it on every piece you do not sell." As long as the selling price remained higher than the expense for wages and materials, all the old factories would continue to compete. Even if ownership of the firm changed hands by foreclosure, the concern would continue to operate. However, no new competition would enter the field unless the price were sufficient to afford a liberal profit after paying all charges on fixed capital. "Thus prices, instead of constantly tending to gravitate toward an equitable figure, oscillate between two extremes." Hence the rate of production at figures yielding a fair profit would usually be either much larger than the rate of consumption, or much smaller. In the former case the producer would fare badly, in the latter, the consumer. "The average price resulting from such fluctuations might be a fair one; but the wide changes in price are disastrous to all parties concerned."

This has sometimes led, he said, to industrial units necessary for the proper utilization of labor becoming so large as to produce actual monopoly, particularly in such distributive industries as water, gas, telegraph, and railroads. Even in cases where the need for concentrated management was not so marked as in railroads, "competition of different concerns always involved a loss, from the need of maintaining too many selling agencies, the expense of unnecessary advertising, and the lack of proper utilization of fixed capital." This latter phenomenon, Hadley noted, was often mistakenly assumed to indicate industries of "increasing return" in contrast to industries of diminishing return; but actually it indicated unused capacity, for when a certain relation was established between output and fixed capital, the current expenses per unit of production increased very rapidly.

This problem of unused capacity, Hadley added, also cast doubts on the traditional doctrine of savings. In the beginning of civilization scarcity of capital had been a serious economic danger, and at that time anything that induced people to save and use their savings productively was good for society. In modern times, according to his analysis, the tendency to invest capital in machinery rather than to purchase consumers' products reduced the demand for the product of machinery. If one man, in his effort to save, converted his capital into permanent investment, he could accomplish his end, but if all did the same thing, the expected profit would not be realized because of the overproduction of plant, and a commercial crisis would follow. Certainly, he agreed, the increased utilization of existing capital which followed any stimulus to consumption was apt to be more conducive to general prosperity than a corresponding increase in the amount of investment without such stimulus; but unfortunately the methods used to stimulate consumption, such as currency inflation, were transient in their nature and led to a stronger reaction.

Hadley further pointed out that the synchronization or equilibrium between investment of capital and price of products, posited by practically all leading economists, in fact confused mercantile and industrial competition. In a large part of modern industry, he said, the times of active capital investment have been times of advancing prices. True, the additional investment would soon produce a reaction, but these movements were not those posited by the theorists. In their view "the capital movement and price movement must be simultaneous. . . . The equilibrium will become a wholly unstable one if the two are separated." Prices in good and bad years might on the average vary but little from cost of production, but the average was composed of widely divergent quantities and the "mercantile conditions in industries using large capital favor such variations instead of preventing them." [4]

Not least of Hadley's insights was his use of labor unions as an illustration of the baneful effects of cutthroat competition. He assumed that the price of labor, like that of any other commodity, was determined largely by competition, and he compared a workman on starvation wages to a factory or a railroad running merely for operating expenses. In prosperous periods, he said, the workman received comparatively good wages, he married and supported a family in reasonable comfort. This family became a fixed charge upon him; and it was important to society that he should be able to meet this charge. But during depressions wages fell to a starvation level and rose again only after long years of misery. The workman, therefore, sought relief in combination. This theory led Hadley, and others, he thought, to have a friendlier feeling toward unions. Just so with the pools, he continued. If capitalists and workmen could see the analogy between starvation wages and cutthroat competition, they might arrive at a better understanding of each other's position.[5]

Hadley's fundamental social philosophy was revealed when he explained why economists were not government advisers. In part, he said in 1899–1900, this was because the American government had become too responsive to popular clamor. The system of representative government, with its currying to the demands of local constituents, had proved unsuccessful in conducting public business. A strong executive administration, with the power to carry out its policy, would naturally use economists as guides, but this country did not have that. For centuries the people had been "busy devising constitutional checks of the royal prerogative," and consequently the executive had insufficient powers for good government and was at the mercy of the legislature with its local interests. The growth of the "trust" idea, he thought, promised a healthy change, because with industrial and political progress, old-fashioned competition and representative government could not safeguard the public interest. "Business has," he concluded, "become a trust, in a sense far different from that which the accidental application of this word has carried with it."

Similarly, he said, the management of colonial empires with their weak inhabitants had infused into the managers the notion of public office as a public trust. The more completely our undertakings, whether private or public, industrial or political, took the character of trusts, the more impossible it became for the authorities to represent personal or class interests without grossly violating the dictates of sympathy or justice. When this should take place, the American people, with the aid of economists, would meet the needs of industry and government with a "true collectivism of spirit" rather than with "superficial collectivism or socialism, which, like the individualism which it strives to supersede, often makes too much of mere political machinery, and believes that men are to be saved by their institutions rather than their characters." [6]

This social doctrine was based in part on what Hadley felt to be his permanent contribution to the field of economics, the "method of making connections between economics and ethics by the application of the principle of natural selection." Judging by the illustrations he cited, however, he apparently failed to realize that the time had passed when the principle of natural selection could be simply identified with the modern regime of property rights and business practices and the operations of a crude Malthusian doctrine.

On the other hand, his *Railroad Transportation*, which he deprecated as "valuable chiefly as a collection of facts that give clearness to other people's theories rather than as a set of new theories of my own," [7] turned out to be enduring and fertile. In this treatise and in his textbook he threw the spotlight on those important problems that are now thought of generally as "overhead costs." Also, by his suggestion that the workman be enabled to meet the fixed charges of his family, he doubtless opened that line of modern thought which calls for consideration of labor as an "overhead cost" or "fixed charge" on society.

FRANK WILLIAM TAUSSIG

The difficulties of economic terminology and the fluidity of its theory are well illustrated by Hadley and Taussig. Hadley claimed that classical economics in general, and Ricardo in particular, were obsolete because free competition was obsolete. His friend, F. W. Taussig (1859–1940), although reaching much the same practical conclusions, insisted on the substantial validity of the classical school. The difference in the two was largely one of personal taste.

Taussig was born in the border state of Missouri, the son of a successful St. Louis businessman. [8] He had all the opportunities a wealthy and cultured family could provide. He went to Harvard, where he studied economics under Charles F. Dunbar, and was graduated with honors in history. Then he made the customary grand tour of Europe. He stayed long enough to spend a winter at the University of Berlin studying political economy and Roman law. On his return to the United States he became secretary to President Eliot of Harvard and began his work for a doctorate in economics. For his dissertation he turned out the admirable *Protection to Young Industries* (1883).

Taussig was as yet undecided as to whether he would make law or economics his life work. He took over some of Dunbar's classes during the year 1882–83, while the latter was away, but on Dunbar's return he entered the law school. He continued his writings on economics and gave a course on tariff legislation. After receiving his law degree in 1886, he accepted an assistant professorship in political economy and henceforth devoted his energies to economics.

Taussig was interested in the various modern developments in economics, though he was first and last a follower of the classical tradition of Ricardo and John Stuart Mill. Thus as early as 1884 he declared: "I am not a follower through thick and thin of the German school, but there is much truth in the qualifications which they suggest to accepted economic principles." [9] While he was one of the leaders of the "old school" in the 1886 controversy with the "new school," he nevertheless attempted to have reprinted in the United States the famous article "Political Economy," written for the *Encyclopædia Britannica* by the Irish supporter of the "historical school," the Reverend John Kells Ingram of Trinity College, Dublin. In fact, he called on his friend and opponent in the debate, E. R. A. Seligman, to help. "It is an excellent sketch of the history of political economy—the best in our language, by all odds," he wrote Seligman. "It is just what I want, as a book of general reference for the students." [10] At the end of that year he joined the American Economic Association, the first of the "old school" advocates to do so. This was not surprising, for Taussig accepted some of the tenets of the marginal utility school, although skeptical of the fully developed scheme. He approved the doctrine in substance, but he thought it too complex and susceptible to statement in more simple language.

The need, Taussig stated in 1892, was for a "restatement of the general principles of economics which would be accepted, for the time being, as a standard exposition of the present state of political economy, at least for English-speaking countries." It must be a book which "will attain the authoritative place that, in its day and generation, was achieved by John Stuart Mill's recasting the then-accepted doctrines of political economy." When Marshall's *Principles of Economics* appeared, Taussig declared that while it was the most important contribution since Mill, he doubted that it would fill the need. He continued to use Mill "because of its educational value, and because it prevents delusions as to economic questions being easy of solution." [11]

Perhaps the clearest picture of Taussig's views was revealed in his statement of what should be taught in high school economics. While the best-equipped scholars differed on many important questions, he wrote, there was a mass of fundamental matter on which the economists were in agreement and which could be simply taught to the students. "The marvelous division of labor in a civilized community," he said; "the mode in which laborers, farmers, merchants, transporters, contribute to the community's revenue of commodities and services; the nature and functions of money, and the ramifications of the machinery of credit; the position of the businessman as the great middleman of industry, and his relations to hired workmen on the one hand, to consumers on the other; the growth and significance of production on a great scale; the elements of international trade and of taxation; the difference between a regime of private property and one of co-operation or of collectivism—these are matters which can be set forth simply, effectively, and instructively." A good deal of useful and interesting information on the history of industry, especially during the last two centuries, "can be interwoven with the explanation of the principles; while abundant illustration can be found by the competent teacher in the familiar facts of everyday life." [12]

In *Wages and Capital* (1896) Taussig maintained that a wage fund existed in the attenuated sense that the real source of wages was in the recurring supply of finished and consumable goods, and this supply, as the Austrians had also shown, could for the time being be increased but slightly. "All hired laborers got their share of these commodities and their real wages, by having money turned over to them by capitalists and employers. The wages-fund doctrine was right in looking at the advance of funds from capitalists to laborers as the first step in the process by which wages were determined." A considerable and permanent rise in wages could occur most effectively, he said, through increases in the proximate source of the laborers' incomes, "either through directly larger receipts accruing in the hands of active capitalists, or through the less direct process of larger money sums being turned over to the capitalists by investors." In his scheme, therefore, the wages of any particular group depended on what the consumers were able and willing to pay for the commodities produced, and a permanent rise in wages could be obtained by such a group only if the "permanent conditions of the market—that is, of ultimate demand—" were favorable to them. [13]

Taussig's complete theory of wages was substantially like that of

Clark. He believed that wages were "determined under competitive conditions by the discounted marginal product of labor." He agreed that this might be considered simply another way of saying that wages were "determined by the specific or imputed product of labor," and that interest was "determined by the specific or imputed product of capital." But he criticized the Clark version, that "labor gets the specific product of labor," because it implied that this was "all that labor *ought* to get. . . . Whether it is right that every man should get what he himself produces, raises deep-reaching questions as to justice." [14] He tended to think such questions outside the realm of economics. For instance, he thought that the proponents of labor legislation were guided by an excessive humanitarian spirit. The suggestion made by such a highly respected thinker as Laveleye, that the State should indemnify workmen who were left unemployed by the introduction of machinery, seemed especially extreme to him.

But the problems kept arising, and he had to deal with them. He questioned if the pioneering work of the German government in social insurance, providing for disability and old age pensions for all wage workers, would be successful, because of the enormous clerical staff needed. In the United States it would surely be unworkable, he thought, because "we who are used to Anglo-Saxon ways of self-help and self-dependence, look with suspicion on a scheme in which a man partly is helped by others, partly compelled without choice to help himself. . . . These measures . . . leave little room for individual development, . . . for training in character. . . . In practice, the system must reduce itself to something hardly distinguishable from taxation on the one hand, alms-giving on the other." Long after a substantial number of economists were supporting a minimum wage for women, Taussig insisted that it was injurious to the interest of women workers.[15]

Taussig was conservative, as can be seen by his phrasing, but he was not prone to blame every labor dispute entirely on the laborers. In the famous Homestead strike he felt that the manager, Henry C. Frick, should have been more tactful in dealing with representatives of the employees. "No doubt a man of action must fret at the incongruity of a conference with an unwieldy committee of twenty-five slow-headed workmen. But with tact, patience, friendliness of bearing, the cultivation of a spirit of confidence and good-will, it is possible—whether probable, who can say?—that the struggle might have been avoided; and these qualities were conspicuously absent in the manager." Frick had, he said, no conception of any duty to guide and help the workers, and the "responsibilities of wealth and power were in some degree disregarded." [16]

On the question of railroad regulation Taussig's views were summarized in 1891 in his statement that those people who thought a really "effective and detailed supervision of railroad bookkeeping can be looked for" were immature and "utopian." Since most railway costs were joint, he said, the various rates could be determined only by demand, and not by cost of service. This was nothing more than the "general practice of 'charging what the traffic will bear.' That practice is not an accident, nor the result of arbitrary exercise of power by railway managers. . . . It will . . . appear under public as well as under private railway management." It was therefore almost impossible, he felt, to determine "reasonable" rates as the Interstate Commerce Act demanded. On the one hand there was the "extraordinary complexity of the [railway] business, the constant transfer and rearrangement of industry, and the corresponding shifting in the demand for transportation; on the other hand [there was] the monopoly element in the railway business, the extent to which many roads are in the position of rent-yielding natural agents, the enormous vested interests." Thus he felt that the Commission in practice had wisely accepted the existing system of rate-making as on the whole reasonable.[17]

On the great issue of free silver Taussig by his opposition was forced in the course of that long struggle to qualify or attenuate Ricardian economics. He contended in 1884 that there was no permanent tendency toward a decline in prices and that bimetallism, or any approach to it, would result in an undesirable inflationary rise.[18] In the nineties he argued that the fall of prices was due to the extraordinary improvements in the production of commodities. Since money wages and incomes had in all civilized countries shown a tendency to rise rather than fall, he said, the debtors did not suffer a real hardship in repaying the same nominal amount. And, he added, justice demanded that creditors as well as debtors should share the profits of labor's increased productiveness.

To the argument that low prices were ruining business, he replied that only those enterprises which were not sufficiently competent to utilize the improved means of production had failed under the impact of low prices; the wide-awake ones had gained. In fact, to his mind, the immediate cause of the fall of prices had been the increased marketing of goods produced with profit at lower and lower cost. "The business world," he said, "has not been in any state of chronic depression. In the ups and downs of industrial activity there have been periods which seem to confirm the pessimistic accounts of the bimetallist and of other persons malcontent with the present order of things; but in due time the tide has always turned." [19]

True, the Middle Western farmers were suffering from falling prices, admitted Taussig, but their difficulties sprang from phenomena which could not be cured by monetary or government measures. Although caused to some extent by the competition of new producing areas both in the far West and other parts of the world, this merely aggravated the effect of the inefficient methods used by the discontented farmers. A good share of the American agricultural population, having been bred to the easy and careless use of virgin soil, could not, he said, accommodate itself to the intensive methods of rotation and selection of crops, of truck and dairy farming, when their lands began to show signs of exhaustion. The more intelligent and versatile adapted themselves to new conditions and prospered, but a large number preferred to move west. In such periods of transition, he suggested, all sorts of remedies for hard times would appear and have their run.

Taussig concluded that gold performed the functions of a measure of value and of a standard of value with as close an approach to perfection as could reasonably be expected from any monetary system. But to provide an "elastic" currency for the needs of industry, Taussig supported the notion that the national bank notes be based, not on the constantly decreasing public debt, but on the general assets of the banks; and he even suggested as an alternative restoring state bank issues. "Eventually, it may be hoped," he wrote, "that the United States will leave the path of direct government issues, whether paper or silver, and will put the provision of the form of the currency which its paper and silver have supplied into the hands of banks, under a system enabling them at once to put forth an unmistakably sound currency and to offer their services to industry with the minimum of restraint." [20]

His views on taxation were best evidenced by the majority report of the Massachusetts Commission on Taxation in 1897 which was almost entirely his work. It recommended replacing the tax on securities representing ownership of, or interest in, property outside the state, by imposing an inheritance tax and a state tax on dwellings. "In principle," he wrote, "an income tax is said by nearly all writers on taxation to be most equitable," but in this "country, with our political traditions and business habits," it could not be successfully administered.[21]

Beyond all these statements on the problems of the day was the importance of Taussig's work on the tariff. He elaborated his dissertation into the classic *Tariff History of the United States* (1888), and from time to time he added new chapters. Taussig was a freetrader in principle, but in his characteristically judicious manner he allowed room for the infant industry argument and for the need to go slowly in removing tariffs. He approved, he said, of a "moderated tariff." To the frequently heard argument that a tariff was necessary to protect the high wage-scale, he answered that wages in America were high not because of the tariff, but because of the great general productiveness of labor, which, in turn, was due partly to the energy and efficiency of our laborers, partly to the extended use of machinery, and very largely to our great natural resources.[22]

To his profession he rendered an important service by his able editorial supervision of the *Quarterly Journal of Economics*. His catholicity was unparalleled. Although conservative in both economic theory and practice, he was gifted with an ability to discern significant developments. Thus he opened the *Journal* to little-known writers even though he considered their views outside the tradition of sound economics. And on more than one occasion he definitely went out of his way to encourage what he considered a radical variant of economic thought.[23]

Along with this he contributed much through his teaching, and he was quite right in saying: "I do believe I have done some useful and good teaching here in this University, and perhaps have given an undue share of my strength to achieving this."[24] His teaching exercised a tremendous influence on the course of American economic thought and action. Practically every Harvard student of economics studied under him, for he taught and supervised the basic elementary course in the subject. And his most famous graduate course, "Ec. 11," devoted to a critique of classical and neo-classical writers, was the training ground of many economists of the next generation.

He also broadened the subject matter of economics, being largely responsible for developing the study of international trade and related fields in the United States. Taussig worked closely within the lines of the Ricardo-Mill tradition—as his treatise *International Trade* (1927) so well attests—but he gave it definitive shape. His students were among the outstanding contributors to the modernization of the older doctrine—James W. Angell, Frank D. Graham, Jacob Viner, John H. Williams, to name but a few. His influence, however, extended far beyond his students because of the great popularity of his *Principles of Economics* (first edition, 1911), in which he attempted to perform the task of bringing Mill up to date. It was neatly said of the book that "the filling is modern and telling. The shell is traditional." [25] So well did Taussig do the job that his book became authoritative even in England. It was indeed fitting that Taussig should be the only American economist ever awarded an honorary doctorate by Cambridge University; he received the degree of Doctor of Science in 1933.

JAMES LAURENCE LAUGHLIN

Most dogmatically classical among these younger economists of the traditional school was J. Laurence Laughlin (1871–1933).[26] Laughlin's father was a lawyer and one-time mayor of Alliance, Ohio, but young Laughlin was forced to finance his own education at Harvard. This he accomplished partly through a scholarship but largely through tutoring. In 1873 he was graduated with a *summa cum laude* in history. He went on for a doctorate in history under the most famous of the three Adams brothers, Henry Adams; meanwhile he supported himself by teaching at the Hopkinson's Classical School in Boston.

For his degree Laughlin turned out a workmanlike dissertation in 1876 on *The Anglo-Saxon Legal Procedure*. But two years later he was definitely in economics as an instructor under Dunbar. In 1883 he was given a five-year appointment as assistant professor. Near the expiration of that period he suffered a nervous breakdown, which interrupted his academic career.[27] Through his friendship with Edward Atkinson he became secretary and then president of the Philadelphia Manufacturers' Mutual Fire Insurance Company. He continued in the insurance business even after he returned to teaching at Cornell in 1890. When the new University of Chicago opened in 1892, Laughlin became head professor of its Department of Economics.

Laughlin appreciated the need of change in economics, but the changes he visualized conformed to the lines of the older generation of free-trade economists. As early as 1882 he had set about projecting an economic association, which he called the Political Economy Club, to contain as members a few of the leading economists. "It ought," he said, "to be made a dignified body, for it can be authoritative & useful in many ways. . . . We need to be stimulated & to get an interchange of ideas, as much as any body of scholars, & our meetings ought to bring out good work." This association got under way late in 1883, but with the organization of the American Economic Association, which included many of the younger men, his "club" disintegrated. When most of the "old school" came into the American Economic Association, Laughlin still held aloof on the ground that it was too much associated with "Elyism." As he put it, "I do not care to be another rag tied to Ely's kite to steady his erratic movements." [28] Not until 1904 did he become a member.

Though Laughlin's training had been in history, he had little sympathy with the historical school.[29] Nor did he view the mature marginal utility school with much enthusiasm, feeling that it was primarily engaged in metaphysical nonsense. He followed Mill, but without his broad "social philosophy," as Laughlin's popular abridgment of Mill's treatise so well evidenced. Whereas Mill's scope was indicated by its original title, *Principles of Political Economy With Some of the Applications to Social Philosophy*, Laughlin eliminated the "applications" on the ground that "omission of much that should properly be classed under the head of Sociology or Social Philosophy, would narrow the field to Political Economy alone, and aid, perhaps, in clearer ideas." [30]

To Laughlin, the rigidly classical John E. Cairnes was the soundest guide. Laughlin insisted in the opening article of the *Journal of Political Economy* that the study of economics must be true to the reality of the Common Sense position, although not necessarily true to the facts of the existing situation. "Political Economy [is not] a body of concrete truth," he wrote; "it does not pretend to be a statement of fact, or a description of actual conditions, or even of future ones. It is a means of analyzing the play of economic motives, of measuring their force, of discovering and explaining the relations between concrete truths, and of ascertaining their causes and effects. . . . If we could be certain of all the facts affecting the case, we could prophesy; but in the nature of things, we never can be sure of them." [31]

He insisted that he was a firm believer in free competition and that it was legitimate for one enterpriser to gain control of an industry through the workings of free competition. But should such a concern charge a price which it was "impossible to suppose was reasonable," he admitted that government regulation was warranted. Asked if this meant government price-fixing, he said that the regulations should take the form of regulating profits, but he was not ready to say "offhand what disposition should be made of that." [32] To him the successful businessmen, especially bankers, were the greatest force in the intellectual, social, and material development of the nation, and any concessions that he might make for their control were not made with the intention of endangering their dominance.[33]

Much of Laughlin's dogmatism was due to the fact that he began teaching in 1878 just as the Bland-Allison Act was passed. Strongly convinced of the unsoundness of the silver position, he continuously and furiously attacked the silverites. Almost from the beginning he warned the community that the silver money doctors were dealing with a very complicated mechanism, and if their diagnosis was incorrect, persistence in their wide treatment would cause serious damage to the financial body.[34] During the bitter 1896 campaign he attacked Bryan and his supporters in a series of newspaper articles, and provided simple manuals pointing out their "errors." Such procedures hardly made for calm consideration of the issues at stake. But then, to Laughlin, the silverites constituted a serious threat to the Republic.

In a sense, his treatment of the silver question justified Francis A. Walker's complaint that the gold monometallists were constantly changing their arguments. Originally, in 1885, Laughlin had attenuated the quantity theory of money so as to make credit the important factor in determining prices. He had asserted that prices were affected by purchasing power of any kind; that purchasing power or demand for goods arose not merely from the amount of money in the hands of the public, but also from the amount of credit used; that the rapid use of money, banking devices, paper money, credit substitutes for gold and silver, checks, drafts, and book credits, all went to increase the demand for goods, if offered, and so acted to increase prices. Consequently, even if the supply of metallic money were to remain exactly the same, prices would vary, owing to changes in the other factors affecting prices, namely credit. After all, he had argued, since 1873 a great collapse of credit and confidence had occurred; so that it could not be said that prices had fallen because of the so-called scarcity of gold.[35]

Recognizing that his emphasis on credit had been a little too strong, he explained in the following year that the "level of prices depends not solely on the quantity of money or on credit, but on both combined. . . . The fall of prices can be explained by causes wholly independent of the quantity of gold in circulation, but connected with the contraction of credit, as, for example, the fall of profits due to increased competition in certain branches of industry, large production, and the introduction of new processes and improved machinery."

In the nineties Laughlin came out finally against the quantity theory as unsound throughout. In his campaign manual against "Coin" Harvey, he declared that Harvey had erred in holding that all economists admitted the quantity theory; the facts did not support this contention. He, for one, did not. Price, he declared, was a ratio between goods and the standard money commodity—gold. More specifically, the difference between his theory and the quantity theory centered "about the time and the manner of the evaluation process between goods and gold." The evaluation, in fact, he said, went on "antecedent to the exchange operation, since the exchange cannot philosophically or practically take place until the rate of exchange has been settled." Paradoxically, Laughlin's theory of prices was utilized in 1933 by a president who moved in the Bryan tradition, Franklin D. Roosevelt, when in the hope of raising prices he had the dollar devalued. Perhaps the most significant feature of Laughlin's criticism of the quantity theory was his reiteration that to "assign the causes of the changes in prices chiefly to variations in the quantity of money" was both one-sided and ambiguous.[36]

Laughlin was quite aware that he had not made as much of a contribution to the development of economic thought as his capacities warranted. He frankly stated to Ely in 1899 that, having been forced by events to touch on "scattered practical questions," he did not think that there was anything in his writings on money or on value and distribution that was of "sufficient value to recall." [37] But he contributed more than he knew. His *History of Bimetallism in the United States* was, and is, a useful study of the legislation and the controversies. And his voluminous writings on money and banking made these issues more vital. While Laughlin at times oversimplified the banking process, especially when he described it as a "refined system of barter," he clearly showed its defects from the standpoint of the banking and business community. Through his intensive activities in the press and in his teachings, he helped to bring about some needed banking reforms. Notable among these endeavors was his *Report of the Monetary Commission of the Indianapolis Convention of Boards of Trade, Chambers of Commerce, Commercial Clubs, of the United States* (1898), which contained one of the most able presentations of the asset currency scheme.

He encouraged his best students to subject the quantity theory of money to a thorough "inductive" as well as "deductive" criticism. Thus Sarah McLean Hardy wrote a notable dissertation which caused considerable controversy. This led to a reformulation of the quantity theory and, perhaps more important, helped to emphasize the need for more thoroughgoing investigation of the actual business process in the formation and function of prices.[38] And it is most commendable that Laughlin filled his department with pioneering spirits, some of whom had had difficulty in obtaining positions. Mention need only be made of Thorstein Veblen, Wesley C. Mitchell, Herbert Joseph Davenport, and Robert Franklin Hoxie. Isaac Hourwich, who had participated in Russian revolutionary activity, taught statistics in the department and wrote articles defending Marx's views against the Austrians for Laughlin's *Journal of Political Economy*.

These three outstanding university men contributed their most original thought to specialized fields: Hadley to railroads, Taussig to international trade, and Laughlin to money and credit. On those subjects they either opened up a new area for investigation or made significant new suggestions. But that explains only a little of the influence of Taussig and Laughlin; their most important contribution was in their remarkable careers as teachers, for from their classes and departments, administered with a catholic tolerance encouraging both liberal and conservative, came many of the leaders of the next generation. Furthermore, and this was also true of Hadley, their services on a variety of important public bodies helped to spread in the community a keen awareness of the need for thoroughgoing analysis of economic problems.

CHAPTER XIII

The Voice of Dissent

WEIGHTING more heavily than most the new social factor in the economic formulas, a number of well-trained economists devoted much of their attention to the social implications of economic doctrine; conversely, by examining the social order, they arrived at significant modifications of their economic opinions. Chief among these men were John R. Commons, whose work may usefully be examined in detail, and J. Allen Smith and Thomas Elmer Will, whose contributions, although of lesser influence, deserve notice.

THE SAGA OF JOHN ROGERS COMMONS

Commons (1862–1945) was a Middle Westerner, born in Ohio and reared in Indiana.[1] He was a restless intellectual soul. This was in good part due to his heritage, which was that of reformers and heretics. He was named after the famous sixteenth-century divine, John Rogers, who was burned at Smithfield by Bloody Mary. His father's family left North Carolina because of their hatred of slavery. His Vermont mother was a graduate of that hotbed of abolitionism, Oberlin. Both parents were active in the Underground Railway for the escape of slaves to Canada. They took opposite sides, however, on evolution versus theology. His father went from Quakerism to Darwinism and Spencerianism; his mother remained a strict Calvinist.

The family fortunes hardly fitted in with the father's Spencerian social philosophy. He acquired enterprises by "swapping" but could never operate them successfully. From his father's last venture, a newspaper, John R. Commons learned to set type, which was later to be of real service as a craft to fall back on, but that was the only profit obtained. The mother supported the family by taking in boarders.

In the hope that Commons would become a minister, his mother sent him to Oberlin in 1882. He supplemented the family income by working as a printer and at that time became a member of the printers' union. The educational scheme of Oberlin was that of the old theological New England colleges. Economics was taught by the professor of political science and modern history, James Monroe, who taught Carey's economics but with extreme tolerance. He allowed Commons and some of his classmates four sessions in which to expound the virtues of Henry George's views. Owing to a nervous breakdown, Commons took six years to complete the course. After his graduation in 1888, Professor Monroe persuaded two of the college trustees to lend him money for graduate work, and he entered Johns Hopkins University because he wished to work under Ely.[2] Soon Commons was helping Ely to complete the latter's *Introduction to Political Economy*.

However, failing in 1890 to obtain a fellowship to finish his doctorate, he had to look for a job. With the departure of Woodrow Wilson to Princeton, the Wesleyan University authorities divided the chair of history and political economy, and Commons was given that section that fell into a department of economics and social science. With the rank of tutor, and a salary of $1000, he taught "Political Economy," "Currency and Finance," and "Social Science," which included study of the State, the family, pauperism, charities, and prisons. Commons was not reappointed at the end of the term because, according to him, President Frederick Raymond wanted a "man of name and years." Commons then obtained an associate professorship of political economy at Oberlin at $1200 and taught "American Institutional History," "Sociology," and "Political Economy." In the elementary course in economics he used Andrews' treatise and in the advanced class he used Marshall's *Principles* and Böhm-Bawerk's *Positive Theory of Capital*.[3]

After a year Commons moved again, this time to Indiana University. Here his salary was $2000 and his rank was professor of economics and social science. At Indiana, Commons matured. Influenced by his mother and by Ely, he saw in religion one of the mighty instruments of reform. He and Ely organized in 1893 an American Institute of Christian Sociology, composed of "earnest Christian men" who saw the need for "encouraging . . . among the people of America the study of social questions from both the scientific and Christian standpoint."[4] Along these lines he published a number of works, including *Social Reform and the Church* (1894).

Although Commons' basic economic interest lay in the implications which the science had for the social and spiritual life of the people, he was professionally trained and entirely ready to grapple with technical problems. Thus, during the nineties, his chief concern was with the monetary question. His position was quite moderate, though he supported Bryan in the presidential elections. He opposed free silver, approved the repeal of the Sherman Silver Purchase Act, and supported a scheme to allow silver as a money of redemption only at its market value. According to this scheme, a National Monetary Commission would establish a general price barometer to determine fluctuations in the price level. When prices fell, the Commission would expand the currency by buying silver bullion in exchange for legal tender bullion notes; when prices rose, the Commission would contract the currency by selling bullion for notes.

To take care of "emergency" situations, especially "speculation," which reduce prices, he proposed in addition that the Commission have power to issue a limited amount of notes without purchasing bullion. These would be deposited in selected banks, and the government would share in the banks' profits from their use as reserves for loans. More concretely, these deposits would particularly be made with New York banks whenever a "money panic" raised the interest rate to 8 per cent.

Commons wanted an elastic currency to maintain a stable level of prices. He contended that this could not be achieved by national bimetallism, and that we must adhere to the international standard of values—the gold basis—because our foreign trade was a vital part of our industry. A bimetallic standard would, in effect, put us on the silver standard and thereby reduce us to the level of Mexico, China, and India.

In this connection Commons presented in 1893 an elaborate and in some ways novel analysis of fluctuations in prices. He prepared a chart showing the range of average prices of staple wholesale articles in the London market measured in gold for the last century. He declared that special factors had affected the supply and demand of each article and had caused its price to fluctuate. But a general cause, the change in the supply of the standard money, had affected all the articles in the same direction. This was revealed by averaging the prices of the several commodities, which eliminated individual peculiarities.

The chart, Commons declared, presented two sets of movements. The first, a "secular movement," extended over long but unequal stretches of time and exhibited a "majestic far-reaching tendency." It rose and fell for long periods. The second, the shorter "credit cycle," was superimposed, as it were, upon the "more majestic swell of the secular movement," and made its rounds in six to ten years. He illustrated the credit cycle as follows:

Starting with low prices, a revival of confidence and enterprise created new demands for commodities, and prices began to rise. In this period speculation abounded, and debts were incurred on the prospect of increased prices and increased business. However, the increases failed to occur within the hoped-for limits, and the failure of a large enterprise brought down with it several banks from which it had borrowed funds. The ruin then spread, a collapse of credit occurred, and demand for articles, and thus prices, fell everywhere. This continued until the weaker concerns disappeared, and then the cycle again began its upward movement.

According to Commons, when the money supply was increasing, as from 1850 to 1873, an upward movement of credit acted cumulatively and prices leaped forward. If credit should contract during this secular movement, the fall of prices would be short, recovery would be prompt, and the "next apex" would be carried above the preceding one. But if the secular movement was downward, the opposite effects would occur. With each panic, since 1873, prices had fallen lower than in the previous cycle until currently prices were the lowest in the century. "These credit cycles with their respective panics, indicated by the successive pinnacles in the mountain chain of prices," he concluded, "have each their own peculiar history." But they have the common features which the "trade journals call overspeculation—overtrading, overproduction, and final collapse."

Industrial reform, Commons continued, had done much already to reduce the extreme fluctuations that characterized the credit cycle. And the rise of powerful trusts was an attempt to eliminate falling prices and overspeculation. As fast as industries were monopolized they were removed from the field of overproduction and placed in that of regulated production. Because trusts were organized on a "scientific basis," the line of prices did not show such extreme fluctuations as in earlier years. Several other reforms, Commons added, would be necessary to eliminate overspeculation. First corporation laws should be so revised that business accounts would be given publicity whenever an enterprise had become a monopoly, and second, the government should take over the "necessary monopolies."

The more basic movement, the secular one, was caused, he said, by changes in the money supply. The credit cycle derived from changes in the credit supply, which, in turn, was dependent upon the quantity of available money. Monetary reform was therefore all important. An elastic currency should be provided for; that is, currency at all times should be sufficient to maintain a stable level of prices, and here he felt his bimetallic scheme was the real answer.[5]

Beyond these specific studies, Commons developed a broad economic philosophy that many felt was socialistic. Commons was not a socialist, although he was frequently accused of "wildly radical views." In fact, among the last articles he wrote while at Indiana was one in which he attacked socialism as unworkable and espoused "progressive individualism." His private letters indicate the same position; he wrote Ely that socialism ignored the need of individual regeneration and proposed to "elevate the laboring class as a mass rather than as individuals." [6] He pointed out that calling a principle socialistic did not make it so. If governmental control stimulated the self-reliant energies of the people, opened new avenues for private enterprise, equalized and widened the opportunity for employment, and prevented monopoly, then for him the government was not socialistic but was supplementing the highest individualism by achieving free, open, and fair competition. To do this, he said, the government must undertake certain reforms. To those already suggested, he added others. There should be, for one thing, tax reform. This would include a protective tariff, for, if properly levied, a protective tariff would stimulate invention and diversify industry, thereby furnishing the most varied outlet for the abilities and capacities of all individuals. Commons also favored progressive inheritance, income, and land taxes, but not such heavy ones as to discourage enterprise and economy.[7]

Commons agreed with Gunton's philosophy that working hours might be reduced for the benefit of labor, business, and the community; but he thought this should be achieved through the influence of public opinion, especially that of the consumers. He strongly urged the need for improving the housing conditions of the working class. "Tenement house reform involves more than inspection," he said. "It involves demolition." [8]

In 1893 Commons presented a comprehensive treatise on economic theory, *The Distribution of Wealth*, based on a very elaborate form of Austrian marginal utility economics. The theory of value, he declared, was the doorway to the theory of distribution, because the share of an individual or class in the social income was a "problem of the ratios at which the various products are exchanged." Behind value, he wrote, lay marginal utility, the "quantity or utility or pleasurable sensation afforded by the last increment of commodity actually enjoyed." Value arose from the limitation of supply relative to the demand, and important institutions, as well as the niggardliness of nature, could limit the supply. For control of the supply situation, as created by human factors, he thought that we must look to the law. Lacking that supreme authority with power to define and enforce the rights and duties of individuals, modern industry to him would be impossible. These rights and duties might or might not be based on ideas of justice, he said, but they must be definite, because the arbitrary rulings of individuals must be avoided.

The most important personal right, Commons maintained, was the right to life. Not only must the individual be protected against unlawful violence by his fellows, but he must be furnished with a share of the social product equal to his minimum of subsistence. In medieval times, he said, the State had guaranteed the right through slavery and serfdom; today the right found a new recognition through public poor relief. Another bundle of rights he subsumed in the term liberty, which should enable the laborer to obtain the highest possible share of the social product in return for his personal abilities. To Commons this return was, like all commodities, subject to the law of marginal utility. As he expressed it: "If the number [of laborers] is large compared with the wants supplied, the marginal utility and the wages will be low."

Limitation of their numbers by the formation of labor unions, according to his analysis, was one of the workers' most important rights, which included restriction of the admission of apprentices and the exclusion of non-union men from the opportunities of the trade. While the expansion of free contract enabled the laborer to obtain a share of the surplus of the social product above his minimum of subsistence, he pointed out that this bargaining power applied only to those laborers who could keep their marginal utility above the minimum. Thus freedom of contract benefited the skilled, the intelligent, the educated, the gifted laborers, but not "the unskilled, unorganized, redundant laborers who have a low marginal utility."

Laborers could also maintain the marginal utility of their labor, he said, by "finding new opportunities where the marginal wants for their labor are more intense." This, too, was dependent upon certain personal legal rights of freedom, and took the form of the right to employment. This right was, to him, simply a "new application, under modern conditions, of the old right to freedom of industry." Free industry in the past, he said, meant essentially free access to nature for the production and acquisition of wealth. It applied only to organizers, promoters, and employers; to laborers it meant only the right to leave the rank of wage receivers and join the profit receivers. The right had practical value, he thought, up to the last quarter of the century, when industry had been unorganized and abundant opportunities for investment had prevailed, when a vast public domain had been available on generous terms, and when small business had been characteristic. Now, however, he said, free industry benefited only the wealthy capitalist, because of the immense capital needed to become an entrepreneur.

In his view even agriculture and retail merchandising were rapidly moving toward monopoly, so that the great mass of workers would necessarily remain employees. Consequently only through the right of employment could the mass obtain access to nature for production. This right should therefore embrace security of tenure against arbitrary discharge of honest and efficient workers, and government provision of work for the unemployed.

The introduction of Civil Service reform, with its purging of political influence, signified to him that the right to security was being recognized. The guarantee of this right in private industry would be worth millions to the country, he thought, for it would eliminate the waste of strikes, lockouts, and class antagonism. The right of tenure would then be enforced by government-created arbitration commissions, which would also adjudicate wages, hours, and conditions of work. As long as industry remained prosperous, he said, the laborer would be as independent in his right to employment as in his right to life.

But this, Commons declared, would not solve the involuntary idleness caused by depressions and technological advance. The answer, he felt, lay in recognizing that all rights depended on economic progress—the increased production of wealth. This was occurring with the growth of monopolies, which were, he said, "the greatest economic invention the world has ever known." Since depression was caused by overproduction, his theory went on, trustification would eliminate its causes and make work regular, and government employment bureaus and public works would remedy the unemployment created by technological changes.[9] Through a proper system of taxation, unimproved lands and natural resources held for speculation could be made available to laborers. By eliminating the chronic excess of laborers over opportunity, the right of employment would raise the marginal utility of the laborers and thus would raise all wages. Commons added the important qualification that the practicability of these suggestions could be determined only after a "multitude of experiments and years of patient, scientific thought."

It has been pointed out that Commons' thought often went far afield, centering primarily around social questions. This, in one instance, led to an extreme and curious opinion. He argued that one right of freedom, marriage, was mischievous for the laborer, for, unrestricted, it allowed the poor, uneducated classes to contract marriage before they were financially and mentally ready. Since competition reduced the wages of the class increasing most rapidly by lowering the marginal utility of the last laborer, the unrestricted right of marriage could account in large part for the material and mental poverty of the lower classes.

He was on a little more solid ground in his analysis of monopoly profits, arguing that the enormous returns could be tapped for the benefit of labor and legitimate enterprise. He gave as the reasons that such profits, having arisen from monopoly privileges such as land sites, patents, franchises, trusts, good will, etc., were the returns not of industry but of certain fixed social relations and rights; that, like rent of land, they tended to engross all the gains of progress; that they differed from the true entrepreneural profits because the latter arose from the ability and risks of the entrepreneur and were temporary and contingent; and that permanent monopoly profits might originally have been the personal profits of the entrepreneur, but, when capitalized, became permanent profits.

On the other hand, the profits which arose from economies, inventions, widening of markets, should go to the entrepreneurs, Commons declared, for they were personal or temporary profits, the reward of their enterprise. Although society might, without injuring industry, appropriate permanent monopoly profits through taxation, "sufficient margin should be allowed for the wide play and scope of the pure entrepreneur's profits." He concluded that the "so-called conflict between capital and labor" was at bottom "a conflict between capital and labor on the one hand, and the owners of opportunities on the other. . . . Tax reform should seek to remove all burdens from capital and labor and impose them on monopolies. Public policy should leave capital and labor and business ability free and untrammeled, but endeavor to widen and enlarge the opportunities for their employment."

Commons, in developing his theory of monopoly profits, or "surplus value," presented an expansion of the law of diminishing returns that subsequently was taken over into the main tradition of economics. The law of diminishing returns, he argued, would be seen to be a universal law, applicable to all industries, except for the fact that it was viewed from one standpoint in agriculture and from another in manufactures. In agriculture, the standpoint was that of a given amount of ground; in manufacture, it was that of an entire industry or of a single undertaking regardless of the area it occupied. But if the standpoint of area was always taken, the law would be applicable to manufactures and to every industry.

At the same time Commons restricted the concept of rent of land to the return from location and excluded the original Ricardian meaning of return for the "original and indestructible powers of the soil." He contended that soil was capital, and that its returns were governed by the same law governing returns from machinery. Ricardo and his followers, he said, developed their law of rent from the circumstances of a country with abundant and fertile new lands. "But," he pointed out, "new land is not the normal condition of agriculture. After the first generation of settlers the original qualities have been worn out and whatever remains is due to the productive power of labor and capital. This must be renewed and repaired every year like machinery."

The profession did not take kindly to the *Distribution of Wealth*. Taussig turned down a request for a review with the statement that it was an "unbaked" performance. Hadley in the *Yale Review* said the author was ignorant of economic history and criticized him for basing his theory on the fallacy that men "make money by hurting society. He has gone back from the conception of trade as a means of service to that of trade as a means of extortion; and stands on substantially the ground which has proved such a source of weakness to trade-union leaders in every age." Richmond Mayo-Smith of Columbia University stated that Commons' method was not scientific, and that his socialist bias would be more excusable if he had not attempted to conceal it. Second, a scientific author, in considering legal and social relations as factors in the distribution of wealth, "should describe them as they are, not as he thinks they ought to be." Third, Commons, in discussing the right of employment, obviously violated the canon and introduced "purely subjective notions into a scientific discussion." Professor A. C. Miller of the University of Chicago, in the *Journal of Political Economy*, after pointing out that Commons made monopoly the central point, went on to bemoan his perversion of economic theory and concluded that the whole essay was a "disguised attempt to found a scientific basis for a theory of socialism." [10]

Such criticisms appear to have disturbed the Indiana University authorities, and they wrote to Henry C. Adams asking what he thought of Commons. Adams replied that "an attempt to investigate a professor of Political Economy for doctrines held would do more than anything else to check the conservative influence which [the] writings of economists are exerting upon the general social and industrial question." But this did not settle the matter. More serious consequences came from the newspaper attacks on Commons' views as expressed in his public speeches in 1894–95. Commons was greatly disturbed by the charges that he "favored socialism, single tax, free trade, Populism." To Ely's warning that he be more prudent, Commons replied: "I believe fully in what you say regarding the *timeliness* of expressions of advanced views, and I recognize that on some occasions I may have seemed needlessly to have aroused antagonism. It is difficult to combine opportuneness with exposures of injustice, but I believe I am getting more cautious." [11] And when an offer came from Syracuse University for the new professorship of sociology, President Joseph Swain encouraged him to take it. Commons would have preferred to stay at Indiana, but he had no alternative.[12]

Commons' fixity of purpose at the time he made this change is well illustrated by his correspondence. His chief concern was with his principles of sociology: "I am planning my work to center around the legal aspects of sociology—expanding the doctrines in my *Distribution of Wealth*. I am moved to it especially by the curious productions of Patten and Giddings, neither of whom in their treatises on sociology gives more than passing notice to the two great features of society, law and education." [13]

But this was to be a fifteen-year project, and Commons had too active an interest in the manifold practical problems of the day to restrict himself. He continued to expound rather moderate reform views. For instance, he proposed that local governments hire their own day laborers rather than deal with contractors. Although he favored municipal ownership of local industries requiring a municipal franchise, he presented the case in moderate fashion. Government, he said, should not undertake experiments on a large scale, that is, operate new modes of manufacture or services. Such ventures, involving incalculable and speculative risks, he did not consider safely the business of government. Instead, private parties should be encouraged to engage in untried fields, so that, if they were unsuccessful or ahead of the time, they and their dependents alone would suffer from failure and bankruptcy. He pointed out that a large-scale failure, involving repudiation or oppressive taxation, would produce "a popular revulsion, and deep-seated distrust of government itself," possibly resulting in anarchy. He thought, however, that such municipal utilities as electric lighting plants, which were successful under private enterprise, could be taken over.

But municipal government machinery should be improved, Commons stated, in order to prevent corruption and achieve efficient management. The state should supervise the cities by providing uniform accounting systems and by authorizing sound financial arrangements. An unsalaried municipal board or commission should replace the usually corrupt Board of Aldermen as the administrative body. The initiative and referendum should be used in the purchase, sale, or lease of plants. Finally, an improved Civil Service system should be established so that superintendents in charge of various municipally-owned utilities would be "appointed on merit and held personally responsible and then . . . be entirely free to appoint and remove all subordinates without interference from an outside Civil Service commission." [14]

His general views on the structure of society quite naturally led Commons to specific ideas for political organization and action. Thus, ever since his Oberlin teaching days, Commons had believed that social problems could be solved by proportional representation. His argument was that in a system of government where all classes and interests were represented by their leading spokesmen, social invention would proceed not by State coercion but by mutual concession. A city council, based on the principle of proportional representation, would be a "perpetual board of arbitration, possessing many powers of sovereignty, but not compelled to use them." Strikes and boycotts

would be settled by mutual agreement between authorized negoti-
ators. In state and national affairs, the legislatures and Congress would
fill a similar office. These assemblies would be composed of moderate, sensible, earnest men, because the people were so. The extremists and idealists would be controlled by hard contact with the
practical difficulties of ideal legislation, and the overwhelming majority of moderates would be forced to realize that ideal conditions
must be considered equally with the rude facts of the present.

These leaders, declared Commons, would pass such well-considered
laws that the people would willingly accept the measures. They would
bolster their acts with references to science, comparative legislation,
and history. Instead of jumping back and forth from revolution to
reaction, there would be a steady march toward social reform. By
mutual concession a basis would be established for the brotherhood
of capital and labor and the gradual solution of the main social problem. Thus the legislature could safely be the sovereign organ of government and the promoter of social reform.[15] After all, he said, the
direction law should take would be "determined by compromise between antagonistic interests of society." Commons even pushed the
doctrine so far as to suggest its use by trade unions in their organization, and he utilized its logic in demanding that the State protect
the interests of minority stockholders.[16] He also used the doctrine of
proportional representation or representation of all affected interests
in presenting the composition of his Monetary Commission for maintaining a stable price level. Agriculture, manufactures, and banking
would each have a representative, and two "monetary experts" would
complete the membership.

Commons reiterated this doctrine at the American Economic
Association meeting in 1899. Congress, he said, should be composed
of representatives of organized classes. This was his plan: Let the
labor unions, irrespective of locality, come together and elect their
candidates just as they elect their officials. They would probably
elect such men as Gompers and Debs, the "true representatives of
the wage-earning class." Let the bankers elect their own men, and
they would doubtless choose men like J. P. Morgan. The trusts
would elect Rockefeller, Carnegie, or perhaps attorneys like Joseph
Choate. The railroads would choose Chauncey Depew. The farmers' organizations would send their presidents; the anti-trust league
would send its president, and so on. "In such a Congress these
various interests might send economists—men like . . . Hadley and

Taussig on the one side, and men like . . . Ely, Henry George, on the other." Each class would be represented by its ablest and "authenticated spokesmen." From these true leaders would result "broad-minded, patriotic compromises." [17]

Commons had used even more startling language at the previous annual meeting (1898) when he stated that George and Marx represented the thought of the class that was rising to dominance and political power, i.e., the "radical classes," as against "the capitalist and banking classes" and the "commercial classes." Shortly after this address Commons was notified by the chancellor of Syracuse, the Reverend James Roscoe Day, that his chair of sociology was abolished.[18]

Five years outside the academic world followed. Commons occupied himself with free-lance activity, primarily miscellaneous research for government and private bodies. He first arranged to work with that reformer in general and silverite in particular, George Shibley, to assist him on a salary basis for a year and a half, or two years if he did not find a place to teach. They were to collect and publish news on "live questions."

In this enterprise Shibley and Commons were joined by another of Ely's exiles from academic halls, Edward W. Bemis. They appealed to the Buffalo Political and Social Conference to sponsor their proposed combination information bureau and correspondence school, a "college of Social Science" modeled on the Chautauqua system. They planned to have a Board of Regents composed of from twenty to twenty-five men of a "liberal standpoint, great and deserved prominence in business or professional life, and . . . either possessed of some wealth or likely to have influence in procuring the donations." [19] Such a wealthy group could not be obtained, but the projected College of Social Science became a branch of Bliss's short-lived Social Reform Union, of which Commons was a member.[20]

The trio meanwhile set themselves up in New York as the Bureau of Economic Research to investigate practical subjects in economics, statistics, and politics from a "non-partisan but progressive viewpoint." Among other things, the Bureau published two quarterly bulletins in 1900, primarily devoted to an index, constructed by Commons, showing that prices were falling as the silverites contended. But by the fall of 1900 Shibley ceased to have any monetary interest in the Bureau, which had already cost him $3000.[21] Shibley moved to Chicago to supervise the preparation of the campaign text-book for the Democratic National Committee. The Bureau soon folded up, after which Commons fortunately managed to obtain work with the United States Industrial Commission.

Upon the problems such a commission faces, Commons had some-what modified his views. He still advocated compulsory arbitration for disputes between labor unions and employers, but he insisted that neither party should be compelled to accept the awards. "It ought to be . . . a compulsory conference of the two sides, and they ought to make the decision. . . . [The judge] should simply preside and bring them . . . to the point where they agree on something."

He still insisted on the desirability of an eight-hour day but justi-fied it primarily on the ground that it would enrich American citi-zenship by providing more time for studying and for exercising the rights of freedom. He strongly questioned the validity of the eco-nomic argument for the eight-hour day as a cure for unemploy-ment. To his mind a mere reduction of hours would simply spread the same amount of wages over a larger number of men. He pointed out that Malthus and the proponents of the eight-hour day had the same general economic theory but differed in the remedy. The eight-hour day position was based, he said, on the theory of under-consumption; that is, that the producers' earnings were insufficient to buy all they produce. Where Malthus believed that the cure for unemployment was increased expenditures on luxuries by the wealthy, the eight-hour-day advocates, Commons pointed out, be-lieved that increased consuming power by the masses was the essen-tial need. He thought the similarity held for the argument that the working classes obtain only sufficient to live hand to mouth, while the rich, having surplus incomes, invest their savings in productive enterprises so that productive capacity is increased beyond what the market can bear.

This general doctrine held that either the wealthy must spend their surplus income on luxuries rather than on mills and factories, or the workingmen be given higher wages, so that extraordinary profits would be absorbed. These higher wages would be used for building their homes, or otherwise consumed, rather than placed in banks or invested in new enterprises. Thus if the working classes could increase their consuming power, the multiplication of indus-tries and overproduction would be impossible. Malthus' remedy was not then generally held, he said, and the specific formulation offered by the eight-hour day proponents also had somewhat the same defect, for should total wages be raised as hours were reduced, costs would increase, and the resulting loss in sales by business would mean less employment. The real remedy, to his mind, still was variations in the monetary supply to maintain stable prices.[22]

Commons also asserted that the concentration of wealth in "combines" was beneficial to the extent that it improved the quality of products and services, lowered their price, widened their use, and raised the standard of living of the employees. Although patent rights and trade-marks were special privileges, they benefited the public, for the former reduced costs of production and the latter improved the quality of goods. To his mind the most dangerous special privilege of concentrated wealth was that which gave it power over currency and banking. "Without a central bank," he said, "managed by the government or by the merchants, as in Europe, and able to relieve a money panic by extra issues of emergency paper, the business community is at the mercy of powerful raiders." [23]

After the Commission completed its work in 1902, Commons collaborated for a short period with the wealthy Socialist William English Walling in his projected "Economic Year Book." After this he obtained a good opportunity to put some of his ideas on arbitration and economic councils into practice, for he became an important negotiator on labor disputes for the National Civic Federation, of which he was secretary and later statistician, at a salary of $4000.[24] This body, organized in 1900, was composed of representatives of employers, wage earners, and the public.

After five years in exile he returned to university teaching. In 1904 Ely raised a substantial sum from wealthy philanthropists to establish at the University of Wisconsin the American Bureau of Industrial Research. In this organization he hoped to work with Commons on a "History of Industrial Democracy in the United States." But Commons had been outside the academic world for some time, and it was not easy to bring him back. Ely obtained eloquent testimonials for the authorities from outstanding economists, not least of which was one from John Bates Clark. The University finally agreed to give Commons a three-year appointment as professor of political economy. His salary would be $3000 a year, of which the private fund would pay $2000.[25] In this way, Commons at the age of forty-two returned to academic halls, and during his permanent teaching career at Wisconsin he made that institution a leader in American economic thought.

He soon had complete charge of the project. With the collaboration of able graduate students he published his most important work, the eleven-volume *A Documentary History of Industrial Society* (1910–1911) and the two-volume *History of Labor in the United States* (1918). At this time, too, Commons began to publish rather realistic studies on labor. Much of their value was the result of his carrying out the advice he had given his Indiana students to visit the workingmen in their homes and to join a labor union, for only then could the needs and aspirations of the universal class, the working class, be really understood.

The illustrious authorities in economics, he pointed out, had denounced the demands of workingmen as all wrong, but if they had gone among the workingmen themselves, they might have found that these workingmen were more nearly all right. Though they knew little of abstruse books, he said, they were in daily contact with things, and soon felt where the shoe pinched. He held that there was some deep reason in the boycott, in the refusal to work with non-union men, in the complaints against women and child labor, against the introduction of machinery, and against contract and prison labor. What these reasons were the books did not teach, he said; and the educated man did not know. If the latter would study them at first hand, he might not be convinced by the workingman's arguments, but he would begin to comprehend that these were real evils which they should seek to avoid.[26]

Commons soon became the great pioneer in the serious study of current labor problems as well as in the history of American labor. He continued to promote reforms. He proved invaluable to Robert La Follette in making Wisconsin a leading state in liberal legislation, and he trained a most distinguished group of students of labor. Commons' reformism, especially in factory legislation in Wisconsin, was in the last analysis based on Henry C. Adams' notion of raising "the plane of competition." But where Adams held that the State should enforce a reform in industry only when the great majority of, if not all, the interested businessmen agreed, Commons argued that the State should enforce such reforms when the progressive employers had shown that the change was practicable; the progressive employers might be relatively few, but their success with the reform showed that it was not a speculative "ideal" or "theory" but a workable, profitable proposition; that is, it was reasonable in the minds of employers as well as in the eyes of the law.[27]

Commons continued to advocate that commissions and conference bodies conform to the spirit of his basic notion of proportional representation. He felt that government commissions should follow the administrative principle used in Germany for railway rate-making. There, he said, "all parties concerned get together in conference and adjust rates to the best interests of the community. But our commissions have regulated without reference to the interests affected. The practice has been to collect facts at the office of the [Interstate Commerce] Commission, work out a theory, and then issue orders. Our commissions have not gotten the idea of calling together representatives of all parties concerned, including the public, and adjusting differences in conference." [28]

With the passage of time Commons became more cautious in desiring that the "coercive" power of the State should operate in labor reform. In 1912 he stated that minimum wage legislation was the final step of a system of labor legislation. In such a system the administrative machinery must first be perfected to handle it. Provision must be made for the prevention of accidents, then prevention of industrial disease, then the restriction of hours. After those preparatory laws were effectively enforced, the State might take up the minimum wage. Commons held the minimum wage to be essential for the protection of labor, the only question being whether it should be established by law or by labor organizations. Perhaps, he said, the government should avoid the field except in the case of the most oppressed laborers, those not in a position to organize. Concerning government and business, he finally concluded in 1917 that the "regulation of wages for all classes of labor must eventually lead to compulsory arbitration and prohibition of strikes—a strain on our political institutions which we are not prepared to meet." [29]

Broadly speaking, Commons was convinced, at least for his time, that economic conflicts could be remedied by eliminating "machine" politics. From his point of view the conflict between the employing and wage-earning classes was not inevitable and could be avoided by the will of a third group, the public, which he didn't consider a class, if this group were given the power to determine the issue through direct nomination, direct election, initiative, and referendum. Class antagonism would not disappear, he said, as long as there was wealth to distribute. But if it could be "transferred to the jury of the people," then social classes might be expected "to state their case in the open and to wait on the gradual process of education rather than plunge into battle." [30]

Commons' strength and weaknesses were those that flowed from a fertile mind ceaselessly occupied with formulating definite social policies. He was always writing and negotiating in particular matters. He had little time to bring general systematic order into his thoughts, to engage in what might well be called consecutive thinking. He constantly attempted to show that his specific policies resulted from a general economic theory; as often as not, that general theory was little more than a rationalization for action, dressed up in the ever-changing terminology of one or more variants of "orthodox" doctrines.

In a fundamental sense Commons' inconsistencies and shifts were the by-products of a mind groping with the utmost sincerity for ways and means of achieving the harmonious working together and progress of the various interests in the complex modern money economy. He was moving for reform on all fronts. Throughout all this, his work evidenced that conflict, often unconscious, so characteristic of the reformer-intellectual of the United States. When Commons discussed labor and similar problems, his analyses usually ran in terms of an economic order in which trusts and monopolies were here to stay; when he discussed money, transportation, and the like, his analyses ran in terms of achieving the ideal order of free competition. And sometimes, in a large theoretical work such as *The Distribution of Wealth*, both views were presented. Reviewers could not be altogether blamed for being confused into harsh attacks.

What saved him from brilliant superficiality was his habit of constantly "investigating." Although his "researches" were generally constrained by the requirements of immediate use in policy, few economists were as aware as he of the need to come to grips with the facts of the economic scene, if society was to progress. His emphasis on what he called the "observational" method made him successful with able students and with men of affairs. He was giving adults what he once called the crying need for high schools, "observational" treatises and teaching by the "observational method." His concept was that if instructors could see that economics was the "practical, everyday neighborhood problem of getting a living," and consisted "mainly of the simple matter of comparing facts instead of squirming over theories," then they would be aroused to its importance and be "inspired to teach it to their pupils." [31]

With a mind so closely attuned to the movement of events, it is not surprising that Commons underwent change and development in his views. He continued extremely active in the period that goes beyond the confines of this volume. It would do him little justice, under the circumstances, to discuss those later views at this juncture without the setting that will be presented in the sequel volume.

Although in the minority all his life, and always having to fight for a hearing, Commons was not alone. Among the reform economists of the nineties there were several who, on one specific issue or another, went even further than Commons. Outstanding among these were J. Allen Smith and Thomas Elmer Will.

JAMES ALLEN SMITH: ADVOCATE OF CONSTITUTIONAL REFORM

J. Allen Smith (1860–1924) was a graduate of the University of Missouri.[32] After practicing law in Kansas City, Missouri, for five years, he decided in 1892 to do graduate work in economics at Michigan under Henry C. Adams. Like Adams, he believed that while in certain industries the "socialistic principle" should apply, for the larger part of industry competition was an effective regulative principle. But he differed from Adams in that he believed that the essential cure for economic ills was a proper monetary standard, and he made this the topic of his dissertation for the doctor's degree.

This thesis, "The Multiple Money Standard," was extremely suggestive. It showed, though in a disjointed fashion, that modern industrial society operated on a money rather than a commodity basis. Smith stated that a monetary standard, based on a single commodity, such as gold, caused fluctuations in general prices; and that those fluctuations, by disturbing the normal relations among the interest, wages, profits, and rent existent in a barter economy, brought about panics and depressions and all the evils connected with falling prices. According to his theory, falling prices placed an oppressive burden on the entrepreneur. Therefore the "interests of society at large demand that the entrepreneur, who assumes the initiative in production, should not be artificially burdened for the special benefit of the [interest-receiving] class who take no active part in industry. The effect of the whole system is to discourage production, and to make a bond a more desirable investment than an entrepreneur's interest in capital."

In order to maintain stable prices, Smith advocated a variant of an old principle of monetary reform. Basing his principle on Newcomb and others, he demanded the establishment of a "multiple standard" which would cause the money economy to conform to the ideal or barter economy. The circulating medium would be government notes convertible into specie—even gold alone—but the price of the specie would be variable. It would vary inversely with general prices. Thus if prices rose the currency would be contracted, and if prices fell the currency would be expanded.

To render the process more efficient, the government might add to the currency by purchasing good securities on the open market until the demand for currency was met; to eliminate excess currency, the process would be reversed. Whatever method was used to contract the currency, it ultimately must take the form of taxation. Contraction, therefore, would be achieved by collecting in taxes more than the government expended, while expansion would require only that the revenue should be less than the expenditures.

But Smith had to face the fact that the multiple standard would be only a national standard, in effect a "non-exportable medium of exchange," and would therefore lead to fluctuating exchange rates. To these criticisms he answered that "the crucial test" of a good monetary standard was not "steady rates of foreign exchange, but the existence of a practically constant relation between the monetary unit and commodities generally." Besides, he said, since the great bulk of American commerce was domestic, the money question should be viewed from this angle rather than from a foreign-trade viewpoint.

The multiple standard would, he contended, protect the United States from those grievous commercial disturbances and panics which arose abroad, and which under the single gold standard affected the entire commercial world. The government need merely raise the price of gold as soon as it began to be exported. No change would occur in the relation of money to commodities or in the market rate of interest. As it was, he said, the gold standard countries checked the loss of capital by raising the interest rate to a point where commercial disaster resulted, but under the multiple standard the United States could prevent disaster simply by raising the price of one commodity. In this way foreign panics could be shut out effectively.

Perhaps the most significant point for subsequent analyses was Smith's view that the co-ordination of the various industrial forces was effected through the instrumentality of prices, and it was the failure of prices to show the actual situation that led to irregularity in production. He based his analysis on the "crucial test of normal distribution," i.e., the maintenance of "efficient demand." In a "progressive society," that is, one where capital is accumulating, he said, efficient demand could be maintained only through "a continuous rise in the rate of wages and a continuous fall in the rate of interest." The maintenance of a due proportion between the demand for subsistence, therefore, and the demand for capital investment would operate to "give wages a continually increasing proportion of the total product." Such insights perhaps outweigh his reiteration that the competitive control of industry had heretofore been a failure, because of the imperfections of the monetary system.[33]

The study, which appeared in 1896, attracted considerable attention, but intervening circumstances prevented Smith from developing the work. In 1895 he went to Marietta College as acting professor of economics and sociology with a salary of $900. He found it hard to adjust himself to the prevailing mood of the academic world. In his course on economics Smith began with Mill's treatise as a textbook and then went on to an elaborate discussion of the defects of laissez faire, especially monopolies and the gold standard; and, even more unusual, he gave a lengthy presentation on panics and the wastes of depressions. He soon felt that he would not remain long at that college since, as he wrote Adams, those controlling the Board of Trustees strongly favored the "gold standard, McKinley protectionism, and non-interference with monopolies. Nothing short of a miracle would make it possible for me to keep on terms of good fellowship very long with such a combination." [34]

He was prophetic; he was dropped at the end of the first semester of the academic year 1896–97 on the ground of retrenchment.[35] From Marietta he went to the University of Washington in Seattle, having been appointed by its Populist president as professor of history and political science at the salary of $1500. Here he used Francis A. Walker's book for the elementary economics course and Alfred Marshall's treatise for advanced work. Yet here, too, Smith was troubled by the political atmosphere. He wrote to Adams in 1899 that the Board of Regents contained some peculiar members, "when you consider that they are appointed by a Populist governor, and are supposed to be in sympathy with reform." The manager of a large Standard Oil property, he declared was the "dominant factor on the Board. The Populists of this state seem to be completely dominated by the very interests they profess to be fighting." Disturbed by this situation, Smith began devoting all his "spare time . . . to the study of government rather than to economics." [36] The result was his famous *The Spirit of American Government* (1907), which exercised a profound influence on the liberal movement of the twentieth century.

By vigorously asserting that the Constitution had originally been promulgated by a reactionary propertied interest, and that radical changes should be made, the book caused considerable stir. Oddly enough, Smith's economic interpretation of the Constitution was very similar to that first formulated by the Federalist opponents of Jefferson and his party during the War of 1812,[37] which later became the standard interpretation of the Federalist and Whig historians. This was the view that the Constitution was the work of the wealthy, conservative class. But while the original propounders considered that the action of the wealthy imposed highly desirable restraints on the democratic hordes and thus increased the wealth and power of the nation, Smith argued that this "spirit" in the Constitution was very undesirable both socially and economically.

The forces working "silently and unconsciously" toward democracy, that is, political rule by the majority, had gained their impetus in the American Revolution and found expression in the Declaration of Independence, wrote Smith. But the conservative, wealthy class had regained its domination through control of the Constitutional Convention. The Constitution was therefore an economic document deliberately devised to prevent majority rule and aimed at achieving a centralized government for the protection and extension of the interests and privileges of the wealthy and well-born.

This aristocratic spirit was apparent, he wrote, from the whole system of checks and balances, the almost insuperable difficulties of amendment, the nature of the Senate, especially the selection of senators by the state legislatures, the restraints on the states, and, above all, the veto power over legislation held by the irresponsible

Supreme Court. In his analysis, universal suffrage did not imply popular rule, for it was counteracted by "indirect election, official independence, and the rigidity of the constitutional system as a whole." This made possible graft, corruption, and favoritism for private corporations. Prevailing evils, therefore, could not be attributed to democracy but to the lack of it.

Smith did not recommend that the Constitution be scrapped nor that the national authority be strengthened. On the contrary, he feared the extension of national power and held that reform must come through the states and the municipalities. The evils would be largely eliminated once the local legislatures were made responsive to the popular will through the establishment of the direct primary and the initiative. Then, with the state legislature directly nominated and subject to removal through the recall, it would necessarily select as United States senators the popular choices, just as the electoral college ratified the popular choice for president. With the Senate thus democratized, the Supreme Court could be prevented if necessary from thwarting the will of the majority by the power of the president and Congress to name additional judges.

Critics paid little attention to Smith's concrete proposals, but they showed considerable interest in his description of the Constitution as a reactionary document and of the judicial veto as a subversive "monarchical survival." In fact, both the Progressives and Democrats used it in their campaigns of reform.

Smith himself, it turned out, was less concerned with the development of popular rule than with what he and Henry C. Adams called "national centralization." In later years he sharply opposed an amendment to the Constitution prohibiting child labor,[38] and in his posthumously published volume, *The Growth and Decadence of Constitutional Government* (1930), he stated: "Since the majority have come to regard themselves as the final source of political power, their attitude toward the theory of individual liberty has profoundly changed." It was to their advantage in the "eighteenth century to defend the rights of individuals against the State. Having accepted the idea of popular sovereignty, however, they now regard individual liberty as a check on their own power." Smith contended that there was much to be said for the "conservative view that in a democracy personal liberty is more likely to be abridged than under a government in which the people have less influence." A government which is supposed to represent and has the support of the majority, he said, is more "confident of ability to override all opposition" than one which, not recognizing the right of the majority to rule, must avoid the danger of "arousing too much popular opposition." In an undemocratic State the possessors of authority recognize the need for a "cautious moderate policy—one which will as far as possible conciliate all important elements in the population and thus safeguard the country against the danger of revolution." Governments' respect for the "rights of individuals is due in much larger measure to this balance of opposing interests within the State than . . . to formal constitutional guarantees."

By 1930 Smith's early reformism had become a vigorous force in American thought. The whole approach to politics as a balance of economic forces has been so widely discussed in recent times that his statements have a peculiarly modern flavor. And his monetary views anticipated later respectable schemes, such as Irving Fisher's "Compensated Dollar."

THOMAS ELMER WILL: POPULIST

The other figure who attracted wide attention for his heterodox views was Thomas E. Will (1861–1937). He financed his college education by teaching in the country schools of his native Illinois. After receiving his Bachelor of Arts degree from Harvard, he was granted a fellowship, and in 1891 he obtained his Master of Arts degree. His first college teaching position was at Lawrence University (now Lawrence College) in Wisconsin. But two years later he was back in Boston as secretary of the Christian Socialist organization, The Boston Union for Practical Progress. In 1894 he went west again, this time to Kansas State Agricultural College (now Kansas State College of Agriculture and Applied Science), where he took over President George T. Fairchild's courses in the social sciences.[39] Three years later, when the Populist-dominated Board of Regents terminated the services of all employees of the institution, Will was made president, and he promptly brought in a number of academic exiles.[40]

Will boldly proclaimed the social reformers' faith. "We are steadily democratizing government, religion, education, social privilege and rank," he informed the farmers in 1899. "The time will come when we will democratize wealth; when that which all aid in producing all will enjoy; when immoderate wealth and debasing poverty will disappear, and existence for the average man will be more than a mere struggle for bread." To achieve these objectives, he said, people must realize their resources and strength, "learn how to adapt means to ends." To succeed in this, "I commend to them the candid and impartial study of economics." [41]

Will used as a textbook Andrews' *Institutes*, but in his writings he went beyond Andrews in the clear-cut expression of his views. Originally he had been an ardent supporter of Henry George and the single-tax movement,[42] but at Kansas he felt that the basic solution of economic ills was a currency that would make for a stable price level at all times. Will took his stand on the "Ricardian formula" of the quantity theory of money, modifying it slightly to meet the "requirements of changed economic conditions." He argued that a statistical investigation of the course of the price level revealed a double movement—an oscillatory movement, violently fluctuating through short periods, as months, years, and decades, and a general trend which since 1873 had been a terrific downward movement. Both these movements he considered vicious: the oscillatory movement fostered the speculative spirit, turning business from "the work of producing for the satisfaction of consumption into that of 'betting on the market,' " while the steady downward trend of prices also tended to the abandonment of the "legitimate arts of production," since businessmen would not produce against a "falling market." It led instead to an increasing demand for safe investments, such as government securities.

The answer, however, was not rising prices, he said. True, they benefited debtors, but sometimes the creditors were the poor and weak, and the debtors were the rich and powerful; for example, the poor widow who invested her little estate in bonds. Natural laws could not be circumvented by eliminating rising prices through price-fixing; rather, the procedure should be through reduction of the supply of money.

To achieve stable prices, two reforms were essential, according to his theory: first, a government commission to compile and publish at stated intervals the statistical and diagrammatic record of the double movement of prices; and second, the maintenance of a stable price level by government buying and selling of its own call bonds or other securities, by issuing paper money to expand the currency and contracting it by receiving these notes in taxes on ground rent, monopoly incomes, and inheritance of large properties, and by remitting at the same time tariff taxes, personal property taxes, and the like. In addition, if it was necessary to control credit in order to maintain a stable price level, the government should enter into the banking business and make loans at 2 or 3 per cent.[43]

Another plank in Will's creed was government ownership of trusts. All other methods of handling the problem he declared inadequate. He agreed that the economic advantages of trusts were considerable, but he felt that trusts under private management would never be popular, for the people would never accept the idea of monarchy even in industry. The only virtue in the proposals to destroy trusts, he said, lay in the fact that the ensuing agitation would stimulate thought and action to a more practical line. Heretofore anti-trust legislation had succeeded in making the trust disappear in one form, only to reappear in another, more highly organized and of more formidable proportions. And those who administered the legislation soon realized that instead of the legislature controlling the trusts, the trusts sooner or later controlled the legislature. Public ownership, therefore, was to him the only solution, for public ownership had none of the disadvantages of trusts in private hands, and all the advantages: production to order and on a vast scale, better and cheaper goods, unified management, the elimination of competitive warfare with its correlative waste and savagery, and industrial democracy in place of irresponsible mastery.

Critics, he said, argued that public ownership of the trusts would tend to complete socialism, claiming that industry tended to monopoly, monopoly to public ownership, and public ownership to complete socialism; but this was hardly a strong argument, for all growing bodies tended to infinity in size and weight, but they stopped before attaining too great a size. At certain times in American political history, the nation had moved strongly along the Jeffersonian line, at other times as strongly along the Hamiltonian, he argued. And just as there was in man, in varying ratio, the elements of egoism and altruism, of regard for self and regard for others, so there were in him, in a ratio varying with circumstances and influences, the principles that at one time would impel him toward socialism and at other times toward individualism. If, then, a society, certainly an Anglo-Saxon one, should find it had pushed public ownership and employment so far as to interfere seriously with individual liberty, the majority sooner or later would as eagerly vote itself out of it as it had voted itself into it.[44]

In 1899, when the Republicans won control of Kansas and the Board of Regents, Will along with his major appointees was removed. He then became successively president of Bliss's correspondence school—the College of Social Science—dean and professor of social sciences at Ruskin College in Trenton, Missouri (1900–1903), and president of the American Socialist College at Wichita, Kansas (1903–1905). In 1905 he obtained a position with the Census Bureau.

All the while Will actively supported Debs' Socialist Party. He contended that those critics who believed the aim of the party was the complete collectivization of industry on the day it obtained political power through the ballot misread its platform and spirit. In fact, the party held, he declared, an evolutionary viewpoint substantially similar to that of the Fabians. Will's sharpest attack was directed against Bryan, who asserted that socialism sought collective ownership through the State of all the means of production and distribution, a development that would diminish incentive, restrict freedom, and hamper the expansion of individualism. If Bryan's premise were sound, his conclusions would have some force, said Will, but Bryan had as badly misunderstood the socialist position as Bryan's own position had been misunderstood in the past.

Will's statement of the socialist position was as follows: Socialists believed that collectivism should keep pace with industrial concentration. In other words, industries which through their great size and monopolistic character became social in fact should be socially owned and operated, while industries which through their small size and competitive character continued to be individual in fact should be individually owned and operated. Socialists considered collectivism as a means, not an end. The end was a social State from which exploitation would have been extirpated and in which opportunity, initiative, freedom, and fellowship would be possible for the least and the lowest. To the extent that collectivism would further this end, it was desirable. Thus the socialists believed in individualism in its best and broadest sense: "love of liberty, the desire to develop one's powers and individuality, to live a complete life, to realize one's largest possibilities, and fulfill one's destiny."

We must also achieve, he went on, equal rights to the use of land

and of tools. Any measure needed to make the race fair should be utilized; even, when necessary, a graduated income tax, inheritance tax, franchise tax, and a tax on land values, as well as State insurance, pensions for aged and exhausted workers, complete education for all children and the free administration of justice. Socialism, he said, did not seek to convert society into a great penitentiary. It was not bureaucratic but democratic, demanding an equal chance for the poor and oppressed. A socialist was an individualist who could see no "scope or opportunity for true individualism short of socialism." [45]

Will did his most influential work in pushing the new movement for conservation of the nation's forests. As secretary of the American Forestry Association and editor of its journal, he carried on a tremendous campaign through the press and on the platform. On relinquishing his posts in 1910, he declared that the movement was but a phase of the broader and deeper movement whose end was the "conservation of the equal rights, liberties, and opportunities of all the people, and the establishment and maintenance of conditions under which the least and lowest may live an unfearing and complete life." [46] In all his activities he professed the same ideals. For the next quarter of a century Will was engaged primarily in real-estate developments in Florida, where he pioneered in the settlement of the Everglades region. That his interests were more than personal pecuniary gain is attested to by his forceful emphasis on permanent settlement and adequate self-sufficiency rather than tourist traffic.[47]

CHARLES AUGUST TUTTLE AND THE EXPLOITATION THEORY OF MARGINAL PRODUCTIVITY

A few Americans showed acquaintance with a variant of the marginal productivity theory, better known in Europe than in the United States, which held that the marginal productivity determination of wage rates was not fair to labor. Among these was Charles A. Tuttle (1865–1935), an Amherst product with a Heidelberg doctorate. On his return from Germany in 1886, at the age of twenty-one, he began teaching at Amherst. In 1893 he left his associate professorship to accept a full professorship of history and political economy at Wabash College in Indiana. On his departure in 1913 for Wesleyan University in Connecticut, Wabash awarded him an LL.D. That all the learned journals accepted Tuttle's articles gives evidence of his abilities.

Tuttle was a great admirer of John Bates Clark and his methods,[48] but he felt that Clark's version of marginal productivity was too simple. In his privately printed volume of lectures given at Wabash in 1894, while he accepted the doctrine that all units of labor received the same pay as the final unit, he held that this did not mean that there was no exploitation. On the contrary, the entrepreneur received as a part of his income-profits all that surplus which "earlier" units of labor had created, just as the landlord received the rent yielded by supra-marginal grades of land. Laborers as a class, he insisted, could obtain the entire product of their labor only by combination. When perfectly organized they could, by withdrawing their labor from the market, that is, by strikes, increase the rate of wages from the increment of product on the "poorest opportunities" necessary to employ all the labor, to the increment which results from the use of labor in "average opportunities." The surplus product of the units of labor in better opportunities, which in the absence of labor organization went to the profit receivers, would make up for the deficiency of those units working in poorer than average opportunities. To achieve this end and give labor its entire product was the legitimate goal of labor organization in regard to wages.[49]

Tuttle also criticized the fact that economists in extolling economic progress overlooked the accompanying unemployment. On this problem he created a stir at the meeting of the American Economic Association in 1901. After asserting that Clark had not fully appreciated the consequence of his statement that a "dynamic society keeps a certain number of men in transit from one employment to another," Tuttle went on to argue, as Commons had, that the displaced laborers should not be compelled to bear the burden of technological advance. Since the movement created first a special profit for the entrepreneur, he said, and only "ultimately an 'elevation of the level of human life,'" the displaced laborers should be indemnified through funds drawn in part from the general tax revenues and in part from a special tax on the entrepreneur. The indemnity to the laborer might take the form of "free public employment bureaus, and perhaps free railroad transportation." Whatever the method, it should be recognized as the "workman's economic right, and not as a form of public charity." [50]

Tuttle's concrete propositions were viewed by participants in the discussion, with the exception of Commons, as a threat to the foundation of the social order. They declared that the scheme would reduce initiative, the State would eventually have to enforce compulsory employment, the government would become the sole employer, and slavery would be necessary. Finally, William W. Folwell of Minnesota declared: "The practical difficulties of working any such scheme are too great, and we have merely been engaged in a purely academic and theoretical discussion." [51]

There was doubtless, therefore, a good deal of justification for Ely's statement that the "theoretical work of the decade has as a rule lacked sufficient boldness. We have been too timid, and have in some cases spent much time in petty refinements while essentials have been overlooked." [52]

Broadly speaking, the tradition of John Stuart Mill still held chief authority. Winthrop M. Daniels, professor of political economy at Princeton, expressed the view of the economics profession in his delightful "A Letter to John Stuart Mill":

I never knew one of the existing race of political economists who had not some pet grievance against your Political Economy. . . . Still, when all abatements are made, candid judges will, I think, allow that there still remains of your economic labors, a coherent theoretical framework, containing nearly all that was best in your predecessors, and much more besides—without which economic science both in substance and form would today be immeasurably the poorer. . . . No successor with an undisputed title has succeeded you upon the economic throne.[53]

While the general accuracy of this statement cannot be questioned, there came to be more and more individual deviations under the impact of the changing economic and social scene. The teaching of economics was definitely broadening; thus one notes that at the University of Georgia, in 1891, Francis A. Walker's treatise was the textbook, with Mill, Ely, and Marshall as the reference works.

Under the mellow light of this broadened subject matter, the insights of such heterodox thinkers as Commons, Smith, Will, and Tuttle, seemingly so dangerous when introduced, looked less and less startling as a new generation became familiar with them. As the new synthesis inevitably suffered academic formalization, it benefited to some extent by this leaven introduced by events in the social scene.

PART IV

The Promise of the New Century

CHAPTER XIV

The Spirit of Reform

ALTHOUGH economists were slow to catch it, the political mood of the early part of the twentieth century was definitely one of reform. Now that most people were interested, there were endless suggestions as to the scope and the character of the measures necessary. President Theodore Roosevelt was in tune with this mood and played an important part in creating it. Vigorous and enthusiastic, he had just that breadth and vagueness to give him great popular appeal. He was in everything everywhere. As one of his sons was supposed to have said: "The trouble with father is that when there is a wedding he thinks he is the bride and when there is a funeral he thinks he is the corpse." [1] This very quality of showmanship helped him to take the public pulse and prescribe the medicine. His bedside manner was peculiar but effective.

In a sense, the keynote of the period was set by the work of the Industrial Commission. Its nineteen volumes of testimony and reports were epoch-making. For the first time the federal government had undertaken a comprehensive survey of the country's pressing economic problems, and this published report provided an insight into the functioning of modern business. At one extreme the Commission recognized the need for the competitive system and for the removal of all clogs which might hamper its efficient operation; at the other, it recognized labor problems and the need for a solution to them. But how these difficulties, intensified as they were by new developments, could be overcome, was not very clearly determined.

COMBINES, TRUSTS, AND MONOPOLIES

The formation of the billion-dollar United States Steel Corporation in 1901 ushered in an era of great combines. The battle for

control of the Northern Pacific Railroad Company between the
J. P. Morgan and James J. Hill interests on the one hand, and the
Harriman and Standard Oil interests on the other, was finally settled
when the contestants formed a far-reaching holding company, the
Northern Securities Company. Buttressed by such success, Morgan's
will became "law" with most of the Wall Street capitalists and
institutions. He "publicly avowed his belief in creating corporations
with capital stock so large that existing managements could not be
unseated." [2]

An all-out defense of the modern business development was supplied by Charles A. Conant, eminent authority on banking and
treasurer of the Morton Trust Company of New York. The technique of the holding company undoubtedly increased the power of
the big financiers, he said, but it introduced "unity" into an "in-
coherent and incompetent" management and enabled the financiers
to proceed with farsighted plans to meet the requirements of national and international trade. The "voting trust" too was designed
to "put properties into the hands of competent and responsible persons," for business was developing along the lines of banking. The
concentration of banking resources, together with the ability to act
resolutely in times of crises, based on the co-operation of the banks
and a few powerful leaders, were to him among "the most potent
factors in our recent industrial progress and our present financial
security." [3]

The tremendous importance to economic prosperity of the few
great masterminds in industry—the inventor, the captain of industry,
the resourceful authors of new financial combinations—was, according to Conant, too little appreciated; their ability to work unfettered
in a free economic field determined whether a nation should be
great or little. Even some of their "questionable" operations should
not be restricted by law lest their entire activity be restricted. In
the last analysis, he said, the people could be protected only through
economic education; they should be taught to invest wisely. Unwise
restrictive legislation might relieve the citizen of the obligation to
look out for himself, but it would promote a condition of dependence upon the State which would be detrimental to genuine economic progress.

In line with this he suggested in 1907 that legislation be passed
to permit the issue of bank notes based on general assets; that is,
restrictions should be lifted on the extension of bank note issues for

business needs. Otherwise, he said, American prosperity would be arrested, and we would suffer in competition with foreigners both abroad and at home. Commerce, not the government, should determine the note issues and bullion needed.[4]

In substantial agreement with Conant, Charles R. Flint, the promoter of combines, insisted that the centralization of wealth through large-scale manufactures and the corporate system evidenced cooperation, not monopoly. To him, centralized manufactures would permit the largest utilization of special machinery, and the subsequent benefits would be distributed to the great body of the people. The great fortunes worked under the same natural law for the public good, he said, because they existed as shares held in corporations, were subject to the will of the majority of shareholders, and were guided by "leaders of superior intelligence and experience." Should these fortunes be inherited by degenerate descendants, no harm would be done; in fact, he said, fortunes usually fell apart "in such a way as largely to benefit the charities and other beneficent institutions and to qualify and embellish the commercial spirit of the times." [5]

Even Herbert Croly, the liberal journalist, defended trusts as the symbols of true democracy. In the name of "progressive democracy" he demanded the repeal of the Sherman Anti-Trust Act. Public interest was not promoted by the expensive attempt to save the small competitor, he said. He also disapproved of giving the Interstate Commerce Commission the power to fix railroad rates because he felt that reasonable rates were insured by the desire of the corporation to develop traffic.[6] Walter Weyl, another influential journalist, declared in *The New Democracy* (1912) that the trust encouraged "internal competition." For example, factory managers competed among themselves, inasmuch as a factory manager who produced more goods at less cost than a rival manager would receive an appropriate reward.

The message of President Roosevelt to Congress in December 1901 developed the economic concept that it was only just that the largest producers be given greater gains. This was so because such big enterprises were of benefit to society and could exist only if adequate prizes rewarded success. Unrestricted business action was essential to maintain the country's lead "in the strife for commercial supremacy" among nations. Disaster to great business enterprise was most damaging to the wage earners, said the President, since the capitalist lost his luxuries but the laborer lost his necessities. But, should the large combinations show harmful tendencies, then they should be subject to reasonable control through publicity.

The immortal "Mr. Dooley" summarized the message in the following fashion: " 'Th' trusts,' says he [Roosevelt], 'are heejoous monsthers built up by th' inlightened intherprise iv th' men that have done so much to advance progress in our beloved counthry,' he says. 'On wan hand I wud stamp thim undher fut; on th' other hand, not so fast.' " [7]

In accordance with Roosevelt's views, a Federal Bureau of Corporations was set up in 1903 in the newly established Department of Commerce and Labor to make diligent investigation into the organization, conduct, and management of any corporation, except railroads, engaged in interstate commerce. The Bureau could either publish the information or turn it over to the President. At the same time Roosevelt wanted the Sherman Anti-Trust Act revised in order to retain "reasonable" combinations as against "unreasonable" ones.

The Northern Securities Company was in his eyes an unreasonable one, and he inaugurated a successful campaign to end it. The Supreme Court in 1904 ordered its dissolution as in restraint of interstate trade. In 1911 the Court, in dissolving that "monster holding company," the Standard Oil Company of New Jersey, took a definite stand in favor of Roosevelt's philosophy by declaring that "reason" or "undue restraint of trade" should be the criterion in judging whether combinations were monopolies or not. Since the Court allowed the chief stockholders of the dissolved holding company to receive proportionate shares in the underlying concerns, large in themselves, there was considerable doubt in the public mind whether concentrated control had been destroyed.

In the same year the House of Representatives ordered an investigation of the United States Steel Corporation, "the greatest industrial concern" in the nation. Lengthy hearings were held. The majority report of the investigating committee declared that daring financiers used the steel industry as a basis for fabricating securities, not goods, by a "monotonous repetition of the old process of the inflation and exchange of securities." The committee accused them of practically paying themselves out of the securities which were so lavishly issued in disregard of the rights of the stockholders or the welfare of the industry. In short, the interests in control derived a greater profit from operations in the stock market than from the manufacture of steel. By collusion at the top competition was prevented. But unionization at the bottom was prohibited. A study made by the United States Commissioner of Labor showed that of the 153,000 employees in the blast furnaces, steel works, and rolling mills, 50,000 worked seven days a week, and 20 per cent worked eighty-four or more hours a week—a twelve-hour day, including Sunday. Even with those hours wages were barely enough to provide subsistence.

The corporation, moreover, made heavy contributions to political parties, particularly to maintain the protective tariff against competing items. In this activity it co-operated with the whole industry, which was easily done since the management was highly centralized. As the report went on to emphasize, the "inside management" or system of interlocking directorates, whereby a few powerful individuals controlled several corporations, sometimes damaged the corporations themselves, but more often harmed the general public.

The report recommended that full publicity be given to the operations of the Steel Corporation and similar organizations; it wanted the laws enforced against the use of "cunning devices" to secure unfair advantages over competitors, and it demanded that industrial concerns be prohibited from owning an interstate carrier.[8]

In 1911 too, the Senate Interstate Commerce Committee held a full inquiry into federal policy toward business. The president of the United States Steel Corporation, Elbert H. Gary, gave the familiar defense that healthy competition was needed, but that a return to unrestrained cutthroat competition would mean a return to the order of the survival of the fittest, and the elimination of the weaker, poorer concerns, thereby ending in monopoly. "We of the United States Steel Corporation," he declared, have "by our connections . . . our dinners, etc., endeavored to establish relations which would expand, not suppress, trade, build up competition, not destroy it." Restrictive proposals such as limiting the percentage of business, prohibiting interlocking directorates and holding stock of other corporations, said Gary, were ill advised. "If large aggregations of capital are beneficial," then it is questionable whether there is a point "beyond which you can say they are not of an increasing benefit. It is just as necessary to . . . protect those who are influenced on the outside by capital."

To alleviate the existing evils Gary suggested that a federal commission be set up to license corporations engaged in interstate and international business. This commission should have the power to regulate prices in order to prevent monopoly and restraint of trade, but all acts of the commission should be subject to review by the courts. He proposed this because "the salvation of the country really is in the courts. . . . If a judge is independent of the people, if he is an educated man selected because of his merits, as the judges usually are—I do not think we will have any trouble from the courts." Gary added: "[Some] think my individual opinion, in view of my connections, is somewhat radical and extreme. I have often been accused of being a socialist." However, "what I suggest is the way to prevent the bad results which would come . . . from socialism, so called, carried to . . . its extreme."

George W. Perkins, a former Morgan partner, suggested more conservatively that the commission should be "composed largely of experienced businessmen," and that publicity should be the essential feature of its rules and regulations. He bluntly stated that the bigger the corporation the more efficient and the more socially desirable it was. In fact, the time might come when a single large business in an industry would be the rule.

Opposing them, Louis D. Brandeis, the brilliant Boston lawyer, speaking for liberal opinion, declared that trusts and huge corporations were dangerous and inefficient and could survive only under conditions of unfair competition and discrimination. For every business concern, he said, there must be a point of greatest efficiency. That point would differ with varying conditions, but clearly an organization might be too large for efficient management as well as too small. Anything big, simply because it was big, seemed to be good and great to the people. However, "we are now coming to see that big things may be very bad and mean."

A federal interstate trade commission with extensive powers of investigation and publicity might be satisfactory, Brandeis agreed, since it would provide an opportunity for competition. But he thought it should not yet be given any mandatory functions. Most of the violations of the anti-trust law, to his mind, had resulted from the general belief that the government and perhaps the American people themselves were not sincere in the desire to prevent monopoly and to insure competition. But the moment Congress, with the approval of the American people, gave the assurance that the law would be enforced, a very large part of the difficulties would disappear.

In discussing the relations of government and business Brandeis outlined the theory that the government should have a definite duty to regulate competition in order to prevent destructive practices which could lead to monopoly. It could aid competition by undertaking industrial research, just as it conducted agricultural research. Industry should receive research benefits, just as the merchants received the results of expensive consular inquiries and information distributed through the Department of Commerce and Labor.[9]

The business community was beginning to think, however, not in Brandeis's terms of competition between small units, but in terms of co-operative self-regulation. Arthur Jerome Eddy, the Chicago lawyer and journalist who first came to public notice in the eighties as an ardent free-trader, created quite a furor in business circles in 1912 with his book *The New Competition*, which went through five editions in three years. Eddy contended that the "old competition" which the Sherman Anti-Trust Act sought to restore was cutthroat competition; that true competition was "co-operative competition," the competition embodied in sound trade associations —for a number of which he was the attorney. His ideal scheme of trade association was one where members did not agree on prices, output, or division of the market, but simply exchanged information on these and related business matters. This sort of association he described as an "open price association," that is, open information to the members. It did not lead, he said, to "arbitrary or unfair advance in prices," but to "stability of prices at fair levels." In a sense the scheme would give that full knowledge of the market which was a premise of the traditional doctrine of competition; except that Eddy was very vague as to whether customers as well as sellers were to have the information. As for government and business, Eddy vehemently complained that manufacturers and dealers were ill treated by government, while other interests were fostered. The Department of Agriculture, he said, had as its primary object better crops and prices for farmers; the Department of Commerce and Labor sought to obtain better terms and wages for labor, and so there ought to be some department to help dealers and manufacturers get better returns for better products. But the only interest in them manifested by government was to "force them to sell at the lowest prices under the most adverse conditions."

This was not the mood of the public, however. Senator Francis G. Newlands seemed to express the general temper of the country when he pointed out that nine-tenths of the witnesses before the Senate Committee were insistent that the Sherman Anti-Trust Act should be retained and supplemented. As the period ended, Francis A. Walker's able son, Francis Walker of the Bureau of Corporations, summarized the situation by saying that the United States still lacked "a general system of corporation law, while the state corporation laws have been extremely lax, and in particular have placed little restraint on the formation of holding companies." [10]

There seemed to be a rising public insistence that something should be done. But whenever anything was done, the influential financial and business interests complained that government intervention was the chief cause of the current depression in business. It was a case of "politics" interfering with the natural laws of the economic order. This charge aroused the ire of the outstanding conservative commentator on business conditions, Alexander D. Noyes, financial editor of the *New York Evening Post*.

Depressions are explainable by purely economic causes, rather than by politics, he wrote in February 1912. "There are such things as cycles of prosperity: rising and receding waves of industrial activity." He took as an example the world-wide political upheaval of 1848. In that very same year, he said, the world was in a business depression, which was the outcome of the panic of 1847, the result of the same wild financial excesses that preceded all great crises of this sort. And the political events of 1848, which "aroused such dismay and despair in the minds of rigid conservatives of the day, in and out of the [London] Stock Exchange, have long since been placed by the verdict of sober history among the great forward movements of the century. We know now, as the frightened bankers and business men of 1848 did not, that the political upheaval of that year was both necessary and inevitable, unless the social and political institutions of the period and probably its financial institutions with them were to enter on a chapter of decay. There are always excesses and misjudgments somewhere in a worldwide movement of the sort, but they are corrected in the long run; for there is a vast deal of hard common sense in the people as a whole. Time sets right even the judgment of timid and suspicious financiers. . . .

"Possibly, after a reasonable lapse of time, when what is now controversy has become settled history, even the most conservative and old-fashioned of us will understand why, in the normal course of human progress, it was necessary that in 1911 . . . the United States government should demand the dissolution of industrial combinations, which in the wild 'promotion period' of the past ten years had acquired absolute or potentially absolute dictatorial power over American industry." [11]

THE RAILROADS

The railroad problem, which had been the original cause of the combination issue, was still a burning one, but there were definite signs of increasing effective control, in spite of terrific opposition. One important critic, railroad attorney Walker D. Hines, in addressing the American Economic Association in 1902, warned that the country's material welfare would be impaired if the Interstate Commerce Commission were given "tremendous and dangerous power," which was "necessarily involved in the power to make rates." The Commission, he said, was necessarily composed of superannuated politicians. They were rarely practical railroad men and usually entered the Commission with elaborate theories which, not being based upon experience, were probably incorrect, and then they attempted to make railroad practices conform to their theories rather than to readjust their theories to the practical necessities of the transportation business.

To this Chairman Charles A. Prouty answered that until he had been appointed to the Commission he "had been merely a railroad lawyer, just like my friend Hines. I knew no more about these matters than he does now." But since then he had devoted six years, the seventh part of an average business life, to studying them. "The most stupid man in that time should acquire some little knowledge of traffic conditions," he said, "and three of my associates are older in service than I am." He recalled that the caliber of the men who composed the first Interstate Commerce Commission had been great largely because they had been charged with great responsibilities. "The discharge of a great duty draws to itself great ability. . . . If the personnel of the present Commission be small, it is because its functions have been belittled. Make the Interstate Commerce Commission what it was once supposed to be and what it should be, and you will have no criticism to pass upon the members of that body or the manner in which its duties are discharged." [12]

With the passage of the Hepburn Act (1906) and the Mann-Elkins Act (1910) the Commission was granted wide scope and more effective rate-making powers. There was as yet, however, no definite basis for determining "reasonable" rates. To amend this, the liberal Republican senator from Wisconsin, Robert M. La Follette, following the suggestions made by Henry C. Adams, demanded that provision be made for a "physical valuation" in the nature of "reproduction cost" of the railroads. The presidents of the various railroads and other spokesmen for the carriers strongly opposed this. One critic of the proposal continued to maintain that the real value of a railroad was an outcome from its earnings. "It obviously cannot be possible to derive rates from value, when value itself is actually the final consequence of rates," he said. Another critic stated more succinctly that the value of a railroad was nothing but its "earning power capitalized." Consequently valuation had nothing to do with cost. Furthermore, cost of construction could not be used to evaluate the "intangible assets," which included the possession of "exclusive privileges, franchises, and territorial monopolies."

Frederick W. Whitridge, learned corporation lawyer and executive, declared that if the value of property measured by the cost of reproduction was less than the value of a property measured by its income, any attempt to limit the securities to the amount shown by the first method would be in effect confiscation. Also, any proposal limiting the income of a property by reducing the amount of its securities in which the income was to be paid—the "theory of the arch and senatorial Wisconsin philosopher"—appeared to him to be "undiluted nonsense." [13]

In 1911 President Taft, at the request of Congress, appointed a Railroad Securities Commission, with Arthur T. Hadley as chairman, to investigate the issuance of railroad securities. The Commission suggested that the railroads should not oppose a "physical valuation" by the Interstate Commerce Commission, for such opposition would give "countenance to exaggerated estimates of the amount of water in railroad stocks"; that it should be recognized that this valuation would not necessarily be the controlling element in value, but merely one element in determining fair value. The physical valuation would not be used as a basis to cut down the amount of securities nor to prohibit the issue of additional securities, even if the amount outstanding exceeded the "physical valuation," for such action would destroy the investors' confidence.

The Commission reported that investors lacked confidence in railroads primarily because the public failed to understand the folly of protecting the interests of the shippers by taking away the rewards of the investors. Finally it stated that the evils resulting from compelling railroads to secure authorization from a government agency to issue any securities were "too serious to warrant its adoption at the present time." However, the government should insist on "accurate knowledge of the facts concerning the issue of securities and the expenditure of their proceeds." [14]

Notwithstanding the fear and trembling with which it was begun, regulation of railroads had made such progress by 1913 that Professor William Z. Ripley of Harvard could say that he had the pleasure of hearing the "foremost railroad presidents of the United States approving a policy of federal government regulation, which, when I approved it on paper ten years ago, was characterized in a letter from a leading railroad man to the president of my university as 'pernicious.' " [15]

GOVERNMENT INQUIRIES AND REGULATION OF BUSINESS

As society began to feel its way to an adjustment of government regulation and free enterprise, the states took up the search for information and proper organization of control. The pioneering advances in public utilities regulation were made by Wisconsin through its Railroad Commission. This Commission had been set up by La Follette with the aid of Commons. Balthasar H. Meyer, its chairman was Commons' departmental colleague. With this expert leadership, the Commission had no difficulty in bringing its views within the form of current economic doctrine. It declared that "in a general way the reasonable return [upon investment in public utilities] may be said to be that rate of return at which capital and business ability can be had for development. Theoretically it cannot be lower than this, for in that case no capital would enter the field." Under free competition it could not in the long run be higher, for the supply of capital would be increased, thereby reducing the rate of profits and interest. But free competition was out of the question because such utilities were monopolistic in their nature. Consequently, in their case, a "reasonable" return should be substituted for the standard otherwise established through competition. Since competition did not exist, the state must supply the regulating force through absolute legislation, and this regulation would be guided by what was reasonable under the circumstances. "To determine what is reasonable in any given case is a matter of investigation and judgment." [16]

New York went beyond the restricted area of public utilities into the study of large-scale business generally, especially "the money power." In 1906 the New York State legislature ordered an investigation into the abuses of life insurance companies. Under the skillful direction of Charles Evans Hughes, the committee soon revealed the close relationship among insurance companies, banks, large corporations, the stock market, and politics, which worked for the benefit of a "few insiders" under the headship of the so-called "money trust." As a result of its findings the investigating committee recommended, among other things, that no officer or director of an insurance company be permitted to engage either as principal, co-principal, agent, or beneficiary in any purchase, sale, or loan made by the corporation except to obtain a loan on his personal policy. No opportunity should be afforded for a conflict between his private interest and his official duty.[17]

Two years later Hughes, as governor of New York, appointed a committee to investigate the abuses of the New York Stock Exchange. The chairman of this committee was Horace White, and John Bates Clark was a member. Its report suggested various means by which stock-exchange authorities could check the notorious abuses practiced by members upon customers; however, it discouraged the idea of incorporating the exchange so that its actions might be subjected to more complete supervision by the public authority and courts. According to the report, under the current voluntary organization, stock-exchange officials had unlimited power to take instant disciplinary action against any errant member; but if those misdeeds had to be submitted to the courts, delays would result and discipline would be impaired. It considered even periodic government examination of the books of the members unwise.[18]

Congress in 1912 followed New York' lead and wrote a grand finale to this period's dramatization of the "money power" in the report of the famous Pujo Committee. The Committee accepted the fact that concentrated financial power and its leaders had rendered invaluable service in developing the country's prosperity. "There should be no disposition to hamper their activities," it said, "if a situation can be brought about where their capital, prestige, and connections can be independently employed in free and open competition," but it had reached a point where it levied a tribute on other people's money, and on every form of enterprise. For example, the report pointed out, it forced railroads into bankruptcy in order to realize the profits of reorganization. By their control of credit this "inner group" had been more destructive of competition than anything done by the trusts, for they struck at the "vitals of potential competition in every industry . . . under their protection." If this was allowed to continue, the report went on, it would not be possible to restore "normal competitive conditions in the industrial world." If the clogged arteries of credit "are opened so that they may be permitted freely to play their important part in the financial system, competition in large enterprises will become possible and business can be conducted on its merits."

As a partial means of freeing these arteries, the Committee recommended that no person should be "permitted to be a director in potentially competitive financial institutions, or in competitive industrial, railroad, or other corporations." It declared against a corporation's making contracts in which one of its management had private interests. This prohibition, however, was limited to bank officers and did not include even bank directors. It also protested against "security" holding companies as adjuncts to banks, but was rather vague about a remedy. The Committee did specify, however, that the issue of interstate railroad securities should be supervised by the Interstate Commerce Commission and that their sale should be subject to competitive bidding; but it thought that the power of Congress to regulate the sale of securities of industrial corporations engaged in interstate commerce was more doubtful and no recommendation with respect thereto could be made at this time.[19]

Brandeis insisted that the Committee had not gone far enough. It should, he said, have at least extended the prohibition against interlocking directorates to all bank and trust companies. "The Money Trust," he declared, "cannot be destroyed unless all classes of corporations are included in the prohibition of interlocking directorates and of transactions by corporations in which the management has a private interest."[20]

In 1912 the National Monetary Commission, which Congress had created in 1908, completed its report on banking reforms. The Commission was headed by the conservative Rhode Island senator, Nelson W. Aldrich, an outstanding Republican party leader. He conceived it to be the task of the Commission to secure an organization of capital and credit by which confidence could be firmly established and credit maintained under all circumstances. The research was done in good part by economists, headed by Professor A. Piatt Andrew of Harvard University. Its findings, comprising over forty volumes of published material, contained much valuable information on the state of money and banking in the United States and abroad.

The Commission's solution to the banking problem was in effect the re-establishment of the Bank of the United States, with extensive powers over the banking and monetary system of the country. The proposed institution, which would be called the National Reserve Association, would have headquarters in Washington and fifteen branches throughout the country. Its capital would be subscribed by the national banks, state banks, and trust companies. Government control would be limited. Of the forty-six members of the Board of Directors, thirty-nine would be chosen in a rather complex manner by the subscribing institutions, so that the National Reserve Association would be a "corporation with private stockholders," although its principal powers would be of a public or semi-public character. The primary reason for its existence would reside in its "ability at all times to sustain the public credit." [21]

Popular opinion was generally hostile to the National Reserve Association plan. In fact, it soon became obvious that the public was "determined to see nothing good in anything with which the name Aldrich is connected." [22] One of the proposal's most ardent supporters, Professor E. W. Goodhue of Colgate University, feared that the plan would be discarded because the "average citizen sees nothing in it but a scheme to still further entrench the so-called 'money trust.'" Such organizations as the American Bankers Association, he declared, had made commendable efforts to "educate the people along banking reform lines," but while large sums had been spent for propaganda, the work of education had just begun.[23] Goodhue's fear that the specific plan would be discarded was quickly enough realized, but many of its features and suggestions were later embodied in the Federal Reserve Act.

RESOURCES: NATURAL AND HUMAN

During this era, too, the national policy of conservation, begun on a slight scale in the nineties, was extended. Large areas of public lands containing great forests were set aside for the use of the entire nation, and public lands containing valuable minerals were withheld from sale. Irrigation projects and the reclamation of swamp lands were undertaken. In 1903 President Roosevelt vetoed a bill for the private construction of a power station at Muscle Shoals, Alabama, on the ground that the ultimate effect of granting such privileges should be considered in a comprehensive way, and that "a general policy appropriate to the new conditions caused by the advance in electrical science should be adopted under which these valuable rights will not be practically given away, but will be disposed of with full competition in such a way as will best substantiate the public interest." [24]

The conservation of human resources also showed signs of progress. Under the impact of public opinion aroused by the exposé of packing-house conditions in Upton Sinclair's novel *The Jungle*, Congress passed a Pure Foods Act. Labor legislation had harder sledding. State laws limiting hours were not readily accepted by the Supreme Court. While the legislation limiting hours for women was finally approved in 1908, when the Court upheld the Oregon ten-hour law for women, legislation limiting hours for men was accepted more reluctantly.

The Supreme Court was a good weathervane for indicating the winds of doctrine. In 1905, in *Lochner* v. *New York*, the Supreme Court declared unconstitutional the New York law limiting labor in bakeries to sixty hours a week. The Court declared that there was no "reasonable ground for interfering with the liberty of persons or the right of free contract, by determining the hours of labor, in the occupation of a baker. . . . The act is an illegal interference with the rights of individuals, both employers and employees, to make contracts regarding labor upon such terms, as they may think best or which they may agree upon with the other parties to such contracts." Twelve years passed before the Court practically reversed itself by upholding another Oregon ten-hour act.

Most liberals contended that the voiding of the labor legislation by the Court reflected its arch-conservatism. John R. Commons, however, insisted that the Court's lag was due in good part to the fact that the attorneys' briefs for desirable labor legislation were inadequate, because they emphasized the legalistic arguments. The Oregon ten-hour laws, he declared, had been approved because Brandeis, Felix Frankfurter, and Josephine Goldmark in their briefs had extensively utilized medical evidence to show the danger to health of long hours and the beneficial effect of short hours.

Along with the drift toward humane hours, the notion of a "living wage" was rapidly gaining momentum. This was popularized in the English-speaking world by the Fabian Socialists Beatrice and Sidney Webb in their *Industrial Democracy*. Much of the interest shown in the United States was due to the enthusiasm of the Reverend John A. Ryan, professor of ethics and economics at St. Paul's Seminary (later at Catholic University). The living wage, he declared in 1906, was to be achieved not only by moral suasion but also by "social effort," including the "activity both of private associations, such as labor unions, and of the State." Ryan vigorously pushed state minimum wage acts. These measures, he wrote, introduced a new principle into American labor regulations, because heretofore wage regulations had been regarded as something "too sacred to be touched by the profane hand of the legislator." In his opinion, legislation establishing decent minimum wages was fundamental and far-reaching because it affected almost all other standards and requisites of reasonable living and working conditions. If proper minimum wage laws were enacted, there would be no need to worry about such matters as housing, child labor, and social insurance.[25]

The Massachusetts Commission on Minimum Wage Boards sharply denied in its report of 1912 the existence of "an economic law which, by some mysterious but certain process, correlates earnings and wages." It asserted that "wages among the unorganized and lower grades of labor" were mainly the "result of tradition and of slight competition."[26] The upshot in Massachusetts was the passage in 1912 of a non-mandatory measure limited to women and minors. The following year, however, other states passed mandatory measures for these classes.[27]

These limited legislative measures failed, however, to reach the heart of labor difficulties. In 1902 the Pennsylvania anthracite coal strike revealed what these difficulties were. In that year plants were forced to shut down for lack of fuel. The Pennsylvania state militia was sent into the strike area, but no coal was obtainable. John Mitchell, president of the United Mine Workers of America, said that he would accept the decision of any arbitrators appointed by President Roosevelt. The operators, however, led by George F. Baer, refused arbitration and called upon the President to send federal troops to suppress the strikers. Roosevelt wrote Senator Marcus A. Hanna that the belligerent and uncompromising attitude of the operators would "beyond a doubt double the burden on us while standing between them and socialistic action." Ex-President Cleveland informed Roosevelt that he was "especially disturbed and vexed by the tone and substance of the operators' deliverances" and expressed sympathy with the idea that the government proceed against the operators under the Sherman Anti-Trust Act. Finally Roosevelt sent his Secretary of State, Elihu Root, to confer with J. P. Morgan, and three days later Morgan informed the President that the operators would agree to a President-appointed arbitration commission. Organized labor demanded representation on the commission, but the operators "were prepared to sacrifice everything," President Roosevelt said later, "and see civil war in the country rather than acquiesce." Roosevelt solved the problem by appointing as the "sociologist" member Edgar E. Clark, who was in reality Grand Chief of the Brotherhood of Railway Conductors.

The miners' legal representatives, among whom were Henry Demarest Lloyd, Clarence Darrow, Isaac Hourwich, and Louis D. Brandeis, arranged for more than two hundred human products of mining conditions to appear before the Commission. So terrible was the testimony of this "moving spectacle of horrors" that the Commission would not hear all of it.[28] The miners won a large part of their demands, but industrial peace seemed as distant as ever, for bloody strikes continued to sweep the nation.

As a result of such violence the problem of bringing labor and management together was forcibly brought to public attention. While arbitration boards were more widely used to settle wage disputes, it was hard to find any definite principles for guidance. The boards sought light from the established principles of political economy without much success. As one board succinctly summed up the case, it had searched vainly for "some [effective] theoretical relation, for a given branch of industry, between the amount of the income that should go to labor and the amount that should go to capital." [29]

To gain a better bargaining position labor pressed for the closed shop. Brandeis, although sympathetic to labor unions, opposed the closed shop because he felt it tended toward monopoly and no court could enforce it. But he favored strong employers' associations and strong labor organizations as the best means for amicably settling the conditions under which the men would work.[30] In opposition to the open shop Hourwich said before the Industrial Commission that the demand for the "recognition of the union" was the heart of unionism. Although regarded by the employers as an encroachment upon what was technically known as "the freedom of labor," if the men were to meet the employers on equal terms, the union must be able to represent all the workingmen. If it represented only half, the agreements would be only slightly respected by employers. A union could "sooner concede a reduction in the rate of wages than waive this fundamental demand." [31]

The Christian Socialist W. D. P. Bliss, sarcastically declared: "The open shop means, we are told, liberty, opportunity, Americanism, and individuality. It will give to the laborer freedom to work long hours, opportunity to accept such wages as employers please, chance to labor on the terms the masters make, liberty to become hand and soul the master's man. It will free the oppressed employer from that . . . socialistic legislation which is today limiting child labor, decreasing the employment of women by night, entailing needless expense for the safety, the modesty, the convenience of the workers. 'From all these and other evils may the good Free Shop deliver us,' so runs the siren song." [32]

In general, such an attitude as that of Bliss seemed to be getting a larger hearing, for the Socialist Party was growing. Its vote in presidential elections rose from 94,000 in 1900 to 875,000 in 1912. In part this was probably due to the fact that socialism was still essentially reformist, or, as some of its leading theoreticians said, "opportunist." John Spargo, a member of the party's National Executive Committee, declared: "Not human equality, but equality of opportunity to prevent the creation of artificial inequalities by privilege is the essence of socialism."

Spargo was peculiarly effective in enrolling under the banner of socialism many sincere seekers for social justice who had heretofore been disturbed by the notion that socialism was anti-religious. "The overwhelming majority of religious believers," wrote Spargo, "want, under the title of the Kingdom of God, a social order based on economic justice in which fraternalism shall rule, a social order not essentially different from that which the Socialist seeks to establish under the title of the Co-operative Commonwealth. It is to be hoped, then, that the Socialist movement will drop its hostility to religion; . . . that it will not charge against the free democracies of organized religious life in America today the evils of religious autocracy of other lands and other times. . . .

"On the other hand, religion needs the great spiritual passion, the exalted idealism and the faith with which the Socialist movement vibrates. . . , The Kingdom of God for which Jesus prayed, as did the older prophets of Israel before him, involved social justice and equal opportunity. . . . The two movements have a great common purpose: each cherishes an ideal of personal and social righteousness which requires for its attainment a social democracy." [33] By stressing these similarities, he said, perhaps the public mind could be prepared for socialism, without which the movement could not come into power.

This brought up the question of the relationship of American socialism to Marxism. Morris Hillquit, who presented the accepted socialist position, declared: "Socialism is a modern progressive movement, engaged in practical everyday struggles, and it cannot escape the influence of changing social conditions or growing economic knowledge. The international Socialist movement is still Marxian, because the fundamental social and economic doctrines of Karl Marx, his collaborators and disciples still hold good in the eyes of the vast majority of Socialists; but in the details of its methods and mode of action the Socialist movement today is quite different from what it was in the days of Marx." [34] And the lawyer Louis Boudin, who claimed to hold to the letter as well as the spirit of Marx, interpreted him in a manner contrary to the older tradition. In *The Theoretical System of Karl Marx* (1907) he declared that "Marx did not consider the growing poverty of the working class a *necessary* result of the evolution of capitalism." [35] In short, class war was being redirected toward class collaboration.

H. Gaylord Wilshire, publisher of the most widely read socialist journal, *Wilshire's Magazine*, presented a rather suggestive mixture of radical doctrines. Wilshire, who had for a time attended Harvard University, engaged in socialist journalism and socialist politics as his life work. He was active on both coasts of the United States as well as in Canada and England. At the same time he engaged in real-estate ventures on the Pacific Coast and gold-mining ventures in South America and California. Comments of prominent newspapers that he was a millionaire, the owner of several cattle ranches, a member of the billboard trust, a stockholder in the Standard Oil Company, and a bank president, he duly reprinted in his own journals as testimony of his financial wisdom.

Wilshire's most important essay was *The Solution of the Trust Problem* (1900). In it he worked out the following analysis: The stream of wealth flowing to the rich divides itself into two. One stream endeavors to satisfy the gluttonous expenditures and can be described by the general term "spent money." The other stream, which can be designated as "saved money," goes to building new instruments of production. This second channel, "saved money," has been the great sluiceway for carrying off the surplus product of labor and has avoided the constant menace of a money plethora in the present industrial style. But the rich, despite their luxurious tastes, have been forced to save increasing amounts, because of their inability to devise new means of spending. In fact, for them it requires more labor and pain to spend than to save. And this, together with the fact that the income of the masses is barely sufficient for subsistence, results eventually in "overproduction."

Wilshire admitted that the trust was a great instrument for efficient production but asserted that it could not permanently eliminate unemployment; and while American capitalists needed foreign fields for investment of their capital more urgently than did European capitalists, this outlet was the most illusory of solutions. According to his theory, trusts prevented the rising flood of surplus capital from swamping domestic industries, but they could not keep the flood from rising. Imperialism was a means of diverting to foreign shores the threatened deluge of domestic savings. The trust was not only a protection against undue competition, but also a highly effective labor-saving device. The increased industrial efficiency of the trust, together with its elimination of the wasteful duplication of machinery, would hasten by so much the completion of the world's industrial outfit.

At that point, capital would vainly seek profitable investment. Interest, determined by the amount of gain received by the last amount borrowed, would fall to zero, and banks would have idle money on their hands. "The last incentive for the poor man to be 'thrifty' will perish." The workers previously engaged in producing new machinery would join the unemployed in regiments. The trust would be defenseless against the new phase of industrial strife, for there would be no demand, because the unemployed would be without wages. This he considered inevitable, and the capitalist could do no more than temporarily stave off the time by such means as an eight-hour day.

Under these circumstances, he said, the best device for bolstering up the capitalist system would be a first-class war between the great powers followed by a prolonged civil war, with a great destruction of life and property. The need to replace the destroyed industrial equipment then would provide unlimited employment and an excellent source for investment of savings. But war could not last forever. The final disappearance of capitalism, therefore, was inevitable. And Wilshire, like Douai before him, prophesied that the growing difficulty of finding a profitable return would eventually end with the Rockefellers and Morgans handing over their holdings to society.

John A. Hobson, the noted heterodox English economist, saluted Wilshire for his exceptionally able account of the relation between capital and imperialism. "For many years," Hobson wrote Wilshire, "I have been striving, in vain, to drive into the dull or biased brains of our economists this analysis of 'overproduction' or 'underconsumption,' which is the connective tissue of these two cancerous growths upon the body politic. I wish you better luck in addressing the open ears of the people." [36]

Hobson, on his visit to America in 1903, made in his own right some rather interesting comments on the future of socialism. Hobson was not considered a socialist, but his books, especially *The Evolution of Modern Capitalism* and *Problems of Poverty*, were the most widely quoted works in socialist propaganda in England. He doubted at this time that there was much hope for a definite socialist movement in England or even in America, for the Anglo-Saxon people would not readily take to socialism of the "continental kind." They were not built that way. There were relatively few men of intellectual prestige—scientists, authors, artists, college professors, and the like—in the organized socialist movement in the Anglo-Saxon world, whereas in Germany and Italy it was the reverse. There they were accustomed to a more positive government policy than were Englishmen and Americans. Rightly or wrongly, the current view of socialism, to which many doctrinaire theorists seemed to subscribe, he said, was that of a huge bureaucracy in which there would be no opportunity for individual development or enterprise. To them he pointed out that side by side with the great concentration of various industries, new industries were constantly springing up, and these should be encouraged as private enterprise. True, some socialists disclaimed any intention of destroying private property in its entirety. But Hobson claimed that his quarrel with the socialists' method was precisely because they did not make this clear. They persisted in publicly demanding the socialization of everything when they meant only some things. They should discriminate between things which could, and things which could not, be privately owned with safety. In England the socialists were too rigid, in the continental fashion, and they repelled instead of inviting support. If they were more tolerant and practical, a strong alliance might be built between them and the more progressive labor unions and the advanced radicals. They could be gotten together in a program including some measure of land nationalization, government ownership of the railways, some means for the security of the trade unions, and, most important of all, government banking. Alongside this a sound municipal policy might be pursued.

The affected industries, he said, should not be confiscated, but purchased at a compensation agreed upon. This would not lead, as some claimed, to a tremendous interest-bearing public debt. Suppose a number of important enterprises were socialized on the basis of compensation for a period of over thirty years. When the initial payment was made, the receivers would look for some form of safe investment, and all they could do would be to invest in public stock. Consequently the rate of interest might easily fall to zero, in fact become a minus quality altogether.[37]

Pierrepont B. Noyes, son of the founder of the famous religious communistic Oneida Community in New York, and himself largely responsible for that very profitable offshoot, "Oneida Community Plate" silverware, made the interesting prophecy in 1903 that large-scale communism would very likely establish itself first in Russia rather than in the Anglo-Saxon world. In *Wilshire's Magazine* he wrote: We hear of "communism discredited on the grounds of common sense and history," that customs, habits, prejudices, and institutions preclude a change. But the Anglo-Saxons might well ponder whether they were not, after all, posing as judge in a case where they would prove to be only helpless observers of the growth of a great new power. "For two hundred years the genius of enlightened selfishness has been carrying civilization forward as never before in the history of the world, and the Anglo-Saxon as the embodiment of this principle has necessarily been the leader of the movement. . . . To expect a people who have achieved their supremacy by the efficiency of their selfishness to become the leader of a movement based on individual unselfishness may prove futile, but if so, then that point in commercial history where the competitive principle has reached the limit of effective development will be the exact point in evolutionary history where natural selection will pick from among the races one more altruistic then the rest and force it inevitably to the front as a new leader of the nations."

It is asserted, he wrote, that no power can stop the trusts because they make for superior economy and efficiency. For the same reason, and with the same lack of resistance, communism will make its way. If the Slavs have a temperament which will permit them easily to unite in communal organizations, and find individual enjoyment in the welfare of the whole community, they are the race of the future. Communism's ability to produce wealth, both for the individual and the nation, having been demonstrated in one or two instances, will spread like the "trust" epidemic in the United States. Nothing will stay its advance or compete with its products. America will certainly awake to find herself industrially at the mercy of Russia, just as Europe today finds itself unexpectedly at the mercy of the United States.[38]

To the conservatives, the growing audience for the socialist theories seemed bad enough, but when the labor movement seemed to be taking them up, the danger of action became critical. In 1905 the Industrial Workers of the World (I.W.W.)[39] was organized; it was soon judged to be a movement akin to revolutionary socialism. It had as its philosophy a combination of the notions entertained by the defunct Knights of Labor, the philosophical anarchists, and the earlier Socialistic Labor Party, but it was more militant. It was basically an attempt to found a labor organization, embracing industries as units, on socialist principles. In effect, it would be the labor arm of the socialist movement. It would be prepared to operate industry and undertake the necessary administrative functions on that day when socialism achieved victory and the State as a guardian of capitalism was eliminated. Among its sponsors were the two rival socialist leaders, Debs and De Leon, and the militant socialistic labor leader "Big Bill" (William D.) Haywood.

The organization proclaimed in its constitution that an uncompromising struggle must continue between the working class and the employing class until all "the toilers come together, on the political as well as on the industrial field," to take and hold that which they produced by their labor, "through an economic organization of the working class, without affiliation with any political party." De Leon, in *The Preamble of the Industrial Workers of the World* (1905), explained that the ballot was an essential weapon because the people were accustomed to universal suffrage. But the moment labor should acquire political power, the need for geographic voting would cease and society would appear in its new administrative garb of organization by industries. But if labor achieved political power, and was unprepared to operate industry, a social catastrophe would result. Under such circumstances, with capitalists still controlling industry, production would cease.

The organization had been in existence little more than a year when major defections took place. The difficulties lay partly in the conflict of personalities and partly in differences as to tactics. De Leon was expelled, and Debs withdrew. The phrase "political field" was eliminated from the platform, which now read that the class struggle must go on "until the workers of the world organize as a class, take possession of the earth and the machinery of production, and abolish the wage system." Yet Haywood, who was now the dominant figure in the I. W. W., was still serving on the National Executive Committee of the Socialist Party and was ardently supporting its presidential candidate, Eugene V. Debs.

The leaders of the I. W. W. increasingly stressed in their literature the need for "direct action," which was supposed to be distinguished from political action and to mean the "organized industrial power of the workers." They introduced the colorful French word "sabotage," which was almost interchangeable in their literature with the none-too-clear concept "direct action." One I. W. W. official defined sabotage as implying the "withdrawal of efficiency from the work." A contemporary student of the I. W. W., John Graham Brooks, who lectured at leading universities, declared that in substance sabotage was as old as the strike, and that trade unions were as familiar with it as with other weapons. It was a "specialized form of making trouble for the employer." It included such practices as clogging machinery and literally carrying out rules so as to impede production; in fact, almost anything that would severely damage the employer without resulting in the employee's loss of his job. More broadly, "sabotage" or "strike on the job" was "any practice designed to slow up or impede productive industry." [40] However, according to the outstanding authority on the I. W. W., Professor Paul F. Brissenden, while there was much talk of direct action, the organization avoided violence and sabotage. [41]

In *Industrial Socialism*, written in collaboration with Frank Bohn, a highly educated leader in the movement, Haywood in 1911 presented the I. W. W.'s interpretation of Marxian socialism. [42] The treatise appears to have been influenced as much by the current climate of American reformism as by Marxism. For instance, in explaining how wages had gone down while profits had risen, the authors declared that prices had risen and would continue to rise, not because the trusts could arbitrarily set prices, but because the currency in use had been diluted. The capitalist government had printed paper currency far in excess of the gold reserve, and as a consequence the cost of living was soaring. Wages did not rise proportionately because the increasing use of machinery under capitalist control resulted in greater competition for jobs by labor.

The authors broke with the usual American socialist view by emphasizing the doctrine of "economic determinism." According to their account, Marx showed that an "individual or a nation or a class will finally come to think that right which is to his material advantage. . . . When the worker, either through experience or a study of Socialism, comes to know this truth, he acts accordingly. He retains absolutely no respect for the property 'rights' of the profit-takers. He will use any weapons that will win his fight. He knows that the present laws of property are made by and for the capitalists. Therefore he does not hesitate to break them."

A sharp controversy arose over whether this paragraph was sound socialism. Debs declared that all socialists were agreed on principles but differed on tactics. As a revolutionist, said Debs, he could not respect capitalist property law, nor scruple against violating it. "If I had the force to overthrow these despotic laws, I would use it without an instant's hesitation or delay," but not having it, he was a law-abiding citizen—under protest; that is, he said, he abided by the law but bided his time. By the same reasoning, Debs proposed that the Socialist Party declare against sabotage and every form of "violence and destructiveness suggested by what is known as 'direct action.' " [43]

This reluctant reformism finally won the victory over revolutionary direct action. At the convention in 1912 the Socialist Party passed a resolution that "any member of the party who opposes political action, or advocates crime, sabotage, or other methods of violence as a weapon of the working class to aid in its emancipation, shall be expelled from membership in this party." [44] Haywood was removed from the National Executive Committee by a referendum vote. The *International Socialist Review*, however, pointed out that the applause of the "capitalist" press misrepresented this action. The editorial emphasized that the weapon of industrial unionism was a strike at one time by all workers in a given industry in order to force higher wages, shorter hours, and an ever-greater degree of labor control over shop management. Industrial unionism did not propose to destroy factories by dynamite, but to operate them for the benefit of the working class. It was "Socialism with its 'working clothes on,' to use Haywood's phrase." [45]

Many Socialists could not forget that Haywood and his group had gone out into the field and factory to organize the unskilled, the casual and migratory laborers, and that they had led the recent dramatic struggle to better the intolerable labor conditions in the textile mills in Lawrence, Massachusetts. A large group of New York Socialist intellectuals protested that the anti-sabotage clause made for persecution and was anti-democratic. They protested in particular "that we know Comrade Haywood to believe in political action, and to have been of great service to our party in helping it to solve the difficult problems that confront the working class upon the industrial field. Instead of exaggerating inevitable differences of opinion, instead of reviving De Leonistic tactics of personal incrimination, heresy-hunting, and disruption, we should make use of the special talents of every member within our ranks, and in this way secure loyal service and co-operation. We believe in a united working class." [46]

The most stinging criticism came from the gallant Helen Keller in her plea for harmony. She deeply regretted the attack made on Haywood: "It fills me with amazement to see such a narrow spirit, such an ignoble strife between two factions which should be one, and that, too, at a most critical period in the struggle of the proletariat. What! Are we to put difference of party tactics before the desperate needs of the workers? Are we no better than the capitalist politicians who stand in the high places and harangue about petty matters, while millions of the people are underpaid, underfed, thrown out of work and dying? While countless women and children are breaking their hearts and ruining their bodies in long days of toil, we are fighting one another. Shame on us!" [47]

This desire to get on with the work of reform was present in all camps. Even so strong an opponent of the Populist movement as Frank LeRond McVey, president of the University of North Dakota, admitted in 1912 the change in the political climate. In his words: "The nation is now attempting to find a way to preserve its republican character and to continue the maintenance of democracy. We have gone a long way since the creation of the Constitution and the establishment of the federal government, a long way from the view that things can be accomplished by letting them go their own way. Little by little regulation has come about; the theory of non-interference has been abandoned, and we are setting up here and there various types of governmental machinery to protect the interests of the common people. But this development which is to be seen at the present time is not going on in accordance with the socialistic view. The tendency is toward a new type of communism whose attitude is determined by the question of expediency or the wisdom of the courts. Labor disputes and arbitration, the regulation of immigration, the judiciary control of railway rights, interference in matters that affect the health of the community, the establishment of building regulations, all point to a new view of government." [48]

WOODROW WILSON: THE SPIRIT OF THE NEW LIBERALISM

The 1912 presidential campaign testified to this widespread desire for reform, with every candidate including something of its spirit in his platform. Republican President William Howard Taft, seeking re-election, declared that the party was opposed to special privileges and monopoly. The platform pointed out that the Republican administration had passed the Interstate Commerce Act and the Sherman Anti-Trust Act and favored legislation supplementing the Sherman Act so that those seeking to obey the law would have a guide. "Certainty should be given to existing law, . . . prohibiting combinations and monopolies . . . in order that no part of the field of business opportunity may be restricted by monopoly or combination, that business success honorably achieved may not be converted into crime, and that the right of every man to acquire commodities, and particularly the necessaries of life, in an open market uninfluenced by the manipulation of trusts or combinations may be preserved." The platform also called for a federal trade commission to take over functions now exercised by the courts, and thus promote promptness in administering the law.

The Progressive Party, that faction of the Republican Party which chose Roosevelt as its standard bearer, called for a number of labor reforms. On trusts, it too wanted a federal trade commission, to do for industrial corporations what the Interstate Commerce Commission did for railroads. Roosevelt proclaimed the need for the "social regeneration" of business to prevent insurance, banking, and railroad scandals. The concentration of modern business, in some degree, he said, was both inevitable and necessary for national and international business efficiency, but the power had been abused. "Wherever it is practicable," he continued, "we propose to preserve competition; but where under modern conditions competition . . . cannot be successfully restored, then the government must step in and . . . supply the needed control." [49]

Curiously enough, however, under the presumably conservative President Taft the government had been more active in "trust-busting" than under Roosevelt. The fact that a former Morgan partner, George W. Perkins, was one of Roosevelt's chief sponsors suggested, as Brandeis claimed, that the Progressives viewed private monopoly in industry as not necessarily evil.

The Democratic Party, in the language of Brandeis, declared that "competition can be and should be maintained in every branch of private industry; that competition can be and should be restored in those branches of industry in which it has been suppressed by the trusts"; and that no "methods of regulation ever have been or can be devised to remove the menace inherent in private monopoly and overweening commercial power." [50]

Because of the split in the Republican Party, the Democrats won the election. The Democratic candidate, Governor Woodrow Wilson of New Jersey, was a new phenomenon, a scholar in politics. After receiving his doctorate in political science in 1886 at Johns Hopkins, Wilson began an academic career that culminated in the presidency of his alma mater, Princeton, in 1902. In his background the conservative note was predominant, but there were also views to suggest that he was open to humanitarian trends. At Princeton he had thoroughly imbibed Lyman Atwater's conservative economic teachings, but at Johns Hopkins, as a graduate student, he had studied under Ely.

Wilson's ideas were of mixed quality. In one essay he both praised Francis Bowen for his proper historical spirit and sound appreciation of American circumstances, and expressed unstinted admiration for Francis A. Walker's work.[51] His use of Walker's treatise as an economics textbook and his high praise of the progressive spirit of John Bates Clark's *Philosophy of Wealth* suggested that he was taking into account new insights in economics. As another Ely student put it in 1902: "Isn't it fine that Woodrow Wilson is to be President of Princeton? He is, of course, pretty conservative, but nevertheless the various social sciences ought to stand a pretty good show under his administration." [52]

After his election as governor of New Jersey, Wilson embarked on a program of curbing the excesses of corporation finance. But in accepting the Democratic nomination for president he specifically declared that "competition cannot be established by law against the drift of a world-wide tendency," nor is "business upon a grand scale by a single organization—call it corporation or what you will— necessarily dangerous to the liberties, even the economic liberties, of a great people like our own, full of intelligence and of indomitable energy. . . . We shall never return to the old order of individual competition, and . . . the organization of business upon a grand scale of co-operation is, up to a certain point, itself normal and inevitable. . . . I am not afraid of anything that is normal." [53]

However, Wilson was no clearer than other economists as to just where the line was to be drawn between large business and monopoly. But he did say that "the government must intervene . . . to take care of the beginner, . . . of the new businessman, . . . the little businessman, and see that any unfair interference with the growth of his business shall be a criminal offense." And perhaps his general attitude toward business was best expressed by his warm approval of the Wisconsin legislation regulating public service corporations. The men controlling the corporations, he said, fought the regulatory plans of that state as they "would have fought the prospect of ruin; and what happened? Regulation of the most thoroughgoing sort was undertaken, and the result was that the securities of those companies were virtually guaranteed to purchasers. Instead of being speculative in value, they were known to be absolutely secure investments, because a disinterested agency, a commission representing the community, looked into the conditions of this business, guaranteed that there was not water enough to drown in, guaranteed that there was business enough and plant enough to justify the charges and to secure a return of legitimate profit; and every thoughtful man connected with such enterprises in Wisconsin now takes off his hat to the men who originated the measures once so much debated. The chief benefit was, not regulation, but frank disclosure and the absolutely open and frank relationship between business and government." To answer those who thought such measures the first steps toward socialism, Wilson made it clear that he did not believe in socialism. But "if you want to oust socialism, you have got to propose something better. It is a case . . . of 'put up or shut up.' You cannot oppose hopeful programs by negations." [54]

Wilson considered the tariff the real problem. "Every business question in this country," he stated, "comes back, sooner or later, to the question of the tariff," [55] and the tariff, he felt, should be cautiously reduced in such a manner as to revive the energies of the business community. Wilson's first request to Congress, as President of the United States, was for the reform of the tariff.

Having succeeded in obtaining some reductions in it, he then asked for the reform of the banking and currency system. Congress must give the businessmen a banking and currency system, he said, which would enable them to "make use of the freedom of enterprise and of individual initiative which we are about to bestow upon them" through tariff reform. They should create a currency "readily, elastically responsive to sound credit." The control of the new system of banking and of issue must be vested in the "government itself, so that the banks may be the instruments, not the masters, of business and of individual enterprise." [56]

Following the broad terms laid down by Wilson, Representative Carter Glass of Virginia and Senator Robert L. Owen of Oklahoma pushed through the measure that became the Federal Reserve Act. The usual opposition to a central bank was avoided by setting up twelve regional Federal Reserve banks with the stock owned by the national banks in the districts and those state banks and trust companies that joined the system. But at the head of the entire system was the Federal Reserve Board appointed by the President with Senate approval.

Under the scheme a member bank could rediscount at its regional Federal Reserve Bank short-term commercial paper and paper issued for the purpose of carrying on trading in federal securities, but rediscounting of paper issued for carrying on other trading in stocks, bonds, or investment securities was prohibited. Through rediscounting, the member banks would receive a new currency, the Federal Reserve notes. These notes the Federal Reserve Bank could obtain by pledging with the Federal Reserve Agent—who would also be chairman and a director of the Federal Reserve Bank—a 100 per cent collateral consisting of gold and paper eligible for rediscount. The Federal Reserve Bank would have to maintain a 40 per cent gold reserve against Federal Reserve notes in circulation, but the gold given as collateral for the notes could be considered part of the reserve. These new notes would be similar to the "asset" currency so long demanded by Laughlin and many other economists.

Bryan, who was Secretary of State, had always objected to asset currency as "undemocratic" and a free gift to bankers of the public money.[57] But Wilson convinced him that as obligations of the government the Federal Reserve notes were actually government currency. The situation became amusing when some staunch Republicans and Progressives, sounding strangely like greenbackers, denounced the bill as playing into the hands of the "money trust," while that former ardent free silverite, George H. Shibley, highly extolled the measure as the fruits in good part of his labors in the days of the Bureau of Economic Research.[58]

The main point of controversy was over the demand of the banks that they be directly represented on the governing board. Glass himself had in his first draft given the banks a minority representation, but Wilson ruled it out. When Glass brought a delegation of bankers to see the President, Wilson challenged the bankers to "point to a government commission in the United States or any civilized country of the earth upon which private interests had representation." Glass reported, "The bankers were dumb, and I was converted." He agreed that in the end there might be too many bankers on the Board rather than too few.[59]

The measure seemed to please practically all interests, and Wilson, in signing it on December 23, 1913, expressed surprise at the sudden almost unanimous acceptance of this measure by public opinion: "I say 'surprised' because it seems as if it had suddenly become obvious to men who had looked at it with too critical an eye that it was really meant in their interest." [60] Wilson's amazement was justified in the light of the many decades of bitter argument which had raged over many of the monetary issues the new system was attempting to solve.

There was considerable opposition, however, to the third main step in Wilson's reform program on trusts and monopolies. "Private monopoly is indefensible and intolerable," Wilson declared. His program, he hoped, would be "comprehensive but not a radical or unacceptable" one, and the items of reform would be those changes which "opinion deliberately sanctions and for which business waits," such as preventing "interlockings of the personnel of the directorates of great corporations—banks and railroads, industrial, commercial, and public service bodies." This would bring a "new spirit of initiative, new blood, into the management of our great business enterprises." Furthermore, since businessmen now recognized the injustice the financiers had committed against the railroad systems, the country would, he thought, willingly accept a law empowering the Interstate Commerce Commission to superintend and regulate the financing of railroad development. Another forward step would be an explicit legislative definition of the existing anti-trust law. Nothing hampered business so much as uncertainty, he said; monopolistic practices, having been abundantly exposed, should be explicitly and specifically forbidden by statute. An interstate trade commission should be established, not to make terms with monopoly or assume control of business, but to serve only as an indispensable instrument of information and publicity, as a clearing house for the facts by which both the public and the managers of great business undertakings could be guided. Holding companies should be prohibited, and holders of large blocks of stock in a number of companies might be allowed voting rights only in one company.[61]

Congress refused to extend the power of the Interstate Commerce Commission, but it was willing to establish a Federal Trade Commission. This Commission, which superseded the Bureau of Corporations, was given the authority to order business engaged in interstate commerce to cease "unfair methods of competition" in commerce; that is, the Commission had the power to issue "cease and desist" orders, and it was authorized to seek aid from the courts when business failed to comply. Along with this, Congress passed the Clayton Act, which limited common directorships and forbade a variety of practices, including the acquisition of stock by one corporation in like enterprises in commerce when its effect "may be to substantially lessen competition . . . or tend to create a monopoly." It also declared it illegal for anyone engaged in commerce within the jurisdiction of the United States to discriminate in price between different purchasers of commodities "where the effect of such discrimination may be to substantially lessen competition or tend to create a monopoly in any line of commerce." The proponents recognized that "fair competition" was a shifting concept, but to them this was no serious disadvantage, for the Commission would be composed of economists as well as lawyers and men experienced in industry.[62]

Labor made distinct gains during the Wilson administration. One event, the importance of which has generally been overlooked, was the establishment of a separate cabinet department of labor, which was "to foster, promote, and develop the welfare of the wage earners of the United States." The first Secretary of Labor was a founder of the United Mine Workers of America, William B. Wilson. The creation of the post marked the official recognition of the existence of a permanent wage-earning class. Furthermore, Wilson had written into the Clayton Act a declaration which Samuel Gompers described as labor's "Magna Charta." In summary: "The labor of a human being is not a commodity or article of commerce"; nothing in the anti-trust laws shall be construed to forbid the existence and operation of trade unions or agricultural cooperatives or to forbid them from carrying out the "legitimate objects thereof"; nor shall they be considered "illegal combinations or conspiracies in restraint of trade, under the anti-trust laws." Also, injunctions were prohibited in labor disputes growing out of the "terms or conditions of employment, unless necessary to prevent irreparable injury to property."

This "Magna Charta" did not immediately grant the kind of freedom that Gompers had hoped for, because it was open to many interpretations, arising in part from public doubt about its advisability. Equally controversial was Wilson's support of an eight-hour day for railroad trainmen. In 1916, after all efforts had failed to arbitrate the dispute between the railroad brotherhoods and the companies, he asked Congress to pass an eight-hour law. "The eight-hour day now undoubtedly has the sanction of the judgment of society in its favor," he declared. The "whole spirit of the time and the preponderant evidence of recent economic experience" clearly support it.[63]

Wilson's position on anti-trust legislation and his advocacy of hours-of-work restrictions, coupled with his support of La Follette's Seamen's Act, which improved conditions on American ships, led to his being charged with radicalism. The imputation also passed from the President to the Democratic Party. Wilson replied by demanding a realistic view of the country's economic position. If radicalism, he said, means a "constant attempt . . . to keep the legislative action of the country abreast of the extraordinary changes of time and circumstances, I can only say that I see no other way to keep the law adjusted to fact and to the actual economic and personal relations of our society. But radicalism is a matter of spirit rather than form, and . . . the truest conservatism consists in constant adaptation." [64]

Wilson, by proceeding on a variety of fronts for reform, was manifesting the view that the development of the nation required balancing manifold interests. It is this that makes him the exponent of the new liberalism.

Thus during the first years of the twentieth century the spirit of reform took possession of the country. The question was not whether to change or not to change, but how to change. Counsels were widely divided between encouraging and destroying the trusts, between centralizing and decentralizing the financial system, between expanding and limiting the labor unions, between stimulating and stabilizing free enterprise. The one premise upon which nearly all reformers agreed, although not always consciously, was the intervention of government in economics, and the economic theorists were increasingly forced to rephrase their subject in terms of political economy.

CHAPTER XV

New Economic Stimulants

THE realm of economics was invigorated not only by political reforms but also by a variety of intellectual movements. New developments in philosophy and psychology had considerable impact on the study of economics, as did also the growth in statistics and economic history. As a result, there were a number of innovations and even radically new viewpoints in economics. The doctrine of marginal productivity remained a focal point but was subject to a variety of interpretations.

ECONOMIC PSYCHOLOGY

In philosophy and psychology the findings of John Dewey and his students at the University of Chicago were attracting considerable attention. Calling their viewpoint "functional" or "pragmatic," they expounded a variant of William James' proposition that the "idea is essentially active." George H. Mead, agreeing with Dewey, stated that instead of a psychical state dependent upon a physical excitation, "investigation shows in every case an activity which in advance must determine where attention is directed and give the psychical state the very content which is used in identifying it. . . . What we see, hear, feel, taste, and smell depends upon what we are doing, and not the reverse. In our purposively organized life we inevitably come back to the previous conduct as the determining condition of what we sense at any one moment, and the so-called external stimulus is the occasion for this and not its cause." [1]

In discussions of social problems the James-Dewey type of philosophy was vague at times, but at least it lacked that extreme conservatism so characteristic of the old Common Sense philosophers in their handling of social problems. And it led Mead to welcome the change in the worker's psychical state. He was annoyed at the failure of European philosophers and psychologists to understand that modern socialism was not Marxian and utopian but reformist and "opportunist." Having lost confidence in "any delineation of the future condition of society," modern socialists, he said, were acquiring better critical standpoints. He felt that socialistic thinking of this type opened the minds of the laborers to the fact that wages and working hours were not the simple dicta of employers but the outcome of the forces creating the fabric of civilization. Also, socialistic thinking had led to the rise of the trained expert who represented the labor union in conference with the employer and recognized the common situation between employer and employee upon which alone any arrangement or compromise could be made.[2]

William McDougall of Oxford, later of Harvard and Duke Universities, created interest among economists by his emphasis on instincts in *Introduction to Social Psychology* (1908). He asserted that traditional political economy was useless and that what economic science needed was a more adequate psychology to replace its hedonism, which was all he thought the pleasure-pain psychology of economics really amounted to. The success of monopolies in reducing prices was illustrative, he said, of defective conclusions drawn from hedonistic premises.

The instinct of pugnacity, according to McDougall, was a leading factor in the evolution of the higher forms of social organization. The "more the pugnacious instinct impelled primitive societies to warfare, the more rapidly and effectively must the fundamental social attributes of men have been developed" in the surviving societies. In such a society the social organization of the warlike tribes was more efficient and stable, because the chiefs attained unquestioned obedience. Each man identified himself with the entire community and loyally performed his social duties. In the higher social organization the instinct of pugnacity was replaced by its derivative, emulation, molded by a severe process of military selection. This desire to "get the better of others, to emulate, to excel," was the driving motive in beneficent commercial activity.

McDougall's instinct psychology was not as radically new as it might seem at first sight; still it helped to direct attention to what have been well called non-economic motives. Even such a sturdy "old school" economist as Taussig was sufficiently caught in the excitement to step for a moment outside the conventional methods of economics to examine the "psychology of money-making." He described his *Inventors and Money-Makers* (1915) as intended to "arouse interest in the important topics that lie on the borderline between economics and psychology and ethics."

ECONOMIC INTERPRETATIONS OF HISTORY

In these same years economic history came into full repute and commanded wide interest. Thanks in good part to the work of such German academic economists as Werner Sombart, and the English thinker John A. Hobson, "capitalism," a suspect Marxian term, became somewhat respectable, its growth a matter of interest, and Marx's materialistic interpretation of history, properly qualified, a source of fruitful leads. Thus Seligman in *The Economic Interpretation of History* (1902) pointed out that his own doctrine was not socialistic and that the staunchest individualist could believe in it. To him the only bond between the doctrine of socialism and that of the economic interpretation of history was that both were originated by Marx. Seligman's book enjoyed a tremendous success because, as Patten explained, it stripped "Marxian doctrines of their materialistic interpretation and gave them a sentimental setting." [3]

Charles W. Macfarlane noted at the time that economists were "wont to cry out for an economic interpretation of history," but failed "to realize, despite the criticism of the 'German historical school,'" that there was "an even more crying need for a historic interpretation of economics." He then presented his own economic interpretation. He referred to Montesquieu's remarkable bit of philosophic insight: "'Capital is protestant.' . . . Only three words, and yet this coupling of an economic phenomenon with a corresponding religious phenomenon contains more of the real philosophy of history than is to be found in whole volumes by other writers."

Macfarlane, asking himself what the sentence meant, answered that perhaps the essential difference between Catholicism and Protestantism was that the former rested on the principle of authority, and the latter on the right of the individual to decide for himself even questions of religious belief. Perhaps, he said, it meant that England, the greatest Protestant country, was also the most advanced industrial nation, and so had the largest investment in machinery or capital goods. In addition, there was the well-known fact that, by revoking the Edict of Nantes, France drove out large numbers of her most valuable artisans and thereby long retarded her development. But Macfarlane wanted to go a little deeper and discover why the artisan or the man with industrial training had been more prone to protest against the authority of Rome than the laborers on the farms held under feudal tenure. When the masses were engaged in tilling land owned by some feudal lord, they were hardly likely, he thought, to develop a strong faith in their individual judgment, even in matters affecting their daily toil. The results of their labor, being subject to sun and season, were beyond their control. Under such circumstances men naturally turned to the power that controlled these elements or to those they thought had a voice potential with that power. This in his theory was what had caused the authority of the Catholic hierarchy to grow and flourish in the days "when the feudal lords sat at the 'seat of customs.'"

With the rise of manufactures and the growth of commerce, according to his interpretation, men changed. No longer were natural elements so important, and no longer could it be assumed that a given effort would invariably be followed by the same result. "Man's confidence in his own judgment grew apace," and this confidence was strengthened by his association with his fellow-man, also an outgrowth of the new type of industrial activity. Soon this self-confidence was extended to the domain of political opinion and religious beliefs, and civil and religious liberty was the outcome. Thus the growth of commerce and manufactures, or of capital goods, modified the psychology of mankind so as to compel a corresponding change in political opinion and religious beliefs.[4]

The growth of combinations, Macfarlane felt, was in accord with his economic interpretation of freedom and advance. These great combinations, however, if they were to stay, must eventually be transformed from stock-jobbing schemes into permanent investment. Those in control must provide conditions resulting in regular and permanent income. When industry had been split among a large number of promoters, each could seek his own advantage without seriously considering whether he was ruining others. But as large portions of industry were brought under control, he said, the effects of this egoism would become manifest. "For this destruction of the purchasing power of others must eventually react on general industry" and cause periods of overproduction.

As for the current situation, he said, in order to supply the abnormal demand of the more active periods, enormous investments had been made in plants that were absolutely idle during the long periods of depression. This created the conditions for a continuing economic development. As he saw it, if the economy in management, which these great combinations effected, was sufficient reason for their existence, then surely the importance of the greater economy resulting from regulating production and the consequent avoidance of unnecessary duplication of plant would not be lost upon those controlling the combines. "They will be constrained to realize that an arbitrary exercise of their monopoly power carries with it the seeds of their own destruction." Furthermore, they will be compelled to deal with their employees in a more "liberal spirit," not merely because of the political and industrial pressure of trade unions, but because they will recognize that "if the products of all industries are to find purchasers, the employees must be allowed the means with which to purchase and the time in which to enjoy these commodities." This does not mean, he said, that the men controlling industry will "suddenly become altruistic or that organized labor will shortly find its occupation gone. On the contrary, the pressure that organized labor can exert will be of growing importance for a long time to come, but it will meet with less intemperate opposition from employers as industrial combinations grow in strength and in that broader policy which the demand for permanent investments will impel their management to adopt." [5]

At this time a greater interest was shown in the economic influences in American history. One of the most popular theories that developed was that of the frontier. This had immediately become widely adopted after the presentation of Frederick Jackson Turner's "The Significance of the Frontier in American History" (1893). To Turner the ever-shifting frontier had been the source of democratic ideals, and had maintained them by providing a "safety valve" for the ever-increasing numbers of the discontented and propertyless that threatened "older" areas. The thesis was by no means new, and many American historians had harbored the notion. But previous historians had generally used the thesis as evidence of the raw, uncouth extreme egalitarianism that was responsible for all that was bad in American society and that must disappear with its maturing. Turner too found much to deprecate in the frontier attitude, but he also emphasized those democratic values which liberal Americans cherished. Much of what Turner disapproved of, especially a proneness to paper money and monetary panaceas, was simply a part of tradition rather than actual historical fact, and betrayed the conditioning of Turner's thinking by the current Populist movement. The frontier thesis also led students to oversimplify some of the basic problems of the modern industrial age, especially that of labor.[6] But it had the merit of counteracting current explanations of American development that ran in terms of divine nepotism or of descent from the ancient forests of Germany.

More specifically economic and even more disturbing to the uncritical idealistic concept of the origins of American institutions was Charles A. Beard's famous *An Economic Interpretation of the Constitution* (1913). Actually this book, along with his earlier *The Supreme Court and the Constitution* (1912), was, in part, an attempt to meet J. Allen Smith's charge that the Constitution was a reactionary document. In the earlier work on the Supreme Court, Beard granted that the Constitution had been formulated and carried through by the large propertied interests, but he claimed that these interests represented the forces of progress. In the chapter called the "Spirit of the Constitution" he argued that it was the radical "populist" philosophy of Jefferson and his distrust of government that had led to the establishment of that weak and inefficient instrument of government, the Articles of Confederation.

In Beard's words: "The makers of the Federal Constitution represented the solid, conservative, commercial, and financial interests of the country. . . . [These] interests, made desperate by the imbecilities of the Confederation and harried by state legislatures, roused themselves from their lethargy, drew together in a mighty effort to establish a government . . . that would be strong enough to pay the national debt, regulate interstate and foreign commerce, provide for national defense, prevent fluctuations in the currency created by paper emissions, and control the propensities of legislative majorities to attack private rights."

In *An Economic Interpretation of the Constitution* Beard elaborated his thesis by drawing a detailed analysis of the economic interests of the Constitutional Convention. He found that for the most part they represented the interests of large mobile wealth, enterprise, and capital; the opposition came from the "little man," the debtors, the landed interests. His main point was that the large enterprising interests were those making for the growth of national wealth and power. He did say that had the men of the Convention been doctrinaires, like those at the Frankfurt Assembly of 1848, they would have failed miserably; but, being practical men, "they were able to build the new government upon the only foundations which could be stable: fundamental economic interests." [7] But such statements were infrequent and were lost in the multiple details so that when the book appeared Beard, like Smith before him, was denounced as subversive.

A little later A. T. Hadley, in *Undercurrents in American Politics* (1915), was able to express Beard's ideas more succinctly. He too brought in the "little man." "A large majority [of the Constitutional Convention] were men of substance; a considerable minority were men of wealth," Hadley declared. "They had viewed with apprehension the readiness of their fellow countrymen to issue paper money, to scale down debts, or to interpret the obligation of contract in such a manner as to render large investments of capital precarious." It was at one and the same time a matter of personal and public interest to prevent this; "of personal interest because acts of this kind would impair their own enjoyment and success; of public interest because it was vitally necessary to America to have its industry and commerce managed in the most efficient and far-sighted way. This fact is of itself sufficient to account for the general tone of the Constitution on matters of property right."

There is no question of the stimulating effect of such broad economic interpretations as that of Smith and Beard. But their theses rested, after all, not so much on a close scrutiny of the complex scene as on the selection of certain traditional "facts," and the selective process was conditioned considerably by the deep engrossment of the writers with the current political scene. Detailed historical research which was being done at the same time, while not drawn on such a broad level as the work of Smith and Beard, at least promised to serve as a healthy corrective. Guy Stevens Callender of Yale pointed out in his *Selections from the Economic History of the United States, 1765–1860* (1909) that leading colonial thinkers supported paper money because of the needs of the expanding economy. This belied the tradition that such demands came primarily from ignorant radical farmers and debtors. Similarly, Joseph S. Davis of Harvard (later of Stanford), in his *Essays in the Earlier History of American Corporations* (1917), showed that the developing business operations cut across the traditional distinction between Jeffersonians and Hamiltonians. Unfortunately Callender passed.off the scene in 1915 before he could develop his insights, and Davis moved on to current economic problems.

A more comprehensive and continuous investigation into the whole range of American economic history was begun with the establishment of the Carnegie Institution of Washington in 1902. Its advisory committee on economics, composed of Carroll D. Wright, Commissioner of Labor, John Bates Clark of Columbia, and Henry W. Farnam of Yale, decided that a comprehensive American economic history would be highly desirable and that the most useful topics for economic research lay in the economic and legislative experience of the states. Since no isolated investigator could handle this diverse and vast experience, or even a limited phase of it, and since government officers were obviously not in a position to treat it with the freedom demanded by science, the Carnegie Institution, with its funds and power to enlist the co-operation of scholars, was equipped to direct the work.

Some of the topics suggested were:

1. The social legislation of the states, which should be critically examined with reference to its results.
2. The labor movement.
3. The industrial development of the states.
4. State and local taxation and finance.
5. State regulation of corporations.

If these and allied topics were thoroughly presented, wrote the committee, the program would constitute a "monumental economic history of the United States."

The Carnegie Institution set up a department of economics and sociology, with Wright in charge, and allotted funds for a five-year project. The department was originally divided into eleven sections, and the research of each was to be supervised and the findings written up by a prominent economist. The sections were:

1. Population and Immigration—Walter F. Willcox (Cornell).
2. Agriculture and Forestry—President Kenyon L. Butterfield (Rhode Island College of Agriculture and Mechanic Arts, now Rhode Island State College).
3. Mining—E. W. Parker (Geological Survey).
4. Manufactures—S. N. D. North (Superintendent of the Census).
5. Transportation—W. Z. Ripley (Harvard).
6. Domestic and Foreign Commerce—Emory R. Johnson (University of Pennsylvania).
7. Money and Banking—Davis R. Dewey (Massachusetts Institute of Technology).
8. The Labor Movement—Carroll D. Wright (Commissioner of Labor).
9. Industrial Organization—Jeremiah W. Jenks (Cornell).
10. Social Legislation—Henry W. Farnam (Yale).
11. Federal and State Finance—Henry B. Gardner (Brown).

In 1906 a twelfth division was added—"The Negro in Slavery and Freedom," headed by Alfred Holt Stone, "an educated businessman from Mississippi." [8]

In view of the pioneering character and magnitude of the enterprise, it was hardly expected that the supervisors could fully appreciate all the problems involved. Of the twelve original supervisors, only one brought his study to something like completion and this one, Johnson's on commerce, was not published until 1915.[9] In the succeeding years only a small part of the program was completed, but the contributions to the history of agriculture, manufactures, and labor were important in spite of their shortcomings, not a few of which originated from the dominant attitude that economic history was merely an adjunct of economics. Wright himself declared that the statistician recognized that his statistical point of view limited him to collecting, classifying, and publishing facts relating to the condition of the people. Their "economic interpretation," he contended, must be the work of another group.[10]

ECONOMISTS AND ECONOMIC CHANGE

Not least of the striking features of the time was the use of a small number of academic economists in high government positions or as advisers. F. W. Taussig was chairman of the recently established Tariff Commission; Thomas Nixon Carver was an adviser to the Department of Agriculture; and A. Piatt Andrew was Assistant Secretary of the Treasury in Taft's administration; Balthasar H. Meyer of Wisconsin and Winthrop M. Daniels of Princeton were on the Interstate Commerce Commission; E. R. A. Seligman advised Cordell Hull, then an influential member of the House Ways and Means Committee, on the income tax and other taxing measures; H. Parker Willis of Columbia was technical adviser to Glass in pushing through the Federal Reserve System.

And economists were beginning to find a function even in business. As Winthrop M. Daniels, a close friend of President Wilson, later put it, the economist's castigation of high protective tariffs was anathema to the "capitalistic upholders of 'rugged individualism,'" and his condemnation of the price policies of "industrial trusts left him 'outside the breastworks' of Big Business." But his views upon "sound money and sanctity of contracts, happening to coincide with the interests of the industrialists, made him not entirely *persona non grata* with the world of practical affairs." Some banks accorded him a recognized professional role, and so did some of the major industries when "public regulation of rates or wages required his expert assistance."

In some ways the economist's practical experience would seem to have reacted upon his thought. While academic opinion staunchly supported the gold standard and emphasized the undesirability of government determination of prices and wages, still it surrendered some of the "peripheral provinces of laissez faire." It generally approved a limitation of working hours, especially for women and children, collective bargaining for wages, and workmen's compensation laws. Economists were also beginning to view with a tolerant eye minimum wage acts and old age pensions. Even economists whose main interests lay far away from the problem of labor reform showed a rather deep concern for the uplift of labor by means of State powers. E. W. Kemmerer of Princeton, an outstanding student of banking, supported minimum wage legislation on the ground that competition worked imperfectly in providing a fair wage for some groups; that ignorance, lack of organization, and immobility made some classes of labor weak in bargaining power. Whereas the employer maintained his machinery at full efficiency by the use of depreciation accounts, in the case of his human machinery—labor—the depreciation charges were not met by the employer but by society, in the form of charities and institutions for defectives and criminals. The social expense of the employer's exploitation of labor, therefore, was a continuing one, since its victims were not only those who had themselves been exploited but also their children.

Roswell C. McCrea, dean of the Wharton School, declared in an address that the "results of many of the newer devices have shown how groundless were the old fears of paternalism, of pauperization, and of subversion of the public order." Or as Jacob H. Hollander of Johns Hopkins put it, the economist repudiated laissez faire but was unwilling to venture upon the uncharted sea of socialism except as a final resort. Hollander turned to constructive social legislation; for this proposed to retain the competitive system of industry, to improve upon it, by "restraint of law and by pressure of public opinion," by such limitations and controls as experience demonstrated to be necessary for the largest social interest.[11]

As the economist began to recognize the need for controls, the necessary concrete basis for them fortunately began to appear. There were great developments in the realm of statistics, both in methodology and in the growth of available data. The Census Bureau was placed on a permanent basis. A government-appointed committee of economists suggested that something similar to the French Central Statistical Commission be established to promote co-operation among the statistical bureaus of the various departments. An interdepartmental statistical committee, composed of a representative from each of the Executive Departments and from independent agencies, would obviate the evils of duplicated results, lack of uniformity of methods, and frequent lack of harmony in the use of statistical terms or principles. The duties of such a committee would be "deliberative and advisory rather than executive." [12] And the ratification of the income tax amendment gave promise of providing material that would make the discussion of national income and wealth a matter of valid objective inquiry. With the publication of price data and index numbers by government and private organizations, discussions of prices became better grounded.

As the facts became more reliable, their significance was analyzed more expertly. Correa M. Walsh and J. Pease Norton of Yale made notable contributions. Walsh's monumental *The Measurement of General Exchange-Value* (1901) was a pioneering study of index numbers. "Values," Walsh declared, "are the quantities with which economics deals; and economics cannot be a science until it can measure the quantities with which it deals." [13] Norton, in *Statistical Studies in the New York Money Market* (1902), developed and improved basic statistical techniques for use in time series. These came to be far more than adjuncts for the "Sumnerian Sociology" with which he avowedly prefaced his studies.

Agricultural economics was growing, and several treatises devoted entirely to this field appeared. The solution of some of the more pressing problems of the farmer looked away from the democratic ideal with which farming had been so definitely identified in the past. Henry C. Taylor of Wisconsin, an outstanding pioneer in the field, declared that with the progress of society an increasing number of tillers of the soil must become tenants, and he pointed to England, where 86 per cent of the land was so cultivated. England's advanced position in agricultural improvement, he thought, was due in good part to the excellent situation between tenants and landlords and proved that land ownership by the farmer was not essential to good agriculture. Edwin G. Nourse, professor of economics at Iowa State College of Agriculture and Mechanic Arts, declared that the "passing of the remarkable democracy of our agricultural class may be the passing of a period of inefficiency, and the emergence of some large incomes for those who do farming in a large way . . . may be a sign that new leaders are beginning to set new standards of attainment in this ancient calling." [14]

THE LOOSENING OF DOCTRINE

The doctrine of marginal productivity continued to be dominant, as has been said, but many of its most ardent exponents tended to give it considerable flexibility. There was, for example, the case of Thomas Nixon Carver (1865–) of Harvard. He had early shown considerable analytical skill by unifying the various orthodox theories of interest. He did this by showing that interest was "the price that measures the marginal productivity, on the one hand, and marginal cost or sacrifice on the other." With either element lacking, therefore, interest would be as impossible as value, if utility or cost were lacking.[15]

From there he went on to the ills of the existing order. In a sprightly article written while he was a graduate student at Johns Hopkins he discovered in Moses a fine economist. By the enlightened view of political economy, said Carver, one set of laws might be very good under one set of circumstances, but very bad under another. Moses' agrarian and anti-usury laws had been excellent schemes for preventing extreme inequality of wealth, which was always accompanied by extreme poverty. But now, though the same problem of "congestion of wealth" existed, such laws were undesirable. All sorts of plans had been proposed to meet it, but no Moses had arisen to supply a simple, direct, and practical solution of the vexing problem.[16]

Carver based his economics on the precept that the great economic virtue was thrift, which consisted in spending money for things which would bring a permanent or a durable advantage. It very often took the form of investing money, he wrote; that is, in buying income-bearing goods, which could be done directly, as when a farmer buys a tractor, or indirectly, as when one deposits money in a savings bank, buys an insurance policy or a corporation bond. In all these and many other cases the saver merely turned his money over to other agencies, and they did the investing; that is, they bought the producers' goods or the income-bearing goods with it. Of course, a community might go too far in avoiding consumption, but such a possibility was so rare as to be unknown. Everywhere there was too little rather than too much thrift.[17]

While Carver supported the marginal productivity doctrine, he pointed out that Clark's specific productivity doctrine related wholly to functional distribution and left the "more vital question of personal distribution untouched." It did not necessarily follow, he argued, that the owners of the factors of production were entitled to the income earned by the factors. Land, for instance, earned its share in the form of rent, but this did not justify giving the rent to the landowners, for land was not the product of human effort. Still, added Carver, there were functions performed by the landowner which justified private ownership in land.

A considerable extension of the land tax, Carver contended, would be good for the nation, because it would force into productive use lands then held for speculation, relieve active production from the repressive tax burden, and finally, and most important of all, would cut off the incomes which then supported capable men in idleness, thus forcing a certain amount of talent into action. In fact, Carver felt that the problem of involuntary unemployment would be solved if means could be found to stop the capable members of the community, those who acquired fortunes most rapidly, from retiring early. The involuntarily idle had received the most attention, he said, but they constituted the least important waste of labor because, first, the least efficient labor normally remained unemployed, and second, the utilization of labor power which was then going to waste at the entrepreneur level would "go a long way toward solving the problem of unemployment at the lower end of the scale." [18]

Roswell C. McCrea (1876–) was another member of the modified marginal productivity school. In his theory the "proof that the laborer gets the value equivalent of the portion of the goods he is responsible for producing is to be found in the demonstration that the value of the *marginal product* (what the laborer is shown to be responsible for) is the community's estimate of the value of that product, and is therefore the value equivalent of what the community gives for that product." [19]

At the same time, however, McCrea expressed considerable sympathy with John A. Hobson's "widening" views on economic welfare. He wrote: "Spend on consumables all that is needed for health, strength, and spiritual outlook—the qualities that beget efficiency; beyond this, save and invest as much as possible, apportioning such surplus wisely among productive uses. Do this to the end that there may be more and more goods to devote to efficiency promotion. . . . There is a growing surplus of goods above the subsistence needs of the moment. The surplus increases at a rate beyond that required for maintenance and healthful growth of social productive capital. The big problem is that of diverting relatively ill-used surplus to the work of bettering living and working conditions. The cumulative results of such a policy will be reflected in enlarging comfort, increasing efficiency, and ever-growing surplus. To view the situation thus throws new light on problems of taxation and State function, of labor unionism, of private benevolence, and of related and subsidiary questions." [20]

McCrea did not work out the implications of this analysis, for, unfortunately for economics, he also had great gifts as an administrator. Consequently most of his energies went into deanships, first of the Wharton School and later of the School of Business of Columbia University.

The intensely humanitarian Henry R. Seager of Columbia accepted a rather rigid view of Clark's law of "competitive distribution" in the first part of his popular *Principles of Economics* (1913), then qualified it as being "merely an aid toward an understanding of the complexities of actual industrial life in which monopoly and change are even more conspicuous than . . . 'normal' conditions," and in the latter part went on to approve of social legislation along British lines with no reference to Clark's law.

Allyn A. Young (1876–1929), who taught at a number of institutions, beginning at Wisconsin and ending at Harvard, accepted the marginal productivity doctrine but more as a general impression than as a concrete reality. "Unless the supply of some productive agent is increasing with undue rapidity," he declared, "nothing can prevent it, as the volume of output grows, from commanding a higher price in the market. . . . The forces working toward the diffusion of the product operate relentlessly and surely. Every bit of ground gained by the rank and file is tenaciously held, and becomes a starting point for yet further progress. This impressionistic picture . . . is in essential harmony with the doctrine of most of the schools of economic theory." But, Young asserted, "general impressions will not suffice." The great need was for a "thoroughgoing and authoritative study of the actual distribution of property and incomes. We lack satisfactory methods of analysis and interpretation, but most of all we lack the facts." [21]

Henry L. Moore (1869–) of Columbia University, an eminent mathematical economist who developed statistical techniques for uncovering the market counterparts on the theoretical demand curves, made some significant qualifications in Clark's doctrine of specific productivity. As early as 1906 he pointed out that though under the hypothesis of perfect competition the laborer should get exactly what he produced, the proposition did not necessarily mean that labor got all it should. "A more just wording would be that labor gets what the assumed property rights and assumed organization of industry make possible, and the important question is not so much whether labor gets what it produces under those conditions, but rather why actual conditions make possible so small a product." Furthermore, he said, the doctrine did not apply in cases of perfect monopoly, nor when the producers of a commodity were few in number, as in oligopoly ("competing monopolists"), nor in the case of the monopoly of one or more complementary producer goods. Then, too, the doctrine must be seriously modified when applied to industries subject to the law of increasing returns.[22]

In 1911, in *Laws of Wages*, Moore undertook a mathematical-statistical verification of Clark's doctrine of specific productivity in its practical conclusions. He recognized that the doctrine did not lend itself directly to statistical proof, and that his statistics were scanty. Behind his procedure lay a traditional social philosophy which found even in the very development of statistical technique a justification of differences in income. "The most marked development of science in the latter half of the nineteenth century," said Moore, "took its point of departure from the study of deviations from the average rather than of the average itself, and economists will, of course, adjust their theories in the light of this newer evolutionary science."

Moore declared that his investigation established that the "law of natural differences in ability between individual laborers" found its expression in the apportionment of earnings among laborers in the present industrial state," and that there was a remarkably close congruence between the "actual distribution of wages and distribution as it should be according to *a priori* theory." He also pointed out that if increased wages did not follow upon the increased efficiency of the laborer, then labor unions could through strikes obtain the increased product. But without the increased efficiency no strikes could permanently increase wages.

Following the Italian economist Enrico Barone, Moore declared that the government of a collectivist State seeking to maximize the national dividend must "apportion the means of production, so that their [the means'] marginal productivity shall be the same in different forms of production." And it must place "values upon the units of the several factors that are proportionate to their respective marginal productivities. The latter principle of valuation is the principle of reward according to specific productivity that tends to be realized in the present industrial state."

David Kinley of the University of Illinois praised Moore's treatment of the laws of wages as one of the most successful illustrations of the statistical verification of theory. It "established statistically the specific productivity theory, and incidentally checked the deductive processes whereby that theory was reached in the first place." On the other hand, Taussig, in reviewing Moore's book, held that the doctrine of specific productivity was true to the extent that capital had increased in modern countries faster than the number of laborers and that consequently wages had risen and interest fallen, but Moore's deduction that labor's share of the country's total income was increasing too ran counter to familiar facts. Taussig's most serious quarrel with the doctrine of specific productivity was that Clark and Moore used it not merely to analyze the existing scheme but to justify things as they were.[23]

Moore's extensive use of mathematical techniques and his abhorrence of literary "types and forms of economics" made his writings difficult to follow. Perhaps Moore's case was most sympathetically presented by an able admirer in describing Moore's *Economic Cycles* (1915): "Of course, there are parts of it I can't read at all, and other parts in which I wish he had offered a little more of the exposition necessary to quell irrelevant objections. But it is a bully piece of work, and I take a huge satisfaction in the fact that such a supremely fine personality as Moore has produced such a supremely significant work." [24]

Though Moore's work appealed to a very restricted circle, his influence was appreciably extended by his most brilliant student, Henry Schultz, in *The Theory and Measurement of Demand* (1938).

While Moore had a high regard for the mathematical method, he was annoyed by the "ridiculous claims" made for it. Thus, after hearing Barone in Rome in 1910, he declared that some of the results that Barone attributed to the mathematical method, he himself had learned from Clark many years before. He expressed the hope that both the mathematical and statistical methods could be combined, for then there would not be a science comparable to economics in beauty and utility. "But is this possible?" he once asked.[25]

This was the basic question posed by the developments in economics. Could all the various new threads be woven together into a pattern that had beauty and utility? Did they require a whole new design for economic theory? Or could they be worked into the traditional pattern? This was the problem upon which the twentieth-century economists were to expend their efforts.

CHAPTER XVI

The Sharpening of the Pecuniary Logic

A GROUP of younger academic figures, young at least in teaching experience, presented what might be called a pecuniary-psychological variant of the Austrian economics. They insisted that economics must be drastically reconstructed to be useful in the modern business age; that the inconsistencies of traditional economics could be overcome only by a more adequate terminology, one that would accord both with the dominant pecuniary phenomena and with the insights that had been supplied by the founders of marginal utility economics. The traditional economic psychology of human behavior that found its expression in the "economic man," the pleasure-pain psychology, was to them part of the anachronistic trappings that must be eliminated, and the emphasis placed on the mechanics of the market. The leaders of this group were Frank A. Fetter, Irving Fisher, and Herbert J. Davenport. Much of their departure was merely in terminology rather than in substance. They refined the old notions, they discovered new elements, but fundamentally they accepted the traditional economic motives. The change in emphasis, however, led them to rather individual solutions to current economic problems.

FRANK ALBERT FETTER: THE "AMERICAN PSYCHOLOGICAL SCHOOL"

Fisher was the dean of the group, but the man who first made their general position prominent was Fetter (1863–).[1] A native of Indiana, he entered the state university in 1876. In his junior year he obtained his training in the philosophical basis of political economy via the customary Common Sense moral philosophy.[2] Had Fetter gone on to the senior year, he would have learned the correlated principles of economics from Perry's textbook. But he was forced to drop out of school because of family obligations. For a short period Fetter engaged in newspaper work and studied law, and then he went into business, operating a large bookstore in his native town of Peru.

Besides an income, the bookstore provided Fetter with a vast library. It carried many of the popular periodicals, which in that day contained the greater part of the ablest writings on economic and social matters. After business hours Fetter read voraciously. Like so many of the intellectually active young men of the day, he was deeply moved by Henry George's *Progress and Poverty*. For a while he became a sort of "philosophic" single taxer. He soon found "errors" in George's views, but, as he said later, the book was the determining factor in making economics his life work.

After an absence of eight years he returned to the university for his senior year. In the interim an important change had taken place in the teaching of the social sciences at Indiana. The textbook in economics was no longer Perry's treatise but Francis A. Walker's, and the teacher was the very popular Jeremiah W. Jenks. Fetter's college career ended very successfully. He achieved considerable local fame by winning the state oratorical contest and then the interstate contest, in which ten states were represented. Jenks, who soon afterward accepted a post at Cornell, obtained a fellowship there for Fetter and encouraged him to go on to Halle, to study with his own teacher, Conrad.

On returning to the United States, Fetter held an instructorship for a year at Cornell and then became professor of economics and social science at Indiana. Here he taught a variety of courses, ranging from "Dependents, Defectives, and Delinquents" and "Socialism and Communism" to "Statistics" and "Economic Theories." After three years at Indiana and an equal period at Stanford, Fetter rejoined Jenks at Cornell in 1901 as professor of political economy and finance. At Cornell, as elsewhere, he was extremely popular; students in engineering and prospective social workers flocked to his courses. In 1911 Fetter became permanently established at Princeton.

Fetter considered Patten and Clark the two men who had proven most fertile in the new economics of marginal utility.[3] But much remained to be done in freeing economic doctrine from "obsolete" theories. "Writers who use in a masterly way the utility and marginal concepts," Fetter wrote, "nevertheless accept as an ultimate standard of value a rejuvenated Ricardian or Marxian labor unit." [4]

In the first edition of his popular *Principles of Economics* (1904) Fetter accepted the old "subjective" pleasure-pain psychology. As he put it, the aim of all economic activity was to attain pleasurable conditions in mind and soul. The value of all goods was "derived from the pleasurable psychic" impressions which they caused, and these psychic effects constituted the psychic income, which was the end of activity. Using this basic motive, Fetter went on to the familiar marginal utility economics. This "subjective" or "psychological" method, he stated before the Congress of Arts and Sciences in 1906, "begins with introspection and pursues the analysis of man's nature and wants by observing and comparing the impressions, the hopes, and the motives that determine acts in relation to gratifications. The method of psychological analysis requires here no defense, and the service of the marginal utility theory, as developed by various writers, will hardly be denied." [5]

In his 1915 edition Fetter made a radical innovation, namely, a "new statement of the theory of value, one in accord with the modern volitional psychology, thus eliminating entirely the old utilitarianism and hedonism which have tainted the terms and conceptions of value ever since the days of Bentham. The basis of value is conceived to be the simple act of choice and not a calculation of utility." He even proposed to abandon the phrase "marginal utility." Actually Fetter merely dropped the word "pleasurable" in most places. He now defined psychic income simply as "desirable results produced in the realm of feeling by valuable objects or by valuable changes in the environment which accrue to or affect an economic subject within a given period. . . . [Anticipated] total psychic income is what motivates our economic activity." [6]

Fetter's new "psychological" theory was modern only in that it attempted to accord with the latest views of the successors of John Stuart Mill's association psychology, notably, E. B. Titchener. Fetter's reformulation consisted in saying that "valuation," the individual's measurement of "gratification," was implied in choice rather than preceded choice. Diminishing utility now became "diminishing gratification," and marginal utility became "marginal desire" and "marginal valuation." To explain this Fetter declared that in a "well-ordered life, in an advanced economic society, the means of gratifying desires as they arise are provided in advance. The changing series of desires is met by a changing series of goods." Clearly following Spencer in defining life as a "constant adjustment of inner relations to outer conditions," Fetter went on to assert that "economic life is therefore like physical life, a constant adjustment; and this adjustment of goods but reflects the shifting and adjustment of feelings."

Since the impulse to seek immediate gratification was rooted in men's nature, in his theory, the gratification of wants at a future date was not as important as present gratification. Thus he found time value pervading the entire economic structure and the capitalization of psychic income a basic process of human nature. Obviously, he said, these applied more to the relatively permanent goods than to non-durable consumption goods. The capital value of any permanent good, therefore, was the sum of the whole series of rents or incomes it contained, discounted at some rate to its present worth; that is, it was the monetary expression of the psychic incomes yielded by the goods.

He then extended the application of this theory. Even differences in pay of different occupations, he felt, could be partially explained in this manner. In many workers' families the difficulty in meeting costs of preparation for their work was so great that even a large increase in future wages would be insufficient to induce the beginner to make the sacrifice. These families had an extremely high rate of time preference. The question here was that of the active investment of capital and the element of uncertainty involved. As he said: "Often the expenses of industrial education are returned many fold in the form of larger labor-incomes to the individual, but in some cases the expense is 'thrown away' because of the incapacity or of the moral weakness of the learner."

For Fetter the rate of interest was the rate of discount implied in the process of capitalization as it emerged from the play of the demand and supply schedules for durable goods. First, he said, capital values were determined through the equilibrium in the market of individual estimations of net worth based on each individual rate of time preference. The rate of interest was but an "index of the ratio inherent in the equilibrium of psychological forces, desires for present and future incomes; that is, time preference." Capital and interest could be expressed in money units but money was "no more their cause than the hands of the clock are the cause of the time of day." Similarly, the borrower was only an intermediary, transmitting to the market of consumers, through the agency of prices, the effect of time preference.

The practical traders, in bidding for capital goods, were only dimly conscious of the logical process of capitalization involved, Fetter asserted. Each trader merely tried to get as much as he could, but the shrewd bargainer was one who could "foresee more clearly than his fellows the changes to come" or who could show "an intuitive sense of the net result. . . . The ability and inability to foresee such changes" make men rich and poor. Future incomes could be maintained, according to Fetter, only through the constant exercise of the faculty of abstinence, which was the great conserving and dynamic influence. Private property was essential to saving, for it forced men to subordinate present desires to the future, to fix responsibility for waste and improvidence, and to multiply the rewards of abstinence.

Fetter stressed greater business ability as the real need, because with the growing division of labor and complexity of industry the workers would require more supervision by men who could foresee the distant results and the future incomes. Through the corporate structure the captains of industry have become the management, safeguarding the interests of the stockholders. Profits were the share of income of the enterpriser for his skill in directing industry and in assuming the risks. Despite complex influences, Fetter considered that this share was determined by the enterpriser's contributions to industry.[7]

Fetter also held that the chief factors tending to raise wages were the "productiveness of industry, peace, order, and security to wealth, honesty in man and master, in lawmaker and in judge, the efficiency and intelligence of the workers, and an earnest effort on their part to get the share that competition will accord them." Chiefly because of this last factor, trade unions played a useful though subordinate part in regulating wages over the whole field of employment. Unfortunately, "with so modest an ideal . . . as the true competitive wage, organized laborers and their leaders cannot always be expected to be content." [8] In fact, as labor claims gained more and more sympathy, Fetter became increasingly disturbed over the tendency of younger economists to lose sight of "the competitive aspects of wage adjustment . . . amid the discussions of the ethical and humanitarian aspects, in such questions as minimum wage for women and children, a 'fair' wage, an ideal standard of living, and the control of wages in the interest of organized labor." After all, "underlying the wage-bargain . . . [is a] competitive force or market price of labor to which the wage-bargain must conform." [9]

Fetter's vagueness on ameliorative programs arose in good part from his strong streak of Malthusianism, which took the form of a plea for eugenics. He thought that "democracy and opportunity" were favoring the process of "increasing the mediocre and reducing the excellent strains of stock. . . . Progress is threatened unless social institutions can be so adjusted as to reverse this process of multiplying the poorest, and of extinguishing the most capable families." The eugenics movement, Fetter explained, introduced "an element of rational direction into the process of perpetuating the race, so that . . . superior capacity shall be increased." [10]

On the question of trusts and monopolies Fetter shifted his position during his career. Originally he was skeptical of the attempts to curb the great combines. But in *Modern Economic Problems* (1916) he unequivocally supported Wilson and the Democratic Party and was critical of the Progressive Party for having a "policy of monopoly-accepted-and-regulated." In *The Masquerade of Monopoly* (1931) he used strong deprecatory language, which had been absent in his *Source Book in Economics* (1912), and he later stated that the growth of monopoly had raised a strong doubt in his mind that capitalism could survive unless vigorous action against monopoly was taken.[11]

Throughout his theory Fetter emphasized that the most progressive business practices should be taken into account. He insisted that in dealing with industry he was discussing the "most developed capitalistic conditions." But in truth his analysis did not differ too sharply from the older theories; he used the terminology of modern business, but he held that the basis of its activity lay in the non-pecuniary forces of desire and nature. Such views, rigorously presented, led Fetter in his treatises to depict human nature in the image of the businessman. No man protested more sharply in articles against making price economics identical with welfare economics.[12] But these protests were not integrated with his main views. Such integration was not easy, for the generation from which Fetter sprang held consciously the social philosophy which he so succinctly had summarized in his prize oration in 1891: "Self, self, self is the axiom of evolution, the postulate of political economy, the rule of human action." [13]

IRVING FISHER: MATHEMATICAL ECONOMIST AND MONETARY REFORMER

Although generally developing his thought in a method similar to Fetter's, Irving Fisher of Yale (1867–1947) more directly and consciously reduced physical and human phenomena to pecuniary categories. He was one of the most colorful figures in the field by virtue of his zeal in pushing various reforms, ranging from the improvement of national health to setting up the League of Nations.[14]

Fisher was the son of a Congregational minister. His father died in 1884, the year he entered Yale, and he took upon himself the burden of supporting his mother and young brother. In spite of his responsibilities, he achieved a brilliant academic record and was class valedictorian. He studied with the eminent Yale mathematical physicist, J. Willard Gibbs, obtained his doctorate in mathematics in 1891, and taught the subject for a number of years at Yale. During his graduate period he also studied economics and was deeply influenced by Sumner. Both interests were manifested in his dissertation, *Mathematical Investigations in the Theory of Value and Prices* (1892). Thus Fisher became the first well-trained American mathematician to make economics his main interest.[15] In a way the dissertation realized Simon Newcomb's hope for the development of a complete formulation of economics in mathematical terms. To Fisher the mathematical method was sufficiently vindicated by having contributed the most fruitful idea in the history of economics—marginal utility.

Fisher's objective was to undertake a "systematic representation in terms of mechanical interaction of that beautiful and intricate equilibrium which manifests itself on the 'exchanges' of a great city but of which the causes and effects lie far outside." The criticisms of philosophers of the hedonistic or pleasure-pain calculus made Fisher uneasy, but he did not question that psychology. He did think that pleasure and pain had important biological and sociological functions, and that for certain ethical and economic investigations it would be desirable to determine how to compare the utilities of two individuals, but it was not necessary for the economist to "envelop his own science in the hazes of ethics, psychology, biology, and metaphysics."

The economist is concerned, said Fisher, with the causes of the "objective facts of prices and commodity distribution," and for that purpose he can strip utility of any connection with pleasure and pain. The "conception of utility has its origin in the facts of human preference or decision as observed in producing, consuming, and exchanging goods and services." The only necessary "psycho-economic postulate" is that "each individual acts as he desires." But to simplify the discussion other assumptions are necessary: (1) The market is sufficiently large to prevent "one man's *consciously* influencing prices." (2) There is a given period of time. (3) "During this period, the rate of production and consumption are equal. . . . (4) Each individual in the market knows all prices, acts freely and independently, and preserves the same characteristics during the period so that the *forms* of his utility curves [his predetermined schedules] do not change. (5) All articles considered are infinitely divisible and each man free to stop producing and consuming at any point. (6) The marginal utility of consuming each commodity decreases as the amount consumed increases, and the marginal disutility of producing each commodity decreases as the amount produced increases. (7) . . . the utility of each commodity is independent of the quantities of other commodities and likewise for disutility."

Given these postulates, he could construct his mathematical theory. Although the individual's estimate of utility might be fitful and ever-changing, and prices might vary from day to day, Fisher declared, the use of a period of time eliminated the sporadic elements. Prices might vary from hour to hour because of excitement and rumor, and from season to season because of weather changes, but these fluctuations were self-correcting.

Considering these assumptions as essential to the competitive situation and operating on a presumed analogy between "mechanical and economic equilibrium," Fisher deduced that "a consumer will so arrange his consumption that the marginal utility per dollar's worth of each commodity shall be the same. . . . The marginal utilities of all articles consumed by a given individual are proportional to the marginal utilities of the same series of articles for each other consumer, and this uniform continuous ratio is the scale of prices of those articles. . . . Prices, production, and consumption are determined by the equality of marginal utility and marginal cost of production." Deviations from the equilibrium are corrected by a "special functionary, the speculator."

Fisher went beyond the usual Jevonian formulation of marginal utility analysis, whose pivotal assumption was that the utility of each commodity is "a function of the quantity of each commodity alone." For Fisher the "utility of a commodity is a function of the quantities of all commodities." This led him into higher mathematical formulations of marginal utility, and the introduction of the concept of the indifference curve. But as Fisher reached the "higher regions" of the general case of a number of interdependent commodities, he found that no such quantity as "total utility or gain" could be determined. Rather, we must conceive the "economic world to be filled merely with lines of force or 'maximum direction.' "

Although stressing the interdependence of markets and prices, for most purposes Fisher felt that the assumption of one commodity as independent of another was a good first approximation, which held fairly well and widely, for in general the interdependence was very slight. And this was especially true if the interdependent commodities were grouped in such a manner as "to eliminate the really important influence of commodities on each other." For elementary teaching and for practical problems Fisher therefore employed the particular (or partial) equilibrium approach of analyzing the market of one commodity at a time.

Fisher was aware of some of the limitations of the mathematical method. Although he admitted that the assumed ideal static condition could never be achieved in fact, he argued that it must be used as a basis. Panics were evidence of a lack of equilibrium, but these, he thought, should be studied in economic dynamics, which should also include the effect of changing tastes and methods and of social organization. But, after all, "normal price, production, and consumption are sufficiently intricate to engage our careful study without the complication of changes in social structure." The ultimate development of economic dynamics, declared Fisher, would reconcile many of the apparent contradictions.

Fisher also dismissed, rather summarily, specific problems raised by large-scale industry. The proper discussion of railroad rates for roads already built, he said, should take no account of fixed charges, but be "formulated as 'what the traffic will bear.'" Similarly, he found that the tendency toward trusts and pools was the result of instability arising in those exceptional cases where the assumptions of decreasing marginal utility with an increase of the commodity, and increasing marginal cost with increase of production, were not true.

Fisher's approach gained little following among economists in the United States, not because they thought the method of the "mathematical school" erroneous, but rather because they thought it required special genius to handle it. His colleague Arthur T. Hadley declared that the mathematical method permitted a man to frame hypothetical conduct and then treated it as rigorously verified principle. Such an error could be avoided only if a man was either an exceptionally good psychologist like Jevons or an unusually good mathematician like Léon Walras or Fisher.[16] Nevertheless, Fisher was highly enough regarded by economists, including those who deprecated the utilization of the mathematical approach, so that when a general Handbook or Cyclopædia of Political Economy was proposed in the nineties, Fisher was assigned the section on the theory of value, while John Bates Clark was to write on the theory of distribution and Franklin H. Giddings on production.[17]

For a short while Fisher zealously pushed the mathematical approach. When the translation of Cournot's book, *Researches into the Mathematical Principles of the Theory of Wealth*, appeared in 1897, to which Fisher contributed a bibliography of mathematical economics, Fisher announced that the drift was toward the mathematical approach and that with its growth economic science would be "divested of those crudities which have made it too often a laughing-stock when applied to the hard and stubborn facts of the actual world." [18] But Fisher realized that the time was not fully ripe; perhaps the next generation might be sufficiently well trained in mathematics to do the task. Therefore, while continuing to point out the merits of the mathematical approach, he himself turned increasingly to less "refined" literary methods.

In this development he moved along lines substantially similar to those of Fetter. Although Fetter insisted that economics was a psychological science, and Fisher stated that it really had nothing to do with psychology and that utility was "mere intensity of desire," they managed to reach substantially the same conclusions since they possessed much the same conceptions of the physical universe and human nature. Where Fetter insisted that the essence of interest was time preference, Fisher, much earlier, had declared that the essence of interest was in "impatience," the desire to obtain gratification earlier than we normally should get it, or the preference for present over future goods. This desire, he said, was a fundamental attribute of human nature and as long as it existed there would be a rate of interest.[19]

Building on this concept of interest, Fisher argued that "enjoyable services (psychic incomes) and objective services are themselves incommensurable," but "their values are not." With proper bookkeeping "the values of the physical elements cancel among themselves and leave as the net result only the value of the psychical elements. It is precisely because of this cancellation, closely corresponding to . . . double-entry bookkeeping, that the harmony between psychic income and the bookkeeper's money income works itself out automatically and not as an empirical make-shift. . . . Psychic income emerges at the end, not as opposed to or discordant with items recorded on merchants' ledgers, but as the ultimate elements up to which those ledgers lead." The aim of his book *The Nature of Capital and Income* (1906), Fisher stated, was to show that the "businessman's concept of income and the economists' concept of income thus dovetail into each other when the proper method of their cancellation is understood." [20]

Possessed of a strong sense of internal logical consistency and symmetry, Fisher declared that capital was all the stock of wealth, "including human capital," and that income included all the flow of services. "The two conceptions . . . are exact and perfect counterparts of each other. All services flow from capital . . . and all capital is the fountain of services. When the flows are all rendered perpetual and uniform, the value-ratio of the income to its capital is identical with the rate of interest."

The ownership of capital, in Fisher's view, had no other significance than the ownership of the anticipated income from that capital. The division of income between different owners was a division of the ownership of the capital yielding the income; the individual shares constituted property rights. But, he found, people had difficulty in appreciating that a real basis, wealth, underlay property rights, especially in the case of securities. The rights were so far separated from the things to which the rights related that people deluded themselves with the notion that nothing need be behind them. Take the case of a manufacturer who was offered by rivals a substantial sum to close his mills and did so. The contract he "made with his rivals constituted a kind of property for them; the wealth by *means* of which his promise was made good was evidently his own person, together with his plant; and the service performed was the inactivity of both." Similarly, real wealth underlay "good will." The firm possessing it owned a "valuable claim upon its patrons; namely, the chance of their continued patronage." These patrons and their wealth were what underlay the property right, because they were "the means to the desired services to which these rights" applied.

Fisher stated quite early that Adam Smith was justly criticized for recommending saving to society as he would to an individual.[21] Yet he felt that there should be no concern over the possibility that unlimited accumulations would reduce opportunities for reinvestment and thereby reduce the rate of interest. According to his analysis, each reduction in the interest rate would tend to check the desire for accumulation.[22]

John R. Commons rather sarcastically referred to Fisher as being along with Fetter, a representative of the new school of economists who preached business economy rather than political economy. Fisher's views, he said, would cut off any attempt at regulation.[23] Fisher retorted that he himself was an ardent critic of laissez faire. And this was indeed true. In fact he felt that the doctrine of laissez faire had been pretty much abandoned and that there had been a return to the older view for which "economics was first named political economy." But such phenomena as government rate-regulation, curbs on corporations, and compulsory workmen's insurance seemed to him to arise from "political" rather than economic considerations, and these developments abroad and at home indicated to him that the country was moving "dangerously fast" toward socialism. He thought that government power and efficiency were limited. To him history showed that even under a socialist regime the ruling class, in order to maintain its position, usurped power, employed oppressive methods, and distributed special privileges; that when one class attempted to rule another, there was always a tendency toward corruption, inefficiency, lack of adaptability, and abuse of power.

Having thus disposed of the "political" side, Fisher turned to the "economic" side and argued that some people needed enlightenment as to where their best interests lay and that others needed restraint because of their lack of self-control in following their impulses. As to the first point, since the world was divided into the educated and ignorant, if progress was to be made, "the former should be allowed to dominate the latter." Thus a law against drunkenness was best for the drunkard. And the lower classes could be taught to appreciate their interests and appropriate conduct by the educational efforts of voluntary associations, such as the National Civic Federation and the Society for the Study and Prevention of Tuberculosis. Once it was admitted that the instructed classes should give instruction to the ignorant, the range of human betterment would be boundless.

Social interest, Fisher declared, required legal restraint on the individual interest in such matters as conservation, irrigation, sanitation, fire nuisances; and he supported compulsory health insurance and workmen's compensation acts. An especially undesirable result of the blind pursuit of individual self-interest to his mind, was cutthroat competition in railroad rates. This had led to government regulation, but he doubted the efficacy of the remedy.[24]

During his whole career Fisher wrote continuously on money, but not with absolute consistency. In the bitter campaign year of 1896 he expressed some sympathy with the silverite view and contended that, on the whole, although debtors had suffered from the fall of prices, the loss was small, for in the long run the interest rate tended to adjust itself to the changed value of money and therefore to offset losses caused by changes in the value of the principal. Furthermore, the loss could not be rectified by monetary legislation, which would seriously weaken the social fabric. It was best not to endanger the ancient principle of the "inviolability of contracts" and non-retroactive laws. "The world has reached these principles through a long and weary struggle," he said. "When once a government has undertaken to 'correct' debtors' losses, it will not stop at one attempt." But he also granted that if a stable and less expensive monetary standard could be found, it would be an "inestimable boon to the civilized world." Such a standard, Fisher held, would largely eliminate not only long-term movements, but short-term movements, booms and depressions. Changes in the price level, whether upward or downward, created a divergence between the market or nominal rate of interest and the real rate of interest because of differences of foresight. This divergence tended to be corrected ultimately, but it was at the heart of the alternating periods of prosperity and depression. When the price level began to rise, businessmen who possessed "superior foresight" realized that they could increase their profits through borrowing at the "money rate" of interest, and lenders were content to lend increasing amounts at that rate. This intensified the rise of prices and caused a boom. The adjustment of the rates of interest was made tardily, and the whole situation changed. When prices began to decline the fall was intensified by the same differences in foresight, for lenders were unwilling to accept a reduction in the money rate to the "real" rate. This analysis of the lag of adjustment of the market rate of interest to changes in the level of prices has become one of the most fruitful suggestions in the study of business cycles.

After the bimetallic controversy ended, and the long-term line of prices had begun to rise, Fisher advocated a standard the feasibility of which he had previously questioned, a legislative standard.

By 1907 he was saying that laissez faire in the form of unbridled "monetary individualism" had been extremely dangerous to the economic system. In fact this was the worst aspect of laissez faire. Nations and individuals failed to realize, he wrote, that an increase in the stock of money was waste, not gain; that the paper money delusion was thoroughly appreciated by the people, but that it must also be perceived that all inflation was vicious, including that caused by an increased gold supply.

His basic remedy was a "stabilized" or "compensated" dollar, which could be achieved by varying the gold content of the standard money inversely with price changes. By 1912 he felt that the current so-called gold standard had wrought untold mischief. For a quarter of a century, from 1873 to 1896, he wrote, the dollar had increased its purchasing power and caused a prolonged depression of trade, culminating in the political upheaval which led to the free silver campaign of 1896, where the remedy was worse than the disease. Since then, there had been a reverse movement, but still the growing clamor of discontent was daily adding to the ranks of the socialists who were ready with quack remedies. The "compensated dollar" was the prescription.

This "compensated dollar" scheme, however, had originally little more than academic interest, since Fisher first stated that its adoption by one nation alone would derange the international exchanges and that it could be effectively established only by international agreement. During World War I he felt that the United States could take the lead in establishing it. Following the tradition of Carey, Fisher bluntly declared that it was essential to put "our own internal commerce on a stable basis; and our internal commerce is probably a score of times as important as our own foreign commerce."

In this scheme Fisher embraced the quantity theory of money, with qualifications, by building upon foundations laid down by Newcomb. The price level, he declared, normally varies "directly with the quantity of money (and with deposits which normally vary in unison with the quantity of money), provided that the velocities of circulation and the volume of trade remain unchanged and that there be a given stage of deposit banking." Or, as he put it in his famous equation which has since appeared in countless textbooks, $MV + M'V' = PT$, where for a given time period P is the general level of prices, T the volume of transactions, M the quantity of money, M' the quantity of deposit currency, V and V' their respective velocities of circulation. The variations in the amount of money remain, as in the old quantity version, the great causal force, "normally." By controlling the amount of money, the price level could be stabilized, according to Fisher.

The adverb "normally" was inserted in the proposition, said Fisher, in order to provide for those "transitional" or "abnormal" periods which he, like Commons, called "credit cycles." Rather unexpectedly, however, Fisher added that since "periods of transition are the rule and those of equilibrium the exception, the mechanism of exchange is almost always in a dynamic rather than a static condition." Yet Fisher considered the quantity theory of money "practically . . . an exact law of proportion, as exact and as fundamental in economic science as the exact law of proportion between pressure and density of gases in physics, assuming temperature to remain the same. Of course . . . in practice, velocities and trade seldom remain unchanged. . . . But the *tendency* represented in the quantity theory remains true, whatever happens to the other elements involved; just as the tendency represented in the density theory remain true whatever happens to temperature." [25]

In good part because of Fisher's work, the quantity theory of money was restored to its old position of dominance in monetary discussion. Fisher's formulation became standard. In fact, his influence became so overpowering on this matter that critical and enlightening work on the quantity theory was treated with scant courtesy in the profession if it failed to dovetail with Fisher's exposition.[26]

In his own mind Fisher felt that critics of the quantity theory of money did not understand that a scientific law is not a formulation of statistics or of history, but a formulation of what holds true under given conditions. "Statistics and history can be used to illustrate and verify laws only by making suitable allowances for changed conditions," he said, and on this basis asserted that he had made statistical inquiries on the subject for the last "ten centuries in the rough and of the last decade and a half in detail. In each case we found the facts in accord with the principles previously formulated."

Fisher had the strong advantage of a lucid style, a trained mind, and the support of tradition. Back of all his work, however, was a rather ambiguous distinction he made between historical and scientific truth.[27] Conceiving scientific truth as not subject to the test of prediction, and the logic of economics as a bookkeeping device for transforming men's efforts and satisfactions into measurable monetary form, it was natural that Fisher's theoretical work should have in great part the nature of a pecuniary logic. It was apparently intended to show how men should, and for the most part do, act under the system of free contract and competition, unless blinded by irrational temporary impulses such as failure to recognize that the dollar may vary in value. Fisher's emphasis on statistics along those lines, though rather rough and "heroic," did much to push the development of statistical inquiry; and his pioneering work on index numbers was of enduring value.

Fisher never claimed that he was extraordinarily original, and he was quick to admit that others had preceded him. Thus, apropos of his "compensated dollar" scheme, he wrote J. Allen Smith that Smith's early scheme for a multiple standard "seems to be almost identical with mine." [28] Although much of Fisher's work was not novel, through his numerous and well-written publications he impressed his ideas on the economists of the day.

Fisher, like John R. Commons, underwent considerable intellectual development after World War I; the developments were so extensive and so closely related to the events of the period that a discussion of them is reserved for the sequel volume.

HERBERT JOSEPH DAVENPORT: CONFLICT OF LOYALTIES

Like Fisher and Fetter, Herbert J. Davenport (1861–1931) felt that the deficiencies of traditional economics could be remedied by reformulating and purifying its concepts.[29] To do this he, more than the others, provided an elaborate presentation of the pecuniary logic.

Davenport was descended from two Puritan statesmen, the Reverend John Davenport and Roger Conant. And in his independence he evidenced some of the characteristic traits of these forebears who had led in the migration to the New World. Davenport had difficulty finding a place in life. In 1882, at the age of twenty-one, he entered Harvard Law School as a special student. After attending two and one-third years, he took and passed the final examination for the full three years, but as a special student he could not obtain a degree.[30]

Davenport turned to a business career, and since his parents had left him a substantial fortune he went west to engage in the real-estate business in Sioux Falls, South Dakota. He prospered, but his intellectual interests were so strong that he took time out in 1890–91 to attend first the University of Leipzig and then L'Ecole Libre des Sciences Politiques in Paris. In 1893 he lost most of his fortune in the panic, and became a high school principal in Sioux Falls, where he stayed four years.

Davenport used to say, half jestingly, that he was attracted to economics because he was convinced that there was something wrong in socialism and he wanted to find out what it was. He began writing on economic topics for the professional journals in 1894. But since he was not likely to be accepted as an economist without a college degree, he registered at the University of South Dakota. He apparently attended no classes, but within a year took all the examinations for the four-year course and received a Ph.B.[31] In 1896–97 he published two "studiously theoretical" textbooks—one for colleges, *Outlines of Economic Theory,* and a condensed version for high schools, *Outlines of Elementary Economics*—both based on marginal utility doctrines.

Davenport defined economics as treating of men's "commercial and industrial activities . . . from the standpoint of markets and values." But man, he said, should be "regarded as standing over against an outside world of fact and circumstance." In his theory capital and land represented the energies of the environment coerced by man's labor—whether as a wage worker or as an entrepreneur—to yield utility. The returns for labor, wages or profits, were enhanced by returns from the environment, interest and rent. The character of the people and the nature of the "opportunity" of the environment explained the nation's prosperity or poverty, the magnitude of its production and rate of wages.

The ethical character of the desires was not a fundamental part of his inquiry. Men labored and underwent privation for "whiskey, cigars, and burglars' jimmies," he said, "as well as for food, or statuary or harvest machinery." As long as men were willing to buy and sell "foolishness and evil," the former commodities would be economic factors with market standing, for utility, as an economic term, meant merely adaptability to human desires. So long as men desired them, they satisfied a need and were motives to production. Therefore economics did not need to investigate the origin of choices.

For Davenport the value of a thing was fixed by the sacrifice, generally in utilities, which it commanded in exchange. For all buyers and sellers, other than the marginal "operators," there was a surplus, a differential advantage—which he, like Alfred Marshall, termed "quasi-rent"—measured from the point of actual market sacrifice. Thus developing the cost doctrine along the same lines (and almost contemporaneously) as did David I. Green in his conception of opportunity costs, Davenport declared that the cost of production of commodities was a "summary of the working out in industry of the social demand for some commodities as compared with others"—that is, "an expression of demand working simultaneously on a number of commodities." [32] Thus the portion of the product received by any laborer or group of laborers was "approximately the measure that his or their production ministers to the social demand."

The employer class was justified, in Davenport's view, because it enabled labor to obtain increased utilities and payments. The employer was the agent or representative of the social demand, engaged in purchasing labor's product and "compelled by competition if effective" to pay laborers approximately in proportion to their services. The competition assumed by nearly all statements of economic law he defined as a "struggle for maximum economic rewards (minimum sacrifice)." Since "any incompleteness or failure of competition" caused "confusion in economic reasoning" and the necessary modifications were awkward to make, economists viewed these discordant features with "scientific and moral disfavor."

Assuming competition on the economists' terms, he wrote that its primary tendencies were toward economies in production, lower prices, and better quality, but occasionally it brought about such wastes as excessive number of retailers, adulteration, false advertising. From one point of view, he said, combination and monopoly were "mere aspects of competition," for the movement toward giant industry at the expense of the small unit was a competitive product; but in proportion as these secondary aspects lacked the "primary competitive characteristics," they were "awkward of treatment to the economist and perplexing to the moralist and legislator." Davenport seemed to feel that the real problem involved was cutthroat competition.

In his general economic outlook Davenport would extend the regulating power of the State to make laissez-faire individualism successful. He approved of an income tax, provided the tax was based on expenditure, such as that upon house rent, the number of servants and horses. The best form of taxation would be based on expenditures for luxury and vice. This seems somewhat liberal, but he was not consistently so, for he was rather dubious of most labor reforms. On the basis of the marginal principle, he questioned the desirability of an eight-hour day and the elimination of sweatshop labor. Child labor, he thought, should perhaps be restricted for the sake of the child's opportunities or the health of future generations; but the regulations should be flexible, for families often needed a child's earnings. The self-respect accompanying independence was a valuable quality, and government protection of children might result in tyranny for both parents and children.

Davenport was clearly not in sympathy with government inter-ference as such; and he leveled against socialism all the arguments accumulated since the days of Aristotle. He warned that the for-tunes of the rich were reserves for meeting commercial depressions. And since the rich were usually busy men of simple tastes, their efforts chiefly benefited the poor. Thus Vanderbilt's great railroad ventures were in reality destined for the greater service of the pub-lic. Besides, the growth of culture was dependent on a wealthy class. This was his broad general defense for the existing system.

To Davenport socialism's strongest argument was that it would end commercial crises, the most noticeable weakness of the modern competitive system. He admitted that if the "commercial crisis" was beyond remedy within the present system then there was little danger of society finding itself worse off in any probable change.

So Davenport was forced to find a solution for these crises. He did so by the following analysis. The phenomenon that gave rise to panic, he wrote, was not the industrial situation, for at the time of the crash that seemed never so "prosperous in thorough efficiency and organization." The difficulty lay in the financial situation; that is, with expanding business currency also expanded, and commonly in a degree more than proportionate to the demand for it. This in-crease ordinarily occurred in the credit element. Without credit "the great expanding business operations would carry with them their own veto in falling prices and vanishing profits." The advan-tages of credit were purchased at the risk of enormous dangers, especially at the full tide of prosperity. For then, if for any reason, "whether of extravagance at some point, or of over-production in some industries, or of failure of harvests in some districts, or of over-speculation or even of business prosperity carried to the point of over-stringency in the loan market," a contraction of credit would begin, and a general crash would follow because debtors could pay only by calling in turn on their debtors. Industry would slow to a stop, not because there was too little or too much wealth, but because the wealth was badly arranged to withstand the flurry of credit.

The remedy lay in discovering a currency effectively flexible in times of need; in other words, asset currency so arranged that it would be withdrawn once the emergency was over. As for the popular scheme of bimetallism, he said that his business friends of Sioux Falls were "stark mad on silver and Populism." [33] Although

he lost his fortune in the Panic of 1893, he remained a Gold Democrat.

His solution through asset currency did not, however, clear his
mind of all traces of doubt. "It is possible," he said, "that something
of ebb and flow in commercial affairs—of that which in philosophic
phrase is termed rhythm—is inseparable from the conduct of business, so long, at least, as the industrial organization retains its speculative features. In this view the question is to some extent a psychological one."

More suggestive was Davenport's explanation of why a depression
was not short-lived. This he attributed to certain dislocations. First,
all prices did not fall equally because goods produced under more
or less monopolistic conditions maintained their prices. Second, since
business indebtedness did not decrease, as measured in money units,
there was tremendous resistance, in many cases a struggle for financial existence, against sale and liquidation at the going levels of
prices. The third and most important was wage rigidity. The first
of these disproportionate declines in prices was not serious; and the
second, indebtedness, could be remedied by an elastic currency system, provided the rigidity of wages could be eliminated; but this
rigidity was difficult to remove because strikes and violence would
prevent competition among laborers, and public opinion would uncritically side with the hired workers. The harassed entrepreneur,
who was merely an intermediate agent buying labor and material for
the purpose of profit, had to produce within the market price. Consequently, according to the marginal principle, those employers
least able or least disposed to continue production on narrow margins would find it more profitable to cease operations. Eventually
the resulting increase of competition among wage earners for employment would reduce in some degree the pressure upon the remaining employees, and recovery would begin.

Although in his analysis labor bore most of the responsibility for
prolonging depressions, it should be noted that Davenport was one
of the first of the respectable economists to give serious attention
to the problem of unemployment. He went so far as to say in *The
Outlines of Economic Theory* that unemployment was the "most
important practically, and perhaps the most difficult theoretically,
of all the problems of economic science. Theory and fact, here," he
said, seemed "somehow out of harmony." Because of invention,
changes of taste, and the like, there was a "normal and in a certain

sense healthful volume of non-employment," but periods of crisis and depression aggravated this condition to a disease. Under the present system the best ameliorative device was to postpone public works to periods of "labor stagnation." The work of men who otherwise would be idle would then cost society nothing. This would save energy. Certainly, he agreed, there was no excuse for public works in periods of brisk employment, unless the need was immediate and acute. In periods of "lax employment," however, the choice lay between "public enterprise, public charity, and suffering." In a period of depression, therefore, the public should borrow for public works and pay off the bonds in time of prosperity.

Doubtless, he added, states had gone too far in providing employment for the "out-of-work," but a certain amount of public work was inevitable. Therefore the choice was merely as to the time at which public works should be executed and to which payments should be postponed. Certainly the public works which in any case would be postponed should be performed at the period of lowest social cost.

After developing these theories in his first two books, Davenport in 1897 still vainly sought a suitable teaching post. Fortunately Laughlin obtained a fellowship for him at the University of Chicago. In one year Davenport did his necessary graduate work, wrote his dissertation, taught elementary economics, and, with Anna M. Emerson, wrote *The Principles of Grammar*. Then he again became a high school principal, this time in Nebraska.

At Chicago he had become a student and warm personal friend of that skeptic Thorstein Veblen, who seemed to be engaged in criticizing the psychology of orthodox economics. Davenport was impressed. In 1902 he declared that "the rapid movement in psychological opinion . . . toward . . . the 'volitional' psychology as distinguished from the passive or associationist point of view—the newer insistence upon impulse and instinct in human activity as against calculating and reflective choice," showed the necessity for reformulating the fundamental assumptions of economic theory. The process of valuation being a psychological problem, the next step in advancing economic theory must come from the psychologists. Until then, he thought, the economists need only recognize that any form of hedonistic theory was discredited. And, he asserted, that although the Austrian school had been using a good deal of Benthamite language, their essential doctrines could, without substantially impairing their economic bearing, be stripped of their psychological or ethical implications. That is, all that remained to be done in the way of a purely economic analysis was to purge the Austrian theory and terminology of its hedonistic origins.

To Davenport these modifications consisted of reformulating the Austrian scheme in terms of "marginal relative utility" or marginal sacrifice. He now thought that only by this concept, i.e., "the individual's comparison of competing marginal utilities," could economists move from "the purely personal and psychological aspects of the problem to the objective and impersonal [market value] resultant," for the marginal utilities of different persons were incomparable.

Davenport further refined the marginal analysis by declaring that the seller's minimum prices or producer's "reserve" prices were in effect "demand" prices, and thus supply represented an implicit demand, in accordance with the logic of the Austrian school. For example, if at a price of $1.00 a seller preferred to withhold from the market a commodity which he would sell at $1.01, his "own demand" for the product was strong enough to make himself a "buyer" rather than a seller at $1.00.[34]

Davenport reiterated that the "opportunity cost" consisted of the sacrifice of alternative opportunities of productive employment or productive investment. True, the actual going concern—the market system under which production occurred and costs were determined—conformed only slightly to any schematic statement, but the enterpriser chose his product in accordance with his estimate of market opportunities. His cost of production was essentially the same as in the isolated Crusoe economy: "Cost is the long-run refusal price below which, as a margin, the advantages of some alternative activity will tip the scales.[35]

Davenport, though now a man of some reputation in "theory," was still considered "eccentric" by chairmen of college economics departments.[36] Fortunately he obtained an instructorship at the University of Chicago. But though he rose to the rank of associate professor he felt that such status and its income tagged him as a "second-class man." [37] Consequently in 1908 he accepted a full professorship at the University of Missouri, and in 1913 became head of its newly established School of Commerce. But he wanted to be in an institution allowing him more scope for graduate work. The opportunity came in 1916 when he was called to Cornell.

During this time Davenport became increasingly convinced of the need to cleanse economic theory of its crude apologetic notes. Toward this end he prepared a critical volume on the development of economic thought, one of the most comprehensive of its kind— *Value and Distribution* (1908); and in 1913 he published a new text under the title of *The Economics of Enterprise.*

Superficially the books seemed to cut across well-established traditions. Economics, he declared, must cease to be apologetic, must eschew such erroneous doctrines as "specific productivity," the "social organism," and the description of "capital" as purely "technological." It must recognize that the present competitive system, with its institutions of money, exchange, and private property, was not grounded in nature, but was merely a stage in the evolution of society. It must not hide behind the doctrine of Adam Smith's beneficent unseen hand, but fearlessly study economic life from the private, acquisitive point of view, from the "standpoint of the phenomena of price" as the central factor in economic life. Thus even "production" must be viewed as simply the securing of an income, so that the successful thief is productive. At this point Davenport contributed a lengthy sentence which has since become classic: "All labor, therefore, that commands a price, though it be the poisoning of a neighbor's cow or the shooting of an upright judge, all durable goods commanding a rent or affording a valuable service—lands, machines, burglars' jimmies, houses, pianos, freight cars, passenger cars, pleasure boats—all patents, privileges, claims, franchises, monopolies, tax-farming contracts, that bring an income, all advertising, lying, earning, finding, begging, picking, or stealing that achieve a reward in price or a return which is worth a price— are productive by the supreme and ultimate test of private gain."

Davenport had closed his earlier treatises by parrying the criticisms of the existing order; he now closed with a bill of particulars against it. The use of a different style and emphasis—and new expressions drawn primarily from the idiom of Veblen—created confusion in Davenport's readers. He repeated his basic philosophy of man and environment. The truths of economics remained valid, he said, so long as the fundamentals of human nature remained unchanged; namely, the existence of human needs and desires, the dependence of aggregate consumption on production and the dependence of production on men's efficiency, instrumental aids, and environment. Institutions were subject to change, but were "good or bad according to the degree of human development." And "only that government was good which both governors and governed were fit for." Consequently private property, individual initiative, competition, the money system, and production for the market were "present adjustments." Since exchange was a socially productive process, a money economy meant merely that a particular commodity had been specialized to perform the intermediate exchange function.

In Davenport's entrepreneurial analysis product prices were explained by the factor prices, and the prices of the factors would in themselves be explained by the prices of the products. Opportunity costs, the alternate opportunities of the entrepreneur, related entrepreneur costs to the actual facts of business; but they provided no escape from the circle, for the opportunity foregone was merely to produce another thing at a price, and this still left price undetermined. The entrepreneurial analysis therefore concerned itself with the last item in a long series of causal connections, based on the ultimate forces of human desires for products and the productive capacities of human beings and their instrumental equipment. Market value emerged as the adjusting point for all the forces engaged.

According to Davenport, what from the social point of view was expressed in the relative scarcity or plenty of products was from the competitive point of view expressed in higher or lower money costs of production. To take the entrepreneur's point of view as ultimate would involve circularity, he declared; that is, a foundation could not be laid in the real forces of which prices and costs were the pecuniary expression. The circularity involved, Davenport illustrated in a rhyme.

> The price of pig
> Is something big;
> Because its corn, you'll understand,
> Is high-priced, too;
> Because it grew
> Upon the high-priced farming land.
>
> If you'd know why
> That land is high,
> Consider this: its price is big
> Because it pays
> Thereon to raise
> The costly corn, the high-priced pig!

To resolve the circularity Davenport elaborated this view: "Prices have their setting in a great moving equilibrium, all the parts of which are related to all the other parts, and are in close interdependence with them. As one part changes, others and then still others change. The lines of causation are not easy to trace or even the direction of them easy to establish. . . . We start with the entirely correct assumption that the market price of any one commodity is determined by the demand for it and the supply of it, and that this price is the equating point between the demand and supply. But note that this way of formulating the price problem concerns itself with only one commodity at a time. Prices are tacitly taken for granted as already fixed for all other lines of production." In this, as a commentator has remarked, Davenport, though inept in mathematics, verbally performed a "difficult mathematical feat—to avoid 'circularity' in handling the neo-classical price problem—by a procedure equivalent to simultaneous equations." [38]

Like John Bates Clark, Davenport now found that land must be treated as capital, that higher rents were paid for the same reason that higher wages were paid. Rent was the hire of any item of capital; interest was the same hire expressed in terms of the percentage of the money value of the capital. Rent therefore was a cost, indistinguishable from all other costs.

Because of the law of diminishing returns, which Davenport christened the law of proportion of factors, there was to him no intrinsic difference to the entrepreneur between costs for labor and costs for capital. Because of the never-ceasing possibilities of substitution, cost outlays could not be allocated into rigid categories. In the market process they were all price shares in a homogeneous fund. The entrepreneur by the process of competitive bidding was bound to pay approximately all he could afford for any item's gain-yielding capacity, but the gain as a cost was ultimately traceable to its relative scarcity.

Davenport defined production as anything yielding an income, but he stripped this conception of much of its apparent heretical implication by distinguishing between primary and secondary distribution. Primary distribution, he said, accompanied the production of goods and services, for it was the income of the instruments and labor which created the aggregate psychic incomes. Secondary distribution was merely a redistribution of the primary income and essentially "predation or parasitism." The "rigging" of the stock market, through "bear" raids, artificially low dividends, or by "declaration of unearned or bookkeeping dividends" furnished examples.

Thus, while not all income was "received by title either of independent production or of co-operative contribution to production," there was "a distribution by right of productive contribution." Many of the "mere rights of tribute" were included in the productive process, and ranked as a valuable market advantage or opportunity for individuals controlling these rights—for example, royalties on patent processes. But since there was no way to bring these classes of facts "within the orderly sequence of economic laws," Davenport said they might well be dismissed from the discussion "merely stopping, however, to note that the incomes upon them—to the extent that these incomes are so far vested as to promise future revenues—are capitalized under the discount principle, are saleable like other acquisitive goods, are wealth for all individual ends of gain or of social prestige, and carry with them the right to participate in the enjoyment of the social product."

In general, Davenport contended that the imperfections incident to the competitive system referred not so much to the "primary—the production—distribution, as to the political and property institutions" under which the secondary distribution occurred, and to the modifications of the primary distribution because of the reacting effects of the secondary distribution. By similar reasoning he argued that despite the importance of monopoly and corporations they were not of theoretical interest for they did not warrant any "change in the traditional theory and terminology of the science."

Davenport's books, especially the *Economics of Enterprise*, aroused a furor in the profession. Fetter said that what little was sound in it had long been stated by the American Psychological School (by which name he designated his own doctrines.) He declared that Davenport was guilty of radical expressions. "Loose women with their flaunting appeals appear so often that they make some chapters . . . appear like an evening at the uncensored movies." He added that Davenport, noting that private capital did not always correspond with social welfare, became a doctrinaire and, like Marx and Henry George, engaged in "indiscriminate denunciation" of the present order, which he carried "well nigh to the length of radical communism." He criticized Davenport for overlooking the "grounds of social history, social expediency, and social productivity of a big institution," such as private property.[39]

Fisher, on the other hand, warmly praised Davenport's *Value and Distribution*. He felt that Davenport had independently and by literary methods reached the conclusions of the mathematical economists, including Jevons and Marshall; though, had Davenport been better acquainted with the mathematical school, he would have avoided certain difficulties. Fisher gave great credit to Davenport, however, for successfully adopting his theories, as a sound economist should, to the ideas and methods of the practical businessman.[40]

Perhaps the best comment among the mixed reception was made by John Maurice Clark in a personal note to Davenport. As a strict logician and grammarian, Davenport had been a stickler on definitions. So Clark was justified in saying: "I think you must suffer in the eyes of economists from your attitude towards terms and definitions. One moment you are fighting for the only correct usage, and the critic might say: 'He's dogmatic and he doesn't know what definitions are for in a scientific discussion,' and the next moment you are using the terminology of the other school and the critic might say: 'He's shifted his terms after establishing them: he isn't playing the game through as he began it—again he doesn't know what terms are for.' "[41]

Beyond stirring up controversy, Davenport left his permanent imprint on the development of economic doctrine. Perhaps his most novel and suggestive lead was his elaboration of the loan-fund doctrine of capital. This fund, he declared, comes primarily from the commercial bank's creation of circulating credit, that is, deposit currency rather than savings. Commercial banking is, therefore, essentially an underwriting of borrowers' credits. The "problem of the supply of the loan fund and of the interest rates is, for any given time and situation . . . a banking problem. [It is more] a question of the volume of circulating medium and the uses for which it is offered, than a question of the aggregate wealth of society, of the source or nature of it, or of the abstinences conditioning the existence of any part of it." The fixing of interest rates, he flatly declared in expanding his thesis in 1916, is "exclusively a banking phenomenon," and their fluctuation is "almost entirely a matter of banking policy." The thing borrowed, deposit currency, is primarily of banking origin. "Capital is furnished to the businessman by the loan to him of the banker's credit. The derivative funds as they fall into the hands of individuals disposed to lend them are ordinary loanable funds, . . . are capital to the borrowing customer, and are funds which are capital assets to any holder disposed so to employ them." When banks have easy reserve conditions, the offer of funds increases and interest rates fall.

To analyze interest without attention to the phenomenon of banking, as was done in most treatises, Davenport denounced as futile. The bankruptcy of current interest theory, he explained, could be seen in the world situation after the outbreak of the European war. Although interest rates were extremely low and credit was easy in both Europe and America, with "abstinence and consumption perspectives" still the standard explanations of interest, "economic authority and theory," he said, "have become a joke and a byword." [42]

Along similar lines was Davenport's questioning of the traditional doctrine of savings. He asked how in the existing economic organization this saving occurred. His explanation was that when the railroads have unused capacity, "they will not borrow to construct more. When the dividends are falling, new railroads will not be built." If businessmen and corporations will not extend their operations, savings in any considerable volume become an impossibility because there is no market for them. He concluded that the "limit of rational savings is set by the prospective elasticity of consumption," that is, current savings, and decrease in consumption should be undertaken only with an eye to the future increase in consumption. But, following the older tradition, he condemned savings which manifest themselves not in the increase of the productive equipment, but which flow into consumption loans or into financing fiscal deficits.

In his correspondence of this later period Davenport was, at one and the same time, far more critical than in his books and yet skeptical of any specific reforms in the existing order. Stirred up by what he considered Arthur Twining Hadley's blunt demand that economists be conservative, Davenport wrote in 1909 that the time was long overdue for thoughtful men to get radical. He thought, however, that he could be most useful in helping to eliminate "our outworn and apologetic Political Economy—the Hadley sort." The laws, he said, also "need changing and the judges even more—but I have not much belief in these things as fundamental causes or that affairs would go very differently if these intermediate facts were changed. . . . What little I have seen of the Initiative and the Primary in the West has not won my faith. But, of course, I am still further away from thinking that bad economic doctrine is fundamental. . . . Each of us must keep hitting and hacking away at whatever good work is nearest him. For my own part, I have not much confidence in any of it; I suspect that it all comes too late." [43]

Yet Davenport declared that Fisher's scheme to stabilize the dollar led logically to the conclusion that no reason existed for gold coinage. "In the present situation," he wrote, "this sort of talk would be dangerous and inexpedient, but . . . some day the practice . . . ought to come to this." Although the financial interests would oppose the scheme, if they thought it might lead to something like government banking, yet it was "true that there is no need for the American people to have two billions of dollars invested in gold bullion used as money." [44]

In his correspondence Davenport stated that employers should not expect a lowering of wage costs. This, in the long run, would be as "undesirable as it is unpromising." Furthermore, no lasting welfare could come to society, even if it could be accomplished, from any general restriction of consumption and saving of incomes on the part of the laboring classes. "If products are to be produced someone will have to consume them; else business stagnation will necessarily attend the savings program. The entire doctrine of the meaning and limitations of savings in our competitive society I believe to have been wrongly held by the classical economists." [45]

Much as he tried, Davenport could not completely divorce his ethics from his economic science. He found he could not complete his book on taxation because of his desire to resolve the question of the ethical basis of taxation, which led him to the ethical basis of the State. His close friend, the historian Carl Becker, tried to convince him that the State was simply a form of power resulting from the conflict of wills and interests. But Davenport was not convinced. "He felt profoundly that some things were instinctively judged right and wrong and apart from convention and custom; but he could never find any social basis for this instinctive individual feeling," wrote Becker.[46] Yet it was this tacit but rigorous emphasis on individual feeling that perhaps accounts for Davenport's success in developing the logic of the ruling price economics.

Davenport was a gifted teacher. He was merciless in the classroom with anyone who questioned his doctrine; but the cross-examination of the luckless doubter was always conducted on a high intellectual level. Curiously, he would encourage the dissenters to discuss their views with him in private conference, and he would turn out to be most anxious to push the inquiries of anyone who thought he found something wrong in his ideas.

He was essentially a simple, forthright man. Asked to contribute to a volume in which each American economist was to present a summary statement of his own doctrines, he replied:

> I don't think I like the plan. I have never seen but one specimen of its working out. . . . It seems to me in the very worst of taste. I should not like to report just what I think of my own theories. At the best fist I could make of it, I don't see that it would do any good, and I should get ill in the process. So count me out.[47]

Davenport engaged young instructors in economics who to him were not actually "theorists" but rather students of bordering subjects such as philosophy, psychology, sociology, and ethics. Thanks to Davenport, they had the opportunity to follow their interests, and several of them became outstanding economists of the succeeding generation. Through this practice Davenport did much to expand the scope of economic inquiry, while by his own intellectual formalism he attempted to narrow it. This is not to deny that his formal analysis was not valuable; it was extremely important, for it was a courageous attempt to eliminate the apologetics that so easily crept into economic analysis.

Each of these men—Fetter, Fisher, and Davenport—worked out the inherent logic of the competitive system as a rational order. Each also saw defects in the system, but they gave little attention to the integration of these with the logic. With Fisher, the removal of the defects awaited some future day when analysis would be powerful enough to cope with them; with Fetter, the defects could be expected to disappear in the course of progress; with Davenport, they merely evidenced the inherent limitation of the true science of economics.

In spite of the fact, however, that they tried to create a logical pattern for the seemingly illogical behavior of human society, they approached its brute facts more nearly than any of their predecessors. They attempted, with remarkable success, to walk the ridge between economic formalism and expedient business practice; this gave their thought an alertness and a nimbleness that requires much intellectual agility to follow. This also accounts for the fact that, despite their emphasis upon the mathematics and logic of monetary measurement, they appear flexible, and rather as seekers of truth than followers of an established faith. Their theory suggests the rational skepticism of the eighteenth century.

CHAPTER XVII

A Study in Contrasts

THE capacity of the American university to encourage and foster diverse views has seldom been more clearly demonstrated than at the University of Michigan. There two first-rate social scientists, Fred M. Taylor and Charles Horton Cooley, were influential teachers. Each took his doctorate at Michigan, and each spent almost his whole active career at that institution. And yet, during their long years of service, Taylor and Cooley developed along almost diametrically opposed lines. Taylor became an expert analyst and purifier of "orthodox" economic thought; Cooley emerged as an innovator, particularly in his belief that valuation is a social process.

FRED MANVILLE TAYLOR: SYSTEMATIZER OF DOCTRINE

Fred M. Taylor (1855–1932) was a native of Michigan. His undergraduate work was done at Northwestern University,[1] and after graduating in 1876 he taught and headed an Illinois high school for three years. Then he became professor of history and belles-lettres at Albion College in Albion, Michigan (1879–92).[2] His studies in history and political science left on him a stronger and more conscious impression than on most teachers of economics; for Taylor, in the beginning, was primarily interested in political philosophy. In fact, while teaching at Albion, he completed his doctorate at the University of Michigan in political philosophy under the Hegelian philosopher George Sylvester Morris.

Taylor's dissertation, *The Right of the State to Be* (1891), was

Hegelian in form. It was avowedly an attempt to defend the order of "natural law" or the law of nature against attacks from "zealous reformers." It characterized the critics of natural law and natural rights as engineers who would abolish weight and friction as a necessary prelude to constructing a stone fortress. "While law sets limits to the range and method of our activity," Taylor wrote, it is essential to the stability and reality of our work. In the past fanatical revolutionists, inspired by that "half-mad, uneducated child of genius," Rousseau, had appealed to natural law to achieve quickly the improvement of man, but they ignored its two bases: the nature of man, and the circumstances at the given time. Thus the "absolute order" of natural law, when properly conceived, was established not by opinion but by nature, and was consequently supreme over every order of human design and was the best antidote to fanaticism.[3]

By the time Taylor's dissertation was published, he was expounding the doctrine of "natural law" in the field of economics at the University of Michigan.[4] He made his debut as a writer on economics supporting the gold standard in the free silver controversy of the nineties. He was keenly interested in monetary matters and planned as his first textbook a work on money and banking. To this end he printed privately for the use of his students *Some Chapters on Money* (1906). Tampering with the established monetary standard, he argued, could only bring disaster. A good standard was a stable one, but stability required first of all that the mechanism be the product of "natural evolution," and not something "highly artificial, originating in human ingenuity." Such a system would be hard to overthrow, for it had behind it permanent abiding forces— "a claim proved by the fact that it has been evolved." On the other hand, a system which resulted from the special efforts of men contending against "natural tendencies" would be weak, because men's conscious ideals, opinions, and desires changed easily, and thus the forces on which such a system depended would in turn change.

Basically Taylor stood for the gold standard because to him the most important requisite of a good standard was internationality. Since the ideal, a world standard, was impossible to achieve, he said, a standard like the gold standard, which was the same as that of the countries with which we maintained the closest commercial and banking relations, was best. Such a common standard, first of all, would provide a constant par of exchange a matter of the utmost significance to trade. Second, it would facilitate the international movement of capital, by reducing the risk element and in some cases rendering the burden of debt easier to bear. Third, the common standard, by permitting the free flow of money in and out of the country, would permit a country to rectify any deficiency in its stock of standard money by importing it; a surplus would be eliminated by exports. Finally, the common standard would be far more constant in value than one limited to a few nations.

On the other hand he did not maintain that the standard should depend on concerted international action, but simply on national action. Systems which depended on international concert he considered inherently unstable. "Nations are free to change their minds in dealing with each other; they are likely to have abundant reason for doing so; and all experience shows they frequently yield to the temptation." He said that he was not against nations agreeing on a common standard but that the standard should not be one depending for its stability on the agreement. Taylor avowedly aimed this at international bimetallism, which, requiring international concert of the great powers, would, even if practicable, be undesirable because unstable. And he also attacked J. Allen Smith's multiple standard as "too artificial, too ingenious."

In addition to the gold standard, Taylor wanted an "elastic" national bank currency, in the form of an asset currency, as the best means of providing for sufficient money in a panic, of mitigating the evils of fluctuations in money in ordinary times, and of protecting the gold reserve. The greenbacks and silver certificates he wanted abolished.

It was in connection with the problem of protecting the gold reserve that Taylor made his most suggestive analysis in the field of money. Under the universal gold standard, he pointed out, the world's monetary stock would tend to distribute itself automatically according to "relative need," that is, relative "resources." When the stock of one country, as compared with another, was small in relation to the money work done, its bank reserves would be deficient. The discount rate would then rise, and money would flow in for investment. Furthermore, the high discount rate would cause the prices of securities and staples to fall, resulting in a further inflow of money. Should a country have excess money, the reverse process would correct the situation.

He qualified this, however, by saying that in some circumstances a conscious control of the movement of money would be desirable in order to maintain the stability of the credit system. In our modern monetary structure, composed largely of credit money and bank money, he wrote, the standard money was actually the basis of the whole system. Consequently every extensive movement of standard money must be jealously watched, for while in the long run the excessive drain would correct itself, we could not afford to wait, for meanwhile serious consequences might occur. The loss of the reserve would overthrow the standard; even the beginnings of a serious depletion would so disturb the business world and so injure industry as to precipitate a panic. Under such circumstances active and vigorous measures to prevent a drain must be taken.

He pointed to European practice as an example. To protect the reserve, the great European central banks had developed an elaborate series of checks, the most important of which was the discount policy, a device for hastening the operation of the natural correctiveness of a drain. When gold exports became serious, the Central Bank raised its discount rate, and if this proved ineffective, the rate was raised still higher. Soon the mobile capital of neighboring countries was attracted, and gold outflow, to that extent, was stopped.

Taylor was even willing to allow a country to suspend specie payments to protect the gold reserve, as had France after the opening disaster of the Franco-Prussian war of 1870. The specie of the great bank reserve of France, he wrote, was being drawn for export. To prevent the loss, the government ordered the Bank of France to suspend specie payments. "This policy was of course seriously objectionable in that it involved a temporary overthrow of the standard of value, and a setting up of a fiat money standard," but the paper money was so judiciously handled that the change in the standard was comparatively small and the evil effects insignificant compared to its achieving the stoppage of the specie outflow.

Taylor himself specifically limited the "conscious" control of gold movements or "stay measures" to drains caused by great wars and the drains arising from unwise statutes, like the Sherman Silver Purchase Act, or other "artificial conditions" which at the very best could not be changed for a considerable time. But his logic was capable of expansion beyond the limit he set.

Taylor's general theory of money and prices was along the lines of Laughlin's anti-quantity theory position, but it was not so extreme. He agreed that it was almost indisputable that the price level tended to vary with the quantity of money, provided sufficient emphasis was put on "tended." But he added that "under normal conditions the influence of changes in the quantity of money" in general was "so slight as scarcely to deserve consideration." The majority of changes in the price level could primarily be explained by conscious readjustment to a changed standard, or by the real cost of producing goods, or by changes in business confidence. The first, which in an expanded form was Laughlin's position, happened when the public had fairly conclusive evidence of the occurrence and extent of a change in the value of the standard. In such cases an almost immediate "direct readjustment of general prices would take place, i.e., of the value of money to the changed standard." The clearest example of this was one which could hardly arise in any "decently governed modern country"; that is, where a formal change was made from the standard consisting of a specified amount of one metal to that containing a different amount of the same metal. Suppose, he wrote, the American government should substitute for its present standard of the dollar, 25.8 grains of gold, a standard half as large, 12.9 grains, "surely no one can doubt that there would at once be a prompt readjustment of prices to the cheaper unit." That is, every dealer would immediately double the prices of the goods. "No one would think of waiting till the result was worked out by natural processes. Each [dealer] would see that readjustment was effected without delay." This being an unlikely case, Taylor considered the most important cause of variations in the price level to be changes in the real cost of producing goods. Perhaps his most interesting analysis dealt with the third cause: changes in business confidence which cause alternating periods of excessive trading and industrial stagnation. As long as credit and confidence increased, he said, demand was "constantly overtopping supply and so raising prices"; with a decline in these factors, supply would overtop demand and so depress prices.

This analysis Taylor based on the causes of variations in the price level in the "short-run period." According to him, the only way changes in the quantity of money influenced prices was by influencing the demand for goods. But the demand for goods was not caused by the quantity of money available, but by the desire to possess these goods. Now the people whose desire was significant in these matters were the dealers, and they would buy only if the prospect for profit was good. That is, according to Taylor's analysis, changes in demand primarily depended on changes in the dealers' estimate of business prospects. Of course, the dealer must have available buying power, but this was only a condition. The primary cause of the buying was not the possession of the buying power but the inclination to buy, "due to supposed prospects of profit." To assume that the money was the cause was like assuming that a man decided to move because a moving van happened to be in front of the door.

Taylor, being completely wrapped up in defending the gold standard, contended that even if a monetary standard could eliminate booms and depressions, this would be of doubtful value. The early rise and later decline in prices which characterized them, he said, were "perfectly natural phenomena, expressing the real facts of value as determined by demand." In the physicians' language, they were physiological rather than pathological. "The presumption surely is that, being perfectly natural, they have some part to play in industrial life and should be let alone."

Taylor did not consider his attacks on the quantity theory as a departure from tradition, for he asserted in the end that his criticisms were directed against the "crude quantity theory." [5] As the controversy over bimetallism petered out, Taylor devoted increasing attention to preparing a general treatise on economics. His standard of self-criticism was high; he had seven editions of his *Principles of Economics* privately printed for his students before he permitted a commercial edition. It presented a most rigorous treatment of the principles of economics and an evaluation of the current system from an "orthodox" standpoint.

Most noteworthy was Taylor's comprehensive statement of the laws of return. He held that increasing returns to variable factors of production prevailed only when the indivisible fixed factors were themselves under-utilized. This implied that more of the indivisible factors were on hand than would be technologically desirable with full divisibility. Taylor stressed his point by an elaborate numerical and tabular presentation, which has since served as the basis of modern statements of the law. He "demonstrated" that if all factors were assumed divisible, and if additional units of a variable factor were added to a fixed amount of a divisible factor, then any tendency to increase marginal products of the variable factor would imply a negative marginal product of the constant factor. This would indicate the presence of too much of the latter, relative to the amount of the variable factor. Taylor went on to show that with all factors costing something and with full divisibility, diminishing returns would characterize the use of all factors.

Taylor admitted that the increase in the size of plants, as distinguished from the proportioning of factors with a given size of plant, might be another cause of efficiency and of diminishing unit costs; but he believed this law of decreasing costs, the "economies of large-scale production," to be temporary.[6] In the face of limited resources, human and inanimate, he said, the normal law was that of "increasing costs," although for long periods "constant costs" might characterize an industry. Normally, he thought, plants could not grow into giant monopolies; and therefore so-called monopolies should be distinguished from efficient large-scale units.

In accordance with the views of "mathematical" economists, Taylor held that the prices of all goods were interdependent because the prices of products and their costs must coincide, and because almost all goods were "reciprocal substitutes" for one another. Equilibrium, therefore, would inevitably occur when the price of each primary factor or "cost good" coincided substantially with its "marginal significance," and if it involved a disutility factor of human origin, it coincided substantially with the marginal disutility of supplying that factor. If the prices of the factors expressed their "marginal" or specific significance, utility, production would be correctly guided by these prices both in respect to the choice of goods and in proportioning the factors in the production of goods.

Furthermore, if the prices for the factors should happen to be incorrect in the sense of not expressing their marginal significance, immediate reaction would eliminate the mischief. If, for example, some factor had an abnormally high price, entrepreneurs would reduce their use of the factor; its demand would fall below the stock or natural output; and the superfluous stock would cause a fall in its price to its natural level. Therefore only the prices for primary factors which expressed their marginal significance would maintain themselves under the "automatic working of economic forces."

Although Taylor did not credit entrepreneurs with the ability to determine the "precise amount of product imputable to each factor in joint processes," to him the policies they tentatively but spontaneously adopted in each situation tended "automatically, in spite of the ignorance of their authors . . . to establish the correct factor prices, the price expressing their marginal significance." [7]

Though rent had no original disutility cost, it had an equivalent, what he called "derivative disutilities." Since the market price of land equaled the capitalization of its net income, persons seeking to become rent receivers would invest in land as if it were a producible commodity and thereby assume the "ordinary capitalistic disutilities, abstinence, waiting, and risk taking." Thus under free competition, he wrote, "every individual tends to get approximately that income which expresses the marginal significance of the natural supply of the type of contribution made by himself or his property to the sum of utilities, and which at the same time expresses approximately the marginal disutility involved in making that contribution." This he held to be the "service value" principle underlying the current scheme of distribution.

Although a stickler for objectivity, he sought it by peculiarly narrowing his field of investigation. Such practices as predatory competition, favoritism, stock-jobbing, he would completely exclude from "a purely scientific analysis of economic principles." The extent to which they modified economic principles belonged in ethics or sociology. But he felt called upon to defend wealth, saying that thrift after all was still essential to acquire and maintain large fortunes. If moralists deprecated the large fortunes created through government grant of resources, they ignored the fact that this public liberality had been justified as part of the price of the country's extraordinarily rapid development.

In general Taylor was against government intervention. He opposed price-fixing because he felt it would intensify the underlying difficulties of scarcity by taking away the stimulus to increase production. But if certain prices were unreasonably high from the standpoint of the public welfare, the government might purchase the goods and resell them at reduced prices to the classes especially injured by the high prices. Production in the affected fields would be insignificantly reduced, since the producers would bear only a slight share of the taxes required to pay for the goods. The socialist contention that "public initiative" would eliminate the "so-called industrial cycle" was fairly reasonable, he wrote, but of lessening importance as the leaders of industry were learning to control the cycles. To those who contended that a shortage of purchasing power existed which culminated in depression, Taylor countered with perhaps the best textbook statement of Say's law.

Taylor staunchly declared that, compared to other forms of economic organization, the present system was the best, at least for the moment. He took pains to point out the defects of socialism. To begin with, he said, the principle of equality of income was undesirable because it would prevent society from making the best use of its resources. To avoid wasting important factors in unimportant commodities, each primary factor must be assigned a price under socialism as well as in the present order of free initiative and private enterprise. But whereas under the present system the assigning occurred automatically, socialism would require a complete system of bookkeeping. And "when each person has been credited with the true value of his contribution, would not that person under any system remotely practicable have to be paid that value or something approximating it?" Indeed, a truly benevolent "dictator in a collectivist state . . . would choose to retain the present system." [8]

Taylor conceded and even emphasized that production in a socialist state need not necessarily be guided by arbitrary principles; it would be on a sound theoretical foundation if it followed the fundamental principles of economics he had laid down. "If the economic authorities of a socialist state would recognize equality between cost of production on the one hand, and the demand price of the buyer on the other, as . . . the only adequate proof that the commodity in question ought to be produced, they could . . . [guide] production, with the well-founded confidence that they would never make any other than the right use of the [community's] economic resources." [9]

But to Taylor the demonstration that a socialist State could rationally operate the economic mechanism, that is, follow "orthodox" principles, by no means proved that the socialist State was just as good as, let alone better than, the present system. On the contrary, the demonstration would merely show the universality of the fundamental "orthodox" principles, and would also show that the current system closely approximated the ideal of rational economic organization. In line with this he presented the following problem to his advanced students:

"How about getting help from the study of value under . . . [a communistic order], in trying to understand the concept of economic value in the present order? If we find in such a study that real values under a communistic order coincide with the values which ideally perfect conditions . . . [in the system] of free private initiative would tend to embody in prices, we should surely have a strong presumption in favor of the idea that the present system tends to establish the economically correct prices. Defend that statement." [10]

Taylor's demonstration that socialism could follow orthodox principles was eventually hailed as a major contribution by those writers who, accepting the tenets of the dominant theory of value, wished to "modernize" socialist economic doctrine.[11] Taylor considered himself not an innovator in economics but a˙systematizer; not an inquirer into actual conditions but a formulator of the logic of why the current system had an underlying harmony. "My particular capacities and tastes," he declared, "added to earlier training in Philosophy, made it natural for me, as a teacher of Economics, to devote myself to theory, with only so much attention to the concrete as was necessary to furnish the background required for theoretic analysis. My chief ambition was to restate what might be looked upon as generally accepted economic doctrine brought down to date—that restatement to be more organic and self-consistent than is usual." [12]

In later years Taylor made some striking exceptions to tradition. In edition after edition of his *Principles* he had sharply denounced the heresy of general overproduction by vigorously presenting Say's law that the "demand for goods produced for the market consists of goods produced for the market, i.e., the same goods are at once the demand for goods and the supply of goods; so that, if we can assume that producers have directed production in true accord with one another's wants, total demand must in the long run coincide with the total product of output of goods produced for the market." But in his ninth and last edition, in 1925, he made a significant qualification in his characteristic manner. He still asserted the truth of Say's law, but it now became a long-run principle in more than the usual sense of long run.

His analysis was based on his qualification that in modern society every exchange of product was divided into two parts; first, a product was exchanged for money or bank credit; then the money or credit was exchanged for another product. And there was always a time interval between the two operations. Thus the second part could be postponed for a long period, even indefinitely, thereby reducing the general demand for goods, though the amount of production was not cut down. But when such discrepancies between demand and output became quite general, that is, a general decline in demand, this of necessity meant a "general slackening of productivity all along the line." Such a situation was characteristic of the depression that followed a business crisis. Should the government at such times undertake a large public works program, total demand would be increased considerably, thereby increasing general prosperity.

This conclusion was startling, coming as it did from a man who had earlier insisted that the phenomenon of boom and depression was simply a reflection of natural law. But it was still of so little theoretical importance in Taylor's mind as compared with the fundamental truth of Say's law that it was not even given a question in the list appended at the end of each chapter. It cannot be said to indicate any significant change in Taylor's fundamental tenets.

These he held to tenaciously and dogmatically in both teaching and writing. A former colleague complained that "the defect of the elementary course under Professor Taylor was that it was . . . an exercise in logic, rather than instruction in the practice of the scientific method of determining premises. The result was to make young students who had been exercised in the artificially simplified cases used in the course unduly sure of themselves." [13] To such contentions Taylor frankly admitted that he considered a dogmatic presentation the best foundation for sound thinking, and that he wished to discourage reading of other men's theories until the students had been thoroughly drilled in his principles.[14] He even prepared a book of selections, *Some Readings in Economics* (1907), with proper introductory and editorial notes, pointing out the passages that supported his theories. For the benefit of instructors he prepared a *Key to Problems in Principles of Economics* (1921), which gave the "proper" answers to the questions asked in the treatise. Taylor's particular drill-master technique, with its printed questions and readings, achieved such a vogue outside of Michigan that department heads at leading institutions proposed similar systems, lest Taylor's system envelop the field.[15]

Outside the classroom and his published work, surprisingly, Taylor advocated a variety of social reforms. He supported organizations favoring child labor legislation and, in the presidential election of 1924, backed the third-party candidate, Robert M. La Follette. The explanation of this seeming contradiction is revealing; Taylor was convinced that political and social matters belonged in the realm of "imponderables" and were not amenable to scientific analysis. The "ponderables" were those factors that accounted for the working of the modern economic system.

And behind Taylor's theoretical scheme lay the notion, expressed in his first published paper, that the great safeguard and the "ultimate foundation of society—security for life, liberty, property, honor, etc."—was moral training. Enlightened self-interest, he argued, is inadequate since the majority of men are not enlightened but are guided by emotion and by immediate appetite rather than the thrift that cares for the morrow. Consequently enlightened self-interest breaks down in the time of trial, and the "torrent of passions sweeps away in a moment the work of a lifetime." [16]

A further paradox might be added to what is already involved enough by tracing the "radical" use to which Taylor's conservative economic doctrines were later put by the New Deal. The old order, which Taylor thought he was defending, bitterly criticized the New Deal devaluation of the dollar, public works program, and sale of commodities below cost to people on relief—all of which could be defended by reference to Taylor's economics. It is ironic that his few lapses from tradition would seem to have had such far-reaching effects. But this is largely fantasy, for the New Deal economists were scarcely followers of Taylor.

Irony also permeated Taylor's teaching career. The administrative system in his own courses indirectly permitted the growth of heresy. Gifted young men, already touched with heterodoxy but of limited means and interested in acquiring doctorates, accepted the low-paying temporary instructorships at Michigan. These men soon mastered a technique of giving their students a good but rapid drilling in "Freddy's economics" so that class grades were high, and then the instructors used the remaining time to expound what doubtless would have sounded to Taylor like rank heresy. In fact the very men whom he had considered among his best teachers became in later years outstanding critics of the main tradition.

CHARLES HORTON COOLEY: CRITIC OF "ATOMISTIC" INDIVIDUALISM

Heresy at the University of Michigan in part arose from the influence of another teacher, Charles H. Cooley of the Department of Sociology. Cooley (1864–1929) was the son of the conservative

Judge Cooley, but like his father he was an independent spirit. In his undergraduate years at Michigan he was interested primarily in engineering. After a year of post-graduate work in that field he entered government service, working first with the Interstate Commerce Commission and then with the Census Bureau. Having a broad scholarly bent, he returned to the university in 1892 to teach half-time as an instructor in Adams' Department of Political Economy, and to work for a doctorate in economics. He obtained the degree in 1894, with a dissertation on "The Theory of Transportation."

In this study Cooley approved of government control, but not government ownership, of railways. Control, he declared, was more elastic, permitted the trial of various methods, and was "more in agreement with historical tendencies." And the first instrument of control should be publicity.[17] In that same year, in an essay on transportation written in collaboration with his father, Cooley declared that "the most natural solution" for the abuses of the railway companies would be regulation which should include the determination of controversies by representatives of the roads acting under the supervision of public authority. "One feature of such regulation must be the revival of the pooling principle, accompanied by such modifications and restraints as would render it more effectual than formerly and at the same time prevent its operating injuriously to the public interest."[18]

Cooley soon transferred to the new field of sociology, which he had offered as a minor for his doctorate. In good part Henry C. Adams was responsible for this move. While Cooley was walking along with Adams and Taylor one afternoon in 1892, Taylor made some suggestions for extending the work of the department. Adams replied that "he would rather see a course in sociology offered." Cooley told Adams that he would like to offer such a course, and Adams encouraged him to prepare for it.[19] In 1894 he introduced the course, and from that time on devoted himself exclusively to the subject.

Cooley's work as a sociologist enabled him to subject the notions which he entertained as an economist to a broader type of criticism. In the tradition of Henry C. Adams, he was quite skeptical of some of the rigid dogma of orthodox economics. His position on the type of economics associated with Taylor was most clearly stated in a lecture in 1911 on "Political Economy and Social Science." The treatment of process in the textbooks, he said, was "almost wholly a short-range study of mechanism, remarkable for elaborateness" in a narrow area, but it lacked breadth and shed little light on the "wider economic and social significance of the mechanism of which" it treated. The economic theorist, therefore, was like the man who observes "only the second hand of a watch: he counts the seconds with care, but is hardly in a position to tell what time it is." Cooley wanted an economic theory that "without losing any of the substantial results of current economics shall so broaden them as to meet in some degree the requirements already suggested."

The economic theorists, he said, started with consumer "demand as a datum"; and though demand was quite properly taken as a datum for the purpose of intensively studying market processes, in practice this method unfortunately amounted to assuming that demand was justified, and thus justified all the economic conditions effectively contributing to supply it. But "demand," protested Cooley, "is simply an expression of economic power and will as determined by all the existing conditions. It is as much the effect as the cause of the actual state of the economic system. Like all our inheritance it comes down from the past in a turbid stream, bearing with it those struggles and compromises that make up human history. All the evils of the economic system, except those which are added in the market process, are already implicit in demand, and of course are transmitted to production and distribution." The acceptance of this system as pure is like a city expecting to avoid the effects of polluted water by using clean pipes. "The pipes—that is, the process connecting demand and supply—are a matter of great solicitude to the economist, the source comparatively little."

Cooley did not subscribe to any economic interpretation in terms of a rigid class theory. But he did make the incisive observation that demand was largely a class phenomenon. Thus demand, according to him, was preponderantly determined by the economic power and will of a fraction of the population. But this did not necessarily make the concentration of it bad. While it meant waste and misdirection of social resources, it meant also the fostering of "important interests which a more equal distribution of power might possibly neglect." So demand, Cooley reiterated, expressed all the vices and virtues of the actual social system: it called just as loudly for prostitution, child labor, and corrupt politics as for better things. "In one sense it is the outcome of the inherent corruption of human nature"; in another it is the "outcome of the economic process itself."

The theorist, Cooley went on to say, peculiarly failed to show that competition was a part of a process of "progressive organization in which competition and combination are complementary phases of social adaptation." Competition was the very heart of the economic process, but the economist by abstracting it from other phases of the social movement conceived it in a "highly individualistic sense, and erected this narrow conception into an ideal." The theorist regarded combination as a disturbing condition and fitted it into the scheme by so-called "doctrinal patching." Yet far from being a "natural" development under so-called static or settled conditions, free competition could exist only as far as it was made a "conscious object of public will." It could be preserved only if in the first place certain "dynamic elements exist, such as the inequalities of individual capacity," and if it were deliberately fostered by such methods as "free public vocational education and the public control of great industries."

And the same comments were to his mind applicable to the economists' attitude toward government intervention. They treated the doctrine of public control also as a patch, he said, as alien to the economic process; whereas we should see public control as a "normal and inseparable part of the economic process; always growing with it." In the same way the economic theorists of the dominant school ignored the role of philanthropy and ethics. A social science which was not also in its basic principles "an ethical science," was "unfaithful to its deepest responsibility," that is, aiding general progress. Where this obligation was observed by the economists, it came from their "untutored good sense and good feeling . . . rather than from the principles of their science." In their textbooks the ethical considerations were "admittedly patches, not organic parts of the doctrine."

Cooley granted that the economist must necessarily specialize in the economic aspect of progress, but maintained that the economist should not do so by separating the principles of his science from those of social ethics. In short, he said, current economics dealt with social process, "almost wholly in its immediate and somewhat transitory aspects—such as that of market valuation—and is not, in a large sense, a science of process at all." [20]

Cooley thought that the economics of his day admirably explained the determination and workings of market valuation, but did not comprehend the underlying forces behind supply and demand. More deeply, he felt that it emphasized the material, pecuniary forces as agents of progress rather than the higher ethical forces. Its impersonal exactitudes, to his mind, left no room for those deeper insights into the individual and society that were requisite for social progress.

Primarily on these grounds he attributed much the same role to statistics as to orthodox economics. Although he had engaged in statistical work and had taught statistics, both "theoretical and practical," at Michigan at the beginning of his career, he considered it secondary even to traditional economics.[21] "Exact prediction," he declared in Social Process (1918), would be possible only when the general social situation remained unchanged or changed in ways not involving new problems of choice in the specific field of inquiry. The more the question was one of intelligence, the less the numerical method could cope with it. Students of the principles of sociology should be less concerned with seeking primary facts than with their interpretation, because at present the latter was the more difficult task. Facts were easily available which, "if fully digested and correlated, would be sufficient to illuminate" the whole field. It was, he said, as in economics, whose principles had been primarily worked out by "closer study and interpretation of facts, which, as details, every businessman" knew.

Cooley quite frankly stated in Social Organization (1909) that the principles of justifiable government undertakings were those advocated by Jevons. The real basis of most State functions was the need for them and the existence of no other adequate way to perform them. This held not only for the "primary ones of waging war and keeping order, but of issuing money, building roads, bridges, and harbors, collecting statistics, instituting free schools, controlling monopolies, and so on." But government undertakings should be "susceptible of comparatively simple and uniform methods," because the mechanism of the State was clumsy. The reasons justifying a State in running a post office or a telegraph, for example, were not necessarily sufficient for its assuming the far more complex railroad business. Again, any business taken over by a State should be watched at least by some "powerful group steadfastly interested in efficiency and capable of judging" whether it was attained. Thus the monetary and financial functions would be "safeguarded by the scrutiny of the commercial world." But in the case of the protective tariff, the lack of an effective balancing interest similar to that of the business community produced what he considered practically class legislation.

Consequently, said Cooley, the municipal sphere was the most favorable for the extension of government function. "Municipal socialism," he wrote, "has the great advantage over other sorts of State extension of being optional by small units, and of permitting all sorts of diversity, experiment, and comparison." It had nothing of that "deadening uniformity and obliteration of alternatives involved in the blanket socialism of the State. The evils we suffer from private monopolies . . . are as nothing compared with those to be feared from an all-embracing State monopoly."

The most far-reaching of Cooley's contributions to economics was his emphasis, reiterated from time to time, on the necessity of going behind pecuniary demand to realize that this was itself "no trustworthy expression of the human values actually working in the minds of men at a given time." At the same time he undertook to show how human values might progressively be given market standing; that is, become objects of pecuniary demand. "In general values can be expressed in the market only as they have become the object of extended recognition in some exchangeable form, and so of regular pecuniary competition." To attain such a position they must be accepted by the organized opinion of a considerable social group, who would supply the competitors. "They must also, in a measure, be standardized; that is, the degrees and kinds of value must be defined, so that regular and precise transactions" would be possible. New values seeking pecuniary expression must achieve a system; in other words, the "progress of market valuation . . . is a translation into pecuniary terms of values which have already become, in some measure, a social institution."

According to Cooley, the question of social improvement in terms of valuation was largely, therefore, that of imparting such "precision and social recognition" to those "psychical values" we believe evidence improvement, as "shall give them pecuniary standing, and add the inducement of market demand to whatever other forces may be working for their realization." More broadly, a better pecuniary valuation of men, said Cooley, required that service values be developed along with the social organization necessary to appreciate and define these and obtain their pecuniary recognition. No social manipulation could compel people to pay high prices for poor service, nor would good service obtain an adequate reward without support from a social structure. The natural process was "one of the concomitant development, though a continuing group, of service values and pecuniary appreciation." [22]

In the last analysis, Cooley held that economic phenomena should be viewed and studied as merely one phase of that organic whole which he called the social process. While Cooley was less heretical in detail than some of his broad propositions might indicate, their very breadth and his emphasis on social change within the framework of the existing system helped to feed the stream of liberal economic thought. He deeply influenced a rising group of liberal economists, not only through his writings, but also through personal contact with them in their formative years. As one of them, Walton H. Hamilton, put it, "he forced us to give up our Common Sense notions, led us away from an atomic individualism, made us see life as an 'organic whole,' and revealed to us 'the individual and society' remaking each other in an endless process of change." [23]

In a sense Taylor and Cooley were complements of each other; Taylor stressed the perfections of the market mechanism, and Cooley stressed its imperfections. But in a deeper sense they reflected something of an impasse in the field of economics; each more or less assumed as a major premise what the other was trying to establish as a conclusion. Although the fact that these two theorists could be teaching side by side speaks well for academic freedom of thought, the problem of determining the relative importance of the factors each stressed remains an enduring one.

CHAPTER XVIII

Innovators within Tradition

IN THE period from 1900 to 1918 a number of writers were successful in producing an essentially positive criticism of the established tradition in economics. Important new ideas emerged from the use made of the old, especially in the fields of money and banking, savings and investment, and the relations of government and business. These economists, trained in the old school, with the exception of Johannsen, modified the tradition in their attempts to apply it more closely to the observed facts.

NICHOLAS AUGUST LUDWIG JACOB JOHANNSEN: THE "AMATEUR ECONOMIST"

N. Johannsen (1844–1928) of New York presented one of the sharpest critiques of the doctrine of savings in its relation to depressions. Heretofore little has been known of him, yet some of the ideas he expounded contained the germs of modern developments.[1] Perhaps this can be accounted for by the fact that Johannsen was one of the strangest characters in American economics. He was of German birth and retained a keen interest in German matters, publishing in German as well as in English. He had little formal education. For many years he was an executive with a New York export and import firm, and his letter books indicate that he engaged extensively, and rather successfully, in stock-market operations. Johannsen's first writings appear under pseudonyms, a fact which he explained on the ground that his employer might think that he could not pay full attention to business and write on financial topics at one and the same time.

Johannsen began writing as early as 1878, publishing a pamphlet, *Cheap Capital*, under the pseudonym "A. Merwin." In this he stated that depression hung on because business could not obtain "cash capital" or "cash funds" at low interest rates. The depression, therefore, could be alleviated if the withdrawal of greenbacks were stopped, but in the end the increase in amount of greenbacks could not achieve prosperity, for greenbacks had no adequate security behind them. Rather, cash capital should be expanded through the increase of national bank notes backed by government bonds, these notes to be redeemable in greenbacks. While such expansion was inflationary, he contended that it would be safe if it were continued until the long-term rate of interest fell to appoximately 2 ½ or 3 per cent.

A rather interesting point was Johannsen's presentation of the *modus operandi* of panics. If all property were owned free of debt, he said, the pressure to sell, characteristic of panics, would not occur. However, since most property was encumbered with debt, in many cases nearly to its full value, any decline in price, started by the most casual occurrence or some important event, would eliminate the margin owned by the nominal owner of the property, thus forcing its sale. This process originated in the stock exchange and spread to all other property.

Around the turn of the century Johannsen began working on a theory of depression that constituted a significant contribution to the literature. In 1908, at the age of sixty-four, he published his basic theory, *A Neglected Point in Connection with Crises*. In this work, and later in the condensed pamphlet *Business Depressions* (1925), he argued that the true cause of depressions was in an " 'impaired' form of savings." Primarily and immediately, by reducing demand, the act of saving tended to create unemployment. When, however, savings were invested in productive equipment or other durable wealth, full employment resulted, and such use of savings constituted "normal" savings. He used as an example a community with an income of $100,000,000, of which he assumed that 85 per cent was expended for consumables and 15 per cent for investment in the construction of new productive equipment. About 85 per cent of the population, then, were engaged in producing consumables for all, while the 15 per cent saved went to the construction workers as income for their services and for the production of the raw materials. Thus all workers were fully employed.

"Impair savings" differed from "normal" savings, he wrote, in that while the latter when disbursed came to the receivers in the form of earnings, the "impair savings came to them over the bridge of their own impoverishment." Suppose of the $100,000,000 of the community's total annual earnings, 15 per cent had no opportunity for useful investment, "there being already productive capital in the community up to the saturation point sufficient to produce all consumables" for which there was a sale. Then the construction workers who ordinarily earned $15,000,000 in the aggregate remained unemployed. These workers would be forced to meet their living expenses by using up their savings accounts, selling their securities, taking mortgages on their homes, or borrowing from friends.

The saver, then, had extracted money from the community as income, but had been unable to return it to the community. His savings thus became "impair" savings. Should he subsequently return the funds either through extending loans or purchasing the properties of needy people, his investments would become "impair investments." These loans and purchases would bring partial relief, but only after his savings had caused unemployment, retrenchment, and destitution. Johannsen's analysis was unique in that it demonstrated a peculiar multiplication of this primary cause, achieved by the reaction of one trade upon another. This principle Johannsen called the "multiplying (or cumulative) principle" and originally presented it in 1903 in his brochure *Depressions-Perioden,* published under the pseudonym J. J. O. Lahne. In *A Neglected Point* Johannsen explained that the baneful effects of impair savings extended beyond those who ordinarily constructed the new capital goods, for unemployment in these lines would reduce the demand for consumable goods, thus creating further unemployment. One group of workers after another would be affected until finally even the incomes of the savers would be decreased. Thus the people's income might decline two or three times the amount of the impair savings. On the other hand, savings promptly invested to create new capital or wealth would bring full employment and progress, as well as increased demand, for a dollar saved and usefully invested would cause two dollars' worth of demand for consumables.

In the later condensation, *Business Depressions,* he wrote that building activity, expanding auto production, and heavy purchases of foreign bonds would provide the investment opportunities to prevent a slump, but that these fields could not expand indefinitely. During and since the war, he said, United States exports had enormously increased, creating employment for American workers at the expense of workers in other countries. When American capitalists invested their savings in foreign securities, these funds, actually paid to the home producers of the surplus exports goods, had the same effect as savings invested in domestic productive capital. Exports increased business activity and the country became richer, but at the expense of other countries, which through their indebtedness became poorer. When the time should come to adjust the disproportion between exports and imports, when the country's tremendous building activity should settle down to normal, and the auto and radio industries reach the saturation point, this country would be ripe for a severe depression. And the situation would be aggravated should the debtor countries repay their war debts in cash, thus increasing American investment-seeking cash funds.

In his chief treatise, *A Neglected Point,* Johannsen declared that the only solution he could offer was that old, well-developed countries should attempt to have a lower saving propensity than new, progressive countries, and that perhaps the wealthy should purchase more luxuries.[2] But in the same year, 1908, in an article in the *Journal of Commerce*, entitled "How to Relieve the Depression," he offered a more concrete suggestion: that proper financing of the railroads could help bring about a revival. The railroads needed enormous cash funds for developments, he said. With a surplus of cash funds in the money market, the roads could not obtain capital, at a reasonable rate of 4 or 4½ per cent, because investors distrusted the roads. This distrust was due in part to the predatory practices of railroad magnates. It could be overcome if a syndicate of bankers, with the power to veto any measure of management, would guarantee the interest on new railroad bond issues, in return for a slight fee. Furthermore, the syndicate could buy up the roads' high-yielding short-term notes, which were, of course, more attractive to investors than 4 per cent long-term bonds. It could obtain funds to buy these notes by following the procedure of stockbrokers who charged their customers 4 per cent on margin accounts and borrowed from the banks on call at 2 per cent. The sellers of the notes, having cash, would naturally be tempted to buy the bonds.

The expanding roads would create employment, increasing income, and consumption, thereby creating further employment. "And the well-known interplay of activity and reaction, thus started," Johannsen concluded, would help relieve depression. Thus, while in "How to Relieve the Depression" Johannsen approved of increasing bank credit under "extenuating circumstances," he deprecated its use in normal times because it tended to take the form of a permanent investment. In *A Neglected Point* he asserted that only a small part of "bank money" originated from loans made on commercial paper, and that most of it was issued on the security of stocks and mortgages; in other words, banks did not confine their loans to their "legitimate sphere," the discounting of commercial paper, but branched out into the field of permanent investment. True, these loans were not "normally of a permanent nature, being put out on 'call' or on short term." But in reality they constituted permanent investments, for their aggregate did not diminish but expanded, and debtors paid the maturing loans by making new ones, "shifting them from one bank to the other and from one holder of the securities to the other."

Johannsen did not give up his effort to find a cure for depression. While in 1908 he tackled the problem by encouraging investment, in 1913, in his German publication *Die Steuer der Zukunft*

("Taxes of the Future"), he endeavored to meet the problem through discouraging savings and encouraging consumption. He suggested that the government should issue as the circulating medium a paper money which would bear an annual tax of 50 per cent, payable at the rate of 1 per cent a week for the first fifty weeks. Thus, whereas other taxes by reducing purchasing power tended toward a depression, this taxed currency would promote spending. In sending copies of the volume to leading German economists, Johannsen explained that the scheme would stave off the threatening and seemingly inevitable socialist revolution.

Johannsen's scheme was similar to the "stamped money" scheme developed by Silvio Gesell in the nineties, which acquired a certain popularity in America in the thirties and was promoted by Irving Fisher. But there were certain differences in detail between the two plans, especially on the rate of taxation. Furthermore, Gesell meant the scheme to achieve the abolition of rent and interest; but Johannsen, while he contended that his own scheme would lower interest rates, felt that some interest was essential, and he opposed the attack on rent.[3]

In 1920, in *The True Way for Deflation*, Johannsen stated that the inflation was due primarily to the excessive demand for new construction, and he suggested that the Federal Reserve Board determine when member banks may make loans for construction. But the force of his argument was weakened by his insistence that stock-market speculation continue unhampered, and by his deprecation of any attempts to curtail bank credit for purchases of stock on margin.

On the whole, economists considered Johannsen a crank who did not grasp the ABC of economics. But the exceptions were notable. Elmer H. Youngman, editor of the *Bankers' Magazine*, encouraged him and opened the journal to his writings. John Bates Clark saw merit in Johannsen's theory that the savings of one class were used to acquire the property of another, and he felt that Johannsen's study of the causes and effects of depressions threw light on the problem. Johannsen's presentation of the mode in which a loss of employment by one group led to loss of employment by another group was also suggestive, Clark thought; although to his mind Johannsen failed to recognize all the limitations of this process of multiplication of the original disaster and overestimated the amount of enforced idleness indirectly caused.[4]

The less orthodox students of economy were more enthusiastic and responsive to Johannsen's ideas. John A. Hobson and Wesley C. Mitchell strongly stressed the merits of his theory in their major works; and the old Fabian Socialist George Bernard Shaw informed Johannsen that the "category of impair savings is a valuable corrective to the ridiculous optimism of our capitalist economists." He hoped that Johannsen would probe deeper into "our frightfully wasteful way of dealing with our capital." [5]

This mixed reception in no way discouraged Johannsen. In the year of his death Johannsen, intellectually vigorous despite his eighty-four years, was still pushing his "specialty, impair savings due to saturation of productive capital," and hoping that after a "long line of disappointments, my endeavors may still reach a successful end." [6] In reality, they had done so theoretically, for, despite his deficiencies and inconsistencies, there is no question that Johannsen had an acute insight. His general theoretical analysis of saving contains many a germ present in more recent analyses of the problem of unemployment.

HAROLD GLENN MOULTON: CRITIC OF TRADITIONAL BANKING THEORY

Johannsen's audience was limited by the fact that he was a pseudonymous and itinerant writer, but the heterodox views of Harold G. Moulton (1883-) had the imprint of the best academic sources. While teaching at the University of Chicago (from which he went later to the presidency of the Brookings Institution), he threw more light on the doctrine of saving and the theory of capital formation. Moulton worked in an atmosphere surcharged with feeling against the complacency of existing traditional economic thought; he was deeply stirred by Cooley, Veblen, and Davenport. He found it shocking that an introductory treatise on economics should present "eternal verities and lead the student to believe that the present industrial order is about all that human wisdom could hope to evolve." On the contrary, he said, "if society is to be made to serve the best interests of nations and peoples, we shall have to study the system as it is, and endeavor to reveal its weaknesses, as well as its points of strength, to the end that its glaring defects may be intelligently remedied." [7]

More concretely, Moulton built upon the banking suggestions of Davenport.[8] Like Davenport, he questioned that saving—thrift—was at all times beneficial for the community under the present pecuniary system. He went further to question the whole structure of capital formation, pointing out that traditional economic theory failed to understand that commercial banking was the most important institution related to capital formation. Guided by the general theory of value and distribution, he said, economists were treating commercial banking not in relation to the whole economic system but in isolation, merely as a guarantor of personal credit. An institutional treatment, however, would show that expanding bank credit, made possible by the gradual perfecting of a credit machinery, was the agent of rapid industrial progress. To him, those of a "mathematical inclination . . . disposed to view the economic organization in equilibrium rather than in process" failed to see that the expansion of bank credit, rather than the restriction of consumption, made possible a more rapid capital formation. Failing to differentiate between primitive society and the modern specialized pecuniary organization motivated by profits, these economists could not see that new capital goods would not continue to be created in the face of a lagging consumption demand. Therefore, to a certain degree, thrift, according to his theory, would always retard the rate of capital formation.

The historical result had been, he said, that rapid capital formation had accompanied rapid consumption. This anomaly, from the standpoint of classical economics, had been made possible because we were gradually perfecting our banking mechanism, whereby the system as a whole could make loans and investments to the extent of sixteen times the cash reserves. The expansion of bank credit had thus enabled businessmen to secure the funds with which to induce the otherwise large amount of unemployed human energy to create capital goods, without having to rely on previous saving by consumers.

But this analysis, said Moulton, applied to the formation of capital during a "transitional period," in which, to use his words, the "use of the commercial banking machinery has been growing more universal and in which the banking frontier has been gradually disappearing." This period was, he thought, drawing to a close, and the time would eventually come when the ratio between cash reserves and loans and investments could not further be decreased. Although the organization of the Federal Reserve System had somewhat extended the length of the transitional era, and might extend it much further, we must sooner or later face the problem of capital formation under conditions where an expanding banking currency would no longer provide the funds without the need of preceding consumption. Thus capital formation must, in the "absence of some new motive force to production—that is, some force other than relatively short-run profits—eventually proceed at a substantially retarded rate." Of course, even if "society could once strike the 'happy medium' between spending and saving (but this would be a mere chance strike)," not everyone could find employment in producing either capital goods or consumer goods.

Although Moulton's views were a shrewd thrust at traditional economics, the qualifications satisfied specialists in banking. Harold L. Reed of Cornell approved them enough to summarize them in 1919 as follows: "The production of indirect goods takes place most largely in periods of heavy, rather than in periods of light, consumption of direct goods. Lessened consumption of direct goods may destroy the profit possibilities of the production of the indirect. It is not from thrift or individual saving that the bulk of the investment funds has been obtained in periods of rapid construction of equipment goods. In large part such funds have represented the expanding credit grants of commercial banks. The labor for the production of the indirect goods must not be considered so much a subtraction as a virtual addition to that utilized in the production of direct goods resulting in less unemployment and more enthusiasm on the part of both the entrepreneur and the laborer."

It was quickly enough recognized that Moulton's views argued by inference for the inflation of credit to prevent unemployment. Thus Reed stated on the basis of Moulton's theory that with funds from the bank, the liquid capital necessary for the production of durable productive agents could be obtained, and "rising prices for consumption goods would stimulate entrepreneurial seizure of opportunities" for the creation of the capital goods.

While banking specialists were not worried by Moulton's criticisms, direct and implied, of the traditional doctrine of no general overproduction, more general economists were. Among them was Myron W. Watkins, then of the University of Missouri (later with the Twentieth Century Fund). "An attempt to explain the relation of specific institutions, habits, and immemorial precepts to the fundamental processes of economic society is praiseworthy at any time," he declared. Moulton had helped to advance economics by his "discussion of the relation of loans and discounts to the cash reserve," by his "reference to the investment feature of commercial banking, and [by] his directing attention to the lack of any theoretical analysis of the institutional processes by which savings are converted into productive equipment." But to Watkins the heresy of general overproduction had long since been demolished by J. B. Say. So Watkins could not accept Moulton when he argued that saving was not always socially desirable, because what was saved would not under all circumstances eventuate in an increased supply of capital equipment. Although Watkins granted that individuals and institutions might engage in some hoarding, that some friction might occur in the process of converting savings into capital equipment, that banks sometimes acted like misers; and that even entrepreneurs were occasionally subject to peculiar psychological states of which doubtless much could be learned by a careful, concrete, and comprehensive study, nevertheless, abstract inquiry did not require that explicit allowance be made for the modifying conditions of "imperfect economic machinery" and "illogical actions among the economic prime movers."

Thus, unfortunately, a discussion that might have led to a fruitful inquiry into the nature of the institutions of investment and saving got tangled up, on the one side with the immediate objective of modifying the legal limitations upon the Federal Reserve banks in rediscounting; and on the other with the objective of showing what Watkins called the error of neglecting "logical assumptions" and of emphasizing "modifying conditions." [9]

BENJAMIN MC ALESTER ANDERSON, JR.:
SOCIAL VALUE AND THE THEORY OF MONEY

Working along lines similar to the heterodox notions of Johannsen and Moulton was B. M. Anderson, Jr. However, he had a more comprehensive theoretical framework. Anderson (1886–1949), scion of a politically prominent Missouri family, received his undergraduate training at the University of Missouri.[10] In 1911 he presented for his doctoral dissertation at Columbia University, *Social Value*, and its reception among economists promised Anderson a meteoric career. While preparing his thesis Anderson was deeply impressed with Cooley's work in sociology, but he was also impressed with Clark's *The Philosophy of Wealth* and *The Distribution of Wealth*.

And he listened intently to John Dewey and Franklin H. Giddings, both of whom had become permanently settled at Columbia University.

Anderson claimed that he based his position on a "pragmatic" or "utilitarian" philosophy; namely, truth is what "we find will satisfy our desires and needs." Since desires and volitions were the common ground of our intellectual life, a similarity between individuals must exist on the desire-feeling-volitional side. After this reformulation of the pleasure-pain psychology, Anderson went on to state that value was a "quantity of motivating force, power over the actions of man, embodied in an object," and not the subject. Within the realm of individual psychology, according to him, the whole system of values—ethical, religious, economic, aesthetic—was "constantly tending toward equilibrium . . . all asserting themselves and finding their place in the scale and getting their 'margins' fixed, extensive margins and intensive margins." This, Anderson declared, was "merely a generalization of well-known economic laws." But a further point, Anderson added, was that since this equilibrium holds among all values, any object of value may be used to measure the value of any other and is thus the "price" of the other.

To him these laws held for social values as well as individual values. Thus, at any given moment, "there is an equilibrium between . . . the forces tending to correct and to perpetuate the inequalities in the distribution of wealth. . . . The legal value of private property— one of those great social 'absolute values'—checks at an early stage many of our well-meant but badly planned efforts at justice." For example, at the margin a struggle occurs between the entrepreneurs on the one side, endeavoring to produce at a minimum expense irrespective of the health of their employees, and law and morals on the other side, attempting to restrict them. "The money prices of the products reflect the marginal equilibrium attained."

Unfortunately, said Anderson, the economist too often neglected the non-economic moral and legal values, which he held to be constant. But the practical businessman studied these factors, tried "to estimate their force in quantitative price terms," and adjusted his plans to them. Thus, when agitation for rate reductions occurred, the manufacturer of railroad equipment planned to reduce his output.

The reviewers generally expressed admiration for Anderson's

ability, but several questioned that it differed substantially from current "orthodox" economics. Alvin S. Johnson, an outstanding student of J. B. Clark, in reviewing *Social Value*, said that Anderson's doctrine made "exchange ratios correspond in all cases with underlying social value." Thus it was a "mere redefining of terms—a restatement of a problem." [11]

Anderson's claim that he followed Cooley in good part was doubted by a number of economists equally conversant with Cooley's work. One critic pointed out that while Cooley attempted to study "real facts and forces," Anderson attempted to "formulate and adopt a concept," and thus got "into doubtful ground of logic and dogmatism." [12] A student and former colleague of Cooley, Walter W. Stewart of Amherst, asserted that Anderson's theory held that economic utilities "ought not to be left in the mind of the individual, and so he converted them into an attribute of the commodity and named them 'social value.' Thus the theory drops the concept of the economic man, who reflected the institutions of the eighteenth century, and adopts the concept of social value which makes the goods reflect the habits of men. Either method is equally fatal to an interpretation of institutions in their own right." And Anderson's claim to be a follower of John Dewey was also denied by a critic, who pointed out that Anderson's performance moved in a philosophical tradition that Dewey was combating—that of Hegel with his Absolute.[13]

The book, meanwhile, won an important national prize in the profession, the Hart, Schaffner & Marx prize, and in 1913, at the age of twenty-seven, Anderson, who had been an instructor at Columbia, was promoted to assistant professor. He accepted, however, a more tempting offer from Harvard.

In 1917 he elaborated on his "social value" in *The Value of Money*. Here he attempted to show the concrete bearing of the doctrine on the pecuniary system. That values were the outcome of society's will, not the result of arbitrary whim of individuals, he declared, was well illustrated by great financial operations. The head of a great banking house possessed large power in deciding whether to underwrite an issue, but he could not exercise it capriciously, for should investors suffer, he would lose prestige. Thus, like the judge, he was a social instrument. Similarly, in the great speculative markets, the stock and produce exchanges, buyers and sellers were "primarily interpreters, students, of impersonal social forces, seeking to adjust themselves to these forces." The speculators knew that if they ran counter to the facts, they would lose money.

Anderson went on to argue that credit transactions were a part of the productive process and increased values. The function of credit, he said, was to universalize the characteristics of money, high salability, "to 'coin' so to speak, rights to goods on shelves, lands, etc. etc., into liquid rights, bearing the dollar mark." Thereby they would become much more salable than they had been in their original form, and often would become "as salable as money itself, functioning perfectly as money."

From this analysis Anderson drew two "practical conclusions." First, that contrary to the complaints of many farmers, merchants, politicians, and even scientific writers, Wall Street did not drain our commerce of its life blood—money—but rather prevented that life blood from coagulating. Second, the provision in the Federal Reserve Act forbidding Federal Reserve banks from rediscounting stock-exchange paper should be eliminated. The member banks should be free to grant loans with stock-exchange securities as collateral. By closely limiting liquid assets to gold, he thought, the power of the Federal Reserve banks to help commerce was greatly weakened. Furthermore, in periods of financial crises, the Federal Reserve banks could provide no effective relief, for if stock-exchange loans lost their liquidity, all other bank loans would certainly be in the same position.

Technically speaking, Anderson directed his work on money to an attack on the quantity theory of money, and in that connection he made a most illuminating suggestion in an address before the Harvard Economic Seminar in 1914. According to the minutes, Anderson contended that "while the quantity theory assumes that it is the quantity of money in existence that is important, the thing of real significance is the quantity of income in the country measured in terms of money." [14]

In 1918 Anderson was offered a full professorship at the University of Michigan, but by the time the offer arrived he had accepted the position of economist for the National Bank of Commerce on the ground that Wall Street had become his laboratory. "The past three or four years," he wrote Seligman, "have convinced me of my ability to get along pleasantly and effectively with bankers and brokers and businessmen, and have, moreover, convinced me that Wall Street is more interested in scientific truth about economic facts and tendencies than any other set of men I have met. . . . It is refreshing to deal with men who cannot afford to be deceived, who really want the truth because they need it in their business." [15]

Anderson's concrete objective was not unlike that of Moulton and Johannsen—a demand for easing bank discount policy in favor of "permanent investment"—and there is no question that Anderson's *Social Value* was a powerful force in broadening the realm of economic inquiry. An entry in Charles H. Cooley's journal at the time is quite enlightening on the point:

> I have this fall a Saturday morning seminar of young instructors, three men engaged as assistants to [Fred M.] Taylor and one man from the Philosophy Department. They are eager and able and are working on the reconstructions—the foundations of Political Economy, from a larger standpoint. A new book on "Social Value" by B. M. Anderson is much occupying them just now.[16]

ALVIN SAUNDERS JOHNSON:

A COMBINATION OF ORTHODOXY AND REFORMISM

Johannsen, Moulton, and Anderson primarily questioned notions of saving and banking, but their questions naturally led into broader areas of economic and social reform. One of those who looked for answers in these broader areas was Alvin S. Johnson (1874–).[17] He has been held in high regard by circles representing the dominant viewpoint of formal economic theory, but his active mind, especially in matters of practical proposals, has often enough cut across that tradition.

Johnson's father was an immigrant Dane, and Johnson was born and reared on a Nebraska homestead. Not satisfied with the intellectual diet of the district school, he read Charles Dickens, Edward Bellamy, Henry George, and "Coin" Harvey, and he became sufficiently interested in reform to lecture for the local lodge of the Farmers' Alliance in 1890, at the age of sixteen. On entering the University of Nebraska, however, Johnson's interests were primarily in the classics, and after graduation in 1897 he taught the subject for a period. In 1898 he went to Columbia University to do graduate work in economics. There he soon fell under the influence of John Bates Clark. His attachment to Clark was personal as well as intellectual. Clark employed Johnson as his secretary and, from Johnson's account, the secretaryship entailed more work for Clark than for himself.

Johnson's doctoral dissertation, "Rent in Modern Economic Theory" (1902), showed unusual skill in solving problems by the dexterous use of classification. Many thinkers, he said, were impressed by economic developments which seemed to foretell a new monopolistic order of society. Actually, competition had simply changed its form. "Competition is less keen," he said, "among industrial establishments which create one and the same kind of commodity; but it is far keener than formerly between industrial groups which create, not like commodities, but commodities yielding like amounts of satisfaction, from which the consumer selects according to his estimates of utility and cost."

Again, Johnson divided incomes into productive and exploitative. In his analysis the former represented wealth obtained by the owners of the agents used in its production; the latter represented an element secured by other parties in distribution. "Exploitative incomes depend upon friction," he wrote, "and frequently exist by virtue of different degrees of resistance to economic laws in different social media." These incomes "vary so greatly in permanence and in the laws of their development that they hardly permit of scientific classification." The same holds for incomes arising from "abnormal productivity which favored industrial units may secure. According as exploitative and abnormal incomes are more or less permanent, they are usually classed as monopoly return or profit. But at present a completely satisfactory analysis of such incomes is not possible." However, for normal productive income, "a general law of diminishing returns renders possible a scientific explanation of their nature and a description of the laws of their development." [18]

Johnson's textbook, *Introduction to Economics* (1909), presented the reigning orthodoxy so well that teachers complained that it left nothing for them to discuss. His faith in traditional principles never wavered so far as textbook presentation was concerned. In his articles, however, he often developed variants, one example of which was his defense of protectionism. Suppose, he said, a tariff were levied on goods used primarily by wage earners. A large part of the wage-earning class saved nothing, whether wages were high or low, because standards of consumption tended to absorb any surplus of income which might accrue. Thus a duty borne by the wage earner would not check accumulation, and by diverting income from a lower thrift class to a higher one would be an impetus to the formation of capital. Such, he said, had been the tendency of modern protection, which by diverting income from a "lower to a higher thrift class" had played a part in equipping modern society with its present vast stock of capital goods. Johnson concluded that protective duties should be given to rapidly developing industries; when an industry ceased to develop rapidly, the duty should be removed.[19]

Johnson's theory of protectionism was more generous than this view might offhand suggest. "I lean toward protectionism," he declared, "as an instrument of nationalism, a movement whose historical mission I consider far from fulfillment. I accept the work of the free-trade economists as establishing once for all the fact that a protected industry is an expense, of course. But I regard it as an expense very often worth assuming, if it is a part of a systematic development policy, adopted not in blind prejudice against the foreigner nor in subservience to greedy private interests, but with a self-conscious political economic purpose that is quite alive both to local circumstances and international relations." [20]

Although accepting the essential soundness of Clark's marginal productivity theory of distribution, Johnson in an essay attempted to show that, contrary to Clark, labor-saving devices did not in all cases favorably affect wages. For example, if through "improved financial methods" capital could be easily withdrawn from established uses for employment in a new field, or the natural increase of capital from old fields be diverted to the new, it would become impossible to hold the view that labor saving was "invariably a force making for high wages." [21]

Johnson called attention to the fact that while economists insisted that the vast accumulation of capital had made possible an increase in material welfare, they failed to make any study of the development of habits of saving in society. One aspect of the question, the effect upon saving of variations in the rate of interest, had received some attention in recent years, he declared, but otherwise there had been little advance beyond the position of John Rae in 1834.[22]

Johnson's attempt to attack this problem with new knowledge resulted in this theory: the laborer's "fundamental demand upon society is that the daily earnings of every able-bodied and willing worker shall be sufficient to satisfy all reasonable desires. Accident, sickness, and old age require provisions; and it is most reasonable that he should desire to accumulate a reserve against these contingencies. But how shall the reserve be accumulated; by individual saving or by collective saving? Obviously the latter method makes the least demand upon the daily income of the laborer; it is therefore likely to become the prevalent one." This explains, too, said Johnson, the increasing demand for governmental workmen's insurance.[23]

Johnson from time to time expressed dissatisfaction with the limitations of "orthodox" economics. He objected to the fact that economists disposed of the standard of living by treating it as a "force affecting the supply of labor, and hence affecting wages." Yet in bargaining for labor, he said, there was a "considerable margin between seller's minimum and buyer's maximum and . . . the course of the negotiations [was] likely to be affected by even the personal appearance of the worker." He also thought prevailing economics offered only a formal solution for much of the phenomena in the field of commodity values. Thus it did not take into account such facts as sturgeon, costing a few cents in Chesapeake Bay thirty years before, currently being sent to France where it was artistically packed for its return to this country as caviar, at ten dollars a pound. Its rise in value was, of course, primarily due to its extraordinary vogue as an article of "fashionable consumption." This problem, therefore, could be translated into terms of an equilibrium of demand and supply, or into the "more seductive terms of a balancing of utility and cost," but such translation shed no "light upon the real problem of the rise in price of caviar." In short, to his mind, the great deficiency of prevailing economics was that it excluded from analysis "all the problems of value and distribution that are refractory to the supply and demand analysis, that persist in all their original perplexity despite their subjugation under supply and demand equations." [24]

Johnson also protested against the economists' tacit or avowed opposition to ameliorative labor legislation, especially the minimum wage for women. The economists, he said, while in fact opposed to the minimum wage, had hesitated to place economic theory and the minimum wage in mortal combat, for fear that economic theory would emerge second best. Taussig, he continued, had the courage to do so, and the opposition to him revealed that the economic theory which dismissed the minimum wage doctrine was essentially static. It assumed out of existence changes in the supply of labor, along with so many other vital matters which stubbornly existed nevertheless.

Although he thought there was no early prospect of a nation-wide minimum wage law, there was, to his mind, no real economic reason why the existing state laws should not be both successful and satisfactory. The newer states could prevent slums or sweat-shops—through minimum wage laws—from taking root. Every manufacturer contemplating the erection of an establishment in such a state would have to decide whether he could pay the state minimum. Every worker contemplating moving to that state must calculate whether he could earn the minimum. The inefficient employer who lived by virtue of starvation wages, the inefficient worker who was satisfied with crumbs, would avoid such a state. The development of industry might be slower, but it would surely be sounder. In the long run it would even itself out, for in the long run efficiency was cheap.[25]

Johnson broke with tradition again when he supported the federal tax on corporations in 1909. He disagreed with those editorial writers who contended that the tax would be shifted to consumers. They assumed, he wrote, that cost of production, including interest on capital, governed prices. This theory might have been true in an earlier epoch but was not then generally applicable. It held for agricultural products and for the products and services of many small manufacturing and mercantile establishments. In the wider field the principle of charging what the traffic would bear operated. Corporations in areas where costs controlled prices were relatively few and generally so small as to be exempt from the tax. But corporations which set prices according to the "tolerance of the market" could not add all or even a perceptible part of the tax to their already full price.

Johnson further contended that it was too often assumed that only the very large monopolies and the relatively small group of proprietors of patented processes and registered trade marks fixed prices according to the tolerance of the market. In truth, the practice prevailed extensively even in the retail trade. For example, grocers in rich districts of the city charged higher prices than grocers in the poorer districts, for consumers in the former could afford to pay the higher prices. Since they already paid what the traffic would bear, their prices would not rise when the grocer was taxed on his net income.

Johnson thought this principle could be expanded to explain some supposedly anomalous aspects of the theory of price. For example, import duties on certain raw materials had been reduced, but the prices of the finished products had not fallen. The explanation was simply that, somewhere between the producer of the raw material and the final consumer, an enterprise had the power to exact what the market would bear. Wherever such power rests, he said, there a tax may be laid without seriously burdening the consumer.[26]

Another significant analysis by Johnson was his proposal in regard to the railroads. Utilizing J. B. Clark's notion of inappropriables, he pointed out that there were many districts without railroad facilities in which the advance in all values, the increase in opportunities to make a living, would far outweigh the cost of railway construction; but private railway companies could not take into account the general improvement and increase in wealth, but must wait upon sufficient prospects of traffic.

He thought the ideal solution would be public ownership, not because there was any particular magic in public ownership, but because eventually the government must address itself very seriously to the task of making the most of the nation's resources, human and material, and must in the process make full use of a properly developed railway system, which would require it to go beyond immediate pecuniary considerations. The system need not be completely public-owned at the start, but the public need for railways should be determined by the public authority. Private capital might be called upon either under a guaranty of earnings or under some form of partnership arrangement by which the government would supply as much capital as could not be assured a pecuniary return.[27]

Johnson was by no means a radical; he believed that reform could be achieved without subverting the foundation of the social order. There was a need to get rid of unsocial investments, he declared, but this should be done not through confiscation or expropriation of the property involved, but rather through compensation. He declared that in countries where security of property had long been established there was a progressive sensitiveness about the human rights of non-propertied man. In such countries one found recognition of a universal right to education, to protection against violence and protection against epidemic disease, to relief from the misery of destitution. He added, "These are perhaps meagre rights; but they represent an expanding category." The development of such rights is, he said, not only compatible with "security of property, but it is, in a large measure, a corollary of property security. Personal rights shape themselves upon the analogy of property rights; they utilize the same channels of thought and habit. One of the most powerful arguments for 'social insurance' is its very name. Insurance is recognized as an essential to the security of property; it is therefore easy to make out a case for the application of the principle to non-propertied claims." [28]

What gave his economic writing unusual qualities was Johnson's many-sided, subtle character. He was an accomplished classical scholar before he became an economist, and he was one of those rare figures whose literary ability was on as high a level as his intellectual caliber. He wrote novels with the same ease that he wrote on the theory of value. His uncanny insight into the potentialities of exceptional students at the various institutions where he taught—note particularly Walton H. Hamilton, James Harvey Rogers, and Frank H. Knight—and his efforts to encourage their bent, whatever it might be, resulted in the nourishing of a number of outstanding although diverse scholars. And in the last phase of his active career, as director of the New School for Social Research, he rendered a memorable service to the republic of learning by greatly developing the concept of adult education and by providing a haven for a large number of European scholars removed from their posts by authoritarian governments.

GUSTAV ADOLPH KLEENE: RICARDIAN SOCIALIST

The uses of the classical school were not by any means exhausted by the conservatives. This was proved by Gustav A. Kleene (1868–1946), who armed his critique of the existing order with the weapons of the older classical school.

Kleene received his Bachelor of Arts degree from Michigan in 1891 and began graduate study in 1893. He attended Berlin, Tübingen, Columbia, and finally Pennsylvania, from which he received his doctor's degree in 1896. After working for a short period for the Charity Organization Society of New York, and then as a teacher of history and civics in Illinois high schools, he obtained an assistantship at the University of Wisconsin in 1901. A year later he became an instructor in economics and social science at Swarthmore College, and in 1903 he was appointed assistant professor of economics at Trinity College in Hartford, Connecticut. There, four years later, he attained the rank of full professor.

In his first publication, which appeared while he was teaching in his native town of Peoria, Illinois, Kleene sharply attacked Marx and praised the reformist or "revisionist" socialists in Europe. Marx's views, he wrote, were materialistic, international, cosmopolitan, and hostile to the existing State and to State socialism. Neither Marx nor his followers had grasped the true theory of value, which was that of marginal utility; reformist socialists, on the other hand, more or less accepted it. Contrary to Marx, he thought that recent events led to the expectations that social democracy on the Continent would become a democratic rather than a purely proletarian movement. Since this modern socialism did not represent one class, it would make moderate demands and lay less stress on class war. "With strong social reform parties representing the common people in local and national politics, and with vigorous trades unions and co-operative societies, the social movement on the continent will resemble more closely the great English-speaking democracies," Kleene concluded.[29]

Hardly had Kleene taken up his post at Trinity when he came forth with concrete proposals for social reform. First of all he advocated free medical care for all. While on the whole public opinion had approved some kind of medical relief to the indigent, he found, nevertheless, that charity workers and students of poor relief deprecated the rapid extension of free medical aid. The theory of general relief inherited by the charity organization societies from the English was thus based on an individualistic social philosophy. In his words, it brimmed over with a fear of pauperization and was distrustful of all aid not "bristling with tests and deterrents." The free dispensary in particular had been fiercely attacked. But the arguments to limit free medical aid, said Kleene, were specious. He denied that "generous and indiscriminate medical aid" pauperized; on the contrary, it prevented physical degeneration, and thus pauperization, by saving those who were struggling to maintain their economic independence. Nor would it hinder the development of more desirable methods of medical treatment. Too many persons lacked the means to pay a private practitioner for expensive specialist service.

The chief opposition to the free dispensary, he pointed out, came from the private physician. This arose from the fact that the economic interests of the profession were at variance with the interests of society as a whole, for the more sickness the wider the physician's market and the larger his income. Some physicians were not above the temptations of this situation, and some of them used clearly dishonest methods to get a practice. In consequence, he said, "it is not an ideal system that leaves to individual enterprise the commercial exploitation of human suffering." In the art of healing, unlike the ordinary processes of industrial society, progress had not been the result of the competitive spirit. The scientist, the humanitarian, the man working for a salary rather than the man hunting for a fee, had been the discoverers and inventors. The profession had adopted new methods not because of the presence of competition, but because of the teachings in the medical colleges.

The proposed extension of medical charity, Kleene said, might be either public or private, according as society tended toward aristocracy or democracy. Long strides already had been taken in the direction pointed to by the socialists. Medical service was not merely performed gratuitously by public authorities, but in some cases forced upon unwilling recipients. It had become a question of degree not of principle. That the physicians' services would become as free as those of the teacher or librarian was not to be expected in his generation. But the time had come for the charity expert to cease opposing the "slow but inevitable 'drift of things' and to adjust his mind to the expectation of a new order."

In 1907 Kleene went on to criticize the methods of charity organizations and to call for State unemployment and old age relief as well as for free medical aid. The charity organization societies, he pointed out, had for their aims the co-ordination and more efficient operation of relief agencies. They insisted on rigorous and detailed investigation of applicants for relief; they operated in good part too on the principle that the wealthy contributor should uplift the poor by visiting them as a voluntary service, and they expended much of their efforts in attempting to suppress mendicants. All this seemed to Kleene a forbidding machinery.

The callousness of the investigators appalled Kleene into protesting. Perhaps if charity dealt with a class of hereditary paupers only, investigation might proceed without regard to feeling. Or if society were divided into castes, and the poor were resigned to their lot, they might submit to investigation as one of the inscrutable ways of the "social gods above them." But the belief in democratic ideals even among the destitute made them regard the prying investigations as offensive and caused them to shun the charity organizations. Detailed, particular investigation should be restricted to exceptionally peculiar cases; for the majority there should be uniform, easily understood methods which in themselves would constitute a test to sift out the impostors.

The attempts of the charity organizations to suppress mendicancy directly was to his mind a striking example of the conflict of these organizations with popular feeling. Their attempts failed because the people believed that among the beggars were worthy but unfortunate men. "Certainly in times of industrial depression at least," he said, "[this idea] contains a measure of truth." He held that this notion would persist until sufficiently large and complete measures were taken to give work to all. And until the public should be convinced that there was no longer any excuse for begging, such public employment measures would have to be in excess of private employment. In any event, relief should be geared to periods of depression as well as prosperity, for the unemployed as well as for the aged poor.

Finally Kleene opposed having the "aristocratic" supporters of the charity organization act as friendly visitors to their beneficiaries. "In a society divided into rich and poor, educated and uneducated, bathed and unbathed," he argued, "the only satisfactory relation conceivable between classes" was that of "forbearance and the mutual respect of strong class organization." Therefore this visitation should be left to salaried, experienced workers, not to voluntary inexperienced agents.[30]

Such ideas marked Kleene as somewhat ahead of his time with his social program. Then, beginning with an article in Taussig's *Quarterly Journal of Economics* in 1912, and culminating with his book *Profit and Wages* in 1916, Kleene presented a formal theory of distribution, whose avowed roots in Ricardo and Marx recalled the Ricardian socialists.

Kleene took full advantage of the criticisms made against the regnant economic theory, especially by continental socialists who claimed to be elaborating and modernizing Marx. He granted that the Austrian doctrine provided a better theory of value than its predecessors, but the theory of distribution was a distinct and separate phenomenon, as the old classical school held, and the followers of the marginal utility school denied. Kleene extended to Marx the tribute of coupling his name with Ricardo's as the source of his own doctrine.

Kleene formally reinterpreted the classical wage-fund doctrine and went on to the residual-claimant theory of profit, in which he included interest. This theory, he said, as worked out by Ricardo and Marx, concerned itself with profit in the sense of a residual income remaining in the hands of the capitalist class as a whole, after they hired the laborers and acquired whatever the laborers produced in excess of the amounts paid them. Kleene introduced a modification. In the old theory, he said, the supply of laborers was determined by a fixed and low standard of living, and varied in numbers in such a way that laborers received in the long run the wages which accorded with their low standard of living. This, according to Kleene, held true in such backward areas as Central Europe. It did not hold in its entirety in capitalistic countries, but a modified application was still valid. Wages in the United States, for instance, were not determined by any standard of living among the established American laborers, but by the standard of living and the natural wages of immigrants, who brought with them the standard of the backward areas of the pre-capitalistic old world.

Kleene quickly and sharply disposed of the established theories of wages and profits. The productivity theory at best, he said, could only help to explain comparative rates of remuneration, but the absolute scale of payment, "the general level," could be explained "only by a reference to the total of purchasing power directed to the employment of labor." As for the time-preference theory, the expectations, hopes, and fears suggested by the phrase were not "sufficiently definite and powerful to be given a place in a carefully formulated general theory of the rate of interest." As for the abstinence theory, great amounts of investment funds were accumulated without thought and effort. This was especially true of the recipients of large incomes and of the managers of corporations who accumulated surpluses out of earnings without consulting the willingness of the stockholders to abstain from consumption.

The classical economists, Mill especially, he said, seriously considered the possibility of a rate of profits falling to zero and analyzed the preventives. According to Kleene, Mill gave as the first cause of such a situation the waste of capital in periods of "overtrading and rash speculation" and the succeeding "commercial revulsions." And to this factor Kleene added destruction and waste of capital by militarism. On Mill's second cause, improvement in production, Kleene commented that up to then it appeared that capitalism had been saved by waste and progress. Mill's third cause was that the perpetual overflow of capital into colonies or foreign countries indicated that the day of reckoning might be postponed by the extension of capitalism into new territory. Kleene observed that despite the vast economic expansion, which had been uninterrupted since Mill's day, the chief worry still remained idle capital.

The term "exploitation" Kleene deprecated, although to him it correctly suggested that interest grew out of a portion of the product of labor withheld from the laborer. "Exploitation," however, carried an ethical connotation which it would have been well to keep out of economic theory. Such emotional content in words had in recent years tended to cloud the issues, and there the earlier economists had the advantage. Of course, it would be absurd to insist, declared Kleene, that the classical school had said the last word on all questions of distribution, but the "strategic points of attack on fundamental problems were more clearly perceived by Ricardo and his generation than by the majority of their successors. Not given to academic refinements and subtleties, nor led by radical attacks on property to bend scientific inquiry in the direction of an apologetic of capitalism, their thought moved directly and with single aim upon the significant and fundamental features of the industrial system before them."

Kleene's treatise received little attention. It was viewed as merely a complete return to the old-fashioned classical tradition. Only Taussig seemed to have any sympathy for it. "Kleene is a bit infected by Marxism," said Taussig, "but is a keen and interesting chap who deserves more attention than he has received." [31] Encountering difficulty in finding a reviewer for the *Quarterly Journal of Economics*, Taussig did the job himself. In his review he praised Kleene's scholarship and critical abilities and his lack of fear of the term "wages fund." But Taussig thought that "the specter of immigration and of a standard of living debased by immigration hovers in the background of Professor Kleene's picture almost as much as in that of some anti-immigration extremists." Kleene's doctrine of wages was, according to Taussig, basically unsatisfactory because it led to the conclusion that the outcome for this and other countries of "advanced" civilization was an "impassive unregulated impact." In it, the determination of wages and profit became simply a matter of the "gathering accumulation of investment meeting the gathering number of laborers, with no ultimate determinant of wages or of profit and no 'normal' return for either."

Perhaps we must come so some "such agnostic doctrine," added Taussig. "If we give up the notion of a regulating rate of 'time preference,' or the similar one of a minimum return necessary to induce abstinence and saving, we have no 'normal rate of interest.' And if we give up also the notion of any 'natural' wages, settled by a standard of living, what have we left? Specific productivity cannot be demarcated; and the productivity of industry at large bears merely on the national dividend as a whole, not on its apportionment between the different factors of production. Nothing seems to be left but the Ricardo-Marx conception—this admittedly is Professor Kleene's—of a surplus, essentially fortuitous, grabbed by those who now control industry, and soon to be seized (the suggestion lies at hand) by those who are rapidly acquiring control." [32]

Later Kleene went a step further, presenting a "collectivist" economics and using in a novel manner Moulton's doctrine of the role of bank credit in capital formation. The traditional doctrine that the necessary abstinence was that of voluntary savers and investors was, he reiterated, misleading. A considerable and increasing proportion of the reduced consumption had been supplied unconsciously and unwillingly and without reward, not by hopeful investors, but by the discouraged recipients of fixed or slowly changing incomes. The expansion of bank credit to entrepreneurs and the consequent rise of prices had forced the necessary abstinence on the same unfortunate classes, not on the creators or users of credit. The increase of currency distributed by the banks was not distributed over the entire population but was at the disposal of businessmen who could use it to increase industrial equipment. When the productive forces were fully employed, this increased demand for industrial apparatus could be realized only by reducing the facilities for producing consumers goods. The businessmen and bankers who successfully employed an expansion of currency, reaped the gain of the involuntary unrewarded abstinence of fixed income receivers and of a large proportion of the wage earners.

Besides the large business and banking interests, he pointed out, governments could press the economy toward investment in productive apparatus. Like the banking interest, they could levy a toll on the recipient of fixed incomes by currency inflation and thereby enforce the necessary reduction of consumption, essential, for instance, to conduct a great war. Whether this was done by issuing Treasury bills or by public borrowing with a "permissive or an encouraging attitude" toward the expansion of bank credit, the effect would be to throw the economic cost of war on those whose money incomes did not increase with the rising price level. But an alternative method to increase a government's wartime spending power and to reduce consumption would be the imposition of heavier taxes.

In the same way the business environment led governments to resort to public credit rather than to taxation to provide for large public enterprises, such as docks, railways, and canals; that is, they appealed to voluntary saving, to the capitalist investors and the creators and users of bank credit. In the future, Kleene thought, the State might call upon the citizen to contribute to a greater degree to the "construction and maintenance of the equipment required by the collective interest, in proportion to his ability and without special reward." [33]

These five men—Johannsen, Anderson, Moulton, Johnson, and Kleene—demonstrated, in their attempts to make the classical theory cover the ground which modern observers had cleared, that the "old school" principles could not be stretched so far without losing their original shape. What they did was to cast doubt, even while using classical doctrines, that those doctrines could meet modern conditions. It is in their innovations that these men are significant. In the study of saving and investment the theories of Moulton and Johannsen are the ground of modern argument. Kleene's discussion of the relationship of business to government is the ground of modern politics. Anderson in his social value theory, although narrowly applied by him, calls attention to the uncertain psychological foundations of economics. And Johnson illustrates vividly the paradox of the brilliant codifier of the classic school being driven by his humane interests into innovation.

CHAPTER XIX

The Disturbing Voice of Thorstein Veblen

AT THE turn of the century a deeply disturbing influence appeared in American economics in the person of Thorstein Bunde Veblen (1857–1929).[1] Yet he had neither high academic position nor popular journalistic appeal. He had uncomfortable things to say, and he said them in so strange a manner that men still differ over the meaning and even the validity of his work. The unfolding course of events will eventually supply the answers, but a glimpse into his life history throws some light on his meaning and gives consistency and coherence to an apparently miscellaneous list of publications.

Veblen was born in the United States, but for all practical, or rather cultural, purposes he was an immigrant and might as well have come to this country at the age of, say, sixteen. His life presents the head-on conflict of two cultures. His family heritage was that of rural Norway, with its sharp separation in custom and language from the dominant city population of officeholders and businessmen. The Norwegian settlements of his youth, in Wisconsin and Minnesota, were "little Norways" of relatively self-sufficient farmsteads, and they regarded the "Yankees" as no different from the masters or the townspeople they had known in their European home. But as Veblen reached manhood, the centuries-old insulated self-sufficiency was being smashed by the technological changes in flour production, which turned his area into a one-crop country, brought the railroads, and extended the scope of the money economy.

In 1874, just one year after a severe depression had set in, Veblen, knowing very little English, left Nerstrand, Minnesota, and entered near-by Carleton College, which was designed especially for the children of the "Yankees" and for the propagation of New England ideals in religion and morals. Thus began a process whereby Veblen was stripped to a considerable degree of the preconceptions of his own culture, although his heritage prevented him from assimilating the ideals of the dominant pecuniary culture. Intellectually homeless, he saw more vividly than the general run of his contemporaries the changes in technology and economic organization that were transforming the country into a mature product of the money economy.

His skeptical bent became highly developed in this theologically saturated college, and Veblen soon learned the technique of dissecting men's most cherished views without annoying people to the point of calling forth punitive action. His reading fed his skepticism. Although the college library was made up largely of theological works, Veblen managed to obtain books seldom read by his fellow undergraduates, ranging from the works of satirists like Jonathan Swift to the philosophic treatises of Kant. The work of Herbert Spencer, which was denounced for undermining theology —and thus law and order—Veblen read thoroughly. For a graduating oration he chose John Stuart Mill's *An Examination of Sir William Hamilton's Philosophy*, a work in high disrepute in dominant circles in American academic philosophy because it attacked the relatively naïve Common Sense philosophy which had ruled in the American colleges for over a century.

Veblen was subjected to the customary doses of moral philosophy and political economy, but his teacher was John Bates Clark, who was then developing his doctrine of specific productivity. Consequently Veblen had the advantage of an early acquaintance with the most mature product of the main tradition of American economics. While the rest of the faculty and most of the student body were decidedly doubtful that Veblen would become a useful citizen, Clark soon discerned his promising intellect.

The skeptical Norwegian rustic was compelled to overcome innumerable adversities before he could make his contribution; in the process he matured early. Upon graduation in 1880, Veblen taught for a year in an elementary school and then entered Johns Hopkins. He stayed less than a term. He then went to Yale to major in philosophy, although he retained his deep interest in economics. Yale at the time was the most conservative center in the country. President Noah Porter was making a last effort to save Yale from Spencerianism and German Idealist philosophy. William Graham Sumner, who ruled the social sciences, was fighting for Spencerianism. Veblen felt the full shock of this mighty conflict of social orders and the clash of principles of knowledge. Permanent victory went to Sumner, and the once-suspect Spencer was established as the philosopher of the social sciences. Doubtless it was then that the skeptical Veblen began to question whether the contrast Spencer drew between status and contract was as sharp as Spencer imagined, and whether the progress of civilization was toward his ideal system of free contract.

Veblen fell into another movement that was causing a storm in the intellectual world of Europe but hardly a ripple in America. His favorite philosopher was Kant, and he could not fail to be affected by the tremendous "Back to Kant" movement which was protesting the Absolutism of Hegel. Its proponents held that Kant had glimpsed the true doctrine of evolution, and that the evolutionism which Spencer so well typified was, in contrast to the teachings of modern science, "anthropomorphic teleology." The great leader of this movement, Frederick Lange, declared that nature proceeds in a way radically different from human purposefulness; her most essential means, if measured by the standard of human understanding, "can only be compared with the blindest chance." He particularly pointed to the rationalistic teleology of political economy, with its insistence on harmony of interests. Based on dogmatic egoism, he said, it attempted to "show that the progress produced by the restless struggle of Egoism . . . improves the position of the most depressed strata of the population." But to him this ignored that "comparison with others which plays so great a part among the rich." Since this emulation or desire to surpass others was capable of increasing *ad infinitum*, "an enormous development of power and wealth is taking place while the circumstances of the laboring class show no decided advance, and without the haste and greed of acquisition in the propertied classes being in the slightest degree moderated." Since these egoistic feelings had been developed into a system of daily life, they exerted their influence even upon those who personally were not without noble impulses.[2]

Veblen's generation showed a strong philosophical preference for Hegelianism as a better intellectual defense of "Puritan morals and religion" than the relatively naïve Common Sense philosophy. Not so Veblen. Abolutism and Hegelianism, he held, had established an external standard—history, or the State—to which man was more or less enslaved, whereas Kant, by emphasizing the individual conscience, gave courage to liberalism. The Absolutes were as uncongenial to Veblen as they had been to Hume and Kant. Hume denied man's capacity to know ultimate truth or God and was driven to rest in the arms of feeling, custom, and habit for appreciation of experience, but Kant discerned a rational pattern. It was this viewpoint of order that appealed to Veblen's scientific bent.

To Veblen the importance of Kant's philosophy lay in its emphasis upon the human subject. Unlike the primordial first truths of the Common Sense philosophy, Veblen pointed out, Kant's *a priori* elements were "relational functions, . . . activities dynamically creative." While the principles of Common Sense were the very guarantees of absolute truth, Kant's "*a priori* forms" were merely "brute conditions of our experience." The supreme principle in "the development of knowledge" was the "activity of the experient subject itself." When all was said and done, there was the "moral law within." For Veblen, as for Kant, "the origin of the Critical Philosophy" was "in Morality—responsibility for action." [3]

The tribulations that Veblen underwent after obtaining his doctor's degree in 1884 were hardly calculated to moderate his skepticism. Though he had letters of the highest praise from Clark, Porter, and Sumner, he could find no teaching post, for academic openings were scarce. Complaining of ill health, he returned to the family farm, where he passed seven years in loneliness and frustration. That was the Golgotha of his career. He used this enforced and bitter leisure to think down to the roots. He read widely and followed the movements of discontent. After reading Edward Bellamy's utopian novel *Looking Backward*, he turned his attention definitely to economic questions and away from the realm of formal philosophy. He emerged into the world doomed to personal misery, but ripened for intellectual combat. After 1891 Veblen's views underwent no fundamental change.

Family pressure forced Veblen out of retreat. He entered Cornell in 1891 as a graduate student, and, of all people, the conservative J. Laurence Laughlin, who was then head of the Department of Economics, became sufficiently impressed to obtain a fellowship for him. When Laughlin went to Chicago the following year, Veblen went along, but still as a fellow. He became an instructor in 1896, and several years passed before he was appointed an assistant professor. In 1906 he obtained a position as associate professor at Leland Stanford University, but after little more than three years he was again forced to move on. Herbert Joseph Davenport brought him to the University of Missouri, but in a temporary post as professorial lecturer. Veblen's failure to establish himself in the academic community was due, not so much to his views, as to his being a poor pedagogue in the conventional sense and to his matrimonial troubles. When the United States entered World War I, he found a haven in the Food Administration, but his work gained little approval and in 1918 he went on to the recently established New School for Social Research. He was no more successful there, and in 1925 his academic career ended.

Veblen is not an easy man to comprehend, standing as he does halfway out of society. Observing that technology and capitalism had become intertwined, he rejected the latter as predatory and wasteful yet accepted the former as fruitful and productive. But here also at certain points he was not completely at home with the whole Western emphasis on material development. He was thus armed with a double weapon for a critique of both his particular age and civilization as a whole. He was the man from Mars and at the same time a man at home in the factory; indeed, sometimes he seems a typical American gadgeteer. Such was his philosophical bias, and the tool he employed to elaborate it was a wide and deep-ranging distinction between "business" and "industry" and a broad view of the nature of "institutions."

Veblen discerned that the high command of the "institution" of modern capitalism was vested in the most powerful of financiers, who by controlling the flow of credit to important industries were able to manipulate them for their own ends. In the process the ordinary and sometimes even the larger investor was a passive figure, and the industrial operator or distributor was more directly concerned with the material contribution of society. In this high command was reflected most clearly and extremely the spirit of pure gain (monetary) or pecuniary profit, entirely abstracted from material efficiency or service.

On the other hand, the all-important "institution" making for material progress was "technology," the state of the industrial arts. The industrial arts, in Veblen's sense, were not only the arts proper but the habits, skills, transmission of skills, and the opportunity to develop and advance them. It was not physical capital or labor, let alone funds, which were to Veblen the great productive factor, but the cumulative growth of the technological habits of thought that comprised the machine process; without this intangible element physical instruments and labor would be of little use. Productivity was therefore an indivisible social phenomenon, not an individual one, a function of the given technology. Such was Veblen's "institution" of the "industrial arts."

Henry George had made physical land the source of the great "unearned increment," yielded to landowners through the growth of society and population; Karl Marx had found the capitalists' return in the exploitation of labor through the ownership of the capital goods; Veblen went further. He held that the source of "unearned gain" was in the ability of the large businessman to engross the community's technological knowledge, through the control of the funds essential to acquire the capital goods by means of which the all-important technological knowledge could achieve its end. Veblen thereby neatly presented the business classes as making no contribution to material progress but living off the industrious.

The machine technology under the regime of private property seemed to Veblen to have given rise to the dominance of corporation finance, which obeyed a logic of its own. The aim of finance was to increase funded money values, pecuniary gain, he said; while the aim of technology—reduced prices—disrupted the only values that business knew. Since corporation finance was master, industry obeyed business; and the community suffered the convulsions of crises and depressions, of restricted output, unemployment, and imperialistic ventures. Thus the acquisition of money did not register man's success against nature, or the individual's reward in the great contest, but a complex of pecuniary "institutions" which made profit not the means of life but its end. Pecuniary values, Thomas Carlyle's "cash nexus," therefore repressed material values, and business conflicted with industry.

To Veblen the money economy was "institutional," and not a natural requirement of humanity. He used "institution" in a broad and new sense, as a method of action arrived at by habituation and convention and generally agreed upon. Most "orthodox" economists would have agreed with this, but they presumed that "institutions," in the ordinary sense of the term, arose in response to men's needs and represented the state to which man had progressed in his struggle with nature. Veblen criticized this view as ignoring what the institution had become, an end rather than a means.

To him "institutions" of price, property, and contract were active forces rather than passive embodiments of nature to which man adjusted himself by pleasure and pain. "Institutions" were them-

selves the embodiments and channels of the activity of man. Habits
of thought were created by habits of action. Money, therefore,
could not be viewed as a medium of exchange, and the successful
large businessman ceased to be merely an intermediary in the efficient organization of industrial forces to satisfy men's wants. With
money and securities made ends in themselves, or, more accurately,
with the complex of "institutions" comprising modern business
given an active or creative role, corporation finance became the
main character in the drama. On its side, the machine technology,
which comprised the industrial "institutions," could not be viewed
merely as an element of production, different only in degree from
artisan labor, but as a comprehensive and delicate process with a
distinctive life of its own. Now the objective of the pecuniary experts was neither the supplying of goods to the consumer nor the
efficiency of industry, but the accumulation of funded wealth, the
making of money. Every step in the never-ceasing integration of
industry, however, provided them with greater opportunities to
achieve their ends, and these in their turn disturbed the arrangements of industry.

These untoward results came, according to Veblen, from the inevitable transformation of responsible ownership into the corporate
organization, with its dissociation of nominal property rights and
actual control, and consequent creation of competing feudal dynas-
ties. The captains were not tied permanently to any industrial unit
but constantly shifted their interests and thus gained by corporate
losses as well as successes.

Veblen therefore turned from the conventional inquiry to a study
of business or profits as an "institution" in itself. His was an inquiry
into the economics of enterprise, with enterprise conceived in terms
of the only realities it recognized, pecuniary realities, money profits,
and with the modern enterpriser, who wields discretionary power
in the economic order, occupying the seat of Kant's ultimate responsibility. In place of the successful functioning of industry
through a competitive struggle to serve the public, Veblen's investigation found industry disorganized as a consequence of the struggle
of competing captains to overreach one another in a purely imperialistic pursuit.

Capital in modern business enterprise, Veblen said, was funded
wealth, the values of the stock market, with no definite relation to
hard material values. Capital items were items of control of in-

dustry, and their value was determined not by material cost of production, nor by capitalization of "psychic incomes," nor even of actual earnings, but by the capitalization of their putative earning capacity; that is, their earnings, in the larger businessman's strategy. They were consequently an ever-varying, rather intangible magnitude. Thus the most valuable assets were the intangible assets of a monopolistic or quasi-monopolistic character. They signified the differential or monopolistic gains of the greater enterprisers at the cost, proximately of other businessmen, ultimately at the expense of the community, because business men were not bearers of the technological knowledge of the community.

The whole imbecile procedure of pursuing essentially imaginary values was not recognized as such, continued Veblen, for it proceeded on the preconception or "institutional" fact of the stability of the money unit, the notion that money measured productive contribution, that the success of business enterprise measured industrial advance, that the acquisition of funded pecuniary values represented an increase of material assets. To him this growth of capitalization in symbols acted as a dead hand on the country's material fortunes; for with the continued technological advance and integration of industry and its depressing effect on price, business was constrained to restrict output in order to maintain its nominal capital values. The result was recurrent crises and depressions. The inflationary periods were always stimulated by extraneous, essentially wasteful forces, such as war or land booms. Thus Veblen introduced a study of recurring periods of prosperity, crises, and depressions, not as abnormal phenomena, but as integral if not dominant factors of the economic order.

Here Veblen's theory became a theory of business cycles, or, rather, a theory of the nature of corporation finance. It was a theory of modern credit, the credit of the capital markets, not the credit of the corner grocery story or the refined system of barter. Prosperity and depression were first of all prosperity and depression in pecuniary values, and only secondarily in industrial values. To illustrate this, Veblen pointed out that when business was sanguine, the competition for credit raised the apparent value of the assets of the community without so much as touching their real value. Then we were ready for still more credit. Many financial people took a lot more money without anyone's making or consuming anything more. Since this could not go on forever, eventually the real or actual profit was spread thin over the huge desert of securities; eventually wages and other costs caught up with the inflated prices produced by inflated credit. For Veblen, the discrepancy between nominal and effective capitalization arose because returns on the ever-increasing nominal capitalization could be met only by increased funds in the hands of consumers of consumption goods, and this could not be achieved because it would mean eliminating the gains of the inflation to the corporate financiers.

In liquidation, Veblen continued, a redistribution of ownership occurred in which the issuers of credit, the corporate financiers, acquired the greater share of the assets and the real owners suffered. Having profited from prosperity, they now profited from depression. But to Veblen chronic depression was the rule rather than the exception in modern business, because the increasing efficiency in technology and the competition of reorganized concerns kept prices too low to meet the fixed charges of nominal capital. His analysis found the notion that one must make more and more money so ingrained that even when the value of money rose in terms of goods, and therefore less money might mean greater real wealth, the larger business community nevertheless insisted on maintaining its high nominal capitalizations.

In Veblen's theory the future was not bright. According to it, schemes for maintaining "reasonable prices" would threaten business enterprise in the end. Thus an increase in the ever-growing monopoly of industry might prevent the cutthroat competition now caused by partial monopoly, but to be effective it must embrace all industry, and thus would eventuate in a bitter conflict between organized labor and organized capital. On the other hand, the inordinate productivity of industry, which reduced capital values, might be satisfied if the business community would waste more than it did now; but it could never waste enough, for the habit of saving was ingrained. War, colonies, foreign investments, could only temporarily help to waste the surplus.

Of course, Veblen granted that neither businessmen nor most economists considered business fundamentally a pecuniary "institution." But then he insisted that observation of the actual day-to-day operations as distinguished from official pronouncements or claims would confirm his views. Such an observation would involve not only looking at ledgers, business correspondence, profit and loss statements, and the stock market, but also, for the sake of a broader perspective, a study of other cultures and folklore, history, anthropology, psychology, ethics, aesthetics, and the like. This principle of study led him to direct his students to study actual business operations on the one hand, and to read widely on the other hand in the above-mentioned fields.

In Veblen's imaginative mind the argument became allegory and symbol. The contrast between business and industry, between pecuniary and industrial "institutions," became a contrast between different "disciplinary" systems, between the spirit of industrial and pecuniary employments. The pecuniary employments resting on the natural right of property were concerned with bargaining; they disciplined its adepts, the businessmen, in the personal self-seeking animistic logic of acquisition by seizure.

With a twinkle in his eye, Veblen here, as in many other places, gave a humorous and playful expression to a serious analysis. The process of valuation, he said, ran in terms of salesmanship and all the traits of character that depended for their success on taking advantage of people's weaknesses. It gave rise to a pragmatic point of view, with "pragmatic" meaning the agent's preferential advantage at the expense of others. But industrial employment also "disciplined" its adepts, the industrial population in general and engineers in particular, in the impersonal logic or cause and effect of the machine process, which was a more sober method. Its process of valuation ran in terms of the use of the inanimate forces of nature, not in the use of man by man in a cannibalistic struggle.

In Veblen's clash of industry and finance the respective employments lost touch with each other, since individuals worked either in one or in the other, and the differences in employment created fundamental differences in outlook that in effect represented different cultures. Men in the contrasted occupations thought differently because they acted differently. In the pecuniary occupations the faith in the punctilios of modern private property, in funded wealth, became more dogmatic and unswerving, while in the industrial occupations the faith in property tended to wane. Since the "institution" of private property, moreover, could not be stated in terms of cause and effect, it was threatened by a decay in "devout observances." The only effective cure for such unconventional conduct, which might work out in strikes and revolutions, was a counter "discipline" which would undercut the mechanistic logic. This might be supplied by recourse to warlike raids and imperialistic ventures, for training in warfare was antithetical to the training of peaceable industry. But the recourse to the counter "discipline" would bring a full flowering of the military genius; business enterprise would become merely an instrument of warlike power; and the economic order would turn into a feudal order.

To Veblen, the "natural decay" of business enterprise was certain; but the time element was important. Modern business enterprise was a transient phenomenon in the manner of a biological "sport," and must give way either to an industrial republic in conformity with the machine process, or freeze into a feudalistic dynastic regime. Modern property rights could be saved only by scrapping the machine process.

This "occupational" approach was not Veblen's only device to bring out or to dress up the meaning of the conflicting dictates of "business" and "industry." James' and McDougall's work on instincts had created a furor; everybody was talking of instincts. Veblen promptly contributed an instinct of his own, the instinct of workmanship. The unsophisticated instinct of workmanship characterized industry, he said, and the "institution" of property perverted it into the instinct of sportsmanship.

Veblen even utilized conventional economic theory to bring out the distinction. The people of traditional economics who said that economics was evolutionary, meant, he said, that techniques and processes of business and competition were natural and useful; or, in other words, they constantly adapted themselves to the need of society. This to Veblen was begging the real question, which was whether traditional economics was adapted to modern requirements; or more particularly, whether modern business enterprise was adapted to the technological and material needs of the community.

The grimmest and most elaborate analysis and portrayal of his mighty theme was contained in his celebrated *The Theory of the Leisure Class* (1899). The book appeared in a highly expansive period of business development and prosperity. It was Veblen's first book, but its roots went back to his first writing, "Some Neglected Points in the Theory of Socialism," which dates from his re-entry into academic halls at Cornell in 1891. He gave it great care and attention, taking at least five years to complete it. The title was peculiarly apt, for leaders in the social sciences constantly bemoaned the country's lack of an aristocratic or leisure class corresponding to the English to check the inherent greed and commercialization of life. They hoped that the captains of industry who were largely responsible for the nation's progress would form a substantial element of such a select group.

The book contains one of the most withering dissections of contemporary capitalism yet penned. The nature of the control of the captains of finance over the material welfare of the community was worked out in terms of the canons and activities of the gentleman of leisure and his apparent prototype, the barbarian chieftain (read "modern businessman"). The system of free contract became the system of status; the system conforming to the machine process became the industrial republic. The commercialization of life with its poisoning of the springs of survival and advance was traced, not to men's concern with material production, but to its antithesis, pecuniary exploitation.

Veblen's "anthropological" discussions were in fact contemporary delvings into the nature of the modern money economy under the guise of anthropology. His description of the barbarian's standard of success in terms of skulls led up to his description of the modern man's standard in terms of money. And modern ownership, as in effect an ownership and enslavement of persons by pecuniary masters, he analyzed most sharply under the guise of a discussion of the barbarian status of woman as a chattel of the ferocious warrior.

The contrast between "business" and "industry" was worked out in the strangest guises—dress versus clothing; the higher learning versus the lower learning; pecuniary beauty versus economic beauty; pecuniary canons of taste versus aesthetic canons of taste; predatory dogs versus peaceful cats; medicine men versus modern scientists; athletic combats versus physical education; criminals versus the industrious; the patriarchal family versus the household of the unattached woman; and, most sharply of all, the ferocious barbarian age versus that "earlier" stage, the presumptively primitive age of peaceable and free savages.

The free savage suddenly seemed superior; Veblen, on top of all else, was something of an anarchist. At least intermittently he showed a lack of sympathy for the "animated slide rule" or "finikin skeptic" of modern science, and for the impersonalization of large-scale industrial and social organization. An occasional pessimism regarding progress crept through; and he waxed eloquent on how man's inherited human nature was being restrained to meet the requirements of modern technology. He had an undercurrent of sympathy for that golden age when man, if he was not completely rational, was at least not predatory.

"As seen from the point of view of life under modern civilized conditions in an enlightened community of the Western culture, the primitive, ante-predatory savage . . . was not a great success. Even for the purposes of that hypothetical culture to which his type of human nature owes what stability it has . . . this primitive man has quite as many and as conspicuous economic failings as he has economic virtues—as should be plain to anyone whose sense of the case is not biased by leniency born of a fellow-feeling. At his best he is 'a clever, good-for-nothing fellow.' The shortcomings of this presumptively primitive type of character are weakness, inefficiency, lack of initiative and ingenuity, and a yielding and indolent amiability, together with a lively but inconsequential animistic sense. Along with these traits go certain others which have some value for the collective life process, in the sense that they further the facility of life in the group. These traits are truthfulness, peaceableness, good-will, and a non-emulative, non-invidious interest in men and things."

One of the most important facets of Veblen's character was his anthropological objectivity, which sharpened while it deepened his insights. He generally managed to write in the terse impersonal manner of a man from another planet and prosaically dissected the pecuniary foundations of modern society. Even his personal affairs he discussed in this way. For example, in 1913, when seeking a permanent post where he could continue his investigations into Baltic and Cretan antiquities, he wrote to one of his closest friends:

Do you happen to know whether President Vincent of Minnesota [formerly of Chicago]—our old friend George Vincent, as you no doubt know—is inclined to regard me with suspicion or any degree of ill will? This question is not prompted by sentiment, and an answer to it would stir no emotions but would afford valuable information.

He is, as you are aware, in a community in which, as he is apparently just beginning to appreciate, the Scandinavian element has to be catered to by anyone who seeks popularity, as he is doing. . . . So it occurs to me that this antiquarian proposition of mine might well appeal to him as the right sort of thing to encourage, in case I am not *persona non grata* to such an extent as to make me impossible. I may add that I stand well with the Norwegians in Minnesota, largely on the ground of the very exten-

sive popularity of an elder brother of mine [Andrew A. Veblen]. . . .
As you are probably aware, the point of departure for the inquiry would
be the Scandinavian antiquities, and the greater part of the inquiry would
be within the Scandinavian field. And Minnesota has plenty of funds.

Please let me know what you think of it. The whole thing is too close
to my interest to allow me to see it in perspective and judge of its practicability, besides which I have no means of knowing the state of Mr.
Vincent's sentiments.[4]

One final word must be said on Veblen. His critique of the traditional economic doctrine and of the established economic order is
extremely severe, and one can sometimes detect a motivation rooted
in personal distress. Nevertheless, his free intelligence was fundamentally positive and richly suggestive of new and powerful ideas.

SOME HEIRS OF VEBLEN

A number of the younger generation of economists, especially at
the University of Chicago, were sufficiently impressed with Veblen
to attempt to follow his line of thought, and some sought to revise
the philosophical and psychological assumptions of economic theory.
Ablest of this group was Henry Waldgrave Stuart (1870–). Trained
in Hegelian philosophy and Austrian economics at the University
of California, he came to the University of Chicago in 1894 as a
fellow in economics and became devoted to both Dewey and
Veblen.

With Veblen's encouragement and leads, Stuart published a series
of articles that promised to break new ground for an interpretation
of economic organization in terms of the activity of businessmen.
In his first article he criticized the assumption of Hadley and Patten
that "subjective valuation is a process of calculating pleasures and
pains, after the manner . . . specified by Bentham and his disciple
Jevons." Stuart said that "pleasure (or the desire for pleasure) is
. . . not itself a primary fact of consciousness. Pleasure is the feeling
concomitant of certain states or modes of activity." Pleasure, in
other words, would result from attaining some already existing end
of action. It was not in itself an end. Man always pursued actual objective ends.

In subsequent articles Stuart elaborated the argument, asserting
that all the variants of "orthodox" economics were based on hedonism, an unknowable pleasure-pain calculus, instead of the simple
basis of the businessman's activity. The seller's valuation, he said, is

as real a fact and is itself and for its own purposes "as 'ultimate' and 'natural' as any other valuation in the complex economic process." But the orthodox economists avoid it by the inscrutable concept of "normal value," which is in reality market value. According to the Austrians, "the value of goods is not the use which their possessor may make of them, not what he may do with the goods, but what the goods are able to do to him, and this conception of well-being, whether in this case consciously so or not, is essentially hedonistic. Subjectivity, then, according to the Austrian usage, implies a virtual reference to sensation, and subjective exchange value, *qua* subjective, must accordingly be expressed in terms of future enjoyment."

The older classical school represented by Mill also had a hedonistic point of view according to Stuart, since it regarded "seller's valuation as in the long run the resultant and accurate representation of the more ultimate or 'original' valuations which labour and abstinence place upon the suffering and irksomeness which they respectively involve." This hedonistic standpoint "prevented an interpretation of capitalist's cost and valuation as self-centered psychological phenomena," an interpretation in terms of the "universal process of the pursuit of Ends and the adaptation of Means thereto." Stuart, in concluding, declared: "Pain is incidental to a discrepancy, pleasure to the degree of correspondence, between the end ideally in view and the end which the means at hand are adequate to secure." [5]

Though Stuart later formally shifted his main interest to philosophy,[6] he retained a deep interest in economics. In his doctoral dissertation in philosophy, *Valuation as a Logical Process* (1903), he pointed out that essentially the principle of marginal utility reflected the "conservative function of valuation." According to that principle the value of the unit quantity of a stock of any commodity is "measured by the least important single use in the schedule of uses to which the stock, as a whole, is to be applied. Manifestly, then, adherence to this valuation placed upon the unit quantity is in so far conservative of the whole schedule, and the marginal value is a 'short-hand' symbol . . . of the value of the . . . complex purpose presented in the schedule. Moreover, the increase of marginal value concurrently with diminution of the st k through consumption, loss, or reapplication is not indicative so uch of a change of purpose as of determination to adhere to so nuch of the original program of consumption as may still be possible of attainment with the depleted supply of the commodity." [7]

In a much later essay, "Phases of the Economic Interest," he elaborated his position more definitely along Cooley's lines, and more concretely. He contended that marginal utility economics applied simply to routinized behavior, but was not applicable to ever-rising, newly developed situations. The latter called for "constructive comparison" or "creative intelligence."

Perhaps Stuart's most striking point was his emphasis on the logical and psychological continuity of the ethical and economic problems. Suppose, he wrote, that labor legislation for an industry were passed and the community approved the law even to the extent of cheerfully paying the additional cost. It would then be arbitrary to insist that the old price was still the economic one of the commodity, and the additional cost merely the price of a quiet conscience. Actually the old basic labor cost had become obsolete. Stuart therefore protested against "*a priori* and wholesale condemnation of such legislation as merely irresponsible, 'ethical,' and 'unscientific.' "

After all, the egoism of man, he wrote, "is not fixed and unalterable fact. . . . As an actual social phenomenon egoism is merely a disclosure of a certain present narrowness and inertness in the nature of the individual which may or may not be definitive for him. It is precisely on a par with anemia, dyspepsia, or fatigue, or any other like unhappy fact of personal biography."

It has been argued, Stuart said, that such measures as insurance against old age, sickness, industrial accidents, and unemployment lead to systematic pauperization. But this type of criticism "assumes a permanent incapacity in 'human nature,' or in most actual beings therewith endowed, to recognize as seriously important other interests than those upon which hinge physical life and death." The criticisms assume that ordinary man is held back from "moral Quixotism [as well as] from material extravagance by the fear of starvation alone; and . . . no other interests in the 'normal' man . . . can or ever will be wholesomely effective to these ends." Even if what is alleged be true, he thought it less a "proof of original sin and 'imperfectibility' than a reproach to a social order whose collective tenor and institutions leave the mass untouched and unawakened above the level of animal reproduction and whose inequalities of opportunity prevent awakened life from growing strong. And second, the democratic society of the future, if it exempts the individual in part or wholly from the dread of premature physical extinction, must leave him on higher levels of interest similarly dependent for success or failure upon his ultimate personal discretion. And is it inconceivable that on higher levels there should ever genuinely be such a persisting type of issue for the multitude of men?" [8]

William R. Camp gave promise of another significant line of development. He studied under Veblen at Stanford and followed him to Missouri for graduate work. His dissertation, "The Limitations of the Ricardian Theory of Rent," was so well regarded that it was published in the *Political Science Quarterly*.

Camp pointed out that the Ricardian theory of rent was drawn in terms of a land monopoly. The only differential advantages contemplated—soil and location—were to accrue to the landlord. Such advantages were considered sufficient to centralize wealth in the hands of the owners of agricultural land. But technological changes, especially the rise of the railroads, brought such "differential disadvantages" to the farm-owning class that wealth became centralized in more powerful hands. Such factors as credit facilities, transportation rates, marketing facilities, became important.

Camp did not mean to question Ricardo's logic. Rather, he wished to point out that Ricardo could not be "expected to explain conditions which he could by no power of prescience forecast." A new theory, therefore, was needed to explain the centralization of wealth in the hands of others than the owners of agricultural lands.[9] Camp hoped to produce it; but he experienced great difficulties in adjusting to an academic career, and as a result the promise of his dissertation was dissipated in frustration and bitterness.

Several of Veblen's students chose a concrete field of economics for detailed inquiry and found themselves moving gradually into ever-widening realms. Veblen had had the effect of stripping them so thoroughly, though unconsciously, of their complete confidence in the old way, that they tended to base their inquiries closely upon the existing facts. And their appreciation of Veblen increased as they proceeded in their detailed inquiries.

Robert Franklin Hoxie (1868–1916)[10] was one of this group. Hoxie had a brilliant mind and an exceptionally warm and generous nature. But it took him a long time to find his bearings. While an undergraduate at Cornell he became a disciple of Laughlin and followed him to Chicago. After numerous changes in his teaching posts, he returned to Cornell in 1903. Here he thought that perhaps Fetter's psychological approach to economics offered the true light, especially since its "reduction of actuality to psychological terms gave its conclusions a sense of finality." [11] Then he made his final change by accepting a post at Chicago. By that time he thought he was at the end of his quest, for here he came definitely under the influence of Veblen, who appeared to him to supply all the answers.

In an address in 1907 before the American Sociological Society Hoxie declared that the contrast between the industrial and pecuniary disciplines definitely proved the inevitability of class conflict. Hoxie held that these differences in discipline could not be obviated since they were a necessary aspect of the developing life process in society. "Without these differences no division of labor, no specialization, no development of efficiency and individuality could exist. To obviate them, we should have to accept the simplicity, stagnation, and atrophy of the communistic community." [12] However, as Hoxie turned his attention more directly to the concrete details of labor union organization, he realized that Veblen's distinction between industrial and pecuniary employments was a guiding principle of search rather than an explanation; that Veblen's apparently methodological criticisms of academic economics were more vital than the mere charge that the dominant economic theory was unconscious apologetics for things as they were. Thus Hoxie turned to a more effective examination of labor, in terms of the spirit of workmen's organizations, of workmen's ideals and aspirations under the pervasiveness of business principles; and at the same time he manifested a sympathetic understanding of the employers' attitude.

Hoxie's posthumous publication, *Trade Unionism in the United States* (1917), still stands as one of the few permanent contributions to the theory of labor organization by an American economist. Most interesting was his elaborate "functional" analysis of trade unions. In practice, he found, these functional types did not represent any particular union organization or group, for no union organization functioned strictly and consistently according to type. But as representing fairly alternative programs of union action, these functional types were real.

The first and most recognizable type, in Hoxie's analysis, was "business unionism." This was characteristic of local and national craft and compound craft unions, because it expressed the wishes of the workers in a craft or industry rather than of the working class as a whole. A business union sought to attain immediate objectives for its members, in terms of higher wages, shorter hours, and better working conditions. It accepted the existing capitalistic organization and the wage system, and, regarding unionism mainly as a bargaining institution, worked toward its goal through collective bargaining. Thus it was generally exclusive, limiting its membership, by means of an apprenticeship system and high initiation fees and dues, to the more skilled workers. In harmony with its business character, it tended to emphasize discipline within the organization, to develop strong leadership, and to become somewhat aristocratic in government. In method, this type of union was temperate and economic. It favored voluntary arbitration, deprecated strikes, avoided political action, but refused arbitration and resorted to strikes if it felt such actions would increase its bargaining power. The railroad brotherhoods, Hoxie thought, best exemplified this type of union.

His second functional type was friendly or "uplift unionism." Because of its idealistic viewpoint, it sought the greatest degree of mutuality and democracy. For this it employed collective bargaining, stressed mutual insurance, and advocated political action, cooperative enterprises, profit-sharing, and other idealistic plans for social regeneration. The nearest approach to this type of union, according to Hoxie, was the Knights of Labor, which was just passing out of the picture.

A third type was revolutionary unionism, which was either socialistic or quasi-anarchistic unionism. He quickly passed over it to a discussion of his final type, "predatory unionism," characterized by the ruthless pursuit of immediate ends. Predatory unionism, Hoxie divided into two types, "hold-up" unionism and "guerrilla" unionism. The first superficially appeared to be conservative, professed "a belief in law and order," and operated "openly through collective bargaining." In reality it had no consistent principles, was monopolistic, boss-ridden, and corrupt, with the members blindly following the leaders as long as they delivered the goods. Frequently it joined "with the employers in a double-sided monopoly . . . to eliminate both capitalistic and labor competition, and to squeeze the consuming public." The other type, "guerrilla unionism," like "hold-up" unionism, lacked fixed principles and ruthlessly pursued immediate ends by means of secret and violent methods, but it differed from the "hold-up" type in that it could be bribed.

With an analysis of the functional types as a starting point, Hoxie went on to give an illuminating interpretation of the growth and development of trade unionism in America.[13] He then came to the latest industrial conditions facing labor. His analysis of "scientific management," that is, job analysis, ably grasped underlying considerations. He declared in *Scientific Management* (1915) that such management would damage labor unless certain controls should be established. Otherwise scientific management, by breaking down established crafts and craftsmanship and eliminating skill, would make all labor competitors for almost any job. Such a situation would destroy the current form of unionism and render collective bargaining impossible in matters which the unions considered most essential. As a general rule, he said, "unskilled workers cannot maintain effective and continuous organization for dealing with complicated industrial situations." Yet collective bargaining required such an organization. By time study the employer could constantly initiate new methods and conditions and reclassify workmen's jobs. Thereby he could easily evade the unions' efforts to "establish and maintain definite and continuous standards of work and pay."

True, scientific management, said Hoxie, increased the efficiency of the relatively unskilled and enabled them to earn more. But the native efficiency of the working class would suffer from the neglect of apprenticeship unless other means of industrial education were forthcoming. Furthermore, the whole scheme of scientific management, especially the gathering up and systematization of knowledge formerly possessed by the workmen, would tend to add enormous strength to capitalism, that is, to the employer. This fact, together with the greater ease of replacement, would increase the insecurity of employment.

Scientific management in itself, Hoxie pointed out, did not eliminate strikes and establish industrial peace. So long as union men "believe, as they seem warranted in doing, that scientific management means the destruction of their organization, . . . unionism will doubtless continue to oppose it energetically." The need was not so much for repression and direct control, he thought, as for "social supplementation and increased knowledge," for a frank recognition of the trend of events, and for a method whereby the worker's life would have the "content which he is losing as the result of increased specialization and the abandonment of the old apprenticeship system."

In accordance with the functional approach, Hoxie insisted that in the broader realm of doctrine and practice an understanding of the current situation required a knowledge of the history of its development. Thus he wrote in his unpublished "History of Economic Thought":

> To understand men and institutions in any practical sense, i.e., to understand them in such a manner that you can depend upon their reactions, that you can make the best of them as they are or modify them in the interest of social betterment, we must know their past history. What is true of men and institutions is true also of economic theory. It is not a thing merely of the present—a true reflection and explanation of the present economic situation. Wipe out all economic texts and traditions, put a new set of men unacquainted with these traditions at work to recreate the body of economic doctrine and precept, and it is quite possible that the new creation would bear no striking resemblance to that body of doctrine which we are prone to regard as the "true" explanation of the existing economic situation and a true guide to action. This is because the men who write economic texts and discuss economic problems build upon the work of their predecessors, who in turn build upon theirs, and because also these economic writers bring to their study of the economic situation their own inherited preconceptions and prejudices. Our present-day economics is a mosaic of survivals and is based to a very great extent upon postulates, preconceptions, and precepts which have their genesis in the past and under different circumstances.[14]

Hoxie's death in 1916 cut down not only a promising career, but also a potent force for meliorating the ever-increasing drift toward distinct schools of economists, for he had enjoyed the respect and devoted friendship of many outstanding leaders. Perhaps a more serious loss can be seen in the fact that the path Hoxie was breaking in his investigations "was one that might lead the economist to a position where it was possible for him to act as an arbitrator between opposing camps, or at least as a moderator of hostile opinions, capable of allaying the bitterness needlessly attending inevitable conflicts of interest." [15]

Veblen and his students made traditional economic doctrine stand trial, putting it through a severe cross-examination. The classic economists did not come out of the ordeal with shining success. Veblen brought the whole constitutional basis of economics into question—the motives by which and for which men live, the character of their institutions, and the pattern of their development. All of this was completely unsettling, and there were few economists who cared to face the responsibility of reconstructing a new body of law. Veblen, unlike Marx, did not elaborate his theory into an alternative system. In view of what has happened to Marx, this was probably a good thing. So his greatest influence was that of a critic, a skeptic who helped shake economic theory down to bedrock.

His writing is suffused with a congenital distrust of the economic society of his day. His sharp break with the traditional and customary approach, and even with style, forced him out of the web of society, and he was able to see it with unusual clarity, as a whole, from the outside. This is the function of uncommitted intelligence. It repudiates the debt of myopia that accepted theory pays to society. But in his bird's-eye view he failed to see the organic interdependence that those rooted in their society feel most deeply; he was condemned to loneliness. It was left to his successors to go to the market place and apply his vision to the life around them. Henry W. Stuart studied the quality of individual motives; Robert F. Hoxie analyzed trade unions; and Wesley C. Mitchell charted the tides and currents of economic flux.

CHAPTER XX

Wesley C. Mitchell: Scholar of Business Cycles

WESLEY C. MITCHELL (1874–1948) was the foremost intellectual heir of Veblen.[1] He was no slavish disciple, for Veblen suggested leads that Mitchell found fruitful in developing his own bent in economic inquiries. In so doing, Mitchell added a new dimension to American economics as well as to popular thought. Before him the "business cycle" with its alternations of prosperity and depressions had been emphasized by such critical social thinkers as Marx and Veblen, but in academic traditional thought the cycle was an exception more interesting than important, a temporary deviation in the transcendent regularities of demand

and supply. Mitchell brought diligent academic research to bear on the concept of the cyle. In the process he made a real contribution in his organization of statistical and empirical data.

Mitchell was first of all a sanguine American. He was heir to the cultural tradition of New England. His grandparents were farmers in pre-Civil War Maine and Western New York. His father, though originally a physician, was incapacitated by a wartime wound and eventually turned to fruit farming in Illinois. A farmer's children were expected to help with the work, and Mitchell as the eldest son had a special responsibility. He came to know the problems of farming and developed a facility in the mechanical arts.

Mitchell's self-reliance came into play in connection with the family plans for his college career. While he was still a junior in the local high school in 1891, the opening of a new university in near-by Chicago was announced for the following year. It would be sufficiently close to home so that Mitchell could help on the farm during vacation periods. Finding that his high school training would not equip him to pass the entrance requirements, he spent his senior year studying by himself.

At the University of Chicago he was particularly influenced by three teachers: John Dewey in philosophy and Thorstein Veblen and J. Laurence Laughlin in economics. While Dewey was studying men's actions to understand their thought, Veblen was checking economic rationalization against behavior; while on the whole Dewey tended to accept the world, Veblen dissected the world largely to reject it. Guided by Dewey and Veblen, Mitchell delved into psychology and history to obtain a broader perspective of human nature than that offered by traditional economics. Laughlin, by his extreme dogmatic individualism in laying down the principles of economics and social policy, tended to make Mitchell more receptive to Veblen.

After Mitchell's graduation Laughlin obtained for him a series of fellowships. He received his doctor's degree *summa cum laude* with a major in economics and a minor in philosophy, and in 1900 was added to the staff of the University of Chicago as a junior member. At the suggestion of Laughlin, Mitchell did his doctoral dissertation on a solid topic, the history of greenbacks. In it he set out to determine objectively what had happened to the country when greenbacks were the currency. Seven years after he had begun the task he published a portion of that history, dealing with the Civil War period, under the title *A History of the Greenbacks with Special Reference to the Economic Consequences of Their Issue: 1862–1865* (1903). With this very first book Mitchell struck out along lines different from those of both of his teachers.

Mitchell had no special statistical training; furthermore, at the time the teaching of statistics was in a rather primitive state and the available material was not of the best. Yet through the use of such statistical material as he could obtain, he developed a new insight into the price system and particularly into its peculiar deviations and fluctuations. In order to study the true source of fluctuations he first weighted carefully relatively fixed payments, such as carfares and contracts, indicating those lags and barriers—psychological, institutional, contractual—which affected responses generally considered automatic and spontaneous adjustments of supply and demand. He declared that persons whose products or services did not immediately rise in price, opposed, so far as they could, changes which increased their money expenditures. Laborers might demand a rise to compensate for the increased cost of food, but the employer could not grant it, without injuring himself, until the price of his goods had advanced. If he sold to other dealers, they would object to paying higher prices unless they were sure the increase could be "shifted onto others." And consumers objected to paying higher prices, especially if their own money incomes did not rise.

From a detailed study of political, military, and financial events in the business annals, Mitchell found that the gold value of the greenbacks had roughly varied in accordance with the ebb and flow of public confidence in the Union's victory; that is, on the probability of ultimate redemption of the notes. Finding from his statistical study that the course of commodity prices corresponded, with a lag of several months, to the course of the gold premium, he concluded that both changes were largely due to a common cause: the varying esteem in which the government notes were held.

Having determined the fluctuations of the price level, Mitchell now endeavored to determine the fortunes of the various income receivers. But this in turn required that the precise fluctuations of those money incomes be determined as accurately as possible. He therefore began separate discussions of wages, interest, rents, and profits, utilizing the available statistical materials on the subject. He found striking fluctuations not only in each broad category, but also in the subdivisions. In 1908 he published *Gold, Prices, and Wages under the Greenback Standard,* a comprehensive statistical study of the material on the entire greenback period.

After he finished the first volume on greenbacks Mitchell went to the University of California as an assistant professor. His main interest shifted to a consideration of modern economic society. It began with his course "Economic Origins," moved on to plans for a comprehensive study, which he sometimes called the "Theory of Prices," at other times "The System of Prices," and at still other times "The Money Economy," and resulted finally in his classic *Business Cycles* in 1913.

By this date he had transferred to Columbia University, where he was willing to accept $700 a year for the privilege of teaching a graduate course on "Types of Economic Theory" and with no undergraduate assignments. Though he had received tentative offers of full professorships at Harvard, Yale, and Cornell, he preferred to be in New York, the center of financial life, where he could more effectively study the workings of the money economy.

It was in his course in "Economic Origins" at California that Mitchell first elaborated a broad attack on the current conception of the mechanical nature of economic life. He attacked the conception of man as a "lightning calculator of pleasures and pains," the conception of the law of supply and demand as merely a pitting of aggregate commodities against the mountain of demand, the result of which was price, and the similar mechanical notion that the general line of prices varied directly with the amount of money. Traditional economic theory, he declared in his outlines of "The Money Economy," did not take account of basic human motives—impulses and habits; consequently it missed the most substantial fact, the conflict between the logic of the price system and these human motives, and ignored the profound influence of the money culture in economic life.

Economists, he said, have not been bold enough to show the logic of the money economy, but they have pushed to an extreme the pecuniary logic of human behavior. Failing to distinguish sharply between the two, they presented the hedonistic psychology as a reflection of pecuniary motives and in this way conceived of economic life as naturally controlled by a balance sheet. In their view income and outgo in utilities and disutilities balanced so that each man got his product. Hardly any attention was paid to human valuations, "to the habits of men in using money, to the considerations that weigh with men in spending the money in their pockets." The price system, however, was less like a piece of machinery which men perfectly control and more like a "natural force which men have learned to harness and direct but which retains a refractory character of its own and is ever and again escaping control and throwing into confusion the whole process of which it forms a part."

Statisticians, compilers of index numbers, and writers on crises were the most fruitful contributors to a more satisfactory theory of prices, Mitchell asserted. He found little statistical information available, and that little was unorganized by an indifferent economic profession. Therefore he opposed the spokesmen for traditional economic theory who claimed that at best the office of statistics "is purely that of supplementing the data for analysis derived from individual observation and experience, and that the only question arising in determining the desirability of applying statistical methods in any specific investigation are: (1) Are the facts with which it deals sufficiently well ascertained? and (2) if not, are they susceptible directly or indirectly of quantitative statement?" To him such a view rested upon very crude psychological notions, and such inferences regarding the actual uses of statistics were contrary to fact. "Can we draw the assumed line between the presentation of facts and their explanation?" he asked. "Is not such a notion contrary to the favorite theory of modern psychology: that all perception is apperception? Are not the processes of discovering facts and explaining them so closely interwoven in consciousness that they cannot be separated except by an artificial analysis?" Anyone who has used statistics extensively knows that "figures may often be used to explain our problems, to discover causal relations, to correlate different parts of our knowledge, as well as to supply the material for analysis." [2]

To him the use of statistics was much more far-reaching. Index numbers, he thought, provided relatively full and exact knowledge of the character of price fluctuations, and rendered many ideas more precise and definite. In consequence, economists could be better informed about the differences and the similarities of the price changes of different articles in the same market and of the same article in different markets—the relations between wholesale and retail prices, and between the prices of raw materials and manufactured articles. Again, the extent of the influence of "cycles of business activity" on prices as against that of changes in the production of precious metals could in some measure be determined from index numbers. Furthermore, index numbers could reveal more definitely than armchair speculation the correspondence in the movement of the price level in different countries. Finally, the price tables helped, at least in part, to show the interrelations of the parts of the price system—the influences which fluctuations in the price of one good exercised upon that of other goods.

Like the compilers of index numbers, writers on crises, Mitchell said, had the advantage of starting with a concrete problem. "To them the price movements are one phase of a general dislocation of economic relations, intimately connected both as to cause and consequence with such other phenomena as changes in investment of capital, business failures, shrinkage of production, lack of employment, variations in the reserves of banks, etc. They are concerned moreover with those phenomena as parts of a process in which all the inter-related facts develop together. These facts lend to their discussions a realistic air. . . . Their explanations, so far as they succeed in giving them, are explanations of economic experience, not explanations of what would happen under unreal hypothetical conditions." [3]

Mitchell's analysis of prices began with the distinction between goods bought for consumption and those bought and sold for profit; that is, between consumers' prices, i.e., retail prices as a rule, and business prices, i.e., wholesale prices, and prices of production goods. The businessman's estimates of probable fluctuations in market price were largely ignored, according to Mitchell; for the businessman figured differently from the consumer, and the dominant marginal utility school, overemphasizing the importance of consumption goods, did not realize his importance. That school, in consequence, gauged business demand in terms of consumption.

After distinguishing between business and monetary, including money market, factors, Mitchell declared that business demand prices—considerations of business expediency affecting buyers in deciding questions of prices—depended on the prospect of profit on a given purchase and the financial ability of businessmen to make the necessary purchases. The prospect of profit depended on the anticipated future prices of both purchase and sale of the goods, anticipated volume of trade, and the anticipated prices of the other elements in manufacturing and handling the goods. Similarly, business supply prices depended upon the prospect of profit from sales and the need of funds; the prospect of profits from sales depended upon the anticipation of future price and the cost of goods. It was these supply and demand prices in transactions among businessmen, as distinguished from consumer prices, that explained the "tolerably brief and regular rises and falls in prices covering periods of varying length" which were revealed by tables of index numbers.

Behind the price system, declared Mitchell, was the money culture with its commanding logic and techniques. In his analysis, "getting and spending" money was a social habit, the outgrowth of centuries of development. Continual preoccupation with money-making drilled the pecuniary habit of thought into men. Here a psychological element entered. Men were not thoroughly rational. Their ancient tribal habits and the instincts of primitive societies have never been thoroughly eradicated. This helped to explain the unreasoning optimism of investors and businessmen in periods of prosperity and their panicky pessimism in periods of depression. The money economy as a cultural factor therefore produced its own kind of human being who did not harmonize with, but exercised a cumulative influence upon basic human nature. "We still distrust this alien's ways, we still think his cold logic inhuman, we still hope he will not make us like himself, but in the meantime we make constant use of him."

This money economy, Mitchell pointed out, had a productive as well as a destructive aspect, for the use of money had been a potent force in developing individual responsibility and freedom and achieving superiority in production over any known realized scheme. Doubtless credit for this superiority, he added, should be directly attributed to the various factors summarized as "the machine process," but its adoption and elaboration occurred only in a society where economic relations were based on money prices. In such a society the price system with its flexibility supplied three indispensable conditions: (1) a simple and effective method of controlling complicated economic activities by accounting in terms of money cost and money income; (2) a strong motive for individual enterprise; and (3) a basis for extensive co-operation between men of the most diverse capacities and aptitudes in accomplishing tasks of great magnitude.

To Mitchell, as has been said, this was not an unmixed blessing;

for the making of goods and the making of money were not the same thing. On the business side, the price system led to opportunities whereby individuals could make money at the expense of society, to a situation in which workingmen as well as employers would be less interested in efficiency, to monopoly, to imperfect co-ordination of productive efforts, to emphasis on money power rather than human or social needs, and to a cumulative disparity in wealth beyond any natural differences in industry, skill, thrift, intelligence, and physical environment.

He thought that legislation or better business organization might remove many of the defects. Waste of natural resources and the evils of child labor could continue to be checked by government regulation. Unfair methods of securing the property of others could be subject to severe penalties. Restraining laws could prevent abuses. The integration and reorganization of corporations could reduce many wastes of competition. Standards similar to Civil Service rules could enable larger enterprises to obtain the best brains for directing economic activity, and the gradual extension of government supervision could mitigate the dangers of monopolistic exploitation.

None of these particular reforms would appreciably change the economic organization, according to Mitchell, for the economic relations among individuals would remain in the form of voluntary price agreements. But in the aggregate these reforms, if they continued, might ultimately "effect by their cumulative influence an important change . . . for they represent an increasingly conscious effort" by the community to overcome the conflicts between making money and making goods. Intelligence must guide, he said, and the need was for knowledge comparable in certainty and definiteness to that which has been the basis of industrial advance.[4]

Mitchell felt that with *Business Cycles* he had definitely narrowed his interest in the workings of the money economy to one specific aspect, the "technical exigencies" of the price system. But the whole picture of the money economy became clearer as a consequence. The center was modern business enterprise with its corporate organization and machine technology. Here Mitchell dealt with the characteristic pulsation of modern industry and business, rather than with the varied crashes and booms of history. The latter were sporadic, he said; the former increasingly regular and predictable in their broad features.

The pursuit of money profits was Mitchell's guide for analysis;

and the considerations which entered into businessmen's calculations of profits, and which operated as both causes and effects in the interlocking system of prices, were the categories for organizing the data. The "method" he had attributed to students of crises became formally his method of studying "business cycles." "The theory of business cycles presented," he said, "is a descriptive analysis of the processes of cumulative change by which a revival of activity develops into intense prosperity, by which this prosperity engenders a crisis, by which crisis turns into depression, and by which depression finally leads to . . . a revival of activity."

In basic outline, Mitchell's study followed his previous drafts of the theory of prices, but whereas formerly he had begun with the contributions to the theory of prices by general economists and specialists, he now utilized a survey of the various significant current theories of "business cycles." All the data and ideas, he wrote, fitted into a framework provided by the basic fact of money economy, that the industrial process of making goods was subordinate to the process of making money. Since the scope and intensity of the phases of business cycles depended on the extent and perfection of business organization, the center of interest was the inner world of business comprised by the highly organized enterprises in wholesale trade, transportation, manufacturing, lumbering, banking, and finance.

Mitchell held that any theory of modern prosperity must deal with these business conditions, and with their pecuniary aspect. Just as the ever-recurring changes within the system of prices affected business prosperity and, through it, national welfare, he said, so changes in business prosperity reacted upon prices, in an interminable series of readjustments, flexible in detail yet stable in the essential balance of the interrelations, "a system like a living organism in its ability to recover from the serious disorders into which it periodically falls." Although engineers guided the technical side of the money economy, higher authority was vested in those skilled in money-making, the businessmen, whose policies in turn were subject to review by lenders, especially the larger capitalists. And government had the role of protecting the public welfare against the excesses of making money.

This money economy was, Mitchell thought, unquestionably the best system men had yet practiced in organizing economic activity. Its defects arose from the lack of a general plan of production. The primary defect was lack of effective co-ordination of effort among independent enterprises. Civilized nations, having as yet failed to develop intelligence to cope with the problem, continued to rely on the "badly co-ordinated efforts of private initiative." Second, since guidance by pecuniary profit meant guidance by purchasing power, the satisfaction of the most important needs of the community was warped by this artificial aim. Third, from the business point of view, prospective profit was an uncertain guide because its components, profit margins and volume of sales, were related in unstable fashion and each was subject to changes from a multitude of unpredictable causes. Even the shrewdest profit calculations could be upset by unanticipated conjunctures. Finally, the hazard of chance grew greater with the extension of the market and the increasingly heavier investment of capital for future production brought about by the progress of technology. These defects caused the recurrent disorders constituting crises and depressions.

Mitchell pointed out that, contrary to orthodox economics, a state of change in business conditions was the only "normal" state. The business world was always undergoing a cumulative change, always passing through some phase of a business cycle into some other phase. Statistical data were organized this way, from the standpoint of their bearing on changing business profits. Even an introductory study of economic organization, said Mitchell, revealed the chief factors affecting profits and solvency, but the problem was "to follow the interaction of these factors through all the permutations which heighten or darken the prospects of profits and make easy or difficult the maintenance of solvency."

Since business cycles were conceived to be a continuous round, he continued, the analysis could begin at any stage. Commencing with the revival phase, Mitchell found as a legacy from depression low prices and costs, narrow profit margins, liberal bank reserves, conservative capitalization, moderate stocks, lending at low ebb, and cautious buying. These conditions, he felt, tended to a cumulative expansion of the volume of trade. Although the change from dullness to activity was effected slowly, it was often hastened by some event outside of domestic business, such as an exceptionally profitable harvest, heavy government purchases, or heavy exports. Even if the revival were limited at first to a few industries or a single section of the country, it would soon spread to other parts of the business field, through purchases from other enterprises, and so on without assignable limits. The active enterprises borrowed money, employed more labor, and made larger profits. Family incomes increased, consumers' demands spread in ever-widening circles to all classes of goods, stimulating afresh the demand for both consumer and producer goods. This instilled an optimism among businessmen which for a time justified itself and heightened the forces that generated it by making everyone ready to buy more freely.

As the existing facilities were fully utilized, Mitchell said, prices rose because less efficient resources were called into play. The expectation of such a price rise hastened it, for the buyers hurried to purchase at the existing low levels. The rise spread rapidly, for every advance put pressure on others to recoup themselves by a compensatory advance in the price of what they sold. But the resulting price changes were irregular. Retail prices lagged behind wholesale, staple consumer goods behind staple producer goods, and finished products behind raw materials. Of the raw materials, mineral products reflected the changes in business conditions more regularly than the others. "Wages rise often more promptly, but always in less degree than wholesale prices; discount rates rise sometimes more slowly than commodities and at other times more rapidly." Interest rates on bonds were more sluggish, while the advance in the prices of stocks, especially common stocks, both preceded and exceeded those of commodities. The causes of these differences were partly in the organization of markets, partly in the technical conditions affecting the relative demand for, and supply of, the several classes, and partly in the adjustment of selling prices to buying prices.

These Mitchell considered the fundamental maladjustments which could be alleviated but never removed. In the great majority of enterprises profits, he wrote, result from these divergent price fluctuations because of the lag in the price of labor and the fixity for the time being of overhead costs. Profits swelled and investments were encouraged by the mutual stimulation of the increases in the physical volume and prices and the spread of optimism. Theoretically, a balance could be maintained if the demand for goods kept pace with the rising supply despite rising prices; if the cost of raw materials did not increase excessively as compared with the selling price of the manufactured products; if bank reserves expanded with demand liabilities and the cost of living did not rise much faster than money incomes; if banks and investors could supply business's increasing need for funds, etc. If a serious maladjustment should occur in the rate of growth of any of these factors, some businesses would suffer losses, and the injury would spread just as prosperity did. Thus the very growth of business prosperity caused a cumulative growth of the stresses and strains in the system which disrupted the balance.

The very forces which brought about rising prices, therefore, turned prosperity into a crisis, he continued. First, the costs gradually increased. When firms contracted for all the business they could handle with their standard equipment, the decline in overhead costs per unit would end. Thereafter unit costs would rise. A further expansion of business now required the use of less efficient equipment. Prices of raw materials, wage rates, and interest rates increased rapidly when business enterprises were avidly competing for supplies, labor, and loans. Furthermore, it was difficult to maintain a high standard of operating efficiency when overtime was common, discharge was an insignificant penalty, and everything was done in a hurry. The strain in the money market arose from the tendency of reserves to decline; the reserves fell to the limit fixed by law or prudence, while demand liabilities expanded. The high interest rates, especially of call loans, were a symptom of the weakened technical position of the banking system. A strain in the market for investment goods was caused by the rise of construction costs and interest rates, which led investors to postpone their projects.

Disaster could be postponed, said Mitchell, only if prices rose indefinitely. This could not happen if for no other reason than that the insufficiency of cash reserves forced banks to cease expanding loans. But even before this stage was reached, the price rise would be halted by the consequence of its own inevitable inequalities. Certain prices were fixed by law and custom; others depended on the incalculable chances of the harvests. In some instances the construction of new equipment had increased capacity faster than the demand for products had expanded under the repressing influence of high prices. Unwillingness of investors to let fresh contracts threatened loss to contracting firms and their suppliers. The high interest rates checked not only the demand for goods, but also efforts to maintain prices by withholding goods. Finally, the success of some enterprises in raising prices aggravated the difficulties of those in trouble. Since credits were based on the capitalization of present and prospective profits, cautious lenders refused extensions and renewals. Prosperity merged into a crisis. Liquidation was rapid, for everyone became alarmed and put pressure on his debtors. Businessmen concentrated on husbanding their financial resources.

A period of cumulative depression resulted. The mass discharge of labor and the reduction of other sources of family income started a cumulative decline in consumer buying and hence of the physical volume of production. Prices fell cumulatively with decline of production, for with idle capacity there was keener competition for business. As with the rise of prices accompanying revival, so the fall accompanying depression was characterized by regularly recurring differences in degree. Wholesale prices fell faster than retail; producers goods faster than consumer goods; raw materials faster than manufactured products, with the fall in minerals showing more regularity than other raw materials. As compared with general wholesale commodity prices, wages and long-term interest rates declined in less degree; and while discounts and stock prices fell in greater degree, the prices of high-grade bonds rose during depression.

The decline, however, also initiated processes of readjustment overcoming depression. Operating costs were reduced by the rapid fall in prices of raw materials and bank loans, by the greater efficiency of labor in a period of scarce employment, and by closer economy exercised by the enterprises. Fixed charges were cut by reorganization, the writing off of bad debts, the writing down of depreciated properties, and by the effective recapitalizing of business enterprises on the basis of lower profits.

After two or three years of depression the demand for goods began to expand slowly. Current consumption began to require current production; consumers' supplies of semi-durable goods, machinery and the like, which had begun to wear out, required replacement. A larger population must be fed, and new tastes appeared. Most important, the demand for industrial equipment revived, for the drop in foreclosures and reorganizations limited these sources for bargains to investors; capitalists became less timid, low rates of interest on bonds encouraged borrowing, accumulated technical improvements might be utilized, and contracts let on favorable terms. Once the physical volume of trade expanded, the process became cumulative, though growth would be slow for a while because of the continued sagging of prices. Profits did not rise rapidly, but business prospects became brighter. Old debts were paid, inventories absorbed, weak enterprises reorganized, and the banks were strong. Revival would begin when some fortunate circumstance gave a "sudden fillip to demand, or, in the absence of such an event, when the slow growth of business has filled order books and paved the way for a new rise in prices."

Thus the waxing and waning of prosperity were fundamentally due to processes that run regularly within the world of business itself. But such cycles might be accentuated or distended by important external events. Such events, for example, were changes in gold output and technological improvement, war and peace, alteration in monetary standards, or changes in government policy toward corporations. These, however, entered the situation not as leading causes, but as complicating or disturbing factors from outside. Moreover, cycles varied with changes in business organization and practice and the importance of different industries. Thus the violence of panics and the extravagances of booms were mitigated by the better organization and knowledge and firmer policies of the banks.

Mitchell found that the patterns of these cycles, though similar to one another, were not identical. Thus the development of manufacturing and the decline of railway building made the business cycles of 1900–1910 different from their predecessors. The great rise of corporations had made the securities markets more influential than in the day of family enterprises. Other changes reacting on business cycles were the extension of monopoly, industrial integration, the "organization of labor with its standardization of wage rates, and in general the readjustment of business to changes in the material, political, or social environment." Such changes had to be taken into account in any future study.

Since these broad changes were inevitable, "the economists of each generation will probably be forced to recast the theory of business cycles which they learned in their youth." To Mitchell, however, the very regularity of business cycles gave promise of progress in economic organization. Prosperity, he thought, was short-lived, because men lacked the knowledge and skill to prevent the accumulation of stresses and strains. He hoped for progress by bettering the forecasts of business conditions. Consequently, he said, one way of increasing social control of economic activity was to "democratize the knowledge of current business conditions" then possessed by a favored few. Private services were highly defective because too frequently they could not obtain accurate information. Government service was therefore necessary.

In conclusion Mitchell declared that the effect of business cycles on social well-being revealed the double personality of the creatures of the money economy. The pecuniary institutions imposed the artificial ends of money-making for the individual and business prosperity for the nation. "Beneath the one lie the individual's impulsive activities—his maze of instinctive reactions partially systematized into conscious wants, definite knowledge, and purposeful efforts. Beneath the other lie the vague and conflicting ideals of social welfare which the members of each generation refashion after their own images. In this dim inner world lie the ultimate motives and meanings of action, and from it emerge the wavering standards by which men judge what is . . . worth while. The money economy has not supplanted, but it has harnessed, these forces."

To Mitchell, thinkers like Georg Simmel, Werner Sombart, and Veblen had partially worked out how money imposed upon men's thinking its own formal logic, efficient within limits, but pernicious when pushed to extremes. His own task, Mitchell said, had been merely to detail how the technical exigencies of the money economy subjected economic activity to continual alterations of expansion and contraction. But Mitchell's volume was more than a mere detailing of the technical exigencies of the money economy. While he held that the philosophers of the money economy had dealt with the basic problems, still he felt that these thinkers had not determined the relative importance of the various and often conflicting factors involved. His book was therefore in good part an attempt not only to furnish a test of their views, but to reformulate the vital problems raised by the philosophers of the money economy, so as to make them capable of analysis in terms of the actual behavior of the money economy.

The volume was the first step in a reorientation of economic theory, for henceforth the ebb and flow of business activity furnished the theme and the categories for inquiries into the nature and onward movement of the money economy as it manifested itself in interactions constituting the price system. The modern economic order came to be understood in terms of the changing phases of the business cycle. Instead of crises being an exception to the equilibria of economic theory, the equilibria became merely theoretical goals and statistical indexes, because of the logic of inevitable change. By emphasizing the dependence of the community on "expansion" and "contraction," Mitchell neatly reformulated the problem of the economic order and economic theory. Since his analysis there has been less place for systematic treatises based on the assumption of a secure body of stable principles of human nature; traditional "human nature" has been transformed to fit an unstable money economy.

The test of a pioneering work lies in its ability to impose itself on currents of thought in such a way that it forces both present and future generations to face the problems it has exposed to view. *Business Cycles* was such a work. It increasingly forced men to think in terms of the mighty, though perhaps unpleasant, reality of the ebb and flow of "business" as an activity. Henceforth the literature of economics was to speak of "business cycles," [5] not of commercial crises or industrial fluctuations.

In Mitchell's formulation of "business cycles" lurked, however, certain dangers for the future of inquiry. His conception of the "business cycle" contained the expectation of satisfying two great ideals: first, the achievement for the first time in economics of the principle of scientific law as then understood, of regularity or uniformity in sequence, so as to be subject to the test of prediction; and second, by virtue of that same test, the hope of controlling the undesirable workings of the money economy on the welfare of man. This could easily lead, on the one hand, to the exclusion and ignoring of pertinent phenomena of change, for the sake of emphasizing the certainty of prediction; and, on the other hand, to personifying the concept of "business cycles" into something like Herbert Spencer's "unknowable" guiding force of evolution which brought all the good or evil. But no man of his generation was more aware of the dangers than Mitchell himself; and he testified to his working realization of these possibilities by constantly pleading for more data on the system of prices and for the perfecting of techniques. Of all the efforts being made to extend our knowledge of the system of prices, none seemed to him so certain to prove fruitful as the "effort to record the actual prices" at which transactions occur, for these would supply essential material to the investigators and test their insight. "Long after the best index numbers we can make today are superseded," he said, the original data "will be among the sources from which men will be extracting knowledge which we do not know enough to find." [6]

Except as a contribution to economic statistics, the pioneering character of the book was little appreciated at first. For this, Mitchell's phrasing was partly responsible. Mitchell wrote in simple everyday language rather than in the specialized language of the prevailing "orthodox" economics. This was partly because, as he said, he wrote for businessmen as well as for economists, but more fundamentally, because he felt that the categories of "orthodox" economics tended to obscure the importance of money. It tended to treat the "business cycles" as merely the problems of crises and then to dismiss them as an abnormal feature. Second, Mitchell's procedure of "descriptive analysis" was confused by the traditional economists with mere narrative accounts. Third, Mitchell's insistence that his analysis rested primarily on statistical data, and that his interest in various theories was not to test them but to utilize their suggestions in a more adequate account, was taken literally to mean that Mitchell had merely borrowed his views and supplemented them by statistical data. Finally, such a study based on the conception of cumulative change and especially on the price system as a loose though orderly system of ever-shifting relations and ramifications appeared unusually indefinite—and even erroneous—as compared with so-called rigorous deductions from specified premises.

Herbert J. Davenport's reaction was perhaps typical. He stated in a review "that like most economists, I have believed that the high prices make the products high or the high products make the costs high. Either view would by the test of [Mitchell's] statistics appear to be untenable, but especially the latter." Davenport concluded that out of his "laborious and brilliant statistical investigations Professor Mitchell has deduced certain distributive doctrines which are not merely unverified by the available data, but are also beyond the possibility of test by statistical methods, at the same time that they are theoretically incredible." [7]

But the book sufficiently caught the trends of development in economic life to become itself a force in that development. In this sense, the theory of "business cycles" was Mitchell's creation. It was not imposed on economists, however, by dogmatism. Not a little of the enduring character of Mitchell's work flowed from his genuine intellectual humility and working faith in the growth of knowledge as the means of the progress of knowledge. These attitudes were neatly expressed in a letter to a colleague in 1944:

I incline to discount heavily the dependability of "wisdom," and in that I think I am wise. By this I mean that I don't believe that accumulated experience over many years is so safe a guide in managing affairs as objective knowledge, when the latter can be attained. The older I get, the more conscious I become of the fallibility of my opinions insofar as they are based upon the residue left in my mind by my contacts with other human beings. . . .

What I really have come to think is man's best prospect of improving his lot is knowledge resting upon analysis of human behavior as we can observe its manifestations objectively in large groups of people. . . . Business cycles are repetitive phenomena which give one an unusually favorable opportunity to gather, analyze, and interpret observations of actual behavior. If I can demonstrate (and I think I can) that we learn a great deal more reliable and useful knowledge concerning the failures of an economic organization based on the making and spending of money by taking this line than by speculation, I may contribute something useful on one set of problems and encourage others to adopt the methods of inquiry that seem to me most promising. If what I do does not impress others as worth its heavy cost, I shall at least have made an experiment, the negative result of which is not without instruction.[8]

This seems too modest a statement. His book *Business Cycles*, with its method of "descriptive analysis," in a broad sense marked the first significant bridging of the gap between orthodoxy's denial of the possibility of general overproduction and the business community's equally insistent assertion that overproduction was the chief cause of depression. And what is more, as the eminent French economist Charles Rist wrote in the 1948 edition of his *A History of Economic Doctrines*, largely because of Mitchell's work and example, the field of business cycles became less concerned with what might happen and mysterious explanations of the phenomenon, and more concerned with what actually happens.

The depression of 1920–21 drew the eyes of the profession and business to the appositeness of Mitchell's book, and by 1927 John Maurice Clark could say: "[It] is a monumental example of comprehensive induction transforming the current way of looking at an outstanding group of phenomena"; and the "result is sufficiently realistic to afford a more practicable basis for policies of control than had yet been achieved." [9]

With the onset of the great depression in 1929, Mitchell's book was still considered the outstanding study of the problem; for it had "opened up the discussions which culminated in the policies inaugurated by the government during the depression of the early thirties." It had "demonstrated that depression unemployment was due to forces more basic than the management of individual businesses, and that the alleviation or prevention of such unemployment called for social controls." [10]

Mitchell's place in the history of economic theory is secure. His pre-eminence has long been recognized. In 1937, as a testimonial to the state of economics as a science and Mitchell's role in developing it, the American Association for the Advancement of Science chose him as president. This had happened to a social scientist only once, and that thirty-five years before.[11] A decade later, Mitchell was the first recipient of the Francis A. Walker medal, an award established by the American Economic Association; it was to be given at intervals of no less than five years to a "living American economist who has in the course of his life made a contribution of the highest distinction to economics."

This was peculiarly fitting, for Wesley C. Mitchell bespoke a reorientation in tradition and a broadening of economics with emphasis on empirical research, a movement which Walker had initiated in the seventies.

CHAPTER XXI

The Impact of the War

THE First World War brought this country face to face with its first major international responsibility, and there was inevitably a great deal of confusion in every area of thought and action. For economics, in the broadest sense, it was only slowly seen that national mobilization must go beyond the mustering of men to effective use of the nation's whole industrial resources. Furthermore, in carrying out this mobilization, it was in time evident that "common sense" was not enough; recourse was therefore had to the services of men whose professional interest had led them to study the economy of the country.

The utilization of economists by the government in the 1917-18 period was often grudging and inefficient; their advice, when accepted, was not always put into effect. The government and the public, nevertheless, made some important discoveries: they felt the effect of a concerted national effort, which was in part the result of planning, and in this they found an added usefulness for the services which could be rendered by professional economists.

The country was in the midst of a recession when war broke out in Europe in 1914. Then the financial machinery of the world became disorganized; the New York Stock Exchange was closed; an emergency bank note currency provided for by the Aldrich-Vreeland Act of 1908 was issued for the first time. When the financial disturbances subsided, the depression intensified. Not until the middle of 1915 was a revival apparent.

This depression seems to have made the country conscious, for the first time, of the recurrent character of periods of widespread unemployment, aptly described as that "national pest which corresponds in our day to the famines and black plagues of medieval times." The Chicago social worker Graham Taylor stated that the nature of the widespread unemployment was "at last, thank God, beginning to dawn through . . . our 'concrete heads.' Therefore we must admit that unemployment is both periodic and chronic." Despite the fact that periods of unemployment had occurred time and again, he said, the public was always caught unprepared, but with the war there was a decided difference. Although it should be just as possible to mobilize for peace as for war, he found that it was not done, and there was truth in the statement that the "only thing men really plan for is war." [1]

For some years, however, a plan of compensatory public works had been touched upon as a palliative for depressions,[2] and at this time the idea became of immediate interest. John R. Shillady, secretary of the New York City Mayor's Committee on Unemployment, proposed as a remedy the planning of "public expenditures to compensate for decreased private employment during business depressions." He declared that these "periodic trade disturbances," which occur approximately every ten years, were due to fundamental, deep-seated, but remediable causes. Pending industrial and economic reconstruction, widespread unemployment could be prevented by a planned long-term program—say, ten years—of "public improvements and expenditures and those of quasi-public bodies, such as the railroads." In each normal year of the decade a variable percentage of such an expenditure program would be deferred. These accumulated deferred improvements and purchases would constitute an "employment reserve" to be used during the period of decreased private employment. Thus unemployment would be prevented both "directly, through increased public employment and purchases, and indirectly, through an increased stimulus to private business." The construction of the deferred projects would be performed exactly as was "customary in the most efficiently administered governmental departments and would not be in the nature of relief work to 'employ the unemployed.' . . . In accelerating or retarding public improvements and purchases, no deviation is proposed from accustomed methods of employment at regular wages, regular hours, and under whatever safeguards heretofore have been adopted." [3]

Professor Henry R. Seager of Columbia preferred a modest and limited form of unemployment insurance. He pointed to the scheme recently adopted by the British government and insisted that there was nothing in American conditions to prevent its introduction here. He stated, however, that the scheme was just getting started when the war broke out in Europe, and dejectedly commented: "Who will say what may befall this and other European plans of social insurance before the titanic struggle is over? These plans are not suited to a world of men gone mad with the lusts and hates of war. . . . The war has temporarily eclipsed the forward movement of social reform in Europe." He hoped that the United States would rise above this paralyzing influence.[4] But such a sign of character was not necessary; the revival of business and America's entrance in the war nipped the discussion of the question. Nevertheless, a beginning had been made.

European demands, especially for war supplies, were great. American producers asked prices which would quickly repay their investments in new plants, and the belligerents needed the supplies at any price. Productive capacity expanded rapidly. In finance, contrary to the "best-informed opinion" in 1914 that the lower reserve ratio provided for by the Federal Reserve Act would not create inflation because the gold holdings of the banks would be reduced, the influx of gold from Europe combined with the low reserve requirements tended toward heavy expansion of loans. The usual checks of high interest rates and, more important, the difficulty of securing bank accommodations were not present;[5] so inflation began early.

The government had definitely embarked on a defense program

as early as 1916, but little of a concrete nature was accomplished. The Naval Consulting Board appointed a committee to make a comprehensive survey of the industrial plants of the country, but it did not "appear to have been as useful in practice as might have been expected." [6] Congress provided in the same year for a Council of National Defense, consisting of six members of the cabinet, to co-ordinate "industries and resources for the national security and welfare" and to create relations which would make possible "in time of need the immediate concentration and utilization" of the country's resources. The act at the same time provided for an advisory commission appointed by the President on the recommendation of the Council. For some time little more than conferences occurred. But with the approach of war large numbers of subordinate committees were established, composed primarily of business executives who served without pay.

Though this variety of organizations covered the entire economy, a systematic plan was lacking. Even after the declaration of war in April 1917 there was no effective co-ordination among the numerous supply divisions of the Army and Navy. In the Army alone ten separate procurement agencies were bidding against each other for supplies. And purchases by the Allies increased the confusion. Bernard Baruch, chairman of the reconstituted War Industries Board, recalled later that the various Army contracting agencies "fought each other as bad as they fought the Germans, and then they fought me just as hard, and fought the Navy just as hard." In fact, it took more than a year to achieve some sort of effective co-ordination.[7]

The problem of essential industries became very perplexing. Every business considered itself essential, and so many priorities were issued that by 1918 there was danger of breakdown.[8] In general, the business community wanted changes in the economy to be gradual. The New York *Annalist* stated that while the notion of "business as usual" should not be allowed to interfere with winning the war, still labor should not be taken from one industry until another was ready for it.[9]

For some time after the United States entered the war the railroads were left to their own devices. They attempted to meet the need for unified action by a voluntary organization, called the Railroad War Board, composed of five railroad executives. This proved ineffective, and in December 1917 President Wilson commandeered the roads. In July 1918 the government took over the telephone and telegraph lines; later the cables, and just a few days before the Armistice, the express business was placed under government operation.

Even after the War Industries Board was given sweeping powers in March 1918, its activities were still governed by "expediency in individual instances" rather than "by an established policy for which the whole administration took responsibility." [10] In an attempt to bring about unity, more and more boards were created. The quality of many of these boards gave rise to the *bon mot*, "A board is long and narrow and wooden." [11]

In recalling this period, Baruch stated that "the greatest deterrent to effective action" during the war was the lack of facts.[12] For prosecuting the war, as Professor Allyn Young said, the government required statistical information for the "measurement of our national resources . . . ; the determination of our actual and potential output of the immense variety of things that are important directly and indirectly in the conduct of the war; the gauging . . . of our own needs and those of our allies and of the other countries that have to be recognized as in some measure dependent upon us," but when the country entered the war our "federal statistics were woefully incomplete and inadequate." Remedying the defects was no easy task. There was a real need for a central statistical commission to supervise and co-ordinate the work of the numerous independent statistical bureaus and to supplement their activities. Only in June 1918 was a Central Bureau of Planning and Statistics established, with Edwin F. Gay of Harvard as chairman. It set up a clearing house of statistical activities, appointed contact men to keep in touch with the statistical work of the war boards and certain of the permanent departments, and to supervise questionnaires in an effort to eliminate excessive duplication. In the end Mitchell could say: "When the Armistice was signed we were in a fair way to develop for the first time a systematic organization of federal statistics." [13]

THE BALANCE BETWEEN CONTROL AND FREEDOM

The needs of the government for prosecuting the war and the complaints by consumers of rapidly rising prices resulted in ever-widening government control of prices. But the system of control, as in other fields, was developed in a piecemeal fashion as "expediency dictated." After all, government price-fixing ran counter to the habits of the business community and some of the most firmly entrenched doctrines in political economy.[14]

A Special Price Committee of the Council of National Defense had recommended on May 5, 1917, that the President inform the country that "Price regulation should not be necessary. Production should be adequately stimulated, and industry and business enterprise fairly and justly rewarded, if the channels of distribution are kept free and open and any practices of speculative manipulation or withholding for speculative purposes are prohibited. Fair and just prices involving fair and just profit to producers and manufacturers would naturally follow, and with such guarantees of open, unmanipulated market, maximum production need not hesitate. This will be the government's policy." But the President felt that this was too great a commitment.[15]

The question was debated at great length. Professor W. C. Clark of Canada expressed the opinion of economists skeptical of price-fixing. Price-fixing, he said, fails to check waste and unnecessary consumption; it drives the commodity from the market and discourages production; it throws out of balance the sensitive mechanism of the price system; it involves endless frauds, with a general lowering of moral standards of the community. It therefore aggravates the conditions which it seeks to remedy, and if pursued far enough will inevitably drive the government to other drastic measures. For arbitrary prices determined without regard for competition must be supplemented by arbitrary regulation of production and consumption. The State, then, must control and direct the production of the different commodities, either by a system of compulsory labor or by a graduated scale of rewards, which would drive the requisite proportion of laborers to the different industries. Further, consumption would have to be controlled by a system of rationing. Such a control of production is obviously impossible, Clark declared, and the bureaucracy required to enforce rationing would be so tremendous as to make it impracticable.[16]

But many leading American economists recognized the need for some form of price-fixing. Taussig, a member of the Price-Fixing Committee of the War Industries Board, argued that price-fixing was justified in wartime because when government purchases absorb such a large share of the output, the ordinary formulas of demand and supply no longer apply. Government must have the goods irrespective of the price. Technically speaking, "demand is virtually inelastic; the demand curve is almost perpendicular; there is no such thing as a determinate equilibrium price." This, he said, explained the soaring prices, sharp fluctuations, speculative shifts, the quick response to rumors of government policy.[17]

One notion, "the bulk-line or marginal cost" method of price-setting, came into vogue and enjoyed favor with both the Price-Fixing Committee and the Fuel Administration. The bulk line of production was the indispensable amount of a commodity required by the war program; and the bulk line of cost was the unit cost to the producer of the last unit lot required. The cost to the "marginal" or "bulk-line person" was the usual basis for price-fixing, and both administrations attempted to set a price high enough to assure the output of about 85 to 90 per cent of the country's "absolute maximum production." [18] In simple language the price fixed was supposed to cover the bulk of representative producers, those who commonly produced without loss. The cost to the most expensive producers (the remaining 10 or 15 per cent), it was thought, need not be considered; they ordinarily produced at a loss either because of inefficiency or some abnormal condition. But while the bulk-line concept stimulated a reconsideration of the nature of costs and competition, it was never too clear.

Taussig admitted that the bulk-line concept was not the orthodox conception of marginal cost, which applied to the long-run period and to variations of cost due to natural or physical causes, rather than to differences in managerial capacity. The justification for focusing attention on the bulk-line producer, he said, was the need to maintain output. This was the reason for bolstering the marginal producer.[19] He attempted in a rather ingenious fashion to apply the concept to moderate the demands of the logging industry, which he felt overstated its case even on its own figures. In the ordinary course of business, the bulk-line producers did not flourish, he declared. They neither lost nor made big money. Persons at that stage were entitled to a return upon their capital and would in the ordinary course of business get a return, although not a handsome one. True, this return, about 6 per cent, was less than the average return the producers in the industry would expect to get. Therefore it would be fair to fix the price at something like the bulk-line figures.

But R. A. Long of the Long Bell Lumber Company, not to be outdone, claimed that, on the contrary, the most efficiently managed concern had some high-cost mills, owing to natural difficulties such as "the roughness of the country." Consequently he would accept a price of not less than 10 per cent on capital calculated on the bulk-line producer. The colloquy between Taussig and Long in attempting to arrive at a fair price was quite revealing.

> Mr. Long: Doctor, is it your idea that no industry should make any more profit during this war than it made [normally] prior to the war? . . .
>
> Dr. Taussig: I should say so.
>
> Mr. Long: Then I would like to ask you, Doctor, how you would expect to finance the war, if you confine the industries down to where they would make no more money. . . .
>
> Dr. Taussig: Unfortunately, it has too frequently been that a considerable number of people have made money out of wars, but a great bulk of the population inevitably could not. . . . We are trying, if possible, in some way to bring about a better order; . . . that nobody shall make money out of the war, because everybody cannot make money out of the war. . . .
>
> Mr. Long: In all your talk about this fact that the boys across the sea are giving their lives for the salvation of this country, and we ought to give what we have for their support, we agree to the limit, but when it comes to the matter of general business, these things must be treated on a commercial basis, as you treat other commercial businesses.[20]

That the use of the bulk-line concept in fixing prices would in any event give those above the bulk line a large profit was of course recognized, but it was expected that taxation would take care of those gains—an expectation that was not fully realized. In fact, this whole bulk-line concept was not a realized theory but rather a rationalization of practice; for in practice government price-fixing was guided more by convenience than abstract principles or deliberate policies. In the main, declared Taussig, it was "opportunist, feeling its way from case to case," but it was the only policy possible.[21]

The price-control program did, to some extent, prevent runaway prices. An index number of 573 commodities brought under price control at various dates from midsummer 1917 to the Armistice dropped from 209 in July 1917 to 189 in June 1918. Thereafter, with moderate advances permitted, the index rose again, but it did not rise to the pre-price-fixing point.

As Professor Mitchell has well said, the price-fixing authorities might have accomplished more had they "realized their power earlier, brought more commodities under control, and insisted upon more drastic reductions." But he thought that their success demonstrated that within quite wide limits the price level was susceptible to direct control by the government when supported by public opinion.[22]

As for war financing, there was a danger at the start that the government would to an overwhelming degree have recourse to loans rather than taxes; and taxes of a character primarily in the nature of excises and custom duties rather than income and excess profits taxes. On the eve of America's entrance into the war Senator Simmons of the Senate Finance Committee was reported to have said that it had been the country's custom to pay its war bills by bond issues and he saw no reason for a shift in that policy.[23] But this attitude soon changed. This modification of policy was in great part due to the vigorous campaign instigated by O. M. W. Sprague, professor of banking at Harvard. Sprague was, in general, a conservative, and was not even an expert in public finance. Yet he aroused the public and the profession to protest against the original congressional policy. He began his campaign as early as 1916, with a speech before the American Economic Association. The objection to financing the war primarily on loans, he said, was that loans had the defects of paper money. Individual borrowings for the purchase of bonds and bank investments in bonds would occasion expansion of the volumes of credit, thereby tending toward inflation. While a taxing policy would reduce demand for unnecessary consumption, and hold down the money costs of war, easy monetary conditions, needed to float loans, would enable many to borrow without reducing consumption; and the resultant uneven advances in prices would give rise to undesirable variations in income, to "undeserved and temporary gains" for extravagance in consumption.

Sprague pointed out with some asperity that a loan policy gave higher consideration to property than to life. Since modern warfare required the conscription of men, he said, it should logically and equitably require conscription of all income above that absolutely necessary. Under the loan policy the stay-at-home could convert his surplus into an interest-paying loan, to which the soldier, if fortunate enough to return, would have to contribute. Furthermore, the stay-at-home very often received a higher income and a better position, while the returning soldier would find it difficult to secure his old position or its equivalent.

It might be argued, he granted, that if income could not be saved for investment, essential war plants could not expand. But the experience of war economy so far proved conclusively to him that war's needs were too great and immediate to wait upon the "slow processes of the adjustment of facilities of supply to demand working through prices and business profits." As a result, he pointed out, the belligerent governments had given financial guarantees and advances, and had in many instances taken direct control of plants and production not only of munitions, but of other indispensable articles.

Sprague emphasized that during wartime patriotism, not profits, should be the incentive to secure persistent effort and to take business risks. In any event, the risk was slight, since industry was directed to supply the war demand and other essential needs. Finally, a policy of no economic benefit from war would stimulate the efforts of the vast majority of workers, because it would eliminate the discontent arising from the large gains and the extravagance of the few. He then left this high ground and came down to disagreeable facts and figures. For illustrative purposes, Sprague suggested a tax starting with 5 per cent on incomes of $1200 or $1500 and rising gradually to 50 per cent on incomes of $40,000 and 100 per cent on incomes in excess of $100,000.[24]

Upon the entrance of the United States into the war Sprague, through every kind of journal, called for what became known as the "conscription of wealth," to parallel the conscription of men. And more and more economists began to fall into line. Just about a month after the declaration of war an imposing memorial embodying Sprague's views was presented by economists to Congress. It urged that substantially all war profits accrue to the government by a tax; that the income tax be substantially increased and a heavy tax placed on luxury goods.[25] Henry W. Farnam of Yale wrote in a letter that while the Yale signers did not agree with all the arguments, they felt that it was important to put themselves on record as favoring taxation as against loans, and as the tendency of Congress was so strongly the other way, it was perhaps better to overstate the case than remain silent. And Professor Roy G. Blakey of the University of Minnesota, one of the most active sponsors of the memorial, reminded the public not to forget that "we now look upon our former wars . . . and condemn Congress, our financiers, and the people for not adopting vigorous taxation at the beginning. The next generation may condemn us . . . for short-sightedness, inability to learn from experience, and unwillingness to do social justice." [26]

Professor Thomas S. Adams of Yale, then working with the Treasury, frankly said: "Had I been told in August 1914 that England would soon be levying a normal income tax of 25 per cent, progressive income taxes which carried the upper limit of 42 per cent, and excess profits taxes rising to 60 or 80 per cent, I should have repudiated the whole proposal or program as revolutionary, and should have done it with much heat and certainty. The event has proved, however, that the common legislators of England were wiser than students like myself." [27]

Though the tax program as enacted did not come near the "fifty-fifty" idea which was the real heart of the Sprague demand, it was generally acknowledged afterward that the vigorous expression of the proposal at an opportune time had brought salutary results. It is noteworthy that Seligman, one of the most vigorous opponents of Sprague's viewpoint, wrote that, with all its faults, the Revenue Act of October 1917 (with its heavy income and excess profits taxes) was based on "democratic principles hitherto unrealized in fiscal history. To impose the great burden of taxation on wealth and luxurious consumption rather than on the expenditure of the mass of the people was to take an appreciable forward step in the direction of realizing the principle of ability to pay." [28]

Each successive revenue measure raised the tax rates, with especial emphasis on personal income taxes and excess profits taxes. Thus in 1916 the normal income tax rate was 2 per cent, with a surtax on incomes exceeding $20,000 ranging from 1 per cent to 13 per cent on incomes in excess of $2,000,000. By 1918 the normal rate was 6 per cent on net incomes up to $4000 and 12 per cent on higher incomes, with a surtax ranging from 1 per cent on incomes exceeding $5000 to 65 per cent on incomes over $1,000,000. The business and financial community did not let this "dangerous tendency" toward "excessive taxation" go unchallenged. The Chicago banker George M. Reynolds complained at the time of radicals urging excessively high taxes to relieve the middle class and little business. He said: "Do they not know that if the wealthy and big business are oppressed and harassed through excess taxes and price reductions that are beyond reason, and depression is brought upon us, the poor and middle classes and little business will be the chief sufferers? Having less power of resistance, they will be the first to feel the pinch of hard times. It will be like a panic or fire. The strong are able to care for themselves, but the weak go down in the crash." And Mortimer Schiff of Kuhn, Loeb and Company declared that the government must not hamper enterprise by "unwise or too onerous taxation." Capital as well as labor must be permitted, according to him, to earn a fair return. The government must also offer a fair return of interest on its bonds, reasonably close to other prime and readily salable investments. The Federal Reserve System should provide additional currency to support both government and industrial needs. As he outlined the situation, current savings were inadequate; the various classes must borrow from their banks to invest in government bonds; the banks, in turn, must rediscount their customers' notes with the Federal Reserve banks. The money thus received the government would return to the people through the channels of trade and would again become available for investment in government bonds. This pyramiding process was sound, he thought, for it would be self-liquidating as the people would repay their debts from savings and from the proceeds of their production.[29] But in spite of the heavy increases in taxation and of numerous pronouncements from President Wilson on down that there should be no profits from the war, substantial profits were reaped, for, as Taussig pointed out, the legislation was not created with the expected speed nor on the expected scale.[30]

Control of labor was even more gropingly applied. The need for unified administration of the labor supply and for centralized treatment of labor questions was belatedly recognized. The government had to face the problem of the I. W. W. pacifism, and attempted to solve it by mass arrests of the leaders. Upon this Alvin S. Johnson, in discussing why America lagged in the war effort, commented that labor in the Northwest was pretty well infiltrated with I. W. W. ideals, and it was necessary to employ I. W. W. men and their sympathizers to obtain the essential wood supply for airplanes and ships. "And it is worth noting that those I. W. W. laborers have done important pieces of our war work in record time. The actual producers have found it not impossible to do business with men of I. W. W. leanings and to get them to agree to sink their private predilections for sabotage for the country's good." Yet the Department of Justice fell upon their leaders with indictments of conspiracy. "Believe what you will against these I. W. W. leaders; many of them were to be counted on to hold labor in line; and the rank and file of workers in sympathy with the organization now feel suspicious of the government and all its works." [31]

In general, however, the government was not hostile to labor unions, and they flourished. There was a proliferation of boards— for mediation, policy, and labor standards—but only toward the end of the war was the machinery becoming comprehensive and fully effective. Despite the slow method of trial and error the government's experience was of great value for subsequent action.

Perhaps the most drastic proposal for running the war came from Harold G. Moulton. His scheme visualized a thoroughgoing industrial conscription, managed by a committee of experts who would be in complete control. He pointed out that all the European countries had realized that the only workable plan was to have a central board allocate capital and labor. The Germans had their scheme long prepared, and their success was due in good part to such a plan. In choosing a method of industrial reorganization, he said, this country should remember that it was competing with Germany. The present method rested not on the concentrated effort of a board of experts imbued with the national point of view, but upon individual self-interest and the unreasoned impulses of the mass. After all, self-denial and economy did not come easy. Since price-control would run up against the great difficulty that, as increasing war supplies were needed, prices must be constantly raised to cover the costs of the marginal producer plus his "usual profits," he proposed that the government conscript industry, fix nominal prices but underwrite the loss of those unable to cover costs, thereby guaranteeing "reasonable profits." [32]

Speaking generally of the economic mobilization in the war period, and remembering the stupendous tasks involved, the absence of relevant data to begin with, and our insufficient experience in government control, it was a successful effort. For a large number of economists, their experience seemed to justify the application of social intelligence to economic problems. The mistakes did not discourage them, and they had real optimism that the lessons of the war would not be lost in the peace that followed.

THE PROMISE OF THE FUTURE

The meaning of the war effort, however, was not the same for all economists. Even while winning the war was occupying most of their energies, they were deeply concerned with the state of affairs in post-war America. Many vague proposals for reconstruction were advanced, calling merely for a national point of view and the dethronement of selfishness and excess individualism.

A goodly number of economists seemed to feel that the war was merely an interlude. For instance, concerning foreign trade, Taussig declared that the machinery of equalization and settlement of international trade had broken down, but whatever the course of the war and the changed conditions of international trade afterward, "we must expect an eventual return to the normal conditions of peaceful trade." A redistribution of specie among the different nations of the world might conceivably occur for a period after the peace, but sooner or later the mechanism of foreign exchange would again be at work, the flow of specie be reduced to a minimum, and exports pay for imports.[33] E. W. Kemmerer of Princeton University felt that high interest rates constituted a serious problem for the future. This could be solved if for some years the people would "restrict rigorously their consumption of luxuries, hold down their standards of living and save." Savings were the raw materials from which capital was built, and interest rates would not fall until capital became plentiful.[34]

However, one segment of economists felt very strongly that the economic changes brought on by the war would force the United States out of its "shell of isolation." "The United States will remain for a long time by all odds the wealthiest country of the world," Seligman declared. Instead of being a debtor country, the United States would become an outstanding creditor nation. Also, instead of supplying the old countries of Europe with raw materials and receiving in return their manufactured commodities, the United States would become increasingly a competitor of the European industrial nations, primarily of Great Britain, in the foreign markets. Most important of all, the United States would increasingly become a competitor of the European nations in foreign investments.[35]

The possibility of vast immediate unemployment upon the cessation of hostilities received considerable attention. *The Journal of Political Economy* stated in an editorial that the initiative of employers, impelled by anticipated profits, could not be relied upon to prevent a glut of the labor market, for the war's end would be a threat to their profits. It was foolish to expect an "aggregate demand" to replace immediately the huge cancellation of government contracts. Industries supplying war needs as well as those supplying raw materials would be affected. And, as the markets collapsed and prices fell, business would be discouraged, and a serious depression would occur. Furthermore, it continued, within the period of demobilization ordinary business practice would not be able to secure a proper distribution of materials and men among the different industries. Sooner or later the system would absorb all the available capital and labor, but such a readjustment by a process of trial and error was wasteful.

The editorial also indicated that a positive government plan was needed to provide buffer employment for the surplus labor discharged from the Army and to stimulate the resumption of peacetime industry as rapidly as was consistent with stability. A system of public works, such as railroad improvement and extension, irrigation, highway construction, housing, etc., would take care of buffer employment. The stimulation of industry should be effected by removing the unnecessary uncertainty and by quickening the expectation of profits. One effective device would be government indemnity of business risks.[36]

Alvin S. Johnson suggested that the returning soldier be given an opportunity to buy reclaimed land at moderate cost. He visualized communities rather than individual settlers, and pointed to the experiments with community settlements in Australia and California to show that such a plan developed a healthy agricultural life. A community would enjoy much cheaper money, both for improvements and working capital, than isolated farmers could command, and furthermore, could afford a competent agricultural adviser. Such a community should consist of a select group of literate and energetic men willing and able to avail themselves of technical advice. And with tenure in the community conditional upon satisfactory performance, the force of personal emulation would operate far more powerfully than in the old-fashioned rural district. Finally, co-operation would find a fertile field. Co-operative buying would enable the participants to have pure-bred stock and would make available expensive machinery. Co-operation, and efficient marketing and purchasing, could make possible a variety of production not economical under current conditions.

Critics might contend, asserted Johnson, that as the first enthusiasm of community formation was exhausted the farmers would permit their lands to sink back into the traditional rural condition.

But a community of independent farmers would not die easily; a community could be killed only by "absenteeism and tenantry, engrossing of fields and landlessness; the infiltration of undesirable elements through land sales." Against such evils he thought appropriate tenures an adequate safeguard. Under his tenures a candidate for farm holdings, having served a sufficiently long probationary period to exhibit his real qualities, might have tenure for life and might pass his farm on to his heirs, provided that they lived on, and continued to cultivate, the land.

Thus it would be economically possible, according to Johnson, to establish communities whose members would enjoy far better opportunities than were then open to men with small capital, and without taint of charity or confiscation. But the scheme could be workable only when the American people realized that the settlement of soldiers would require an infinite amount of expert work, involving the mobilization of a great variety of talent—legal, engineering, agronomic, and financial. If the American people were incapable of making the effort "essential to set the mobilization process in motion, let us not count ourselves among the farsighted nations who are planning to build a sounder and more fruitful economic system upon the foundations remaining unshaken by war." [37]

Several younger economists who had matured during the war period looked upon the war as something of a milestone of social change and therefore of social thought. They became quite vocal in demanding a reconstruction of traditional economic doctrines and policy. They wanted more attention paid to psychology in economics and to social control. These newer economists had brilliant pens to support their ability. Among them was Carleton H. Parker (1878–1918) of the University of Washington. Parker was distressed by the failure of government officials to understand the dissatisfaction of labor during the war, and he blamed the economists for this. He made his point clear in a stirring address before the American Economic Association in December 1917.[38] "Why are economists mute in the presence of a most obvious crisis in our industrial society?" asked Parker. "Why does an agitated officialdom search today in vain among our writings for scientific advice touching labor inefficiency or industrial disloyalty, for prophecies and plans about the rise in our industrialism of economic classes unharmonious and hostile?" The answer, said Parker, was that "economists are not curious about the great basis of fact which dynamic and behavioristic psychology has gathered to illustrate the instinct stimulus to human activity."

He then outlined what he thought was relevant to economics in the current psychology. Current psychology described "present civilization as a repressive environment." Those with open eyes could see a "deep and growing unrest and pessimism." Unfortunately the economists viewed "economic inequality and life degradation" as phenomena outside the science. Their value concept was "a price mechanism hiding behind a phrase." If economists were to play a vital role in the social readjustment immediately ahead, they must put human nature and human motives into their basic hypotheses, and provide a concept of value that would be a yardstick for measuring just how "fully things and institutions contribute to a full psychological life. . . . We must know more of the meaning of progress." The great evil of the domination of society by one economic class, he said, was that it thwarted the "instinct life" of the subordinate class and perverted that of the upper class. "The extent and characteristics of this evil can only be estimated when we know the innate potentialities and inherited propensities of man, and the ordering of this knowledge and its application to the changeable economic structure is the task before the trained economists today." [39]

Parker perhaps unduly emphasized instincts. In fact, he reduced behavior to a catalogue of instinct unit characters, but the stir and enthusiasm which the address aroused among the old as well as the new generation of economists was itself a sharp indication that economists were sorely troubled by the deficiencies of older points of view.

Louis B. Wehle of the legal staff of the American Emergency Fleet Corporation, a subsidiary of the United States Shipping Board, showed deep concern over the need to stabilize employment in postwar America. He considered the insecurity of labor the outstanding element in the labor problem, the basic source of the hostility between labor and capital and the rest of the industrial and civic world which was aligned with capital.

The employer would not strongly oppose the stabilization of employment and wages, he felt, if he could be shown that he would not be hurt more than his competitor. Suppose, he said, government specified industries "capable of regularization," and in these industries regulated speculation in the raw materials they used, imposed special taxes for days the plants were idle, or required that except by special ruling employment should be upon an annual basis. The result would be a considerable increase in productivity of capital in these industries, a great improvement in their labor relations, and a "scientific standardization of production based upon reckonable demand and supply over long periods of time." Of course many kinds of industries and a certain portion of every occupation would always remain upon a casual or a seasonal basis; but even here the condition would be improved by the stabilization achieved elsewhere, and the laborer would receive higher wages because of the greater element of risk. At the same time labor exchanges run by the State or by labor unions could effect the transition with minimum losses through idleness. But these changes "would require a long period of public education and of preparation." [40]

Wesley C. Mitchell, as he prepared to enter government service, closed his lectures at Columbia University in May 1918 by saying: "The war has demonstrated the feasibility of considerable and rapid changes under the pressure of circumstances. In the past the social sciences have viewed civilization as extremely slow moving. . . . We have held that we must trust to a slow evolution for social improvement. But the war has impressed the fact that when the eyes of the community are turned to attaining one great goal, when there is some object which appeals to the masses as of transcending importance, then within a short period far-reaching social changes can be achieved.

"The need for scientific planning of social change has never been greater, the chance of making those changes in an intelligent fashion . . . has never been so good." The peace would bring another set of problems, but, he said, "it seems impossible that the countries concerned will attempt to solve them without utilizing the same sort of centralized directing now employed to kill their enemies abroad for the new purpose of reconstructing their own life at home. . . . It seems probable that for a long time to come, perhaps always, we shall increasingly use intelligence for guiding the social economic forces, relying more and more on trained people to plan changes for us, to follow them up, to suggest alterations." [41]

To John R. Commons the lessons taught by the war, which he thought had accelerated American democratic development, can be summed up as follows: The so-called inefficiency of government could easily be rectified; for when the American people realized that liberty and property depended upon a competent Civil Service and expert administration, they made sacrifices and strengthened that administration. Thousands of successful businessmen, professional men, and labor leaders, through their government service in wartime, had learned both the vital importance of public business and the reasons for its incompetence. Government officials had learned that they could not "administer public business without the aid of these same representative private citizens." By a new state of mind the United States was already building up great public interests that required, and were beginning to get, the co-operation of private interests.[42]

For Thorstein Veblen, however, the issue was much bigger than merely the problem of international finance and piecemeal adjustments. In *Imperial Germany and the Industrial Revolution*, published in 1915, Veblen examined, from his anthropological viewpoint, the basic character and essential differences of two warring economies. He saw that in one—that of England and the English-speaking countries—the development was purely in response to the market, both national and international. In the other, the government was from the beginning the stimulant. It sought to use the modern machine technology, notably railways, for the additional purpose of military strategy and territorial expansion. That, indeed, explained its greater apparent strength: while the liberal countries frittered the gains of technology away in wasteful private expenditures, Germany used them for military purposes. This applied even more clearly to newer feudal industrial systems, like Japan.

The situation of Imperial Germany, that of an organization whose industrial technology was modern but whose scheme of controlling institutions was old-fashioned, belonged, according to Veblen, to a past and antiquated technique of thieving. German technology had been borrowed from England, but the scheme of free institutions which was the concomitant of that technology had not been brought with it.

The English culture differed from the German in its preoccupation with material realities, or the mechanistic conception, as distinguished from the romantic preconception of status and differential dignity. The English businessman was an acquisitive individual, rationalized; the dynast, the Junker, was a robber baron. To Veblen the economic position of the common man was not necessarily more secure in the liberal than in the dynastic society, but there was much more hope for his real dignity and the dignity of the race in the modern liberal state. The success of the dynastic state meant a reversion, a destruction of Western civilization. And he closed *Imperial Germany* by suggesting that unless Germany's peculiar and anachronistic order was destroyed, the liberal states would be compelled to accept its feudalist and war-minded policy in order to counter its strength.[43]

The main issue between the Allies and Germany, he declared in *The Nature of Peace* (1917), was the paramount issue of a peaceful or warlike civilization. His bases for an enduring peace with Germany, if the Allies won the war, were as follows: (1) definitive elimination of the imperial establishment and of the subsidiary orders of the privileged classes; (2) removal or destruction of all warlike equipment; (3) cancellation of the public debt of the empire; (4) confiscation of such industrial equipment and resources as had contributed to carrying on the war; (5) indemnification of civilians in invaded territories by confiscating all estates in the defeated countries exceeding a certain maximum, say, all estates in excess of those owned by the poorer three-fourths of the population.

If, on the other hand, "gentlemanly" government in Germany should be maintained after the war, the pecuniary burdens placed on the defeated peoples would be shifted to the underlying population without touching the responsible parties. This would merely feed the patriotic animosity and "offer a new incentive to a policy of watchful waiting for a chance of retaliation."

But the bill of particulars for the defeated dynastic states was only Veblen's first step toward enduring peace. The opponents of the dynastic states, he said, must establish a neutral league, "or pacific league of neutral peoples," embodying the principle of neutralization and of the rights of citizenship, including the preferential claims of investment and trade and the elimination of privilege and royalty. This league, which would include America and the defeated nations, would assume all debts incurred by the entente belligerents or by neutrals for the prosecution of the war, and distribute them impartially among the members of the league. It would eliminate the war-making power of the individual nations, but cultural integrity or solidarity would not be impaired. Colonies as conventionally understood would have no place; and the economic resources of the so-called backward peoples, wherever they might be, would not be exposed to the ravages of unrestrained business enterprise.

Veblen's league would conserve the natural resources of the backward countries with a view to the least exhaustion of the resources that were so taken over in trust. This supervision would apply to economic penetration of undeveloped countries as well as to the special case of those outlying virgin resources of the savage world.[44] It had been uncritically assumed, he said, that the fastest and most comprehensive development of all hitherto idle resources was best for the inhabitants of the countries possessing those resources and for the citizens of the enterprising nation. But the history of colonization was testimony to the fact that such penetration and conversion to use might be too swift for the continued well-being of the native population. The pacific league, in order to hold fast to what was good in democracy, the policy of peace and good will, must not allow exploitation of helpless wards and dependent neighbors.

Stated very broadly, the "neutral" powers must do themselves what they demanded of Germany; they must eliminate all undemocratic institutional survivals. Finally, they must considerably attenuate, if not virtually abandon, the system of managing industry or investment for a profit, for the private gain of the captains of finance. If the victorious Allied powers did not want to do this, but wished to maintain the current pecuniary scheme of competitive gain and competitive spending, the promoters of peace should make only such "a peaceable settlement as would result in a sufficiently unstable equilibrium of mutual jealousies; such as might expeditiously be upset whenever discontent with pecuniary affairs should come to threaten this established scheme of pecuniary prerogatives."

The war period made clear to the public and the government of the United States that economic science could be of great use in a national emergency. The economists were equipped with information and ideas; and when their recommendations were tried they proved to be reasonably useful and productive. Unfortunately it was also evident that in many instances they had been summoned too late or inadequately supported by those in political power.

In its effect upon theorists the war defined the position of economic thought and emphasized the superior attractiveness of the liberal economic tradition. Thus Mitchell, in summing up the realm of economics for 1918 could state: "One prevalent trait may be mentioned; most writers approve a policy of conscious social control through government agencies. That practical bias is another indication that the preconceptions of economic theory are changing." [45]

The future looked promising; intelligence was at work. Many economists seemed to think that their position as guides for that future was secure. What they failed to give adequate weight was the fact that, as Graham Taylor said, this country could accept planning only as a necessity of war, and that the war itself created an unusual economic morale favorable to planning. Lacking any permanent provision for a high level of economic civil service, it was not surprising that the government called the economists into the war effort belatedly, used them sparingly and inefficiently, and was predisposed to drop them without regret. Their utility in the war certainly enhanced the prestige and the authority of economists. They had come quite a distance on the long way from their relative obscurity in the Civil War. But the habits developed over a century were not easily broken. The relevance of their theories to economic practice in peacetime was still questioned; the motives behind their thinking still seemed suspect; and the value of their authority remained equivocal. Yet the experience of World War I was invaluable for any future crisis. It was a proving ground for the relations of government and business, for large-scale administration, and for tools and techniques in social control. It brought also the hope that the nation, with this new sense of power, could face any crisis and consciously promote its material welfare.

APPENDIX

NO. I. CLARK ON JEVONS

The Jevons theory assumes that increments of some commodity are offered in succession to a consumer and that, as his desire for them is gradually satiated, he attaches less and less importance to them, and the last or "final" increment consumed is the one that figures in the adjustment of values. I had not myself made use of just this supposition, but had thought of the consumer as measuring the importance to himself of different articles already in his possession and adjusting his purchases in such a way that articles of the same cost have the same "effective utility" to him and this may be measured, either by working to replace one that is worn out or lost, or by going without it and measuring the reaction on his enjoyments so occasioned. It amounted to a *final utility* theory, but was cast in a somewhat different form.[1]

NO. 2. CLARK'S ESTIMATE OF HIS CONTRIBUTION TO ECONOMICS

Clark's reply [2] to Ely's request for a statement of his contribution is interesting not only for its succinctness, but also for the flavor of the man:

November 23, 1899.

I am willing to do what you suggest, though what I write must have the color of egotism. I naturally see my contributions as others do not see them, though I do not know that there is in this a reason for necessarily estimating them too highly. In any case I trust to your discretion, and, in the confidence of long-standing friendship, will talk a little more freely than I am in the habit of talking to anyone.

In so far as I know, no one has preceded me in the demonstration of the principle that labor tends to get as wages what it specifically produces, and that capital tends to get as interest what it separately produces. After I had elaborated my theory I discovered in V. Thünen [3] a statement of one part of the law. V. Thünen shows that each unit of labor tends to get what the final one produces, and that each unit of capital does the same. Careful reading shows that he viewed the action of this law as an exploitation of labor and even of capital. Some units of labor, as he seems to view the matter, create more than do others; but they get only the same amounts. The theory of imputation, as Wieser would call it, or of economic causation, as I prefer to call it, is as essential as is the final productivity principle. In my view the apparent surplus in one man's output over another's is due to an excess of capital in the one man's hands and is a product of capital and not of labor. The exploitation does not take place. Labor as a whole tends to get what it creates; and so does capital as a whole. All units of each productive agent get what they specifically create. The law is, in general, one that fixes rewards by the principle of *specific productivity*.

It is social capital and social labor that figure in the problem. The rates of return are general; and the agents that earn them are apportioned, in nice proportions, among all the groups and sub-groups of the industrial system. The law that effects this apportionment is a part of the more general law.

It is essential to the system that capital and capital goods should be distinguished; the one being a permanent and mobile thing, which produces continuously and without "periods of production," while the other produces in such periods. In my view the theory of Professor v. Böhm-Bawerk is based on a study of capital goods, and I can see a way so to extend it as to make it to become a theory of true capital and its earnings.

Underlying my conception of the action of the final productivity principle is a recognition of the fact that static forces and dynamic forces are working together in society as they are in physical nature; and that they must be studied separately. "Natural values," "natural wages," etc., are static values—wages, etc. In dynamics the thing that is natural is a rate of movement, while in statics it is a quantity, such as a dollar and a half, as the product of a day's labor, an amount that will be constant—till conditions change. I think that this involves a rearrangement of the framework of the science. It makes provision for a science of economic friction and disturbance. In particular does it furnish the means of relegating historical economic studies to their proper place. They should, in the end, be the inductive part of Economic Dynamics.

Shall I say more? I hope to do more continuous new work in the department of Dynamics than it has been practicable to do in Statics. I am presenting from year to year a system of Dynamic Theory; and it is taking a more nearly systematic shape each year. I cannot say that I value any discovery above the one that establishes the natural identity of the reward of labor with its contributory share of the social product, and the reward of capital with its contributory share.

If I am to add a list of specific points that seem to me to be new and true, or to have been new when I first hit on them, I should be led into an even greater appearance of egotism; for I should have to make the list a pretty considerable one. I hesitate to say even this; but I waive delicacy in all this general statement.

Finding the basis of distribution in the universal rather than the social laws of economics is one such point. The elaborating of a number of methods of identifying the specific products of labor is another. The application of the principle of rent to the products of all concrete agents, and the identifying of rent with static income and of profit with dynamic income is another point; and another is a considerable enlargement of the value law. This last involves a study of *qualitative* increments rather than of merely quantitative ones in consumers' goods and in producers' goods.[4] The tracing of the concrete sources of incomes, the synchronization of industry and its product, the relation of all rents to values, the delimitation of what may properly be treated as "society," and, in short, rather more than even in my present capacity of egotist, I feel like enumerating, would have to be named in a more complete enumeration.

NO. 3. A HUMOROUS NOTE

In amplification of his value theory, Clark sent the following amusing post card to William W. Folwell.[5]

November 12, 1892.

How is this?

Individual subjective value = condition of competition

Competition = mechanism of adjustment of ratios of exchange ("objective value")

Ratios of exchange express *social* subjective value

Gulf between subjective and objective values not bridged by Austrians, except by B. Bawerk, and by him thus:

NO. 4. STUART WOOD'S VERSION OF MARGINAL PRODUCTIVITY

Stuart Wood, a prominent Philadelphia businessman who, it is believed, held the first doctorate in economics in this country, from Harvard, worked out at about the same time as Clark a suggestive variant of the marginal productivity doctrine, but the comprehensiveness and relative simplicity of Clark's doctrine captured the imagination of economists and dominated both the economic literature of his day and the attention of successive generations of teachers. Wood's contemporaries attributed importance to his work, while noting resemblances to that of Clark.[6] Interestingly enough Clark's son, John Maurice Clark, initiated a revival of interest in Wood's work.[7] Professor George Stigler has presented biographical data and a sympathetic analysis of Wood.[8]

The following is Wood's own abstract of his basic paper, "Theory of Wages," which he delivered before the American Economic Association at the same time that Clark presented his own basic paper.[9]

The history of modern socialism and its allied movements shows the need of a true theory of wages to replace the old wage-fund theory. The price of all labor is regulated by its final utility, the utility of that portion which comes into use last and is least highly valued. But in most kinds of production labor may be replaced by capital. Hence the law: "The price of a given amount of labor is the same as the price paid for the use of such an amount of capital as would replace that labor in those employments where labor and capital are interchangeable and where either can be used to equal advantage." But since the problems of wages and interest are inseparable the law merely serves to show the conditions with which price must comply so as to equalize demand and supply. The rates of wages and interest move on sliding scales, which may rise or fall, either conjointly in accordance with the law of supply and demand, or inversely, according to the relative utility of equivalent portions of labor and capital. In one kind of production capital will be most profitably employed; in another, labor. Between these extremes lies a region of variable interchangeability which sets the law for the whole. Special modifications of this law are necessary wherever the state of perfect competition and absolute mobility of labor and capital do not exist.

Bibliographic Notes

CHAPTER I

1. Hugh McCulloch, *Report of the Secretary of the Treasury . . . for the Year 1865*, 39th Cong., 1st sess., House of Representatives Ex. Doc. No. 3, p. 9.

2. Edward Atkinson to McCulloch, November 1, 1868, McCulloch Papers, the Library of Congress. Atkinson was now as heartily opposed to greenbacks as he had been in favor of them during the Civil War. For Atkinson's earlier views, see Joseph Dorfman, *The Economic Mind in American Civilization, 1606–1865* (New York: Viking, 1946), Vol. II, pp. 966, 971.

3. George C. Clark to McCulloch, November 14, 1865, McCulloch Papers.

4. J. A. F[erris], *A Searching Analysis of the Action of Paper Money Upon the Trade and Prosperity of the United States* (San Francisco, 1868), pp. 68–70. This pamphlet, in addition to its separate paging, had continuous pagination with the author's *The Financial Economy of the United States, Illustrated,* (San Francisco: Roman, 1867) and is to be found attached to some copies of that work. Ferris (1806–1874) had some pretensions to learning. He was a graduate of the University of Vermont and the translator of De Florian's *Numa Pompilius.*

5. J. N. Cardozo, "Essay on Banking and Currency," *The Bankers' Magazine,* March 1869, pp. 673–97; "Systems of Banking and Currency," *The Southern Review,* April 1870, pp. 392–93 (for Cardozo's authorship see *The XIX Century,* May 1870, p. 98). "The Tariff and a Redundant Currency," No. 6, *Charleston Daily Courier,* April 23, 1870. For earlier activities of Cardozo, see Dorfman, *op. cit.,* Vol. II, pp. 551–66, 572–73, 847, 852–62, 939, 985–87.

6. George Walker, *Considerations Touching Mr. Randall's Bill for the Suppression of the National Banks* (Springfield, Mass., 1867), p. 12 [pamphlet].

7. G. S. Merriam, *The Life and Times of Samuel Bowles* (New York: Century, 1885), Vol. II, p. 53; Atkinson to McCulloch, October 27, 1866, in Atkinson Letterbooks, Massachusetts Historical Society.

8. *The Nation,* October 16, 1879. For a discussion of Carey's earlier activities, see Dorfman, *op. cit.,* Vol. II, pp. 789–805, 825–26, 959, 971, 975.

9. Henry C. Carey, *Contraction or Expansion?* (Philadelphia, 1866), pp. 12–13 [pamphlet].

10. Carey, *The Public Debt* (Philadelphia, 1866), pp. 11, 15 [pamphlet].

11. *Report upon the Relation of Foreign Trade to Domestic Industry and Internal Revenue,* 39th Cong., 1st sess., House of Representatives Ex. Doc. No. 68, Special Report No. 10, p. 9. For earlier activities of Colwell, see Dorfman, *op. cit.,* Vol. II, pp. 801, 809–26, 880, 971–75; for Wells, *ibid.,* pp. 808–809, 969–70, 975.

12. These were the *Report . . . upon Over-Importation and Relief* and *Report Upon High Prices and Their Relations with Currency and Taxation.*

13. *Report of the United States Revenue Commission,* 39th Cong., 1st sess., House of Representatives Ex. Doc. No. 34, pp. 27, 36.

14. Horace Greeley, *Essays Designed to Elucidate the Science of Political Economy* (Boston: Osgood, 1869, 1875), pp. 267–68. For earlier activities of Greeley, see Dorfman, *op. cit.,* Vol. II, pp. 669–71, 686, 691, 693, 806, 848.

15. Atkinson to Henry Wilson, July 7, 1866, Atkinson Letterbooks.

16. Herbert Ronald Ferleger, *David A. Wells and the American Revenue System, 1865–1870* (New York: privately printed, 1942), pp. 155–56.

17. David A. Wells, *Report of the Special Commissioner of the Revenue for the Year 1866,* 39th Cong., 2d sess., Senate Ex. Doc. No. 2, pp. 29, 31, 34.

18. Wells to Atkinson, March 6, 1867, Atkinson Papers; Wells to Arthur Latham Perry, March 11, 1867, in Ferleger, *op. cit.,* pp. 175–78.

19. Wells, *Report of the Special Commissioner of the Revenue for the Year 1867,* 40th Cong., 2d sess., House of Representatives Ex. Doc. No. 81, pp. 28, 29.

20. John Stuart Mill to Charles Eliot Norton, March 18, September 24, 1868, in "Letters of John Stuart Mill to Charles Eliot Norton," *Proceedings of the Massachusetts Historical Society,* Vol. L (1916–17), pp. 12–14; "John Stuart Mill on National Faith," *The Nation,* October 15, 1868.

21. Report of Hicks's speech in the *Charleston Daily Courier,* April 13, 1870; C[ardozo], "Dr. Hicks' Lecture on the Protective System," *ibid.,* April 14, 15, 16, 1870.

22. Atkinson withdrew from active public support of free trade after 1872 on the ground that his support had hurt him personally and that "if we avoid controversy . . . we shall secure good sound legislation by consent of both sides."—Atkinson to Wells, November 11, 1875, Wells Papers, Library of Congress (unless otherwise cited, later references are to the papers in this library).

23. Atkinson to Wells, April 11, 1866, Atkinson Letterbooks.

24. Cardozo, "Cotton," *Savannah Republican,* February 10, 1870; "A Financial Crisis Deferred, But Not Improbable," *Charleston Daily Courier,* March 5, 1870; "The Gold Question," *ibid.,* March 11, 1870.

25. Horace White to Atkinson, September 25, 1867, Atkinson Papers.

26. George Opdyke, *Letter on National Finances* (New York, 1868), p. 20 [pamphlet]. On the basis of his doctrine Opdyke in 1878 approved the resumption of specie payments set by legislation for January 1879, but he also contended at that time that the soundest paper currency was one issued exclusively by the government rather than one composed of government and bank notes.— Testimony of Opdyke, April 27, 1879, *Resumption of Specie Payments,* 45th Cong., 2d sess., House of Representatives Misc. Doc. No. 62, p. 240.

27. Silas M. Stilwell, "Specie Payments," *New York Herald,* November 25, 1865; "Our National Debt and the Currency," *The Bankers' Magazine,* April 1868, pp. 784–85; *A Report of Two Interviews with Hon. Silas M. Stilwell* [by the Chicago *Inter-Ocean*] (Chicago, 1874), p. 15 [pamphlet].

28. Charles Francis Adams to Ethan Allen, Cyrus W. Field, B. B. Sherman, March 19, 1874, in *Proceedings of the Mass Meeting of Citizens in the Cooper Institute . . . On National Finances* (New York, 1874), p. 54 [pamphlet]; Brooks Adams, "The Supreme Court and the Currency," *The International Review,* June 1879, p. 641.

29. Henry Bronson, *The Money Problem,* p. 28, originally printed in September 1873 for private circulation, and attached essay, "The Money Problem Again," separately paged (New Haven, 1877), pp. 73–74 [pamphlet].

30. Gamaliel Bradford, "The Treasury Reports," *The North American Review*, January 1870, p. 209.

31. [Horace White], "Secretary Richardson and Commodore Vanderbilt," *Chicago Tribune*, September 23, 1873.

32. *Congressional Record*, 43d Cong., 1st sess., p. 2533.

Charles Francis Adams, Jr., spoke of the panic as one of those "financial storms, incident to the modern high pressure system of conducting business, and which are common to all civilized countries and to every monetary system."—Adams, "The Currency Debate of 1873–74," *The North American Review*, July 1874, p. 111.

33. Thomas W. Olcott to Wells, April 18, 1874, Wells Papers. Olcott (1794–1880) was described by *The Bankers' Magazine* as a man of "eminent ability and large experience." His bank weathered all financial embarrassments of the country. During the Civil War, he served as an adviser to the Secretary of the Treasury, Samuel P. Chase; he advocated both the use of greenbacks and the establishment of the national banking system, and though later he was opposed to greenbacks, he was an ardent supporter of bimetallism. (Obituary Note, *The Bankers' Magazine*, April 1880, p. 820).

34. Wells, "How Shall the Nation Regain Prosperity?" *The North American Review*, July–September 1877, pp. 128, 130, 287.

35. Stilwell to Gordon L. Ford, March 4, 1875, Stilwell Papers, New York Public Library.

36. For Kellogg's views, see Dorfman, *op. cit.*, Vol. II, pp. 678–81, 978–80.

37. Wendell Phillips, "The Outlook," *The North American Review*, July–August 1878, p. 109.

38. Testimony of Carsey, August 3, 1878, in *Depression in Labor and Business*, 45th Cong., 3d sess., House of Representatives Misc. Doc. No. 29, pp. 56–57.

39. While the resumption bill was pending in 1875 Carey declared that the provision to substitute small silver coins for the fractional currency would benefit exclusively the selfish silver kings of Nevada.—Carey, *The Senate Finance Bill* (Philadelphia, 1875), pp. 5–6 [pamphlet]; *Monetary Independence* (Philadelphia, 1875), pp. 3, 10 [pamphlet]. The greenback parties also shifted and included a free silver plank in their platforms.

40. *Report and Accompanying Documents of the United States Monetary Commission*, 44th Cong., 2d sess., Senate Report No. 703, Vol. 2, p. 433.

41. *Ibid.*, Vol. 1, pp. 30, 138.

42. This idea achieved considerable respectability and prominence as the basis of the famous idea of "symmetallism" of the eminent British economist Alfred Marshall. See Marshall, "Answers to Questions on the Subject of Currency and Prices Circulated by the Royal Commission on the Depression of Trade and Industry" (1886), reprinted in Marshall, *Official Papers* (London: Macmillan, 1926), p. 14.

The notion appears to have been presented originally by a prominent eighteenth-century mercantilist, Sir James Steuart; see his *An Inquiry into the Principles of Political Oeconomy*, reprinted in *Works* (London: T. Cadell and W. Davies, 1805), Vol. II, pp. 294–95.

A proposal was also presented in Congress by Senator Alexander Stephens, formerly vice-president of the Confederacy, for a "goloid" dollar containing both metals, but it never got beyond the committee stage. Phillips pointed out that this notion was deemed impracticable because of the dangers of counterfeiting. See J. P. Phillips, *Social Struggles* (New Haven: Tuttle, Morehouse & Taylor, 1886), p. 270.

43. Olcott to Wells, July 20, 1877, Wells Papers.

44. "The New York Stock Exchange," signed "Wall Street" [the paper's regular correspondent], *Boston Daily Advertiser*, February 23, 1869; "Public Sentiment Against It," *Mining and Scientific Press*, October 11, 1879 [editorial].

45. Wells, "How Will the United States Supreme Court Decide the Granger Railroad Cases?" *The Nation*, October 29, 1874.

46. Stephen J. Field to Wells, June 29, 1877, Wells Papers, New York Public Library.

47. Thomas McIntyre Cooley, "Limits to State Control of Private Business," *The Princeton Review*, March 1878, pp. 270–71.

48. Charles Francis Adams, Jr., to Wells, January 14, 1869, Wells Papers; "Chapters of Erie," 1869, reprinted in Charles F. Adams, Jr., and Henry Adams, *Chapters of Erie, and Other Essays* (New York: Osgood, 1871), p. 3; *The Regulation of All Railroads Through the State-Ownership of One* (Boston, 1873), pp. 9–14, 18, 19, 21 [pamphlet]; testimony of Adams, August 23, 1878, in *Depression in Labor and Business*, p. 215.

49. Charles Francis Adams, Jr., "The Granger Movement," *The North American Review*, April 1875, p. 400; "The State and the Railroads," No. 3, *The Atlantic Monthly*, July 1876, pp. 81, 84; *The Federation of the Railroad System* (Boston, 1880), p. 21 [pamphlet].

50. Adams, "Railroad Consolidation," in *Chapters of Erie*, p. 395.

51. O. B. Bunce, "Over-Consumption or Over-Production," *Popular Science Monthly*, July 1877, p. 315. In the controversy that ensued Bunce said that while he agreed with economists in their view that in the long run production adjusted itself to consumption and that the periods of speculation and prostration were only perturbations, still the problem of reducing their intensity and duration remained.—Bunce, "Causes of Commercial Distress," *ibid.*, September 1877, p. 616.

52. R. G. Eccles, "The Labor-Question," *Popular Science Monthly*, September 1877, p. 611.

53. Albert S. Bolles, *The Conflict Between Labor and Capital* (Philadelphia: Lippincott, 1876), pp. 199–204. Bolles, among other things, later became editor of *The Bankers' Magazine* and taught at Boston University and the University of Pennsylvania.

54. William Elder, *Questions of the Day* (Philadelphia: Henry Carey Baird, 1871), pp. 329–30. For a systematic discussion of Elder's ideas see L. L. Bernard and Jesse Bernard, *Origins of American Sociology* (New York: Crowell, 1943), pp. 443–57. For earlier activities of Elder, see Dorfman, *op. cit.*, Vol. II, p. 975.

55. For Steward and his views, see Dorfman, *op. cit.*, Vol. II, p. 980.

56. Testimony of George E. McNeil, August 6, 1878, in *Depression in Labor and Business*, p. 121; W. Godwin Moody, *Our Labor Difficulties* (Boston: Williams, 1878), pp. 69–96; testimony of Moody, August 21, 1878, in *Depression in Labor and Business*, pp. 153–67; *Land and Labor in the United States* (New York: Scribner, 1883), p. 260.

57. Carey, "Capital and Labor," *Debates of the [Pennsylvania] Convention to Amend the Constitution of Pennsylvania, 1872–1873*, Vol. V, p. 473.

58. Atkinson, *Labor and Capital Allies, Not Enemies* (New York: Harper, 1879), p. 38. Atkinson was willing, however, that his projected cotton manufacturing company help its employees purchase houses—but at a return to the company. "I do not believe in philanthropy toward the able-bodied that does not pay 6 per cent," he wrote.—Atkinson to Wells, October 12, 1875, Wells Papers.

59. Testimony of White, August 23, 1878, *Depression in Labor and Business*, p. 569.

60. [White], "The Nature of the Panics," *Chicago Tribune*, October 1, 1873; testimony of George Walker, August 26, 1878, in *Depression in Labor and Business*, pp. 272–73, 280, 282–83; White, "Commercial Crises," *Cyclopædia of Political Science, Political Economy and of the Political History of the United States*, edited by John J. Lalor (Chicago, 1882), Vol. I, p. 530 (hereafter referred to as Lalor's *Cyclopædia*).

61. Testimony of Gage, July 28, 1879, in *Causes of General Depression in Labor and Business*, 46th Cong., 2d sess., House of Representatives Misc. Doc. No. 5, p. 13; *Chinese Immigration*, 46th Cong., 2d sess., House of Representatives Report No. 572, p. 29.

62. A. Maxwell, "Will the Negro Relapse into Barbarism?" *DeBow's Review*, February 1867, p. 179.

63. George Fitzhugh, "Virginia—Her Past, Present, and Future," *DeBow's Review*, February 1866, pp. 178–84; "What's to be Done with the Negroes?" *ibid.*, June 1866, pp. 577–81; "Camp Lee and the Freedmen's Bureau," *ibid.*, October 1866, pp. 346–55. For earlier activities of Fitzhugh, see Dorfman, *op. cit.*, Vol. II, pp. 929–34, 984.

64. Editorial, "The Labor Convention," *Unionville* [South Carolina] *Times*, reprinted in the *Charleston Daily Courier*, November 29, 1869; editorial, "Social Equality," *ibid.*, January 10, 1870; editorial, "They Come," *ibid.*, March 3, 1870.

65. Cardozo, *Reminiscences of Charleston* (Charleston: J. Walker, 1866), pp. 9–10.

66. [A. T. Bledsoe], "De Tocqueville on the Sovereignty of the People," *The Southern Review*, April 1867, p. 332; "What is Liberty?" *ibid.*, April 1869, pp. 264–66, 284. For Bledsoe's authorship, see *Authors of the Articles in . . . "The Southern Review*," photostats of ms. prepared at Vanderbilt University, Library of Congress.

67. B[radley] T. J[ohnson], "Is Virginia Bankrupt?" No. 1, [Richmond] *Daily Dispatch*, January 16, 1875.

CHAPTER II

1. For the earlier phase of the movement, see Dorfman, *op. cit.*, Vol. II, pp. 684–86.

2. Edward Thomas Peters, "The Land Question," *The National Standard*, September 2, 1871.

3. Josiah Warren, *Response to the Call of the National Labor Union* (Boston, 1871), p. 3 [pamphlet]. For earlier activities of Warren, see Dorfman, *op. cit.*, Vol. II, pp. 671–75, 960.

4. "Free Love," *The Word*, August 1874 [editorial].

5. William B. Greene, *Mutual Banking* (Columbus Junction, Iowa, 1850, 1896), pp. 37–39, 66 [pamphlet]. For the Massachusetts land bank scheme, see Dorfman, *op. cit.*, Vol. I, p. 149.

6. Ezra H. Heywood, *The Great Strike* (Princeton, Mass., 1878), p. 3 [pamphlet].

7. Joshua K. Ingalls, *Periodical Business Crises* (New York, 1878), p. 12 [pamphlet]; *Economic Equities* (New York, 1887), p. 56 [pamphlet]; "Ethics and Economics," 1890, reprinted in *Reminiscences of an Octogenarian* (Elmira, New York: Gazette Company, 1897), p. 175.

8. Benjamin R. Tucker, "Supply and Demand," *The New Age*, July 15, 1876;

"State Socialism and Anarchism," 1888, reprinted in his *Instead of a Book* (New York: privately printed, 1893, 1897), pp. 8, 14; "Does Competition Mean War?" 1888, *ibid.*, p. 405.

9. Heywood, *op. cit.*, pp. 5–6; Heywood to Wells, March 28, 1871, Wells Papers; Greene, "Address of the International," 1873, reprinted in his *Socialistic, Communistic, Mutualistic and Financial Fragments* (Boston: Lea and Shepard, 1873), pp. 243–50.

10. Stephen Pearl Andrews, "Address to the Inhabitants of the United States of America and of the World at Large upon the Slavery Question" and "Objects of Pantarchy," ms., Stephen Pearl Andrews Correspondence, Wisconsin Historical Society; "Objects of Pantarchy," *Woodhull & Claflin's Weekly*, September 30, 1871. For earlier activities of Andrews, see Dorfman, *op. cit.*, Vol. II, pp. 675–77; William C. Andrews, "Sketch of the Life of Stephen Pearl Andrews," *Woodhull & Claflin's Weekly*, December 9, 1871.

11. Charles Moran, *Money* (New York: Appleton, 1863), pp. 227–28; "Government," No. 2, *The New York Social Science Review*, July 1865, pp. 293, 300, 301—for Moran's authorship, see pamphlet reprint *Government*, New York, 1879; "Political Economy," No. 7, *New York Commercial Advertiser*, December 27, 1866—for Moran's authorship, see Montague R. Leverson, *Common Sense* (New York: Authors' Publishing Co., 1876), p. 100; *Banking and Money . . . A Reply to Mutual Banking* (New York, 1871), pp. 15–16, 30–31 [pamphlet]; testimony of Moran, October 28, 1876, in *Report . . . of the United States Monetary Commission*, Vol. II, p. 241

12. *Woodhull & Claflin's Weekly*, December 30, 1871. A copy of this rare issue is owned by Frederick B. Adams, Jr., of New York City.

13. Victoria C. Woodhull, *A Speech on the Principles of Finance* (New York, 1871), p. 23 [pamphlet].

14. Central Committee to the General Council, October 1, 1871, in John R. Commons, *et al.*, *A Documentary History of American Industrial Society* (Cleveland: Clark, 1910), Vol. IX, pp. 367–68.

15. For an amusing biography of the sisters, see Emanie Sachs, "*The Terrible Siren*" (New York: Harper, 1928).

16. "An Unemployment Manifesto during the Crisis of 1873," with editorial note by Alexander Trachtenberg, reprinted in *The Communist*, June 1931, p. 571.

17. Testimony of Isaac Bennett, August 2, 1878, in *Depression in Labor and Business*, p. 27.

18. C. Osborne Ward, "Individualism vs. Socialism," *The Socialist*, May 27, 1876; testimony of Ward, August 3, 1878, in *Depression in Labor and Business*, p. 59. Ward was the brother of the noted sociologist Lester F. Ward.

19. [Adolph Douai], "Karl Marx's *Capital*," *The Socialist*, May 27, 1876.

20. Testimony of Douai, August 2, 1878, *Depression in Labor and Business*, pp. 30, 35, 36, 39; testimony of Douai, September 20, 1883, *Report of the Committee of the Senate upon the Relations between Labor and Capital* (Washington: Government Printing Office, 1885), Vol. II, pp. 708–709, 718. This report will be referred to hereafter as *Report on Labor and Capital*.

21. Testimony of Ward, August 3, 1878, in *Depression in Labor and Business*, p. 58; *The Socialist*, June 10, 1876.

22. John Francis Bray, "Industrial Reorganization," *The Irish World and American Industrial Liberator*, November 28, 1880; "Planks for the Future," *ibid.*, December 4, 1880. For Bray's earlier activities in England and the United States, see Dorfman, *op. cit.*, Vol. II, pp. 686–89, 961–62.

23. *The Socialist*, May 27, 1876 [editorial].

24. Wendell Phillips, "The Outlook," *The North American Review*, July-August, 1878, p. 112.

25. "Communism Here," *The Public*, July 25, 1878 [editorial].

CHAPTER III

1. Wayland's treatise, which was extremely laissez faire in tone, was still generally read, although it was published originally in 1837. For a discussion of Wayland and his work, see Dorfman, *op. cit.*, Vol. II, pp. 758–67. The other two first appeared in 1866.

2. Amasa Walker, *The Science of Wealth* (Boston: Little, Brown, 1866, seventh edition 1874), pp. xvi, 13, 269, 273; *The Science of Wealth . . . Condensed for Popular Reading* (Philadelphia: Lippincott, 1872), p. vii; "Labor and Capital in Manufactures," *Scribner's Monthly*, August 1872, pp. 460–64. For earlier views of Walker, see Dorfman, *op. cit.*, Vol. II, pp. 749–52, 969.

3. Walker, "Majority Report," *Reports of Commissioners on the Hours of Labor*, Massachusetts, House Document No. 44 (Boston, 1867), p. 31; "Legal Interference with the Hours of Labor," *Lippincott's Magazine*, November 1868, pp. 527–33.

4. Walker, *The Science of Wealth . . . Condensed for Popular Reading*, p. 442.

5. Walker, *The Science of Wealth*, pp. 65–66.

6. Walker to Salmon P. Chase, August 31, 1861, Chase Papers, Historical Society of Pennsylvania; Speech, January 19, 1863, *Congressional Globe*, 37th Cong., 3d sess., pp. 391–92; Walker to McCulloch, December 8, 1867, McCulloch Papers; "Claims of the Bondholders," *Lippincott's Magazine*, August 1868, p. 207; "Commercial and Monetary Interests of California," *The Overland Monthly*, June 1873, pp. 566–68; "Our National Currency," *The International Review*, March 1874, p. 243; "The Money Problem," *ibid.*, March 1875, pp. 251–53, 263–64; "French and American Currencies," *Scribner's Monthly*, December 1875, p. 227.

For Walker's views on deposits, see Walker to James A. Garfield, June 6, 18, December 29, 1868, March 18, 1869, Garfield Papers, Library of Congress; see also A. L. Perry to Garfield, May 30, 1868, July 11, 1871.

7. Walker, *The Science of Wealth*, p. 160. Earlier, in 1859, Walker wrote: "While human nature remains what it is, there will doubtless always be times of competition, excitement and over-trading; but without the maddening intoxication of a fictitious currency, such terrible revulsions as we have heretofore witnessed would never occur. Panics would be unknown. There would be nothing to make panics of, since they arise . . . from the inherent weakness of a mixed currency."—Walker to Hamer Stansfeld, Nov. 2, 1859, in Stansfeld, *Money* (London, 1860), p. 34 [pamphlet].

8. Walker, *The Science of Wealth*, pp. 105, 468; *Co-operative Associations*, an address before the Sovereigns of Industry at North Brookfield, July 21, 1874 [pamphlet].

9. For earlier views of Perry, see Dorfman, *op. cit.*, Vol. II, pp. 981–83; Perry's textbook, *Elements of Political Economy* (New York: Scribner, 1865), later called *Political Economy*, had twenty-two editions. Editions used here are *Elements of Political Economy*, third edition, 1868, and *Political Economy*, nineteenth edition, 1887.

10. McCulloch to Perry, August 17, 1867, printed in *Springfield* [Massachusetts] *Weekly Republican*, October 12, 1867; Perry, *Williamstown and Williams*

College (New York: privately printed, 1899), p. 697. On Perry's prominence in Cleveland's circle, see Perry to Cleveland, December 24, 1884; Perry to Colonel Daniel S. Lamont, October 27, 1885; Perry to Francis L. Stetson, October 28, 1885, Cleveland Papers, Library of Congress.

11. Perry, *Political Economy*, pp. 99, 102; *Recent Phases of Thought in Political Economy* (Boston, 1868), p. 9 [pamphlet].

12. Perry, *Elements of Political Economy*, p. 123; "Professor Walker at Amherst," *The Financier*, August 1, 1874.

13. Perry, *Political Economy*, p. 457; Perry to G. W. Smith, July 11, 1871, in *Official Report of the Proceedings of the National Insurance Convention of the United States* (New York, 1872), Vol. II, Appendix, pp. 14–15.

14. Perry, *The Foes of the Farmers* (Lincoln, Nebr., 1874), pp. 16–17 [pamphlet]; *Free Trade Lesson from the New Testament*, 1882, [pamphlet].

15. Petition of Ely, *et al.*, dated July 3, 1883, *Bulletin of the National Association of Wool Manufacturers*, 1883, p. 180; Perry, "Preparation for Citizenship," *Education*, April 1889, p. 518.

16. Perry to Wells, October 16, 1882, Wells Papers, New York Public Library.

17. Perry, *Elements of Political Economy*, p. 24; *Political Economy*, pp. 79–80; "Preparation for Citizenship," p. 514.

18. Francis Bowen, *Gleanings from a Literary Life* (New York: Scribner, 1880), Preface; "Malthusianism, Darwinism and Pessimism," *The North American Review*, November 1879, p. 472. For earlier activities of Bowen, see Dorfman, *op. cit.*, Vol. II, pp. 743, 735–44, 957, 978.

19. Bowen to McCulloch, December 19, 1867, McCulloch Papers.

20. F. W. Taussig, "Economics," *The Development of Harvard University*, edited by Samuel Eliot Morison (Cambridge: Harvard University Press, 1930), p. 188.

21. Charles Franklin Dunbar, "Economic Science in America, 1776–1876," reprinted in *Economic Essays*, edited by O. M. W. Sprague (New York: Macmillan, 1904), p. 29. For biographical data on Dunbar, see Taussig's "Introduction," *op. cit.*, pp. vii–xvii.

22. [Dunbar], "Hasty Conclusions," *Boston Daily Advertiser*, January 17, 1860; editorial on proposed eight-hour law, *ibid.*, January 2, 1867.

23. [Dunbar], "Sumner's History of American Currency," *The North American Review*, October 1874, p. 415; Dunbar, "Deposits as Currency," 1887, reprinted in *Economic Essays*, p. 181.

24. J. Laurence Laughlin, "Professor Dunbar," *The Journal of Political Economy*, March 1900, pp. 235–36.

25. Notes of William Graham Sumner's course in the history of finance, politics, and political economy in the United States, written by R. L. Bridgman, dated July 27, 1876; conspectus of course of lectures, 1875–1876, p. 136, in Yale University Library. For biographical data on Sumner, see Harris E. Starr, *William Graham Sumner* (New York: Holt, 1925).

26. Sumner, "The Concentration of Wealth: Its Economic Justification," 1902, reprinted in his *The Challenge of Facts and Other Essays* (New Haven: Yale University Press, 1914), p. 90.

27. Sumner, "Socialism," *Scribner's Monthly*, October 1878, pp. 887–88; *Andrew Jackson as a Public Man* (Boston: Houghton Mifflin, 1887, 1891), p. 225; testimony of Sumner, August 22, 1878, in *Depression in Labor and Business*, pp. 203, 207–208.

28. Lester F. Ward, "Professor Sumner's 'Social Classes,'" 1884, reprinted in his *Glimpses of the Cosmos* (New York: Putnam, 1913), Vol. III, pp. 303–304.

29. Sumner, "The Theory and Practice of Elections," 1880, reprinted in *Collected Essays in Political and Social Science* (New York: Holt, 1885), pp. 138–39.

30. Lyman H. Atwater, "The Labor Question in Its Economic and Christian Aspects," *The Princeton Review*, July 1872, pp. 447, 485, 491; "The Late Commercial Crisis," *ibid.*, January 1874, pp. 123–24; "Our Industrial and Financial Situation," *ibid.*, July 1875, pp. 521, 524; "The Currency Question," *ibid.*, October 1875, pp. 741–42; "The Great Railroad Strike," *ibid.*, October 1877, pp. 723, 732, 733, 743; "Political Economy, A Science–of What?" *ibid.*, June 1880, pp. 423, 434, 435, 441; "The Regulation of Railroads," *ibid.*, May 1881, pp. 427–28; "The Future Paper Money of This Country," *ibid.*, January 1882, p. 20; *Ethics and Political Economy, from Notes Taken in the Lecture Room of Lyman H. Atwater* (Trenton: printed for private circulation, 1878), p. 97. For earlier views of Atwater, see Dorfman, *op. cit.*, Vol. II, pp. 705–706, 956, 970. The Princeton University Library possesses a series of volumes comprising Atwater's signed and unsigned magazine articles.

31. Julian M. Sturtevant, *Economics* (New York: Putnam, 1877, 1881), pp. 101–102, 241, 271, 296; "Method in Economic Science," *The New Englander*, January 1879, pp. 27–28, 30. For earlier views of Sturtevant, see Dorfman, *op. cit.*, Vol. II, pp. 957–58, 967–68. For biographical information, see *Julian M. Sturtevant; An Autobiography*, edited by J. M. Sturtevant, Jr. (New York: Revell, 1896).

32. Wayland, *The Elements of Political Economy*, recast by Aaron L. Chapin (New York: Sheldon, 1878), pp. 387, 390. Chapin also wrote the article "Political Economy" in *Johnson's New Universal Cyclopædia*, edited by Frederick A. P. Barnard and Arnold Guyot, (New York: A. J. Johnson, 1877), Vol. III, pp. 1317–19.

33. Aaron L. Chapin, *First Principles of Political Economy* (New York: American Book Company, 1880), p. 83; "The Relation of Labor and Capital," *Transactions of the Wisconsin Academy of Sciences, Arts, and Letters*, Vol. I (1870–1872), pp. 60–61; "The Nature and Functions of Credit," *ibid.*, Vol. V (1877–1881), pp. 64–65.

34. Van Buren Denslow, *Principles of the Economic Philosophy of Society, Government and Industry* (New York: Cassell, 1888), pp. 368, 380. To the charge of a reviewer that the *Principles* contained "too many inaccurate statements" (J. B. Clark, in *Political Science Quarterly*, December 1888, p. 693), Denslow replied that "inaccuracies in the statement of fact will be likely to increase almost in an equal ratio to the number of facts accurately stated, in any inductive economic work appealing to statistical and historical evidence."– Denslow to J. B. Clark, March 13, 1891, Clark Papers, in possession of J. M. Clark.

35. John M. Gregory, "The Problem of the Unemployed," *The Independent*, November 10, 1887.

36. James H. Canfield, *Taxation* (New York: The Society for Political Education, 1883), pp. 35–36; Alvin S. Johnson, in *Spiritual Autobiographies*, edited by Louis Finkelstein (New York: Harper, 1948), p. 41. Canfield was the father of Dorothy Canfield Fisher and the revered teacher of William Allen White.

37. George Frederick Holmes, "Aspects of the Hour," *DeBow's Review*, April-May 1867, pp. 337–38; *The Science of Society*, (Charlottesville: privately printed at the Miller Manual Labor School, 1883), Lecture xvii, p. 12. For earlier views of Holmes, see Dorfman, *op. cit.*, Vol. II, pp. 920–28.

38. William Preston Johnston, *Report . . . to Board of Administrators, on Plan of Organization of Tulane University* (New Orleans: A. W. Hyatt, 1883),

p. 28; *The Perils of Universities* (1884), p. 7 [pamphlet]. For biographical data on Johnston, see Arthur Marvin Shaw, *William Preston Johnston* (Baton Rouge: Louisiana State University Press, 1943).

39. Robert Ellis Thompson's *Social Science and National Economy* (Philadelphia: Porter-Coates, 1875), was promoted far and wide by the powerful protectionist Industrial League of Pennsylvania. For biographical detail, see "Memorial Meeting in Honor of Robert Ellis Thompson," *The Barnwell Bulletin*, February 1925, pp. 3–23; James H. S. Bossard, "Robert Ellis Thompson, Pioneer Professor in Social Science," *The American Journal of Sociology*, September 1929, pp. 239–49.

40. Andrew D. White, *Autobiography* (New York: Century, 1905), Vol. I, p. 381. For earlier views of Wilson, see Dorfman, *op. cit.*, Vol. II, p. 808.

41. James Burrill Angell to David A. Wells, December 24, 1873, Wells Papers.

42. "The Prize Question in Political Economy," *The Publishers' Weekly*, March 18, 1876 [editorial].

43. Jerome D. Greene to Edwin F. Gay, December 16, 1907, in files of the Department of Economics of Harvard University, supplied by courtesy of Professor Arthur H. Cole of Harvard University.

CHAPTER IV

1. Jevons enjoyed high repute in the United States as well as in his native England for his eminent statistical work on money and prices. His *Elementary Lessons in Logic* was used extensively in the colleges.

2. As in Europe, there were a number of forerunners in the United States of the "utility" analysis. Embryonic versions of marginal utility analysis were given as early as 1812 by Justus Erich Bollmann. See Dorfman, *op. cit.*, Vol. I, p. 494.

3. For earlier views of Newcomb, see Dorfman *op. cit.*, Vol. II, pp. 977–78.

4. Simon Newcomb, "Jevons' Theory of Political Economy," *The North American Review*, April 1872, pp. 436–38; "The Method and Province of Political Economy," *ibid.*, October 1875, pp. 260, 265–66 (in this article Newcomb worked out his own variant of mathematical economics); *Principles of Political Economy* (New York: Harper, 1886), pp. 202–203.

William Graham Sumner also expressed admiration for Jevons' treatise and declared that its mathematical form assured its permanency. But, unlike Newcomb, he felt that there were "no positive data in economics from which results may be deduced, as unknown are derived from known quantities."– *Political Economy and Political Science*, reading list compiled by Sumner, *et al.* (New York: The Society for Political Education, 1884), p. 3; Sumner, "Wages," 1882, reprinted in *Collected Essays in Political and Social Science*, pp. 41–42.

5. Newcomb, "The Silver Conference and the Silver Question," *The International Review*, March 1879, p. 333; "The Standard of Value," *The North American Review*, August 1879, pp. 223–37; "Two Schools of Political Economy," *The Princeton Review*, November 1884, p. 301; *Principles of Political Economy*, pp. 213, 338, 383–87; "Has the Standard Gold Dollar Appreciated?" *The Journal of Political Economy*, September 1893, pp. 503–12; "The Carnegie Institution," *The North American Review*, February 1904, p. 177. For a comprehensive history of the equation of exchange, see Arthur W. Marget, *The Theory of Prices* (New York: Prentice-Hall, 1938, 1942). Pro-

fessor Irving Fisher of Yale, whose own equation became the most famous one, declared that Newcomb was the great pioneer.–Fisher, "Simon Newcomb," *The Economic Journal*, December 1909, p. 642.

6. "Political Economy in Europe," *Commercial & Financial Chronicle*, July 24, 1875 [editorial].

7. Thomas Edward Cliffe Leslie, "The History of German Political Economy," 1875, reprinted in *Essays in Political and Moral Philosophy* (Dublin, 1879), p. 177.

8. Emile de Laveleye, "The New Tendencies in Political Economy," translated by George Walker, *The Bankers' Magazine*, February, March, April 1879, pp. 601–609, 698–706, 761–67.

9. [Edwin L. Godkin], "The New German Political Economy," *The Nation*, September 9, 1875 (authorship supplied by *The Nation*); William Allen, "The New German Economists," *The Nation*, September 23, 1875. Allen was professor of Latin and history at the University of Wisconsin. A similar letter in the same issue was from Brinton Coxe, the wealthy Philadelphia mining engineer and owner of coal properties, who advocated free trade and "sound" money.

10. [James Morgan Hart], "Political Economy in Germany," *The Nation*, November 4, 1875 (authorship supplied by *The Nation*).

11. Charles Francis Adams, Jr., "The State and the Railroads," No. 2, *The Atlantic Monthly*, June 1876, p. 692.

12. Roscher to Louis Wolowski, in Laveleye, "Bi-Metallic Money," *The Bankers' Magazine*, March 1877, p. 703, translated by George Walker.

13. *The Bankers' Magazine*, February 1879, pp. 645, 648.

14. William Watts Folwell, of New England descent, was graduated from Geneva (now Hobart) College in 1857. While teaching mathematics, Greek, and Latin there, he studied law, but in 1860 he went to the University of Berlin to study philology. After serving in the Civil War as a lieutenant colonel of Engineers, he returned to academic pursuits as professor of mathematics and engineering at Kenyon College, and then went in 1871 to the University of Minnesota. Here Folwell's Department of Political Economy included international law and civil government. After resigning the presidency in 1884, Folwell, as professor of political science, also taught economics. For biographical details, see *William Watts Folwell*, edited by Solon J. Buck, (Minneapolis: University of Minnesota Press, 1933).

15. Folwell to Wharton, Lea and Sellars, c/o Henry Carey Baird, February 26, 1872, copy of letter in Folwell Papers, University of Minnesota Library.

16. Folwell, "The True Method of Political Economy," *Bulletin of the Minnesota Academy of Natural Sciences*, December 1882, pp. 239–58; "Money Notes," 1885, ms., Folwell Papers; "Distribution and Exchange: Syllabus, 1890–1891," *ibid.*; *The Wages Question*, The University [of Minnesota] Extension Series, 1894–1895, copy in University of Minnesota Library; "Evolution in Paper Money in the United States," *Minnesota Law Review*, June 1924, pp. 577–78.

17. "We have a Political Science Club here [Minneapolis], which is quite a 'live' affair–but the Yale and Princeton influence is so strong that we find discretion necessary."–Folwell to Richard T. Ely, November 24, 1886, Ely Papers, Wisconsin Historical Society.

18. *Annual Report of the President [of the University of California] for the Board of Regents, 1881–82* (Sacramento: State Printing Office, 1882), p. 8.

19. Bernard Moses, "Social Science and Its Method," *The Berkeley Quarterly*, January 1880, p. 11; [Moses], "Notes and Comments," *ibid.*, April 1881,

p. 198; [Moses], "Henry George's Refutation of Malthusianism," *ibid.*, p. 194; [Moses], "Russia as a Socialistic State," *ibid.*, p. 200; Moses, *Social Infelicities of Half-Knowledge* (Berkeley, 1888), p. 8–9 [pamphlet].

20. Moses, "The Communism of Early Christianity," *The Berkeley Quarterly*, July 1880, p. 219; under the pseudonym of Richard Hassel, Moses wrote "The Historical Foundations of Modern Society," *ibid.*, July 1881, p. 375. For Moses' authorship, see *Biennial Report of the President of the University* [of California], 1886, p. 134.

21. Moses, "The Conditions and Prospects of Democracy," *University* [of Chicago] *Record*, August 7, 1896, pp. 299, 300.

22. Atlanticus, "The Dynamics of Finance," *The New Nation*, June 11, 1864; [Delmar], "Money Article," *The New York Leader*, April 16, 1864. For Delmar's authorship, see Hamilton Willcox, *The Life of the Hon. Alex. Del Mar* (New York, 1898), p. 35 [pamphlet]. For earlier views of Del Mar, see Dorfman, *op. cit.*, Vol. II, pp. 975–76. For a sympathetic discussion of Del Mar's doctrines, see Earl Hicks, "Alexander Del Mar: Critic of Metalism," *The Southern Economic Journal*, January 1940, pp. 310–32.

23. A[lexander] D[elmar], "The Growth of National Wealth," *The New York Social Science Review*, July 1865, p. 202; Emile Walter, "History of the Rate of Interest in Great Britain and Elsewhere," *ibid.*, October 1865, p. 370; Delmar to H. S. Olcott, May 1872, in *Official Report of the Proceedings of the National Insurance Convention of the United States*, Appendix, p. 217. This theory of interest was, in a less developed form, found in earlier writers, notably Turgot and Adam Smith's teacher, Francis Hutcheson.

24. [Delmar], "Loan Assurance—A New Project for Capitalists," *Commercial & Financial Chronicle*, August 12, 1865. For Del Mar's authorship, see Delmar to H. S. Olcott, *op. cit.*, p. 214.

25. Atlanticus, "The Dynamics of Finance." He probably got this example from Henry Thomas Buckle's *History of Civilization in England*.

26. Delmar to Messrs. Bryant and Godwin, June 27, 1868, Bryant-Godwin Collection, New York Public Library.

27. Del Mar, "The Evolution of Words and the Theory of Value," *The Mining and Scientific Press*, February 1, 1879.

28. Del Mar, *The Science of Money* (New York: Macmillan, 1885, 2nd edition 1896), pp. 139–40; *History of Monetary Systems* (Chicago: Kerr, 1895), p. 21; *Story of the Gold Conspiracy* (Chicago, 1895), p. 5 [pamphlet]; *Speech . . . at Cooper Institute on the Occasion of the Recent Bimetallic Meeting* (New York, 1896), p. 7 [pamphlet]; "The New Gold Supplies," *The Bankers' Magazine*, September 1905, pp. 388–93.

29. For biographical details and bibliography, see James Phinney Munroe, *A Life of Francis Amasa Walker* (New York: Holt, 1923).

30. Francis A. Walker to Carl Schurz, June 20, 1878, Schurz Papers, Library of Congress. Walker incidentally pointed out that the census of manufactures could not be considered complete since the counts taken "do not, and cannot, obtain the whole, or even the major part, of the production of the artisans of the country who work in small establishments."—Walker to Henry C. Carey, June 6, 1872, Carey Papers, Historical Society of Pennsylvania.

31. Walker, "American Industry in the Census," 1869, reprinted in *Discussions in Economics and Statistics*, edited by Davis R. Dewey (New York: Holt, 1899), Vol. II, p. 25.

32. Walker, *Money* (New York: Holt, 1878), p. 405

33. [Gamaliel Bradford], "Currency and Banking: English and American,"

The Bankers' Magazine, November 1869, p. 328. For Bradford's authorship, see Bradford to David A. Wells, April 30, 1869, Wells Papers.

34. Walker, "Remarks at the International Monetary Conference," 1878, reprinted in *Discussions in Economics and Statistics*, Vol. I, p. 166; *Money in Its Relations to Trade and Industry* (New York: Holt, 1879), pp. 136, 194; "The Monetary Conferences of 1867 and 1878, and the Future of Silver," *The Princeton Review*, January 1879, p. 45.

35. Walker pointed out that his father and J. B. Say had originally stressed the importance of the entrepreneur, but that contemporary orthodox economics had ignored their contributions and continued to identify the entrepreneur with the capitalist or to consider him simply a superior laborer.

36. Walker, *The Wages Question* (New York: Holt, 1876), pp. 142–44, 391, 405–406.

37. Walker, "The Present Standing of Political Economy," 1879, reprinted in *Discussions in Economics and Statistics*, Vol. I, p. 318. In 1876 Walker wrote that "Pol[itical] Econ[omy] is, as yet, not much of a science, anyway."—Walker to Henry Holt in Munroe, *op. cit.*, p. 186.

38. Walker to Richard T. Ely, April 30, 1884, Ely Papers.

39. Walker, *Political Economy* (New York: Holt, 1883, 1888), p. 419; "Mr. Bellamy and the New Nationalist Party," *The Atlantic Monthly*, February 1890, p. 259; "The Tide of Economic Thought," *Publications of the American Economic Association*, January-March 1891, pp. 36–37.

40. Testimony of Walker, October 17, 1883, in *Report on Labor and Capital*, Vol. III, pp. 340–41; "The Wage Fund," Lalor's *Cyclopædia*, Vol. III, p. 1077.

41. Walker, "The Source of Business Profits," 1887, reprinted in *Discussions in Economics and Statistics*, Vol. I, pp. 371–75.

42. Edwin Cannan, *A Review of Economic Theory* (London: King, 1929), p. 358.

43. Walker to J. B. Clark, May 8, 18, 1891, Clark Papers.

44. F. Y. Edgeworth, review of N. G. Pierson, *Leerboek der Staathuishoudkunde*, 1897, reprinted in *Papers Relating to Political Economy* (London: Macmillan, 1925), Vol. III, p. 89.

45. Joseph Cook, *Socialism* (Boston: Houghton Mifflin, 1880), p. 87.

CHAPTER V

1. See the statement of the congressman and industrialist Joseph H. Walker, *A Few Facts and Suggestions on Money, Trade and Banking*, 1882.

2. N. A. Dunning, "The Volume of Currency," *The Arena*, November 1892, p. 722.

3. For biographical detail on Crocker (1843–1921), see Dan W. Peery, "Colonel Crocker and the Boomer Movement," *Chronicles of Oklahoma*, September 1935, pp. 273–96.

4. Henry Demarest Lloyd, "Lords of Industry," 1881, reprinted in *Lords of Industry* (New York: Putnam, 1910), p. 46.

5. C. E. Perkins to Atkinson, June 15, 1881, Atkinson Papers.

6. James F. Hudson, *The Railways and the Republic* (New York: Harper, 1886), p. 312, ft.

7. [Joseph Bucklin Bishop], "Mr. Blaine on 'Trusts,'" *The Nation*, August 23, 1888. Authorship supplied by *The Nation*.

8. "Trusts," *Commercial & Financial Chronicle*, July 28, 1888 [editorial];

[Horace White], "The Competition of Trusts," *The Nation*, December 20, 1888. Authorship supplied by *The Nation*.

9. Testimony of Jay Gould, September 5, 1883, in *Report on Labor and Capital*, Vol. I, pp. 1080, 1081; testimony of Albert Fink, September 17, 1883, *ibid.*, Vol. II, p. 468.

10. Hudson, *op. cit.*, p. 225.

11. Henry C. Adams, "Administrative Supervision of the Railways under the Twentieth Section of the Act to Regulate Commerce," *The Quarterly Journal of Economics*, May 1908, p. 365.

12. Speech of Leland Stanford, January 10, 1887, *Congressional Record*, 49th Cong., 2d sess., p. 491.

13. Cooley was a member of the Advisory Commission of the Trunk Line Executive Committee, of which Colonel Fink was the Commissioner.—Fink to Cooley, January 25, 1882, Thomas McIntyre Cooley Papers, University of Michigan Library.

Cooley, in fact, did not want the Interstate Commerce Commission job. He wrote his wife when rumors of his appointment appeared: "I really begin to think I am in danger of being named on the Railroad Commission. . . . I don't think there is anything in it for me to feel elated."—Cooley to Mrs. Cooley, February 11, 1887, Cooley Papers.

14. For biographical detail on Wright and a bibliography of his writings, see S. N. D. North, "The Life and Work of Carroll Davidson Wright," in *Publications of the American Statistical Association*, September 1909, pp. 447–466, 550–61.

15. John Lamb to William W. Folwell, October 3, 1888, Folwell Papers, Minnesota State Historical Society.

16. Testimony of Gould, September 5, 1883, *Report on Labor and Capital*, Vol. I, p. 1084; testimony of Miller, September 7, 1883, *ibid.*, Vol. II, pp. 25–26; testimony of Medill, September 26, 1883, *ibid.*, Vol. II, p. 987.

17. Cooley Diary, entry April 7, 1888, Cooley Papers.

18. William Ashley to Richard T. Ely (around 1888), Ely Papers.

19. "Editorial Notes," *Our Day*, December 1888, pp. 524–25.

20. Testimony of Samuel Gompers, August 18, 1883, *Report on Labor and Capital*, Vol. I, p. 374.

21. Testimony of Adolph Strasser, August 21, 1883, *ibid.*, p. 460.

22. Testimony of Frank Foster, August 27, 1883, *ibid.*, p. 668; Gompers to Folwell, April 21, 1889, Folwell Papers, Minnesota State Historical Society. Gunton's pamphlet was a condensation of his exceedingly popular *Wealth and Progress* (New York: Appleton, 1887).

23. Carroll D. Wright, *Industrial Depressions*, 46th Cong., 1st sess., House of Representatives Ex. Doc., Vol. XV, No. 1, Part 5, pp. 257, 286–89; *Problems of the Census* (Boston, 1887), p. 20 [pamphlet]; "The Relation of Production to Productive Capacity," *The Forum*, November 1897, p. 290; February 1898, pp. 671, 673–74.

24. Uriel H. Crocker, *The Depression in Trade and Wages of Labor* (Boston: W. B. Clarke and Carruth, 1886), p. 27. Crocker (1832–1902) wrote a large number of pamphlets and newspaper articles attacking the orthodox doctrine that no general overproduction can occur.

25. F. W. Henshaw, "Commercial Crises," T   Berkeley Quarterly, January 1881, pp. 82–90. For biographical data, see   e *San Francisco Chronicle*, June 9, 1929, the *San Francisco Examiner*, June   1929.

26. Frederick B. Hawley, Address to Tariff Commission, August 14, 1882, 47th Cong., 2d sess., House of Representatives Misc. Doc. No. 6, Part 1, p. 410;

reprinted as "The Determination of a Tariff Policy by a Scientific Formula," *Bulletin of the National Association of Wool Manufacturers*, Vol. XII (1882), pp. 324–25. For biographical data, see *Williams College Bulletin, Alumni Obituary Record*, April 1930, p. 3.

27. Hawley, "The Ratio of Capital to Consumption," *The National Quarterly Review*, July 1879, p. 116.

28. Hawley, "The Fundamental Error of *Kapital und Kapitalzins*," *The Quarterly Journal of Economics*, April 1892, p. 286; "The Risk Theory of Profit," *ibid.*, July 1893, pp. 461, 473–76; "Enterprise and Profit," *ibid.*, November 1900, p. 75. Hawley in 1917 published a more elaborate and systematic discussion of his views, *Enterprise and the Productive Process* (New York: Putnam, 1917). Simon N. Patten had earlier presented a somewhat similar theory of monopoly gains.

29. Hawley, "Edward Atkinson's Economic Theories," *The Forum*, May 1889, pp. 303–304. Hawley's views on business cycles are presented in Paul Barnett, *Business-Cycle Theory in the United States, 1860–1900* (Chicago: University of Chicago Press, 1941), pp. 33–47.

30. George Basil Dixwell, "Review of Bastiat's Sophisms of Protection," *Bulletin of the National Association of Wool Manufacturers*, Vol. XI (1881), pp. 251–52. For biographical data, see "Obituary," *ibid.*, Vol. XV (1885), p. 96.

31. Wells to Atkinson, January 12, 1888, Atkinson Papers.

32. A popular "orthodox" statement at the time was that of the free-trade, hard-money journalist, Richard R. Bowker: "What we miscall 'over-production' [or] 'under-consumption' is largely the misdirection of labor—overproduction of the wrong thing and under-production of the right thing. . . . What we know as 'hard times,' 'bad trade,' etc., seem to depend upon the directors of industry as affected by the margin of profits."—Bowker, *Economics for the People* (New York: Harper, 1886, fourth edition, 1893), pp. 177–78, 182.

33. [D. MacG. Means], "Wells' *Recent Economic Changes*," *The Nation*, December 5, 1889, p. 454 (authorship supplied by *The Nation*); J. Laurence Laughlin, "David Ames Wells," *The Journal of Political Economy*, December 1898, p. 95.

34. Judson Grenell to Bray, May 31, 1883, Bray Papers, Columbia University Library.

35. Joseph A. Labadie to Richard T. Ely, December 12, 1886, Ely Papers. Labadie later became a philosophical anarchist.

36. *Report of the Proceedings of the Sixth National Convention of the Socialistic Labor Party* (New York, 1887), pp. 14, 15 [pamphlet].

37. Albert F. Brayton, H. Puck, P. Peterson, to William W. Folwell, September 10, 1888; W. G. H. Smart to Folwell, September 16, 1888, Folwell Papers, Minnesota State Historical Society.

A draft of Folwell's reply, dated September 1888, stated that the questions presented an embarrassing dilemma: if the writer denied the Ricardian statement of the iron law of wages, he would be called an "unorthodox economist"; agreeing with it, he would be called illogical if he asserted that protection probably might prevent or modify the operation of the law.

38. Smart to Folwell, September 28, 1888, Folwell Papers.

39. Johann Most, "Why I Am A Communist," *Twentieth Century*, May 22, 1890.

40. "No Room for Socialists," *Minneapolis Tribune*, September 26, 1887 [editorial].

41. Graham Taylor, *Pioneering on Social Frontiers* (Chicago: University of Chicago Press, 1930), p. 136. For a comprehensive study, see Henry David,

The History of the Haymarket Affair (New York: Farrar and Rinehart, 1936).

42. Benjamin R. Tucker, "General [Francis A.] Walker and the Anarchists," 1887, reprinted in *Instead of a Book*, p. 386.

CHAPTER VI

1. For biographical detail on George (1839–1897), see Henry George, Jr., *The Life of Henry George* (New York: Doubleday and McClure, 1900); see also the biography George's daughter, Anna George De Mille, published in *The American Journal of Economics and Sociology*, beginning with the April 1942 issue; see also Charles A. Barker's very suggestive "Henry George and the California Background of 'Progress and Poverty,'" in *California Historical Society Quarterly*, June 1945, pp. 97–115.

2. *Report of the Commissioners Appointed by the Governor* [of New York] *to Revise the Laws for the Assessment and Collection of Taxes* (Albany, 1871), pp. 101–108; for George's opinion of the report, see his *Our Land and Land Policy* (San Francisco, 1871), pp. 39, 48 [pamphlet].

3. George to Wells, September 19, 1871, Wells Papers.

4. Del Mar complained: "My fellow townsman, Mr. Henry George, in his work on *Progress and Poverty*, has adopted the author's postulate with reference to the origin of interest, but has nowhere given him credit for it. As to the uses which have been made of this postulate, by associating it with wages and other foreign subjects, the author entirely dissents both from Mr. George's methods and conclusions."—Alex. Del Mar, *The Science of Money*, p. 98, ft.

5. For the strong influence of Mill on George, see George to Mill, July 16, 1870, Mill Letters, Hutzler Collection, Economic Classics, Johns Hopkins University Library.

6. Michael Flürscheim, *Rent, Interest and Wages* (London: Reeves, 1892, third edition, 1895), p. vii; Thomas E. Will, "Henry George," *The Industrialist*, November 15, 1897, p. 220.

7. George Basil Dixwell, *Review of "Progress and Poverty"* (Cambridge: Wilson, 1882), p. 46; William Lloyd Garrison, "Why I Am a Single Taxer," *Twentieth Century*, May 1, 1890.

8. Philip H. Wicksteed to George, October 26, 1882, George Papers, New York Public Library.

9. Samuel B. Clarke, *Current Objections to the Exaction of Economic Rent by Taxation Considered* (New York, 1889), p. 30 [pamphlet]. Clarke wrote a suggestive essay on property as power, *An Examination of Some of the Bases of Current Economic Theory* (New York, 1909) [pamphlet].

10. Marx to John Swinton, June 2, 1881, in "Unpublished Letters of Karl Marx and Friedrich Engels to Americans," translated and edited by Leonard E. Mins, *Science and Society*, Spring 1938, p. 227; Marx to Sorge, June 30, 1881, translation in George Raymond Geiger's *The Philosophy of Henry George*, (New York: Macmillan, 1933), p. 238.

11. W. T. Harris, "Henry George's Mistakes about Land," *The Forum*, July 1887, p. 435.

12. Frank Crowell to Folwell, January 29, 1889, Folwell Papers.

13. C. Osborne Ward, *A Labor Catechism of Political Economy* (Washington: privately printed, 1877, 1892), p. 272.

14. For an excellent biography of Bellamy, see Arthur E. Morgan, *Edward Bellamy* (New York: Columbia University Press, 1944).

15. Edward Bellamy, "What 'Nationalism' Means," *The Contemporary Review*, July 1890, p. 18.

16. Bellamy to William Dean Howells, in Morgan, *op. cit.*, p. 192.

17. Bellamy to J. B. Clark, July 1, 1889, Clark Papers; Baxter to Richard T. Ely, March 14, 1894, Ely Papers.

18. "Nationalist Declaration of Principles," in Richard T. Ely, *Socialism* (New York: Crowell, 1894), p. 380.

19. Caro Lloyd, *Henry Demarest Lloyd, 1847–1903* (New York: Putnam, 1912), Vol. I, p. 141.

20. Morgan, *op. cit.*, p. 389.

21. Burnette G. Haskell, "Why I Am a Nationalist," *Twentieth Century*, May 15, 1890.
Haskell had in 1883 attempted unsuccessfully to unite the philosophical anarchists, the anarchists of the deed, and the political action socialists on a common platform of revolutionary action.—Haskell to Joseph A. Labadie, September 12, 1883, Labadie Collection, University of Michigan Library. A comprehensive discussion of, and documents on, the matter is in C. M. Destler, *American Radicalism* (New London, Conn.: Connecticut College, 1946), pp. 82–104.
The following year Haskell proclaimed that money was the essential problem of socialism and proposed "labor notes" like those of the philosophical anarchists. More concretely he argued like the greenbackers that the government should issue a currency amounting to not less than $100 per head of the population.—Haskell, "Supplemental Chapter," in A. J. Starkweather and S. Robert Wilson, *Socialism* (New York, 1884), pp. 77–81 [pamphlet].

22. Gronlund to Folwell, February 28, 1891, enclosing circular, dated February 22, 1891, Folwell Papers. Gronlund to Richard T. Ely, April 16, 1891, enclosing a circular, Ely Papers.

23. The movement had its roots in the earlier short-lived Christian Socialism of the late forties and early fifties in England, led by the Reverend Frederick Denison Maurice, professor of English literature and history at King's College, London. The earlier movement was composed of "social conservative critics" of capitalism and classical political economy. It attempted at the same time to meet the challenge of the "un-Christian socialism" of the French revolution of 1848.

24. W. D. P. Bliss, "Why Am I a Christian Socialist?" *Twentieth Century*, October 2, 1890.

25. Bliss, "Workingmen in Politics: The Prophecy of an Industrial Democracy," *Work and Wages*, June 1887, p. 1.

26. Bliss, *What is Christian Socialism?* reprinted from *The Dawn*, January-February 1890, pp. 39–45; "Constitution of the Union Reform League," in *What to Do: A Program of Christian Socialism*, p. 14 [pamphlet]; neither place nor date of publication is given; it probably was San Francisco, around 1898, since he organized the league there in 1898. Bliss advocated trade-union rates and hours at least as early as 1892. See *The Dawn*, April 1892, p. 11.

27. Bliss to Richard T. Ely, March 30, December 2, 1891, Ely Papers; *The Dawn*, December 4, 1890, p. 7, and April 1892, p. 11.

28. *The American Fabian*, February 1895 [editorial].

29. [Bliss], "Fabian Socialism," *The Encyclopedia of Social Reform* (New York: Funk & Wagnalls, 1897), edited by Bliss, pp. 578–80.

30. Thomas Davidson to Morris R. Cohen, May 29, 1899, in *Memorials of Thomas Davidson*, collected and edited by William Knight (London: Unwin,

1907), pp. 142–43; see also Davidson, "The Single Tax," *Journal of Social Science*, October 1890, pp. 8–14.

31. *Statements of Objects, Results and Action of the National Social and Political Conference Held at Buffalo, New York, June 28 to July 3, 1899,* circular in Ely Papers; Bliss, "The Social Reform Union," *The Arena*, August 1899, p. 272; "A Plea for Union or What Is the Social Reform Union?" *The Social Forum*, September 1899, p. 128.

CHAPTER VII

1. A biographical account of James and a bibliography of his work appear in "Personal Notes," *Annals of the American Academy of Political and Social Sciences*, January 1896, pp. 78–86, and March 1901, pp. 318–21.

2. E. J. James, "Views of the Economists on the Silver Question," *Science*, March 19, 1886, Supplement, pp. 267–68; "Recent Labor Legislation," *The Labor Movement*, edited by George E. McNeill (New York: Hazen, 1888), p. 65; "Socialists and Anarchists in the United States," *Our Day*, February 1888, pp. 93–94.

3. For biographical detail, see Richard T. Ely, *Ground Under Our Feet* (New York: Macmillan, 1938).

4. Richard T. Ely, "The Past and the Present of Political Economy," *Johns Hopkins University Studies in Historical and Political Science*, March 1884, pp. 143–202. The monograph centered its attack on orthodox economics by criticizing Mill's rigid conception of the economic man in the first part of Mill's early paper, "The Definition of Political Economy." But he used Mill's later *Principles of Political Economy* as a textbook, and even after he published his own treatise he recommended Mill to his students to "expand such doctrines as rent, etc."—John R. Commons to Ely, September 8, 1890, Ely Papers.

5. Ely to the editor, *The Home Missionary*, October 1884, p. 227; "Open Letter from Prof. Ely," *The [Baltimore] Sun*, March 9, 1886. For an illuminating account of the role of religion in Ely's economics, see John R. Everett, *Religion in Economics* (New York: King's Crown Press, 1946), pp. 75–98.

6. Ely, *French and German Socialism in Modern Times* (New York: Harper, 1883), p. 173; "Pullman: A Social Study," *Harper's New Monthly Magazine*, December 1884, pp. 452–66; "The Baltimore and Ohio Employés' Relief Association," *Harper's Weekly*, July 4, 1885; "The Growth of Corporations," *Harper's New Monthly Magazine*, June 1887, pp. 71–79.

7. [Simon Newcomb], "Dr. Ely on the Labor Movement," *The Nation*, October 7, 1886. For Newcomb's authorship, see R. C. Archibald, "Simon Newcomb, 1835–1905; Bibliography of his Life and Works," *Memoirs of the National Academy of Sciences*, Vol. XVII (1924), p. 60.

8. *Science*, October 29, 1886. "Of course the common assertion that I favor socialism is absolutely without foundation. It is a wilful, deliberate lie. It is a mean, cowardly method of attack."—Ely to John Bates Clark, December 1, 1886, Clark Papers.

9. Andrew D. White to Ely, July 6, 1885, Ely Papers.

10. [Charles Lee Smith], "Richard T. Ely's Career," *Indianapolis News*, December 26, 1890. For Smith's authorship, see his bibliography in "Herbert B. Adams: Tributes of Friends; With a Bibliography of the Department of History, Politics, and Economics of the Johns Hopkins University, 1876–1901,"

Johns Hopkins University Studies in Historical and Political Science, Vol. XX (1902), Supplement, p. 126.

11. Frank A. Fetter, "John Rogers Commons," in *The American Philosophical Society Year Book,* 1945, p. 362.

12. Ely staunchly upheld the doctrine of rent at the time. "No doctrine in political economy is more firmly established than that of rent. It has been attacked innumerable times, but the result of every attack has been simply to strengthen it in every essential point. English, French, and Italian political economists all equally accept it, while even the most daring German criticism has never shaken this stronghold of economic science."–Ely, "Land, Labor, and Taxation," No. 1, *The Independent,* December 1, 1887.

13. For a biographical account of Adams, see S. Lawrence Bigelow, I. Leo Sharfman, and R. M. Wenley, "Henry Carter Adams," *The Journal of Political Economy,* April 1922, pp. 201–11 (this includes a selected bibliography); "Memorial to Former President Henry C. Adams," *The American Economic Review,* September 1922, pp. 401–16. Lazar Volin has presented a sympathetic critique, "Henry Carter Adams: Critic of Laissez Faire," *Journal of Social Philosophy,* April 1938, pp. 235–50.

14. Henry C. Adams, *Outline of Lectures upon Political Economy* (Baltimore: privately printed, 1881), pp. 12, 35–36; (second edition, Ann Arbor: privately printed, 1886), pp. 23–25, 43–44; Adams' review of John Bates Clark's *The Philosophy of Wealth,* in *Political Science Quarterly,* December 1886, p. 689; Adams to E. R. A. Seligman, May 14, 1904, copy in Adams Papers, in possession of Mrs. Henry Carter Adams, Ann Arbor, Michigan.

15. Adams, "The Labor Problem," *Scientific American Supplement,* August 21, 1886; see also Adams' statement in *The Labor Problem,* edited by William E. Barns (New York: Harper, 1886), pp. 62–63.

16. See Henry W. Sage's comments on Adams' address in *Scientific American Supplement,* August 28, 1886; see also "Memorial to Former President Henry C. Adams," *op. cit.,* p. 405.

17. Adams, "Relation of the State to Industrial Action," *Publications of the American Economic Association,* January 1887, pp. 471–549. Adams later stated explicitly that any "reasoning upon wages must rest upon the opinion that the matter is very largely one of diplomacy and controversy between organized interests. The theoretic question . . . proceeds no farther than to lay down certain very loosely defined limits beyond which the contending parties cannot go in their encroachment upon the dividends demanded by the others."–Adams to J. B. Clark, no date but probably around 1907, Clark Papers.

18. Adams agreed that the classification of diminishing, constant, and increasing returns was that of Mill except so far as the law of increasing returns was substituted for Mill's consideration of monopoly prices. But he felt that the phenomena of increasing returns had been little discussed previously.–Adams to Charles J. Bullock, April 14, 1902, Adams Papers.

19. Adams, *Public Debts* (New York: Appleton, 1887), p. 394.

20. Adams, "Suggestions for a System of Taxation," *Publications of the Michigan Political Science Association,* May 1894, p. 60; "Publicity and Corporate Abuses," *ibid.,* pp. 116, 119; Adams to George W. Knight, August 28, 1894, copy in Adams Papers.

21. Adams to Seligman, June 7, 1901, in "Seligman Correspondence," No. 2, edited by Joseph Dorfman, *Political Science Quarterly,* June 1941, p. 274.

22. Adams, "Interstate Commerce Act–Discussion," *Publications of the Michigan Political Science Association,* May 1893, p. 143; "Commercial Valuation of Railway Operating Property in the United States, 1904," in Bureau of

the Census *Bulletin* No. 21 (Washington, 1906), p. 8; "Valuation of Public Service Utilities," *Publications of the American Economic Association*, April 1910, p. 193.

23. Adams to Seligman, June 1, 1896, in "Seligman Correspondence," No. 2, p. 273.

24. Cited in Eric F. Goldman, "J. Allen Smith: The Reformer and His Dilemma," *The Pacific Northwest Quarterly*, July 1944, p. 197. "I believe in international bimetallism because I think that a gradually depreciating monetary standard is necessary to continued prosperity."—Adams to F. V. Brooks and R. H. Morrow, July 10, 1896, copy in Adams Papers.

25. Adams, *The Science of Finance* (New York: Holt, 1899), p. 350. This theory of depressions Adams used to offer some theoretical validity for progressive taxation. He defended it by saying: If now it is true that such taxation imposes a "higher payment upon realized success than upon effort," thereby tending to check the further "concentration of industrial property and to weaken the motive to industrial expansion on the part of the most successful," then a more equitable division of industrial incomes will result. "This in turn will cause a diffusion of purchasing power in the community and act as a relief to the stocking of the market."—*Ibid.*, pp. 350–51.

26. Statement of Adams, in Ely, "Report of the Organization of the American Economic Association," *Publications of the American Economic Association*, March 1886, p. 21.

27. C. S. Walker to J. B. Clark, November 19, 1886, Clark Papers; see also Walker, "The Future of the Organization of Labor," *Work and Wages*, March 1887. For biographical information on Walker, see "Charles Swan Walker," *Bulletin of Yale University*, October 15, 1933, pp. 7–9.

28. C. S. Walker, "The Farmers' Alliance," *The Andover Review*, August 1890, pp. 127–40; "The Farmer Movement," *Annals of the American Academy of Political and Social Science*, March 1894, p. 792.

29. John Bascom, *Sociology* (New York: Putnam, 1887), pp. 225–26, 230–37; "The Gist of the Labor Question," *The Forum*, September 1887, pp. 92–95; *Social Theory* (New York: Crowell, 1895), pp. 420–21; *Things Learned by Living* (New York: Putnam, 1913), p. 157. For earlier views of Bascom, see Dorfman, *op. cit.*, Vol. II, pp. 572–75, 957, 967.

30. Before becoming president of Brown University in 1889, E. Benjamin Andrews was Professor of Homiletics at Newton Theological Institute, 1879–82; Professor of History and Political Economy at Brown University, 1882–88; Professor of Political Economy and Finance at Cornell University, 1888–89.

31. Andrews' original scheme is embodied in "An Honest Dollar," *Publications of the American Economic Association*, November 1889, pp. 401–43. A year before publication he submitted the monograph to the Cornell authorities in applying for the Cornell position.—Henry C. Adams to Seligman, December 23, 1889, Seligman Papers, Columbia University Library. For his free silver view, see "The Fall of Prices," in *An Honest Dollar* (Hartford: Student Publishing Co., 1896), p. xxviii; for his change, see the *New York Evening Post*, May 25, 1903.

32. Andrews, *Institutes of Economics* (Boston: Silver, Burdett, 1889), pp. 15, 24, 166–67, 170; review of Achille Loria's *Analisi della proprietá capitalista*, in *Political Science Quarterly*, December 1890, p. 719.

33. Andrews, "Trusts According to Official Investigations," *The Quarterly Journal of Economics*, January 1889, pp. 150–52; "The Economic Law of Monopoly," *Journal of Social Science*, February 1890, p. 6; "Symposium upon the Relation of the State to the Individual," *The Dawn*, November 1890, p. 300;

"Are There Too Many of Us?" *The North American Review*, November 1892, p. 607; "Individualism as a Sociological Principle," *The Yale Review*, May 1893, p. 27; *Wealth and Moral Law* (Hartford: Hartford Seminary Press, 1894), pp. 48–49, 133.

34. For biographical details, see "Memorial Addresses on the Life and Services of Simon N. Patten," *Annals of the American Academy of Political and Social Science*, May 1923, pp. 333–67; Rexford G. Tugwell, "Notes on the Life and Work of Simon Nelson Patten," *The Journal of Political Economy*, April 1923, pp. 153–208. For bibliography and analysis, see James Lane Boswell, *The Economics of Simon Nelson Patten* (Philadelphia: privately printed, 1933).

35. For the clearest though somewhat overcritical analysis of Patten's protectionism, see Ugo Rabbeno, *The American Commercial Policy* (London: Macmillan, 1895), pp. 384–411.

36. Copy in author's possession.

37. Patten to Franklin H. Giddings, August 27, 1897, Giddings Papers, Columbia University Library.

38. Patten, *The Premises of Political Economy* (Philadelphia: Lippincott, 1885), p. 59.

39. Patten, "The Stability of Prices," *Publications of the American Economic Association*, January 1889, p. 428.

40. Patten, "Economics in Elementary Schools," *Annals of the American Academy of Political and Social Science*, January 1895, pp. 24–25.

41. Patten to Giddings, August 19, 1895, Giddings Papers; Patten believed as ardently in the gold standard as in the protective tariff. See Patten, "Wells' Recent Economic Changes," *Political Science Quarterly*, March 1890, p. 91.

42. Patten to Folwell, May 27, 1889, Folwell Papers, Minnesota State Historical Society.

43. Patten, "Malthus and Ricardo," 1889, reprinted in his *Essays in Economic Theory*, edited by R. G. Tugwell (New York: Knopf, 1924), p. 31; "The Interpretation of Ricardo," 1893, *ibid.*, p. 159.

44. Ely to Clark, May 2, 1902, Ely Papers.

45. Patten to Giddings, March 24, 1898, Giddings Papers; Patten to Roswell C. McCrea, April 7, 1909, McCrea Papers, in author's possession.

CHAPTER VIII

1. For a bibliography of Clark's work, see *A Bibliography of the Faculty of Political Science of Columbia University, 1880–1930*, compiled by Milton Halsey Thomas (New York: Columbia University Press, 1931), pp. 77–90. A volume of lengthy extracts from the writings of John Bates Clark and his prominent son, John Maurice Clark, has been published by Emile James, *John Bates Clark et John Maurice Clark* (Paris: Librairie Dalloz, 1948). For the most detailed discussion of Clark's views, see Paul T. Homan, *Contemporary Economic Thought* (New York: Harper, 1928), pp. 17–103.

2. Julius Seelye to James Buell, October 31, 1879, copy in Wells Papers, Library of Congress; Seelye to William F. Warren, July 10, 1875, Clark Papers.

3. Daniel C. Gilman to Clark, September 1 [1876], Clark Papers. Clark did not have a German doctorate, but Amherst awarded him an honorary Doctor of Philosophy in 1890.

4. Clark to E. R. A. Seligman, September 26, 1895, in "Seligman Correspondence," No. 1, edited by Joseph Dorfman, *Political Science Quarterly*, March 1941, p. 115.

5. Clark had the conception in an embryonic form as early as 1875, according to lecture notes of that year, especially Lecture IV, Clark Papers.

6. Clark, "The Unit of Wealth," *Staatswissenschaftliche Arbeiten: Festgaben für Karl Knies* (Berlin: O. Herring, 1896), p. 3; see also Clark to Seligman, September 6, 1906, in "Seligman Correspondence," No. 1, p. 117.

7. Clark, "The New Philosophy of Wealth," *The New Englander*, January 1877, pp. 170–72, 174; "Unrecognized Forces in Political Economy," *ibid.*, October 1877, pp. 713, 719, 722, 723; "Business Ethics, Past and Present," *ibid.*, March 1879, p. 161; "The Nature and Progress of True Socialism," *ibid.*, July 1879, pp. 577, 579; "The Philosophy of Value," *ibid.*, July 1881, pp. 464, 467; "Non-Competitive Economics," *ibid.*, November 1882, pp. 843–45.

8. One of Clark's rare deprecating utterances about specific persons was directed against Sumner. "He [Sumner] is a prominent man, but if he is a great man I have never done him justice. He seems to me to be chiefly what Pres[ident Francis A.] Walker once called him, a cantankerous man."–Clark to Ely, May 30, 1889, Ely Papers.

9. Giddings to Clark, October 24, 1886, Clark Papers; [Giddings], "Economic Notes," *Work and Wages*, November 1886.

10. Folwell to Clark, November 7, 1886, Clark Papers; Clark to Folwell, November 9, 1886, Folwell Papers, Minnesota State Historical Society.

11. [Arthur T. Hadley], "Recent Works on Economic Theory," *The Independent*, February 10, 1887; Hadley to Clark, February 19, 1887, Clark Papers.

12. Horace White to Ginn & Company, November 24, 1886, copy in Clark Papers.

13. Woodrow Wilson to Clark in *John Bates Clark, A Memorial* (privately printed, 1938), p. 20; Henry C. Adams' review of *The Philosophy of Wealth*, in *Political Science Quarterly*, December 1886, p. 688; C. S. Walker to Clark, November 19, 1886, Clark Papers.

14. Clark considered the confiscation feature of George's plan as "essentially the whole of it, and that I never can see as anything but an inequity."–Clark to Ely, January 24, 1888, November 13, 1890, Ely Papers.

15. Clark to Members of the Committee of the American Economic Association on Economic Theory, 1890, ms. in Clark Papers.

16. Clark, "Capital and Its Earnings," *Publications of the American Economic Association*, May 1888, pp. 88–149.

17. Clark, *The Distribution of Wealth* (New York: Macmillan, 1899), p. viii.

18. Clark, "Possibility of a Scientific Law of Wages," *Publications of the American Economic Association*, March 1889, pp. 37–69; Clark to Seligman, May 30, 1891, in "Seligman Correspondence," No. 1, p. 114. For the most succinct statement of Clark's theory of distribution, see his "Distribution, Laws of," *Dictionary of Political Economy*, edited by R. H. Inglis Palgrave (London: Macmillan, 1894), Vol. I, pp. 599–602. This is not in the printed bibliographies.

19. Clark, "The Crisis in Colorado and Its Lessons," *Business America*, June 1914, pp. 502–504.

20. Clark, "Is Authoritative Arbitration Inevitable?" *Political Science Quarterly*, December 1902, pp. 566–67; "The Theory of Collective Bargaining," *Publications of the American Economic Association*, April 1909, p. 38; George E. Barnett, "The Theory of Collective Bargaining–Discussion," *ibid.*, p. 47; Thomas S. Adams, *ibid.*, p. 53.

21. Clark, "The Dynamics of the Wages Question," *Publications of the American Economic Association*, February 1903, pp. 141–42.

22. Clark, English ms. copy of introduction to Japanese edition of *The Phi-*

losophy of Wealth, Clark Papers; "The Study of Economics," *University Extension*, February 1894, p. 253 (this article is not in the printed bibliographies).

23. Clark to Adams, August 12, 1901, Adams Papers.

24. Adams to Seligman, June 1, 1896, "Seligman Correspondence," No. 2, p. 274.

25. These works were Karl Rodbertus' *Overproduction and Crises*, translated by Julia Franklin (London: Sonnenschein, 1898), and Werner Sombart's *Socialism and Social Movements in the 19th Century*, translated by Anson P. Atterbury (New York: Putnam, 1898).

26. Clark to Seligman, April 6, 1892, in "Seligman Correspondence," No. 1, p. 115; Clark, "The Referendum in the United States," *The Independent*, February 20, 1902.

27. Clark to Ely, February 1, 1888, November 3, 1890, March 17, 1891, Ely Papers.

28. Clark, "The Modern Appeal to Legal Forces in Economic Life," *Publications of the American Economic Association*, October-December 1894, pp. 483–84.

29. "New tools promote centralization, and centralization calls for new tools."—Clark to McCrea, January 26, 1901, letter pasted in McCrea's copy of *The Distribution of Wealth*, in author's possession.

30. "The opening of foreign countries means not only a chance to sell goods with profit, but a chance to invest our own capital with an even larger and more permanent profit."—Clark, review of Charles A. Conant's *The United States in the Orient*, in *Political Science Quarterly*, March 1901, p. 143.

31. Clark, "The Necessity of Suppressing Monopolies While Retaining Trusts," *Chicago Conference on Trusts* (Chicago: The Civic Federation of Chicago, 1900), p. 408. This suggestion was made somewhat earlier by the editor of the *Economist* of Cincinnati, Grover Pease Osborne. He declared that if the monopolist "can be compelled to sell everywhere at the same price, his power to obtain excessive prices is partly or completely destroyed." Osborne also suggested that through advertising or other devices for building up a "good name" a manufacturer could obtain a species of monopoly; that is, charge a higher price for his product than another manufacturer, or, in fact, prevent any competition at all for a substantially identical product.—Osborne, *Principles of Economics* (Cincinnati: Robert Clarke and Company, 1893), pp. 375–77, 384.

32. Testimony of Clark, December 11, 1911, *Hearings Before the Senate Committee on Interstate Commerce*, 62d Cong., Vol. I (1912), pp. 974, 975, 983, 985.

33. Clark, "The Gold Standard of Currency in the Light of Recent Theory," *Political Science Quarterly*, September 1895, p. 395.

34. John Maurice Clark to author, November 8, 1947.

CHAPTER IX

1. "The Constitution of the Society for the Study of National Economy," in Richard T. Ely, *Ground Under Our Feet*, Appendix 3, pp. 296–99.

2. John Bates Clark to William W. Folwell, June 25, 1885, Folwell Papers, Minnesota State Historical Society.

3. Ely, "Report of the Organization of the American Economic Association," *Publications of the American Economic Association*, March 1886, pp. 6–7.

4. Ely to E. R. A. Seligman, June 9, 1885, in "Seligman Correspondence," No. 2, p. 281.

5. Simon N. Patten to Ely, July 13, 1885, in Ely, *Ground Under Our Feet,* p. 137.

6. Statement in Ely, "Report of the Organization of the American Economic Association," *op. cit.,* pp. 21–22, 26, 27, 29, 35.

7. Francis A. Walker to Seligman, September 24, [1887], in "Seligman Correspondence," No. 1, pp. 109–10.

8. Simon Newcomb, "Aspects of the Economic Discussion," *Science,* June 18, 1886.

9. Edward Clark Lunt, *The Present Condition of Economic Science* (New York: Putnam, 1888), p. 113.

10. *Publications of the American Economic Association,* July 1889, p. 314.

11. Seligman to Ely, January 29, 1887, Ely Papers; Ely to Seligman, October 22, 1890, "Seligman Correspondence," No. 2, p. 282.

12. The work of the subcommittee on consumption is in the Folwell Papers, University of Minnesota Library, with a covering letter from Clark "To the Members of the Committee on Terminology," dated March 17, 1890.

13. "Contributions to Theory: Report of the Committee," *Publications of the American Economic Association,* January–March 1891, p. 50.

14. George P. Garrison to Ely, December 24, 1888, Ely Papers.

15. *The National Revenues,* edited by Albert Shaw (Chicago: McClurg, 1881), p. 220. The contributors were Albert Shaw, William W. Folwell, Henry C. Adams, Richard T. Ely, Richmond Mayo-Smith, Robert Ellis Thompson, Edwin R. A. Seligman, Jesse Macy, J. B. Clark, Woodrow Wilson, Anson D. Morse, Irving J. Manatt, Arthur T. Hadley, Francis A. Walker, James H. Canfield, Arthur Yager, Edward W. Bemis, J. Laurence Laughlin, Carroll D. Wright.

16. D. Collin Wells, "Sociological Notes," *The Andover Review,* January 1889, p. 91.

17. William Jewett Tucker, "The Outline of an Elective Course of Study," *The Andover Review,* October 1889, p. 437.

CHAPTER X

1. *Congressional Record,* 54th Cong., 2d sess., p. 11.

2. *Chicago Conference on Trusts,* pp. 210, 219, 222, 285, 329–30. Gunton had a magazine, *The Social Economist* (later changed to *Gunton's Magazine*), and an Institute of Social Economics to spread his views, but former liberal benefactors, such as Professor Seligman, attributed Gunton's lack of influence to his being in the "pay of a great corporation."—Hayes Robbins to E. R. A. Seligman, July 14, 1904, Seligman Papers.

3. Cited in J. Laurence Laughlin, "The Study of Political Economy in the United States," *The Journal of Political Economy,* December 1892, p. 3.

4. *United States Strike Commission Report,* 53d Cong., 3d sess., Senate Ex. Doc., No. 7, pp. xxxi, 193; Caro Lloyd, *op. cit.,* p. 147; Allen Nevins, *Grover Cleveland* (New York: Dodd, Mead, 1933), pp. 611–28.

5. "Revolutionary Statesmanship," *Harper's Weekly,* November 24, 1894 [editorial].

6. Carroll D. Wright, "The Chicago Strike," *Publications of the American Economic Association,* October–December 1894, pp. 511–12; *ibid.,* March 1895, Supplement, pp. 62–64. Wright delivered the paper before the Association be-

cause it enabled him to bring before the public some novel points without being subject to the "criticism of talking through the press, which I have persistently avoided."—Wright to Seligman, December 21, 1894, in *Political Science Quarterly* files.

7. Testimony of Gompers, April 18, 1899, *Report of the Industrial Commission*, 56th Cong., 2d sess., House of Representatives Ex. Doc. No. 495, Vol. VII, p. 599.

8. Cited by John D. Hicks, *The Populist Revolt* (Minneapolis: University of Minnesota Press, 1931), p. 323.

9. Morrison I. Swift, "An Open Letter to the United States Senators and Representatives of Massachusetts," *Twentieth Century*, April 19, 1894. Swift wrote a number of utopias.

10. "Sociology," *Eleventh Annual Report of the Kansas Bureau of Labor and Industry* (1896), pp. 185–86; Edward A. Ross to the Bureau, March 28, 1896, *ibid.*, p. 198. Among the other economists who replied were Thomas Nixon Carver of Oberlin College, John Bates Clark of Columbia University, Willard Fisher of Wesleyan University, Herbert E. Mills of Vassar College, W. G. Langworthy Taylor of the University of Nebraska, W. F. Willcox of Cornell University, Frederick C. Clark of Ohio State University, and Frederick C. Hicks of Missouri State University.

11. *Twenty-Sixth Annual Report of the [Massachusetts] Board of Railway Commissioners* (Boston, 1895), p. 13.

12. "An Address By the National Executive Committee of the People's Party to the Citizens of the United States," *The Dawn*, September 1891, p. 9; "Platform of People's Party of Massachusetts," *ibid.*, p. 13.

13. Leland Stanford, "Government Loans on Real Estate," speech, March 10, 1890, *Congressional Record*, 51st Cong., 1st sess., pp. 2068–69; James B. Weaver, *A Call to Action* (Des Moines: Iowa Printing Co., 1892), pp. 328–29; Hicks, *op. cit.*, pp. 234–35.

14. "Repeal of the 10 per cent Circulation Tax," *Rhode's Journal of Banking*, August 1892, p. 855 [editorial].

15. Brooks Adams in 1879 had asserted that the Supreme Court had abdicated its high conservative role in upholding the constitutionality of the legal tenders, the "most painful and most humiliating chapter of American judicial history." —Adams, "The Supreme Court and the Currency," *The International Review*, June 1879, p. 641. Now he was blaming the bankers for eliminating the highly useful Bank of England inconvertible notes after the Napoleonic wars.

16. J. Laurence Laughlin, " 'Coin's' Food for the Gullible," *The Forum*, July 1895, p. 576.

17. H. C. Emery, review of Arthur Kitson's *A Scientific Solution of the Money Question*, in *Political Science Quarterly*, December 1895, p. 733; Arthur Latham Perry, *Williamstown and Williams College*, p. 697.

18. Michael D. Harter to Daniel Coit Gilman, February 16, 1892, in *Historical Scholarship in the United States, 1876–1901; As Revealed in the Correspondence of Herbert Baxter Adams*, edited by W. Stull Holt (Baltimore: Johns Hopkins Press, 1938), pp. 181–82.

19. Marcius Willson's *The Road to Prosperity and Philosophy of Bimetallism* (1896) was published under the auspices of the Democratic Congressional Committee. For early views of Willson, see Dorfman, *op. cit.*, Vol. II, pp. 767–69.

20. Edward Tuck to Manton Marble, May 17, 1900, Manton Marble Papers, Library of Congress.

21. "Bryan's Place in History," *The Bankers' Magazine*, November 1925, p. 69 [editorial].

22. William Jennings Bryan, "The Silver Question," *Speeches of William Jennings Bryan*, revised and arranged by Bryan (New York: Funk & Wagnalls, 1913 edition), Vol. I, pp. 262, 274, 279.

23. George F. Hoar to Francis A. Walker, July 5, 1893, Walker Papers, Library of Congress.

24. Frederic C. Howe, *The Confessions of a Reformer* (New York: Scribner, 1925), p. 147; John R. Commons, *Myself* (New York: Macmillan, 1934), pp. 82–83.

25. Paxton Hibben, *The Peerless Leader* (New York: Farrar and Rinehart, 1929), p. 201; Harry Thurston Peck, *Twenty Years of the Republic: 1885–1905* (New York: Dodd, Mead, 1913), p. 511; John P. Altgeld, "The Election of 1896," *Live Questions* (Chicago: Bowen, 1899), p. 691.

26. William Dean Howells to Aurelia H. Howells, April 13, 1898, in *Life in Letters of William Dean Howells*, edited by Mildred Howells (Garden City, N. Y.: Doubleday, Doran, 1928), Vol. II, p. 90.

27. William Jennings Bryan and Mary Baird Bryan, *The Memoirs of William Jennings Bryan* (Philadelphia: United Publishers of America, 1925), p. 123; Bryan, speech at the New York Reception, August 30, 1906, in *Speeches of William Jennings Bryan*, Vol. II, p. 75.

28. Benjamin R. Tucker, "The Attitude of Anarchism toward Industrial Combinations," *Chicago Conference on Trusts*, p. 261.

29. Tucker, "Edward Atkinson's Evolution," 1891, reprinted in *Instead of a Book*, pp. 282–84.

30. John F. Bray, entries in log books, June 26, 30, December 31, 1893, January 1894, in Columbia University Library; "Steps to Reform," 1894, ms. in Columbia University Library.

31. Michael Flürscheim, "Gold, Silver, Paper," *Twentieth Century*, September 5, 1895; Flürscheim to editor, *ibid.*, January 1896. For biographical data on Flürscheim, see Adolph Damaschke, *Geschichte der Nationalökonomie* (Jena: Fischer, 1905, twelfth edition, 1920), Vol. II, pp. 382–85.

32. Fred Heath and Edward H. James to Daniel De Leon, October 22, 1897, printed in Marvin Wachman, *History of the Social-Democratic Party of Milwaukee: 1897–1910* (Urbana: University of Illinois Press, 1945), p. 77.

33. *Proceedings of the Tenth National Convention of the Socialist Labor Party* (New York: New York Labor News Co., 1901), pp. 16, 86.

34. George D. Herron, "A Plea for the Unity of American Socialists," *The International Socialist Review*, December 1900, pp. 324–25. Herron was formerly professor of Applied Christianity at Iowa College (now Grinnell). He married the daughter of wealthy Carrie A. Rand, who had endowed his chair at Iowa College, and later left a bequest for what became the socialist Rand School for Social Science in New York in 1906.

35. George Shibley to Ely, March 20, 1900, in Ely Papers. Shibley was a Chicago lawyer, who, after accumulating a fortune as sales manager of a law publishing firm, became a publisher on his own and a reformer in general.

CHAPTER XI

1. David Kinley, "University Extension and the Workingman," *University Extension*, January 1894, p. 208.

2. Edward Thomas Devine, *Economics* (New York: Macmillan, 1898), pp. 358–59, 362.

3. F. W. Taussig to Ely, June 21, 1900, Ely Papers.

4. William W. Folwell, "The Higher Education of the Business Man," *Proceedings of the Tenth Annual Meeting of the Minnesota Bankers' Association* (1899), pp. 18–32.

5. Frederick R. Clow, "Economics as a School Study," *American Economic Association Publications, Economic Studies*, June 1899, p. 199.

6. Charles J. Bullock, "Political Economy in the Secondary Schools," *Education*, May 1891, pp. 541–42. Bullock's most significant theoretical contribution was a paper more precisely formulating the laws of return.–Bullock, "The Variation of Productive Forces," 1902, reprinted in *Economic Essays* (Cambridge: Harvard University Press, 1936), pp. 84–120.

7. R. H. Jesse to Ely, December 5, 1891, Ely Papers. The successful candidate was Frederick C. Hicks, who received his doctorate under Henry C. Adams at Michigan. He later went to the University of Cincinnati where, after serving as dean of the College of Commerce, he became president.

8. Cited from *Chicago Journal* in *Public Opinion*, October 17, 1895.

9. Charles H. Hull to E. R. A. Seligman, August 6, 1897, "Seligman Correspondence," No. 2, p. 285.

10. A split in the Association threatened in 1895 when the central states organized an additional and broader organization. This was primarily a protest of Western members against the "domination" of Eastern members in the American Economic Association.–Jesse Macy to Ely, April 19, 1895, Ely Papers; Henry C. Adams to J. B. Clark, January 14, 1895, Adams Papers. The threatened break was healed when the American Economic Association held its 1895 meeting in Indianapolis and elected Henry C. Adams as president.

11. William Ashley to Ely, November 25, 1899, Ely Papers.

12. Folwell, "The New Economics," *Publications of the American Economic Association*, January 1893, p. 25.

13. Thomas G. Shearman, "Statistics of Capital in Industry–Discussion" *American Economic Association Publications, Economic Studies*, April 1899, Supplement, p. 69.

14. Ashley, "The Relation of Sociology to Economics–Discussion," *Publications of the American Economic Association*, March 1895, Supplement, p. 117.

15. On the committee during its two years of study sat William Cunningham, E. C. K. Gonner, H. S. Foxwell, J. N. Keynes, Henry Higgs, F. Y. Edgeworth, L. L. Price, and J. Shield Nicholson.

16. Tentative report of the committee, "The Methods of Economic Training in This and Other Countries," in *Report of the Sixty-third Meeting of the British Association for the Advancement of Science* (1893), pp. 571–72; E. C. K. Gonner, "On the Methods of Economic Training Adopted in Foreign Countries . . . ," in *Report of the Sixty-fourth Meeting of the British Association for the Advancement of Science* (1894), p. 381.

17. C. F. Bastable, Presidential Address before Section F, in *Report of the Sixty-fourth Meeting of the British Association for the Advancement of Science*, pp. 722, 725–28.

18. Emily G. Balch, *Outline of Economics* (Cambridge, Mass.: privately printed, 1899), p. 30.

19. Sidney Sherwood to Ely, November 23, 1891, Ely Papers. The historian Carl Becker much later made his reputation by developing a similar line of analysis.

20. Sherwood, "The Formulation of the Normal Laws with Especial Reference to the Theory of Utility–Discussion," *American Economic Association Publications, Economic Studies*, April 1896, Supplement, pp. 129–30; "The

Philosophical Basis of Economics," *Annals of the American Academy of Political and Social Science*, September 1897, p. 226.

21. Eugen von Böhm-Bawerk, "Macvane's Political Economy," *The Quarterly Journal of Economics*, April 1890, p. 332.

22. Silas M. Macvane, "The Prospect of a Gold Premium," *The Nation*, March 13, 1884.

23. Macvane, "Marginal Utility and Value," *The Quarterly Journal of Economics*, April 1893, p. 269; "The Austrian Theory of Value," *Annals of the American Academy of Political and Social Science*, November 1893, p. 358. For a modern statement of this old controversy, see L. M. Fraser, *Economic Thought and Language* (London: Black, 1937), pp. 92–104.

24. The eminent Cambridge economist Alfred Marshall took over the term "waiting" from Macvane and perpetuated it in economic literature.

25. In this emphasis on the cost and consequences of "waiting," Macvane antedated his more renowned colleague, Taussig.

26. Macvane, "Analysis of Cost of Production," *The Quarterly Journal of Economics*, July 1887, pp. 483–86.

27. Macvane, "The Theory of Business Profits," *The Quarterly Journal of Economics*, October 1887, p. 12.

28. Green was a graduate of Alfred University, where he taught Latin for two years. Ely unsuccessfully tried to find a suitable post where Green could display his talents and erudition.–Ely to Herbert C. Spencer, May 23, 1892; Green to Ely, January 1, 1893, copies in Ely Papers. In 1894 Green became superintendent of the Charity Organization Society of Hartford, Connecticut. Twenty-five years later, in 1919, he became professor of economics and sociology at Kenyon College.

29. Green, "Pain-Cost and Opportunity-Cost," *The Quarterly Journal of Economics*, January 1894, pp. 218–29. Frederick B. Hawley had made some suggestions of an opportunity cost theory which in some respects were more realistic than those of Green, but had not worked them out in Green's systematic fashion. See Hawley, "The Fundamental Error of *Kapital und Kapitalzins*," pp. 301–302.

30. Böhm-Bawerk, "The Ultimate Standard of Value," *Annals of the American Academy of Political and Social Science*, September 1894, p. 176, ft.

31. Green, "Wieser's *Natural Value*," *Annals of the American Academy of Political and Social Science*, January 1895, pp. 69–70. Green's doctoral dissertation followed Newcomb's defense of the gold standard by adopting the "labor standard for comparing the subjective value of the monetary unit to different individuals and to different generations."–Green, "Value and Its Measurement," *The Yale Review*, February 1899, p. 404.

32. Green, "Ethics and Economics," *The Sabbath Recorder*, October 1, 8, 1891. "Extreme privation and want in England as well as in America are due to exceptional conditions or to improvident expenditures."–Green, "The Poverty of an English Town," *The Yale Review*, February 1903, p. 360. See also Green, "The Charity Organization Movement," *Public Opinion*, February 20, 1896.

33. E. R. A. Seligman, "The Next Decade of Economic Theory–Discussion," *Publications of the American Economic Association*, February 1901, p. 248; Fred M. Taylor, *ibid.*, p. 251.

34. Adolph Wagner, "Marshall's Principles of Economics," *The Quarterly Journal of Economics*, April 1891, pp. 319–38.

35. Arthur Burnham Woodford, "Political Economy for Moderns," *The Dial*, October 1891, p. 176.

36. W. G. Langworthy Taylor received his Bachelor of Arts degree and Law degree from Harvard in 1880 and 1883 respectively and then studied for several years in Europe.

37. Taylor, *Write Your Own Political Economy* (Lincoln, Nebr.: University Publishing Co., 1900), pp. 22, 69–70; "Values, Positive and Relative," *Annals of the American Academy of Political and Social Science*, January 1897, p. 100; "Protection, Expansion, and International Competition," *ibid.*, January 1904, p. 42; "The Kinetic Theory of Economic Crises," [Nebraska University] *Studies*, January 1904, p. 19; "Financial Legislation in Principle and in History," *ibid.*, July 1909, pp. 241, 243–44; "Monopoly in Law and Political Economy," delivered November 23, 1906, in *Proceedings of the Nebraska State Bar Association, 1906–1909*, pp. 136–37.

38. The Canadian John Davidson, professor of Political Economy at the University of New Brunswick, declared that competition between masters for labor was set aside by the fact that the "development of the capitalist regime has created a surplus of irregularly employed labor on which much of the force of the competition between masters for labor is dissipated."—Davidson, *The Bargain Theory of Wages* (New York: Putnam, 1898), p. 155.

39. Charles William Macfarlane, *Value and Distribution* (Philadelphia: Lippincott, 1899), p. 158.
Macfarlane (1852–1931) received an engineering degree from Lehigh University in 1876; then for fifteen years he was an engineer and architect; in 1891 he studied economics with Patten and James at the University of Pennsylvania; the next two years he spent with Professor Eugen von Philippovich at Freiburg, where he received his doctorate. For biographical information, see *vita* at end of his doctoral dissertation, *The History of the General Doctrine of Rent* (Leipzig: Gustav Fock, 1893); and *Science and Literature*, edited and arranged by Kathleen Selfridge Macfarlane (Philadelphia: Penn Publishing Co., 1931), pp. v–ix.

40. Seligman, "The Next Decade in Economic Theory—Discussion," *Publications of the American Economic Association*, February 1901, p. 248.

41. Henry R. Seager, "The Fallacy of Saving," *American Economic Association Publications, Economic Studies*, April 1896, Supplement, pp. 134–38; Edward W. Bemis, *ibid.*, p. 138. For a bibliography of Seager's writings, see *Labor and Other Economic Essays of Henry R. Seager*, edited by Charles A. Gulick, Jr., with an introduction by Wesley C. Mitchell (New York: Harper, 1931), pp. 406–21.

42. For biographical material, see *Edwin Robert Anderson Seligman, 1861–1939. Addresses Delivered at the Memorial Meeting . . . At Columbia University* (Stamford, Conn.: privately printed, 1942); for bibliography, see *A Bibliography of the Faculty of Political Science, Columbia University*, pp. 25–43; see also Seligman's autobiography with bibliography, "Edwin R. Seligman," *Die Volkswirtschaftslehre der Gegenwart in Selbstdarstellungen* (Leipzig, 1929), Vol. II, pp. 117–60.

43. F. Y. Edgeworth, "Minimum Sacrifice versus Equal Sacrifice," 1910, reprinted in *Papers Relating to Political Economy* (London: Macmillan, 1925), Vol. II, p. 241.

44. Seligman, "The Theory of Progressive Taxation," abstract in *Publications of the American Economic Association*, January 1893, pp. 52–54; Ely, "Discussion," *ibid.*, p. 55; Seligman, "Progressive Taxation in Theory and Practice," *Publications of the American Economic Association*, January–March 1894, p. 214.

45. Seligman, "Is the Income Tax Constitutional and Just?" *The Forum*,

March, 1895, p. 56; "Progressive Taxation in Theory and Practice," *Publications of the American Economic Association*, 3d series, Vol. IX (1908), p. 874; *The Income Tax* (New York: Macmillan, 1911), pp. 671–72; "The Federal Income Tax," *Political Science Quarterly*, March 1914, p. 14.

46. Ely, *Socialism*, Syllabus of Six Lectures, University of Wisconsin Extension Department, No. 4, 1892.

47. "Professor Ely Replies to the Charges Against Him," *Public Opinion*, August 23, 1894.

CHAPTER XII

1. For biographical detail and bibliography see Morris Hadley, *Arthur Twining Hadley* (New Haven: Yale University Press, 1948); see also Irving Fisher, "Arthur Twining Hadley," *The Economic Journal*, September 1930, pp. 526–33.

2. In an article which appeared about the same time, Hadley appeared to apply the point to practically every type of modern business. The businessman, he wrote, cannot withdraw "when he fails to make the expected profit, without sacrificing a great part of his invested capital and losing the chance of ever again doing business on the same terms. . . . In hard times he will actually produce at a loss to save his capital and connections in the hope of a better future."—Hadley, "Profits," in Lalor's *Cyclopædia*, Vol. III, p. 376.

3. Hadley, "Transportation," Lalor's *Cyclopædia*, Vol. III, p. 931; "Political Economy," in *Johnson's Universal Encyclopædia*, new edition, edited by Charles Kendall Adams (1895), Vol. VI, p. 692.

4. Hadley, *Economics* (New York: Putnam, 1896), pp. 147, 151–54; review of Walras' *Eléments d'économie politique pure*, in *Political Science Quarterly*, December 1889, pp. 680–81; review of Clément Juglar's *A Brief History of Panics*, in *The Yale Review*, November 1893, p. 328.

5. Hadley, *Railroad Transportation* (New York: Putnam, 1885), pp. 78–79.

6. Hadley, "The Relation between Politics and Economics," 1899, reprinted in *The Education of the American Citizen* (New York: Scribner, 1901), p. 81; "Economic Theory and Political Morality," 1900, reprinted in *ibid.*, pp. 96–99.

7. Hadley referred to paragraphs 30–40, 50, 54, 126–29 of his *Economics*, for his permanent contribution. Hadley to Ely, November 24, 1899, Ely Papers.

8. Redvers Opie, "Frank William Taussig, 1859–1940," *The Economic Journal*, June and September 1941, pp. 347–68; J. A. Schumpeter, A. H. Cole, E. S. Mason, "Frank William Taussig," *The Quarterly Journal of Economics*, May 1941, pp. 337–63. For bibliography of Taussig's work, see *Explorations in Economics: Notes and Essays Contributed in Honor of F. W. Taussig* (New York: McGraw Hill, 1936), pp. 535–39. This does not include all of Taussig's semi-popular articles.

9. Taussig to Wells, May 23, 1884, Wells Papers, Library of Congress.

10. Taussig to Seligman, May 15, 1886, "Seligman Correspondence," No. 1, pp. 120–21. The Ingram article, elaborated, appeared in book form as *A History of Political Economy* the following year, with E. J. James writing the introduction for the American edition. Later Taussig led the movement to have Adolph Wagner's *Grundlegung der politischen Ökonomie* translated—Taussig to Seligman, January 12, 1891, "Seligman Correspondence," No. 1, p. 122; Taussig to Giddings, June 24, 1891, Giddings Papers.

Taussig had good things to say for even the major treatise of the most extreme advocate of the historical method, Schmoller's *Grundriss der all-gemeinen Volkwirtschaftslehre.*—Taussig, "Economic Theory," in *A Guide to Reading in Social Ethics and Allied Subjects,* edited by Francis G. Peabody, (Cambridge: Harvard University, 1910), p. 8.

11. Taussig, "Value and Distribution as Treated by Professor Marshall," *Publications of the American Economic Association,* January 1893, p. 100; "Methods of Teaching Economics—Discussion," *American Economic Association Publications, Economic Studies,* Supplement, February 1898, p. 109.

12. Taussig, "The Problem of Secondary Education as Regards Training for Citizenship," *The Educational Review,* May 1899, p. 436.

13. Taussig, "The Wages-Fund at the Hands of the German Economists," in "Handbook and Report of the Sixth Annual Meeting," *Publications of the American Economic Association,* Vol. IX, 1894, pp. 69–70; *Wages and Capital* (New York: Appleton, 1896), pp. 106–107, 117.

Taussig in 1917 succinctly stated his doctrine of the wage fund. "The proximate influence determining the general range of wages," he said, "is the quasi-mechanical impact of total wages fund, or profit-seeking free funds, against the total supply of laborers." By this time Taussig had come to feel that the term "wages fund" was of doubtful expediency, but he still felt that the explanation he had given originally of the mechanism determining wages and profits was essentially valid.—Taussig, "Kleene's *Profit and Wages,*" *The Quarterly Journal of Economics,* August 1917, p. 708.

Taussig did feel that Chapter 2 of *Wages and Capital* "is bad."—Taussig to Ely, November 26, 1899, Ely Papers.

14. Taussig, "Outlines of a Theory of Wages," *Publications of the American Economic Association,* April 1910, pp. 142–53. Seligman noted the inconsistency in Taussig's *Principles of Economics* (New York: Macmillan, 1911) between his "acceptance of the doctrine of specific productivity as applied to capital and his refusal to accept it in the case of labor, even though it is far easier to disentangle the specific product in the case of labor than it is in the case of capital."—Seligman to McCrea, December 23, 1911, in "Seligman Correspondence," No. 4, *Political Science Quarterly,* December 1941, p. 599.

15. Taussig, "Introduction" to Emile de Laveleye, *The Elements of Political Economy* (New York: Putnam, 1884), p. xvii; editorial note, unsigned, *The Quarterly Journal of Economics,* October 1889, p. 79; "Workmen's Insurance in Germany," *The Forum,* October 1889, p. 169; "Minimum Wages for Women," *The Quarterly Journal of Economics,* May 1916, p. 422.

16. Taussig, "The Homestead Strike," *The Economic Journal,* June 1893, pp. 311, 318.

17. Taussig to Giddings, July 7, 1891, Giddings Papers; Taussig, "A Contribution to the Theory of Railroad Rates," *Publication of the American Economic Association,* January and March, 1891, p. 54; "A Contribution to the Theory of Railway Rates," *The Quarterly Journal of Economics,* July 1891, pp. 457–58.

18. Taussig, "Supplementary Chapter," to Laveleye, *op. cit.,* p. 284.

19. Taussig, *The Silver Situation in the United States* (New York: Putnam, 1893; 3d edition, 1898), p. 112.

"The alternations of prosperous activity with halting depressions in trade and industry, which recur at almost regular intervals in modern times," he wrote, "seem to be the inevitable results of the complications of exchange and the sensitiveness of credit."—Taussig, "Industry and Finance," *The United States of America,* edited by Nathaniel S. Shaler (New York: Appleton, 1894), Vol. II, p. 551. Also, "The essential cause of the recurring eras of depression seems to lie in the complications of the division of labor."—Taussig's review of Edward D. Jones, *Economic Crises,* in *Political Science Quarterly,* March 1901, p. 162.

20. Taussig, *The Silver Situation in the United States,* p. 132; "The International Silver Situation," *The Quarterly Journal of Economics,* October 1896, pp. 33–34.

For a "sober and conservative" community, the best scheme is to "enlarge the base on which the national bank notes rest and so enable them ultimately to attain a dominant place in our everyday paper currency." Such a scheme will "present no temptation to currency tinkering" and will grow without trammels as the needs of the community spontaneously call for increase."— Taussig, "What Should Congress Do about Money?" *The Review of Reviews,* August 1893, p. 151.

21. *Report of the [Massachusetts] Commission Appointed to Inquire into the Expediency of Revising and Amending the Laws of the Commonwealth, Relating to Taxation* (Boston, 1897), p. 86. For Taussig's authorship of this report, see Opie, *op. cit.,* p. 13.

22. Taussig, "Supplementary Chapter," to Laveleye, *op. cit.,* p. 276.

23. Taussig not only opened the *Journal* to Thorstein Veblen, but suggested to the president of the American Economic Association—Ely—that Veblen be asked to give a paper at the 1900 meeting. This, "Industrial and Pecuniary Employments," turned out to be the most famous of Veblen's papers—Taussig to Ely, January 17, 1900, Ely Papers.

24. Taussig to Ely, November 26, 1899, Ely Papers.

25. Comment of Roswell C. McCrea at end of Vol. II of Taussig's *Principles,* in author's possession.

26. For biographical detail and a selected bibliography, see Alfred Bornemann, *J. Laurence Laughlin* (Washington: American Council on Public Affairs, 1940). For a penetrating study of Laughlin's character, see Wesley C. Mitchell, "J. Laurence Laughlin," *The Journal of Political Economy,* December 1941, pp. 875–81.

Laughlin's *The Elements of Political Economy* (New York: American Book Co., 1887) was widely used in the colleges as well as in the secondary schools. J. B. Clark used it along with his own *The Philosophy of Wealth* at Smith College.

27. Oliver Wendell Holmes to Frederick Pollock, March 4, 1888, in *Holmes-Pollock Letters,* edited by Mark De Wolfe Howe (Cambridge: Harvard University Press, 1941), Vol. I, p. 31.

28. Laughlin to Atkinson, April 11, 1882, January 29, November 11, 1883, Atkinson Papers; Laughlin to Seligman, July 11, 1890, Seligman Papers.

29. [Laughlin], "Roscher's Political Economy," *The International Review,* June 1879, pp. 707–10.

30. Laughlin, *Mill's Principles of Political Economy, Abridged, With Critical, Biographical, and Explanatory Notes, and a Sketch of the History of Political Economy* (New York: Appleton, 1884), Preface.

31. Laughlin, "The Study of Political Economy in the United States," *The Journal of Political Economy,* December 1892, p. 6.

32. Testimony of Laughlin, December 11, 1911, in *Hearings before the Committee on Interstate Commerce,* Senate, 62d Cong. (1912), Vol. I, pp. 1000-1001.

33. "The ablest and most competent men are, by the operation of our social development, drawn into the service of business. Had the scholars of today the driving energy and intellectual quality of their industrial brothers, scholar-

ship would advance by leaps and bounds, far faster than it does now."—
Laughlin, "The Monetary Commission," *The Forum*, November 1897, pp.
310–11.

34. Laughlin, "Views of Economists on the Silver Problem," *Science*, Supplement, March 19, 1886.

35. Laughlin, *The History of Bimetallism in the United States* (New York: Appleton, 1885, 1900), p. x.

36. Laughlin, *Facts about Money* (Chicago: Weeks, 1895), pp. 110–11; *The Principles of Money* (New York: Scribner, 1903), p. 362; "A Theory of Prices," *Publications of the American Economic Association*, February 1905, p. 68. Other prominent critics of the quantity theory were William A. Scott of the University of Wisconsin, Fred M. Taylor of the University of Michigan and Jacob Schoenhof, the New York lace manufacturer who had held a diplomatic post in Cleveland's administration.

37. Laughlin to Ely, December 8, 1899, Ely Papers.

38. Sarah McLean Hardy, "The Quantity of Money and Prices, 1860–1891: An Inductive Study," *The Journal of Political Economy*, March 1895, pp. 145–168. She argued that the quantity theory was a "hypothetical deductive law" and that the statistical evidence for the period revealed that prices fell with the increase of money. E. F. Kemmerer's *Money and Credit Instruments in Their Relation to General Prices* (1907), one of the most notable reformulations of the quantity theory, was a direct outgrowth of the Hardy publication.—Kemmerer to Bornemann, in Bornemann, *op. cit.*, pp. 71–72.

CHAPTER XIII

1. Commons wrote a delightful autobiography, *Myself* (New York: Macmillan, 1934). For an illuminating, incisive, and sympathetic account of Commons and his views, see Selig Perlman, "John Rogers Commons: 1862–1945," *The American Economic Review*, September 1945, pp. 782–86.

2. Monroe wrote Ely: "I write this note to introduce to your favorable regard my friend and recent pupil . . . Mr. Commons, . . . the leading mind in a large [graduating] class. His character is irreproachable, his scholarship accurate and thorough, and he has a strong taste for the class of studies in which you and I are especially interested."—Monroe to Ely, September 29, 1888, Ely Papers.

3. Commons to Ely, March 26, 1891, January 18, 1892, Ely Papers.

4. "Institute of Christian Sociology," *The Cyclopedic Review of Current History*, edited by Alfred S. Johnson, Vol. III, p. 636.

5. Commons, "Economic Reform," *The Voice*, September 14, 1893.
Commons' colleague, the historian James A. Woodburn, was more radical. He declared that with silver altogether eliminated as money, the basis for credit transactions—which was only 10 per cent—had been dangerously narrowed. Narrowing the base increased the facility by which men who controlled the gold could cause a panic. Panics would recur so long as businessmen were compelled to operate on a credit basis out of all proportion to the ultimate money.—Woodburn, "The Present Aspect of the Money Question," *Indiana Student*, November 21, 1893.

6. Commons to Ely, January 30, 1894, Ely Papers.

7. Commons, "Progressive Individualism," *The American Magazine of Civics*, June 1895, pp. 561–74.

8. Commons, "Shorter Hours for Clerks," *Indiana Student*, January 9, 1894, p. 5; "Temperance Reform," *Fifth Report of the Board of State Charities Made to the State Legislature* (Indianapolis, 1894), Part II, p. 47.

9. In the last year of the decade Commons suggested that a step in the right direction for solving technological unemployment was the German scheme of social insurance, with government, employee, and employer contributing an equal share of the premium. As for unemployment caused by depression, he suggested the creation of employment bureaus, labor colonies, and public emergency work.—Commons, "The Right to Work," *The Arena*, February, 1899.

10. Taussig to Seligman, December 23, 1893, Seligman Papers; Hadley, review of Commons' *The Distribution of Wealth*, in *The Yale Review*, February 1894, pp. 439–40; Richmond Mayo-Smith, review in *Political Science Quarterly*, September 1894, pp. 568–72; A. C. Miller, review in *The Journal of Political Economy*, June 1894, p. 464.

11. Adams to Seligman, August 28, 1894, in "Seligman Correspondence," No. 2, *Political Science Quarterly*, June 1941, p. 273; Commons to Adams, April 16, 1895, Adams Papers; Commons to Ely, May 6 [1895], Ely Papers.

12. According to the historian of Indiana University, Professor Woodburn, "Commons had been made a little uneasy by some newspaper criticisms of some of his public addresses. . . . The reporters failed to understand him or misrepresented him. . . . President Swain in a spirit of timidity did not encourage Commons to stay."—James A. Woodburn, *History of Indiana University* (Bloomington, Indiana: Indiana University, 1940), Vol. I, p. 440.

13. Commons to Ely, March 3 [1896], Ely Papers. Commons presented a short outline of his sociology in an article, "Natural Selection, Social Selection and Heredity," *The Arena*, July 1897, pp. 90–97.

14. Commons, "Municipal Electric Lighting," in Edward W. Bemis, *et al.*, *Municipal Monopolies* (New York: Crowell, 1899), p. 180. The essay was the result of an investigation Commons made of municipal ownership in some of the smaller New York towns. It was financed by John S. Huyler, the candy manufacturer and a trustee of Syracuse University, who established Commons' chair at Syracuse and favored municipal ownership. See Commons, *Myself*, p. 53.

15. Commons, *Proportional Representation* (New York: Crowell, 1896), p. 231.

16. Commons, "Political Economy and Law," *The Kingdom*, January 24, 1896; "The Sociological Theory of Sovereignty," *The American Journal of Sociology*, May 1900, p. 821; *Representative Democracy* (New York: Bureau of Economic Research, 1900), p. 87.

17. Commons, "Economists and Class Partnership," 1900, reprinted in *Labor and Administration* (New York: Macmillan, 1913), pp. 58–59.

18. Commons, *Myself*, p. 58.

Shortly afterward Commons lashed out against private colleges and churches, as "conservators of what has been accepted, not innovators." The only sensible solution, he said, was the establishment of state or national universities, preferably the latter, and "founded in such a way that different sides of living questions should be studied and taught by men who represent the different sides. Experts differ and scholars differ, and truth comes not from one man who speaks for all but from conflict of thinkers."—Commons to editor of *Social Forum*, December 1899, pp. 222–23.

19. Commons to Ely, March 2, 1899, and Bemis to Ely, August 11, 1899,

Ely Papers. Shibley in 1897 had already planned to start an educational movement similar to the Chautauqua system, in which the social sciences would be popularized.–Shibley to Adams, February 23, 1897, Adams Papers.

20. Commons as a member of the "college" staff prepared "Proportional Representation," in *Publications of the Social Reform Union,* October 28, 1899; he also prepared for the Social Reform Union "Direct Legislation in Switzerland and America," which appeared in *The Arena,* December 1899, pp. 725–39.

21. Commons, "Index Numbers of Prices, Freight Rates, etc.," *Quarterly Bulletin of the Bureau of Economic Research,* July 1900, p. 9; "Wholesale Prices, 1896 to 1900," *ibid.,* October 1900, p. 41; Shibley, *Stable Money, New Freedom, and Safe Banking,* 63d Cong., 1st sess., Senate Doc., No. 135, p. 76; Shibley to Ely, August 6, 1900, Ely Papers.

22. Testimony of Commons, November 12, 1900, *Report of the Industrial Commission,* Vol. XIV, 57th Cong., 1st sess., House of Representatives, Ex. Doc., No. 183, pp. 36, 47, 48.

23. Commons, "Concentration of Wealth, Its Dangers," *The Independent,* May 1, 1902.

24. Commons was also engaged in drawing up and promoting tax reform bills for the organization.

25. Ely to Commons, January 20, 1904, copy in Ely Papers.

26. Commons, "The Educated Man in Politics," 1893, reprinted in *Social Reform and the Church* (New York: Crowell, 1894), pp. 64–65. At that time Commons urged that the students join the Knights of Labor, for which they would be eligible since only lawyers and saloonkeepers were barred.

27. Commons, "Investigation and Administration," 1913, reprinted in *Labor and Administration,* pp. 405, 411–12.

28. Minutes of the University of Wisconsin Seminary in Economic Theory, April 4, 1916, Ely Papers.

29. Commons, "The Theory of the Minimum Wage–Discussion," *The American Labor Legislation Review,* February 1913, p. 92; "Eight-Hour Shifts by Federal Legislation," *ibid.,* March 1917, p. 152.

30. Commons, "Is Class Conflict in America Growing and Is It Inevitable?" *The American Journal of Sociology,* March 1908, p. 764.

31. Commons, "Political Economy and Sociology in High Schools," *The Inland Educator,* December 1895, pp. 297–99.

32. For a general study of Smith and a bibliography of his writings, see Eric F. Goldman, "J. Allen Smith: The Reformer and His Dilemma," *The Pacific Northwest Quarterly,* July 1944, pp. 195–214; see also "James Allen Smith," *The Industrialist,* July 15, 1897.

33. Smith, "The Multiple Money Standard," *Annals of the American Academy of Political and Social Science,* March 1896, pp. 215, 217, 222, 232. Smith pointed out that Carey had shown the advantages of a non-exportable medium of exchange.

34. Smith to Henry C. Adams, June 27, 1896, Adams Papers.

35. For Smith's side of the controversy that followed, see "The Case of James Allen Smith," *The Industrialist,* September 2, 1897, p. 180.

36. Smith to Adams, April 18, 1899 and August 9, 1906, Adams Papers.

37. See Dorfman, *op. cit.,* Vol. I, p. 346.

38. Smith to John A. Kingsbury, February 6, 1923, cited by Goldman, *op. cit.,* p. 211.

39. Fairchild was a follower of Perry. He supported free trade and the gold

standard, deprecated trade unions and usury laws, and asserted that the rent of land represented effort. See George T. Fairchild, *The Science of Wealth* (Manhattan, Kansas, 1885), p. 7 [pamphlet].

40. Julius Terrace Willard, *History of the Kansas State College of Agriculture and Applied Science* (Manhattan, Kansas: Kansas State College Press, 1940), pp. 98–99, 125.

41. Thomas E. Will, "Why the Farmer Should Study Economics," *The Industrialist*, March 1899, p. 149.

42. Thomas L. Brown [pseudonym of Will], "Rent: Its Essence and Its Place in the Distribution of Wealth," *The Arena*, December 1893, pp. 81–95. For Will's authorship, see "Personal Notes," *Annals of the American Academy of Political and Social Science*, November 1894, p. 416.

43. Will, "Stable Money," *The Journal of Political Economy*, December 1898, pp. 86–87; "Outlines of the Financial History of the United States," No. 1, *The Industrialist*, January 1898, p. 8; "Scientific Money," *Publications of the Social Reform Union*, May 7, 1900.

44. Will, "Public Ownership and Socialism," *The Industrialist*, October 11, 1897, pp. 197–98.

45. Will, "Individualism through Socialism," *The Arena*, October 1906, pp. 362, 363.

46. Will, "A Personal Word," *American Forestry*, February 1910, p. 111.

47. "Thomas Elmer Will," *Harvard College Class of 1880*, Report No. 9 (Norwood, Mass.: privately printed, 1940), pp. 198–99.

48. Charles A. Tuttle contributed an essay to the volume celebrating J. B. Clark's eightieth birthday in 1927; see Tuttle, "A Functional Theory of Economic Profit," in *Economic Essays Contributed in Honor of John Bates Clark*, edited by Jacob H. Hollander (New York: Macmillan, 1927), pp. 321–36.

49. Tuttle, *Outline of Course in Economic Theory*, (Crawfordsville, Indiana: privately printed, 1894), pp. 92–93. Tuttle's doctrine of exploitation, though not his practical conclusion, was along the lines of Johann Heinrich von Thünen's *Der isolierte Staat*, which Clark questioned (see Appendix).

50. Tuttle, "The Workman's Position in the Light of Economic Progress," in *Publications of the American Economic Association*, February 1902, pp. 209, 210.

51. "Discussion," *ibid.*, p. 230.

In 1837 the conservative Reverend Joseph Alden of Williams College had suggested that an indemnity to labor displaced by machinery was desirable in Europe, and while not a serious problem as yet in the United States would ultimately be felt here also.—[Joseph Alden], "Wayland's Political Economy," *The New York Review*, October 1837, pp. 386–87. For Alden's authorship, see *Publications of the President and Professors of Williams College, 1793–1876* (North Adams, Mass., 1876). In his treatise of 1879, *First Principles of Political Economy*, Alden ignored this problem.

52. Richard T. Ely, "A Decade of Economic Theory," *Annals of the American Academy of Political and Social Science*, March 1900, p. 255.

53. Winthrop M. Daniels, "A Letter to John Stuart Mill," 1900, reprinted in *Essays* (New Haven: privately printed, 1943), p. 76.

CHAPTER XIV

1. F. W. Taussig to Roswell C. McCrea, December 21, 1908, McCrea Papers.
2. Alexander Dana Noyes, *Forty Years of American Finance* (New York: Putnam, 1909), p. 334.
3. Charles A. Conant, *Wall Street and the Country* (New York: Putnam, 1904), pp. 32, 34. Conant at the same time raised the criticism that while orthodox economics as represented by Mill's treatise was sound in a frictionless world, orthodoxy refused to recognize friction. Thus, contrary to the teachings of the "old school," imperialism was justified by the modern intense industrial competition.—Conant, "The Influence of Friction in Economics," *Science*, January 17, 1908.
4. Conant, [Banking Reform] Address before the American Association for the Advancement of Science, *Science*, April 12, 1907.
5. Charles R. Flint, "Centralization and Natural Law," *The Independent*, May 1, 1902.
6. Herbert Croly, *The Promise of American Life* (New York: Macmillan, 1909), pp. 359–65.
7. Cited from Mark Sullivan, *Our Times* (New York: Scribner, 1911), Vol. II, p. 411.
8. *Investigation of United States Steel Corporation*, 62d Cong., 2d sess., House of Representatives Report, No. 1127, pp. 58, 129, 211.
9. Testimony of Elbert H. Gary, November 29, 1911, in *Hearings before the Committee on Interstate Commerce*, Senate, 62d Cong., Vol. I, pp. 695, 702, 704, 706; testimony of George W. Perkins, December 13, 1911, *ibid.*, pp. 1091, 1109; testimony of Louis D. Brandeis, December 14, 16, 1911, *ibid.*, pp. 1147, 1272, 1278.
10. Francis G. Newlands, "Review and Criticisms of Anti-Trust Legislation," *Annals of the American Academy of Political and Social Science*, July 1912, p. 291; Francis Walker, "Policies of Germany, England, Canada and the United States toward Corporations," *ibid.*, pp. 200, 201. See also Oswald Knauth, "The Policy of the United States toward Industrial Monopoly," in Columbia University's *Studies in History, Economics and Public Law*, Vol. LVI (1914), pp. 403–404.
11. Noyes, "Politics and Prosperity," *The Atlantic Monthly*, February 1912, pp. 193–95. Noyes succeeded Horace White as financial editor of the *Post*.
12. Walker D. Hines, "Legislative Regulation of Railroad Rates," *Publications of the American Economic Association*, February 1903, pp. 95, 102; Charles A. Prouty, "Public Regulation of Railroad Rates—Discussion," *ibid.*, pp. 128–29.
13. Ivy L. Lee, "Railroad Valuation," *The Bankers' Magazine*, July 1908, p. 87; Ray Morris, "Tendencies in American Railroad Development," *The Atlantic Monthly*, August 1907, p. 162; Frederick W. Whitridge, "Official Valuation of Private Property," *Publications of the American Economic Association*, April 1910, p. 250.
14. *Report of the Railroad Securities Commission to the President*, 62d Cong., 2d sess., House of Representatives Documents, No. 256, pp. 16, 32, 37.
15. William Z. Ripley, "Are Our Railroads Fairly Treated?" in *Year Book of the Economic Club of New York* (1916), Vol. III, p. 209.
16. "In *re* Menominee & Mariette Light & Traction Co.," *Opinions and Decisions of the Railroad Commission of the State of Wisconsin* (October 16, 1908, to August 3, 1909), Vol. III, p. 793.

17. *Report of the Joint Committee of the Senate and Assembly of the State of New York Appointed to Investigate . . . Life Insurance Companies. . .*, Assembly Doc. No. 41 (1906), p. 388; Charles J. Bullock, "Life Insurance and Speculation," *The Atlantic Monthly*, May 1906, p. 638.

18. *Report of Governor Hughes' Committee on Speculation in Securities and Commodities* (Albany, 1909), pp. 8, 10.

19. *Report of the Committee Appointed Pursuant to House Resolutions 429 and 504 to Investigate the Concentration of Control of Money and Credit* (Washington: Government Printing Office, 1913), pp. 142, 151, 159, 161.

20. Brandeis, *Other People's Money* (Washington: National Home Library Foundation, 1914, 1933), pp. 58–59.

21. *Report of the National Monetary Commission*, 62d Cong., 2d sess., Senate Doc. No. 243, p. 14.

22. Myron T. Herrick to J. Laurence Laughlin, December 12, 1912, Laughlin Papers, Library of Congress.

23. E. W. Goodhue, "Banking Reform–Discussion," *The American Economic Review*, March 1913, Supplement, p. 80.

24. Cited in Henry F. Pringle, *Theodore Roosevelt* (New York: Harcourt, Brace, 1931), p. 431.

25. John A. Ryan, *A Living Wage* (New York: Grosset & Dunlap, 1906, 1911), p. 330; "Standard of Living and Labor," in *Proceedings of National Conference of Charities and Correction* (1913), 40th sess., p. 225.

26. *Report of the [Massachusetts] Commission on Minimum Wage Boards* (Boston, 1912), p. 18.

27. A decade later the Supreme Court declared such legislation unconstitutional.

28. Elsie Glück, *John Mitchell* (New York: John Day, 1929), p. 147; Theodore Roosevelt, *An Autobiography* (New York: Macmillan, 1913), p. 508; Roosevelt to Marcus A. Hanna, October 3, 1902, Roosevelt to Cleveland, October 4, 1902, in Joseph Bucklin Bishop, *Theodore Roosevelt and His Time* (New York: Scribner, 1920), Vol. I, pp. 203, 204.

29. *Report of the Board of Arbitration in the Matter of the Controversy between the Eastern Railroads and the Brotherhood of Locomotive Engineers*, November 2, 1913, p. 47.

30. Testimony of Brandeis, *Hearings before the Committee on Interstate Commerce*, Vol. I, pp. 1180–83.

31. Testimony of Hourwich, December 8, 1900, *Report of the Industrial Commission*, Vol. XIV, 57th Cong., 1st sess., House of Representatives Ex. Doc. No. 183, p. 154. Hourwich was then employed as a translator by the Bureau of the Mint. He had been counsel for the United Brotherhood of Cloak Makers.

32. W. D. P. Bliss, "Nuremberg, the City of the Closed Shop," *The Outlook*, March 17, 1906.

33. John Spargo, *Socialism* (New York: Macmillan, 1906), p. 236; *Marxian Socialism and Religion* (New York: Huebsch, 1915), pp. 175–78.

34. "Socialism, Promise or Menace? A Debate Between Morris Hillquit and John Augustin Ryan," *Everybody's Magazine*, October 1913, p. 487.

35. On the other hand, the engineer and diluted Fabian James Mackaye, in *The Economy of Happiness* (1906), elaborated socialism on the basis of the marginal utility economics. He was praised by one "orthodox" economist as laying the foundations of socialism on the "economics of the modern school."– Thomas Nixon Carver, "The Economics of Socialism," in *A Guide to Reading in Social Ethics and Allied Subjects*, pp. 171–72.

36. John A. Hobson to H. Gaylord Wilshire, in *Wilshire's Magazine*, February 1903, p. 53.

37. Spargo, "Talk with Hobson, the English Economist," *Wilshire's Magazine*, April 1903, pp. 44–48.

38. Pierrepont B. Noyes, "A Russian Possibility," *Wilshire's Magazine*, January 1903, pp. 66–71.

39. For a detailed discussion of this movement, see Paul F. Brissenden, "The I. W. W.," Columbia University's *Studies in History, Economics and Public Law*, *Vol.* LXXXII (1919).

40. John Graham Brooks, *American Syndicalism* (New York: Macmillan, 1913), p. 140; William E. Trautman, *Direct Action and Sabotage* (Pittsburgh: Socialist News Co., 1912), p. 26 and *The Truth About the I. W. W.* (New York National Civil Liberties Bureau, 1918), p. 7.

41. Paul F. Brissenden, "Industrial Workers of the World," *Encyclopædia of the Social Sciences*, edited by Seligman and Johnson (New York: Macmillan, 1932), p. 15.

42. Frank Bohn, after doing graduate work at Wisconsin and Columbia Universities, obtained a doctor of philosophy degree from Michigan in 1904.

43. Eugene V. Debs, "Sound Socialist Tactics," *The International Socialist Review*, February 1912, pp. 482–83.

44. Nathan Fine, *Labor and Farmer Parties in the United States: 1828–1928* (New York: Rand School of Social Science, 1928), p. 273.

45. "Praise from the Enemy," *The International Socialist Review*, August 1912, p. 171 [editorial].

46. "Resolutions of Protest," *The International Socialist Review*, February 1913, p. 623. Among the signers were Walter Lippmann, James P. Warbasse, Osmund K. Fraenkel, Margaret K. Sanger, Max Eastman, Helen Marot, William English Walling, Anna Strunsky Walling, Rose Pastor Stokes, J. G. Phelps Stokes, Louis B. Boudin, and Herman Simpson.

47. Helen Keller, "A Call for Harmony," *The International Socialist Review*, February 1913, p. 606.

48. Frank LeRond McVey, "Social Tendencies in the United States," address given at the University of Christiania, September 1912, *Quarterly Journal* [of the University of North Dakota], July 1915, pp. 136–37. McVey, (1869–) was formerly professor of economics at the University of Minnesota and is president emeritus of the University of Kentucky. For a biography and bibliography, see his *A University is a Place . . . A Spirit*, addresses & articles collected and arranged by Frances Jewell McVey (Lexington, Ky.: University of Kentucky Press, 1944).

49. Theodore Roosevelt, "A Confession of Faith," 1912, in *The Works of Theodore Roosevelt*, edited by Hermann Hagedorn (New York: Scribner, 1926), p. 282.

50. Brandeis to Woodrow Wilson, September 30, 1912, cited in William Diamond, *The Economic Thought of Woodrow Wilson* (Baltimore: Johns Hopkins Press, 1943), pp. 106–107; see also Alpheus Thomas Mason, *Brandeis* (New York: Viking Press, 1946), p. 380.

51. Woodrow Wilson, "American Economists," ms. copy in Library of Congress. Wilson was associate professor of history and political economy at Bryn Mawr, 1885–88; professor of history and political economy at Wesleyan, 1888–90; professor of jurisprudence and political economy at Princeton, 1890–95. After that date he ceased teaching economics.

52. Edward A. Ross to Ely, June 10, 1902, Ely Papers.

53. Wilson, acceptance speech, 1912, *The Public Papers of Woodrow Wil-*

son, edited by Ray Stannard Baker and William E. Dodd (New York: Harper, 1925), Vol. II, p. 464.

54. Wilson, "Government in Relation to Business," *Year Book of the Economic Club of New York* (1912), Vol. II, pp. 179–81.

55. Wilson, *The New Freedom* (Garden City, N. Y.: Doubleday, Page, 1913, 1916), p. 136.

56. Wilson, Address to Congress, June 23, 1913, in *Congressional Record*, 63d Congress, 1st sess., pp. 2132–33.

57. William Jennings Bryan to Francis G. Newlands, June 19, 1911, in Laughlin, *The Federal Reserve Act* (New York: Macmillan, 1933), p. 155; see also the editorials in Bryan's organ, *The Commoner*, April 12, October 18, 1907.

58. Speech of Victor Murdock, September 10, 1913, *Congressional Record*, 63d Cong., 1st sess., pp. 4667–68; speech of Horace Mann Tower, September 13, 1913, *ibid.*, p. 4898; George H. Shibley, *How the New Currency Law Affects Me* (New York: Ogilvie, 1914).

59. Carter Glass, "Fundamental Questions in Banking and Currency Reform, with Special Reference to the Currency Bill," *Year Book of the Economic Club of New York* (1914), Vol. IV, pp. 71–73.

60. Cited in Carter Glass, *An Adventure in Constructive Finance* (Garden City, N. Y.: Doubleday, Page, 1927), pp. 230–31.

61. Wilson, Address to Congress, January 20, 1914, *Congressional Record*, 63d Cong., 2d sess., pp. 1978–79.

62. Speech of Senator Francis G. Newlands, June 25, 1914. *Congressional Record*, 63d Cong., 2d sess., p. 11113.

63. Wilson, "The Eight-Hour Day," August 16, 1916, *The Public Papers of Woodrow Wilson*, Vol. IV, p. 265; Message to Congress, August 29, 1916, *ibid.*, pp. 268–69.

64. Wilson to John B. Knox, October 30, 1916, in Ray Stannard Baker, *Woodrow Wilson, Life and Letters* (Garden City, N. Y.: Doubleday, Doran, 1937), Vol. VI, p. 111.

CHAPTER XV

1. George H. Mead, "The Definition of the Psychical," *The Decennial Publications of the University of Chicago* (Chicago: 1903), First Series, Vol. III, p. 98.

2. Mead, review of Gustave Le Bon's *The Psychology of Socialism*, in *The American Journal of Sociology*, November 1899, pp. 405–406, 409.

3. Simon N. Patten, "The Reconstruction of Economic Theory," 1912, reprinted in *Essays in Economic Theory*, edited by Rexford G. Tugwell (New York: Knopf, 1924), p. 278.

4. Charles W. Macfarlane, "The Place of Philosophy and Economics in the Curriculum of a Modern University," 1913, reprinted in *Science and Literature*, pp. 15, 21.

5. Macfarlane, "The Three Primary Laws of Social Evolution," 1902, *ibid.*, pp. 108–109.

6. On the Turner thesis and labor, see Carter Goodrich and Sol Davidson, "The Wage Earner in the Westward Movement," *Political Science Quarterly*, June 1935, pp. 161–85, March 1936, pp. 61–116, and "The Frontier as a Safety Valve: A Rejoinder," *ibid.*, June 1938, pp. 268–71.

7. For a more detailed analysis of Beard's position, see Joseph Dorfman's

review of Charles A. Beard and Mary R. Beard, *The American Spirit*, in *The American Economic Review*, September 1943, pp. 644–47. Beard, at least as late as 1917, staunchly advocated the doctrine of primacy of economic interest in history. He wrote: "Personally I think most political history . . . is meaningless without the economic content."–Beard to Seligman, December 23, 1917, Seligman Papers.

8. Carroll D. Wright, *et. al.*, "Report of Advisory Committee on Economics,"*Carnegie Institution of Washington Year Book*, 1902, p. 1. Wright, "Report of the Department of Economics and Sociology," *ibid.*, 1904, p. 55; *ibid.*, 1906, p. 158.

9. In 1938 appeared the posthumous publication of another original supervisor, Henry W. Farnam's *Chapters in the History of Social Legislation in the United States to 1860*. After the Carnegie Institution discontinued the Department of Economics and Sociology in 1916, Farnam in good part financed its offshoot, the Board of Research Associates in American Economic History.

10. Wright, "An Economic Interpretation of the History of the United States," in *Publications of the American Economic Association*, May 1905, Part 2, p. 179; "Science and Economics," *Proceedings of the American Association for the Advancement of Science*, 54th Meeting (1904), p. 349.

11. Jacob H. Hollander, *The Abolition of Poverty* (Boston: Houghton Mifflin, 1914), pp. 43–44; statement of E. W. Kemmerer in *Fourth Report of the [New York] Factory Investigating Commission* (Albany, 1915), Vol. I, pp. 615–16; Roswell C. McCrea, "The New Optimism in the Viewpoint of Economists," *Old Penn*, March 27, 1915; Winthrop M. Daniels, "The Passing of the Old Economist," reprinted in Daniels, *Essays*, pp. 8, 11.

12. *Statistical Reorganization: Report of a Committee Appointed by the Secretary of Commerce and Labor to Inquire into the Statistical Work of the Department* (Washington: Government Printing Office, 1908), p. 21.

13. Correa M. Walsh, *The Fundamental Problem in Monetary Science* (New York: Macmillan, 1903), p. 360.

14. Henry C. Taylor, *An Introduction to the Study of Agricultural Economics* (New York: Macmillan, 1905), pp. 320–21; Edwin G. Nourse, *Agricultural Economics* (Chicago: University of Chicago Press, 1916; reprinted in 1919), p. 869.

15. Thomas Nixon Carver, "The Place of Abstinence in the Theory of Interest," *The Quarterly Journal of Economics*, October 1893, p. 43. Carver, born in Iowa, received his Bachelor of Arts degree from the University of Southern California in 1891, then did graduate work with Richard T. Ely and John Bates Clark at Johns Hopkins. After receiving his doctorate at Cornell in 1894, he taught for six years at Oberlin. He came to Harvard in 1900. Carver taught sociology as well as economics and was keenly interested in rural problems.

16. Carver, "Moses as a Political Economist," *The Methodist Review*, July 1892, p. 605.

17. Carver, "Thrift and the Standard of Living," *The Journal of Political Economy*, November 1920, pp. 785–86.

18. Carver, "Clark's *Distribution of Wealth*," *The Quarterly Journal of Economics*, August 1901, p. 579; *The Distribution of Wealth* (New York: Macmillan, 1904), p. 203; *Principles of Rural Economics*, (Boston: Ginn, 1911), p. 185; "The Single Tax," *Essays in Social Justice* (Cambridge: Harvard University Press, 1915), p. 303.

19. Statement by Roswell C. McCrea sent to Thomas Nixon Carver and returned with Carver's approval, December 8, 1905, McCrea Papers.

20. McCrea, "Recent Books on the Principles of Economics," *The Quarterly Journal of Economics*, February 1911, p. 375.

21. Allyn A. Young, "Do the Statistics of the Concentration of Wealth in the United States Mean What They Are Commonly Assumed to Mean?" *The American Economic Review*, Supplement, March 1917, pp. 146–47, 155. It was unfortunate that Young never brought to fruition what was to have been his first book, "The Theory of Surplus Value." This would have included a "discussion of differential gains, monopoly gains, etc., in their relation to the development of economic thought, to the theory of socialism, and to present-day problems."—Young to Ely, February 5, 1902, Ely Papers.

22. Henry L. Moore, "Paradoxes of Competition," *The Quarterly Journal of Economics*, February 1906, pp. 216, 229. For a bibliography of Moore's work, see *A Bibliography of the Faculty of Political Science of Columbia University*, pp. 104–105. For a sympathetic critique of Moore's method see Henry Schultz, "Henry L. Moore's Contribution to the Statistical Law of Demand," in *Methods in Social Science*, edited by Stuart A. Rice (Chicago: University of Chicago Press, 1931), pp. 645–61.

23. F. W. Taussig, "Moore's *Laws of Wages*," *The Quarterly Journal of Economics*, May 1912, p. 518; David Kinley, "The Service of Statistics to Economics," 1914, reprinted in *Government Control of Economic Life* (New York: Gregg, 1930), p. 128.

24. Alvin S. Johnson to John Bates Clark, December 23, 1914, Clark Papers.

25. Moore to Seligman, January 8, 1906, May 27, 1910, Seligman Papers.

CHAPTER XVI

1. For biographical material, see "Princeton's New Recruit," *The Survey*, August 19, 1911, pp. 744–45; "Personal Notes," *Annals of the American Academy of Political and Social Science*, January 1895, pp. 588–89.

2. The textbook for the course was the popular *Handbook of Moral Philosophy* by Henry Calderwood of the University of Edinburgh.

3. Frank A. Fetter, "An American Economist," *The International Monthly*, July 1901, p. 129; "The Nature of Capital and Income," *The Journal of Political Economy*, March 1907, p. 146.

4. Fetter, "The Next Decade of Economic Theory," *Publications of the American Economic Association*, February 1901, p. 240.

5. Fetter, "The Fundamental Conceptions and Methods of Economics," *Congress of Arts and Science*, edited by Howard J. Rogers (Boston: Houghton Mifflin, 1906), Vol. VII, p. 16.

6. On the question of psychology the following quotation is pertinent. Professor Josiah Royce, the Harvard philosopher, in addressing the Harvard Economics Seminary in 1911, attempted to meet the problem of measurability of utility. He declared, according to the minutes: "The subjective phenomenon of economics were quantities insofar as the possibility of arranging them in the order of their magnitude or of their intensity is concerned . . . but . . . they are not quantities in the sense that they may be added to or subtracted from each other or accurately measured. In the terms of logic they are 'intensive' but not 'extensive' quantities. . . . They are incapable of definite measurement."—Report of Royce address, "The Theory of Measurement," November 27, 1911, Harvard Economics Seminary Records, 1908–1911, Harvard University Library.

7. Fetter, *Economic Principles* (New York: Century, 1915), pp. 27, 28, 271,

312–13; "Interest Theories, New and Old," *The American Economic Review*, March 1914, p. 90.

8. Fetter, *The Principles of Economics* (New York: Century, 1904, 1913), p. 256; *Modern Economic Problems* (New York: Century, 1916, 1919), p. 313.

9. Fetter, "Amerika," in *Die Wirtschaftstheorie der Gegenwart*, edited by Hans Mayer, Frank A. Fetter, Richard Reisch (Vienna: Julius Springer, 1927), Vol. I, p. 57. The mimeographed copy of the translation bears the title "Present State of Economic Theory in the United States of America."

10. Fetter, *Economic Principles*, pp. 421–22.

In 1898 Fetter suggested that the "excessive" amount of public relief expenditures should be reduced by eliminating outdoor relief, subjecting able-bodied recipients to a "strict work test," and disfranchising recipients of any form of public poor relief.–"The Improvement of Our System of Township Poor Relief," *Indiana Bulletin . . . of . . . Charities and Correction*, June 1898, pp. 73–74.

11. Fetter, "Can Capitalism Survive?" Address at the University of Illinois, November 12, 1935, mimeographed copy.

12. Fetter, "Price Economics versus Welfare Economics," *The American Economic Review*, December 1920, pp. 719–37.

13. Fetter, "The Heir Apparent," *The Indiana Student*, April 1891, p. 144.

14. For biographical detail, see Ray B. Westerfield and Paul Douglas, "Memorials: Irving Fisher," *The American Economic Review*, September 1947, pp. 656–63; Max Sasuly, "Irving Fisher and Social Science," *Econometrica*, October, 1947, pp. 255–78; see also Fisher's autobiographical article with selected bibliography, "Irving Fisher," *Die Volkswirtschaftslehre der Gegenwart in Selbstdarstellungen*, Vol. II (1929), pp. 1–16.

15. Fisher transferred to the Department of Economics in 1895.

16. Arthur T. Hadley, "Recent Tendencies in Economic Literature," *The Yale Review*, November 1894, p. 254.

17. Jacob H. Hollander to Seligman, May 19, 1896, Seligman Papers.

18. Fisher, "Cournot and Mathematical-Economics," *The Quarterly Journal of Economics*, January 1898, p. 138.

19. Fisher, *Elementary Principles of Economics* (New York: Macmillan, 1911, 1919), p. 371. The comprehensive discussion is in the earlier *The Rate of Interest* (New York: Macmillan, 1907).

20. Fisher, "Professor Fetter on Capital and Income," *The Journal of Political Economy*, July 1907, pp. 423–25.

21. Fisher, "The Role of Capital in Economic Theory," *The Economic Journal*, December 1897, pp. 530, 536; *The Nature of Capital and Income* (New York: Macmillan, 1906), pp. 28–29.

22. Fisher, *Elementary Principles of Economics*, p. 486.

23. John R. Commons, "Political Economy and Business Economy," *The Quarterly Journal of Economics*, November 1907, pp. 120–25.

24. Fisher, "Why Has the Doctrine of Laissez Faire Been Abandoned?" *Science*, January 4, 1907, pp. 24–25.

25. Irving Fisher and Harry G. Brown, *The Purchasing Power of Money* (New York: Macmillan, 1911, 1922), pp. 71, 320; Fisher, "Appreciation and Interest," *Publications of the American Economic Association*, August 1896, pp. 426–29; "Standardizing the Dollar," *The American Economic Review*, March 1913, Supplement, p. 27; "Discussion," *ibid.*, p. 48; "Stabilizing the Dollar in Purchasing Power," *American Problems of Reconstruction*, edited by Elisha M. Friedman (New York: Dutton, 1918), p. 389.

26. F. W. Taussig to Herbert J. Davenport, September 27, 1912, Davenport Papers; Davenport to Taussig, October 7, 1912, copy in Davenport Papers.

27. Fisher, "Economics as a Science," *Science*, August 31, 1906, p. 260; *The Purchasing Power of Money*, pp. 320–21.

28. Fisher to J. Allen Smith, November 5, 1914, in Goldman, "J. Allen Smith," p. 198.

29. For an excellent character portrayal of Davenport, see Paul T. Homan, "Herbert Joseph Davenport," *The American Economic Review*, December 1931, pp. 696–700.

30. Records by courtesy of Secretary's office of Harvard University Law School.

31. Records by the courtesy of the Registrar's office, University of South Dakota.

32. Davenport's close friend, W. G. Langworthy Taylor, in reviewing the *Outlines*, suggested that priority for the concept of opportunity cost should not necessarily go to Green. It was already involved, he said, in Marshall's fundamental concept of substitution, and Davenport, he added, had presented the substance of the idea in the article, "The Formula of Sacrifice" (*The Journal of Political Economy*, September 1895, p. 561). Though published shortly after Green's article, the "present writer has knowledge that this theory has been committed by Mr. Davenport to manuscript form so early, at least, as October 1892." (Taylor, "A New Presentation of Economic Theory," *ibid.*, September 1897, p. 523). See also Albert C. Whitaker, "History and Criticism of the Labor Theory of Value in English Political Economy," Columbia University *Studies in History, Economics and Public Law* (1904), Vol. XIX, p. 136.

33. Herbert J. Davenport to Charles H. Davenport, November 10, 1897, copy in Davenport Papers.

34. Philip H. Wicksteed later elaborated this view and described the supply curve as a disguised or reversed demand curve. See his *The Common Sense of Political Economy*, edition of 1910, edited and with an introduction by Lionel Robbins (London: Routledge, 1938), Vol. II, p. 785.

35. Davenport, "Proposed Modifications in Austrian Theory and Terminology," *The Quarterly Journal of Economics*, May 1902, pp. 355, 367, 371, 376.

36. David Kinley to Ely, February 27, 1903; Ely to Kinley, March 3, 1902, copy; Kinley to Ely, March 5, 1902, Ely Papers.

37. Davenport to Robert F. Hoxie, January 13, 1909, copy in Davenport Papers.

38. Morris A. Copeland, "Herbert Joseph Davenport," *The Economic Journal*, September 1931, p. 499.

39. Fetter, "Davenport's Competitive Economics," *The Journal of Political Economy*, June 1914, p. 564.

40. Fisher, "Davenport's Value and Distribution," *The Journal of Political Economy*, December 1908, pp. 661–79.

41. J. M. Clark to Davenport, June 29, 1914, Davenport Papers.

42. Davenport, "Fetter's *Economic Principles*," *The Journal of Political Economy*, April 1916, pp. 350–51. In the same article, as well as in *The Economics of Enterprise*, Davenport pointed out that the banks' easy reserve conditions were derived in large part from the "discounting activities of still other banks." Professor Lloyd Mints, while emphasizing the high and detailed character of Davenport's statement of the process whereby the banking system could multiply credit to the ratio of the reserves, pointed out an earlier but briefer statement in 1893 by the Florida banker D. G. Ambler.—Mints, *A History*

of *Banking Theory in Great Britain and the United States* (Chicago: University of Chicago Press, 1945), p. 206.

43. Davenport to Delos F. Wilcox, April 26, 1909, copy in Davenport Papers.

44. Davenport to C. H. Davenport, October 25, 1912, copy in Davenport Papers.

45. Davenport to A. W. Douglas, January 16, 1914, copy in Davenport Papers.

46. Carl Becker to Paul T. Homan, undated letter (1931?), by courtesy of Paul T. Homan.

47. Davenport to Seligman, January 28, 1930, Seligman Papers.

CHAPTER XVII

1. For biographical material, see Z. Clark Dickinson, "Fred Manville Taylor: 1855–1932," *The Economic Journal*, June 1933, p. 347. Professor Dickinson kindly made letters and other material available to the author.

2. Taylor laid down historical truths, which he firmly impressed upon his students, by means of a mechanical device relating to historical maps. This was his own invention, which he patented.

3. Taylor, "The Law of Nature," *Annals of the American Academy of Political and Social Science*, April 1891, pp. 559, 563.

4. In the academic year 1890–91, Taylor substituted for Henry C. Adams, who was on leave with the Interstate Commerce Commission. In 1892 he was permanently added to the staff as an assistant professor of political economy and finance.

5. Taylor, "Do We Want an Elastic Currency?" *Publications of the Michigan Political Science Association*, March 1896, pp. 1–28; "Maintaining the Gold Reserve," No. 2, *The Home Study Review*, July 1896, p. 115; *Some Chapters on Money* (Ann Arbor: privately printed, 1906), pp. 143–44, 190, 200, 202, 249, 256, 257; Taylor, et. al., "Report of the Committee on Currency Reform [of the American Economic Association]," *Publications of the American Economic Association, Economic Studies*, February 1899, p. 38.

6. For a recent discussion of this point, see Edward H. Chamberlin, "Proportionality, Divisibility and Economies of Production," *The Quarterly Journal of Economics*, February 1948, pp. 229–62.

7. Taylor felt that the Austrian school underestimated the role of real or disutility cost. "The function of disutility cost is to guide the individual in deciding what is the total volume of income for which he can reasonably strive; its function is not to determine the market prices of commodities. On the other hand, the underlying function of money cost or alternative utility cost is to guide the individual in deciding upon the best utilization of his total income— its best allotment among the numerous commodities which he wants."—Taylor to Friedrich von Hayek, February 18, 1930, copy supplied the author by Professor Dickinson.

8. Taylor, *Principles of Economics* (Ann Arbor: 1911; seventh privately printed edition, 1920), pp. 351–53, 365, 367, 370, 425, 530, 532, 533, 537, 582; *Key to Problems in Principles of Economics*, eighth edition (New York: Ronald, 1921), p. 5.

9. Taylor, "The Guidance of Production in the Socialist State," *The American Economic Review*, March 1929, p. 8.

10. Taylor, *Some Leading Problems in Economic Theory* (Ann Arbor: privately printed, fourth edition, 1922), p. 8.

11. See Oskar Lange, "On the Economic Theory of Socialism," originally published in 1936 and 1937 and reprinted with additions and some changes, along with Taylor's original essay, "The Guidance of Production in a Socialist State," in *The Economic Theory of Socialism*, edited by Benjamin E. Lippincott (Minneapolis: University of Minnesota Press, 1938), p. 64.

12. Taylor to Hayek, February 18, 1930.

13. Cited in Z. Clark Dickinson, "The Department of Economics," *The University of Michigan. An Encyclopedic Survey*, edited by Wilfred B. Shaw (Ann Arbor: University of Michigan Press, 1943), Part III, p. 543.

14. For Taylor's own description of his teaching methods, see his "Methods of Teaching Elementary Economics at the University of Michigan," *The Journal of Political Economy*, December 1909, pp. 689, 696.

15. L. C. Marshall to J. Laurence Laughlin, July 20, 1910, Laughlin Papers.

16. Taylor, "The Public Schools and Moral Training," in *The Michigan Schoolmasters' Club*, first meeting held at Ann Arbor, May 1, 1886, facsimile, 1947.

17. Charles Horton Cooley, "The Theory of Transportation," 1894, reprinted in *Sociological Theory and Social Research*, edited by Robert Cooley Angell (New York: Holt, 1930), pp. 112–13. For biographical data, see Edward C. Jandy, *Charles Horton Cooley* (New York: Dryden, 1942), pp. 7–79.

18. Thomas M. and Charles H. Cooley, "Transportation," in *The United States of America*, edited by Nathaniel S. Shaler, Vol. II, p. 116.

19. Cooley, "The Development of Sociology at Michigan," in *Sociological Theory and Social Research*, pp. 3–4.

20. Cooley, "Political Economy and Social Science," first delivered in 1911; printed in 1918, and reprinted in *Sociological Theory and Social Research*, pp. 251–59.

21. "The statistician operates between the primary observer, on the one hand, and on the other, the theorist who demands light on certain hypotheses." He should be likened to a "cook, who neither supplies the food nor consumes it, but is a specialist upon the intervening processes."—Cooley, "The Roots of Social Knowledge," 1926, reprinted in *Sociological Theory and Social Research*, p. 303.

22. Cooley, *Social Process* (New York: Scribner, 1918), pp. 334–47.

23. Walton H. Hamilton, "Charles Horton Cooley," *Social Forces*, December 1929, p. 185.

CHAPTER XVIII

1. The author has obtained personal items and letterbooks from Johannsen's stepson, W. H. Seiler, of Staten Island, New York.

2. An embryonic version of the doctrine of "impair savings" was presented in a privately printed pamphlet in 1892, called *A Fundamental Principle of Political Economy*, by Edgar J. Rich (1864–1948) who became one of the most prominent lawyers in the country as well as a lecturer at the Graduate School of Business Administration at Harvard. Rich sent a copy to Johannsen in 1926, stating that he had written the essay in 1888 in an effort to meet the reasoning of the classical economists.—Rich to Johannsen, July 19, 1926, letter in possession of author.

3. For presentations of Gesell's doctrines, see H. T. N. Gaitskell, "Four Monetary Heretics," in *What Everybody Wants to Know about Money*, edited by G. D. H. Cole (London: Gollancz, 1936), pp. 385–401; Dudley Dil-

lard, "Silvio Gesell's Monetary Theory of Reform," *The American Economic Review*, June 1942, pp. 348–52.

4. John Bates Clark, "A New Depression Theory," *The Bankers' Magazine*, February 1909, pp. 256–57.

5. John A. Hobson, *The Industrial System* (London: Longmans, Green, 1909), p. 292; Wesley C. Mitchell, *Business Cycles* (Berkeley: University of California Press, 1913), pp. 18, 19, 389, 569, 580, 581, and *Business Cycles* (New York: National Bureau of Economic Research, 1927), p. 25; George Bernard Shaw to Johannsen, January 2, 1926, in author's possession. In more recent years John Maynard Keynes also paid some attention to the "amateur" Johannsen.—See Keynes, *A Treatise on Money* (New York: Harcourt, Brace, 1930), Vol. II, p. 100, ft. Friedrich von Hayek of the University of Vienna (and now of the London School of Economics and Political Science) was so impressed with Johannsen's 1928 leaflet, *A Depression Manifest*, that he asked for earlier writings.—Hayek to Johannsen, April 26, 1928, in author's possession.

6. Johannsen to J. W. Martin, March 5, 1928; to Carl Snyder, April 5, 1928, in Johannsen's Letterbooks.

7. Harold G. Moulton, "An Appraisal of Carver's 'Economics,'" *The Journal of Political Economy*, April 1920, p. 331.

8. Moulton declared that he did not differ essentially from Davenport in his emphasis on commercial banks as characteristically creating loanable funds, except in making a different application of the theory.

9. Moulton, "Commercial Banking and Capital Formation," No. 4, *The Journal of Political Economy*, November 1918, pp. 872, 875; "A Rejoinder," *ibid.*, July 1919, p. 592; Harold L. Reed "The Industrial Outlook," *ibid.*, April 1919, p. 231; Myron W. Watkins, "A Criticism," *ibid.*, July 1919, p. 578; "An Answer," *ibid.*, pp. 603–604.

10. Anderson was a precocious youth. In 1905, only nineteen and a senior at the University of Missouri, he became professor of history at the State Normal School at Cape Girardeau, Missouri (now Missouri State College, Southeast). The following year he became professor of English literature and economics at Missouri Valley College. While head professor of history and economics in 1907–1910, at State Teachers College in Springfield (now Missouri State College, Southwest), he obtained an M. A. at the University of Illinois.

11. Alvin S. Johnson, review of *Social Value* in *The American Economic Review*, June 1912, p. 322.

12. John Maurice Clark to Cooley, April 3, 1919, in Charles Horton Cooley Papers, University of Michigan Library.

13. Walter W. Stewart, "Social Value and the Theory of Money," *The Journal of Political Economy*, December 1917, pp. 1001–1002; Henry Waldgrave Stuart, "The Phases of the Economic Interest," in John Dewey, *et al.*, *Creative Intelligence* (New York: Holt, 1917), p. 340, ft.

14. Report of Anderson's address, "Some Aspects of the Quantity Theory of Money," February 9, 1914, ms. "Minutes of the Economics Seminary, 1912–1921," Harvard University Library.

15. Anderson to Seligman, July 28, 1918, Seligman Papers. Seligman was instrumental in obtaining the post for Anderson, as he was instrumental in obtaining the Michigan offer for him through Henry C. Adams. In 1920 Anderson became economic adviser of the Chase National Bank. In 1939 he returned to teaching as professor of economics at the University of California.

16. Cooley Journals, 1911, cited by Edward C. Jandy, *op. cit.*, p. 222.

17. For a partial bibliography of Johnson's work, see *A Bibliography of the Faculty of Political Science of Columbia University*, pp. 144–50. Johnson

taught at Bryn Mawr, Columbia, Nebraska, Texas, Chicago, Stanford, and Cornell, and was on the first board of editors of *The New Republic*. Later he became director of the New School for Social Research.

18. Alvin S. Johnson, "Rent in Modern Economic Theory," *Publications of the American Economic Association*, November 1902, pp. 1001–1002.

19. Johnson, "Protection and the Formation of Capital," *Political Science Quarterly*, June 1908, pp. 220–41.

20. Johnson to Seligman, November 1, 1915, Seligman Papers.

21. Johnson, "The Effect of Labor-Saving Devices upon Wages," *The Quarterly Journal of Economics*, November 1905, p. 109.

22. For John Rae, see Dorfman, *op. cit.*, Vol. II, pp. 779–89.

23. Johnson, "Influences Affecting the Development of Thrift," *Political Science Quarterly*, July 1907, pp. 243–44.

24. Johnson, "Davenport's Economics and the Present Problems of Theory," *The Quarterly Journal of Economics*, May 1914, pp. 420–21.

25. Johnson, "Beclouding the Minimum Wage," *The New Republic*, July 22, 1916.

26. Johnson, "The Incidence of the Federal Corporation Tax," *The South Atlantic Quarterly*, January 1910, pp. 36–38.

27. Johnson, "Instead of Public Ownership," *The New Republic*, April 20, 1918.

28. Johnson, "Unsocial Investments," *The Unpopular Review*, July-September 1914, p. 19.

29. Gustav A. Kleene, "Bernstein vs. 'Old School' Marxism," *Annals of the American Academy of Political and Social Science*, November 1901, pp. 418–19.

30. Kleene, "The Problem of Medical Charity," *Annals of the American Academy of Political and Social Science*, May 1904, pp. 409, 422; "The Limitations of Charity Organization," *The Yale Review*, November 1908, pp. 311, 313.

31. Taussig to McCrea, December 8, 1916, McCrea Papers.

32. Taussig, "Kleene's Profit and Wages," *The Quarterly Journal of Economics*, August 1917, pp. 709–10; see also Kleene's reply: "The Supply Price of Labor," *ibid.*, February 1918, p. 404.

33. Kleene, "Productive Apparatus and the Capitalist," *The Journal of Political Economy*, February 1923, pp. 19–20.

CHAPTER XIX

1. A compact selection from Veblen's writings, with an illuminating introduction, has been published by Wesley C. Mitchell, *What Veblen Taught* (New York: Viking Press, 1936). See also Paul T. Homan, *Contemporary Economic Thought* (New York: Harper, 1928), pp. 107–192. For detailed biography of Veblen, see Joseph Dorfman, *Thorstein Veblen and His America* (New York: Viking Press, 1934). See also R. L. Duffus, *The Innocents at Cedro* (New York: Macmillan, 1944).

2. Frederick Lange, *History of Materialism*, translated by Ernest Chester Thomas (London: Trübner, 1881), Vol. II, pp. 33, 241–42.

3. Kant's *Critique of Practical Reason*, translated by T. K. Abbot (London: Longmans, Green, 6th edition, 1909), p. 260; James Ward, "Immanuel Kant," 1923, reprinted in *Essays in Philosophy* (Cambridge: Cambridge University Press, 1927), pp. 333, 347; René Wellek, *Immanuel Kant in England, 1793–1838* (Princeton: Princeton University Press, 1931), p. 27.

4. Veblen to Wesley C. Mitchell, February 20, 1913, letter in author's possession.

5. Henry W. Stuart, "Hedonistic Interpretation of Subjective Value," *The Journal of Political Economy*, December 1895, pp. 66, 70; "Subjective and Exchange Value," *ibid.*, June 1896, pp. 363, 376, 383, 384.

6. Stuart obtained a fellowship in philosophy and took his doctorate in that department at Chicago. Later he became professor of philosophy at Stanford.

7. Stuart, "Valuation as a Logical Process," in John Dewey, *et al.*, *Studies in Logical Theory* (Chicago: University of Chicago Press, 1903), 337–38, ft.

8. Stuart, "Phases of the Economic Interest," in John Dewey, *et al.*, *Creative Intelligence* (New York: Holt, 1917), 333–37.

9. William R. Camp, "Limitations of the Ricardian Theory of Rent," *Political Science Quarterly*, December 1918, p. 548.

10. For a bibliography of Hoxie's work, see "A Tentative Bibliography of Robert F. Hoxie's Published Works," *The Journal of Political Economy*, November 1916, pp. 894–96.

11. Walton H. Hamilton, "The Development of Hoxie's Economics," *The Journal of Political Economy*, November 1916, p. 867; see also Hoxie's review of Fetter's treatise, which received Fetter's approval before publication, "Fetter's Theory of Value," *The Quarterly Journal of Economics*, February 1905, pp. 210–30.

12. Hoxie, "Class Conflict in America," *The American Journal of Sociology*, May 1908, pp. 779–80.

13. For a critique of Hoxie's work on trade unionism, see Russell Bauder, "Three Interpretations of the American Trade Union Movement," *Social Forces*, December 1943, pp. 215–24.

14. From Hoxie's unpublished ms., "History of Economic Thought," in author's possession.

15. Alvin S. Johnson, "Robert Franklin Hoxie," *The New Republic*, July 8, 1916.

CHAPTER XX

1. For a partial bibliography of Mitchell, see *A Bibliography of the Faculty of Political Science of Columbia University*, pp. 201–205. For detailed discussion of his views, see Paul T. Homan, *Contemporary Economic Thought*, pp. 375–436; and Allan G. Gruchy, *Modern Economic Thought* (New York: Prentice-Hall, 1947), pp. 247–333. For biographical sketch, see Joseph Dorfman, "The President of the Association," *The Scientific Monthly*, February 1938, pp. 194–97.

2. Mitchell, "Statistical Method in the Service of the Social Sciences," unpublished address (1910?), Mitchell Papers, in W. C. Mitchell's possession.

3. Mitchell, ms. outlines of "System of Prices," Mitchell Papers.

4. Mitchell, ms. outlines of "The Money Economy," Mitchell Papers.

5. The English now use the equivalent expression "trade cycles."

6. Mitchell, "The Making and Using of Index Numbers," *Bulletin of the U. S. Bureau of Labor Statistics*, July 1915, p. 30.

7. Herbert Joseph Davenport, "The Distributive Relations of Indirect Goods," *The Quarterly Journal of Economics*, August 1918, p. 663.

8. Mitchell to Robert S. Lynd, May 31, 1944. Letter is in author's possession.

9. J. M. Clark, "Recent Developments in Economics," in *Recent Developments in the Social Sciences*, edited by E. C. Hayes (Philadelphia: Lippincott, 1927), pp. 284–85. *See also* Clark's "Wesley C. Mitchell's Contribution to the Theory of Business Cycles," 1931, reprinted in Clark's *Preface to Social Economics* (New York: Farrar and Rinehart, 1936), pp. 390–406.

10. John R. Commons, *et al.*, *History of Labor in the United States* (New York: Macmillan, 1935), Vol. III, pp. 132, 152.

11. Carroll D. Wright was president in 1903.

CHAPTER XXI

1. Graham Taylor, "Unemployment: Discussion," in *Proceedings of the National Conference of Charities and Correction*, 42nd sess. (1915), pp. 511–13.

2. Mitchell presented a number of schemes in *Business Cycles* (1913), pp. 586–87.

3. John R. Shillady, "Planning Public Expenditures to Compensate for Decreased Private Employment during Business Depression," in *Proceedings of the National Conference of Charities and Correction*, 43rd sess. (1916), pp. 189–90.

4. Henry R. Seager, "Unemployment: Problem and Remedies," 1915, reprinted in *Labor and Other Economic Essays*, pp. 256–57.

5. Wesley C. Mitchell, "Prices and Reconstruction," *The American Economic Review*, March 1920, Supplement, p. 139.

6. Bernard M. Baruch, *American Industry in the War* (Washington: Government Printing Office, 1921), p. 19.

7. Testimony of Bernard M. Baruch, March 27, 1935, in *Munitions Industry: Hearings Before the Senate Special Committee Investigating the Munitions Industry*, 74th Cong., 1st sess., pp. 6264, 6273.

8. Baruch, *American Industry in the War*, p. 54.

9. *The Annalist*, April 30, 1917 [editorial].

10. Curtice N. Hitchcock, "The War Industries Board," *The Journal of Political Economy*, June 1918, p. 560.

11. Cited by Leon C. Marshall, "The War Labor Program and Its Administration," *The Journal of Political Economy*, May 1918, p. 432.

12. Baruch, *Final Report of the Chairman of the United States War Industries Board*, 1919, 74th Cong., 1st sess., Special Senate Committee Investigating the Munitions Industry, March 1935, Print No. 3, p. 44.

13. Allyn Young, "National Statistics in War and Peace," *American Statistical Association Publications*, March 1918, p. 877; Mitchell, "Statistics and Government," 1919, reprinted in *The Backward Art of Spending Money* (New York: McGraw-Hill, 1937), p. 47.

14. Baruch, *American Industry in the War*, p. 72; William M. Duffus, "Government Control of the Wheat Trade in the United States," *The American Economic Review*, March 1918, p. 62.

15. *Minutes of the Council of National Defense*, 74th Cong., 2d sess., Special Senate Committee Investigating the Munitions Industry, Print No. 7, pp. 95, 101.

16. W. C. Clark, "Should Maximum Prices Be Fixed?" *Queens Quarterly*, April-June 1918, pp. 456–57.

17. F. W. Taussig, "Price-Fixing as Seen by a Price-Fixer," *The Quarterly Journal of Economics*, February 1919, p. 210.

18. Paul Willard Garrett, assisted by Isador Lubin and Stella Stewart, *Government Control over Prices* (Washington: Government Printing Office, 1920), p. 400; for a critique of the bulk-line cost idea, see J. M. Clark, "Recent Developments in Economics," pp. 287–88.

19. Taussig, "Price-Fixing as Seen by a Price-Fixer," p. 228.

20. Testimony of Taussig, *Minutes of the Price-Fixing Committee of the*

War Industries Board, 74th Cong., 2d sess., Senate Special Committee Investigating the Munitions Industry, Print No. 5, pp. 637–38, 645–46; testimony of Long, *ibid.,* pp. 637–38, 654–55.

21. Taussig, "Price-Fixing as Seen by a Price-Fixer," p. 238.

22. Mitchell, "Prices and Reconstruction," p. 143.

23. Cited in T. S. Adams, "War Finance," *The New Republic,* April 7, 1917.

24. O. M. W. Sprague, "Loans and Taxes in War Finance," *The American Economic Review,* March 1917, Supplement, pp. 202, 208.

25. Memorial, May 10, 1917, in *Congressional Record,* 65th Cong., 1st sess., pp. 2045–46.

26. Farnam to Seligman, April 17, 1917, Seligman Papers; Roy G. Blakey, "Taxes Upon Income and Excess Profits—Discussion," *The American Economic Review,* March 1918, Supplement, p. 53.

27. Cited in Blakey, "The War Revenue Act of 1917," *The American Economic Review,* December 1917, p. 809.

28. E. R. A. Seligman, "The War Revenue Act," *Political Science Quarterly,* March 1918, p. 31.

29. George M. Reynolds, "Steady Business to Meet War's Shock," *The Nation's Business,* October 1917, p. 54; Mortimer L. Schiff, "War Time Borrowing by the Government," *The Annals,* January 1918, pp. 49–51.

30. Taussig, "Price-Fixing as Seen by a Price-Fixer," p. 222.

31. Alvin S. Johnson, "Why America Lags," *The Unpopular Review,* April–June 1918, pp. 230–31.

32. Harold G. Moulton, "Some Dangers of Price Control," *The City Club* [of Chicago], September 10, 1917, p. 224; "Industrial Conscription," *The Journal of Political Economy,* November 1917, pp. 916–45.

33. Taussig, "How to Promote Foreign Trade," *The Quarterly Journal of Economics,* May 1918, p. 424.

34. E. W. Kemmerer, "The War and Interest Rates," in *American Problems of Reconstruction,* edited by Elisha M. Friedman, pp. 413–14.

35. Seligman, "The Economic Prospects of the United States After the War," *Scientia,* XXI (1917), p. 233.

36. "The Problem of Demobilization," *The Journal of Political Economy,* November 1918, pp. 931–32 [editorial].

37. Johnson, "Economics of Land Settlement," *The New Republic,* October 12, 1918.

38. Parker was most deeply influenced by William McDougall, but Veblen was his idol. He was a graduate of the University of California, taught economics at his alma mater from 1910 to 1916, and then went to the University of Washington as head of the Department of Economics and Dean of the School of Business Administration. His striking personality is well revealed in Cornelia Stratton Parker, *An American Idyll: The Life of Carleton H. Parker* (Boston: Atlantic, 1919).

39. Parker, "Motives in Economic Life," 1918, reprinted in *The Casual Laborer and Other Essays,* edited by Cornelia Stratton Parker (New York: Harcourt, Brace and Howe, 1920), pp. 129, 164–65.

40. Louis B. Wehle, "Capital, Labor, and the State," in *American Problems of Reconstruction,* edited by Elisha M. Friedman, pp. 173–75.

41. Stenographic copy of Mitchell's lectures in "Current Types of Economic Theory" at Columbia University, in author's possession.

42. John R. Commons, "Economic Reconstruction: Foreign and Domestic Investments," *The American Economic Review,* March 1918, Supplement, p. 16.

43. For a more elaborate presentation of Veblen's argument, see Joseph Dorfman's "Introduction" to the new edition of *Imperial Germany and the Industrial Revolution* (New York: Viking Press, 1937).

44. Veblen, "Outline of a Policy for the Control of the 'Economic Penetration' of Backward Countries and of Foreign Investments," 1917, first printed in 1932; reprinted in *Essays in Our Changing Order*, edited by Leon Ardzrooni (New York: Viking Press, 1934), p. 371.

45. Mitchell, "Economics," *The American Year Book, 1918* (New York: Appleton, 1919), p. 380.

APPENDIX

1. Clark to Professor T. Miyajima, February 6, 1927, copy in Clark Papers.

2. In Ely Papers.

3. Johann Heinrich von Thünen, *Der isolierte Staat.* For a recent comprehensive critique of von Thünen, see A. H. Leigh, "Von Thünen's Theory of Distribution and the Advent of Marginal Analysis," *The Journal of Political Economy*, August 1945, pp. 481–502.

4. This "enlargement" referred to Clark's contention that most commodities, comforts, and luxuries, were not simple utilities but "bundles of utilities." For the different items in the bundle of utilities constituting a commodity, different purchasers were marginal. This reinforced his conception of marginal utility as social marginal utility. "When fine articles—composite things, bundles of distinct elements—are offered to society, the great composite consumer, each element has somewhere in the social organism the effect of fixing a part of the total value. In no other way can the article, as a whole, get a valuation. To no individual are all its utilities final. If they were, such goods would generally be much more expensive than they are."—Clark, *The Distribution of Wealth*, pp. 243–44; see also Clark, *The Essentials of Economic Theory* (New York: Macmillan, 1907), pp. 106–13.

5. Folwell Papers, University of Minnesota Library.

6. See Charles William Macfarlane, *Value and Distribution*, pp. 215, 271; and George Gunton, *Principles of Social Economics* (New York: Putnam, 1891), 144–48, 184–92.

7. J. M. Clark, "Distribution," *Encyclopædia of the Social Sciences.*

8. "Stuart Wood and the Marginal Productivity Theory," *The Quarterly Journal of Economics*, August 1947, pp. 640–49.

9. *Publications of the American Economic Association*, July 1889, pp. 272–73.

Index